BOOKS BY EDMUND WILSON

W9-BTA-974

THE FIFTIES

Edmund Wilson, circa 1952

EDMUND WILSON

The Fifties

From Notebooks and Diaries
of the Period

Edited with an Introduction by

Leon Edel

FARRAR, STRAUS AND GIROUX

NEW YORK

First edition, 1986
Printed in the United States of America
Published simultaneously in Canada by
Collins Publishers, Toronto
Third printing 1987
Library of Congress Cataloging-in-Publication Data
Wilson, Edmund, 1895–1972.
   The fifties : from notebooks and diaries of the
period.
   Includes index.
   1. Wilson, Edmund, 1895–1972—Diaries.   2. Authors,
American—20th century—Diaries.   3. Critics—United
States—Diaries.   I. Edel, Leon, 1907–   . II. Title.
PS3545.I6245Z464   1986   818'.5203   [B]   86–9997

Parts of this book appeared originally in *The New York
Times Book Review*, *The New York Review of Books*, and
The Paris Review.

CONTENTS

ILLUSTRATIONS

Acknowledgment is made to George Weidenfeld & Nicolson
for permission to reproduce the photo of Mamaine Paget
Koestler published in *Living with Koestler* (1985); and to
the New York State Museum and Science Service for the
painting by Ernest Smith facing page 484.

EDITOR'S FOREWORD

Edmund Wilson kept his diaries and journals of the fifties with much greater regularity and in a more systematic way than during his earlier years. Age and domestication, regularity of habits and fewer wanderings, contributed to this. Where he used to make sporadic entries at irregular intervals, he now kept track of his dates; by using his calendar as guide he constructed a largely retrospective journal. This means that the dates, when they are given, refer not to the time of writing but to the happenings and encounters of a recent time. Evidence points clearly now to an intention to publish his journals: and he planned, if he had an opportunity, to introduce further retrospective passages, as he did in *The Twenties*, which was incomplete at the time of his death.

The manuscripts comprising the present volume are a mixture of neatness and scribble. There were days when he wrote with copybook care. On other occasions his pen would run away with him; he would be impatient and abbreviate words and reduce names to initials. I have in most cases expanded these abbreviations but without the use of square brackets and other scholarly devices, remembering his original instructions: to edit him not in the ways of scholarship but as if I had a living manuscript to prepare for a publisher. This meant verifying some of his facts (often where he placed a question mark) and checking some of his spellings. Editing often meant unscrambling.

The signs of his aging occur when he often intends to write one word and then writes another, or when he puts down a portmanteau word. I have corrected these silently. Where an interrogation occurs in square brackets it signifies either editorial bewilderment or sometimes illegible writing. Where there is a question mark in parenthesis it means that Edmund himself placed it there to signal researchers at *The New Yorker* or a post-humous editor like myself that verification is needed. Wilson had his special way of transliterating Russian names—Tchaikovsky was Chaikovsky and so on. I wish to thank Professor Larissa Keller of the University of Hawaii for help with the Russian.

The present work was transcribed from the manuscript with the help of a grant from the National Endowment for the Humanities. Edmund Wilson's children have helped me at various times, and in this volume I have had the particular help of Helen Miranda Wilson. Stephen Bretzius gave me considerable assistance in some areas of research and in the deciphering of difficult portions of the manuscript. He is also responsible for most of the notes. I am grateful to him for his conscientious attention to many small details—for this has been perhaps the most difficult of the four volumes edited to date. I have included more notes than in the previous volumes; these may seem superfluous to some, but they are designed for the newest generation of readers now more distant from the time of writers such as Norman Douglas or Compton Mackenzie who, a quarter of a century earlier, would not have required identification. Phyllis Stenger, a lecturer in English at the University of Hawaii, kindly carried out earlier researches into the genealogy of Wilson's relations at Talcottville, and Marjorie Edel generously read the completed book to help remove slips of pen and typewriter. I am grateful also to Pat Strachan, my editor at Farrar, Straus and Giroux, for assistance and counsel beyond the line of duty.

L.E.

EDMUND WILSON IN THE FIFTIES
La Douceur de la vie

"Nothing but deaths" Edmund Wilson writes in his journals at the beginning of the fifties, when he was haunted by a fantasy that he too might die before his time. Edna Millay had just died—she had seemed dead when he visited her during the 1940s. Christian Gauss, his mentor at Princeton, had dropped dead in Pennsylvania Station while waiting for the Princeton train. His mother had died, recently, of old age, her life in a manner fulfilled. She at least had known "duration." Edmund had been distanced from her early by her chronic deafness; but even without her poor hearing she had proved too prosaic for her overbright son. She would have liked him to be a quiet, ordinary boy who might go with her to the football games and do all the conventional things in their corner of New Jersey. She hadn't approved of his being a writer and never read him. She was devoted to her gardens; she had her house, her car, her chauffeur, her loyal servant, and had lived into her eighties. Edna Millay had been Edmund's troubled and troubling early love, and the ups and downs of their intermittent affair are reflected in his novel *I*

Thought of Daisy and in the memoir he now wrote about her. Assembling his literary writings of the twenties and thirties, which he called *The Shores of Light*, he let the memoir stand as an epilogue, a kind of final shutting of the gate on his passionate past. At the beginning of the book—as a prologue—he placed his tribute to Gauss, who had made him feel the importance of human expression in literature, made him aware of continental writers and the power of language and symbol. In his epitaph for Gauss he quotes Dante's lines to his teacher, Brunetto Latini, *la cara e buona imagine paterna**—"the dear and kind paternal image"—thus naming Gauss as a kind of second father, the father of his intellect. The two memoirs enclose the "shores of light" —the precious decades that had forged Wilson's critical power—as in a felt and permanent embrace.

With his mother's death, Wilson inherited the family's upstate house—the Stone House, as it was called. Situated in Talcottville, a village of some eighty persons, in the lower range of the Adirondacks, it had been begun in 1800, the year after George Washington's death, and completed in 1804. Its huge beams showed ravage; there were the inevitable accumulations of cobwebs and mildew; in places the plaster on the Sugar River limestone, from the ancestral quarry, was crumbling. But it was a splendid, solid house, with large rooms and chaste and elegant fireplaces; there were two stories of wide windows and a full-length veranda on each story. The house had survived, in its rural grandeur, from the childhood of the American Republic.

At certain periods in its history it had served, in the midst of being a dwelling, as a town hall, a post office, a social center. Outlying buildings had included a dairy,

* *Inferno* XV, 83.

a quilting room, and a spinning room where three maids once spun constantly. There had also been a large ballroom. In addition to their homespun clothes, the ancestors had produced their own nails and candles and other household necessities. They dealt in land, built a mill, sold grist from their harvests and produce from the farms. With his usual curiosity, Edmund started reading local history and talking to family relations in the neighborhood. Once he had put up work space in the house, he began to study deeds, genealogy, real estate records, wills. Everything about his mother's family interested him. In one of his Christmas poems sent to his friends he told the family history:

> The Talcotts, Tories at that date,
> Resided here in feudal state . . .
> Another role was Thomas Baker's,
> Who broke and sold the Talcott acres.

There had been disputes, squabbles, litigation. The Talcotts and the Bakers feuded like the Montagues and Capulets but without the Shakespearean mayhem, and some of them finally reconciled proprietary differences in various intermarriages.

His father, Edmund Wilson, Sr., a successful lawyer, had bought the Stone House for his wife. She was descended from a third family, the Kimballs and Mathers, including the celebrated Cotton Mather, and she always called herself Helen Mather Kimball Wilson. The family had brought Edmund Jr. to Talcottville long before he had learned to speak, and as he grew he found the Stone House "a magical world." He remembered bedtime stories in the hushed country twilight and the active days of his boyhood roaming in the wild woodland. Later when he was in prep school, the Adirondacks bored him; he wanted to be with his schoolmates. His mother had continued to summer there during her widowhood, but Edmund returned upstate now to find that the old magicality was reasserting itself. As he crossed the threshold he felt that he walked not only into his personal past but into almost two hundred years of American history. His books were still on the shelves. On the tops of the bookcases he could see his old trophies of travel—some Mexican gods; a plaster gargoyle lugged home from Paris; models of various animals; a stuffed yellow bird bordered with blue and orange beads bought from an Indian woman in Canada. These relics of his younger self made him feel acutely that he was a part of continuing history. He had ceased to be a detached and roving bohemian.

Periodically he sorted out the accumulations—they were a kind of repository of ancient domesticities: combback chairs, bed quilts in bright and faintly phallic patterns, engravings of George Washington, a clutter of spinning wheels, a stuffed heron. There were perforated tin boxes, the foot warmers of another day used during sleigh rides or the Sunday sermon, like those in Balzac's *Eugénie Grandet*, and all kinds of bric-a-brac: dried rose leaves in glass jars, an old wooden flute, bootjacks that had been handled by ancestral hands and—most amusing of all—a convenient little footstool with a little wooden flap. When you pressed the flap you found it contained a cuspidor.

By the middle 1950s, the Stone House, renovated and partly modernized, had become a fixed part of Edmund Wilson's life. His frame house in the New England style at Wellfleet was the center of his achieved domestication during his fourth marriage, to his European wife, Elena Mumm. It had comfortable rooms and to the rear a very large room, which was his library, and an adjoining study. Here he spent autumns and winters and early spring.

When the northern winds from Canada ceased and the ground thawed, he was driven (for he had never learned to drive) to Talcottville, a seven-hour trip, to spend his summers as of old, in the house of his ancestors. The many pages in these journals devoted to his Adirondack life were turned into a book a dozen years later—*Upstate*—which tells in considerable detail this phase of Wilson's life during his later years.

In the journals, we can spend long indolent afternoons with the contented Edmund Wilson. He is in a deck chair between two trees and commands an affectionate view of the distant blue hills. In the foreground, he lazily watches a butterfly catch the sun's blaze in its wings as it flies high into an elm filled with swallows. His eyes follow the squirrels or chipmunks across the roof of the Stone House and he feels an extraordinary freedom—"of that realm of treetop, roof and sky"—a soaring into high space and timelessness. This kind of relaxation and beatitude is new to him—the French sometimes speak of it as *la douceur de la vie*, the Italians *la dolce vita*. Wilson's mood is classical; he might be a writing Roman with his large senatorial head and thick body, escaping from the Imperial city for rustication. Edmund had never dreamed of such harmonies in his crowded Greenwich Village days, or during his subsequent troubled marriages.

Elena Wilson did not like the Stone House. Far from finding *douceur* in it, she complained of the altitude; it made her nervous and indeed she probably suffered from high blood pressure. Moreover, she was a sea person and she missed the smell of the ocean and the swimming at Wellfleet. Edmund, on his side, expressed delight at escaping from the Cape's tourist wave, the cars pushing their way to Provincetown during summers. Elena insisted she saw ghosts; and the house smelled too much of the dead past. She never stayed very long, but retreated to Wellfleet feeling a little as if Edmund were being unfaithful to her in burying himself in the post-Revolutionary past. *Upstate* candidly describes this annual awkwardness between the two, their divided loyalties in their two houses. But for Edmund, Talcottville was more than a place to unwind; it was a place where he could reclaim his selfhood and do "prodigies of writing." That too was a part of the *douceur*.

Edmund Wilson wrote only two books during the fifties but five others were brought together, containing earlier periodical writings and some new material. These were scrupulously edited and revised and had the double effect of shoring up his scattered work while generating much-needed revenue. His arrangement with *The New Yorker* brought in substantial income, but he traveled to other parts of the country, and his trips to Europe—there were two in the fifties—were invariably depleting, financially. And then he had perhaps too cavalierly (deploring the small earnings of serious writers) refused to bother with record-keeping in behalf of the Internal Revenue. His struggle with the I.R.S. belongs to later consideration with his book on the cold war and the income tax; but, with the threat of prosecution and the heavy penalties imposed, he seemed committed, to the end of his days, to reducing a formidable debt of the kind Mark Twain had to reduce by lecturing and Walter Scott by incessant production.

The five collections of earlier writings were *Classics and Commercials* (1950); *The Shores of Light* (1952); *Five Plays* (1954); his "studies in four civilizations," *Red, Black, Blond and Olive* (1956); and his political and social reportage, *The American Earthquake* (1958). In addition he wrote *The Scrolls from the Dead Sea* (1955) and a miscellany of essays, *A Piece of My Mind: Reflections at Sixty* (1956). He was also working at two other books, his ongoing study of the Civil War and his book about the Iroquois.

It was as if he was putting his house of letters into order, as well as the house of life. A feature of these books was Wilson's willingness to acknowledge previous errors and correct them, his tendency to add passages enlarging old ideas, and his general flexibility when compared with certain eminent critics who carefully guarded their "consistency," seeking to be always in the right. Only a man with a distinct personality and a large interest in all facets of human life and endeavor, possessing Wilson's intensity and dedication to the search for truth, could give his past writings this kind of importance. The integration of his writings, their vivid reorganization as "literary chronicles," which gave them historical significance, the infusion of new material, endowed his volumes with distinct values for future generations.

The year of his sixtieth birthday, 1955, was the watershed of his private life during this decade, and *A Piece of My Mind* reflects certain hauntings and anxieties. The disappearance of his own generation brought fantasies of death and a particular poignancy of fear at the moment when he had belatedly taken possession of his little kingdoms on the Cape and in the Adirondacks. The mood of this book is testamentary, a kind of bequeathing of world-weariness, disillusion, the perversities of history, and a declaration of his will to live in spite of his disenchantment. The book inquires into his resistances to the twentieth century and the attractiveness of the eighteenth century—for he not only resisted the new machines, the television and radio, but he felt himself to be locked in "a pocket of the past"—he whose earlier years had seemed so highly contemporaneous. His series of short essays in this book—on war, the U.S.A., religion,

the Russians, sex, the Jews, education, science—are brief
homilies about life's confusion and its *douceurs*. They
read like the work of a liberal newspaper columnist and,
for all their lucidity and charm, are superficial and devoid
of the hard thought to be found in his other writings.
They seem, until one reaches the final essay, the informal
chatter of a mature and meditative man of letters, in his
slippers by his fireside.

The final essay redeems this book and explains its
part in his life of the fifties. Entitled "The Author at
Sixty," it pays only indirect attention to himself, but is
a brilliant sketch of his father, Edmund Wilson, Sr.
The essay seems to me to belong with the significant
writings of the past by sons about their fathers. But
many of these reflect a quarrel between the generations.
Edmund has no quarrel—his portrait is a mixture of
filial affection and a certain bewilderment. He finds it
difficult to reconcile the father he admired, whose probity
and clarity of mind he compares with Lincoln's, with his
frequent lapses into melancholy, during which he committed himself to sanitariums. He paints his father's
aristocratic and gentry leanings, so like his own, and his
democratic roots in the foundations of American history;
his ability to meet people from all walks of life, his deep
sympathy with minorities, not least the blacks, his love
for the American scene, his abiding interest in cities and
men—all these qualities and actions which his son had
carried into his literary and historical writings.

The differences between the father and the son resided
in Edmund Jr. overcoming his own lapse into depression
during his younger years, perhaps because he could lean
on his mother's down-to-earth ways, which made her so
little able to keep pace with the father's active humanism. Edmund Sr. had been Attorney General of New

Jersey. He had jailed the corrupt bosses of the Atlantic seaboard, and President Woodrow Wilson had planned to name him to the Supreme Court, if a vacancy had occurred. He had lost only one case in his entire career. Edmund Jr. describes his father's way of working up his court presentations—very much as the son later worked up his documentary essays. The essay pictures for us not only a successful man undermined by his inner "wound" but the sad and disjointed marriage that resulted and the dilemma it created for its only child. We are given thus the taproots of the son's imagination, his ability to live himself into the past as few historians have done, while maintaining a cool detachment (as his father had done); his supreme power of summary and utterance— qualities of both literature and the law. There is an extraordinary tenderness in the paternal portrait which those who knew the more brusque and cantankerous side of Edmund Jr. may not be able to reconcile or recognize. The writer had exceptional qualities of generosity and benignity. Many younger men now reaching middle age remember how kind he could be and gentle even when he was being highly critical. This generosity was one of his finest attributes, and it seems also to have been a source of his great attractiveness to women. Toward the end of his magisterial essay in *A Piece of My Mind* Edmund lights up for us the deepest reasons that led him to the writing of this book:

My father's career had its tragic side—he died in his sixty-first year. I have been in some ways more fortunate—I am writing this in my sixty-second. And yet to have got through with honor that period from 1880 to 1920!—even at the expense of the felt-muted door, the lack of first class companionship, the retreats into sanitariums. I have never been obliged to do anything so difficult. Yet my own generation in America has not had so gay a journey as we expected when we first started out. In repudiating the materialism and the priggishness of the period in which we were born, we thought we should have a free hand to refashion American life as well as to have more fun than our fathers. But we, too, have had our casualties. Too many of my friends are insane or dead or Roman Catholic converts—and some of these among the most gifted; two have committed suicide. I myself had an unexpected breakdown when I was in my middle thirties. It was pointed out to me then that I had reached exactly the age at which my father had first passed into the shadow. I must have inherited from him some strain of his neurotic distemper, and it may be that I was influenced by unconscious fear lest I might be doomed to a similar fate. I did not recover wholly for years, and there were times when I was glad to reflect that I had covered more than half of my threescore and ten—"on the home stretch," I used to phrase it in reassuring myself. But now I am farther along, I find I want to keep on living.

This then is what haunted Edmund Wilson at the approach of his sixtieth year; this had been the prompting of his autobiographical book. But the ominous deadline had come and gone. He was now older than his father had been at the time of his death. He could take repossession, as it were, of his life. And in a passage in his journals he fills out the thoughts we read between the lines of *A Piece of My Mind*. He had endured. "In my sixty-first year, I find that one of the things that most gratifies me is the sense of my continuity . . . I feel at moments, when I'm living here alone [at Talcott-ville] that it's all myself and nothing else—house, village, and Lewis County. I might get tired of the beautiful view from my door if I didn't feel it was also mine, a part of my habitat, imagination, thought, personality." Those acres which Thomas Baker broke and sold seem to have been recovered: his imagination annexes the surrounding countryside to the durable Stone House and there has been a recovery of selfhood. Edmund Wilson has re-acquired a future, however long or short it may be.

Once, long before, when he was still a small boy, being driven by his parents home from nearby Boonville, he had said to himself, "I am a poet." Then the critic-to-be in little Edmund took over. "No, I'm not quite a poet, but I am something of the kind." And indeed his young self had prophesied his old self—as in a cartoon by Beerbohm—a writer, a polymath, whose prose, as has been said, was always written not "at" but "to" the reader. Now he sits in his upstate realm like an ancient Roman renewing his selfhood and having his *villégiature* —allowing irritations, irascibilities, torments, and frag-mentations to melt together into the mellowness of aging.

Wilson's two journeys to Europe in the 1950s with Elena and his young daughter were in a very particular sense voyages of discovery. He had never known Europe with any intimacy or sought to study it as he had studied Russia in the 1930s when he was writing *To the Finland Station*. Aside from his boyhood trip with his parents, and his glimpse of the First World War shambles as a medic in the American army in 1918, he made only a brief trip in 1921 to England, France, and Italy when he was pursuing the elusive Edna Millay; fourteen years later he passed through Paris homeward bound from Russia; and ten years after that he briefly visited Eng-

land, Italy, and Greece in the dying days of the Second
World War, recording these experiences in *Europe
Without Baedeker* and in his journals published as *The
Forties*. This had been the sum total of his glimpses of
the Continent. He had always been anti-British and more
or less anti-European; he had consistently argued that the
United States had mistakenly fought Europe's battles.
But now he came to the Continent as an established
American man of letters with an international reputation,
accompanied by a European wife, and he found it very
much to his liking. He met a new generation of writers
in England, and looked up lingering Edwardians to whom
he had been devoted in his youth—Max Beerbohm in
Rapallo, Compton Mackenzie in Edinburgh. He gave a
seminar in Salzburg in Max Reinhardt's baroque Schloss
under the auspices of the State Department's postwar
fostering of "American studies" in Europe; he visited
his wife's family in the German wine country near
Frankfurt, a section of his journals that reads like a
Maupassant story in its picture of the decay of a bourgeois family. In England, guided by Sir Isaiah Berlin,
the philosopher and specialist in Russian letters, he
visited Oxford with a jaundiced eye and seems to be
criticizing it for not providing hotel luxuries. He enjoyed Cyril Connolly's gossip and formed a warm friendship with Angus Wilson, relishing his "tart and trim"
pictures of the English upper middle class. He saw
Mamaine Koestler, formerly Paget, with whom he had
fallen in love during his 1945 travels in the Mediterranean (she is disguised as G. in *Europe Without
Baedeker*). He had proposed marriage, but she had
married Arthur Koestler. Still loving her rather wistfully,
he caused Elena some pangs of jealousy, and he mourned
Mamaine when she died suddenly shortly afterwards.
After his painful visits to Johannisberg near Frankfurt

he enjoyed talks in Paris with André Malraux, whom he
had met during the forties. Then he left for his adventures in Israel and his quest for the Dead Sea Scrolls.

On returning to America he wondered why he enjoyed his stay in Europe so much. He had found cities
that were "attractively built" and devoid of American
vulgarities. He thought the Europeans had "good and
quiet manners." He liked the appetizing food and the
universal respect for the arts, and in Paris "the feminine
chic." He discovered that he had some sympathy with
the expatriates who had called themselves "exiles" and
figures like Henry James and his generation who had
chosen to live in Europe. And he asked himself whether
his old hostility hadn't been "unconsciously" his "determination to make something of America." This he
speculated "must have biased me against what was really
good in Europe." When I chided him for his animus
against the British, he replied, "I have a certain anti-
British tradition behind me" and I thought of those
engravings of George Washington he had described at
the Stone House.

At the heart of Wilson's 1950s was his book *The Scrolls
from the Dead Sea.* The most exciting part of his 1954
journey abroad had been his visit to the newly constituted State of Israel to pursue the mysterious scrolls and
write about them on assignment for *The New Yorker.*

The origins of this quest are a part of my memories of
Wilson's sojourn in Princeton during 1952–53. We
walked daily together and one day we came to the
Theological Seminary. I offered my scrap of historical
knowledge that Henry James's father had once studied
here. "I'm studying here now," said Wilson. I was about
to make some remark about my trying to see Wilson in
a clerical collar when he added, "I'm studying Hebrew."

He then told me how, after his mother's death, he had found in her house in New Jersey his Kimball grand-father's Hebrew Bible. Looking at the thick square letters crossing the page from right to left, he had a feeling of being at a great disadvantage. His grandfather had *really* read the Bible, had known the original Genesis. Edmund had a rich store of languages from his early years: his Latin and Greek begun at the Hill School; the French he had spoken fluently and improved during 1918 in France; his adequate Italian, sufficient to read Dante; the Russian acquired in the thirties. Hebrew was foreign to him; and he decided to get its rudiments this winter while giving the Gauss seminar at Princeton. He was in a class of fresh young lads, who brushed their hair, wore sedate neckties and turned-down collars, said prayers, and looked forward to their preaching careers. Edmund cor-ralled me in Nassau Street a few days later. "Lé-on," he said (he was always careful about accents), "I am giving tea to my classmates, the little theologians, and their Hebrew instructor, today. Will you come?" When I asked what I could add to his little class he explained, "They're nice boys but they're teetotalers. They'll be drinking tea. Do me a favor, come to tea and I'll pour you a whisky; then it'll seem quite natural for me to pour some into my glass." I wondered at so much Victorian courtesy for a bunch of modern young re-ligionaries and I murmured something about "Edmund, you are using me!" But I was willing enough to help him out with his late-afternoon thirst and I was curious about his Hebrew studies. The occasion proved charming. The intimate circle of neat, washed and scrubbed youths, encircling Edmund and the instructor, the plentiful cups of tea and cake, and the two glasses waiting on the side before a bottle of whisky. Glass in hand, Edmund fired question after question, about the absence of vowels, the need for gutturals, the packed-in nuances, as if he were at a Jewish parochial school in the basement or ante-chamber of some synagogue. Recalling Edmund's delight in Max Beerbohm's cartoons, I suggested afterwards that Max could do a drawing in the manner of his picture of Robert Browning taking tea with the Browning Society. The caption might be: "Mr. Edmund Wilson learning to read Genesis."

He worked hard at his Hebrew and learned it rapidly, for languages were a passion with him; and in his foraging in various books and his talks with Hebrew scholars he soon learned that there was much excitement about some scrolls found in caves near the Dead Sea in the late forties. But when he made further inquiries he encountered evasion and an absence of detail, and he smelled controversy and anxieties among both the Christians and the Jews. This seemed strange—the discovery of documents preserved for thousands of years was being somehow soft-pedaled. A fire was suddenly lit in Edmund's mind and he had no wish to subdue the blaze. The scrappy but interesting jottings in the daily diaries of his trip tell of soundings, encounters, and the illuminations of the biblical landscapes. He became convinced that neither the Greek nor the King James version did justice to what the Old Testament said, and that there had been much Christian coloring in the translations. The scrolls seemed to offer light on the Essenes, two centuries before Christ. Out of this journey came one of Edmund's most characteristic and fascinating books. Indeed one of his informants (David Flusser) called it "a book which is, from many aspects, a turning-point in the research of the history of religions."

Wilson's imaginative boldness, his ability to summarize complex scholarship, and his skill in cutting across pedantries and shibboleths have nowhere received greater praise than in the remarks of the late General Yigael Yadin, the Israeli archaeologist, who pointed out that the precious scrolls became known through outsiders: roving Bedouins, not archaeologists, found them and they were "brought to the knowledge of the world at large, again not by archaeologists, but by a very scholarly amateur, Edmund Wilson." He had sensed early that the scrolls threw light on the birth and beginnings of Christianity. Reading him, it is not difficult to imagine the ardor with which Wilson pursued his dramatic subject; it was the kind of subject he had always liked best. The notes here printed reveal this ardor, and the history, politics, and ancient lore to which he brought his enormous faculties for imaginative reconstruction and analysis. Scholars had been shy to jump at conclusions and Edmund did not hesitate to discover reasons for their equivocation. In this he had an important influence—as Yadin put it, "he was trying to define the views of some scholars perhaps more boldly than they themselves dared."

In the midst of his work on the Dead Sea Scrolls and his Civil War book, Edmund found still another project. He had always a strong interest in the American Indians —one remembers his fascinating account of the Zuñi in his earlier writings. In Talcottville he was so wrapped up in the earlier life and manners of his ancestors that it came to him as a distinct surprise to discover he was within motoring distance of the Iroquois in northern New York. "I am surrounded at Talcottville," he wrote to Van Wyck Brooks, "by an Iroquois national move- ment—not unlike Scottish nationalism and Zionism— with a revival of the old religion and claims for territory of their own." His fifties journals describe the stages by which he gained access to the Indians, attended their ceremonial rituals, and wrote his vivid *Apologies to the Iroquois*, which was serialized in *The New Yorker* before appearing as a book. The notes here given, on which he drew considerably, are vivid and detailed and convey to us, often poignantly, within their factual content, the sad and long struggle of the upstate Indians for their place in American life. It was perhaps a measure of Wilson's zeal and skill of inquiry—and his capacity for entering into his subjects with fresh enthusiasm—that he made these journal entries during a period when he was beset by painful gout and high blood pressure. And yet he pushed on, refusing as usual to allow physical weakness to interfere with the task he set for himself.

The gout and blood pressure were brought under control, but Wilson's occasional excesses were the habits of a lifetime. He knew he could no longer live at his old pace: still he rebelled at inaction and often ate and drank more than his body could handle. I saw him a number of times in his gouty condition in New York. One evening he arrived at my apartment leaning heavily on his cane and obviously having frequent twinges. I had to leave the room for a moment, and when I came back he was standing on a chair reaching for my top shelves—his searching eye had glimpsed an unfamiliar book. Curiosity got the better of his pain. He brought the volume down with an air of triumph and a low "ouch!"

The end of the decade found him ready for another venture into academe—however reluctant. The Lowell seminars at Harvard offered a substantial sum that he could not resist. Twelve years remained during which he would complete his Civil War book and publish five other volumes. But now in Hilliard Street in Cambridge, among Harvard friends and students, he was face to face with his aging. That encounter would be the struggle of his 1960s, a time in which he demonstrated again and again how strong the creative urge and the drive to action can be—in spite of the defeats of the body. Edmund, to the end, was determined somehow to get to the top shelves, to discover the remotest work.

LEON EDEL

CHRONOLOGY
The Fifties

1950   Publishes *Classics and Commercials*. March–April in New York. Visits old family house at Talcott-ville in upstate New York. Death of Edna Millay.

1951   Death of EW's mother and of Dean Christian Gauss. Inherits the Talcottville house. Winter and early spring in New York.

1952   Publishes selected and revised critical pieces, *The Shores of Light*. Completes removal of his mother's effects from Red Bank, N.J., and spends winter in New York. Summer at Wellfleet. Late in year gives Christian Gauss memorial seminar at Princeton.

1953   Spring visit to Charlottesville. Summer in Well-fleet and Talcottville, where he begins restoration and renovation of the Wilson family Stone House.

1954   In Europe, first in London, where he meets new generation of writers; then Paris. Lectures at

Salzburg seminar in American studies, and visits Elena Wilson's family near Frankfurt. Goes to Israel to research Dead Sea Scrolls, then again to Paris. Late spring in Wellfleet and summer at Talcottville doing "prodigies of work." *The Scrolls from the Dead Sea* appears in *The New Yorker*. *Five Plays* published.

1955   *Scrolls* published as book. Summer in Talcottville. Completes his "reflections at sixty."

1956   Publishes *Red, Black, Blond and Olive* and *A Piece of My Mind*. Attempts to settle income tax penalties with I.R.S. Summer in Europe, visiting Paris, Munich, and then Paris again, recognizing for first time the effect of Europe as a "more gracious civilization." Autumn in Wellfleet.

1957   Winter in Cambridge, Mass. Summer in Wellfleet and Talcottville. Begins visits to upstate Iroquois reservations.

1958   Revises *The American Earthquake*, his book on the 1930s. Devotes summer to Iroquois series.

1959   *Apologies to the Iroquois* published in *The New Yorker*. Summer in Wellfleet and Talcottville. Accepts Lowell lectureship for 1959–60 at Harvard and begins assembling his book on American Civil War writings—on which he has worked since 1948.

1950–1954

"NOTHING BUT DEATHS," 1950–1952

June 8, '50. Walk to Wellfleet just before dinner, stimulated by miscellaneous drinks. This walk, which had come to bore me so that I could hardly face it, seemed suddenly full of beauties: our three or four poppies, which I hadn't seen this spring; the sun was sagging like a great red pie-cherry above the dry mauve of the marshes; the little green and pale blue butterfly blinds on the third stories of the bigger houses; new-painted house in the town (many houses seemed to have been new-painted) a pretty pale blue with white; Ellery Newcomb's big white horse with the wild cape field stretching to the wooded dune hills behind him; George Williams complaining that the new road, in circum-venting the town, took the motorists past so that they did not know there was a liquor store in Truro and were soon confronted with the North Truro one; gray trunk of big old half-dead elm, with leaves in spare tufts, by the old unpainted house that belongs to somebody queer who doesn't live here and refuses to sell or rent it; another tree all mossy with little leaves; the unpleasant

3

people who kept their red cocker a solitary captive,
rushing out with brooms, as Elena said, like witches, to
beat off our dogs when we came by at a time when they
were letting her out for a brief and severely supervised
airing—black-haired people, the man dark, the woman
pale; the stray dwindled pinks (and other pink and
white flowers), a garden as if in caps sprinkled on the
bank by Carl Gross—there are the remnants of some
garden in that meadow-swamp, disregarded, like the
dead unburied skunk by the roadside, and like the old
telephone pole left leaning askew in the half-filled-in
swamp opposite our house.

Trip to Talcottville, June 16–18, 1950.[1] New Hampshire with its schools and dense trees: ponds, big dark
pines, twilight bats and birds, sober old red brick buildings and vesper service at St. Paul's, quietude upholstered
by shrubbery, distinguished and kept up to a certain
standard (the school) but rather uninteresting—there is
a St. Paul's type: quiet, well-bred, slightly stooping and
tanned (doctor or lawyer, serious), sun-reddened and
breathing drinks (businessmen), conviction of superiority
without, necessarily, much serious substance, Kittredge's
dry vein: Harvard accent superimposed on Barnstable,
boy soprano, little golden-haired girlish type (not the
soprano); Andover, Newport, Sunapee.
    —Vermont: green hills crowded close together, furred
as thickly as caterpillars or chestnut burrs—primitive—
crass little towns, almost no attempt to make a show for
tourists, maple-syrup signs, degenerate people up in
hills—
    —After this, New York State opens out: wide cow
pastures, with their stone fences, first glimpse of the
Adirondacks, quite different from the Green Mountains,

more mysterious, grander, more interesting. —Then Glen
Falls, big town full of factories, area of cheap modern
houses and general cheapness and tarnishment; tacky
lower end of Lake George, steamboat waiting for an
excursion, big restaurant-bar, with Italian-looking barmen
and Polish-looking waitress, hard and crass little street
of stores. —But after this, the Adirondacks: blue range
behind blue range, with sharp broken ridges, not furred
—spaces, opening-away non-New England horizons (not
cramped); road through the North Wind, a few camps
and places to stay, but miles through the woods and the
lakes, without passing a car or even seeing a human
habitation (dwelling): Raquette Lake, Blue Mountain
Lake, the early stage of the Hudson, still a shallow river
with gray stones that runs beside the road for a time
(Hudson Falls), Bad Luck Pond, Death Creek, Blue
Mountain Lake—

—At last you emerge into the country of Oneida and
Lewis Counties—it was misty, just at sundown, and
beautiful, the mist lying along the green silky fields,
the green silky elms rising dimmed, the blurred orange
light in the sky (the next day, clear, liquid and bright—
white and yellow and orange)—it always gives rise in
me to a kind of noble thought: dignity and beauty of
the country which somehow has ennobled the lives of
the people and all that old story of their immigration
and living, away from New England, among the hills
and the fields, where they were all alone, but independent and free, flourishing—their human relationships and
labors against the non-human grandeur of that setting—
riding along those up- and downhill roads, a man behind
a horse in a buggy, a farm wagon or carriage, under the
high heavens with fluid orange light or dark blue
thunder clouds.

—Otis:[2] only person left who represented the original upstate race; came in from the movies with open-throated white shirt and no tie—broad farmer with big stomach, but not fat—brawny; self-assurance; ease in authority—looked well in his good clothes—brown suit and tie—when we went there to lunch next day. Bare farmer's living room, tidies on backs of chairs, deer heads in dining room shot by Otis and Thad [his father]—two large trout caught by Thad "on successive casts," painted by Doig.[3] Fern brought out picture of hers made by her father for her—caught in Lost Lake. Her father had had a cheese factory. He had had all the animals he shot stuffed. When he died, they had put them in the attic—there they had lost their luster, and she decided to burn them up, but the wildcat for some reason didn't burn, so the boys put it up on the stone fence—four or five neighbors came and shot it. —The old graveyard on the hill that was not cared for any longer—the church was gone, burned down?—covered with wild roses and devil's paintbrush, a chipmunk, reddish brown and black-striped, on one of the tombstones—the Reuel Kimballs[4] with their Saras and Cleanthes clustering around their family obelisk in the foreground or at the back, half in the woods, Hezekiah Talcott leaning askew, and the Augurs.[5] Not enough people related to these families to raise money to get the graveyard cleaned up. In the Talcott-ville graveyard it was noted that one of the Munns had been cremated.

—Along Sugar River on the way to Flat Rock, forget-me-nots, big white anemones, big purple columbine, an almost bearish-looking woodchuck living in a hole among the stones.

—Return: You lose the glamorous country as you come down on Utica—Mohawk Valley has its grandeur, but is partly industrialized, big chewing-gum plant at

Canajoharie, deer crossing and falling rocks carefully announced—the Berkshires loom: green clotting or inspiration of the rich fields and large trees—Pittsfield, Lenox—the suburban environs of Boston: undecorativeness, lack of taste.

L'Engles:[6] By the late forties, Brownie was not any longer a slightly formidable character possessing a certain prestige. The disagreeable things she said were taken as a matter of course, as unfailing and now almost as monotonous as physical reflex reactions. Her sharpness never failed but it was fading out. At the Seldeses'[7] wedding anniversary party, she was obviously disappointed that there had been nothing serious the matter with my throat; and to Elena, in connection with Henry,[8] she said that there was a professor from MIT who came up here in the summer, but added quickly and with gratification that this summer he had gone to Mexico. Told Elena that they were the only people there who knew French and wanted her to listen to her old French songs (had lately learned to play the guitar—during the last winter had addressed herself to abstract painting)— she finally captured the Biddle boy and Elena saw her on the outskirts of the party giving him the whole program. (Concerts with George Biddle's flute.)

—Old stories: walking into the Dos Passoses' South Truro house while Dos was taking a nap upstairs: Why, this isn't as bad as people say! —To Nina, during the war, when David had been sent to Alaska: What, Alaska in the winter! —Nina said he was not going there to find a winter resort. (Attitude of Paul[9] to Brownie's guitar; made fun of her and perhaps a certain rivalry involved.) —Party many years ago at which Niles Spencer[10] had kept telling her that there was something he wanted to say to her—she was very eager to hear and when nearly everyone had gone she insisted that he could no longer refuse: Brownie, you're a son of a bitch!

Artur Schnabel,[11] out of piety to Beethoven, playing something that seemed wrong in one of his sonatas, though other pianists had accepted a correction that seemed obvious. Eventually he found out that it was an old misprint in the music.

Labor Day '50. The black and wrought-iron lace strength and distinctness of our little tree beside the drive, standing up against the still-bright but long-fading buff and beige and soft gray of the first September sky.

October 19, '50. Our buildings and trees and garden, in the dim pink and gray of the sky, as I came out of the Gull Pond Road, looked like mushrooms and bushes and grass lodged on the humps of the dunes—mist in the pinkish swamp, pinkish but dull as ash.

Phito:[12] Rosalind's[13] difficulties in Boston when he came to see Houghton Mifflin. He had, as usual, over-prepared with drinks. When she tried to explain that Stanley Hillyer had not been able to come, because he had to get injections and be vaccinated—demonstrating with gestures—he thought she meant he was having himself tattooed and said, "I shouldn't like that," etc.

Laura [Kimball] marries. When she got married to Jack Johnson, she had Gilbert and Sullivan played on the organ.

Picnic with Elena at pond near Spiegels', October 21, '50. Little pond in the low woods in the serene mid-October noon—the sand of the little margin that com-

bined a mild and self-contained and salt-white coziness
with the bareness of the outer beach—the leather-red
and lemon-yellow of the small underbrush bushes below
the permanent green of the scrub pines—the reddened
sprigs of tiny plants among the faded grass of the shore—
and the pond, the secluded and quiet pond, with its
dark but not deep shadow, its modestly shimmering
mackerel blue. —Everybody is gone, the sand is heaped
firm but the sea is quiet—here is peace, dry but not
bleak—beneath a blue uniform cloudless sky. —The
shadow in the pond deepens and advances on the further
side of the pond (from the one on which we have been
picnicking, sitting on the log raft), and the sun seems
to concentrate its heat on our side—Elena dozes on the
ground—it seems warmer. I walk all the way around—
it's a comfort to feel that you can—on the narrow white
grass-patched margin. —The black ooze on one end with
its faintly rank smell only sets off the dry white with its
thin delicate grass. —A little lake like a hidden kidney.
—Looking up behind us, one saw the higher pines, with
their rounded cluster-formations and their phallic though
furry tufts, that looked relatively lofty and noble—a few
dried and whitening-gray fallen writhen small limbs
lying on the shore. —A bird or two passed above—an
unseen airplane hummed. —The spare little lines of the
grass that follow the wavering shore. —As the shadow
of the opposite shore extended further across the pond,
it ceased to show deep black, it reflected the trees above
it more and more distinctly, at last painting them mirror-
wise—the water pulsed with a tiny slow ripple—the red
foliage of the low bushes rich but fading autumnal rose
—the molten silver sun has dropped just above the trees
to the left—the tiny ripples are brisker—a bird throbbed
a cry.

When I came back from my walk, Elena had opened

her eyes, and we made love on the sand. I gave her my
old hat as a pillow. Divine—I had had (the new and
better kind of white wine) just enough to drink—no
anesthetizing of sensation in the last moments for me,
as I felt myself driving the charge home.

When we left the pond to go up through the wood,
looking back, we saw the golden and lemon little leaves
almost luminous with the light behind them and the
lake, as if suddenly, dead dark.

Edna's death. [Marginal note: She died about dawn,
October 19, Thursday.][14] I heard that night at the
Waldo Franks',[15] where Katherine Biddle[16] spoke of it,
that the news of Edna Millay's death had been in the
paper the day before. —I have been thinking today
(Sunday the 22nd) of how I first came up here to see
her in Truro and of how my living here was perhaps
due to that visit—though the second time I came, it
was with Mary to Provincetown—partly to see the
O'Neills? Edna's fear and defiance of death in her early
poems—why? New England origin? long-delayed sex
life? She was very neurotic—her fear of crossing streets
alone in N.Y.—but how or why? How little I know
about her. —Strange to think of her going on alone at
Austerlitz, working over her poems, after Gene's death:
nothing more for her in life, it was time to die. —The
night before I heard the news, I had had a long dream
about her—partly erotic, she was in bed and at one point
I was expecting to make love to her—but partly literary,
for I told her at length, and as accurately and fully as
if I had been awake, about John Bishop's relations with
Archie MacLeish:[17] first MacL's lunch in Paris with
Galantière[18] and his saying, when told about Eliot, I'm
glad to know who I have to compete with, then John's
instructing him in Paris—the mushy letters he wrote

John full of maudlin admiration and gratitude, their later estrangement and Archie's finally sending John his own letters back—I thought you might like to have these, the suggestion evidently being that John should send Archie's back—which, however, he did not do. [Marginal note: I had been reading Sartre's *Baudelaire* in bed; and this probably gave rise to the dream.] I think that I thought, in my dream, that it would gratify her, perhaps console her for the neglect with which she had lately been treated, to hear MacLeish exposed—or I may have wanted in my sleep an audience for my literary gossip and someone from old times to talk to. Certainly I had had it on my conscience that I hadn't written to her about Gene's death[19]—I had since been several times almost at the point of writing—when, for example, I read her and George Dillon's[20] translation of Baudelaire early last summer—but had been kept from doing so by the thought she cared nothing about hearing from me, took years to answer if she answered at all, and that the summer before she had refused to see us. But I suppose she has been in very bad shape. (I gather from the *Tribune* editorial that she died during the day. No: story in Friday's paper said that the lights were burning— she was not found for six or eight hours.) —Now I can hardly believe that it is irrevocably impossible to write to her—that she is not there, cannot be communicated with, if I should feel like trying to do so. I had no feeling, as I did with Scott and John, that what I wrote was written for her, as she never read anything of mine, but losing her makes John's absence more complete, as well as cutting off her poetry, which I hoped was reviving after its lapse, and removing her dedicated and noble presence, which was still to be felt in my world. —When we saw them three summers ago, they were both to be dead in a little more than two years' time. —I suppose I feel at the same time a certain satisfaction in surviving her: if I did so much less when I was young than she, I still have the chance to do something good in my own different way.

—Death had already come for them when we saw them summer before last: the faded room, their aging— had given up trying to see people or to live up to much of anything in relation to the rest of the world—her last and desperate attempt to tear herself away from the darkness and realize herself as a poet again (the only way in which she could, perhaps, have ever really been able to). What we had felt was the end, the end that was already there. I had found it hard to imagine that life and then, after Gene's death, to understand her living there alone and to imagine what her future was to be. Of course, there was none.

L'Engles: Conversation about the L'Engles with the Chavchavadzes: they said that Bill was terribly selfish, had never given either of his daughters a single present in their whole lives. I said I thought he had never had a penny, Brownie dispensed the money, didn't she? No! They had found out from his sister that he had always had from their family the same modest income that she had—it was not true that Brownie was stingy, she was actually very generous (I had never seen any evidence of this, her entertaining was anything but lavish—Niles Spencer used to say that she did not give Bill enough to eat).

Mother's death: February 3, 1951. About ten days before, she had done what she was not supposed to do: gotten up at night and gone to the bathroom alone, had fallen and broken her right arm. She did not suffer much from this, but she simply faded out—was already almost blind again—when I was there, did not recognize people and was sometimes confused about what was going on. Later, they say, she cleared up. The morning of her death, she had asked Rosalind about her beaux: "A lot of writers, I suppose. Don't marry one or you'll never have any money!" Rosalind had told her—everything now had to be written out very clearly—about the child that Peggy Hill had adopted. Mother said that she would soon be adopting another one. Rosalind explained that she had no such intention. Mother insisted that people who adopted one child always adopted two. A little later, Peggy arrived and told Rosalind that they were thinking of adopting another child. In the afternoon, she had been having coffee with Rosalind and the nurse, had been joking with them—they had propped her up—then she lay back and died: 4:45. —Elena, Esther, Susan, Charlotte, Margaret, Jenny,[21] Gerda, and William were present at the funeral. Though her face showed the wear and tear of the illness of the last year and her nose and chin seemed sharpened and pulled toward one another as her mouth had shrunk, she had returned, as dead people do, to an earlier, less aged phase: Elena remarked on her noble brow and straight fine little nose. The flabbiness of the last year was gone, and her pale face no longer seemed discolored. Extreme old age is a humiliation, and one felt that she was asserting her dignity: the determination, pride, and rectitude, the fortitude in adversity, the endurance through dissatisfaction, that had sustained her through her whole life. Strange to think that the mold of her features had been printed by those of my grandparents, born in 1828 and 1833 respectively, and that she had been born in 1865, just after the Civil War, had grown up in its aftermath. —Jenny, when she came to say goodbye to her, put her

cheek against that of Mother's and afterwards gave her
the Catholic sign of the cross. She said that she had lost
her "old sidekick," and when I went back at the end
of that week, she told me, though now quite unhysteri-
cal, that she couldn't get over Mother's death and would
never get over it as long as she lived. She had come to
Mother when she was sixteen, had been with her as
long as I could remember.

May 6, '51. Jenny in the hospital: She said that, before
she had come there, she had had a dream in which she
thought she was going into a hospital that was still being
built, and that she was received by nuns all in white
and that inside, on "a big slab" with a table, she found
Mother, also in white, and she said to her, "What are
you doing laying there? You'll catch your death of cold!"
Then she woke up. I said that it must have been heaven.
She said that, whatever it was, it was a funny thing—
because soon she had moved into Riverview, which was
also being built.

She told Rosalind the same story: "She says before
she went to the hospital, she had a recurrent dream in
which she entered a large room, where lots of nuns and
workmen were moving around. In the middle was
Grandma, lying on an altar. All the nuns tried to keep
Jenny from her; but she got past them and said to
Grandmother, who was alive in the dream and wearing
only a thin bathrobe, 'Do you want to catch your death
of cold?' and then she would wake up."

The night before her operation the priest came and
wanted to give her communion, but that would involve
confession, and she didn't want to bother with that—she
said that she "didn't feel sinful." I told her that she

hadn't committed any sins, and she said that even if you
hadn't they expected you to make some up. She refused
the sacrament. —She told me afterwards, though, that at
some point she had had it.

After the operation, when she was getting well, she
became extremely impatient (Monday morning, May 21)
because the doctor had told her he "wanted some action,"
wanted her to do a little walking and the hospital hadn't
provided crutches—she made one of her Irish scenes,
with an eloquent Irish oration, which always went right
on, if they hadn't attained their climax, when the problem had been disposed: This is my leg! This is my life!
—and this is my torture! The nurse said, You just want
to feel sorry for yourself.

Margaret Rullman—dinner with bluefish May 21
(Elena said the house smelt fetid—I couldn't make out
why it did: medical office and food and tropical bird
and little black dog and old stuffy things from her
mother's and aunts' and grandmothers' houses?):
    —It had been said of Adeline[22] by some man in town
that she had given away a million dollars' worth of it
before she knew it was for sale.
    —The people in Denver were crazy for culture—they
had the Metropolitan opera in an old miners' theater,
with the original names on the backs of the seats. —Some
woman out there had complained that all the rampage
had gone out of the people.

Jenny told Elena a story about Mother in her late
years: they had been driving in the car. Mother had seen
somebody either outside or through a window of a house
near the road apparently beating some animal. She
stopped the car, got out, and hobbled up to him, brand-

ishing her cane. He turned out to be beating his wife. He stopped, but Mother was so exhausted that she collapsed, and they had to give her a drink.

Gauss's death:[23] *November 3, '51.* Going over to Princeton for his funeral was somewhat less depressing than I had expected. Alice was up in her room, but when one of the girls took me to see her, she told me how Christian had just finished writing an introduction to Machiavelli's *Prince* and had been pleased with it, had felt that he still had something to say. They had gone out for a drive and talked about their trip to Florida. The next day he had gone up to town, had been very cheerful and joking at the publishers, then had gone to the memorial meeting for Hermann Broch (John Berryman[24] told me afterwards, however, that he had wept at this meeting and asked for a glass of water). He had fallen dead outside the gates (I gather) while waiting for the Princeton train in the Penn Station. But Alice had evidently been terribly shaken and sometimes had difficulty in making connections with the girls and the people who came in to see her. —The funeral in the Chapel, evidently at Alice's request—since they were neither of them believing Christians—was conventional, simple, and brief: Love suffereth long and is kind; 23rd Psalm; prayer by retired Dean Wicks, which I thought rather perfunctory and lacking in much feeling for Christian's qualities. Afterwards, the Gauss house on Bayard Lane—with Alice in a green dress (downstairs), making sure that people were getting highballs, and the children and their husbands and wives and children and Christian's relatives and Mrs. Duane Stuart (telling Elena that she hesitated to say it but she couldn't bear Taft) seemed strangely the same as ever. As Elena said, he was still there—they were all there on account of him. The same old sets of French writers and the poster of the Théâtre de la Renaissance (giving *Lorenzaccio*),[25] just as they used to be, before the dean's home, when they lived so quietly and modestly at the other end of town. I felt that a good deal had come and gone, and that they had remained the same and continued to represent the things they had set out to represent. I appreciated particularly today Alice's innocent and faithful spirit, still, pale and aged and shaken though she was, looking out through her glasses so limpidly and brightly, at once shyly and shrewdly and with something almost girlish about it. Their refusal to subscribe to a creed had been a part of the role they had chosen as advanced young people of the nineties, and, in their official position, they had not abandoned it, nor their dislike of the gloominess of funerals. The official element, in fact, seemed to have been so much discouraged that—at least while we were there—few officials (I did not see the president) came to the house; and I was touched to feel that they had naturally reverted to their old position—being a little at odds with the official point of view—as when Christian had gone around in a shabby old coat with a shabby dog named Baudelaire and had made fun of the English Department.

Nothing but deaths through here.

Visit to Sandy,[26] *April 27, 1952.* Wasn't sure I recognized him at first as he sat in front of the television, slumped down, aged and so sunk in depression, in his old farm worker's clothes, with a red checked cap askew on his head and his underlip protruding and horribly swollen. He was thin, and his nose seemed larger and

more salient—hairs were beginning to grow out of it—
so that he looked like his grandmother Knox. When
I said I was Edmund, he said No; when I repeated it,
he said No again. Then when I sat down beside him, he
said, half turning with a smile and his old charm, It's
nice of you to come to see me. —When I would ask him
a question about the family or something, it would
stimulate him for the moment to make a connection with
reality, and he would answer with a quickness (though
in a very low voice) and a grasp of the past that surprised me: he hadn't seen Esther lately, hadn't heard
about her remarriage; said that his mother was dead; I
told him about Mother's death, asked him whether he
remembered Jenny—Of course I do. I said that Father's
family had come from around there; Yes, I went to New-
burgh one day—mumbled something about his grandfather. His grandfather had come from Knoxville, hadn't
he? Oh, no! that's in Tennessee—Knoxboro. —The radio
was "perfectly wonderful." Told me obscurely about
some work he had done there, selling 25¢ books; worked
a little on the farm, otherwise just hung around. —I sat
beside him mostly silent, only occasionally stimulating
him with a question or a remark. [Marginal note: Did
he remember Dorothy Furbish?[27] Yes: what's become of
her? Married to a professor in Chicago! Does she live
out there?] He would mumble to himself. The moments
of making sense didn't last for more than a few seconds
—the rest of the time he was talking out of his schizo-
phrenic dream, like somebody talking in his sleep.
[Marginal note: Had a book by Clemence Dane[28] in
his lap, which he said was about the stage.] Almost
everything he said was introduced by Do you know what
I think? —It's fun not to be sane. Do you think it's nice
to be young? —The man-eating shark and the shark-
eating man. —There was something he kept reverting

to: he seemed to have a delusion that his father and
mother had been Jews. What did I think of (or perhaps
did I like) motherhood? —All of this, however, was not
unlike what had gone in his mind when he was sane,
musings and fancies to which he had occasionally given
a kind of involuntary expression. —When I asked him
the second time about his lower lip, he muttered (as I
thought), Use your common sense. The attendant said
it was due to smoking. It's terrible—he burns his fingers.
(Not allowed to light matches, so they had to light
cigarettes for him.) From time to time, his old smile and
characteristic little giggle as he said something, half
turning away. When I told him that Raymond Holden[29]
had just been married for the 4th time, he said, That's too
much for me! —One of the dim mad old men, sitting
behind us, would occasionally laugh out to himself,
toward the end of the conversation. Another, while Elena
and Henry were waiting, made a speech to them from
the window: They take away our clothes and everything
in our pockets, etc. —One who drove me to the farm
pleasant—helpful; man of farm, polite, but with hard
blue eyes; Irish male nurse when I returned to main
office, very stupid and surly. Hard-boiledness and sullenness of the guards in these places. Horrible that human
beings should be kept alive in these conditions—and it is
bad for sane people to have to spend their lives taking
care of lunatics. Asylum scandals: not unnatural that
nurses should sometimes be brutal. Looking after lunatics
is largely hopeless work. The schizophrenics and similar
incurable cases should be chloroformed after enough
time has elapsed to establish their hopeless condition. —I
felt very depressed and wanted to weep as I was walking
away: all his sensitiveness and attractiveness as a child;
our relation had been a little reserved as I sat beside him;
naturalness of his responses—good breeding underneath

his rough clothes and dilapidated distorted appearance; to some degree the natural gruffish development of his earlier manner in his youth; naturalness of his responses to me; one of my relatives to whom I was closest; except him, I have none left, and I felt it filled a gap and a need in my life to see him even in this condition. —Esther had stopped going to see him, because the presence of a woman upset him, and he had sometimes, she said, attacked her. He said that she had come to see him at Christmas, but this, she told me, wasn't true. She has, in I think a more callous and less graceful way, her mother's way of making a sort of well-bred duty— which they deplore and make you accept on reasonable and even human grounds—of not seeing, not doing things for people who, from illnesses or misfortune or inferior breeding, happened to be inconvenient to them. My mother never did this: she would soundly denounce as bores friends and relatives whom she found a nuisance, but she never let them down or neglected them.

NOTES

1. See *Upstate* (1971), pp. 76–79.
2. Otis and Fern Munn, Talcottville cousins of EW. *Upstate, passim.*
3. Doig, "Boonville portraitist of fish," *Upstate,* p. 78.
4. Reuel Kimball (1778–1847), EW's great-great-grandfather, a Presbyterian minister. *Upstate,* pp. 15–17.
5. Hezekiah Talcott bought and settled (1798) sixteen hundred acres in upstate New York and founded Talcottville; *Upstate,* pp. 47–48. The Augurs, Talcottville relations of EW.
6. William and Lucy (Brownie) L'Engle, watercolorists and Provincetown neighbors of Dos Passos.
7. Gilbert Seldes, author, editor, and playwright. *The Shores of Light,* pp. 156–74.
8. Henry Thornton, Elena's son by her former marriage.

9. Paul and Nina Chavchavadze, Russian friends of Elena and Wellfleet neighbors. *The Thirties* and *The Forties, passim.*

10. Niles Spencer (1882–1952), precisionist artist and industrial architect. *The Thirties, passim; The Forties,* p. 224.

11. Artur Schnabel (1882–1951), piano virtuoso and authoritative interpreter of Beethoven's piano works.

12. Philippe (Phito) Thoby-Marcelin, Haitian poet and novelist. *The Forties, passim.*

13. Rosalind Wilson (b. 1923), daughter of EW and the actress Mary Blair.

14. Edna St. Vincent Millay Boissevain (1892–1950). See earlier volumes in this series and EW's memoir, *The Shores of Light,* pp. 744–93.

15. Waldo Frank (1887–1967), American novelist, essayist, and biographer with special interest in Latin America. Lived near EW on the Cape.

16. Francis Biddle (1886–1968), U.S. Attorney General from 1941 to 1945, and Katherine Biddle (1891–1978), poet. *The Thirties,* pp. 396–97; *The Forties,* pp. 313–14.

17. The poets John Peale Bishop (1892–1944), a Princeton classmate of EW's, and Archibald MacLeish (1892–1982).

18. Lewis Galantière (1895–1977), American banker and man of letters, translator of Saint-Exupéry and the condensed Goncourt *Journals. The Thirties, passim.*

19. Eugene Boissevain, Edna St. Vincent Millay's husband.

20. George Dillon (1906–68), poet and editor of *Poetry* magazine. The translation of Baudelaire's *Flowers of Evil* appeared in 1936.

21. Esther C. Kimball, a first cousin of EW's on his mother's side; *A Prelude* (1967), p. 4. Susan Wilson, Charlottesville cousin of EW's; *The Thirties,* pp. 694–95; *The Forties,* p. 172. Margaret Rullman (née Edwards), friend of EW's early Red Bank years; *A Prelude,* pp. 2, 40. Jenny Corbett was Mrs. Wilson's maid for more than fifty years.

22. EW's Aunt Adeline Kimball. *A Prelude,* p. 34.

23. Christian Frederick Gauss (1878–1951), EW's Princeton mentor, dean of college, 1925–45. *The Shores of Light,* pp. 3–27.

24. Hermann Broch (1886–1951), Austrian novelist, philosopher, and playwright, author of *The Sleepwalkers;* lived at Princeton from 1938. John Berryman taught at Princeton intermittently from 1946 to 1952.

25. Alfred de Musset's play (1834) about the young Lorenzo de' Medici.

26. Reuel B. (Sandy) Kimball, EW's mentally ill first cousin. *A Prelude, passim.*

27. Dorothy Furbish, granddaughter of EW's cousin Grace Reed, married Malcolm Sharp, professor at the University of Chicago Law School. *Upstate*, pp. 55–56, 84.

28. Clemence Dane (1890–1965), pseudonym of Winifred Ashton, English novelist and playwright.

29. Raymond Peckham Holden (1894–1972), poet, novelist, and former husband of Louise Bogan. *The Thirties*, pp. 393–95; *The Forties, passim.*

CHARLOTTESVILLE, 1952

Visit to Charlottesville, May 1–5, '52.[1] Green softly-rolling fields setting off black cattle—ploughed fields of Indian red—one of them, further away, almost the red of rambler roses—a crease, a slit in a field—better, a crack—looked sometimes like prints of a lipstick, unhealthy spots where the grass looked rubbed away, exposing what looked like a sore spot. —Along the "Skyline" to Lexington, white dogwood all through the fields and woods—so many in one place that it looked as if the whole landscape had been lighted up with white. Shenandoah Valley—big soft green expanses and vistas, softly misty hills beyond; only a few abrupt hillocks like teeth; strange to think of those as scenes of the Civil War, Charlottesville secure behind its hills. A few sheep, a few small cabins, pink azaleas in the woods, red flowers, large violets, pansy-like: some light blue, some with the top petal dark purple; cardinal birds.

Monticello: Elena pointed out that Jefferson was not an original architect, had picked up a lot of things he liked and felicitously fitted them together. They did not always come out quite right: cornice that overlapped the

cornice of a door, railing on the outside that could not
go around the brick wall, so was prolonged by a flat
imitation railing, clock that had to be off center outside
over the front door in order to be centered inside, weights,
hung from the clock, that had to go through the floor,
so that Saturday and Sunday they come down below;
columns on the University "Lawn" that Elena counted—
and found that there were not the same number on
either side of the last house on the West—and the two
at the end were closer together than the others. [John]
Dos [Passos], who, with Betty, was with us, spoke of
Jefferson's "slightly finicky good taste." Jefferson's personal and magic touch. *Edgemont* typical: looks small
outside; inside beautiful, Jeffersonian gem, octagonal
room with vista in level green lawn behind that spread
out fanwise from the house proper, the lawn beyond
the fan on either side graded down; garden at the end
with, at left, little graveyard: one upright gray monument, old big gray flat tombstones; on one side a weeping willow. *People who have bought these houses:* They
had taken a good deal of pains with Edgemont, but a
few sour notes: the dark blue heavily flowered linoleum-
like (?) wallpaper in a downstairs bathroom, purple
flowered covers on the beds. —*Estutleville:* this was the
worst. The lady who had lived there, who, as Elena
said, looked as if she had just come from the Riviera:
sandals and a Doberman pinscher, had thought that it
didn't seem right to have the furniture (some of it
splendid: Queen Anne, etc.) all of differently colored
wood, so had had it painted uniformly and repulsive
ivory; miscellaneous collection of antique objects: Spanish, French, everything; cabinets painted white and
covered with supposed 16th-century scenes, like cheap
magazine illustrations. Library full of mostly second-rate
books, mostly with their paper jackets on; in one corner a

closed-off bar: you looked through a black wrought-iron grille and saw the rather second-rate drinking apparatus, messily left about: a bottle of Bellows; a collection of rosaries and crucifixes hung on the wall next to the little grilled window, and a black chain, for some reason not clear, ran from one of the crucifixes to the grille. In the kitchen, an enormous coat of arms of the owner, a large insipid lion painted white, had been installed in the wall; down below, on the kitchen table, a jar of stuffed olives with the top off—this kitchen was sloppy, too. —*Blenheim*: English Gothic, painted white, long low house, with ⌂ windows: lady who lived in it more comfortable and cheerful, middle-class family furnishings, everything more or less ugly in a not too offensive way, big dreary dull-maroon rugs, tasteless pictures. —She hastened to explain that she was no relation to the original people—lots of children and dogs and cats: we found a girl eating in a sort of breakfast room that adjoined the kitchen downstairs, with a white cat in a basket on a chair in the corner, surrounded by her kittens of mixed color—father had evidently been one of those common striped tomcats—the lady offered Susan [Wilson] one—by her accent, I should think, near-Middle Western. —*Morten*: We were politely received by the groom in his little house decorated with prints of horses, given leaflets, drank water in paper cups, saw garden (where a man pretended to be taking pictures, but was actually, I think, on watch to see that nobody stole the flowers), but were not admitted to house, into which, when I was there six years ago, Susan and I had more or less broken. I gathered that a certain awkwardness had arisen between Mrs. Stone, the daughter of Susan's uncle John B. of Richmond, and the Charlottesville Minors: she was the only one connected with the Northern invaders and privileged actually to live in a

Jeffersonian house. Whitney Stone was very rich and had a stud farm at Morten. It had been his mother who erected the garden and, I suppose, made the collections in the house. —*Castle Hill*, since I was there, had been sold, after the death of the old lady, by the nephew, who had also auctioned off the contents of the house (A. K. Davis of the University had bought up a lot of the books, absolutely, so far as I could see, without regard for their contents—since there were treatises in French on physics and chemistry and *la mécanique*, which had belonged to Amélie Rives's engineer father[2]). The towering box hedges had been trimmed, so that they no longer threatened to choke the drive, and the old place had been cleaned up. The house looked rather empty now; the thick atmosphere had been dispelled that had been created before by the sheltered or shaded rooms so full of the family's furniture, their portraits, their ornaments, their silver, their china, their many books, with the old lady dying upstairs and the Negro woman who showed us around. The story about Major Wheeler (?), who had come there for a change of mount on his way to warn Jefferson that the British were coming. The owner had received them when they came with the utmost geniality, given them an elaborate breakfast, including mint juleps, over which they had lingered long; they had measured against the doorjamb— the mark was still there—one of the soldiers, who, his officer boasted, was the tallest man in the British army.

The Farmington Country Club, with an enormous enlargement behind that involved an expansion of the downstairs bar, was becoming more and more like a hotel—Susan said that almost anybody could stay there— and did not make upon me the impression of brilliance that it had when I was there before. Rather than wait for dinner, the younger Venable [Minor] took us out to some other restaurant.

Poe's room at the University was now kept open, with a bar across the door. Someone had printed over the mantel, crookedly and crudely, the word NEVERMORE. Susan said that they had never thought about P.'s room down there—the students had simply lived in it—till the Northerners who came down began asking to see it. Typical of their casualness about their illustrious past— partly natural and attractive, partly a deliberate attitude assumed by their Virginian pride—though, also, un- consciously, an effort to get away from the past's great- ness, which embarrassed them nowadays and put them to shame.

Lyttleton Wickham, lawyer from Richmond—very cultivated, much sharper and more competent than any- body I have seen in Charlottesville—read the Greek and Latin classics, had composed (paraphrasing Cicero) the plaque in memory of Minor, and was anxious, I thought, to stump me, if possible—read French, ordering all his books from Blackwell's, apparently never went to New York—did not like Cabell's[3] work, thought he had met him once—was glad to learn from a book about Bever- idge[4] that B. had come to the conclusion that Lincoln had been wrong *about everything*, declared that L. had eaten with his knife; pointed out that, before the war, the people in Europe had felt that the South was closer to Europe than any other part of the country, more "aristocratic." I felt that he was rather embittered and limited by his Virginian role, a kind of thing that, even down there, must be harder and harder to sustain. He had got *Classics and Commercials* out of the library and had thought a good deal of the subject matter seemed rather thin. I mentioned Shakespeare, Joyce, Dr. John-

son. Yes, but a good many American writers. Davis had
said, When you can't bear him anymore, just let me
know. He talked about [Raleigh?] Minor[5]—I got a pathetic picture. Susan told Elena that his drinking had
really caused his death. Wickham compared him to
Sydney Smith[6]—not, I am sure, very happily—the only
person he had ever seen who could stand in front of the
fireplace and hold people for two hours, making them
laugh all the time. I got the impression that he felt
himself a little at odds with the community. He would
tell about old ladies shrinking from him, crying Eek!, on
account of some unconventionality; he would (Wickham
said) go to as much trouble not to wear evening clothes
as you and I would to wear them. He used to tell stories
on Hippo [his brother Venable] that would make him
absolutely furious. This clowning must have concealed
uncomfortableness. At one time he had nearly studied
for the Church—would have made a good preacher.
—He had not, aside from his education, had much support or inspiration from Father, in his latter years so
much in neurotic eclipse, and Father died before Minor
got out of law school. Wickham said that they thought
Minor was rather henpecked by his fatherless family of
mother and sisters. —Wickham had with him an elderly
and not very appetizing Mrs. Chichester that people
were speculating about his marrying—he had never yet
been married.

   —At dinner with the Minors, Venable at one end of
the table was telling Elena about the Levys'[7] buying and
reconstructing Monticello—V. in an invidious way:
nephew had had the servants address him as Mr. Jefferson (his first name being Jefferson)—while the hostess
or guide was telling me the same story—less invidiously—
at the other end. Susan told Elena afterwards that V.
was "steeped in all that"—but this, I fear, was far from

the case. Polly complained that "no distinction was made" among the throngs that came to see Monticello; guide said she approved of this: some of the most un-likely people took the most intelligent interest; the question that was asked most often was where he got the money to do all that.

Henry was wearing a blue-and-white tie with a Ⓥ on it. I asked him what this was, and he told me it was the insignia of the Vintage Car Club. I thought at first that this was a joke, but it turned out that it really existed. They get together and race and display their old cars to one another. Henry was privileged to belong by virtue of his 1934 Lincoln (black and boxlike, luxuri-ously roomy in back). Later he told his mother that he thought of exchanging it for a Cadillac, but that the C. was so old that he couldn't be certain of being able to get parts for it—and then there was another drawback: it had originally been a hearse.

May 10. Birthday resolutions for my 58th year:

> *New Yorker* articles.
> ~~Mario Praz~~
> ~~Little Dickens Preface~~
> from June 1 — ~~Gogol~~
>   ~~Chekhov~~
>   ~~Grant's Memoirs~~
>   Turgenev?
>   Edward Lear?
>   Owen Wister?
>
>   Frank Norris
>   The later T. R[oosevelt]

Read Lermontov and *Oblomov* and the rest of Pushkin
For Princeton — ~~Harriet Beecher Stowe~~
                        ~~Civil War Memoirs~~
                        ~~Bierce~~ and Lanier

Finish the two more elegiac poems by Christmas. [In time for spring 1954: Book containing Haiti, Zuñi, Russians, Edward Lear and Barham, and Genet.[9]] For book to be published January 1, 1953 [Wilson's *Night Thoughts*].[10]

May 19, 1952, Spectacle Ponds: In light May, a leaden shade, when the other ponds glowed blue.

Book on Siamese cats: The ones with slightly crossed eyes reminded me of *Larry Noyes*,[11] of whom I had lately been thinking.

May 23, '52. Helen saw a little white butterfly and went to look it up in her little insect book. She thought she had identified it in one of the pictures and read out to her mother an imaginary description, as she had heard me read from the bird book: "This beautiful little white butterfly flies through the air with the greatest of ease." When her mother went to put her to bed, she found her trying to look up a fly that was annoying her.

—In New York, she developed a tummy-ache one morning in a way that suggested she did not want to go to school. Later she ate a large candy, and when they said they thought she was sick, she answered, "That piece of candy was weeping to be eaten."

Nina on Balkan royalties: Iliana of Rumania carried around a box of Rumanian soil and always slept with it under her bed. The Greek ones, too. —I said that this was not unnatural: Greece had been a wonderful country. —Oh, it had nothing to do with the Acropolis! It was just the patriotism of Balkan royalties, who were more Greek than the Greeks, etc.

Elena, Helen, and Edmund Wilson, Wellfleet

John Biggs's visit to Honeyboy[12]—*Mayor* [Fitzgerald] *of Boston:* magnificent house; flunkeys in knee breeches in dining room. John said, What a fine pair of legs that man has! Honeyboy said, Hey, come over here!—pinched the man's silk-clad calves: See that? He's got two pairs on. John asked why two pairs. He's a hairy son of a bitch!

NOTES

1. EW regularly visited the Minors, relations on his father's side.

2. Castle Hill was for a time the home of Amélie Rives (Princess Troubetzkoy, 1863–1945), Virginia-born novelist. *The Forties,* p. 169.

3. James Branch Cabell (1879–1958), Virginia-born novelist best known for his originally banned *Jurgen.* See *The Bit Between My Teeth* (1967, hereafter referred to as *BBT*), pp. 291–316, and *Patriotic Gore* (1962), *passim.*

4. Albert Jeremiah Beveridge (1862–1927), author of *Abraham Lincoln, 1809–1858* (1928).

5. Raleigh Minor (1869–1923), professor of law at the University of Virginia.

6. Sydney Smith (1771–1845), philosopher and man of letters known for his exuberant drollery and conversational wit, one of the great letter writers of the period.

7. Uriah Phillips Levy acquired Monticello in 1834.

8. EW crossed out items on this list as he read them.

9. The essays on Haiti, Zuñi, and Russia appeared in *Red, Black, Blond and Olive* (1956); the essay on Canon Barham appeared posthumously in *The Devils and Canon Barham* (1973, hereafter referred to as *DCB*), pp. 77–91.

10. *Night Thoughts* (1953), a collection of EW's light verse.

11. Larry Noyes was EW's roommate at Hill School. *The Thirties,* pp. 341, 344–45.

12. John Biggs, Jr. (1895–1979), Princeton friend of EW and Scott Fitzgerald, later a federal judge in Wilmington; *The Forties, passim.* Honeyboy: John Francis Fitzgerald ("Honey Fitz," 1863–1950), John F. Kennedy's maternal grandfather, mayor of Boston (1906–07, 1910–14).

TALCOTTVILLE, 1952

Talcottville June 4, '52.[1] House faces eastward, and from about five in the morning, I saw from my bedroom window a tree silhouetted on the mist—that gave the effect of a photographic negative, but with the darks and the lights interchanged. Then the light came and, pouring in from behind on that night-wet world, seemed to drench everything: big green elms, a field of yellow mustard (?), beyond it a field of brown ploughed earth, the growth of foliage along the little river, the low blue hills in the distance: bracing and even exalting—rich and fresh and brilliant color of the landscape drenched with light (blazing with light).

—How live the little shallow river seemed.

—Trip from Talcottville to Wellfleet interesting, though it took us—going fast—six hours. At one end, fruity fragrance of the country in the clear bright air, at the other, salty smell of the sea in the dim damp fog. Larger houses of New York—more liberty and spontaneity. Berkshires intermediate (fine and fancy white church at Lee)—closed in and hot, the uncombed

32

mountains hunch their backs, face down, New England older, solider.

—The poor old house run-down, grass and vines and shrubbery all grown up around it—Joe McGuire had done nothing since Mother's death. Dead branches on lawn—only the path worn by the neighbors: moldy-smelling inside—so much of the stuff seemed cheap and rubbishy. But I have very ambitious ideas about it—shall preserve it, yet make it something different, my own. Though I always at first find it smaller and less distinguished than I expected, I now get into the spirit of it and feel that it has its dignity and its amplitude, as I go from room to room and up- and downstairs. It always bucks me up to go there: partly the nobility and beauty of this country, partly because it brings me closer to Father, who enjoyed it so much and did it so well.

Death of Reckie, June 4, '52. I didn't know about it till I got back to Wellfleet. He must have been about twelve, had bad kidneys, enlarged prostate—could hardly move, wouldn't eat, couldn't lift leg to pee and later couldn't hold water to get out of house. Awful, when the vet brought him here to bury him, to see his bloating body and gray eye. His look used to be "at the same time simple and wild" like Tolstoy's wolf: wolfish look when interested in food or listening to something outside with half-raised ears (that were limp at the ends); so childlike and gentle-looking when he lay stretched out on the floor. Always a certain fundamental sadness perhaps. I have remembered what Volodya Nabokov said years ago (when Reckie turned up later on his bed, lying against the clean pillow) about dogs being "mad" —between the animal and the human. And he was such a mixture—I never bred him with a Dalmatian, as I

wanted to, and he only had those wretched local bastards.
—These last weeks, he never even greeted anybody—
would get away behind things and at the end of rooms
in the house—would go into my bathroom—then not
be able to get back up the steps and would have to be
carried. I couldn't bear to see him crawling like a bug.
—Last winter, he was still very active—last summer
would follow us to the ocean. Our old joke about his
traveling faster than sound—he would come in first,
then his bark. I wonder whether he strained himself
running in his old age.

Tates:[2] When the Tates were married the second
time, Caroline wore orange blossoms, and many friends
were asked. They were both staying at the house of a
friend in Princeton. They were asked whether they
would mind sleeping in the same room the night before
the wedding, and Caroline said, Certainly not!

Talcottville:[3] Arrived Friday, July 25, 1952. Strange
feeling I had that the old house had slipped into dimness
and dirtiness—behind the fresh and vital and colorful
countryside, and that I must bring it up with this again.
  —Horrible filthiness of the third floor, with its attics
and cubbyholes—bare skeletons of crinolines, a chest
with old waistcoats—moth-eaten red flannel underwear—
an enormous floppy white hat; pictures: a volcanic erup-
tion painted on a slab of metal, watercolors of flowers
and sheep, Cathedral Driveway from Lakewood, Pandora
opening her box; old magazines rolled and tied up, as if
they had been mailed or were to be mailed; books caked
with thick dry white mold and clotted with spider webs.
  —Elimination of washstand sets and bedroom stoves.
  —Golden moon in the trees, as we sat on the back
porch at night.

—Pink and blue-violet dawn seen from the front windows.

—Swallows that fell down chimney one morning—five little ones, with nest they had outgrown. Malcolm Sharp[4] took them out and put them on trunk of tree, to which they adhered and looked like five black spots. Gradually they moved together till they made one big black spot. The mother and father were also inside fluttering in the curtains, he caught them and put them out, but they did not find the children, flew wildly away and the fledglings in a day or two died.

—Fern: As sure as preachin'.

—Old barroom chair I was about to give to the junk dealer, but the Loomises said it was worth $20.

—Great-grandfather Baker, it seems, made people in Talcottville pay for getting water from his well.[5]

—Great-grandfather Kimball's sermons were so hot that it was said that the corn never froze on Leyden Hill in the neighborhood of his church. The Loomises[6] said this was true! The corn never froze on their place.

—Fern has something: a certain robust but sensitive attractiveness, a little bovine but not too much so; gray eyes. By the cow barn, walking with partly high-heeled black shoes in the mud among the cow and goose manure, in a somewhat smeared bright-violet apron, she had a certain sex appeal. Washed out milk can with hose and filled it with water; we loaded it into back of car.

—*Cape Vincent:* First visit with the Gauses[7] and Sharps: everything seemed so clean, neat, and clear. Old stone Chauvisick house, big square white green-trimmed house characteristic of this part of country. The water and the docks—big buoys on a bar; the islands and the Canadian side: flat with sparse wild trees that seemed sometimes, so narrow was the land, to be growing right out of the water—"By Blue Ontario's Shore"—water was a moiré greenish blue. At hotel a straight walk to the dock through back lawn was bordered with peony plants, bloomed out for the summer, and with at first blue, pink, and white petunias and then with portulacas, orange, yellow, and red. Hotel has bass and muskellunge stuffed and mounted and the names of those who caught them on brass plaques—some flirting jaunty tails that were lifted away from the wooden mount (an improvement, as Tony Edgar said on one later trip), others completely flat; a lampshade with a bear and two cubs on it. Hotel (Carleton) white with green trimmings. Open porch with green chairs and green columns. Plain but not bad meals. "Exhibit of Wild Life" in fishing-tackle store: large collection of stuffed birds: loons, heron, grebes, sparrow hawk, eagles, snow owl, and great horned owl— also fishes and a black bear and its cub. Little white lighthouses—Sackett's Harbor. —Elena, who doesn't much like this part of the world, pointed out on my second trip that there were always old run-down abandoned buildings, dim in their gray and brown (Dorothy Sharp says that she likes to see the gray barns but I prefer them red). —Old high gray stone U.S. Fisheries, with chaletlike 19th-century Gothic green peaked porch and roof—beside it and on the hotel lawn, a clump of small sunflowers, a mountain ash with yellow berries, two poplars. —I took the boys—Reuel[8] and Tony—on a fishing trip on my second visit. [Marginal note: weedy windblown trees; river and lake all frozen in winter— Fern had crossed St. Lawrence in sleigh. Terrific winds that swept across.] Taciturn and expressionless French-Canadian guide—jokes about "You can't pull up that bottom" when hook got fouled on bottom—"Don't pull out that plug or we'll have to walk home—it's just like the bathtub"—"That's what we call real estate." Water too "flat" for good fishing—tried Grenadier Island, small automatic lighthouse, red buoy—finally, just as sun was beginning to drop, we began having great luck near the shore just past the mainland lighthouse in the direction of Sackett's Harbor—Reuel caught a whopping black bass; we all caught a lot of small rock bass, with rather pretty green stripes and spiny dorsal fins, which the guide would kill by knocking them on the side of the boat, because they ate "the same bait" as the black bass, and a few green-and-yellow perch, with orange fins. The black bass were striped where they lived among the weeds, more uniformly dark when they lived on the weedless bottom. —At Grenadier Island, we landed and had lunch. About thirty families had lived there, then all had left the island. We explored an abandoned farm—big barn and house, roof of the farm falling in, and we were almost afraid to cross the threshold of the latter for fear the whole thing would collapse; old oil drums and farm machinery left behind, a tractor wheel in the water where we later fished. I sat for a while at the foot of a tree in the woods behind the house. Reuel took a long swim across one end of the little cove—from time to time doing the "butterfly stroke," something I had never seen—a kind of overhand breaststroke; I took a short one where the cove was flat—otherwise a big gray gravel [beach]—dried myself in the sun and, when I came back, found my clothes surrounded by three small green frogs and a gray rock spider in my drawers. The guide explained to us that the water was wonderfully clean and pure, because it washed continually on the stones. There had been about a hundred head of wild cattle on the island that belonged to a man named [name omitted]. In the fall a lot of people turned out to round them up—they took them onto the mainland and sold them for beef; last year they had to shoot two. (Cup and saucer house.) —Big black or white river

steamer quietly crossing the lake—one white one flying
between Chicago and Norden, flying the Swedish flag.
—Antique store that sold stuff from the Chauvisick
house and the other old house.

—Elena said that the *old glass* in the panes gave a
silky effect to the landscape.

—*Sullivan boy* had to go up to Mrs. Burnham's[9] to
look for calving cow who had wandered away. It turned
out to be a hard birth: they got the vet, but the calf died.

—Malcolm Sharp on *blurred feudalism* of this part of
the world. The basic point of view feudal—hence
Constable Hall, so much more like the South and so
unexpected after New England: a "gentleman's county
seat" looking out over his acres. Hence Aunt Lin's[10]
attitude, which used to be described as that of the lady
of the manor passing among her tenantry. The Bakers,
though they must have had this partly already, may
have acquired it by stepping into the position of the
Talcotts. Hence some of my own instinctive attitudes,
and my satisfaction in functioning here at the center
and, as it were, at the top of the town—not walled off
from everything else, but accessible and admitting a free
circulation between our neighbors and us. I enjoy sitting
at this little desk of Mother's beside the window that
looks out on Water Street, along which old women and
children pass or my cousin Otis Munn may come along
on a farm machine. Everybody knows me and—unlike
New England—almost everybody is good-natured and
comfortable; even the dogs are not yappy and snappy as
they are likely to be in Wellfleet. They visit us, too, and
make friends with Helen. It is easy for me to get things
done: cleaning, lawn-mowing, carpentry, bringing water
from the spring and getting rid of the garbage. The

boys play ball with the village boys on a diamond on
the back lot. The village store—with a better stock than
I remember—is right at hand for canned goods and
groceries. We get green vegetables from Carrie Trennam
across the road, and chickens from the Robertses on the
hill. I even enjoy the feeling of being able to walk down
the road to the cemetery and get family dates when I
need them. But nothing remained here long—the people
went away to the West, to the South, to New Jersey, to
the big New York cities. Talcottville—this is what makes
it so different from anything else I know in America—is
at once a point of permanence (since we always come
back here) and a phase in the flux of American life. It
is typical in a peculiar way. You feel both the struggle
of the settlers to make themselves a place in the wilderness and the spirit—of adventure, of the thirst for
freedom, of the need to make new lives for themselves—
that carried them to other places. The reunions here in
the summers of my childhood of the relatives who had
gone away were the symbols of the equilibrium—that
still existed then but hardly now (except as I am trying
to perpetuate it)—of a movement that ranged all through
the continent with a certain stability tethered among
upstate pastures and mountains.

Talcottville is in a sense typical of America itself:
people always moving on, always making a wider world.
During my lifetime and since my childhood, we have
got beyond the United States themselves, which at one
time contained us completely, upon which, in the
twenties, we determinedly and anxiously concentrated,
as they must have on their early communities in the
early days of Talcottville, but to which we may one day
return from a bigger world as the Bakers and Talcotts
do to Talcottville.

—Loomises' anecdotes: Some of the Collinses[11] had lived in the pentagon house at Constableville. When old Mr. C. had died, they had had to take the casket out a window, because the doors were so small. Mrs. C. had been asked whether she wanted to look at the corpse. No! I've seen him for fifty years. —Some relation had said, Why should I go over to Constableville to see those long-nosed Collins girls when I can find Sally Talcott right here in Talcottville pretty as a pink. He married her.

—One day when I went out on the front porch and shut the screen door, it latched on itself. Elena said it was Sophronia[12] trying to keep me out. —Elena told me that one morning when she came down early, she thought she saw a woman in a pleated old dress going into the smaller living room, with her shoulder emphasized—shoulder just disappearing in doorway—or rather she saw the dress without being aware of any head above it (I had found a small trunk of old clothes in the attic). She said that it gave her a very queer feeling of an experience she had never had before and that remained vividly with her. She has never been interested in ghosts, and when she mentioned it at the Loomises', I thought she was joking, but she afterwards told me it was true. —Dorothy Mendenhall,[13] as Dorothy Sharp told me, had figured that fifty people had died in that house—the only ones who are real to me are poor Bessie Furbish[14] and my father, who must have slept in that same room just before he came back to Red Bank and died. But of course there were, within my memory, Aunt Lin, Uncle Tom [Baker], and Aunt Nelly.

—Excavation of barns and attics: horrible old crumbling pasteboard box that contained something, put away in fern leaves, that looked as if it might be a human scalp, but that Elena said was a tippet. Old toilet seat and magazines rolled up for mailing that had either never been opened or never been sent. Mother, who was always so neat and up to her old age kept everything in such shipshape condition, must have forborne to disturb any of this as long as Uncle Tom was alive and then, after his death, not have had the energy to do anything about it.

—Loomises wouldn't give an inch on the Talcott-Baker affair.[15] When I told them about the 1869 will, witnessed by Aunt Lin and Great-aunt Lan, they said that this wasn't valid, because they [Aunt Lin and Great-aunt Lan] were Bakers; and when I pointed out (showing them my letter from Dorothy) that the Talcotts had dropped their claims three days after the hearing at the probate of the will, they asserted that the Bakers had bought them off. They might have stood to inherit the house, and at one time had tried to buy the house from Mother, which she had resented. On the other hand, when their own house, originally bought from the Kimballs, had burned down, Mother had written them demanding, Why did you let my grandfather's house burn down?

—Last day, September 1, I was there, I walked over to Flat Rock across the fields, trying to find Father's little cane which I had left. In the rainy weather the flowers came out much more vividly (brightly) than they do in the sun: devil's paintbrush, asters, blue bugloss (blue weed)—they really seemed to burn in the grass.

It occurred to *Elena*, on reading my *Modest Self-Tribute*,[16] that both Vogüé and Maurice Baring[17] had been much indebted to the Annenkovas for their knowledge of *Russian Lit.* Vogüé had married her great-aunt, and Baring, she said, had much frequented her mother's family. I am thus indebted to them, too.

NOTES

1. *Upstate,* pp. 79–80.
2. Allen Tate (1899–1979) had remarried Caroline Gordon (1895–1981), the Southern novelist, whom he had earlier divorced.
3. *Upstate,* pp. 81–83.
4. Malcolm Sharp married EW's cousin Dorothy Furbish. See note 27, p. 22, and Richard Costa's *Edmund Wilson, Our Neighbor from Talcottville* (1980), pp. 31–32.
5. Thomas Baker (1779–1883) came to Talcottville in 1825. *Upstate,* pp. 49–53.
6. The Loomis sisters, Huldah and Gertrude, were Talcottville friends of EW's youth.
7. John Gaus taught with Malcolm Sharp at Amherst and was then in the Department of Government at Harvard.
8. Reuel Kimball Wilson (b. 1938), son of EW and Mary McCarthy.
9. Lillian Burnham, longtime Talcottville friend of the Wilson family. *Upstate,* p. 103.
10. Great-aunt Lin (Rosalind) Baker, one of EW's great-grandfather Baker's eight daughters. "To call on her in my childhood was a kind of august ceremony" (*Upstate,* p. 54).
11. The Collinses were Talcottville friends of the Wilsons.
12. Sophronia Talcott, the second wife of EW's great-grandfather Baker. *Upstate,* pp. 50–51.
13. Dorothy Reed Mendenhall, EW's much-admired cousin (her great-grandfather was the brother of EW's great-great-grandfather Reuel Kimball). See EW's chapter on her in *Upstate,* pp. 59–71.
14. Elizabeth Reed (Bessie) Furbish, EW's cousin, who died of TB in 1902. *Upstate,* pp. 55–58.
15. When Thomas Baker married Sophronia Talcott in 1851 he moved his family of eight daughters into the Stone House. Sophronia Talcott made four wills, all but one (the third, 1874) leaving the property to Thomas Baker, not to Sophronia's sister Jannett Talcott. *Upstate,* pp. 49–52.

16. See *BBT*, pp. 1–5.

17. Eugène Melchior de Vogüé (1848–1910), pioneer French scholar of Russian literature. Maurice Baring (1874–1945), author of eight books on Russia and Russian literature; *DCB*, pp. 77–91. Vogüé married Elena's great-aunt Alexandra Mikhailovna Annenkova in 1878; *A Window on Russia* (1972), pp. i–ii.

PRINCETON, 1952–1953

[The two or three Princeton entries in EW's journals
tell us very little of what he did that winter, but I am
able to some extent to fill in the gap with an account
of his stay at Princeton, where he gave one of the
Christian Gauss memorial seminars. We both arrived in
the late autumn of 1952. There were four series of
seminars given in each academic year. Edmund gave his
in November–December and I followed with mine in
late January and February. I had met him only once
before, in New York, at the Gotham Book Mart, where
we had talked briefly of Joyce and James. We resumed
our talks now and they widened into many subjects.
Often I would run into EW and Elena at Lahiere's and
they would invite me to join them at table: I remember
we enjoyed the leek-and-potato soup in particular and
drank a great deal of wine. Presently EW and I fell into
the habit of taking a late-afternoon walk daily, even on
the coldest days. "We will call our walks the Edmund
Wilson seminars for Lé-on," Edmund said—and this
was what they were in effect, for I was given a running
commentary on EW's Princeton days forty years earlier,

with many stories about Fitzgerald, John Peale Bishop, and his work on the *Nassau Lit*. As might be expected, he was far from being the typical alumnus glowing with retrospective memories. He conveyed distinctly a picture of his early loneliness, his isolation from the average young wealthy students who came to Princeton with their servants, and his lack of interest in sports. His undergraduate life had been as distinctly literary as all the years that followed. He expatiated in particular on some of the old Princeton houses and the architecture of the period, and I find in one of his later letters to me the evidence of his meticulous adherence to accuracy by his correcting certain mistakes he had made. He had been mistaken, he wrote, in telling me that the "big yellow house on the corner was called Morton and was a replica of [Alexander] Pope's villa at Twickenham. The original Stockton house, of which this was true, was just beyond that monument to the Battle of Princeton." And he went on with further details.

[He was quite as meticulous in his seminars. It was customary for the guest lecturers to attend each other's, and I attended his group of six and he did mine, always bringing Elena with him. The format had been worked out experimentally in earlier years by Richard Blackmur and Francis Fergusson. This was the period when academe talked smugly of ours being "an age of criticism" and tried to turn each student into a full-fledged critic; the students, lacking background, reading, and saturation, could only be parrots, but the "New Criticism" remained in fashion for a long time and then gave way to the new fashions, structuralism, deconstruction, and all the current intellectualizations of a humane process. EW took little stock in this kind of lawgiving: he followed a text wherever it led him and he valued the idea—if not always the practice—of the Gauss seminars, funded by the Rockefeller Foundation (for which we were handsomely paid). Blackmur's idea had been to bring writers and professors out of their cubbyholes into an active dialogue on critical approaches to literature, art, philosophy, an active interdisciplinary dialogue about subjects that mattered a great deal to them. That winter, for example, Paul Tillich, the theologian, preceded Edmund; the latter devoted his six sessions to chapters from his work in progress on the Civil War. I followed with my studies in the "stream of consciousness" and the subjective modern novel—Joyce, Proust, Dorothy Richardson, Virginia Woolf, and Henry James as their predecessor. The year ended with Irving Howe's work on the "political novel."

[The seminars were wholly professional; a couple of token graduate students working on their doctorates were invited, indeed all the participants came by invitation. The professional character of our meetings, two hours a week in the Poetry Room of the library, can be suggested if I mention some of the individuals who were present at EW's and my seminars—they included John Berryman, Delmore Schwartz and his novelist wife Elizabeth Pollet, Saul Bellow, R. W. B. Lewis, Erich Kahler from the Institute for Advanced Study, E. B. O. Borgerhoff of the Princeton French Department. Berryman, whom I faced across the table during EW's sessions, was writing his long poem about Anne Bradstreet; clean-shaven then, he seemed off on some other planet, and looked like a bright young corporation executive in his business suit, necktie, and glasses. Saul Bellow was working on his *Augie March*—short, slim, with his quick wit that bounced and bounded as if he were playing a fast game of tennis. Delmore Schwartz's interventions with tangential questions nearly always seemed a fireworks display. It was a high-powered group, but EW, calm, unruffled, hesitant in speech, delivered his papers in a low-keyed voice, pondering everything and never allowing his enthusiasm for his work to carry him away. He parried mere cleverness by his solid walls of fact; and he was receptive even when some of those present talked nonsense: he had a way of seeming to want the best of his interlocutors. He was happier with the writers and poets than with the academics, who in turn tended to patronize him. In blinding themselves to the catholicity of Edmund's reading and research, the New Critics missed the best of his work: the skill with which he brought in what they deemed irrelevant, in order to enhance and illustrate questions that hadn't even occurred to them. As can be seen from some of his notes, he resented being treated as a prima donna; but his resentment was mild, and he generated healthy discussion where others wanted to generate controversy.

[On his walks, EW was always cheerfully conversational, and in his home he was a happy outgoing host. We used to attend the parties after each weekly session but generally Edmund put in a very brief appearance. He told me he was getting too old for rooms filled with so much talk and smoke (he never smoked) and that he tended to drink too much, which ruined the next day for him. So he preferred to entertain in his own home and in lesser numbers. I have described how he had his seminar in Hebrew to tea at his house (see xxvi–vii), and in my introduction to *The Twenties* there is an account of an evening when he entertained Elizabeth Bowen, the novelist, and invited John Berryman to read portions of his as yet incomplete poem "Homage to Mistress Bradstreet," which was the talk of Princeton that winter. What struck me was the way in which EW, not usually given to this kind of empathy, helped the poet over highly emotional passages by feeding back, in quiet even tones, lines Berryman's personal shyness or anguish tended to obscure and mumble. One evening, when I was there alone, I carried away a memory that I have to this day: the glimpse of EW climbing the stairs like a soldier, very erect in spite of his rotundity, intent on telling his daughter a bedtime story before joining me. That image of his straightness and squareness, leisurely pacing his march from step to step, was ineffaceable; and when he came down with the same erectness and air of authority, I asked him what stories he was reading to Helen Miranda. "I'm not reading. I make up the stories. I've been telling her from night to night the adventures of a mermaid in the Adirondacks."

[During one of our leisurely walks on an afternoon in which the sun glowed like a monstrous red coal on the snow, EW complained to me that I didn't want to talk to him about his other writings: that I focused narrowly on his criticism. Why didn't I mention his plays (he would soon put them together in a single volume), his novels and short stories, his light verse? I suppose I had been too single-minded and I have always cherished his calling me to order to remind me of his versatility, his real desire to be a successful novelist or playwright, but his having to settle for his supreme vocation—that the public recognized and admired him as a critic. Still, like Sainte-Beuve, he could say that he had attempted the principal literary forms and so had authority when he criticized a novel, a poem, or a play: he had been through that creative mill himself.

[He was not altogether pleased with such meetings as he had with the academic figures on the campus. I was then pondering a university position in my search for new pathways, after my service in the army during the Second World War. He discouraged me. He always began by saying, "I am not giving you advice—but you do have to ask yourself what *has* academe really to offer you? I know what *you* can offer it." His own commitment had been to his writing: and his sallies into universities— as in the case of the Gauss seminars—were simply for the money, and involved little more than his reading from his works in progress. Our paths continued to cross —in 1959–60 we arrived at Harvard at the same time to spend the year there; in the middle sixties I followed him to Wesleyan's Center for Advanced Studies. "Lé-on," he continued to coach me, "writing and the academic life don't go together very well. You will always be re-duced to talking on the level of the young. If you want to teach, that's fine; but if you want to write, I'm not so sure. After a while you'll find yourself thinking on their level. A writer needs to be with his peers." When I argued that the United States was too sprawling a country for writers to meet except along the eastern seaboard—compared with the compactness of London or Paris (where writers seemed to breathe down one another's necks)—Edmund replied that he had actively sought out any fellow writer in America who interested him. To be sure, he had acquired a position of eminence that enabled him to do this. And this is what he did that winter when he fanned out from Princeton to the South to talk with James Branch Cabell and had one of his rare meetings with Faulkner.]

Princeton from first week in October 1952. Soon after I arrived: the western end of the Turners' drive, with a soft light of sunset, seen through illumining trees, faded but equally mellow, reminded me of the rich haziness of Inness's paintings of the Delaware Valley. It is a long time since I had been submerged in the atmosphere of this part of the country, and, after Wellfleet and Talcott-ville, I felt its qualities more clearly.

—Cocktail party at the Turners': Horatio T. typical old enthusiastic Princeton alumnus of a vintage a little before my time—classmate of Arthur Holden and Medina.[1] Wanted us to join his party in a special Pullman to the Yale game. Proud of 250-year-old house, where the judge lived who arranged to have the college located at Princeton. Terrific Princeton snob and something of a climber—complained about new people coming in—in the old days, there hadn't been anybody in the town who hadn't been part of the college community. He had met a woman at dinner who had told him how much she loved living in Princeton; he had tried her on names like the Pynes and it was obvious she knew nothing about them. Burnham Dell and his wife; Norman Walker's son and former wife; former editor of *Ladies' Home Journal*, who thought that Edna Millay's letters should be called *A Lovely Light*. Mrs. Turner, with an insistent, rather hard gaze, and face that, as Elena said, seemed rather whisky-seamed, exclaimed to someone, when I had expressed an interest in the pictures that her mother-in-law or someone had brought from New Orleans: "Oh, he wants to know whether they're Corots or Debussys!"

—That old nasal slightly peevish or priggish college bell that admonished you to go to class seemed to have survived from the time when the Seminary (in the early 1800s) was still in Nassau Hall with the college. This note you still sometimes run into, and it quietly jars with the country club aspect. Woodrow Wilson sometimes sounded this note.

Helen, Nov. 14. Her mother had been reading her the Burgess Thompson (?) books about sea life, birds, etc. She had asked whether Pussinka[2] belonged to the order of the rodents. Elena said that she belonged to the same family as lions and tigers. Helen said, "She's a rural member of that family." —This morning, as she was going off to school, there was some question of her being taken by somebody's colored maid. She said, "I don't like black people—we belong to the order of the pink people."

Helen—about to play in a mud puddle: Mud is my heart's desire.

—When I asked her to pick things up: Am I the housemaid? We couldn't make out where she had heard of housemaids.

NOTES

1. Arthur Cort Holden, author of studies in American architecture, and Harold Raymond Medina, U.S. District and Circuit Judge and professor of law at Columbia.
2. Pussinka was Elena's Abyssinian cat.

/0/6 / 10

RICHMOND AND WASHINGTON, 1953

Charlottesville, March 29–30, 1953. Susan [Wilson]:
I was always very touched but eventually irritated by
her—though it was merely her vagueness and her old-
maidish habits. She would always forget essential things
—such as the fact that we were going back, not to New
York, but to Princeton. —She told Elena that she had
been shy at first when she gave up her job at the hospital, when, as she said, she "went into society." But she
had by this time, we could see, made a good deal of progress in adapting herself to her new kind of life: activity
as chairman of some committee of the League of Women
Voters—they recently being successful in getting a
central registrar—otherwise the country people could
never all vote—couldn't find out where to register or
registrar not at home, etc. Woman on local paper gave
League publicity, in return for which she supplied items
of social interest—I think she rather enjoys all this. —Her
long experience of dealing with idiots, who were likely
to make messes—as well as some special condition of her
own—led her to be continually asking whether people

didn't want to go to the bathroom. She behaved, on our trips in the car, whenever we arrived at a gas station, almost like a dog passing a row of trees—would say that would be a good place to stop if anybody wanted to relieve himself. She also worried about getting reservations on trains—was timid—deferential about crossing the street, allowing people to pass, going into public buildings—even in the case of the house at the University in which the Minors had lived and which was now surely college offices.

—Didn't think that Negroes ought to be let into white residential sections—they ruined the value of the property; but pointed out that in Charlottesville the better Negro section was being squeezed out of existence by the encroachments of small factories and office buildings. —I told her of Gauss's story about his lecture in Richmond, when Negro nurses for the first time were admitted to the back pews of a church. She said that in the old days the Negroes had all been up in the gallery, but nowadays they had their own churches. Still—and at this point she began to sound exactly like our aunt Eliza in the atmosphere of the Presbyterian parsonage—there was no doubt that Christ had made no discrimination between black and white, that the Negro had a soul like the white man and just as much right to be saved.

Richmond, March 31–April 1, '53 [James Branch] Cabell: I realized, with Cabell and his household, how bourgeois in certain ways his life had been. Except for the carved marble fireplace transported from the house in which he had been born and some other details of the dining room, there was no evidence of anything but literary taste: the usual portraits of him and of his relatives were all undistinguished. He had escaped from middle-class commercial Richmond into a fairyland middle ages: the situation presented in *The Cream of the Jest* [1917]. I could see how he had worked in the sterile period of the early 1900s, and how pleased he must have been at the enthusiastic recognition of the twenties. He told me that reading my *Shores of Light* had "rejuvenated" him. (One of the first things I saw in Richmond was a Duryea's furniture store, obviously rather ancient.) He was now writing a book about such people as John Macy and Guy Holt,[1] with whom he had collaborated. How little he had seen of the contemporary world, with which, however, in the twenties, his reputation had brought him in contact. Though he had satirized the South and was far from sharing all its prejudices, he, too, had been encased in its postwar vacuum. Though he could not take quite seriously its pretensions and preoccupations, he had never been able to become involved or even at all seriously interested in anything that happened anywhere else. My respect for him and sympathy have lately—since reading *Let Me Lie* [1947]—been considerably increased. —When we first went into the house, his dwarfed son Ballard—fifty with a mentality of ten—appeared, and before Mrs. Cabell explained him, I had a dreadful impression that it was Cabell, who had somehow physically dwindled along with his reputation since I had seen him in the *Vanity Fair* office in 1920 or '21. —Cabell himself did appear a little shrunk—he had been wearing an overcoat then—with his short legs and thinned face—he was already, I now saw, *fin de race*. He asked me to write my name in Ballard's autograph book. He had had flu and taken Aureomycin, which had given him a heart attack, made him break out in a rash. He was not allowed to go upstairs, and a bedroom had been made up downstairs, which separated him from his most important books, so that he read the old Scribner sets of Stevenson,

Kipling, and Dickens. He said to me as I left that he hoped to live to see me again.

When I told him that I had been doing a seminar at Princeton on the literature of the Civil War, he said that he didn't know there had been any literature of the Civil War. —We call it, he added, the War Between the States. Later, when he referred to it again, he said, I'm afraid I'm not polite enough to call it the Civil War. He had, however, recently, in some connection, had to reread *Uncle Tom's Cabin* and declared that is a very good book; had never read [G. W.] Cable[2] and had never read Faulkner.

Faulkner: I might as well put in here some note on our seeing Faulkner a few weeks ago at Bob Linscott's.[3] He talked more, and more interestingly, than I had been led to expect. Had never read Cable, said he was "unreadable"—though Cable, I suppose, was unique in dealing realistically, before Faulkner, with the problem of the mulatto in the South—shows how little all this period of American literature is known and appreciated. He said that it was significant that none of the Southern generals had written their memoirs of the war. I replied that a number of them had—[James] Longstreet, for example. Longstreet had lived long enough, he answered. He had seen him once, as a child. Longstreet had come to Oxford, and Faulkner had been taken to see him. He remembered an old man with a beard. But Faulkner had promptly piped up: What was the matter with you at Gettysburg? and his parents had whisked him away. In Charlottesville, a young instructor at the University, a South Carolinian, told me that Longstreet had published three different version of his memoirs—in each further minimizing his responsibility for the Gettysburg defeat. As the various generals died and could no longer object to what he wrote, he unloaded the blame on others, till, at last, after the death of Lee, he made Lee mainly responsible.

Cabell again: Cabell, when I spoke of his story of the Indian who had been educated by the Spaniards in Europe and had then, brought back to Virginia, betrayed the Jesuits to his own people, told me that they were now constantly discovering new sites for the massacre of the Spanish, pushing it closer to Williamsburg, because that would be "more convenient."

Characteristic of Richmond that Cabell and Lyttleton Wickham should not even know one another. Wickham had told me that he thought he had met Cabell once. Wickham, they told me in Charlottesville, had now given up his law practice and retired to his house with his books. Had never married—the lady who had been with him when we met him in Charlottesville last spring, we found acting as guide in the Capitol.

Richmond: The handsome Capitol, designed by Jefferson—with its fine classical columns, its painted 18th-century dome (dry patterns in green on dry yellow), its busts of the Virginian Presidents, with the Houdon Washington[4] in the middle—though it dominates a green hill, gives the impression of being crowded by the big blocks of commercial buildings, insurance, etc., that cut off the vista across the lands—as in Charlottesville, Jefferson's vista at the bottom of the University lawn is cut off by the Stanford White building in its too big, somehow badly proportioned brick-and-marble early-1900s style.

Washington, March 28–29 and April 1–2. Washington seems to me to become continually more impressive. I don't exactly approve of the new Jefferson or the Lincoln memorial—the latter, as Mario Praz[5] says, a little too much like the temple of the something-or-other Zeus; but the whole thing, with its monuments to our past great men, the new Supreme Court and National Gallery, and its importance as a world center now, is thrilling as it never was before. One remembers with a certain emotion the days when, in leaving the White House, *"on trébuchait sur les vaches."* (This was true no doubt in Jefferson's time but Henry James is said to have resented it, as of his own time, when it was mentioned to him by some non-American.[6]) It has occurred to me only lately that Washington is on such a scale as no other capital in the world. Praz told me that some official greeter explained to him that the Potomac had once been called the Tiber (this is not quite accurate, I think—the Tiber was some other, smaller stream (?)), expecting, as Mario Praz annoyedly thought, that he would then say that Washington was the new Rome. (Indoctrination of foreign visitors—resented by Praz, made little of by [illegible]—schedule of lectures, etc.: town government, maternity hospitals. This is one of the things, like persecution for guilt by association, that we have probably—regrettably—imitated from Russia.) Tact observed —I suppose, inculcated—in the sightseeing tours at the FBI: young man who took us around explained at one point that he worked in the fingerprint department; but they were made to conduct these tours to give them practice in talking to people and controlling nervousness. Yet he did appear under a certain strain—which we could see him successfully controlling when the girls had made the mistake of climbing the stairs by themselves. He quietly made them go back to the bottom floor and saw to it they took the elevator: Better go down in the elevator—it's seven flights. —Relative

vulgarity of the Capitol, with its enormous historical
paintings and the hall of statuary, in which, as well as
elsewhere, appeared the sometimes grotesquely or monstrously outsize figures of a miscellany of great men and
women (Frances Willard[7]) from all periods of American
history contributed by the various states. But this repre-
sents America, too—as well as the Supreme Court and
Holmes, the National Gallery and its distinguished collection: the Capitol is democratic. Anybody can go to
see it, anybody can go to watch Congress; and as we
sent all kinds of representatives to the Senate and the
House, we can send our favorite heroes and effigies of
bronze and marble to stand in the halls of the Capitol,
the Smithsonian, with its old-fashioned science, the
Freer Museum, with its *fin de siècle* aestheticism.

F.F.: —Felix Frankfurter is at his best in his dignified
house on Dumbarton Avenue, the great door of which
stands high above the street, so that one reaches it by a
long flight of steps. We talked at first about Laski and
Holmes,[8] and he talked carefully, weighing what he said
—trying to put the best appearance on Laski—agreeing,
discreetly, but I think with some gratification, to what I
said about the liberalizing of Holmes. Little taste in his
living room and dining room, but a certain sobriety and
seriousness. Later, Justice Wiener began to effervesce.
"I am appalled at the abyss of indiscretion above which I
stand!" —This prefaced some remarks about a colleague
—evidently Douglas—who allowed his personal feelings
to get into his decisions—accompanied by a sly suggestion that I ought to understand his failure to give way to
this weakness in connection with *Hecate County*.[9] —But
enjoyed him: his enthusiasm for Kingsley Martin's book
on Laski[10] and his loyalty to Laski, his lively interest
in everything (interpretation of the phenomenon of
McCarthy: opinion west of the Alleghenies, fear of

the atomic bomb, Truman's unfortunate remark about dragging a red herring), his aside in connection with Holmes's aristocratic instincts, about his own distaste for the domination of what I understood him to call "anonymities"—all brought me back to the twenties, to the earlier beginnings of *The New Republic*, etc., about which I seem to be nowadays I suppose almost pathetically nostalgic—not from the point of view of too much idealizing that period or wanting its conditions back, but from the point of view of finding its survivors the people with whom I much enjoy talking. Thus Felix, whom I thought of at *The New Republic* as belonging to an earlier phase and whose suggestions I always resented, had now come to seem my contemporary, who spoke my own language and shared my instinctive feelings. —Of the new Republican administration, he said that you couldn't "go to Capri," couldn't regard it as simply four years out. This showed how much his hopes and ideals had been bound up with the New Deal and the Democrats.   */0/19/10*

Richmond. The Confederate Museum: The big old corner house, where Jefferson Davis had lived as President; Lincoln had come there when Richmond surrendered; after the war had been used as a school; then rescued and made a museum. Now crowded with records and relics: flags, portraits, anti-Federal caricatures and broadsides, uniforms, swords and guns, dark volumes of regimental histories. Sad and stale: a room for every Confederate state, crammed from the floor to the ceiling. Lee's uniform, sword, and spurs worn at Appomattox. Touching plaque to Mrs. Surratt.[11] Old custodian, full of Confederate spirit, spoke of Lincoln's having been "killed."

—Splendid and spacious back gardens: beautifully

kept lawns, fountains and statues, iron lacework on porches, effect of compartments (in gardens) that Elena liked. —Elizabethan house, in which Queen Elizabeth was supposed to have slept, transplanted from England by some rich man—now a museum. In back garden, varied primroses and enormous 18th-century (?) stone magots of Mahomet (?) and Louis XIV: Elizabethan box hedges and turf.

Tates and the South: People like the Tates exhibit in a specialized intensified form the typical Southern state of mind (perhaps dying out with the present generation); having grown up trying to believe an impossibility —namely, that the South was not, or ought not to have been, defeated in the war—they go on, having come to the end of their rope with this, to accepting—having had so much training in the *credo quia impossibile*—the Catholic tradition and dogma, which also involve looking back to the past instead of forward to the future. They used to have the Confederate flag in their back room on Linden Place; in their present house they have the crucifix.

Washington, etc., connection here through Catholics, McCarthy: My Washington visit and return to Princeton were brightened by public events, the outflanking of McCarthy,[12] the thawing-out of Russia, the feeling that the Eisenhowers knew what they were doing (also Reuel's growing-up)—one began to have a new confidence that American institutions would prevail and that the struggles for them—as in Felix's case, the *Miracle* decision[13]—had been worthwhile and had their effect.

Reuel, spring '53. He already, at fourteen, has a blond mustache sprouting. I developed early, too, and I hope he will not be obstructed in his sexual opportunities for so long a time as I was. I am glad to see his enthusiasm for dances, which I could never face. He prides himself on his dancing.

I feel for the first time, in this first spring vacation of his being away at boarding school, that he has now reached the age that I remember reaching myself, when the father was to begin treating the boy more manly, as an equal—then, suddenly, it seems, for both, the old man's weaknesses are manifest, he has to admit his uncertainties. The boy, who is no longer so afraid of him, begins inevitably to take him less seriously. It is only later on that he is able to conceive his father's early life and really understand what is behind him and what his significance has been—as I didn't do, really, till after my father's death—though I had begun to from the time when I got back from the war and was no longer in the least in awe of him.

North and South: One has to remember, in connection with the [Allen] Tates and Cabell and others, that they don't have the Republic, or rather the United States, to believe in. Their attitude toward it can be only ironic, as in Cabell's account of his visit to Theodore Roosevelt or Allen's sour reflections in his poems. Thus Felix Frankfurter and I, though he was born in Vienna, have something in common that Allen and I, though we were both born later and both of British families long in America, do not. We talk together more easily (Allen and I), but don't make so much sense.

—The kind of American to whom I am really closest is someone—very rare—like John Biggs.

Washington, Reuel and Elena: Elena and Reuel were a very cunning sight when they walked off to see the

White House, where I dropped them from the taxi: she in her smart beige (?) dress, looking so slim and elegant, but putting down her feet, in their low red shoes with thin backstraps and little bows, in her slightly flat-footed and gawky way; he in his best blue suit with his soft black moccasin-type shoes, his stocky figure lately matured—both hatless, she with her soft brown hair, he with his thickish shock that would not quite lie down behind—walking quietly together with mutual confidence, intent on seeing the White House.

Washington: Paddy Jackson.[14] He was working now for John L. Lewis and I thought was getting to look rather like him: his brow had become more beetling, his eyebrows more bristling than ever. He speaks of almost everyone with the same emphatic enthusiasm. Tells every political story in the same quiet weighty way as if it were of great significance—invariably begins by addressing you by name: "Bunny!"[15] Dodie had produced one of her rich and fattening and admirably cooked dinners, which, as one of the guests said, had usually a touch of the exotic, or at least of the unconventional: cream of corn soup, roast chicken with spoon bread, green salad with tomatoes and avocados, a delicious cream dessert that made a beautiful ring around a pool of stewed strawberries—as Elena said, all the dishes had a certain resemblance to one another. The guests were, beside ourselves, a young and perhaps slightly pansyish correspondent for the New York *Post*, who had graduated from Clark College in Worcester and done graduate work at Harvard; a sort of political journalist (and his tall rather taciturn wife) who had ghosted for Wallace and Tugwell, and now, under David Lawrence,[16] with whom he was far from agreeing, was supplying, I think, some sort of news service; a young Jewish lawyer, smooth-faced and somewhat pasty, a little walleyed behind his glasses, who had been dissolving a small but tight trust, originally organized by Brandeis in his early Boston days before he had become a reformer. A steady exchange of wisecracks; sad tales and apprehensions about the removal of officials appointed by the last administration; what could McCarthy hope?—to make himself President by popular pressure, disregarding machine politics?—I suggested that, if allowed to have his head, he would try to have Eisenhower impeached for treason. They must have had their hopes raised high by Stevenson, then dropped into an abyss of discouragement. Like Schlesinger and Max Lerner,[17] they jump on every move of Eisenhower and Dulles, putting the worst construction on it—to the point where they don't even notice that the problem of McCarthy is being handled well by treating him with politeness but firmly discrediting his pretensions. The fabulous Iowa character who had performed such extraordinary feats in the hybridization of corn and had now invented for cattle some sort of chemical diet which cut in half the cost of feeding them.

The Jacksons have two dogs: a quiet black field cocker with tan above his eyes and an enormous rich spaniel (at once sheepdoglike and poodlelike) that gambolled in an elephantine way, flopping all over everybody and everything. They put him out, but he whined and scratched, and they eventually let him back in. The Worcester correspondent had been asked by some other visitor why "they had to have that beast around," and had replied, "Why, don't you know?—that's their landlord." At one point the dog began drinking out of the bowl of ice for the drinks, and Dodie gave him a large piece of ice. He took this into the front room and crunched it up on the rug, where he left it. Dodie had to go in and clean it up. In the meantime, the smaller dog made himself a nest under my chair and produced a succession of dreadful smells. Paddy told us about the big dog in the same enthusiastic and emphatic way as if he had been one of his Washington characters: they say that after all the other breeds had been made, they took everything that was left over and created the Irish water spaniel! So you have this *clown dog!*

Amens and Highets[18]—a.m. and evening of April 19. Amens seemed to be in dreadful shape. Marion had been in bed and appeared with two black eyes. She patted John on his head and said, Johnny gave them to me— then explained it had really been a fall. John, behind the dissipated disintegration of his face, seemed solicitous and a little pathetic. Both their faces seemed completely *abîmés*, then the German girlfriend came in with her enormous dog and looked equally dissipated as well as discontented and cross; asked me whether I enjoyed writing—Remarque[19] said he hated it, yet had to do it. John said that Francis Biddle was a horse's ass, had been responsible for the dreaming-up of the list of subversive organizations (though when I had said to Biddle something about this, he had given me the impression that it had been done before he got in but that he had had to supply it, if asked), some of which he actually knew nothing about. McCarthy was another horse's ass—had just been in Washington, testifying before his committee —in that case had been acting in harmony with him, though he hated him. Better side of John—his job checking on the loyalty cases was just over—was going up to Maine, where he had just at last made inhabitable a place on the land that his father had left him. Marion and I had been talking about Princeton, when the German lady appeared, and I found that I rather resented her; but I presently made myself more agreeable to her, talking about Haiti, where a German friend of hers, Pless, had a big plantation. She complained about her first husband. I told Marion about the Seminary; she told me about the revival of all the churches—some that she had never heard of—that she had seen in connection with her Girl Scout work. I reflected, when I left them, that I really knew very little about them, had no idea what had happened to them. —I find that Elena is much more sensitive than I to what sort of condition people are in, how they feel about one another, etc.

—The Highets, to whom I then went, presented a striking and amusing contrast. Helen (who had just published a new novel, which Gilbert, in his last book reviews in *Harper's*, said that he regretted he couldn't praise, in view of her being his wife) was wearing a becoming blue dress. I complimented her and went on to make favorable comparisons between Scotch and English women—which started her off on herself—bankers and accountants had tried to marry her, when he was nobody and was making nothing. —He always called her "Duchess." This led to a great glorification of their marriage. They had carried on an affair that had begun seven years before they were married—a rather difficult thing for them to do, when they were going to college, etc.—now they had been married twenty years. At first, Gilbert said, there had been certain shits and sons of bitches who had wanted to take her away from him—but their marriage had lasted, and—his tone implied—weren't they successful and happy! —It turned out that he hated Joyce when I tried to take him to task for what he had said in his book. "I grew up only a few streets away from him." A lot of things were going on in Ireland that he completely ignores in *Ulysses*: railroads were being built, people were succeeding, getting out of their lower-middle-class environments. Joyce had chosen just to wallow in it. —I said that, after all, Joyce took the family seriously. There was not, he replied, in Joyce a single happy family: the Blooms! the Dedaluses! —How about the Earwickers? —Gilbert held his nose—hadn't Earwicker exhibited himself to two soldiers in the park? I asked Gilbert whether he had never exhibited himself to two soldiers. —No! Joyce gave a false picture of Dublin, a subject he pretended to be covering completely. —This showed, on Gilbert's part, some very naïve notions about literature and art in general. The Scotch moral indignation. Yet he was certainly not hypocritical, and it may be that the life that he and Helen have led, the careers they have made for themselves, *do* have a heroic quality, which seems so anachronistic nowadays that at first we cannot quite believe in it. —And yet, on the other hand, in the moral exhilaration of their new American citizenship, not having had to like America or come to grips with the American problems, they don't have any real idea of them. They were very proud of their son Keith, who was at Harvard, writing poetry at a great rate. John Amen has at least been grappling with the struggle for civil liberties.

NOTES

1. John Albert Macy (1877–1932), poet and literary editor of *The Nation*, 1922–23. Guy Holt (1892–1934) was a prominent publisher and editor. Cabell's recollection of them appears in *As I Remember It* (1955).

2. George Washington Cable (1844–1925), New Orleans-born novelist. *Patriotic Gore*, *passim*.

3. Faulkner's editor at Random House.

4. Jean-Antoine Houdon (1741–1828), French sculptor, whose busts of American leaders included the one of Washington.

5. Mario Praz (1896–1982), professor of English language and literature at the University of Rome, author of *The Romantic Agony* (1930). *BBT*, pp. 151–57, 653–68.

6. EW is remembering a passage from Henry James's two-volume life of the sculptor William Wetmore Story (1903), in which the novelist, describing the early days of the city of Washington, speaks of its "queerness and its anomalies, as of a great gay political village or civil camp," and remembers this as "evoked for me long ago in the talk of an old foreign diplomatist who had served there in his younger time." James then quotes the diplomatist (clearly with amusement, not resentment) as saying: *"Je vous assure que lorsqu'on sortait, le soir, de dîner chez le Président on trébuchait sur les vaches couchées à la porte"* (*Story*, I, 239). ("I assure you that when one left, in the evening, after dining with the President, one stumbled against the cows lying at his door.")

7. Frances Elizabeth Willard (1839–98), president of the Women's Christian Temperance Union.

8. See "The Holmes-Laski Correspondence" in *BBT*, pp. 78–101.

9. Felix Frankfurter had disqualified himself from sitting in the case of the banned *Hecate County* (1946) because he was a friend of EW's. *The Forties*, pp. 311–14.

10. *Harold Laski, 1893–1950: A Biographical Memoir* (1953).

11. Mary E. Surratt, who ran the boardinghouse where John Wilkes Booth met with his conspirators. She was hanged with them.

12. McCarthy's abusive interrogation of a brigadier general regarding another soldier's loyalty occasioned a conflict with the Army that emboldened some senators to speak out against him in March 1953.

13. In 1952 the Supreme Court unanimously overruled the New York Court of Appeals' ban on the film *The Miracle*, ruling that motion pictures were entitled to constitutional guarantees of free speech and press. Justice Frankfurter wrote an extensive concurrence with Justice Clark's opinion.

14. Gardner Jackson, nicknamed Pat or Paddy, journalist and fighter for liberal causes. *The Thirties*, pp. 319–20.

15. EW's mother's pet name for Edmund. She let it slip at the Hill School and it stuck.

16. David Lawrence (1888–1973) wrote the daily syndicated column "Today in Washington."

17. Max Lerner (b. 1902), Russian-born political scientist, teacher, and columnist.

18. John and Marion Amen, EW's longtime friends. See previous volumes, *passim*. Helen MacInnes Highet (1907–86), pen name Helen MacInnes, novelist, and her husband, Gilbert Arthur Highet (1906–78), author, educator, and critic. They moved from their native Scotland to New York in 1939 when Highet became professor of Greek and Latin literature at Columbia University.

19. Erich Maria Remarque (1898–1970), author of *All Quiet on the Western Front* (1929).

TALCOTTVILLE, 1953

Talcottville,[1] *April 23–24, 1953.* I had never been there before at this time of year. The weather was more pleasant and warmer, and the fields greener than I had expected. There is a new little train to Boonville—they call it the Bee Line—put on, I suppose, for the ski trade and a great improvement on the old milk train. Whenever a door was opened, one heard a chorus of frogs of a loudness that at first seemed incredible. Driving in to Talcottville, it seemed to me that the landscape toward the Adirondacks had a pinkish look—though this was some trick of the light on the dun and buff fields as seen framed in the light woodwork of the window of the car. After finding things so moldy when I had come back before, I was surprised to find them now so neat and clean; but inside it was as if the whole winter cold had been concentrated and kept in the house, and I had to go out from time to time to get warm. Richly yellow double daffodils I had never seen before blooming where the bushes grow behind the house; the stone bowl and the other stone containers on the porch were full of dark dead leaves like the front steps. Branches that had been blown down strewn all over the lawn.

　　—I had never been upstairs in the Munns' house before. I have never seen any other house that gave me the
same impression. In spite of the unpainted exterior, everything inside was clean and in good condition; but it represented a family in which, fond though they were of one
another, there was in some sense no home life at all: no
taste, hardly any pictures (two heads of deer in the dining
room and the painting of the big trout—two—caught by
Thad), two bookcases, a small phonograph. (Otis, when
we came in, was asleep on the large red couch.) Upstairs
there was a large bathroom without a tub (no hot water,
the pressure wasn't strong enough to keep a heater running) and seven bedrooms that opened out, with Talcott-
ville-type beds in them, almost like a fan; those tube-
contained lights on the walls—that flicker when they are
first lighted. Big kitchen with deep-freeze still containing
some venison, little red restaurant-type table and chairs.
Their meals were most irregular. They got up at six and
milked the cows (Otis asked me whether he was "stunk
up"—they got used to it and didn't notice it), then came
back about eight and got breakfast. Then Fern went to
the coöp in Boonville, where she made out the milk
checks—that winter she had really run the whole thing.
Otis got himself some lunch—opened a can of soup or
made himself some bread and milk. The family came and
went without wasting conversation, but I have never
heard any of them say a disagreeable or even sulky word.
—The Loomises and the Munns obviously do not care
much for one another. The Loomises think Otis lazy and
Fern illiterate; the Munns say that the Loomises will always, if they possibly can, get out of paying anything
they owe, and they will go right through your house,
sticking their noses into anything, without being invited.
—Otis Jr., who resembles his mother—same solid and
rather handsome gray eyes—married the daughter of a

man in the logging business and made $5,800 this year,
beginning the first of January during the weeks when the
logging is going on: about $500 a week, of which, how-
ever, he only makes about $300 clear, on account of
expenses and eventual deterioration of his truck. Has
traveled a good deal by car, but been in a train only once,
when he rode from Boonville to Lyons Falls just to see
what it was like. The truck sometimes overturns—it's
quite a strain carrying a load of logs, but you don't get
hurt because it turns over slow.

—*Cooking:* That evening Fern had to go to preside at a
square dance given to raise money—the third—by the
man whose barn had burned down last summer. I was
sorry to have to miss it, but felt too ill with my cold and
went to bed right after dinner (characteristically perfunctory in the cooking: thick slabs of ham not hot,
enormous Lewis County potatoes still partly hard, green
beans that must have come out of a can, and plum
pudding with whipped cream that must have come out of
a can too—everybody serves himself with his own knife
and fork, in somewhat bad repair—I imagine they use the
dining room rarely). There had been a hundred people
there, including many Poles who did Polish dances. —I
was reading Harold Frederic's[2] Civil War stories—
Marsena and *The Copperhead*—and the life of that country is so well described in them and this life has changed
so little that they easily merged in my mind. In *The
Copperhead*, when old Abner's barn is burned, you are
told that he *cannot* expect the neighbors to raise money
for him by giving a husking bee, on account of his un-
popularity. —In most of these stories, Frederic is interested in showing how American democracy—neighbor-
liness, sharing in a common cause—in the long run asserts
itself over class division (created by more money and
superior education) and difference of opinion. Only

"Marsena" is cynical in the vein of *Theron Ware*—the girls in both these stories are snobbish and insufferable flirts (I think so, in *Theron Ware*, though it is so long since I've read it), a type at the hands of whom Frederic himself must have sustained some wounds. The class line-up appears also in *In the Valley* in its more acute pre-Revolutionary form, and here, of course, democracy triumphs. These stories (not in *In the Valley*) are excellent in their accurate picture of the local life and their consciousness of historical significance. He makes one feel the trauma of the Civil War and how it at once stimulated antagonisms—in the North—and brought people closer together. Old Abner, in *The Copperhead*, is the type of indomitable independent who had stood up to the British in the earlier days and who, in spite of his heretical stand, eventually commands the respect of his neighbors—his kindness and his sense of justice unexpectedly emerge when his barn has been burned and we are prepared to have him swear vengeance. When Frederic makes kindness prevail, we feel—as we don't always with Howells—that he is not entirely trying to meet the demands of the comfortable feminine audience of the nineties but making a serious point about the American society of the time—"My Aunt Susan," for example— since certain of his stories, like "Marsena," admit the possibility, in certain cases, of the triumph of heartlessness. —How would these stories appear to someone who did not know the country? They seem to me in more or less the same category as the neglected stories of Fuller[3]—such as *Waldo Trench and Others*—too sober and unobtrusive, too full of irony, too dependent for their point on social criticism, to have interested the public of their period. Yet in this case the relative cultural poverty of upstate New York may have had something to do with it. You feel the limitations of that life, and its relatively meager history, limitations it still has. People loved to read about New England then: Mary E. Wilkins Freeman, Sarah Orne Jewett.[4]

May 8,1953. Birthday plans for my 59th year (I have crossed out the ones on last year's list that I have carried out):

Book of plays[5] should be ready next week.

By next spring, Oxford book of miscellaneous studies:

Edward Lear?	Zuñi	notes	Russian	underlined
	Haiti	in	Language	have still to
Pornocrats	⌈ Sade	Russ.	Pushkin	be written
	⌊ Genet	Lit.	Gogol	
			Tolstoy	
			Chekhov	
			Nabokov	

Hebraic	Old Testament
Tradition	Hebrew Tradition in America
	Holmes and Laski

Go through notebooks completely

Get well started with novel[6]

Get both Wellfleet and Talcottville repaired as far as possible

Reuel, May 9, '53. He has matured remarkably in the last year. I felt that he got along well with the boys, and that his friends and the younger ones looked up to him. He introduced to me, in the dormitory, a smiling small boy, with a kind of air of proud patronage. He has a perceptible shadow of blond mustache, voice ·seems to have almost completely changed. When I took him to the eye doctor, he talked about the inner structure of the eye: aqueous chamber, etc.; when I asked him later where he had acquired this lore, he said that, in their biology course, they had been dissecting the eye of a sheep. He had read *Crime and Punishment* and was now reading *Anna Karenina*. I spoke of the line-up between Petersburg and Moscow, and he said he had noticed this. As we were passing the Fun-Shop, to which Rosalind had once taken him, he stopped to look in the windows and wondered what he should get to surprise the boys at school. We went in, and he said almost at once: I guess I've outgrown this now, but lingered over some boxes. He said, Sometimes you find something curious. I asked him what he meant by "curious." —Like a cigar that squirts. He had evidently just learned the use of *curious* and used it in several connections. He seemed to be interested in everything that came up in conversation or that we passed on the road, and had ideas about them. More observing and more practical than I was at that age. He had done, for his own amusement, a little landscape of the school-grounds, which was not badly drawn; and he and Bull had borrowed from a school collection two pictures, which, however, for lack of wire, they had hung only a little way below the ceiling, so that it was almost impossible to look at them. Had noticed how they handled the boy in the cow barns at Newport; had definite ideas about the kinds of dogs he liked—liked whippets because they looked so beautiful, chows were not really disagreeable, admired Afghan hounds.

L'Engles: I don't know whether I noted the incident of Brownie passing me one winter or autumn when I was plodding against bad weather on foot to Wellfleet. She waved to me in a debonair way. When I saw her at some party a few days later, she mentioned that she had seen me. I remarked that she hadn't offered to pick me up. —What! With a dog in the car!

She is supposed to have said of the Matsons:[7] They shouldn't have come beyond Eastham.

She has apparently never ceased to regret that she saved Sonya Brown from drowning—told people how much it had cost her to get her watch repaired, because it had been spoiled by the water; and spoke as if she had been swindled when she heard of Sonya Brown's paralysis. Her account of the incident was that when she had saved Sonya there had been "a Negro sitting on her head." This had actually been a colored boy who had tried to go to the rescue.

But Brownie got a rise out of me, after all these years, a couple of years (I think it was) ago, by saying, Why, a critic can't write a play, and other things of the same nature. I finally came out with something like: Brownie don't talk such stupidities—you really are awfully stupid. This delighted her, and I felt that she had heavily scored.

Between sleeping and waking: I was able to seize what goes on in one's mind in a way that I had not been able to do before. I could see how, in the continual shifting of the elements of one's consciousness, an image, at any moment, might be precipitated out. It would always be concrete, but always a different image, since the flux was always changing. It was as if there were an infinite number of infinitely thin leaves of a book. If one inserted a paper cutter at any point (this figure is not quite right: it is more as if one brought to bear a certain pressure) an image would appear that would be something more permanent than the moment of flux—that is, something that could be remembered. —I think I have got hold of something fundamental here. A work of art is an organization of such images—or apprehension of a cluster of such images—and an incorporating of them in materials which will enable them to be experienced by other people. What is the relation of such constructions—which include, of course, all human works—to the stuff of the consciousness and unconsciousness behind them—the continually shifting flux, the infinitely divisible *grouillement?* Human effort cannot all be directed toward a concretization and organization which will eventually result in something static. The relation to the constructed thing also changes: we never read the book the author wrote, etc. The constructions themselves become elements in a flux from which further constructions must be made. Toward what is all this heading? Undoubtedly, a more and more complete re-creation by humanity of itself and the world—which must deal with larger and larger, more and more fundamental phenomena: situation in planetary space, laws of biological development. Impossible to think any farther.

Cabell as a Southerner. Psychology of defeat in the South: Somebody was telling me of a Southerner who never discovered until he went North that the South had lost the war. Somewhere a world where they did not lose. The forms under which this appears in Cabell: Rudolph Musgrave, in *The Rivet in Grandfather's Neck,* tries to give his fiancée away, to his upstart rival; Alfgarius Ecben, having conquered the rival king, resigns to him his throne and kingdom, condemns himself to homeless exile, comes at last to the cave where the gods are honored and kneels (?) before the altar of his own little god (that of Ecben), who has otherwise been forgotten. Here we have the South voluntarily refusing or resigning a victory. Cabell begins with romantic and more or less conventional novels, goes on to satirize the Virginians, exhausts the possibilities of this—you cannot go on indefinitely dwelling among the defeated and merely making wild fun of them—then invents an imaginary country in which he can forget the new middle-class Richmond and still cultivate an unrealistic romance—though he never loses completely his ironical sense of the situation. Later, in the *Smirt* trilogy, he makes fun of himself as a Virginian writing about his imaginary country without really ceasing to dwell in it; and, in *Let Me Lie*, returns to the actual Virginia to destroy the local legends.[8] [Marginal note: Don Quixote element in Rudolph Musgrave and Afgar (second of these names is something like an anagram of the first).]

The Civil War, continued: The North has made a point of forgetting the war: uneasy feelings of guilt, but, above all, desire not to make matters worse; no longer reads Grant's memoirs or *Uncle Tom's Cabin*—just as my grandfather Wilson made it a rule that the war should never be mentioned when Aunt Susan was in the house. The South, on the other hand, has made a point of remembering it—nursing their grievances, reliving it to try to see where they made their mistakes.

"Said the Governor of North Carolina to the Governor of South Carolina: 'It's a long time between drinks.'" Where did this originate? It came to me in a dream that it would be a brilliant idea to write the conversation which would terminate with this remark; but when I woke up, I wasn't so sure of its possibilities.

Cabell: Cabell's affectations of style: no least, not ever, questionless, builded, a little by a little, by ordinary, to the other side.

This Wardour Street English is a Southern trait that, even satirizing the South, he has never been able to shake off (like Silone's Italian rhetoric[9]). It really derives from reading Scott and is a part of the chivalrous feudal tradition that Cabell continues to represent even in making fun of it.

His habit of using continuous tenses—You will be seeing, etc.—is probably derived from Synge and the other Irish writers.

Reuel said to Elena, when Henry was coming back from his basic training, "Henry is quite a libertine, isn't he?"

July, '53. Helen was ill and had to go to bed just before the 4th of July. She said, "Put an ad in the paper and say, 'No fireworks till the little girl is well.'"

Talcottville Program for July 17 till Labor Day:
(perhaps read *Ruth*)   ~~Finish Genesis~~
Read in English the rest of the historical books
Apocrypha   Finish Renan's *Peuple d'Israël*[10]
Read Florida book about H. B. Stowe[11] and do *New Yorker* article about her (H. B. Stowe)
Do *New Yorker* article on Olmsted[12] and perhaps *In Ole Virginia*[13]
Get Xmas card into shape
Type 1930 notes and 1931
Read *Cords of Vanity*[14]   Angus Wilson's *Clocks*
Trowbridge's *The South*[15]   Some Belli with Paolo
Read Harold Frederic, if there's   Milano[17]
     time   Book on Edith Wharton
Get old novel typed in   Yeats's letters to
     Boonville[16]   K. Tynan

Helen at Talcottville: "Little girls like lemon drops, and fathers understand, because they like lemon drops, too—but mothers resist lemon drops."

At Flat Rock, paddling—sitting around in the shallow water: "Oh, this is so enjoyable!"

Talcottville: July 17–September 2. The house had been painted and the balcony and porch repaired, the chimneys had been reconstructed. Helen Augur had given the place a good cleaning and planted flowers in the stone things in front of the house; the grass had been well taken care of and in the bare patches was growing again; Elena had painted the bathroom white last summer and the red linoleum had been laid after we went. It delighted me to see the place looking so well again.

Paolo Milano had just finished a stay at Yaddo, and I had him meet me at Yaddo and brought him up here. We had very pleasant conversations. He is calm and more serious away from New York. We would walk up the hill in the afternoons or sit in the evenings in the front room that opens out on the lawn; he read me Belli and Dante, and I read him Swift and Yeats. It is so quiet, only occasionally a dog barks; at night the Lincks' cow sometimes moans. I like the feeling that I am occupying the largest and most distinguished house in a town of eighty people, that everybody knows me and takes me for granted—that I can say or do whatever I please, with the town at my door and all about me. At night we can sit on the porch and talk while the village people pass.

Helen Augur[18] is a true Baker, more than she realizes, not having seen very much of them: warm and vital voice, capable and energetic bustling, ambitious and instinctively tending to dominate a household. What is pathetic is that she has no household, and has neurotically doomed herself not to have one. In this house, she has become like that female beaver in a book I once read about beavers who, when taken into the beaver fancier's house as a pet, was one day possessed by her beaver instincts and began madly building a dam with mud against the front door of the house. Helen eventually became so tyrannical, undoing everything I did and thwarting whatever I tried to do, putting away things that I needed and snatching other things out of my hands, that I began having acrimonious scenes with her. And her nervousness, which takes the form in all this of ostensible efforts to help which are actually efforts to interfere, eventually drives me crazy. Nevertheless—though she was never here much as a child—one feels she belongs in this house. It has been a satisfaction to me to have her here: the other members of the family hated the Augur connection so that they behaved toward them rather unfairly. But Helen's passion for managing effects are like the same trait in my mother, and—though I like to have her, as I do Susan Wilson, as a kind of substitute sister—I very soon begin to react against her. —The worst of it is that Helen has herself become so convinced of the hopeless inferiority and the screwiness of the Augurs that she has always rather lacked self-respect and has allowed her Baker determination to be put down or shoved aside too easily. The Baker qualities are complicated by something in her that derives from the academic tradition of her father, who had a girls' school in Minnesota, of her grandfather Adams, who was head of Lowville Academy. She is really an intellectual but is not enough of one: the vigorous practical side (except perhaps when she was a foreign correspondent) has never been effectively integrated with the moony and cerebral one. She seems to live a good deal of the time in some adolescent self-centered fantasy, which she cannot exploit as fiction, but which keeps her from grasping clearly what is going on around her. Her sudden sorties out of this among the situations of the outside world always turn out to be at cross-purposes with what people are actually up to and

are likely to be merely annoying. She is always trying to
fill in my sentences before I have been able to finish them,
and I don't remember one occasion on which she has
gotten it right. (Elena often gets it right, but is likely to
supply something obvious, which is not what I was
going to say; Mary had an uncanny instinct for knowing
how my mind was likely to work; she established, in a
peculiar way, very close intellectual and what may be
called sensibility relationships—as when we used to have
dreams that paralleled one another's.) —Helen's self-
indulgence in her dreams, her lack of self-respect, now
appear in her slumping figure, the cigarette always hanging out of her mouth and her yellow upper lip—though
sometimes the pretty Baker woman comes back—reminds
me of how well she looked when I first knew her, married to Warren: blond, plump and pink-cheeked, smiling,
pimpante in clean bright clothes. Today her nice smile is
usually employed to mark some catty remark. —At times,
as when I talked to her the other night in Aunt Addie's
house, she surprises you by being quite lucid and criticizing herself; but usually she gives the impression of not
wanting to face herself and her problems, of having
resorted to all kinds of expedients, the source of her
annoying mannerisms, to divert people's attention from
her weaknesses (her ill-breeding that spoils her cleverness) and protect herself against the world. Mixture of
self-delusion and practical sense, intelligence and utter
idiocy. When she used to come to see me at Stamford, I
tried to get her to go to an analyst; she would promise
me that she was going but could never bring herself to
go. Instead, she had induced some M.D. to indulge her
hypochondriac side by telling her she would never be
well until she had left Warren. She is sunk in her private
dream, does not, as she told me the other night, really
care enough about people; then she tries to make people

notice her by alternately pretending to help them and making spiteful remarks. I can understand all too well her bemused self-enclosed side. She has a different idea every day, just as she did at Stamford, about what she is going to do to give herself a satisfactory life: get a job with children, get a job up here, get a job with flowers and plants (she has had no experience of gardening but has enjoyed pulling up weeds at Aunt Addie's and thinks that, on account of her grandmother and mother, she ought to "have a green thumb").

I am writing on the third floor in the room that looks out toward the old stone barn, and I first saw Helen cross the lawn, at her morning slumpingest and yellowest, on her way from the street to the back door of the house; then, a little while after, Fern Munn got out of her car to go into the store, just behind the barn: she walked, in spite of a figure which is now becoming rather full, with a firm step and straight carriage, looking very handsome. (She tells me that she is a mixture of Irish, New York State German, and Pennsylvania Dutch.) She accomplished her business in the store, then walked back to the car in the same unhurried but purposive and competent way, and drove off with her trailer full of milk cans. This summer she suddenly bobbed her hair (going to a beauty parlor in Constableville), and they left it a little frizzy—I don't like this nearly so well as the great thick old-fashioned bun that she used to wear behind— she says that it reached to her waist. She is the best-dressed woman around here—Elena says she spends more on her clothes than she (Elena) does—and she always has a certain sex appeal. Elena says correctly that she looks like a handsome cow: her big round gray eyes look at you with an innocence that is all the more winning because it seems to contrast with her executive ability and, I think, a certain amount of shrewdness. But this animal

innocence is associated, perhaps, with a slight touch of
Irish coquetry. It is as if she were aware of her attractiveness, of her round erect physique, her mastery of
whatever she is doing, even in the barn at milking time,
in dirty old overalls and boots, walking in the cow
manure, clamping on the milking machine, and shooing
away the bull. She sometimes seems a little shy but has
never any bad self-consciousness like Helen's. At haying
time, driving the tractor with the baling machine attached,
she seemed a figure almost symbolically sexual: bare-
headed, her solid round behind on the seat, with her legs,
in their farmer's pants, apart, and, behind her, the piston
of the pounder working steadily with a movement that
seemed powerfully phallic; the wire-bound square bales
of hay were excreted in close succession from the aperture
behind, and Otis Jr., her broad-shouldered boy, with the
help of a hired boy, piled them up on the platform behind. Round and round the field she drove; imposing the
baler on those big hay-grown fields, mastering all their
produce, packing it away in the barn, between the soak-
ing downpours and the thunderstorms of that high, almost mountainous country, was a serious and challenging
labor. There was something august about it. —Yet she
had fainted in the heat, from the sun, the afternoon of
the day when she came to get me in Utica. —She and
the children have had several dreadful accidents. These
are hazards of farming life; the same sort of thing has
happened to Mrs. Burnham. It may be that the Munns
are clumsy—or it may be that farm life necessitates a
pushing and lifting, a laboring over big areas, a piling-up
of copious products, a filling of enormous receptacles, a
marshaling of large animals, a control of ungainly machines, that let you in for heavy blunders, blunt mis-
calculations; you are handling huge materials by main
force of machinery and muscle, and there are moments

when you will fall off something, not see that something is coming, get at cross-purposes with the cattle.

Helen does not like the Munns. She gave Fern the impression that she had to work and did not care to see people, then made it a grievance that she and Otis had never asked her there or called on her. When Fern was painting the bedroom here, she believed that she kept her from writing and complained that she slopped the paint around. She cannot accept the fact that Otis uses bad grammar; said to Paolo Milano that Thad had married a "peasant" and that Otis had married "another peasant." Actually, however, Fern has rescued the Munns from their decadence. The Munn men seem not to have been able. They started in with their 80,000 acres of land, from which they first sold the timber; by the time of Otis's grandfather and father, they had taken badly to liquor and got along by selling the land. Now Otis has bought back part of the Munn land; he never touches alcohol; he has Fern and four robust children. They are substantial responsible people—though their aims and operations, if you see them in a long perspective, appear to be a little confused. They are always extending beyond their means, taking up new lines and dropping them, selling all their cattle, then a year or so later buying another herd. They do not fit in well with the other farmers, yet they haven't enough education or habit of town life for assimilating themselves to the Boonville bourgeoisie.

—On the second of August, Elena arrived. Rosalind had driven her and [little] Helen, with Bambi[19] and Pussinka, from Wellfleet. Elena cannot make herself at home here and she has a most dismal time. She says that the climate is all right for me, because on the Cape I am too keyed up and Talcottville tones me down, whereas the sea bathing at Wellfleet keeps her toned up and Talcottville lets her down so that she never has any energy and can hardly get breakfast in the morning. The altitude affects her, also, by causing her to begin to menstruate from the very day she arrives, and she seems to feel out of sorts almost all of the time she is here. This summer the first weeks of her stay were full of uncomfortable accidents. There was immediately a thunderstorm, in which one of our big trees (by the barn) was struck by lightning and a huge limb that overhung the street came down on the electric wires and cut off all the current as well as obstructing the road, so that early-morning motorists could not at first get past. The little girl woke up and began to cry; Rosalind says that a sheet of flame seemed to be flowing up that side of the house. I saw a shower of sparks crackling out of the wires on the corner. A day or so later Elena and Rosalind and Helen started out for a picnic at Flat Rock. Elena was wearing a red dress, and Rosalind had on red pants; and, whether by this or by the baskets they were carrying which the cattle took for salt, they attracted the attention of the cows, which—something I have never known them to do—came after them not walking but running, plunged down the steep bank of Sugar River after them and even crossed the river. They dropped their lunch and their bathing suits on a large stone at the edge of the river, scrambled across, slipping in the water, and got under the fence on the other side. Later, when Elena and Helen and I were walking on Leyden Hill, Helen, not looking ahead, suddenly started to cross the road to look at some cows on the other side, and if we hadn't stopped her in time, would have been hit by a speeding car, scaring us all and enhancing the general feeling of lack of coordination. Elena cannot find any field here, as she has been able to do at Wellfleet, for her creative homemaking and charming people. Her spirits sink; she tends to sulk. She imagines that the water is contaminated; complains that the people peer in at the window, that everything and everybody gives her the creeps—though for members of the family all this seems quite natural. Helen loves it, as children have always done, and has made friends with the Green and the Linck children and the little girl from the store, pretty but very dirty, with whom the other children have not been allowed to play. The ostracism of this little girl has aroused very strongly, however, Elena's democratic instincts, and she told Helen that it wasn't right that Marcia should be excluded, so now they all play together. Rosalind, too, likes being here; she says—I suppose, rightly—that it is too absolutely American for Elena to make connections with it. When we would talk about going on a picnic or spending an afternoon at the fair or taking a trip somewhere—a kind of project that she usually welcomed—she would mutter or simply be silent. When Rosalind and I would exclaim over the landscape, she would give the same cool response. On one occasion, on a beautiful evening, driving back from dinner at Constableville, she remarked that she didn't think she liked cows, and when Helen Augur loyally came to their defense and said that she liked to smell them, Elena replied that she did not like their smell—you expected to breathe fresh air and what you got was the smell of cows.

—When Fern drove little Helen and me to the Lowville Fair, I said that Lowville seemed a prosperous town, and she told me that it was full of rich farmers, but that they were very close, "tight as the bark on a tree."

—Mrs. Burnham told me about going to visit the Furbishes in Boston sometime around 1900. She had never been there before, and Bessie took her to see the sights. When she went back to Leyden—it was September—Bessie said she thought it would be a good opportunity for her to visit her mother, since Lillian Burnham could help her, on the train, to look after the three children. There was a storm on her way back to Boston, and Bessie caught cold and died of TB (in the Stone House) two years later.

—The Loomises told me that Talcottville had once been considerably bigger: a place where they made furniture, and a hoop and carriage factory. It was deprived of any future when the railroad, instead of running through it, was put through off in the valley (you cannot even hear the trains here). This confirms Elena's impression, after seeing Cooperstown, where there are many well-kept-up old places along the thickly settled streets, that the Stone House was built for a town, not for a rural community. —Mrs. Seifter has in her Boonville house (née O'Brien, Cousin Nelly's protégée) the portrait of the Talcott girl who married a Daniels. The husband (Seifter) had, the Loomises said, behaved very meanly about it, had no real right to it. He had been involved in the scandal of the subversion of the hospital funds (the hospital was still only half built) and had died when the fraud was exposed.

—The night that Elena and I sat on the front porch and saw the harvest moon, like a partly deflated balloon or a section of a tangerine coming up over the river. This was rather pleasant. She always becomes more humane when the time for departure approaches.

—Gertrude Loomis told a story about Aunt Lin, imitating her accent (they rightly said that Aunt L. behaved as if she were mayor of Talcottville). An impudent boy had climbed up one of the pillars of the front porch: "Aoy spoke to him in a voice of thunderr!" I have only just become aware of this feature of the upstate accent, which is something like the Irish tendency to substitute *i* for *oi* or *oi* for *i*. I believe I have a trace of it myself, which I have never understood before. The New England twang

of Fred Burnham—"The caows are up by the haouse"—
seems to be obsolete, as, so far as I have heard lately, it is
in New England, too. On Aunt Addie Munn's part, the
only trace of accent I remember—which rather used to
surprise me—was saying "wun't" for "won't." Now that
I think of it, I am not sure that Gertrude was imitating
Aunt L.'s accent: she may have only emphasized her
own by bringing out that dramatic sentence. I do not
remember that my grandmother had any trace of that
accent.

—This summer[20] I feel, as I did not last year, that I
have now moved into the house, to some degree taken
possession of it. I fill it with myself and my family: my
work and my mind occupy the big room where Aunt Lin
used to receive and first cousin Grace, then Mother sat in
front of the fire. I remember reading Michelet there, in
one of the not very comfortable chairs, when the fire was
burning at the end of the summer. (On the balcony, in
earlier days, I read Milton and Catullus through and *The
Education of Henry Adams*.) I now throne in the corner,
with the window on either side, in the overstuffed armchair from Red Bank, with my Hebrew apparatus on one
card table, my notebooks and the typewriter on another,
and my correspondence on the desk. I have partly dispelled the past; the house has now entered on a new
phase (the preceding ones were the Talcotts, the Bakers,
the Reeds, Uncle Tom's household after he married Nelly
Kent, my parents). —Though the southwest bedroom
has now been done over in yellow and does not look as
gruesome as it did last year, I still have to struggle, when
I sleep there, against a certain oppression: it is the room
where Cousin Bessie died and where my father slept
before he came home and died at Red Bank. The bed
with the head of Columbus in the southwest room is not,
as I now learn, at the Loomises', the one that has always

been there. It was bought by Mother from Minnie Collins, or given her by Mrs. C. Mother did not want the bureau and the washstand that go with it, which the Loomises now have in Aunt Addie's house. They would like me to take them, but I am not sure I want them. Though I have got used to sleeping in the bed, it rather gives me the creeps, as Elena says it does her—too wide, too amorphous, too flabby. The four-posters of the earlier period, in which I feel perfectly at home, are infinitely preferable to these. The bed in which Huldah Kimball died, in which Huldah Loomis now sleeps, seems admirable today and quite practicable for modern life, where these great sprawling pieces seem antiquated, invoking visions of sprawling sleepers in 19th-century nightgowns. The bed with the Columbus head used to be, the Loomises tell me, in the front room upstairs at the Collinses', where I believe my mother and father used to sleep in it.

—On this bed, on Elena's birthday, I made love to her in the morning when I was still lying in bed and she came in to see me. She was lying across it, not lengthwise; and, with the daylight, the position, and the lack of ceremony, it reminded me, as she had not done before, of my more satisfactory experiences with prostitutes: a simple enjoyable moment. How different this can be from the more romantic, intimate, more personal, or more passionate kind of thing. The next time, above my study in Wellfleet, she was almost as passionate as she had ever been, and I felt deeply peaceful and satisfied for a day and a half afterwards.

—Otis drove us back to Wellfleet. Sitting around the living room at Wellfleet, away from the farm and his family, he talked about his life at length. It began with his saying, as I poured another drink, that he had never been able to bear to drink, because his father's drinking had made his childhood—"really, you might say"—

miserable. He (Thad) had spent all his patrimony, had borrowed from all his friends, used to beg his money from Otis when Otis began to work. Otis did not get much schooling; used to run all the way from Boonville to Leyden Hill; was the fastest hand-milker in the neighborhood. Thad would disappear on sprees, would give all his money away; if, in a bar, he saw anyone badly dressed, he would give them money in a lordly way and tell them to get themselves some new clothes. He climbed into bed with Fred Burnham's sister, carrying a gun (Otis did not tell me these anecdotes), and she said, "Thad Munn: you put down that gun and get out of here!" and he once followed Florence Loomis, saying at intervals, "I love you, Florence!" Twice they had to put him in an alcoholic institution. He was bad when he was drunk, and Otis and his mother would hide behind the house when they heard him coming home at night. He had a gift for drawing—which Otis says his son George has inherited—but never did anything with it. He had had no interest in farming, and it had had to be the whole work of Otis's life to pull the farm together and make it go—he has even bought back some of the Munn land. It had taken him years to pay his father's debts, and some were not paid yet. —I remember how Aunt Addie once told my mother how Thad would come and wake her up at night, demanding money, and sometimes threaten to kill her; "I wish he would and have done with it," she said. Otis tells me that in her later life she did not see him for years. She used to say to us that she would not go to Talcottville even in the summer except for "little Otis." —This is the depressing side of life in this part of the world. The community had not developed—there was no field for superior abilities. The more enterprising men went West. You cannot imagine my Kimball uncles living in Lewis County. In my childhood, Homer Collins was the only

man of his generation from one of the old families still
functioning in Talcottville. He had been to sea instead
of college and seemed quite content to farm. He was
quiet, wonderfully patient and good-natured, and had
the kind of calm authority that the children of the settlers
had. (Otis has it, too.) His relationship with my father
was touching: Father would spread himself and Homer
would smoke his pipe; they would go on fishing trips together. The Munns were more arrogant and spendthrift;
Otis says that it had been bad for them always to be
rich—they had owned 80,000 acres—and never had to
work. Otis now tells me that there were two Loomis boys
—whom I have never heard the sisters mention—who
drank themselves to death. One was quite brilliant, had
been to college, drank and drank till his wife left him,
came back to Talcottville and eventually worked on the
roads. —Otis says that, due to his lack of education, he
can't help a feeling of inferiority and is shy about meeting people, because he doesn't know what to say. His
father was fired from boarding school (I don't know
whether he knows this). He once tried to put one of his
own boys in Exeter, simply took him there, not knowing
he would have to be entered and pass examinations.
None of his children (unless, perhaps, Ann) had even
finished high school. —Mother helped them through the
depression and used to send clothes for the boys, which
had been outgrown by the son of someone she knew.

—Elena had tea with Mrs. Burnham just before she
left. Mrs. B. gave her chocolate cake and explained that
the icing was made by a special and secret method. Her
sister-in-law had had it first, and on her deathbed had
felt an impulse to pass it on to Mrs. Burnham but had
then thought better of it and said, "No, I *won't* tell you!"
After her death, Mrs. Burnham had finally figured it out
for herself. The Loomises had tried to get her to tell how

it was done, and she had always refused; but now she was going to tell Elena: "Don't make it here, though! Just make it in Massachusetts." —When Elena made it in Wellfleet, it turned out to be very thick and rich, almost like some kind of chocolate candy.

Though I find that I remember quite clearly almost everything I have written about in my old notebooks, I often do not remember the faces or names of people who have been to the house here a year ago. Elena, however, seems to remember everybody and everything: how they were dressed, what they said, etc.—even everything I have told her about Talcottville, though this I partly forget myself from one summer to another. This, on my part, is the result of getting older. It is, also, more difficult for me, I find, to respond appropriately to new situations. When Reuel had his chickens last summer—not being used to having chickens around—if I met one of them, with my mind on something else, I would be likely to call it "Pussy Cat." My stereotyped response to a small domestic animal which was not a dog was based on the habitual assumption that it must be a cat. So I sometimes make speeches to people that are merely old phonograph records, with no particular relevance to the person or situation.

In New York (over the weekend of October 18, '53)— as the result, I suppose, of something that had caused me to revert to the mental habits of childhood, I had—what with me is rather rare—a simple and explicit Freudian dream. I thought that I was living with Elena, and that my father, in a quiet and natural way, came to get her to go to bed with him. I at first accepted this, then thought that I ought to resent it; but then had to realize that it was my father who was married to her, and that it was I who, in living with her, was violating his rights.

On my last visit to the Amens (in June '53), they gave me—if anything, worse—the same impression of demoralization. John at one point said to me, in some connection, "There's no good or bad anymore." The Rosenbergs had just been executed,[21] and John thought that I had probably been over in Brooklyn demonstrating at their funeral. The German girlfriend said that she didn't understand how these things were done over here: "In Germany, they would bury them behind the jail. Here you have a public funeral!" John said, "That's America." She had just read Polly Adler's book[22] and thought it was wonderful. John —as I discovered for the first time—had been getting her a divorce.

December '53. I walked to Spectacle Ponds on a bright day: the liquid sparkling of the black water; the fresh soft green moss in the woodland path, with the winter world all around.

Edna Millay: Carolyn Linck[23] said that at Vassar Edna had been very nice to her, but C. had been frightened of her. She had "ruined the lives" of a couple of girls by taking them up, then dropping them. When some girl had thrown herself out the window, Edna had said, Well, they can't blame me for *that!*

Esther Adams[24] told me of Edna's advising her always to be discreet. Once when she was driving in Central Park with a man, the horse had dropped dead. Afterwards, she and the man, who did not want their escapade known, told different stories about it. He had told his wife or whomever that he had had dinner with Edna

Millay, she had told somebody else about the horse dropping dead.

Christmas afternoon, '53, at the Shays':[25] *Ed Dickinson*[26] told me that in his childhood in upstate New York he heard constantly about the Civil War; his father preached about it and men who had been in Andersonville or Libby Prison gave talks about their experiences. Later on, he grew a beard and did a self-portrait in Federal uniform lying dead on the field at Shiloh, with a cannon in the background and his rifle by his side. He also bought the hundred and some volumes of the Civil War history, but had recently sold them for $60.

[At this point EW pasted a clipping in his diary from the New York *Times* headed "Eugene O'Neill at Princeton" and wrote: This is exactly what O'Neill once told me. He said that Fine had been very decent and encouraged him to come back. They had gotten a little tight in Trenton but were having a conversation on a very high level—"one of those conversations about Byron, Shelley, and Keats, in which they were getting them mixed up and talking about 'Kelly and Sheets.' " They had broken the glass insulators in sheer high spirits. —It amused me to hear him say that he thought he might have been in line for one of the food clubs.]

NOTES

1. *Upstate*, pp. 91–95.

2. Harold Frederic (1856–98), Utica-born novelist and short-story writer: *Marsena and Other Stories* (1894, includes "My Aunt Susan"); *The Copperhead* (1893); *The Damnation of Theron Ware* (1896); *In the Valley* (1890). DCB, pp. 48–76.

3. Henry Blake Fuller (1857–1929), Chicago novelist: *Waldo Trench and Others* (1908). DCB, pp. 18–47.

4. Mary Eleanor Wilkins Freeman (1852–1930) and Sarah Orne Jewett (1849–1909) wrote novels and short stories set in rural New England.

5. EW's *Five Plays* (1954).

6. See *The Forties*, pp. 10–25, for EW's notes for his unfinished novel.

7. Norman Haghejm Matson (1893–1965), Midwest-born novelist living on the Cape. *The Forties*, p. 30.

8. Cabell's *The Rivet in Grandfather's Neck* (1915), *The Way of Ecben* (1929), *Let Me Lie* (1947), and *The Smirt Trilogy* (*Smirt*, 1934; *Smith*, 1935; *Smire*, 1937).

9. Ignazio Silone (1900–78), Italian novelist, author of *Bread and Wine* (1937). *The Forties, passim; Europe Without Baedeker* (1947), pp. 80–96, 170–73.

10. Ernest Renan (1823–92), French philosopher and orientalist; *Histoire du peuple d'Israël* (1887–93, 5 vols.).

11. *Mandarin on the St. Johns*, by Mary B. Graff (University of Florida Press, 1953).

12. Frederick Law Olmsted (1822–1903), landscape architect known for his unbiased travel writings in the slave states.

13. Short stories (1887) by Thomas Nelson Page (1853–1922).

14. A novel by Cabell (1920).

15. John Townsend Trowbridge (1827–1916), poet, editor, author of books for boys (pen name Paul Creyton): *The South: A Tour of Its Battlefields and Ruined Cities* (1866).

16. *Galahad*, written in the early twenties and first published in *The American Caravan*, edited by Van Wyck Brooks et al.; reprinted by EW in 1953.

17. Giuseppe Gioacchino Belli (1791–1863), Italian poet, author of over two thousand sonnets. Paolo Milano, Italian writer teaching at Queens College.

18. Helen Vinton Augur, a second cousin of EW's. *The Thirties, passim; The Forties*, p. 24; and *Upstate*, pp. 96–100.

19. The Wilsons' spaniel.

20. *Upstate*, pp. 103–4.

21. The Rosenbergs were executed June 19, 1953.

22. Polly Adler (1900–62) wrote *A House Is Not a Home* (1952), about life in a brothel.

23. Carolyn Linck was a Talcottville neighbor. Her son did gardening for EW.

24. Esther Root Adams had met Edna Millay in Paris in

1921 and later married Millay's close friend and early supporter, the columnist Franklin P. Adams. See note 76, p. 150.

25. Frank and Edie Shay were Provincetown friends of EW. See previous volumes, *passim*.

26. Edwin Dickinson (1891–1978), painter. He was born in Seneca Falls, New York.

LONDON AND OXFORD, 1954

[EW's diary of his stay in England provides a good deal of entertaining—if by now ancient—gossip about his literary and intellectual encounters there during 1954. His last visit had been brief and semi-anonymous; he was writing his postwar reportage for *The New Yorker* recorded in *Europe Without Baedeker* and *The Forties*. This time he arrived with a considerably expanded reputation as a result of the publication of his literary chronicles, *The Shores of Light* and *Classics and Commercials*, and his novel *Memoirs of Hecate County*. He greatly enjoyed his celebrity. London seemed "its old comfortable self," which meant that he took his young daughter to the scenes of his own childhood in the British metropolis— the Tower and the pantomime, the music halls and magicians' shows. He also revisited his own Edwardian past by seeking out writers like Compton Mackenzie whom he had read in his youth, and later, on the Continent, Max Beerbohm. But he had not been long in England before his old and rooted anglophobia reappeared.

[He seems—in general—to have always disliked the British people and their manners out of a sense of his discomfort with them: their class distinctions, hierarchies, reticences, modes of speech, and their potential for bad manners—the kind Henry James had referred to in his aphorism: "As for [British] manners, there are bad manners everywhere, but an aristocracy is bad manners organized." His dislike derived from his own type of isolationism and his set conviction that Britain had involved America in two bloody wars. The very words Lords and Commoners apparently infuriated him. He had his own distinctions, as we know from his gentry style of life at Talcottville. He tended to refer to the traditions of the American Revolution; and his earlier readings of Marx had sharpened his sense of class wars. The result was that he faced his transatlantic confreres with a certain amount of bellicosity. He reveals as much in his diaries when he writes of "my present policy in England of maintaining a discreetly aggressive policy." It wasn't very discreet, and quite often it was explosive. He had, as he noted, "a stock of questions about customs and habits of speech in England" and he fired these at his newly made acquaintances in his brisk cross-examining way, as if to relieve himself of personal curiosity (as well as anxiety), but what it amounted to was a consistent baiting of the British. That this kind of verbal skirmishing should meet with characteristic responses was inevitable —sometimes silence, sometimes polite indifference, and sometimes a retaliatory and ironic thrust. His British peers knew how to deal with him—thus increasing anxiety and tension.

[Arthur Waley, the eminent translator of Chinese and Japanese poetry, reacted to Edmund's chatter about Hemingway's latest escapades in Africa and the possibility that T. S. Eliot might become Britain's Poet Laureate with "devastating deadpan cracks." We have a picture of firecrackers bursting as they talked, although

Waley was reputed to be a shy man. Waley's retort on the subject of Eliot was: "I don't care a pin who is the next Poet Laureate." This was undoubtedly true—given his private laureateship in the realm of Oriental poesy. EW found him "extremely snooty." We have in this instance, however, the testimony of a third party: Celia Paget's remark that EW was "awfully tense" as he talked with Waley. Edmund agreed, but tried to explain it: Waley was "overanxious to live up to his role, and this made me self-conscious." An alternative speculation is possible—for EW doesn't define Waley's "role." His anxiety about his own, amid the Britons, was clear enough: it was that of a rebel who had to work off aggressive feelings.

[He lunches with the editors of the liberal journal *The New Statesman*, and is a bit miffed when Richard Crossman, M.P., teases him at *The New Yorker's* failure to refer to Senator McCarthy's doings, his red hunt being then at its height. However, the occasion has its pleasant side—it reminds him of his old editorial lunches at *The New Republic* and he has some good talk with Kingsley Martin, the editor of *The New Statesman*. He meets the editor of the literary *Horizon*, which had existed during the war in the midst of great difficulties, the rotund epicure and aphorist Cyril Connolly, and they exchange a great deal of domestic and literary gossip. EW notes he is not a good listener and concludes he is too busy polishing his epigrams to listen. Of the newer writers he is happiest with Angus Wilson, whose novels have satirized the British middle class, and with John Betjeman, "a minor poet but a good one," who would become the Poet Laureate later on.

[EW's anglophobic malice extends even to Sir Isaiah Berlin, the eminent philosopher and authority on Russia, whom Edmund had sought out during his postwar visits to the United States and invited a number of times to Wellfleet. Berlin had served in the British embassy in Washington during the war, his Russian expertise being much in demand; his dispatches had attracted the attention and praise of Winston Churchill. At that time EW is said to have avoided meeting Berlin on the theory that he would "surely want to use him [Edmund] for propagandist purposes." The war over, EW made the first gesture and invited Berlin to lunch. They quickly became friends. Sir Isaiah's ease of manner, his well-informed anecdotes, his charm as a raconteur, and his scholarly breadth made him an appealing friend, particularly to such an omnivorous gatherer of table talk as EW. Berlin remembers: "We had very good times together. I used to talk to him about ideas and books, principally English and Russian, with probably my usual vehemence, and it may be, verbosity. He used to reply in fragments, which seemed to come from ideas thrashing about not wholly articulate, always first-hand, original, sometimes deeply moving and always impressive." Berlin also remarks that when EW "missed his target" he could do so "by many miles."

[At Oxford, where he was a Fellow of All Souls, Isaiah Berlin sought to help EW meet various historians and writers, as the diaries show. But EW's anti-British obsession interfered with these amenities. A party arranged by Berlin for the American critic to meet the Oxford critic John Bayley and his wife, the novelist Iris Murdoch, proved a frost—EW pronounced them boring and confused Bayley with Humphry House, a noted Dickens scholar. EW also decided that the Oxford dons were trying to foist certain persons on him and discriminating against others. He seemed disinclined to meet David Cecil, the well-known literary historian and biographer, who was a don at Oxford, because he was an "aristocrat"—Cecil being the youngest son of the Marquess of Salisbury and entitled to be called Lord David. EW compared him with the Sitwells and spoke of him as "one of those noblemen who are touchingly anxious to associate with literary people and to be known as writers themselves." When they did meet, he enjoyed talking with him about the pantomime, but decided this was because as an "aristocrat" he recognized it was a traditional institution which other Britons seemed not to care about.

[In his notes he concluded that there was a clique at Oxford which wanted to introduce him only to their favorites and friends. He reported to Cyril Connolly that he was convinced they "blackballed" certain colleagues— but on the next page of his diary attributes this assumption to Connolly himself—"as Cyril Connolly says, blackballing people from the group of acceptable dons."

[His quest for "class lines" in the Oxford scene is amusingly pursued in relation to the Oxford "scouts"— the men who have the perhaps unenviable but satisfying job of being servants to a parcel of adolescents in the colleges but also the reflected glory of serving some of the world's most eminent scholars. Dining in hall at All Souls and Christ Church, EW develops a curious thesis that the scouts are "disaffected" by the class system. The Oxford young, in the grandeur of their vaulted or arched halls, usually bolt their food and dash away for the evening's fun or study; and the scouts clear up as quickly as possible to salvage some part of *their* evenings. EW complains of the whisking away of food and dishes at the high table, and describes this as "the high-handedness of the class-contemptuous waiters." I imagine this was what Berlin meant when he said EW could miss his target by many miles. "Hall" is invariably a rapid affair. The

lingering occurs in the Common Room, where the dons
go for their port and Madeira. EW seems distinctly unfamiliar with the Oxford tradition and its mores.

[EW came away from Oxford convinced there were
"intramural spites and grudges" and this no doubt was
true. C. P. Snow's *The Masters* has documented Americans on this subject; but the spites and grudges would be
noted by EW later in American colleges as well. EW's old
readings in Marx seemed to be getting in the way of his
enjoying the amenities his friends sought for him. For
the moment he seemed happy to be moving on to egali-
tarian France and his scheduled talks with André
Malraux, who by this time had drifted markedly, in the
De Gaulle camp, toward the right.]

I should have begun this notebook on the boat when
I left New York (we sailed on the *Ile de France* at the end
of December), but am only getting around to it now. I
shall try to fill in all the things that I want to write
down.

Jason Epstein[1] aboard on his Doubleday-paid honeymoon with his nice and touching wife, Barbara. They
were in the first class and had been supplied by Doubleday and other people with more champagne than they
knew what to do with. One night we drank five bottles
with them; met Buster Keaton with them on that "gala"
night—he was going over to perform in the Cirque
Medrano, had told Jason that he expected soon to find
himself clowning at home in a traveling circus. I complimented him on his scene in Chaplin's *Limelight*
[1952] and he said he hadn't seen the picture, evidently
feared to be depressed by finding himself in this minor
role. —Epstein had been working so furiously in New
York that, after the first couple of days, he found the
quiet and idleness maddening, longed for his office at

Doubleday, and began thinking up more plans for his series of Anchor Books.

Thoughts on leaving Wellfleet, and after: Don't talk all the time. It is an error to suppose that other people can have nothing interesting to say. (I had got into the habit in Wellfleet, but got over it in London, where I was interested in what people had to say.)

Nobody is interested in hearing about other people's illnesses.

Nobody is interested in hearing about deaths, unless they can be made pleasing or amusing.

Voyage: perfectly calm sea all the way; during the first days, we would sleep in the cabin for hours.

Jan. 5. We landed in England and went to stay at the Basil Street Hotel in London, where Mamaine [Koestler][2] had gotten us comfortable rooms and left us a potted hyacinth. She came to dinner with us in the hotel.

Mme. Djakelli, old Georgian princess, came to see Elena at 3:30, told Elena of the situation at Dorothy Paget's. Elena hoped that Mme. Djakelli could still be there, so that Olili[3] could stay in London when she came to England, but Mme. Djakelli had to go to Paris because her husband was ill there, and Olili was pretty tied up at Hermit's Wood. They would telephone for her when she was staying with us, and on one occasion, when we came back late at night and found a message from them to call, Elena disregarded it. Dorothy Paget[4] had grown to be a monster, ate enormously and had grown very fat, stayed in bed all day and made her cousin sit up all night playing cards with her. When Henry [Thornton] was brought in to see her, she said at once that he had a dreadful American accent (her mother was a Whitney). Goes out of doors only occasionally for big racing events, where she is flown with great pomp to the track and greeted by the enthusiastic crowd as "good old Dorothy."

Bettina Powell and her husband came to tea. She is a German cousin of Elena's (mother of Dickie); had married a wealthy businessman (quite intelligent, had during the war been sent on a mission to America and traveled all over the country, said that it was more like an empire than a European nation). Then discovered that this cut her off, in England, from the society to which she was accustomed—and which her brother continued to frequent. This annoyed her, and since the war, she has kept going back to Germany to the dissatisfaction of her husband, with whom her relations are now somewhat strained. She has mastered the smart English way of talking: *fahnny, Rahssia, divine, heavenly!* (over Helen's remarks, repeated to her); but Elena feels that it is a little nervous-making: one is afraid she is going to run off the track.

Jan. 7. Went to see Allen[5] in the morning. Planned to see the Tower in the afternoon, and I think this was the day we went: gloomy, implacable, impregnable, the formidable side of the English. I told people afterwards that the two best things to take a child to see, because it could understand them both, were the Tower and the Christmas pantomime: the two poles of the English character. There is something vulturous and horrible about the monstrous ravens, one of which a guard was baiting—it would angrily stretch out its wings and threaten him with gaping beak. Helen at this time was becoming obsessed with the idea of Mary Queen of Scots —demanded to see the spot where her head was cut off,

Barbara and Jason Epstein, Rome, 1954

Mamaine Paget Koestler   *Arthur Koestler*

Elena and Helen Wilson in Salzburg, 1954

then to see the ax. It was growing dark before we left, and our feet were terribly cold; but an appropriate season at which to see it.

Gates[6] came in for drinks, then Connolly and his wife,[7] who had come to dinner. Cyril was conducting a Christmas contest for the best set of Latin verses translating some piece of English verse. He had already discussed this with Sylvester, saying that he was hoping for an elegiac quatrain, and this had started Sylvester trying to make a version of this kind. They talked about his incomplete quatrain and the entries reviewed by Connolly (one by Duff Cooper,[8] Lord Norwich, who was just dead, or some other lord).

Cyril's wife, Barbara, looks, as Elena says, like a Petty girl and, as Mamaine says, is very *farouche*. She said absolutely nothing, but tried a little to vamp me by lingering glances from her brown long-lashed eyes. I wrote Cyril later, when I was leaving England, that she did much to redeem the London literary world from the taint of homosexuality. (Elena's line that the novels of Henry Green[9] and the other current British fiction writers came over to America like batches of delicious little cakes; my line that the homosexual novel had now become the *spécialité de la maison* of contemporary English writing.) We had dinner in the hotel; sat around the fire in the coal grate in our sitting room after dinner. I think Cyril was glad to see us and talk. Like most of the English writers I saw, he was not enthusiastic about Angus Wilson[10]—evidently envied and resented the rapid rise of Wilson's reputation and his accelerating productiveness. When later, after seeing Angus, I told Cyril that he was thinking of giving up his job at the British Museum in order to devote all his time to writing, Cyril said very quickly that he doubted whether anyone who had been

a civil servant so long would be able to give it up.
—Barbara, very determinedly, tried to get Cyril away to
catch an early train; but he managed to miss this.

Jan. 9. We went out to Folkestone for lunch with the
Connollys, because they had invited the Epsteins. I had
phoned Jason to do some business with Cyril and had
briefed Cyril at dinner Thursday. Cyril had brought to
the hotel for me his somewhat deteriorated [coat], which
had been given him by Pearsall Smith.[11] We had a very
good lunch. Cyril, like many wits and raconteurs, never
listens to anyone else's sallies or stories: his mind begins
at once to wander, and when the other person has finished
gives a little nod and smile that indicates he has paid no
attention. Sidney Floris, the photographer, told me that
he had taken a picture of Peter Quennell[12] in conversation with Cyril, with Cyril not listening to him. He is
evidently pleased that someone, in a recent review, had
spoken of him as "a great writer" (but later A. L. Rowse[13]
of All Souls wrote in to the paper to protest against this).
—I found myself totally unable to make any conversation
with Barbara [Skelton] Connolly, though, accompanied by
Barbara Epstein, I walked with her on the path along the
sea cliff, while Jason was talking business with Cyril,
and Elena had taken Helen to the hotel. She came from
one of the Cinque Ports, I found out; and I had the
vision of a small-town pretty girl who had come to London and made her way. Apparently [she] had jumped at
marrying Cyril. She now rules him, obviously, with an
iron hand, and can, I am told, be exceedingly truculent.
On one occasion, when Quennell had kept her waiting
or something, she had rapped him on the head with the
heel of her shoe and made him completely groggy: he
had been reeling in the street. —When, just before
leaving, we all got together, we discussed Epstein's

project for sending Cyril to the South Sea islands. I was surprised at this, and said they had already been overdone, but, being young, he seemed to think that this was all a long time ago, and that it was time to have them looked into again. Cyril said that he didn't like to go anywhere where there wouldn't be a chance of his being able to turn the corner and come upon an old bookshop in which he might find a first edition of Proust. If you could only have Kenya without the Mau Mau, someplace else without something else, etc.! He finally got it around to North Africa, of which, I gathered, one of the attractions was that it would be very easy to reach the Riviera from there. Later I was told that some other publisher had already given him money for a travel book (Riviera, I think). —One reason for the unsatisfactoriness of most of his recent work is that he is primarily an artist, not a journalist. His pamphlet on Burgess and Maclean[14] is not really a pamphlet, and it does not throw much light on Burgess and Maclean: his piece on Bordeaux in *Ideas and Places* [1953] ought to be used as background for a novel: something funny ought to be going on. His reviews in the *Sunday Times* are rarely exactly good reviews. Yet there is always a good phrase or two, a poetic touch of color, in them. I am curious to see his mystery story of the London literary world, which he says he has nearly finished.

—Anecdotes about Cyril: *Horizon* published a plea for contributions of food from America in aid of starving British writers. Later, I was told by somebody that Cyril, himself a deserving writer, was eating up all the stuff that was sent in response to this appeal. I asked Peter Watson[15] about this, when I saw him in New York, and he answered: No—only the *foie gras*.

When Lys[16] left Cyril, she forgot to take her coat, and later sent somebody to get it, but, not wanting to have him encounter Cyril, she chose an hour in the afternoon when she thought he would be likely to be absent—and gave him her key to the apartment. The friend let himself in, quietly went upstairs, and slipped into the bedroom, where he found Cyril lying on the bed naked, "like a great pink Zeppelin." Without turning his head, he said simply: "In the closet."

Barbara—I think after she married Cyril—is said to have taken the fancy of King Farouk, and she and Cyril to have gone to visit him in France. Whoever told me remarked that Cyril and King Farouk had obviously a good deal in common.

I thoroughly enjoyed London, which seemed almost its old comfortable self. Pleasure of getting into the good soft yet solid English beds at the Basil Street Hotel. All my English side has come out and felt at home on this trip. I do not feel myself so much in a strange part of the world as I did at the end of the war, when everything was actually strange, on account of the rockets, etc. —I have, I suppose, been trying to get back to the England of my youth—1908 and 1914—of the Exposition at Shepherd's Bush, the Dickensian waiter who amused my father at the Metropole Hotel, of Maskelyne's[17] Egyptian Temples, of *Pygmalion*, Gilbert the Filbert, our bicycle ride from Scotland taking in all the cathedrals, of our teas in country inns, of our comings and goings to and from the old Langham Hotel (bombed in the last war, I went to look at it in '45), near which the vista of Portland Place used to remind me of *The Golden Bowl*,[18] of the old music halls: Albert Chevalier, Vesta Victoria and Maria and Alice Lloyd. But I cannot get back to this, and the truth is that I have now lived long enough so that the series of my visits to London (and to other places in Europe) now form a sequence of memories each of which is still vivid and can easily be made to present itself as immediate yet of which the earlier ones are somehow so far in the past that I cannot hold them up, cannot anymore include them in any present functioning consciousness, and they seem to topple over at the end of the curve of the lengthened span of my life, even to be lost as actual. If that really means anything to me. I can remember them still with pleasure, yet they do not make part of my present life.

Sometime in the first days, I took Helen to a magic matinee. There was a good English magician, Robert Hardin, trained in the Maskelyne school. The Maskelyne apparatus—and theater, I guess—had been destroyed by the bombing, and there was no elaborate [illegible] but an excellent performance—notably, a new version of sawing the woman in two, in which the woman was not in a box but lying on two or three chairs, and the blade of the saw was seen intact below her after the sawing was done. Hardin made a gentlemanly appearance, quite in the manner of the modern English theater; he had quite dropped the old-fashioned magician's patter, seemed more like the BBC. One felt, also, that he had probably been influenced by experience in the army. —Also, two of the Lupino family—a familiar element of pantomime. —I remembered the London letter in *The Sphinx* in which the British contributor sometimes protests against such ungentlemanly practices as producing borrowed necklaces from the mouth. —Theaters still inadequately heated: we were very cold in the balcony.

—At some point about this time Bill Hughes[19] came in to see us at cocktail time, when Mamaine was there. He has grown heavier and somewhat coarser since Rome and talks in a more self-assured and self-assertive way. This has probably something to do with his legal career: undoubtedly in the courtroom he knows how to make an impression by his loud, positive tones, bullying the witnesses, if necessary. Elena thinks him something of a bounder, and he is not always perhaps in quite the best taste. He seems to be rather vain of his conquests. And I noticed that the laws he went in for usually had a sex angle, divorces and prostitutes, about which he was very explicit. But he was a good deal more fun to see than the ordinary dim English literary man. On a later occasion, he talked about the current homosexuality cases. He said that Gielgud had been drunk when he was arrested for soliciting "just back of where I live." There had also been Lord Montagu. His theory about this was that the police had been out to get him—Lord M., he said, was a rogue—because he had been a nuisance to them so long. (The *Times*' reporting of this was incredible in its language: "The aircraftsman's kits were searched for letters which it was hoped to prove had emanated from Lord Montagu.") He said there [are] two kinds of judges: the kind who said to the offender: "You have been guilty of the horrible crime of buggery. You will never live it down, and your children will suffer. I sentence you to the maximum term of imprisonment that the law admits"; and the kind who said, "I'm very sorry, but the law is on the statute books. I'm giving you the lightest sentence I can." It was very unjust that Gielgud should happen to get caught and be publicly disgraced while Somerset Maugham, for example, who had been doing the same thing for years, was having his eightieth birthday fêted.

We had lunch with him [Hughes] the next day. As if to correct the almost boisterous impression of the afternoon before, when he had had quite a lot to drink, he was rather subdued and formal. He did himself very well in an old mansion—of which he had known the family, "as a matter of fact"—converted into apartments: brass plate outside the door, "William Hughes, Esq.," excellent lunch in a little dining room; rather expensive books. —None-such Shakespeare and Dickens (with plate of illustration from *Bleak House*), Princeton Jefferson, Yale Walpole. His interest in a knowledge of American books is one of the strange things about him. He told us that his grand-father had traveled in America, was interested in the Civil War, and had acquired such rather uncommon books as John De Forest's novels,[20] which Bill now had. I wasn't quite sure that he wasn't lying. He remains enigmatic to me. Who and what is he? When he speaks of his family, it is always in a way not to reveal anything about them, except that they were Anglo-Irish. Cardinal Merry del Val[21] used to visit them. He tends to boast a little, to build himself up: "just back of where I live," knew the family "as a matter of fact." (I tend to do this a little myself.) He knows all the literary gossip, usually says that he has met any literary figure, yet I have never found one who knew him and nobody seems to remember him at Oxford. I got the impression that he is now highly successful, will no doubt soon be "taking silk," and that he is greatly enjoying himself. In telling us about his adventures in court, he would say that the judge or someone liked him. Strange story of the judge who had handed down a wrong decision and then tried to make it up to him, in another case, by awarding his client more damages than he had asked for or something of the kind.

Jan. 10. The Halperns: we went there at 5:30 for supper. Curious to go into a Russian household in Lon-don (it was the same thing later on with Elena's Russian relations in Paris): freedom and informality. I find them easier to get on with than the natives; and they are the same everywhere in the world: Rome, London, Paris, Boston, New York. But in this case Mr. H. is a little on the pompous side and an incompletely defrosted Stalinist

—their daughter, it seems, is a Communist in Paris. I ran into difficulties with him in talking about Ehrenburg and Del Vayo,[22] of both of whom he approves—though he went on to tell me the most damaging things about Ehrenburg. He had accepted an invitation to have supper or something with the H.'s, then, on going, said, "You haven't seen me!" etc. His wife—also, I think, a Georgian princess—was quite jolly and nice—had once been a great beauty and a patron of poets. H. had importuned her to marry him day after day, month after month, and finally she had done so.

Jan. 11. We took Helen to *Cinderella.* The Christmas pantomime is an interesting English institution. Many of its features must go back to Grimaldi's time, if not before. How do the children always know how to come in on the songs and how to answer the questions from the stage? It seems like the special instincts that animals inherit. Fixed features: the principal boy and the principal girl: the principal boy is always a girl whose legs look well in tights; the dame, always played by a male comedian, who undresses at some point, unwinding yards of cloth and revealing unexpected garments: *Cinderella,* which has often been done, offers rich opportunities from this point of view: because, in the stepmother and her ugly daughters, it has roles for three such characters; the scene in which the comedians are lost in a wood and are warned by the audience of some menace behind them, which disappears when they turn around: at the pantomime I saw in 1945, this was simply a bear, but in this new one, it is a space man, has been brought up to date; the lancers danced by the comedian, alone on the stage: Dan Lewis, it seems, used to do this. In this production, the comedian asked the audience whether he should dance the waltz or the rumba or the lancers, and they

cried in chorus, "The lancers!" In '45, this was done—
and better—by the dame. The point of it is the impassivity
with which he walks through the figures, and, at the end,
his being pulled around when the music is stepped up
for the Great Chain.

Elena was struck by the pretty little boys in the audience, said they made one understand the homosexual
tastes of the English, she had never seen anything like
them anywhere else—also, the confusion of sexes in the
pantomime itself.

—Angus Wilson came to dinner, with his "friend,"
whom he had asked to bring. The friend was a very good
example of the current English pansy: good-looking,
though a little bit dead, as they get; did not talk much,
made a little shy, I think, by his position—like a wife
who remains in the background. He is interested in
prison reform. We both liked Wilson and spent a very
pleasant evening with them. Wilson does, as Mamaine
had told me, have the face of a woman (under a lot of
white hair); but in some ways he is not effeminate. He
has positive opinions and a strong Scottish moral strain
that gives vertebrae to his work, and that leads him to
make a matter of principle, as Gide did, of his homosexual habits. He said to me that E. M. Forster was not
really very "courageous"; and I was later confirmed in
my guess at what he meant by his telling me that Forster
had written him about Heinlade a rather guarded letter.
"It was a little too near home." What made our conversation with them different from our conversation with
other people was their interest in the social problems that
the literary world in general seemed completely to have
dropped. When I asked about such slums as White-
chapel, they told me I ought to go there to see how new
housing exploits were being carried out in the midst of
the squalor. Wilson said (either on this or the following

occasion) that, though he still wrote in terms of the social classes, England was heading for a classless society. He told Elena that he had stuck to his job at the British Museum partly because it was useful to him in enabling him to see a variety of types.

Jan. 12. Stephen Spender came to lunch with us. [He] seems less of a prima donna now that he is getting older. His hair has turned quite white since I saw him in New York. He was evidently having his difficulties with Irving Kristol over *Encounter*.[23] Asked me what I thought of it, and I said that the two elements didn't cohere: what Kristol contributed was run-of-the-mill stuff of the type turned out by ex-Communists and the more arid kind of young political intellectual. He was worried at K.'s re-writing these pieces. After lunch, when we were talking in our room, I said that Isaiah Berlin affected me like nobody else I had known; though he was not particularly handsome, I tended to react to him a little as if he were an attractive woman whom I wanted to amuse and please; and this attitude on my part evoked a kind of coquetry on his. This started Spender on his theory of "invisible marriages." There were spiritual marriages that confused one's relations with one's real wife.

—Maika, Natalya's mother, came to tea; then a lot of other people arrived: Mamaine; Sylvester Gates brought John Betjeman, and Betjeman said that he had asked "a jolly girl" with whom he was having dinner to meet him here. This turned out to be some titled lady who was in the news for social work or something identified, after she left, by Maika as "Bedford's son" (I may have the name wrong.) She did not seem particularly jolly. I liked Betjeman, who is quite amusing; has a somewhat clerical look and a perpetual twinkle in his eye—you feel that both these features are deliberate and almost professional.

He was going to give one of his radio talks—I didn't gather whether about church architecture or a real religious talk—he does both, I understand. I later heard a story about his working during the war in some government department and saying suddenly one morning as he was going up in the lift with the other employees in his office: "It's not true what you're all thinking. Lord Woodhull [their chief] doesn't take bribes." On another occasion, Gates told me, when Betjeman had been talking to some earl, he had said suddenly: "Gosh, you're dim! You're the dimmest earl I've ever met!" He had written an essay on Dim Earls. I was surprised at his saying something that implied he was not much read in England. (He seems to pride himself on the obscurity of Murray,[24] his publisher.) I told him that I had supposed he had a considerable reputation. He said that he had had a little more lately; before that, his conventional writing had made him unfashionable. Since Dylan Thomas's death, he is, I suppose, the best poet in England—a minor poet, perhaps, but a very, very good one.

Jan. 13. Elena's old half-English half-American friend from the Oxford Press, Fullerton, came to tea with his wife—nice but far from exciting, some relation to the Princeton [illegible].

Dinner at the Gates'. Isaiah was there in his liveliest London form—though Elena thought—what I certainly failed to notice—that he was conspicuously *abattu* by his father's death. He gave a long description, which I partly failed to follow, of Duff Cooper's funeral, at which he had been and at which some grotesquely inappropriate person had been asked to speak. After dinner, when the ladies had withdrawn, he started telling me about Namier,[25] the historian, whose pompous voice and Jewish accent he imitated. When somebody had asked N. why

he didn't write the history of the Jews instead of the
English parliament, he said that the Jews "had no history,
only a martyrology." I was struck by this saying, which
has something in it: when I read the first part of Cecil
Roth's[26] *Short History of the Jews* [1936], I felt that it
was impressive and that everybody ought to read it, but
when I came to the later part, into its record of disasters
and persecutions, I felt that it was so humiliating that it
was natural not to dwell on it. He went on at such length
about Namier—once started on a story, he cannot stop
giving the whole of his career from the beginning,
pointed up with anecdotes—that he kept us a long time
from the ladies and it took a brusque move to break him
up. After dinner, they read Betjeman's poems aloud. Altogether a very pleasant evening. Just before we left,
when Sylvester was going to phone for a taxi, I went out
with him into the hall in order to ask him about Mayda
and Pearsall Smith's rubber doll. We were laughing about
this latter so loudly that Pauline [Gates], as Elena said,
couldn't stand it and came out into the hall to find out
what was going on. She had already shown her fantastic
suspicions about what Sylvester had been up to, in the
twenties, in the United States—when Mayda's name
was mentioned or when we talked about staying at Hull-
House. I had only been restrained by the presence of the
Gates' daughter from telling her that Hull-House was a
super-brothel that Sylvester and I had gone to Chicago to
visit.[27]

—I had a very good time with Gates this trip, found
him very genial, and we have reached a kind of old-
crony basis, so that I do not have to bother with his
cynicism nor he with my relatively idealistic notions.
Mamaine, however, had told me that she had come to
regard him as "a sinister character." Story about Sylvester's

having refused to let his son keep even one of a litter of puppies and insisting that he drown them all himself. She thought he was very sadistic. The story had been told her by Arthur Koestler, who is always extremely severe on the callousness of other people. —I had been rather depressed, on my former visit, by his public quarrel with Pauline at Henry Green's. His neurotic outbreaks of violence. At "21," in New York, when he didn't move and the proprietor had insisted on talking about hunting, he had picked up the whole table and thrown it into the middle of the room. On another occasion, he had told me, he had thrown a conductor out of a train (in the station, not when it was moving) when he had questioned his ticket or something. M. said that he had socked someone at the Gargoyle bar who had jostled him with his elbow, but that they were always having rows at the Gargoyle.

Somewhere above I have omitted the party for John Lehmann's new *London Magazine*,[28] which is not noted on our calendar. —It was as crowded and deafening as anything in New York and made Elena only want to escape. I saw Louis MacNeice,[29] who was, as usual, nice but not particularly interesting, and met E. M. Forster for the first time and had a curious little conversation. —He is a tiny little man—who might, at first glance, be some kind of clerk or a man in an optician's shop—with spectacles and a small slightly sagged mustache, the mustache of another generation. I said at once that I shared his enthusiasm for his three favorite books: *The Divine Comedy*, Gibbon, and *War and Peace*. —You would, of course. —But, I thought that *Das Kapital* almost belonged in the same category. This seemed to disconcert him a little. He protested something to the effect that Marx didn't have the same kind of literary qualities, did it? —I tried to explain, though the din hardly made conversation possible, that it did have imaginative and literary interest. —How did I feel about Jane Austen? he asked. —I said that this was not the same kind of thing, but that I thought her one of the six greatest English writers (the others, as I did not say, are Shakespeare, Milton, Swift, Keats, and Dickens). We spoke of Jane Austen a moment. Why did the people who didn't like her dislike her so much? I asked. —Oh, because she didn't care about public events, didn't mention the Napoleonic wars. —I suppose he had shifted from Tolstoy and Co. to Jane Austen purposely to try me out on the non-historical kind of author. —Then, although we had talked only a couple of minutes, he said, "Well, I mustn't keep you from other people. I must tell you that your essays have thrown a good deal of light for me on Kipling and other things." —I shook hands with him, and after a moment's hesitation, I said that I had very much enjoyed reading *him*. —"Then that makes everything very nice," he said, and slipped away. —Just as I was leaving, a roguish-looking man, whom I had noticed before eyeing me, waylaid me and became belligerent about Somerset Maugham[30]—asked me if I had changed my mind. —No. —Maugham was a great stylist! —I said I couldn't see it. —At the head of stairs I caught up with Elena. —Stephen Spender, who was guiding us out, had already introduced her to Henry Green, who was standing there. I had thought him rather distinguished-appearing, but, although she had enjoyed his books, she for some reason was disappointed in him, said she thought he had an awful face.

This must have been before the Gates party, because I then told Isaiah about Forster, and he said that, though he and Forster belonged to the same club, he could never get anywhere with him: "He lacks the gift of intimacy." He would have been frightened by the idea of Marx.

Jan. 14. Dinner at Mamaine's: Connollys, John Russell,[31] and us, including Henry, very good little dinner, excellent soup—I had a vision of M. working all afternoon over it. Cyril said that it had turned out that the Latin verses he had given the prize to had one or more false quantities: You noticed how casually I brought them out and discussed them with Gates for your benefit? Well, you were dining with Oscar Wilde just before his arrest! —People had at once begun writing in to point out the winner's mistake or mistakes. —Conversation about use of words: Nancy Mitford's[32] list of things that she said her father had said and that she regarded as the touchstone of good usage. I said that I couldn't remember whether you were or were not supposed to say notepaper. —Cyril said that, since the Englishmen had lost their position, they tried to score over colonials and Americans by putting them in the wrong about speaking the language. He spoke of Pearsall Smith's old lady who made it impossible for visitors to speak correctly: if they spoke of *having tea*, she would say, one has a cold; if of *taking tea*, she would say, one *takes* a dose of medicine (check this in S.'s essay). It was supposed to be wrong to say *car* or *automobile*—you were supposed to say (what?). He and John [Russell] began parodying this. When I asked Cyril if monocles had completely gone out, he answered: One rarely sees *eyeglasses.* I tried to find out about *I say* and *Look.* They constantly say *Look*, which I used to think an Americanism (never saw it written till Dos Passos's early novels), but don't like to admit it—they seem to have a suspicion that it may be vulgar. Some people made a point of saying *an hotel* —I remembered that my father had said this, have forgotten to include it in my list of his language. When the rest had gone upstairs, and Cyril and I were lingering a moment to have a last drink, I said, Since we're playing this game, my father was the only person that I have ever known who said *Zounds!* Have you ever known anybody who said *Zounds?* He said that he never had. —Upstairs, J. Russell said, You had better fetch your greatcoat. I said, My servant does that. —When Cyril disappeared after our arrival at the party and I called attention to this, John Russell said, He may have been waylaid by a footpad. —He reminded me of Bill Mackie[33] when Bill was amusing himself with his exploits in 18th-century language, at college, and his stammer corresponded to Bill's confused way of talking. I got the flavor of his personality as I had not done in '45 when he took me to see Pearsall Smith. Russell seems to be a sort of beau, or perhaps simply confidant, of Mamaine's now. —Cyril didn't know who Henry [Thornton] was, and said to somebody afterwards that he knew M. liked them young but thought that this was going a little far.

—Elena and Henry and I had been to M.'s little house (given her by Arthur Koestler) before, the night when we had tried to go to [L. C. Hunter's] *A Day at the Sea* (the 12th) and found we were a week too early. I had asked her whether it were true that Princess Margaret was a Glamis monster and had webbed feet, and she had answered shortly, Oh, no. Bill Hughes had said that there was one thing that the English of any class liked to talk about: the royal family. For himself, apropos of the coronation, he had hated the whole thing.

—The *Listener* party was enormous—any number of writers and journalists. The program consisted of a pianist playing Chopin and Liszt, a soloist, a lady who, with infinite smugness, read a characterization of the British by André Maurois:[34] your clothes, for the English, mustn't be too new; you had to be absolutely punctual; when they quietly and completely accepted you, you found that you were one of their own. In pursuance of my present policy in England of maintaining a discreetly aggressive policy, I made a little fun of this, with the result that Mamaine, embarrassed, decided she couldn't stand it and went away. When later I saw Arthur Waley and Beryl de Zoete[35] at Celia's,[36] after having met them at this party, they said that they had felt so terribly about what people like Edmund Wilson must have thought of the program. —The best feature was the deadpan humorist who ended the performance by elaborate nonsensical stories, which Cyril tried to think were "a kind of British *surréalisme.*"

Jan. 15. Eliot's *The Confidential Clerk* [1954]—very weak. His characters are pale rubber stamps of characters in Galsworthy novels that he must have read before he first came to England, thinking that he would like, himself, to deal with such splendid Old World types—the old family adviser, the rattle-brained lady of title; and the theatrical technique that he manages to give the impression of having so painfully acquired turns out to consist mainly of having somebody unexpectedly appear just when he or she has been talked about. One doesn't care what he means, what his camouflaged moral is, because the whole thing is on so low a level. But he has got people here buffaloed. Pryce-Jones[37] said to me that he thought the play one of the six very worst he has seen in his life. Yet nobody seems to have reviewed it unfavorably, and it has now been running for months. Eliot is a master showman—if not always on the stage; at least in dealing with his own reputation. (He has this in common with Gide: the well-placed and soberly phrased utterance that takes on the weight of an oracle.) Conrad Aiken has long said of him that he manages to be Trilby and Svengali both; but his supreme achievement is at last to have succeeded in giving the illusion of putting on an

impressive performance when Trilby is no longer there.
(Early compulsive poetry, and thinness and deliberate-
ness of *Four Quartets*.) —The play was also badly acted.
How much did the production of *The Cocktail Party*,
which does not seem to have made so much of an impression in London, owe to the excellent direction and
acting! The text was certainly dreary to read, but the play,
preposterous though in many ways it was, did have something to it: the scene with the divine psychiatrist, the
uncomfortable party of the first act. It seems to me much
his best play—though *Murder in the Cathedral* has merits.

Jan. 16. Drinks with Celia in her own little house, in
a little narrow non-residential street that the taxi driver
had never heard of and where one wouldn't have expected
to find anyone living—as usual, less distinguished than
Mamaine's place, but with identical bird books and other
things, a few volumes on the Paget family (their parents
had both been Pagets). [Marginal note: A mistake: Celia
merely came for drinks. This happened after our return
from Edinburgh—26th or 27th.] Arthur Waley and
Beryl de Zoete were there. This time—after reading V.
Woolf's diary[38] and R. F. Harrod's life of Keynes [1951]
and now that Bloomsbury has become a legend—I observed him from a different point of view than before
and saw in him [Waley] the mannerisms and habits of
Bloomsbury. It was curious that, after they had gone,
Celia had said to me that she thought I might be interested to see him precisely for this reason: that he was
quite a pure specimen of Bloomsbury. He was thought
to look rather Chinese (though he had never been in
China or Japan) and he cultivated impassivity. He had
devastating deadpan cracks and was extremely snooty
about almost everything. —He had done the myths of
the Ainu, about which he had talked in '45. He thought

very highly of the work of the man who had written the
short story on which that Japanese movie was based, and
who had committed suicide. He said that it was all wrong
to think, as people would like to do, that the Chinese
under Communism were different from or independent
of Russia. All the books he had seen were exactly the
same and followed the Russian line. —He was superior
about Hemingway, who had just been much in the papers
on account of his misadventures in Africa. I said that I
was somewhat torn between relief at his not having been
killed and dread of the boasting and blowing he would
do about his exploits and the dangers he had run. Waley
said something aloofly scornful about Hemingway's work,
which I attempted to correct and discovered that he had
not read *The Old Man and the Sea.* I am afraid that one
of the Bloomsbury devices is to snub writers without
having read them. Waley said something faintly ap-
proving about Max Beerbohm, whom he had met—but
added, "His jokes are rather hard to bear." I repeated
Isaiah Berlin's story about Max's remark about Lady
C[unard][39] and he admitted that this was good. He
couldn't remember at first that he had read Masefield's
sonnet about the Queen on the occasion of the coronation, but then remembered he had. I said that I was
afraid that Eliot was going to be the next Poet Laureate.
Waley said icily, with infinite disdain, I don't care a pin
who is the next Poet Laureate! I said that it was somehow
indecent for him to pile up so many honors: it had
already been rather unnecessary for him to turn up to
receive the Nobel Prize with the Order of Merit dangling
from his neck. Waley either said that he did not know
that Eliot had received these honors or succeeded in
conveying that impression. —Bill Hughes was telling me
later that the Bloomsbury people had a gambit for disconcerting people. Virginia W., for example, had said to

David Cecil, Now tell me, what is it like to be a lord? Or they would say, So you're staying at the Berkeley Hotel. I suppose you ride up and down in the lift? Now, tell me, what is it like to live in the Berkeley Hotel and ride up and down in the lift? Bill said that unless you had the gumption to make a comic reply, you would be made very uncomfortable.

I stayed on for a little while after the Waleys had left and Elena had taken Helen back to the hotel. Celia told somebody afterwards that my conversation with Waley had been awfully tense (this was true—I don't know quite why, unless because Waley is overanxious to live up to his role, and this made me self-conscious, too), and it was a relief when they went away. A lady arrived with whom she was going to have dinner. I told Celia that it was hard for me to imagine that she and Mamaine had had real parents, that they seemed to have been hatched out of eggs, like Helen and Clytemnestra. She produced a photograph of her mother, who did not seem pretty and petite like them but a little on the English gawky side. They were early left orphans: their mother died as the result of their birth; their father, who lived in the country and did nothing (Mamaine once said to me that it was hard to understand now how people had once lived in that way), did not survive her many years, though long enough for them to remember him. They were brought up outside London by an aunt—had never, I discovered, been taken to the pantomine.

Dinner with Alan Pryce-Jones. The large house and the splendor in which he lives puzzled me till Elena explained afterwards that his wife, who had died since they came to see us at Wellfleet, had been some sort of Rothschild, and the furniture and interior decorating—Empire motifs I remember—were in typical Germanic Rothschild taste. But for Pryce-Jones they seemed a little incongruous.

He obviously, however, loves living in this way. There was a Lord Kinross,[40] a Scot, who has traveled a good deal in the Near East and has been doing pieces for *Punch*. Compton Mackenzie told me later he was a Balfour and Mamaine (I think) that he was a homo, but no one seemed particularly interested in him or to know precisely what he did. I talked to him about Edinburgh, and he said that more than any city it was divided into social compartments that had no relations with one another. There was also a rather coddled Lady Somebody, who was interested in music and had lived in New York. —After dinner, Pryce-Jones did his stuff in front of the mantelpiece: his vein is probably a mixture of babbling Welsh double-talk with the fashionable incoherence, of which the old-fashioned silly-ass line represented the lower form and this of P.-J.'s the highest, with literary choice of words and its clever placing of phrases.

Jan. 17. Sidney Glass, the New Zealand photographer, came and got me and Helen in a car, drove us to Richmond Park, where Helen fed the deer, then to the cemetery where Whistler and Hogarth were buried and where Foscolo[41] had been buried till they removed his bones to Italy, and then took us to his house to lunch. Special neighborhood—Chiswick beyond Chelsea—for which I did not much care: a kind of more suburban Chelsea—A. P. Herbert[42] and Alec Guinness were his neighbors. I was rather astonished by his household. His wife was a Yorkshire woman, who was dressed in slacks as a fancy photographer's wife—she was nice, I thought, and gave very good attention to Helen. At lunch, she said to me in passing the cheeses, pointing at one with the knife, "Try him: he's *good!*" as Todger's boy in *Martin Chuzzlewit* said to the boarders at Miss Todger's, "The fish has come. Don't eat none of him, though!" A fat little boy who told some of the most dreadful excremental stories (involving also psychoanalysis), using the four-letter word, that I have ever heard from anybody of any age. This seemed, with Helen there, to disturb even his father, who had been telling some pretty high ones himself. Glass had invited me, when I came there, "to put my feet on the mantelpiece," and I was treated with great familiarity, which increased, with the drinks, by leaps and bounds. It got out of hand later, but I didn't know how to control it. In America there would not have been the same kind of problem: in some way, there is more of a uniform standard for different kinds of people; but in England one social world is discontinuous with another. They have the expression *matey*, which doesn't apply in America. There were two friends there, both of whom were supposed to have read my books—which gratified me, although when I meet people who seem very much different from myself, I always wonder what they get out of them. One of them was a composer, who, as Glass told me after he left, did not like my having praised [Benjamin] Britten,[43] whom he resented as one of the homosexual clique. The other resembled some character in Sherlock Holmes, a foreigner of indeterminate origins, who would have turned up in Soho or somewhere. He was a doctor, who had been born in Ceylon; had blackheads on his face and a small pointed beard, and talked very good French to the French maid, who ate with us. He was surprised at my knowledge of English literature, which I told him was quite natural: we were brought up on it in America. He said that it was the same thing in Ceylon, and they had read all the French decadents, too—the colonials, he said, read with a peculiar avidity.

Glass had been most kind and had put himself out for Helen, stopping to buy apples to feed the deer and searching a long time in the park for them—on Sundays, when there were many visitors, they were driven back in the woods—so that she shouldn't be disappointed. But at the hotel he was rather a nuisance—grabbed Elena by the arm on first meeting her and, with Elena and Olili present (she had just arrived that morning), regaled us with a long monologue, in which every other word was *bugger* or *bloody*. It was with difficulty that I finally got him off.

Add to the *Listener* party: I was taken up to see John Hayward.[44] Though I had never met him before, he at once began talking about Eliot in a malicious but amusing way. He never knew where to go for his vacations, so they had finally gotten him off with some people who were going to South Africa—he would be dressing for dinner every night on the ship. He was a Henry James character, full of old-fashioned formalities. I answered that it was true that, when Eliot came back to the States, he seemed less like an Englishman than like an obsolete kind of American. —Hayward is indeed rather dismaying to look at—almost as if he were the frog monster of Glamis—is wheeled around in a chair, has incomplete control of his arms and hands, so that shaking hands with him is rather awkward. He wears spectacles and has a batrachian mouth, of which the lower lip juts forward so far that you see a good deal of the inside of it. —I. Berlin says that it is part of Eliot's Christian role to have a leper to embrace, and that Hayward is Eliot's leper. He (H.) evidently adores Eliot—as one sees by his introduction to Eliot's Penguin prose—in spite of his malice about him.

Jan. 18. Olili is certainly in a very queer state. Though she is four years younger than Elena, she seems older: pale eyes, pale hair, pale complexion. Coolness toward

E.—who later told me that she had been "most disagreeable"—who had obviously been disappointed when O.
did not meet the boat, and then when she did not turn
up till almost two weeks later. She said she had to stay in
Germany for some kind of directors' meeting of the
museum. In England, she lives with Dorothy Paget in a
household that is apparently as bad as Johannisberg—has
to stay up all night playing cards. What I hadn't realized,
however, was that she really runs the racing stable, in
London would study papers on the subject. Paget offered
her the job—with pay, which she doesn't get now, for
taking complete charge of the Irish end of it. I like to
surprise people here by asking them to guess, after she
has gone, what she does: "She runs one of the biggest
racing stables in England." Pauline Gates was amazed:
"I should have thought anything but that!" O. was the
member of the family who had learned about horses from
her father—Elena knows very little. Mamaine had had
about 60; Dorothy Paget has from 200 to 500. She is
certainly in very bad health, has collapses when she becomes more or less unconscious: Elena is afraid to leave
Helen with her. Elena thinks that D.P. is a kind of
perhaps not-practising lesbian. Olili one afternoon brought
in a rather pretty young woman who was D.'s latest
favorite. The girl has a little boy, is a war widow, I
think. She is getting bored at D.P.'s in her anomalous
ambiguous role, but whenever she makes a move to
leave, D. presents her with a piece of valuable jewelry
or something. Elena thinks that Dorothy Paget somehow
came between O. and the man she was once engaged to
marry. She had tried to argue with O. about her position at D.'s, but had made no impression on her. One
factor involved here is that Dorothy supports the Russian
home; the Russian relatives have thus, some of them,
been entirely dependent on her. What Elena doesn't

quite realize, as I afterwards came to see, is that Olili is a person who is always invented by other women. E. is constantly struggling to get her away from the influence of Dorothy or Madeleine[45] and re-create the old O. that she herself invented when they were girls together and called one another Gongeli. —One evening in London, Elena told me, they started talking about things behind their recent falling-out, and it was no use: O. began to become hysterical. Elena told her that there was no point in trying to discuss these matters: they would never agree about them and might as well let them alone. The great rift had been created by Elena's refusing, a couple of years ago, to give Brat a power of attorney to deal with her Mumm interests.[46] She says that he has taken all Olili's share and doles out to her only a pittance while she inhabits a kind of housekeeper's room at Johannisberg.

—I had lunch with the *New Statesman* people, made me quite nostalgic for *The New Republic*.[47] Rather poor and cheap food at a round table in the basement of a restaurant. Crossman[48] immediately challenged me, demanding to know why *The New Yorker* didn't attack McCarthy! I said that they didn't go in for attacking political figures, at which he snapped, "Only novelists!" —Kingsley Martin[49] told me with satisfaction that the *New Statesman* was the only paper of its kind in the West that was self-supporting. —I talked to them about the two phases of Communism in America: the phase when Communist sympathizers thought they were supporting a movement of the international working class, and the phase of people like Remington and Hiss, at the time that the Soviet regime had become completely bureaucratized and the Bolsheviks and the Leninist tradition had been definitely liquidated, when partly idealistic young men somehow saw the Communist Party as a means to a successful career, as a getting-in on the ground floor of a big international bureaucracy—no nonsense in this period about proletarianizing oneself.

Since it was the day of the *New Statesman* staff luncheon and my only chance to see them, I put off lunch with the young Israeli Kanael (an invented name, as Isaiah B. pointed out to me, meaning Jealous God). Simmons and Allen had put me in touch with him: he was towering, spectacled, shaggy-haired, and childlike. He came to see me in the hotel and talked about the Dead Sea Scrolls. He beamed when he saw that I could write Hebrew characters, and at one point in the conversation, when we had only been talking about five minutes, said, "I like you." Afterwards, in a letter he wrote me, he said, "I had already made up my mind that I liked you before I knew who you were."

In the evening, with Olili, Mamaine, and Henry, we went to *A Day at the Sea*, with Ralph Richardson, Gielgud, and Sybil Thorndike—a diluted English Chekhov, to which I was too tired to pay very much attention and did not particularly share Mamaine's amused responses, when I was sitting beside her during the first and third acts. She told me, however, that Henry, who had sat beside her during the second, had appreciatively chuckled at everything.

In the afternoon about three, we went to the Soane Museum,[50] of which I had never heard. Sidney Glass told me about it, and I went to see the paintings of Hogarth's *Rake's Progress* (also found the Election Series). Glass had called up the director, a man named Summerson, who must be the John Summerson who writes about architecture. Glass had called him up, and he took us all through it and told me that a scene during a thunderstorm in Henry James's "A London Life" takes place there. A very strange place, with its mixture of the classical and the Gothic, its panels hung with pictures that swing out from the wall and show other panels of pictures behind, its few good things (Turners, Hogarths) with much second-rate stuff, its elaborate paintings of scenes from Shakespeare, its imitation cloister and crowded basement, its strangely designed rooms (Soane was eventually, it seems, insane), all rather claustrophobic. A curious specimen of the taste of the early 19th century, preserved in its pure state: Soane had it secured by an Act of Parliament, so that nothing could be added or removed.

When we came out, Elena and Helen went home, but I walked to St. Paul's by a route that Summerson had suggested and that took me through Lincoln's Inn Fields and the Temple, up Ludgate Hill, etc.—Dickens's and Barham's London, of which I had a stronger impression, in the deepening gloom, than I remember ever having had before.

In the evening we had dinner (7:45) with Angus Wilson and his boyfriend: dinner at a nearby hotel, where we sat near the music and I felt that W. was trying to get in touch with the spirit of the twenties; after that, went back to their apartment, to which came two of their friends, the literary editor of the *New Statesman* and another man. Very pleasant! I asked Wilson if it were really true that he had never written anything before the stories in *The Wrong Set*. He said that he never had, and that he thought it was perhaps a good thing: he had not been involved in the literary world and had stored up a lot of observation. He had already told me, when I saw him before, that he was trying to do something a little different: "One can't go on being prickly forever." He now talked about the play he had just written: a set of liberals who, in one way or another, were all driven out of their liberal positions, and yet, in the long run, managed to come down on the liberal side. I told him about what Shaw said about the author either directing his play himself or keeping away from rehearsals; how Shaw himself found in dominating his actors the exercise in personal relations that was missing in his private life, would shut himself for rehearsals in the darkened theater as the wild-animal trainer goes into the cage with his animals, never worked with stars, because they were too troublesome, except in the case of *Pygmalion*, when his difficulties with Beerbohm Tree and Mrs. Patrick Campbell finally caused him to walk out in a rage: result, the perfect Shaw production, one in which all the characters were completely subordinate to the play, to Shaw (he always insisted that it made no difference whether or not the actors understood their lines). Wilson said that he thought he might be good at dealing with actors at rehearsal, he had had a good deal of experience in handling people at the British Museum.

I asked them my stock set of questions about customs and habits of speech in England. What about the rolled-up umbrella? (I had been told that, with really smart people, if they ever went so far as to use them, they had to send them to a special place to get them properly rolled again.) Angus Wilson said that formerly, as a civil servant, he had carried an umbrella and worn a bowler, but that he did not do so anymore. —I asked about their habit of saying *Hm*—when did this begin? Nobody could answer this: the habit was universal and evidently quite unconscious. I told W. that I thought he didn't do this, then a few moments after noticed he did. After telling me a long story, Powell, Bettina's husband, said *Hm*. —I tried them on the smart pronunciation, *fahnny*, *Rahssia*, etc. This used to be, in my youth, one of the features of the "Bloomsbury accent," which was definitely lower middle class. Estelle Winwood, the actress, had this pronunciation, and for that reason—this is my impression —could never succeed on the London stage as she did in the United States, where nobody cared if a duchess was made to talk with a "Bloomsbury accent"—it must have been the reason for her permanently living in America. But no English person I have talked to recently has ever heard of a Bloomsbury accent—when I mention it, they think I mean something connected with Lytton Strachey and Virginia Woolf. One of the men at A.W.'s said that that must be what Bernard Shaw in *Pygmalion* meant when he referred to an Earl's Court accent. Angus Wilson agreed with me that this was a significant change. He spoke of the kind of cockney accent that the royal family had. He said that the Queen would speak of "my hahsband and I." —*Pygmalion* (then being revived) was already well in the past for them. When I said I had been in London in 1908 and 1914, W. said, "Henry James's London." He thought certain people now imitated H.J., but I think that he merely elaborated a kind of thing that had long been done. What they called "the aesthetic style" of talking, which I thought had never declined, was already dated for W., and he spoke of a man who talked that way as if he were a museum piece.

I asked what was their explanation of the conversational method of Pryce-Jones and Isaiah Berlin, saying that "P.-J.'s incoherence was very well-written." They agreed that it belonged to the tradition of the G. P. Huntley "nut."[51] Elena does not agree that Isaiah and Pryce-Jones are forms of the same thing, and I was interested to hear, in Paris, from a Jewish friend of Koestler's that Mamaine took me to see, brought up like Isaiah in a Hassidic sect, that the moment he had met Isaiah he had recognized his way of talking as the way peculiar to a certain type of Talmudic scholar (I can't remember the name). When these scholars talk to one another, they have a rapid-fire of unfinished and to the outsider incoherent fragments: they know the subject so well and are so full of it that the beginning of an allusion is all that is needed for them to understand and stimulate one another. Isaiah, with his wonderful adaptability, has exploited this along English lines; but Eloth, the Israeli consul, told me that Isaiah talked Russian even faster than English.*

Jan. 20–21. Olili drove us to Oxford, where Isaiah gave us lunch at All Souls, with Stephen Spender and Stuart Hampshire,[52] who had an enormous reddish-brown fore-lock falling down on his face, and took us a little around the colleges. It had changed very much since 1914, the last time I had been in Oxford. Due to the Nuffield works, the traffic on the High is worse, it seemed to me, than anywhere in America. They have no system of stopping it so that people can cross the street, and the layout of the old medieval town provides no available cross streets or parallel streets. The buildings are also in very bad repair—shabby and crumbling, scrofulous and leprous. I told Isaiah that the Bodleian, which was opposite his windows, ought to be redone and the dome painted green. Max Beerbohm's Roman emperors had crumbled away to a point where they scarcely any longer had faces. He told me later, when I saw him at Rapallo, that they had originally been gray but had turned later to their present yellow. —Elena and Helen drove back to London with Olili, and I spent the night. I was just as glad not to have

---

* EW's speculations on Koestler's friend's remarks seem to have no foundation in fact. Sir Isaiah Berlin was not reared in a Hassidic sect, nor were his parents.

to drive with Olili, who, like Walther,[53] was a speed demon.

Isaiah put me up in Amery's[54] room in All Souls: a dismal little cell like a fourth-rate New York rooming house. The soap dish had evidently never been washed, and the basin had a caked yellow ring of dirt around the inside, which showed that it had never been washed, only emptied out. The curtains were faded and filthy, the bed was rusty. On the door—there was no closet—hung a black college gown, with a tab that said "Right Honourable XX Amery" inside the neck. In one of the drawers of the plain little bureau, his evening clothes were kept. In the morning, the scout came in at eight, pulled the curtains back, perfunctorily rubbed my shoes, and remarked, "It's a damp day, sir." The scouts were obviously disaffected. What I took, the first night at dinner at Christ Church (?) and the second night at All Souls, to be a fine old college discipline turned out to be merely the high-handedness of the class-contemptuous waiters. They would whisk the courses away before we had had a chance to eat them. At All Souls, in the darkened and vaulted room, they suddenly descended on us and stripped the table of its tablecloth, replacing the candlestick; then shoved at A. L. Rowse, the presiding don, the apparatus for the port and the claret. I was told later that the All Souls fellows were now obliged to skip one stage of their ceremonial dinner: they had formerly moved to another room for the port, then to a third for the coffee; but now they moved only for the coffee.

Isaiah was engaged for part of every day in refusing the wardenship of Nuffield College, which was mainly devoted to social studies—which he thought—I'm sure quite rightly—impossible for him.

I had told him at Cambridge [Mass.] that when I came

to Oxford, there were two people I wanted to see: A. J. P. Taylor[55] and Cecil Roth. It was evident that I couldn't have chosen two more totally wrong people. He cried out that they were both impossible—the person for me to meet was David Cecil: Harry Levin had bristled at the notion, but when he had met Cecil, Isaiah just watched him "melting." I told Cyril Connolly about this, that Isaiah and Bowra and David Cecil[56] made themselves a kind of closed group and blackballed people at Oxford. —So I arranged to go to Roth's with Kanael, who shared my admiration for *A Short History of the Jews*, which he said he always carried with him. Roth was most agreeable and helpful, showed me some of his rare books and gave me a pamphlet of his. He is slight, rather birdlike, sensitive—a touch of John Bishop about him. His chair is endowed by rich English Jews, and he does not have many pupils. Evidently nobody knows him; David Cecil seemed never to have heard of him. —After my visit to Roth, Isaiah explained that his criticism of Roth was due partly to a situation that had arisen as the result of the arrival of the Jewish refugees in Oxford. Roth had considered that many of them were not the right kind of people to hold office in the synagogue, and Isaiah had been appealed to, to set in a contrary sense. He had refused, but had held this against Roth. If you are going to be snobbish, he said to me, it's an odd place to begin, don't you think? —Actually, I don't agree. Roth had been behaving just like everyone else who wants to see that his group is represented by "the right kind of people." He is doing what Isaiah does himself when he collaborates with Bowra and David Cecil in, as Cyril Connolly says, blackballing people from the group of acceptable dons.

In the meantime, the afternoon before, just before Elena and the others left, David Cecil had been pro-

duced. He skipped around like a jumping jack, sat down
on a footstool, talked in my face. He is, I think—a little
like the Sitwells—one of those noblemen who are touchingly anxious to associate with literary people and to be
known as writers themselves. He told me—what I had
forgotten—that I had written in *The New Yorker* a good
review of his book on Thomas Hardy. But he did not fail,
at several points, to *faire valoir* his social position. What
was interesting was his account of Bloomsbury (which one
feels at this particular moment—as if with the publication
of V.W.'s diary—to have become a thing of the past
which they can criticize and about which they can be
objective). He said that, having come from "a rich
social world," he had approached the Bloomsbury people
with awe, but that he had presently decided that they were
more removed from life even than his own people. It
had brought him somewhat closer to them when he had
married Desmond MacCarthy's daughter; but their
[Bloomsbury's] relations with their children, for example,
seemed to him awfully queer: the children called their
parents by their first names, and he had been struck by
the parents' blank amazement when he had taken his
own children to the pantomime. He was, I think, the only
English person I met who knew the pantomime well,
since it was for him a traditional institution, and we
talked about it a little.

When he had gone, I told Isaiah that I had had a
very pleasant time with Roth. That evening Isaiah produced, among others, a young don with an impediment
in his speech for which the word *stammer* would be
hardly adequate, since it would throw him into a kind of
convulsion that would stop the conversation for minutes.
This conversation—the impeded don (English), Humphry House, who wrote a book on Dickens, a philosopher

and his wife, a young woman who had written a book on Sartre*—fatigued and bored me extremely. Isaiah afterwards said that he had thought it was "forced and dull." The things that they think about and their way of thinking about them seemed to me to be so removed from everything that is going on. I thought, at the end of the war, that the British intellectuals had been made more provincial by their isolation; but they seem now to be even more so. It seemed all very stale and unreal. I kept thinking how different the things were that had been going through my head from the things that were going through theirs.

My visit to A. J. P. Taylor, the historian, was also agreeable and interesting. I asked him about social changes in England, said that sometimes I thought the class structure was tending to disappear, other times that it wasn't; and he answered that they watched it with the same hopes and doubts. The young people from the social classes who had hitherto not gone to the universities were not having by any means the effect on Oxford he had hoped. They simply, with dismaying rapidity, took over the habits and the point of view that had always been characteristic of Oxford; and he, and those of his middle-aged colleagues who made a sort of radical bloc, found themselves in the queer position of being further to the left than their students: the usual situation was reversed. —He put on his black gown, and we went away to a lecture, which, talking to Isaiah on the phone, I had thought was going to be by Taylor, but which turned

---

* EW here confuses the late Humphry House, the Dickens scholar, who had no speech impediment, with John Bayley, the Oxford critic, author of *The Characters of Love* and other works. The young woman who wrote on Sartre was the novelist Iris Murdoch, Bayley's wife.

out to be an exceedingly dry discourse, like an en-
cyclopedia article, on the beginnings of the Greek
Church.* The lecturer had pronunciations—such as *dis-
pútant* and *mȳth* and *olōgical*—that I had never heard
before. I told Taylor, when it was over, that I had misunderstood Isaiah. "He's very easy to misunderstand,"
said Taylor shortly and tellingly. I had not then seen,
in the *New Statesman*, Taylor's review of *The Hedgehog
and the Fox*,[57] which had rather cast a shadow on Isaiah.
I talked to Taylor about the book as we were coming out
of the lecture, and he said that he felt that Isaiah, when
he couldn't get into his subject, tried to carry things off
"with a burst of words," and that this was what he had
said. There is something in this, I think—I had felt the
evening before, when the conversation became philo-
sophical, as I had sometimes felt with Isaiah before, that
one feels him at moments scraping bottom when he has
sailed into the shallows of his mind; but it is evident
that Taylor, in the plain English tradition, cannot appreciate what they call at Oxford "the Delphic side" of
Isaiah, which is also the prophetic Jewish side. I thought
that the end of the Tolstoy essay, which for Taylor is a
mere torrent of words, was actually quite successful: he
is talking about his own problems: he lives much the
life of the fox but, like all serious Jews, aspires to the
unity of the hedgehog. At this point, he met us, and
Taylor and we had an amiable conversation about the
recent events in Yugoslavia.

The intramural spites and grudges, cliques and snob-
beries, celibate jealousies, rather sickened me—along
with the monastic staleness—even in that short time. Of
course, it was an unattractive season: it had been summer

---

* This lecture was delivered by Steven Runciman.

when I had been there before; but it seemed a long time ago, unrecapturable and unrevisitable, that I had sat on a bench in Magdalene Walk and read English poetry: *Ionica* and J. E. Flecker,[58] or composed *bouts-rimés*[59] in the parlor of the Mitre with Bill Mackie and Frank MacDonald.[60] Though Isaiah tells me that nowadays 80 percent of the dons are married, there is still a definite feeling of women having been excluded, of places where women have never lived, that rather got me down. When I got back late to London, I leapt on Elena, who had gone to bed.

—I was quite proud of Helen at luncheon the day before. She sat at the table quite formally—it was true that Spender talked to her. He has his very good and kindly side.

Jan. 21. Luncheon with Isaiah in London: Cyril C., Shawe-Taylor and Sackville-West[61] and two ladies that I didn't get much out of. Restaurant too noisy to hear what people said. I had just before met Shawe-Taylor in Cambridge, also at lunch with Isaiah. He bubbles and is more cheerful to talk to than I had found the rather dim Raymond Mortimer[62] (and other such literary people) when I had met him in '45 at Hamish Hamilton's.[63] Shawe-Taylor, Sackville-West, and Mortimer all live together.

Too worn-out in the evening to go to Alan Ross's,[64] to which Cyril had invited us after dinner. When I called him up to tell him, I said that I was very sorry not to have had the chance to give him the pep talk I had been preparing. He said, "Well, you've at least succeeded in getting the old icon off the mud"—he seemed at least to have done some business with Epstein. [Marginal note: Getting passport for Israel.]

Jan. 23–25. Trip to Edinburgh: It was terribly cold in the train, and at Kemp Smith's[65] house, otherwise so comfortable, there was no heating in the bedrooms except small electric heaters, and in my bed a hot bottle and in Elena's an electric blanket, which the old Scottish housekeeper warned her she must be sure to turn off before she went to sleep, because a couple of people in Edinburgh had been electrocuted by them. I suffered from the cold myself, and Elena had a dreadful time—I never should have made her come.

Kemp Smith shows his age now—can't walk as he did and has to rest. He doesn't care for logical positivism, says that G. E. Moore's[66] *Ethics* was no ethics at all, because it lets everybody do just what they want (though he was impressed by Moore personally), couldn't understand his friend X's lectures that involved the mathematics of physics. Had heard Isaiah's broadcasts: I asked him how they were, and he said, "Oh, remarkable: it was like a jet from a fire hose; but by multiplying adjectives and saying the same thing in different words, he made himself intelligible."

He took us to lunch at that old hotel, with the Dover Wilsons and Edwin Muir.[67] I get rather tired of doing my stuff—and at Salzburg I was to have to do an awful lot of it—mentioning the national authors and showing off the little I knew about them.

I took Elena to Holyrood, and she said that it reminded her of the South: the Confederate Museum of Richmond and all that. I had been feeling that, too. She complained that Queen Elizabeth had not mentioned in a recent speech that she was Queen of Scotland. They showed us where she had been crowned in Holyrood. This old palace is sinister, with the rooms where Mary Queen of Scots and Darnley lived, and the spot where Rizzio was

murdered. Her rather cooked-up apartment, the grim
views she saw from the window.

—Call upon Compton Mackenzie.[68] He had been
ruined by the results of a suit to get some of his books
(I am vague about this) exempted from the income tax,
would have to sell his moated old house in England
(where Rosalind had visited him), and had moved into
this apartment in Edinburgh, every room of which was
crammed with his books. He had, I thought, queer tastes
in collecting: the complete Loeb classics and the complete
bound files of *Notes and Queries* and the *Illustrated
London News*. —He had been ill and received us in bed,
with—as I thought he would like to feel—the dignity
and beard of Charles I and the wit and grace of Charles
II. A festive Italian bed and above it a crucifix. He spoke
to me about his career with what I suppose was deliberately disarming candor. He had an accent I rather
enjoyed—not of London or Oxford—but perhaps of a
very good actor playing a prince. He had made very
little money out of *Whisky Galore* [1949],[69] had sold
it outright to the films for, I think, £500. He said that he
had made up his mind at a certain time in his youth that
he did not want to be an actor. Maugham and Priestley[70]
had been surprised when they found that their books
were successful, but he had not been surprised: he had
meant to be a success. He made no pretensions, I was
sorry to hear him say: he aimed to be an entertainer. It
was a satisfaction to him that many of his books were
now in print. He wanted to have the Ecclesiastic series[71]
reprinted in one volume: he had meant it to be one novel.
He hoped there was something in the Winds series,[72]
because he had put a good deal of work in it. He had
written to Angus Wilson (W. told me), protesting against
a broadcast of Wilson's in which W. had classed him
with Beresford and Walpole;[73] and he now told me that

when he had reproached Henry James for taking Walpole so seriously in his essay "The New Novel," H.J. replied, "He has never written anything yet."[74] He thought it really ought to be conceded that he [Mackenzie] and [D. H.] Lawrence were in a different category from the other writers dealt with in that essay. —He spoke of his mother's American family[75]—actors, it seemed—there was a portrait of one of his relatives in the Players Club in New York. He inquired about F.P.A. and Monty Flagg[76] —were they still alive? (Betjeman had said to me that Gilbert Harding[77] went with Compton Mackenzie and somebody else, as if this should be enough to place him.) —He was reading a pretty little old two- or three-volume edition of a novel by Paul de Kock, *La Pucelle de XX.*[78] Paul de K. had used to be sold in places that sold sterling douches and such things, but he was really extremely good—the dialogue was excellent. —Mackenzie had not long before, I was told, celebrated his seventieth birthday by a big party at which he had appeared in some kind of very fancy vest and seemed greatly to enjoy himself. The local journalist who brought us there said that it meant a lot to them to have somebody like that in Edinburgh—they weren't used to anything of that kind. —He was doing a lot of hackwork—had just turned out a book on the Savoy Hotel[79] and was now doing one on— what?—the Australian forces in the last world war or something of that kind. —He did also a weekly article in the *Spectator*—I had just read one of them in which he protested, rather *de haut en bas,* against certain pronunciations, contending, for example, that it ought to be ōminous. I told him I had never heard this, and tried on him the, to me, weird pronunciations of the lecturer I had heard in Oxford. He said that he did not pronounce any of those words the way the lecturer had. This self-consciousness about pronunciation is, I think, as Cyril said, a part of the impulse, in proportion as they lose their position as a power, to claim for themselves unique, if unimportant superiorities; and there is also the codifying movement, so foreign to English tradition, and now consecrated by Fowler's *Modern English Usage*. People are surprised to hear that the dramatists, at least through Shadwell (whom I've just been reading), wrote phrases like *between he and I*. And that Ben Jonson in his English grammar, for all his classical preoccupations, says nothing about the objective cases of pronouns following prepositions (in this sentence I have just written, Fowler would say that I ought to have avoided a construction which would not allow "following" to be comfortably preceded by a possessive, and this typical of these false restrictions which the school of Fowler would inflict).

—He says he has always wanted to write a book about Aristophanes.

—I gather that he has always had a tie-up with his sister, the actress Fay Compton, that he is a very rare case of a man who is interested only in lesbians. See Michael Fane and Sylvia Scarlett and *Extraordinary Women*, which, in making the lesbians attractive, contrasts with its companion piece about male homosexuals. —His best book, he thinks—no doubt rightly—is *Guy and Pauline (Plaster's Mead)*: immature, unfulfilled emotion. I asked him about the verses toward the end—"Just one look from the door . . ." (I haven't got it right)— which I had never been able to identify. "I wrote it meself!" he exclaimed—"I wrote a whole sequence of them." —My other general ideas about him I wrote down when I was reading the Greek series.[80]

—His memory is really remarkable. He claims that he wrote the whole Greek series from memory—some of it years after the experiences. Max Beerbohm, when I saw him at Rapallo, thought it a great feat of memory to have remembered all the nuances of seasons and atmospheres at Oxford (he thought highly of *Sinister Street*: he thought it would still hold up, but I told him that, when I had been rereading it ten years or so ago, I had found it rather disappointing).

—I enjoyed Mackenzie and was sorry I could not have talked with him longer—shall always have an affection for his books. Of course he is the complete extravert, who is always improvising and universalizing, reproducing all his impressions. There are very fine things about him that have perhaps partly miscarried in England. The actor, the American, and the Scotsman have produced a combination that does not perhaps find its place here. He has always been playing a role which is not quite in the national drama. Is always buying and living on islands, where perhaps, by himself, he can play it better. But I don't believe he is ever desperate or even sad—he goes on delighting himself by the facility and brilliance of his own performance.

—I asked him if he admired Maugham's work, and he answered, "Not really." I said that M. had no sense of language, and he assented, "None whatsoever!" Maugham, in his malicious way, had once said to him years ago, when C.M. was just making his reputation, "You'd better hurry up. Walpole is getting ahead of you!" Mackenzie had replied, "Look here, Maugham: if you're going to be rude, I can be ruder than you—and when I'm rude, my rudeness is unforgivable" (a very good line, I thought). He said that Maugham had never forgiven him for bringing out *Sinister Street* just before *Of Human Bondage* [1915]. Competition among British novelists must have been fierce in those days. It still is—on a smaller scale, and the stakes are not so high.

—It was also an evidence of his memory that he should have mentioned his conversation with Scott Fitzgerald at Capri, and that this should have confirmed Scott's account. He said that Scott had asked him why his work had gone off and that he had answered—as he says in one of his Greek books—that, after his period of telegram and bulletin writing, he couldn't go back to the least kind of thing that he had written when he got out of Oxford.

10/23/10

NOTES

1. Jason Epstein had inaugurated the paperback series of Anchor Books for Doubleday.

2. Mamaine Koestler (née Paget), to whom EW proposed in 1945. She married Arthur Koestler. *The Forties*, pp. 106–7 and *passim*.

3. Elena's sister Olga was always called Olili.

4. A London socialite who lived with Olili.

5. W. H. Allen was EW's British publisher at the time.

6. Sylvester Gates, banker and longtime British friend of EW. *The Forties*, pp. 152–53, and *Letters on Literature and Politics* (1977, hereafter referred to as *LLP*), *passim*. Pauline was his wife.

7. Cyril Connolly (1903–74), a protégé of Logan Pearsall Smith, attracted wide attention with his early book *Enemies of Promise* (1939). During the war he edited *Horizon*, a review of literature and art. In his later years he wrote a weekly book review for the *Sunday Times*. He was married to Barbara Skelton from 1950 to 1954.

8. Alfred Duff Cooper, Viscount Norwich (1890–1954), Churchill's wartime Minister of Information from 1940 and British ambassador to France after the liberation.

9. Henry Vincent York (1905–73), British businessman and novelist who wrote comedies of manners under the pseudonym Henry Green. *The Forties*, pp. 150, 153.

10. Angus Wilson's fifth book, *For Whom the Cloche Tolls*, had just been published.

11. Logan Pearsall Smith (1865–1946), American-born essayist and aphorist who lived in London for many years, best known for *Trivia* (1902) and *More Trivia* (1921). *The Thirties*, pp. 509–10; *The Forties*, p. 58; and *BBT*, pp. 114–30.

12. English critic and biographer of Byron.

13. Alfred Leslie Rowse, prolific writer on many subjects, especially on Shakespeare and the Elizabethans.

14. Guy Burgess and Donald Maclean were spies in the British Foreign Office who passed atomic secrets to the Soviets, then fled to Russia. Connolly's *The Missing Diplomats* (1953).

15. Writer for *Horizon*, which he helped to found.

16. Lys Lubbock was one of the assistants at *Horizon* and during her intimacy with Cyril Connolly had her name changed by deed poll to Connolly. See David Pryce-Jones, *Cyril Connolly: Journal and Memoirs* (1984), p. 288.

17. John Nevil Maskelyne (1839–1915), illusionist who performed at the Egyptian Hall in London. See *A Prelude*, pp. 26, 72–73.

18. EW is linking *The Golden Bowl* (1904) with Portland Place because of a famous photograph by Alvin Langdon Coburn of this part of London which Henry James used as a frontispiece to the New York edition of this novel (vol. 24).

19. EW met William Hughes in 1945, when Hughes was a staff officer stationed in Rome. *The Forties*, *passim*.

20. John William De Forest (1826–1906), Connecticut-born author of the first realistic novels of the Civil War. *Patriotic Gore*, pp. 669–742.

21. Cardinal Merry del Val (1865–1930), Papal Secretary of State, 1903–14. See EW's satirical poem about the Cardinal in *Night Thoughts*, pp. 187–91.

22. Ilya Ehrenburg (1891–1967), Russian novelist and essayist, and Alvarez Del Vayo, a member of the exiled cabinet of Spain's Republican government. Del Vayo was a correspondent for the *New Statesman* and a commentator for *The Nation* (New York).

23. Stephen Spender and Irving Kristol founded *Encounter* in 1953.

24. John Murray was hardly obscure: the publishing house of John Murray was founded in 1788.

25. Sir Lewis Bernstein Namier (1888–1960), essayist and historian. *The History of Parliament*, vol. 1: *The House of Commons, 1754–1790* (with John Brooke, 1938).

26. Cecil Roth (1899–1970), Jewish historian, then first reader in Jewish studies at Oxford.

27. See EW's "Hull-House in 1932" in *The American Earthquake* (1958).

28. John Frederick Lehmann, poet and essayist, best known as the editor of *New Writing* and manager of the Woolfs' Hogarth Press. The *London Magazine* ran from 1954 to 1961.

29. The poet (1907–63).

30. (1874–1965). EW's essay on Maugham appeared as "Somerset Maugham and an Antidote" (*The New Yorker*, June 8, 1946), revised in *Classics and Commercials* (1950), pp. 319–26.

31. Art critic, translator, and biographer.

32. Nancy Freeman Mitford (1904–73), novelist and essayist. Her comic account of acceptable "upper middle class" usage had appeared in *Encounter* (later in *Noblesse Oblige*, 1956).

33. One of EW's "favorite companions" at Princeton. *A Prelude*, p. 82.

34. (1885–1967), French biographer whose romanticized books on Shelley and Byron were popular in the twenties.

35. Arthur Waley (1889–1966), translator of Chinese and Japanese poets, and Beryl de Zoete, a friend of Waley's and historian of the dance.

36. Celia Paget Goodman, Mamaine's twin sister.

37. Alan Pryce-Jones, then editor of the *Times Literary Supplement*.

38. EW is alluding to *A Writer's Diary* (1953), ed. by Leonard Woolf, extracts from the diaries of Virginia Woolf.

39. See p. 208.

40. John Patrick Douglas Balfour, Lord Kinross (1904–76), journalist, writer, and broadcaster.

41. Ugo Foscolo (1778–1827), Italian poet.

42. Sir Alan Patrick Herbert (1890–1971), novelist and essayist.

43. Edward Benjamin Britten (1913–76), English composer. See EW's "Every Man His Own Eckermann" in *BBT*, p. 591.

44. John Hayward had muscular dystrophy and shared a flat in Carlyle Mansions, Chelsea, with T. S. Eliot for many years. He edited an edition of Eliot's prose for Faber & Faber (1941; 1954).

45. Elena's sister-in-law, Brat's wife.

46. Brat, Elena's brother. The family originally owned Mumms Champagne.

47. EW was associate editor of *The New Republic* from 1926 to 1931.

48. R. H. S. Crossman (1907–74), author, Member of Parliament (1945–74), Minister of Housing and Local Government (1964–66), then assistant editor of the *New Statesman*.

49. Kingsley Martin (1897–1969), essayist and editor of the *New Statesman* from 1931 to 1960.

50. The Soane Museum was founded by Sir John Soane (1753–1837), architect to the Bank of England, and is located in Lincoln's Inn Fields. Sir John Summerson was the curator.

51. G. P. Huntley (1868–1927) was a popular favorite in musical comedy for many years.

52. Professor of philosophy at Oxford.

53. Walther Mumm, Elena's uncle.

54. Leopold Stennett Amery (1873–1955), a close friend of Winston Churchill and outspoken opponent of Chamberlain's policy of appeasement in the days before Britain's involvement in the Second World War. During the war he was Churchill's Secretary of State for India.

55. Alan John Percivale Taylor, the historian.

56. Sir C. Maurice Bowra was then Warden of Wadham College; Lord David Cecil, Goldsmiths' Professor of English Literature.

57. *The Hedgehog and the Fox: An Essay on Tolstoy's View of History* (1953).

58. *Ionica*, a collection of poems (1858) by William Johnson Cory (1823–92). James Elroy Flecker (1884–1915), English poet and dramatist, best known for the play *Hassan*.

59. A sonnet composed by making up a list of end rhymes and then alternating the writing of lines.

60. EW had met Frank MacDonald, then in the English Department at Princeton, at Oxford in 1914. *A Prelude*, pp. 75 ff.; *The Thirties*, pp. 511–12.

61. Desmond Shawe-Taylor, music critic for the *New Statesman* (1945–58). Edward Sackville-West (1901–65), novelist and music critic, a frequent contributor to the *New Statesman*.

62. Raymond Mortimer, a well-known book reviewer.

63. Publisher, chairman of Hamish Hamilton Ltd.

64. Alan Ross, English poet and journalist, editor of *London Magazine* since 1961.

65. Norman Kemp Smith (1872–1958), a Scot who held the chair of moral philosophy at Princeton and who greatly influenced EW when he was there. *The Forties*, pp. 38, 113; *LLP*, pp. 85–86.

66. Cambridge philosopher (1873–1958); *Principia Ethica* (1903).

67. Dover Wilson, the Shakespearean scholar, and Edwin Muir (1887–1959), the poet and translator (notably of Kafka).

68. (1883–1972), prolific writer, author of *Sinister Street* (2 vols., 1913 and 1914), which EW read in his youth and admired.

69. The successful 1949 British film *Whisky Galore*, released in the U.S. as *Tight Little Island*.

70. J. B. Priestley (1894–1984), a prolific writer of novels, miscellaneous prose, and some fifty plays.

71. *The Altar Steps* (1922), *The Parson's Progress* (1923), *The Heavenly Ladder* (1924).

72. *The Four Winds of Love* (6 vols., 1936–45).

73. J. D. Beresford (1873–1947) and Hugh Walpole (1884–1941), novelists.

74. Henry James had discussed recent novelists, including Compton Mackenzie and Hugh Walpole, in two articles on "The Younger Generation" published in the *Times Literary Supplement* (March 19 and April 2, 1914) and included in *Notes on Novelists* (1914).

75. His mother was the American actress Virginia Bateman (1853–1940), who married Edward Compton (1864–1918), the English actor.

76. Franklin Pierce Adams (1881–1960), columnist whose well-known "The Conning Tower" ran first in the old New York *Tribune* and later in the *World*; see note 24, p. 96. James Montgomery Flagg (1887–1960), well-known illustrator.

77. (1907–60), film and television actor.

78. Charles Paul de Kock (1793–1871), immensely successful writer of bawdy and sentimental novels.

79. *The Savoy of London* (1953).

80. Mackenzie's WWI memoirs: *Gallipoli Memories* (1929), *Athenian Memories* (1931), *Greek Memories* (1932).

PARIS

Jan. 28 (?). Left for France. The Gateses had come to see us the night before, when Olili was there—had stayed late and drunk a good deal. Sylvester said the best way to pack and get off was to drink a good deal the night before, then take another drink when you were leaving in the morning.

Trip across the Channel perfectly smooth. Helen seemed to enjoy it: we had breakfast in the dining room, and she looked out the porthole. —But when we had started in the Paris train, and I saw the bombed wreckage of buildings, I was reminded of our trip to Vittel in boxcars in November 1917 and of the bombed towns of Italy in the spring of '45,[1] and I had a sort of sinking feeling of horror and disgust. How sinister Europe had been at the end of the last war. And how futile it now seemed to have twice sent our army to Europe to save them from the German menace, make the world safe for democracy, only to have this part of the world go from bad to worse. Europe has been declining in a sequence of collapses ever since 1918, when it seemed to us still proud and splendid. When we have saved it from the Soviet menace, there will no longer be anything left. I said to Elena then that war was a bad habit that we couldn't yet control; later, when it was brought to my attention how American commercial enterprise was getting hold of Europe, I was driven to fall back again on the importance of the struggle for markets. We lend them money—Italy —to enable them to buy what we make, and now begin to make in their own countries.

Our Paris stay was a disaster. First, the cheap hotel, Passy-Home, to be near Marina's[2] little girl, who, however, was in bed with the flu. Marina said the hotel was like a *maison de passe de troisième classe*. Pleasant evening, the first night, at Marina's, with the Russian relatives—just like Russians everywhere. Marina poured lavish drinks (including much scotch), gave us that night and the next an elaborate Russian dinner. She is well turned out, has small and pretty feet—was previously a model and now works in some department of Dior. Makes more than she lets her family know, so they will not get it away from her. When Elena told her that I had said that Brat and Olili looked as if they had come out of a concentration camp, she said, It's the vicinity of Madeleine.[3] The horrors of the Johannisberg family are one of their chief topics of conversation, and I got a little tired of hearing how dreadful Madeleine is. It is partly that they had all used to visit there and had delightful memories of it, and that they couldn't go there anymore. Marina had been invited to visit the Metternichs and thought that Madeleine would go crazy if she did—she had come into the shop the other day. Her [Marina's] son by her Volkonsky husband was getting to be a problem—just like his father, had the idea that he would never have to work. (He told me that the American Revolution had been made by hunters and soldiers.) Petka also a problem, though he seemed to be better now—was studying singing, and he and his grandmother entertained the delusion that he was going to be another Chaliapin.[4] Elena gets worried by them—by these young men and by Marina's having the little girl in the front room, when she was still sick and constantly crying—we made her put her to bed. She can't resist scolding them, which embarrasses them and of course does no good.

We moved to the Hôtel du Quai Voltaire, where Mamaine was staying. But the cold spell was awful and, combined with other things, made us all sick. I took Helen to see Notre-Dame, and it was even colder than it had been outside—so cold and stale our breath went up in steam—in some ways, I hate these old Catholic churches, with their bereaved people burning candles for loved ones in purgatory. I went to Giraudoux's *Pour Lucrèce* with Petka and Mamaine, while Elena went to see her aunts at the Russian home; and then she had dinner with Nelly de Vogüé, I had dinner with Mamaine. I read Anouilh's[5] *L'Alouette*, and was so disgusted to find it more or less of a plagiarism from *Saint Joan*—scenes, characters, even lines—and was, besides, feeling so rotten the night for which I had bought tickets that I did not even go. When Elena and I set out to see Sartre's *Kean* together, a couple coming away from the doors said, *Vous allez être furieux!*" and explained that Brasseur[6] was ill, so there would not be any performance—we didn't really much care. Olili and Brat and Madeleine had in the meantime descended on Paris; had visited the aunts and made a great fuss over them, in order not to let Elena be one-up on them. Olili was petrified for fear she'd give the others the impression that she was being too nice to Elena, not loyally siding with them. I had the oddest little conversations with her just before I was leaving—would explain that Elena had been terribly ill before we left the Cape, and when I asked her to keep an eye on her, since she was sicker than I was and I should have to let her come on later, Olili would not express the faintest reassurance or sympathy, would say simply, I must go Wednesday morning. She and Brat had the look of phantoms or of the victims of a vampire, who had been drained of blood, while Madeleine had the vampire's bright eyes. The lower part of M.'s face is strong and hard, but discontented to the point of something like anguish, and produces a strange effect of dislocation in contrast to her brown eyes, which are capable of being appealing and on which she depends, I suppose, for her principal ability to charm. General policy they all three had of complaining about everything they do with Elena: the fish at the little restaurant was bad, Olili's bed in the hotel had *toutes les bêtes de l'apocalypse*. When I had put, by mistake, sugar instead of salt on my omelet, Brat said, Somebody might say an American who doesn't know any better than to put sugar on his omelet. Told story of American woman in Europe who demanded chocolate sauce on lobster—chef went crazy and refused, but was finally induced to serve up the two things separately. If I hear this story again, I am going to tell them that I myself like ice cream with hollandaise sauce, a rolled-up anchovy in a half of grapefruit. This family casts a blight, and in Paris its effects were combined with the cold and the current pestilence that everybody got who came here: diarrhea together with a kind of flu. We were ill and in bad humor. Elena, after Mamaine had gone, made me what she later described as "a jealous scene" about her. I was rather surprised and also touched that it was possible for her to think that I could have that much interest in another woman and that she could get to the point of being worried about it. I kidded her about it, but she said that it had seemed as if I were always going off for lunch with Mamaine alone, that she always seemed to be around, and that there being two of them, Celia and M., made it seem as if we were with them all the time. I told her that she misunderstood Mamaine, who didn't have real designs on me, but, having just divorced Koestler, was let down and lonely, and who had hoped to meet John Russell in Paris and, since he had not come, found herself at loose ends. The truth is that she likes to be around married couples, had an American couple at our embassy that she wanted to have us meet, and she likes to bring people together, as she took me, after our dinner, to see Koestler's Hassidic friend, who works at Calmann-Lévy. (I heard from her later that she had gotten sick, too—in her case, it had gone to her lung. She wrote me from a hospital, where she said she had gone to see George Orwell just before he died.) The French themselves and the state of Paris contribute to one's discomfort. As Harry Levin reported, they suffer from the loss of the statues that the Germans melted up. The gilded Jeanne d'Arc is back in the rue de Rivoli; but it is sad to find Voltaire and Condorcet missing from the Quai Voltaire—only the pedestals left with the names. How it thrilled me to see them at the end of the first war when I came down on leave from Chaumont—I wrote a poem about the Voltaire. The English, as Elena says, accomplished their recovery the hard way, by self-discipline, accepting privation, did it from the bottom up; the French have let things go and are suffering now from inflation. They are also demoralized by the discord produced by the German occupation: the atmosphere of suspicion, recrimination, denunciation. There may be something in Paul Chavchavadze's amusing idea that they suffered, after the war, from a sense of frustration for not having themselves had fascism: it would at least have made the situation more clear-cut.

—The night that Elena and I went together to Genet's *Les Bonnes*[7] gave us the coup de grâce. We had a few moments of gaiety having drinks in cafés of the quarter before the performance began, and in the intermission between the two plays, Elena talked about how Paris had thrilled her when she had come here as a young girl and been taken to places like this. But the theater was freezing cold, and the Genet play, though "powerful" and very well acted, poisonously depressing, embarrassing in its probing, by implication—an implication all the more telling because it was no doubt not intended by Genet—into the abject and divided condition of the French. The maids admire and hate the mistress, try to get her lover into trouble. Then decide to poison her— the class angle, but this evaporates: the mistress dashes off to a date, leaving the poisoned tisane. Then the stronger of the two lesbian sisters, who feels that she must poison somebody, decides to poison the other, tells her that, since she wrote the anonymous letter denouncing the lover for murder, the police are now about to catch up with her. When she has thus done the sister in, she tells the audience that she is going to give herself up and then stand up in court and tell them the whole story—the typical Genet gesture—and for the first time express herself. Elena said that it bore her out in her instinctive dislike and distrust of relations between masters and servants. (The Giraudoux play: I had never seen one done in French and was impressed by the way in which the long speeches—very well recited by La Feuillère[8]— sounded very much like the tirades in French classical tragedy. It was curious that Olili, who had been taken to it by Brat and Madeleine, having apparently missed the point that Lucrèce had a yen for the libertine and wanted to believe he had raped her, should have said to me later, in the Goldener Hirsch at Salzburg, that the

play was intended to show how a distorted view of things
prevented one from recognizing realities—just the kind
of thing that Elena had been saying about Olili.)

—Lunch with André Malraux.[9] For this, although
feeling rotten and probably with a temperature, I pulled
myself together. In the cab on the way there, Elena's
solicitude about me reminded me how little she takes care
of herself, how much she devotes herself to other people:
she was very soon sicker than I.

He now lives in a large house, rather modern and
new, quite far from the center of the city. I thought he
was flourishing and happy in a way that he had not
seemed when I saw him on my way back from Russia in
1935. The wife that I met then, Clara, is said to have
treated him badly, and his present one, the widow of his
brother, a very pretty brunette, seemed to both of us
attractive and honest. I think that he is relieved, too, to
be able to relax from politics, which he had on his mind
when I saw him before, and had had constantly and more
heavily on his mind ever since—the Spanish war, the
Resistance, De Gaulle—and devote himself entirely to
writing and art. The Gaullist movement, he said, had
been the only chance for France to get a New Deal but
De Gaulle had now *échoué*. The government now was
nothing—he worried much, as his wife told us later
when she was driving us back to the hotel, about the impotence and nullity, at present, of France; and he told us
that France, having had two great periods of world
importance, in the Crusades and the Revolution, had no
longer at the moment any role in the world, and he had
been writing his work on art partly because the one field
in which France was still supreme was that of art. The
Louvre was the greatest museum in the world. He had
just been in the U.S. for three weeks with his wife, only
New York and Washington. The Metropolitan was *une*

musée de province—the National Gallery was the great one. I asked him whether he had met [Francis] Taylor[10] —said that T.'s review of *Les Voix du silence* [1951] had been idiotic, and he replied with emphasis, *Tout à fait idiot!* —The trouble was that Taylor couldn't cope with a work on that *niveau*. I told him that I thought the preface to the new book on sculpture[11] was one of the best things he had written, and he answered that was what he thought himself, it had been something he wanted to say; but nobody read it: they just looked at the pictures. I said that it was impossible to understand the pictures without reading the preface, and he replied, *On ne comprend pas.*

He has two boys by his present wife, of whom he seems rather proud. I felt on his part a certain satisfaction in living in his large house, in a certain style, and playing the role of family. In a humorous little aside to me, he assumed a complicity of men who knew the inconveniences of family life, and in this and in his way of addressing himself to Elena—whom he always addressed as madame—I felt a deliberate and self-conscious assumption of a certain social role—a kind of thing not usual with educated Frenchmen, for whom the conventional formulas are second nature, a matter of routine; but it is part of what I like about him, of what makes him satisfactory in a way that few modern Frenchmen of the literary world are (Cousteau the deep-sea diver). It is still hard for him to look one in the eye—what is the cause of his reluctant gaze? You must be very direct with him to summon it; and he has substituted for the tic he had when I saw him last—that of spasmodically winking —a different one, a clicking in the throat. He likes to talk on his feet and jump around. His expositions are punctuated by *bon!* and *bien!*, nailing the point just made before rushing on to the next step. —He has some quite remarkable objets d'art—a Buddha (?) of which he told us that it was, I think, the best piece of its kind in France, a reproduction of Fra Angelico, some Hopi katchinas and a New Hebrides mask reproduced in one of his books. (He said that the children liked the former of these but were rather afraid of the latter.) But the house—nor the drinks nor the lunch—did not display much taste of the typical French kind—not that one minded this: a certain effortful bleakness characteristic of Malraux, big spaces, a variety of objects, incongruous one with the other, in which moved continually the vortex of M.'s intense and nervous personality. It was cold, they had just come back and had not yet got the heating going. In the big room, a small electric heater, which was made to play on Elena. —Effect, on Malraux's part, of an intense, energetic, self-kindling, self-consuming force, whirling about without giving heat, but yet generating energy, in something almost like a vacuum: the room, the house, the quarter (extramural Paris, France, Europe).

He was full, as usual, of formulations—some of them brilliantly illuminating, some of them rather inept— especially on the subject of the U.S., which I don't think he understands at all. There had never, he said, been such a phenomenon. People talked about the new Romans, but that was all nonsense. The Romans had been aiming on conquest, at imposing Roman civilization. All that the Americans wanted was *qu'on leur fiche la paix*. There had never been anything like it! Cromwell had known what he wanted; Stalin had known what he wanted; Washington had known what he wanted. But what did modern America want? *Elle ne veut rien*. I tried to remonstrate with him about this. I said that Stalin had not known what he wanted: he was always changing his line—what was involved here was the automatic expansion of power. I tried to explain that in Europe it was impossible to understand American politics. In Europe you had parties with formulated views, based on theoretical principles (difference between American and European papers); at home there was nothing of the kind. He was rather impatient of this: he cannot understand, in his very French way, any movement which cannot be shown to embody an arguable position. And he has also a "mystique" of nations and their role that seems almost Hegelian. He has a Germanic side (he comes from the north of France)—Elena says he writes like a German (is certainly coming to more and more). After lunch, with his queer little air of complicity, he asked me in a lowered voice a question which I did not at first understand, but which turned out to be, on his repeating it, whether I were not a great "partisan of Nietzsche." People expected Americans to be like this—demonstrating with shoulders and fist, i.e., very foursquare and positive. But when on a previous trip (raising money for Spain) he had met the university faculties, he had found them on a high level, but had felt that they were rather timid. —People thought that Americans were materialistic, cared about nothing but money. He is still only in the stage of the first rudimentary reactions to the realities of America. —When I saw him in '35, however, he said one very good thing about the U.S. that showed that he had grasped our position better than most Europeans. I had spoken of the provinciality, compared with our New York papers, of the Parisian press; and he had said, *C'est parce que la France est en Europe, les Etats-Unis sont dans le monde.* When I had left him in the taxi after dinner and asked him whether he would be coming to America, he had replied emphatically, *Je l'espère bien!* But I am not sure that his kind of mind can accommodate itself to us: he would be likely to spend all his time making a series of formulations that would become

more and more incoherent. Strange, I thought, his conception of French culture and his accounting in those
terms for his work on art; can only see his own life and
the life of the nation in terms of one another, and in
terms of some high *intention civilisatrice*.

On literature: He asked about [Alexis] Léger, for
whom he evidently feels a certain admiration as for one
who, like himself, has traveled and known the great
world and has tried to bring it into French literature.
But he said—one of his accurate insights—that the three
distinguished French poets who had come from the West
Indies—Heredia, Leconte de Lisle, and Léger[12]—had all
had in common a combination of sonority and lack of
content. I remembered that Huysmans[13] had called
Leconte de Lisle *le quincaillier sonore*. I agreed that
Léger, though magnificent in rhetoric, as I supposed, in
the handling of French, was desolating, *écrasant*, in the
long run—in a long performance like *Vents*—because
you never touched the man—a lyricism entirely on
parade; and the lines were so full of rare words, like the
labels on exhibits in museums, ethnological, anthropological, zoological, geological, meteorological. (I feel this in
his conversation, too, and sympathize with the comment
of Isaiah Berlin that when he hears Léger doing his
stuff, telling a story in the grand manner, he is likely
to say to himself, as he does at a classical tragedy at the
Comédie, I'm not enjoying this as much as I should.)
—Malraux said that Léger had supported the policy of
Pétain, and that it was undoubtedly on that account that
he had not come back to France. —I asked him whether
Léger was much read in France, said that I thought he
felt that people were not interested in him any longer.
Malraux replied that Léger was read by everybody who
read anything seriously.

I said that I had been disgusted by Anouilh's

L'Alouette, and he told me that the Paris theater was now more or less what Hollywood was with us. They wrote now more and more for money, and pretty much all the dramatists were selling themselves: Anouilh, Cocteau, Sartre—*Kean*, for example. He agreed with me about the badness of *Le Diable et le Bon Dieu* [1951]. —As for Giraudoux, they were trying to make him out to be a great writer, but he was actually a good minor writer. Malraux had been with him the day, or a day or two, before he died. He had not been thinking about *Pour Lucrèce*, which he had drafted some time before, but been occupied with a quite different project. —When I brought up the always embarrassing subject of Genet,[14] and praised *Les Bonnes*—which he said he had read but not seen—he hastily admitted that Genet "had talent," but asserted—I don't quite know what he meant by this —that he had no sense of discrimination. The merits of *Les Bonnes* were due to its having been written when Genet had not "arrived"; it had the intensity of the pressures which had driven Genet to express himself, but he [Malraux?] said he had been weakened by success. I expounded my theory that Sartre had written his enormous book on Genet, dropping his own novel and allowing his gigantic introduction to appear as the "first volume" of Genet's "complete works,"[15] because Genet was the Sartre character which Sartre himself had not had the genius to invent—Malraux: *Sartre n'a jamais inventé rien!*—and that he couldn't get over it, and tried to expound Genet in terms of existentialist philosophy— saying that Genet did not understand himself—not realizing how much more brilliantly he [Genet] had said it himself.

I asked about Michelet's diaries.[16] They would never be published, Malraux said positively. They would cause too much scandal—they were full of his sexual obsessions. But with Genet and Sartre, I said, why should there be any objection to anything Michelet might have written? —*On se fiche de Genet!* he said. But Michelet was in the French pantheon, and the diaries ought not to be published on account of what X, some reactionary paper, would make of this explosion of scandal in connection with the great representative of the revolutionary tradition. I couldn't see this point of view and remonstrated with him about it. It is the political side of Malraux which leads him into what seem aberrations, such as his working for the Communists in the Spanish war. He had told me in '35, when I had asked him whether he had any lowdown on the recent Soviet trials, that he knew no more than I, but that, so far as what the government said went, he was sure that *ce sont des mensonges.* He had told me at that time that I ought to go to see Trotsky, then somewhere in France or Switzerland. (He described to me *le côté Lear de Trotsky,* told me how he had walked with the old man, who had been acting the tragic grandeur of his rejection by his own people and his isolation in exile. He told me also of Trotsky's attitude toward a working-class man who had come to see him— dealt with his business and dismissed him and went back to his conversation with Malraux, as if from an inferior to an equal.) Later on, when he came to America, he was scrupulously observing the Party line, and in the course of a controversy with Trotsky, said, Trotsky lies and knows he lies when he says . . . etc. There may be something of this moral obliquity, the cheating on code in the interests of another, behind his unsteady gaze. —What led up to our talk about Michelet's diaries was his saying, when I asked whether Communism in France derived a good deal of its strength from its followers' connecting it with the French revolutionary tradition, that it was not the real tradition but the myth to which the Communists appealed. French history, he went on to explain, was taught partly in terms of Michelet, partly in terms of the kings, and, in the minds of the children who got this, the two elements existed side by side without contradicting one another. I think he meant to make the point that there was no organic conception of the development of French history, the interaction of forces, so that Communism seemed vaguely familiar, and they did not grasp its real relation to, its incompatibility with, the realities of contemporary France.

I said that Sartre's sense of politics was weak. —*Il n'a aucun sens de la politique! Il ne comprend pas qu'en politique il s'agit soit de faire quelque chose soit de produire un système.* (I probably have the French wrong, but the main phrases are right.)

I asked about the vogue of the Marquis de Sade, and he said that there were three people who owed their reputation to the fact that it was difficult to get at them: Sade, Picasso, Lautréamont.[17] Picasso required an effort in order to be understood; Sade's books were not accessible—if it had been possible to get them and read them, people would not have been interested in them. *C'était un idiot, Sade!* I did not see how Lautréamont fitted into this: he was neither inaccessible nor difficult.

In connection with Michelet's diaries, I felt, as I had sometimes done in reading Malraux's books, that there was something, for a Frenchman, peculiar in his attitude toward sex—something not perhaps puritanical but implying obstructions in his own sexual life: the trait of Garine in *Les Conquérants* [1928] going to bed with two women, the masturbating terrorist of *La Condition humaine* [1933], Malraux's interpretation of *Les Liaisons dangereuses*[18] as a study not in sex but in power. It is a subject on which one feels he is uncomfortable; yet I got a decided impression that his present pretty wife and fairly recent children are doing a good deal to satisfy him. Cf. the passage in Gide's diary where he tells of Malraux, in his earlier marriage, feeling that he was stronger on his own, that he had to get away from his family. This is certainly not the case now.

—In London, I had found, when I went to Verschoyle to sign the contract for my Civil War book [*Patriotic Gore*, 1962], that it was made out for *Studies in the Revolutionary Period*. I tried to explain the difference, but Verschoyle, who was supposed to have seen some of the MS., evidently did not grasp it and did not seem to think it of any importance. Someone else that we talked to seemed to think that I was dealing with the English Civil War—Cromwell, etc. —I told Nelly de Vogüé about this in Paris and discovered that she did not know the difference, either, between the Civil War and the Revolution. Though she had been to the U.S. on business a number of times, the only historical fact she had grasped was that we had a Constitution and she asked when this had been produced.

NOTES

1. *The Forties*, pp. 49–55, 113–29.
2. Marina Schouvaloff, a first cousin of Elena's.
3. Brat and Olili, Elena's brother and sister; Madeleine, Brat's French wife.
4. Fyodor Chaliapin (1873–1938), celebrated Russian basso.
5. Jean Giraudoux (1882–1944) and Jean Anouilh (b. 1910), pre-WWII and post-WWII dramatists, respectively.
6. Pierre Brasseur played the title role in the premiere of Sartre's adaptation (1953) of Dumas père's *Kean* (1836).
7. Jean Genet (1910–1986), novelist, poet, and dramatist; *Les Bonnes* (1944).
8. French actress, the former Caroline Cunati, who married Pierre Feuillère in 1931.
9. André Malraux (1901–76), French novelist and man of

letters; Minister of Culture under de Gaulle. *The Forties*, p. 74;
BBT, pp. 137–50.

10. Francis Henry Taylor (1903–57), director of the Metropolitan Museum of Art, had called the book "pure Apocrypha."

11. *Le Musée imaginaire de la sculpture mondiale* (1952).

12. Alexis Léger (1887–1975), who wrote verse under the pseudonym Saint-John Perse, was born on Guadeloupe; José María de Heredia (1842–1905) was born in Cuba (his mother was French); EW overlooks birth of Leconte de Lisle (1818–94) on the island of Réunion, not in the West Indies.

13. Joris Karl Huysmans (1848–1907), French novelist.

14. Genet was in and out of prisons all over Europe and was openly homosexual.

15. Sartre's *Saint Genet: comédien et martyr* appeared as vol. 1 of the *Oeuvres complètes de Jean Genet* (1952). Sartre was then working on the fourth volume of his novel *Les Chemins de la liberté*, which he never completed.

16. Jules Michelet (1798–1874), the historian. See *To the Finland Station* (1940), *passim*. Publication of his complete *Journal* began in 1959.

17. Comte de Lautréamont, pseudonym of Isidore Ducasse (1846–70), author of the proto-surrealistic *Les Chants de Maldoror*.

18. The epistolary novel (1782) by Pierre Choderlos de Laclos (1741–1803).

10/28/10

SALZBURG

Feb. 4. Elena and Helen were ill, but I was able to travel, so I left Paris the night of Feb. 4 (I think) and got to Salzburg the next afternoon. They followed, still far from recovered, on Sunday (the 7th). I had had a well-warmed *wagon-lit;* in theirs the heating did not work, and they seem to have had a miserable journey. The man who had the lower berth in my compartment was a Swiss doctor who lived in Paris and who was going to Vienna to lecture. He specialized in the alimentary canal and intestines and talked to me about cancer. He had been in New York and said that the Rockefeller Foundation and the other institutions engaged in cancer research were mistakenly concentrating on remedies rather than trying to find out the cause. Food was evidently an important factor: the more complicated the food, the greater the incidence of cancer. More cancer in Switzerland than ever in the U.S.

Feb. 4–March 6. Salzburg: Cold, mist, and illness; lecturing with stopped-up nose and sensitive throat at nine o'clock in morning, after puffing up dark spiral servants' staircase with my folder of notes in my hand. Max Reinhardt's baroque Leopoldskron,[1] with its bogus Austrian portraits and glass and porcelain chandeliers, Austrian-pastry stucco ornaments—painted panels and mirrors, proctic[?] cupids and feminine ecclesiastics of the rooms where lectures were held; big bearded black busts of Romans, with gilded trimmings, along the landing of the upper stairway. In the dining room, heated by a large fireplace, enormous and terrible paintings of Archbishop Firmian willing the schloss to his nephew, with his favorite dog in the foreground; and, opposite, the nephew and his wife, presumably reigning in the castle. Men from the town curling on the lake. Helen practised skating. —My colleagues: Larry Thompson[2] and I gave them at the beginning a blast of Calvinism which some thought preconcerted; Isaac Rosenfeld[3] gave them American philosophy in relation to Am. lit.: it turned out to be mainly philosophy, with an indication of possible parallel developments in the literary field, and I suspected him of giving his regular course; Roy Harvey Pearce, on American poetry, was under the impression that he was operating with a sociological approach, but it seemed to me that what he was giving them was merely a slight variation on the aridities and absurdities of the current *explication de texte*; to listen to him was torture, a drop-dropping of little lead pellets of thought the meaning of which appeared to be nil—a kind of double-talk in a mushy California accent. —The Yugoslavian students were the eagerest, spent a good deal of time in the library devouring American books, not rigorously conditioned like the Russians—there are different nuances of political thought, though they pay a certain lip service to Marxism—tall blond girl who had been, during the war, in a German concentration camp would blush when I criticized it; the man who was translating Hemingway went faithfully to mass. Gaiety of Italians from Genoa, Milan, Turin, Como, Florence, Bologna, Sicily: tendency to sing and dance. —Rex Crawford, excellent linguist, had been cultural attaché in Brazil, lectured in Portuguese and Spanish; somewhat overdid being serviceable, to the irritation of North Carolinian Woodall. Queer to find the very small-town and middle-class Woodalls and Meads in that setting and presiding over that company. Elena thought at first they weren't calculated to give the foreign students a favorable impression of America but later decided they had been chosen deliberately (I'm not sure that this was true) to give everything a sound and prosaic basis: at the discussions, there had sometimes been blow-ups, and they wanted to keep things on an even keel. —We never quite got over our colds and our digestive derangements. The army beds and blankets became a discomfort; the food was depressing in the extreme. In general, the food in Austria is much too sweet for my taste. At the schloss, there was cinnamon mixed with the sugar for the cereal, canned orange and lemonade for breakfast that did not fill the role of orange juice, jam or apple butter. In the restaurants in town—the Goldener Hirsch, where we often went—the tempting-looking hors d'oeuvres would turn out to taste like pastry. The hors d'oeuvres were sweet, the drinks were sweet; they didn't know the use of salt. I never remember to have seen a town with so many pastry shops as Salzburg. In the *Konditorei*, there would seem to be nothing but cakes and chocolate with great gobs of whipped cream on top. The schloss was somewhat battered from having been used as a music school and a barracks, and the *Gauleiter* of the Nazi period had shot himself and his family in the cellar. The *Kastellan*'s apartment was full of pictures of Franz Josef.

Our apartment had two large Chinese grotesque figures and, in the corner of the hall, a wooden female figure holding a skull, her bare toes partly chopped off.

Feb. 12–14. Weekend with the Arthur Mumms: we were ill but got a rest and felt better. Elena's uncle Arthur had moved to Bavaria to get away from Berlin (or Frankfurt) when he foresaw the danger of bombing. Pleasant little farmhouse and stable full of chamois skulls and stuffed (black and red-eyed) caprigellia; heavy and amusing if not charming, somewhat miscellaneous old furniture; amiable conversation and comfortable drinks. Mrs. Mumm, Elena told me, was Jewish, sister-in-law of Sali Horstmann. Arthur's Bavarian costume, ribald jokes at dinner—a touch of the Mumm charm—Elena says he is an awful liar, that she can always tell when he is lying because he gets a certain expression. Usual head-shaking over Madeleine and Brat: Brat had turned up for the first time in years, and they had just sat down for a visit when Madeleine called up from Munich and said that they needed a fourth at bridge, so he had jumped in his car and rushed off. —The Mumm shooting box had been north of Salzburg in the hills.

Feb. 19–25. The next weekend—on Friday, I think— Olgarel[4] and Olili came. More harping on Madeleine. Olgarel has kept herself going as a professional guide in Vienna, conducting tours to other places, writing *Guides Bleus*, etc. They think that she does not really know she is a lesbian, but I rather doubt this. She announced that, on her way through Paris, she had been for the first time to the Folies-Bergères, and that she had been very much disappointed—not a girl was under thirty. She dressed in black like a little woman doctor: short skirts and strong high shoes—hair cut short but, while in Salzburg, she had a permanent, which crinkled it a little. At first, going through the cold museum, the *Haus der Natur*, with Helen, I found it a little hard to take to her: she did not make the usual feminine responses, often would not reply at all; but later I saw that the way to take her was as if she were a little old man who did care to hear conventional chatter. The stuffed animals and things in the museum were decidedly German and different from those in New York: emphasis on the gruesome and noisome, the monstrous: careful reproduction of bear dung, developments of embryos, two-headed calves, elaborate tableau of bodies exposed and eaten by vultures in Tibet. —Olgarel had a wonderful time; I kissed her when she was leaving, and she said to Elena, *Votre mari est le deuxième homme qui m'a embrassé*—somebody, *il ne compte pas*—*votre père et maintenant votre mari!* She sent bread-and-butter letters and postcards every day for a week afterwards. Speaking English, she always said, Methinks. When we were going through the Mozart house, she stopped in front of the portrait of Mozart's son and recited Grillparzer's poem about him.[5] The evening before she left she said to Elena about me (Elena told me): *Ce n'est pas seulement qu'il est intelligent—il est bon.* I was very much touched by this, because I doubt whether I often give this impression.

—Secretary-housekeeper with whom Elena talked: looked back to her years in the Youth *Bund* as the happiest of her life.

—Olili was still heavy going. She and Olgarel came to one of my lectures. She would be full of nervous things she thought she had to do—finding out about her trains, etc. Elena said she recognized the symptoms of her being on the edge of a breakdown. —I saw how she chilled and arrested the talkative and self-assertive Schneditz when he was taking us around the town and she joined

us for a few minutes. Elena thought she did not really
go to see the Arthur Mumms, did not want to be asked
questions or to have her rapport with Johannisberg
broken into by outsiders.

Feb. 28. The next Sunday, the A. Mumms came for
luncheon and dinner, and Franz Höllering[6] from Munich.
Of Franz, I felt at first that it was wrong to see him not
at Stamford, then I came to the conclusion that he was
better off and happier here—was writing and translating
plays, a man around the theater, and had, as I found
when I visited Munich, a very nice woman, a child
psychologist turned novelist, to live with him. —Very
cordial relations with these Mumms, who were not Nazis
(though it was one of A.'s stories that he had flown over
London in a bomber) and didn't worry about the war.

—Visit to Salzburg of sanctimonious spy for Rockefeller (or Commonwealth) Foundation who had himself,
bald-headed and small-eyed, a shrewd and mean look
almost Rockefellerian (former English professor). Elena,
who was sitting beside him, thought he tightened when
I talked, at the evening discussion, about the oppressive
aspects of the big millionaire period in America.

The truth is that I am never at all at home in an
academic environment. I think it is going to be rather
fun, then find that it is mostly uncomfortable. In a
college, one becomes only gradually aware of the at first
invisible hierarchy; and even with professors from different places and far away from their communities, as here,
you and they still belong to different worlds—you and
they belong nowhere in one another's worlds, and,
though ostensibly both concerned with books, you are
concerned with them in such different ways, are working
with such different techniques—and they are, as a rule,
so much more specialized than you—that it is difficult

to get on with one another. On my side, I probably tend to underestimate what they are doing because it is different from what I am doing. To teach a literary subject well (the French 17th century, for example)—as [E. B. O.] Borgerhoff[7] at Princeton evidently does—you have to have more extensive knowledge and permanent mastery of it than I generally do in order to write an essay or even a book. The *kind* of work also is different: teaching something and writing about it demand completely different techniques, ways of living, habits of mind. Relations become sometimes embarrassing, (Incident of Borgerhoff at Princeton apologizing to me for Leon Edel's little speech about Justice Holmes's relations with Henry James, which was one of the only comments on my papers that added anything to them. He evidently thought that we ought to be treated like two prima donnas.)

March 6–8. [Marginal note: written during trip home on the *Ile de France:* April 27–May 31] *Munich:* We stayed at the Vierjahreszeiten Hotel, and had a very pleasant rest and holiday. It was almost like getting out of the army into a good hotel—enjoyment of baths and beds and dinners in the excellent restaurant. Munich, though it had been so flattened out by bombing, was now partially built and made a relatively cheerful impression. We saw Franz Höllering and his girlfriend, with whom he lives. He has made himself—after some time, he says—a sort of place for himself here, translating plays and working for the theater. We went to the theater both nights: first, a highly successful musical show called *Feuerwerk*, the first part of it quite amusing; the second night, a German version of Julian Green's *Sud* [1953], which turned out to be something very odd. They seemed to have cut out most of the references to the historical events of the Civil War. The actor who played the Polish officer, I was told, intensely disliked the part and refused to give it any homosexual accent: he simply stood around and glowered—even when encored at the end. The young humanitarian planter, with whom he was supposed to be infatuated, was costumed and made up more or less like the young Abraham Lincoln. Esther Arthur[8] afterwards told us that in Paris he had been "*très mignon.*" Elena's pansy friend Rouvier said that in Paris the play had been wonderful, that it had been quite evident there that the old planter had been in love with the Pole; but when I came to read the French text, I decided that the planter's secret had been something else—love for a black mistress or sympathy with the North—and that the play contained a historical theme that was not understood in Europe: the officer of the Federal army represented in reality the spirit of the South—arrogant, feudal, cruel; the Southern planter, the humanitarianism of the North. The Pole knew he was doomed and invited his own destruction. The girl from the North, with her rigid moral conscience, admired the relentless Pole more than she did the Southerners.

—Rouvier, an old admirer of Elena's, had wanted to marry her once but she had realized he was really homosexual—now cultural attaché of the French in Munich. I discovered he was half Greek, but did not know Greece well, had only visited Crete from a yacht, and did not care for his mother's family in Athens, who were evidently rather rich, of the French-speaking bourgeoisie of the type of Eva Siphraios's[9] husband's family. He had met Jean Genet and said that he was like a French workman very much preoccupied with his projection of himself in his books. Rouvier agreed with me that such expressions as "*toutes proportions gardées*" in the mouth of Jeanne d'Arc in Anouilh's play were impossible. —Rou-

vier took us to a cocktail party at the house of the American cultural attaché, where we met the actress who had
admirably played the cook in the *Feuerwerk*, a rather
distinguished *von* who spoke excellent English. The
theater in Munich is, as Elena said, all a little like college
theatricals and yet not at all bad: enthusiasm and intelligence have gone into it. The theaters themselves and
the opera were practically all destroyed, and they don't
have much money for productions. The result is that
the actors no sooner achieve reputations than they are
lured away by better pay elsewhere. Not many new
German plays, so they continually do translations.
(*Pygmalion* was being done in London, in Germany,
and in Tel Aviv. A Cinderella play—perhaps the only one
of Shaw's that has this kind of popular appeal.) Hauptmann was very popular; Wedekind no longer done at all
—now seemed quite out of date.[10]

NOTES

1. The 18th-century Schloss Leopoldskron, built by Archbishop
Leopold Anton Firmian (1679–1744), had been owned by Max
Reinhardt (1873–1943), Germany's leading stage director before
WWII.

2. Lawrance R. Thompson (1906–73), Princeton professor of
English and biographer of Frost.

3. Isaac Rosenfeld (1918–56), Chicago-born novelist and
essayist.

4. Olgarel was an old cousin of Elena's.

5. Franz Grillparzer (1791–1872), the Vienna-born playwright
and poet; "Zu Mozarts Feier" (1842).

6. Franz Höllering (b. 1896), the Austrian-born novelist; EW
met him when Höllering was living in New York. *The Forties*,
passim.

7. E. B. O. Borgerhoff (1908–68) taught French at Princeton
from 1930 to 1968; *Liberal Theory and Practice in the French
Theatre, 1680–1757* (1936).

8. EW knew Esther Arthur when she was married to John Strachey, author of *The Coming Struggle for Power* (1933). She later married Chester Arthur, grandson of the twenty-first President. *The Thirties*, pp. 508–09 and passim.

9. Eva Siphraios, whom EW had met in Athens in 1945.

10. Gerhart Hauptmann (1862–1946), the celebrated playwright, winner of the Nobel Prize for Literature in 1912. Franz Wedekind (1864–1918), author of often controversial plays that anticipated German Expressionism.

GERMANY

Frankfurt, March 8–14. We stayed at the Frankfurter Hof, another first-class hotel. Strange to think of having been here with the family in 1908.[1] The river and a church steeple or two seemed quite familiar to me; but the only thing I remember connected with it was seeing, from the hotel window, a drove of old horses being led along the street, being told they were to be used for sausages. The old city had been completely destroyed, intentionally I was told, but the industries outside it had all been spared. New buildings side by side with gruesome ruins; Goethe's house and other things carefully reconstructed. —When I went to the American Express to get my ticket to Israel, I had the impression, in that part of town, where America House (here on a very large scale) and other American headquarters were, that it constituted a kind of American ghetto, where the Germans did not much care to go. The Americans, of course, on their side, were discouraged from fraternizing with the Germans. The young German in the office that handled the tickets at once told me that it was too late. The office was closed. I began talking loudly and peremptorily, and he began scurrying around, saying that he knew the ticket had come, and finally he produced it. Later, I found myself involved in a duel of pomposity and insolence with the Fischer office (the publishers), and I decided that the old complaint about the Germans—that they only respected *Schrecklichkeit*— was still more or less true—an opinion afterwards confirmed by both Elena and Henry. Elena, after I left, found people, she said, most disagreeable. Henry said he always had to be arrogant to get a decent table in a restaurant. I hadn't felt the unpleasant attitude in Munich but did begin to in Frankfurt.

—The Gruniliuses, however, I liked. They were, as Elena said, like the Buddenbrooks in Thomas Mann— one of the men at the supper we went to, with his square face and square mustache, even looked like Mann. His wife was a formidable Chinese scholar, who had for years been director of a museum in China and now taught Chinese at Mainz. I talked to her about Arthur Waley. He had the great merit, she said, of not being immersed in philology, as so many sinologists were—had kept his head above it and appreciated the literature. But she was not without a little of the pedantry of the traditional German professor. —The old Grunilius— eighty-four—was charming, a banker who had made it a point to be something of a man of the world, had traveled in his youth and come to the U.S., where he had visited in Newport. He still took long walks every day. His offices had been bombed, so he had since been doing business in his house—had patiently and shrewdly built the business up again, was now on a very sound basis. There were great cracks in the ceiling and patches of plaster fallen, the result of the bombing which had destroyed the Chinese museum next door; but he had not had them repaired. Elena was impressed by the excellent buffet supper they gave us, because they were proverbially stingy; but we did not eat it in the big dining room above but downstairs in what must have been used as a reception room for clients of the business. The son was at the head of the committee to restore the Goethe house, was the one about whom Elena had told me that he had been in the habit, just after the war, of quietly seizing the food that was sent to them from the States and eating it by himself in his room. The other son had been married to a Jewess, but she had left him and finally divorced him. Their son was there with the family. —The old man was known as Max, the son who now ran the bank as E. Max (Ernst). —The daughter Margaret, Elena told me, now did all the cooking herself and was constantly bawled out by E. Max. She had wanted to marry someone, but had been discouraged by the family, who thought him a social inferior —so she had never married at all. She was rather plain, but the Metzler friend was rather handsome. There were three Jewish families in Frankfurt: the G.'s, the Metzlers, and one other. —The G.'s had never had the house repaired, because they thought it an unnecessary expense. There was, Elena told me, an enormous hole in the stairs; the big salon was so badly damaged that they had had it boarded up. They usually ate in the basement in the servants' dining room, with linoleum on the floor. —I was suffering from my hay-feverish, or whatever it was, sneezing and nose-blowing and eye-watering malady. Elena and Helen had something of the same thing—the eye inflammation, which Elena thought was due to dust from the ruins. But in my case it may have been aggravated by bad anticipations of Johannisberg, which turned out to have been more than justified. I had wanted to go to Israel from Munich, but Elena had asked me to go with her, she thought it would make things easier—

Madeleine, if I was there, would not be able to insult her, as she had done on the previous visit, when she had called her *une sale renégate*. I had told her she ought not to go at all without an invitation and apology from Brat. But Olili maneuvered the whole thing, insisting that Elena should write to Brat—which she resisted at first but finally did—saying she would like to come. Somebody had said to somebody else, "Elena will be too proud to go there." But Elena insisted to me that nothing made any difference: in spite of everything that had happened, she was closer to Olili and Brat than to anybody, that Johannisberg was still her home.

Johannisberg: Olili drove us out, at a terrible rate of speed that reminded me of Walther's driving. I was still completely unable to establish connections with her. I sat beside her in front and tried to "make" conversation. We talked, for Helen's benefit, of the Mouse Tower and the Lorelei Rock, which she said she was to take us to see; and she pointed out the house where Wagner had lived. Elena does not like Wagner, whom she associates with all that is bogus and vulgarly self-assertive in German patriotic romanticism, and I made my usual observation that Wagner is a writer for young people, who ought to be enjoyed at an early age, for his delightful fairy tales—his love stories and exploits of heroes. Olili replied, with her usual coldness—it was evidently a stock comment that she had picked up from somebody —that people who like Wagner usually like Puccini and all of Chaikovsky. I elaborated my idea a little, and she repeated the same opinion in almost exactly the same words.

The Mumm place at Johannisberg was not quite so impressive or attractive as Elena's love for it had led me to expect. It was now rather faded, and the original furniture and decoration had been in rather bad German

taste of the middle of the 19th century, to which Elena's
mother had added objects of the early nineteen hundreds
—fashionable (??) portraits among the ornate wooden
columns and stairway banisters and doorways that made
the rooms rather heavy and dark. The corridors of the
wings upstairs with their rows of doors all on the same
side were like an old-fashioned hotel. (We were put in
the wing that was used for guests in the rooms that had
been used by Bazata,[2] who had had to be moved out.
Thérèse, the old servant of whom Elena was so fond,
told her that there was a great deal of traffic in that
hallway at night—Madeleine coming to see Bazata.)
We were supposedly invited, when we first arrived, for
tea in the central living room, but no tea appeared, and
we sat there with Olili and Brat through one of the
coldest and stiffest, one of the most constrained three-
quarters of an hour or so that I ever remember anywhere.
Elena told Brat about the headwaiter in the Munich
restaurant who had recommended some other brand of
wine, in preference to Mumm Johannisberg, and Brat
replied, "If you'll pardon me, Americans haven't much of
a place for taste in wine." If I hadn't been new to the
household, I'd have said I'd pardon him, because Germans
didn't have much of a place for politeness. At last, Brat
produced some liquor from a cupboard in the wall and
made a gin-and-champagne cocktail—perhaps his own
invention—of which, in any case, he seemed to be
proud.

—The landscape, in March, was pale and the weather
already quite mild: the vineyards on the rounded slopes
stretched away to the Rhine. It was not romantic, not
exciting, neutral and faded like the house.

—Dinner, like all the meals, was meager—visiting
relatives had complained of this. They would have soup
and one dish such as liver. I didn't mind this, however,

since I usually eat breakfast and lunch alone, and dinner in the middle room on trays; sitting up at a table and talking has come more and more to fatigue me. I have finally come to the conclusion that eating and conversation ought to be kept separate. I believe that the Japanese —or somebody—think that it is absolutely disgusting for white people to watch each other eating.

—There were, besides the family, a local count and Joe Bazata. I had met the latter for the first time just before dinner. I observed him with curiosity, because I had never been able to get any clear idea about him from what people said about him. [Marginal note: Little Mumm girl is named Magdalena, and they always call her Alena. Madeleine had her christened a Catholic.] Certainly he and Madeleine are admirably united to one another—both adventurers and rather clever ones. She has nothing in common with Brat, whom she evidently despises. The rest of the family make her uncomfortable, and it must be much more interesting for her to have Bazata around—much more so than the unfortunate Allegretti, who was relatively naïve. I was struck at first by the way in which Bazata was trying to live up to Johannisberg—he was cultivating continental refinement—elegantly holding his teacup and saying *Fránce* and acquiring the British conversational rhythms. He would occasionally assent *oui, oui* to something that was said in French, though I don't believe he knew any French. (The family talk French, English, and German in spells, shifting from one to the other with habitual regularity, just as they change in their letters. This is probably, in some ways, a bad thing for them—though, of course, it is really a part of their whole special situation. Brat, I am sure, is under the impression that he is in some way a Frenchman, and had not been an invader of France. Their multilingual way of talking is one of their means of escaping their responsibility as Germans, they somehow do not think of themselves as responsible to any country. Brat still feels that, by the Rheims champagne business, he is closely bound to France; Olili escapes to England.) But Bazata became gradually recognizable as the kind of tough but somewhat original character that Ted Paramore[3] would have found in a bar and whose stories and boasts would have amused him, but whom his old-fashioned notions of propriety would have prevented him from bringing home. —At dinner, I suppose I challenged him, without being completely aware of it, by holding forth in a clear and authoritative voice on various American subjects: I spoke of the statue to Rumford[4] in Munich, about which, and whom, neither the Mumms nor he knew; and I gave them my theory of American Presidents—the able idealist politicians carrying on the tradition of the Republic (Lincoln, Wilson, the Roosevelts), the machine party politician (Harding and Truman), and the completely non-political expert put in by the big-business interests on the strength of a popular reputation achieved in some non-political field (Grant, Eisenhower, Hoover). At this point Bazata broke in to contend that Hoover had been a very sound President. I said that he had done nothing whatever; Elena reminded him that he had driven the veterans out of Washington. He repeated that Hoover had been "sound," there were times when it was sounder not to do anything, Hoover was a "safe" man—he had had an interview with Roosevelt just before the latter's inauguration, and Roosevelt, for the sake of his own glory, would not let him proclaim a bank holiday, which had been Hoover's own idea. I answered that I knew they had had an interview, but doubted whether Hoover had originated the idea of a bank holiday. Bazata was evidently not in the habit of being contradicted at that table on the subject of American affairs.

—After dinner, the situation went rapidly from bad to worse. We sat in the room next to the dining room, and they played a cheap musical radio program. Under the influence of Brat's brandy, Bazata became cruder and more insolent, and I became more pugnacious. He would help himself and halfway offer it to me, winking broadly and saying, "Wonderful old cognac!" His conversation was full of animadversions to sexual inadequacy —that was the trouble with Dulles, etc.—which were evidently intended as justifications of his position in Brat's household. (Elena had told me, after her previous visit, of his bullying Brat at Ping-Pong or whatever game it was.) Brat had been, pathetically, advised by his doctor to interest himself in a dog, and had acquired an enormous black schnauzer, whom he liked to have beside him and with which, despite Madeleine's warnings, I managed to make friends. The little Mumm girl tried to maul him, and he made a feint of snapping at her. Madeleine hated the dog. She hated animals in general; reverted to French to say how disgusting he was in the house. (Elena had told me of her brutal and embarrassing punishment, on Elena's earlier visit, of the boy, since dead, for his taking his dog or cat to bed with him, against her severe orders, and concealing him under the covers.) Bazata, taking his cue from her, held forth on how much he hated animals—so long as dogs kept away from him! (attitude of mock horror)—had buried a cat in a hole in a field, with stones on it so it couldn't get out. "Buried it alive?" I asked. Yes; and another cat he hit in the face with a spade, hit it till its eyes hung out. Olili, who was nearer me, explained that he liked to pull people's legs, suggesting that it was all delightful— English visitors who had lately been there had been astonished and puzzled at his boasts of parachuting exploits. In the meantime, Brat's young daughter had come to sit beside Bazata on the couch, and he was fondling her hair. It was a part of his superseding Brat. —It was remarkable the way in which Madeleine had indoctrinated both Bazata and Allegretti. When Madeleine and Allegretti had come to the Carlyle in New York, I had, after listening awhile to Elena's rather unpleasant conversation with Madeleine, gone down in the lobby to find Allegretti, who was patiently waiting there, and had been astonished, on inquiring about Germany, to hear him say, with evident approval, that the Germans were reviving Nazism. Now it appeared that Bazata, no longer in the U.S. army, thought that Hitler would have been "fine" if he had succeeded and had nothing good to say about America's role in Europe. Madeleine and Brat were always complaining about the American occupation, and I would say that I sympathized with them and should be all for withdrawing our troops —which of course they did not want. Later, on further provocation, I reminded them that the Germans had occupied a number of countries themselves. Brat said that, after all, as far as France was concerned, the French had twice occupied Germany—Napoleon and Louis XIV. I did try, however, also, to establish good relations with Brat by giving him my regular line (for Germans) of the better relations of the Americans with the Germans than with the French (my memories of Trier in '18–'19) and the mistake we had probably made in getting involved in the First World War. I said, too, that the rivalry had recently been between Germany and England rather than between Germany and France. He eagerly assented to this. He was sitting beside me, and we were having a conversation detached from the rest of the company. I felt that he was very feminine, had the

instinct to agree of a woman, the habit of falling in with
the dominant personality of any company. —Madeleine
said that the only thing wrong about Hitler was that
he had turned out to be insane. This was their regular
line; that he had suddenly, at a given moment, gone mad.
—In connection with this visit, I was having to struggle
with the feeling that there was something sinister about
even Olili. It was as if she had allowed herself to be
made the accomplice to too many crimes. Nothing could
be more curious, or, in the long run, more disagreeable,
than the disdainful and aristocratic tone adopted by her
and Brat in complicity, yet contrasting, with the trashi-
ness and crookedness of Madeleine and Bazata. —Brat
told with satisfaction of his frustration of possible attempts, when the Americans had arrived, to reduce him
to doing ignoble work: a local sheriff or somebody, who
respected his rank, had saved him. They had been, he
hastened at one point to assure me, at first very pro-
American. It had been an American officer who had
rescued Olili and taken her "under orders" to where she
would have proper care, when she had been so ill in the
hospital (it had been bombed nine times). Some of the
American soldiers had been connoisseurs enough (a certain amount of irony in this) to carry off Olili's choice
phonograph records (though Elena had told me they
had deliberately smashed a good many of them). But
of course—he did not refer to this—he had, after all,
spent some months in an American prison camp. The
whole situation here was one of those wretched ones
such as, reading about the Civil War, I had recently
become aware of in the Reconstruction period in the
South: the occupied people become cynical, the occupying force corrupt; each tries to exploit the other. Madeleine and Brat thought they were exploiting the Americans, undoubtedly loved the idea of converting Bazata

and Allegretti to Hitler, had actually done so with Allegretti, who, after they had gotten rid of him, had come clamoring for his bride. Bazata was at present doing well, having, no doubt, the time of his life (though Thérèse had said to Elena, *"Pauvre lui aussi!"* Madeleine was supposed to rule him with a rod of iron). —In connection with my going to Israel, Brat had told some quietly contemptuous story of a Jew who had come back and wanted a job. *10/29/10*

Elena said something about evidence obtained by wire-tapping. Bazata retorted that wire-tapping was a perfectly legitimate device when it was a question of "getting these rats." I said that it remained to be proved who were and who were not rats, and pointed out that Judge Hand, in New York, had thrown out one of the Communist verdicts on the ground that it was based on evidence obtained through wire-tapping. He said that you couldn't worry about doing things politely—probably used the old cliché about "handling with kid gloves." I said that we had, in the U.S., a quite elaborate system of laws (intended to safeguard citizens' rights). He replied that you couldn't stop to bother about whether the means you were using would be shocking to your old aunt—he had been a detective himself (and knew what he was talking about); he had also been a spy. I said, in a somewhat insulting way, that I hadn't realized that what he had been saying was prompted by a special professional point of view. —At a later point, the dialogue got hotter. Apropos of Dulles—what could be expected when our government sent them (Europe) such dopes with no sex appeal?—and in connection with the Mumms' systematic disparagement of everything emanating from America, he declared that the U.S. sent Europe "clowns." I was incensed to the point of replying, "You're not the person to talk, old top: you're

a clown yourself." This shook him a little, but he rallied:
Was or was not somebody or other a clown? I told him
that if he'd stayed in the States, there would be one
clown less in Europe. I had previously said, in connection with the wire-tapping business, that he belonged
with the Hitler Nazis, not in the U.S., and had asked
him whether he were still in the American army. He had
answered no, thank God! I said he belonged right in
Germany, with the other pro-Hitler forces. He replied
with considerable violence: I wish there were *ten thousand* like me in the States! I reiterated that, if he were
at home, there'd be fewer clowns in Europe, wouldn't
there? I don't think, he replied, you really want an
answer to that question. It was true that things had got
to a point at which the logical next step was a fistfight.
He volubly followed up—he was evidently used to out-
talking people and talking himself out of situations, but
I paid no attention and interrupted by getting up and
saying that we had to go to bed. The local count, Elena
told me she thought, was "rather horrified by the whole
thing." Madeleine, she pointed out to me, had actually
been egging us on, loving it and hoping we should lose
our tempers. When we got to our room, I told Elena
that I would not stay another day, had never insulted a
guest in any decent house I had visited. The whole
Johannisberg episode made upon me an impression more
sinister and queer than anything that had happened to
me—like the beginning of a novel of horror.

[Marginal note: Madeleine said something about the
absurdity of Americans coming to Europe to expound
American culture. —At another point, she fired at me
the question: "Who would you say are the three best
American writers of the present time?" I said I wouldn't
know how to answer this question, that I didn't read
many contemporary books. Asked about Faulkner and

Hemingway, I said that I did know their work, had always read them with great interest, because they belonged to my own generation. This way of dealing with the subject caused Olili to exclaim, in lifeless surprise, I thought he was supposed to be the most eminent critic in America!]

The next morning, we explained to Olili that I ought to get back to see Fischer and, in the event of my not hearing from Max Beerbohm, to arrange for an immediate departure by plane for Israel. She quietly but strongly protested, said there were no trains; but I made her produce the timetable. Elena called up Fischer and found out that Hirsch had not come back, so I said I would stay until afternoon, fixing definitely on a train. Olili then tried to sabotage it by insisting that, on account of the fair, we should not be able to get into a hotel. I countered that, in case of emergency, I could go to the American authorities. We found Olili in her two or three little rooms—very much like housekeeper's quarters—that she had in a corner of the bottom floor. Photographs of the family and bookcases of her French books and art books. I told her, when Elena had left us alone, that I couldn't remain in a house—a rather odd reason, perhaps—where I had to insult the guests. She answered that, after all, Bazata *was* Brat's guest, that they had got to like him very much. He was "a brilliant man," she said—had been a war hero, mentioned in several books, and was one of the American soldiers who had received most decorations. I said that I was sure he was a frightful liar, that I thought him "most obnoxious" and didn't see how they stood for him. (Billy von Rath told Elena later, when she went to see him in the country, that he never visited Johannisberg without wanting to throw Bazata out of the house.) I then got up to look at the books and changed the

subject by talking about Vogüé. Olili had never read his
diary. I told her how appalled he was at the panic and
impotence that followed, in St. Petersburg, the assassina-
tion of Alexander II, the complete inability of the Court
to fill the blank void of terror, to set up new machinery
to carry on; and how he was surprised later, and rather
shocked, on seeing Chekhov's plays, at the way in
which the Russians were able to go to the theater and
enjoy and applaud the exposure of their own incapacity
and weakness. To a Frenchman—especially a Frenchman
of the old noble upright type, devoted to the traditions
of his country—this appeared shameful. Olili replied
that a sense of humor had never been the Vicomte's
strong point. It occurred to me, as I was talking, that I
might, without being aware of it, have intended my
reference to the helplessness of the Russians to have
some application to her and Brat, as she had evidently
been getting at the present situation in what she had
said about Giraudoux's play. At some point, old Thérèse
came in, and she, Olili, said, "What's the matter, *ma
belle?*" in a way that, though perfectly calm, implied
a shade of impatience. She is far less close to Thérèse
than Elena is. Olili did not know that her great-aunt
Nelidova had the great liberal salon of Vogüé's period,
nor had she, as I remember, ever read *Le Roman russe*.

In spite of supposed difficulties and actual delays
about driving us to the station, we got off in the afternoon, Brat taking us. Helen did not want to go, since she
was having fun with Alena. Elena thought that Brat was
secretly pleased at my having attacked Bazata. But I
felt uncomfortable about it, since I had him at a disadvantage—he couldn't very well have suggested that
we settle it outside, where he would have had the advantage of me. He had not appeared at lunch, which was
meager as usual—Madeleine was late.

That night, in the hotel, before we went to sleep, Elena told me again how wonderful her mother had been, how attentive, in spite of her snobbery and waspish malicious wit, to the people on the place. She had already told me how she had learned from her *"jamais faire fi de personne."* Elena had enjoyed—"up to a point," as she says—going back and being affectionately greeted by Thérèse and the *Intendant* and his family, on whom we called in their little house. He had been an enthusiastic Nazi. She was pleased when he told her that, when Henry[5] had walked up, he had recognized him as a true Mumm. (On the last of her visits before the war, when she had left Henry for a few days at Johannisberg, Olili had told her, on her coming back, how fine Henry had looked heiling Hitler. It was after this visit that Elena became an American citizen.) She lives so much in people's admiration and affection—it is a necessity for her. She fails to realize that, as I told her, the attitude of Olili and Brat is inevitably somewhat sour—when she returns a U.S. citizen, with an American husband and an American son in the army of occupation in Germany. Olili—and not simply, I think, out of nervousness, as Elena said—would keep alleging reasons why she could not come to see us, do things with us, why she had to go away or could not get a car to drive us. That morning we had taken a walk to the Metternichs' schloss, and— "to my horror," as Elena said afterwards—Olili had called Elena "Madeleine." But she seemed to be genu- inely distressed as I obdurately took them (Elena and Helen) away. At the moment we were leaving, she said, "But you haven't had Brat's wine—we were going to have it tonight!" I did not see her again.

Frankfurt: Elena took us in a taxi to the old Mumm house on the outskirts of Frankfurt, now some sort of municipal offices: it was bigger than I expected, as big, I think, as the biggest houses of American millionaires. The grandfather had left it to Walther, who had eventually sold it, but in the meantime the Mumms and the Radowitzes had lived in it, but on a special floor.

I went alone to Strauss's *Salomé* at the Opera, had never seen it before and did not like it. The night I was taking the train we all went to the Bartók *Mandarin* ballet, preceded by a *Hamlet* and followed by the *Nutcracker* ballet. The Bartók quite effective, with its macabre characters and its "constructivist" and "expressionist" setting. They alternate in their entertainments between the gloomy and morbid and the light Viennese kind of thing—as Richard Strauss does in his own work. —Elena was reluctant to have me go, and I was touched to feel that I meant that much to her—especially after failing to help make things easy at Johannisberg, and, on the contrary, as she kept saying, having "made everything more complicated." She said, "You'll come back, won't you?" The last night she let me know that she wanted me to make love to her, though I found she was almost dry. I wanted her, and making love to her, though rather queer, with cold cream, under these conditions, was nevertheless delightful, slowed up and deliberate—each stroke was a separate pleasure. Yet afterwards it was one of the things—as well as the Johannisberg situation, to which she was the next day returning—that made me sad at leaving her and made me think, on my journey, about making it up to her later when we should be together again. She wondered about the bad shape I was in, but my ailments soon cleared up. I had all the best of it in getting away from Germany, with its problems, and finding good weather and a warm climate in Italy and Israel. Elena and Helen spent three days at Johannisberg, then went for a rest and a holiday to Sankt Anton in Austria, then to Bohlingen to be near Henry, where Elena found the American camp more cheerful than the town, then to Frankfurt again and Johannisberg—at some point they visited the Radowitzes. Helen had another cold in Frankfurt, which prevented their getting to Paris before I arrived. On her second visit to Johannisberg, Elena felt that she had established somewhat better relations between herself and Brat and even Madeleine—was able, as she said, for the first time to see Madeleine as a miserable hysterical woman—in the light in which I had described her. Madeleine had talked to her about the boy who had died, and this had partly melted Elena's heart, though no doubt it was a calculated gesture.

—Frankfurt–Milano; Milano–Genoa (that dreary oppressive city reminded me of a night spent there in the summer of 1921, the only unattractive town, all commerce and big buildings).

NOTES

1. See *A Prelude*, pp. 23–25

2. Joe Bazata, a guest of Brat's who had fought with the American army.

3. Ted Paramore was EW's old disorderly, fun-loving friend. See previous volumes in this series, *passim*.

4. Benjamin Thompson, Count Rumford (1753–1814), American-born physicist and philanthropist. He met the Elector of Bavaria during his travels on the Continent and was made a count of the Holy Roman Empire.

5. Henry Thornton was stationed in Germany at the time.

RAPALLO AND MAX BEERBOHM

Visits to Max Beerbohm, March 15 and 16, 1954.[1]
He was just getting over an attack of the flu and received
us sitting in a chair before the little fire. —Coming in,
we had seen in another room little portraits of his grandfather and grandmother, both of whom resembled him,
both had a smiling look, the grandmother *l'oeil espiègle*,
only thing suggesting Jewish stock the somewhat flat
nose of the grandfather; between them was a miniature
of the father, who, Sam Behrman[2] said, had been called
Superbo; the grandparents were like idealized characters
in 18th-century operas—I almost suspected Max, with
his love of hoaxes, of having invented them himself;
but when I met him the moment afterwards, I felt that
he must have had a family background of elegance and
fine wit. (There was also in this great room a brightly
painted Italian inn sign, with a harlequin who somewhat
resembled Max, standing beside a mask that lay on, I
think, a tambourine, and that so much resembled a
bearded face that one took it at first for a decapitated
head, like that of John the Baptist in *Salomé*—this
picture is described in *Yet Again* [1909]. I was shown

later, in a room across the hall, a harlequinesque dressing
gown made, like a patchwork quilt, from bits of material of different colors.) —I was principally struck, on
this first visit, by his distinguished appearance and manner. His head seemed bigger and stronger than I had
expected it to be: something rather Germanic about his
nose and jaw and blond mustache. He later showed us
a caricature he had made where somebody had told him
he looked like Bismarck: with a weak chin and mild
dreamy gaze, he was wearing an Iron Cross; but I felt
that in the modest and wispy figure he always presents
in his caricatures he had considerably played himself
down. He is very Edwardian still, and his way of saying
"Don't you know" would seem dated to Angus Wilson,
though to me it seems perfectly natural—we used to
say "Don't you know" in my youth. But in general I
felt about his personality that it was continental rather
than English. His round blue eyes had big red circles
around them—Sam Behrman had warned me about this,
and said that Max was very conscious of them, but I
didn't see any evidence of this. His hands were quite
astonishing—unlike any I had ever seen: instead of
being slender and tapering as one might have expected
them to be, the fingers were long and of uniform thick-
ness, almost like the legs of a spider crab, and sharpened
at the end as if they were pencils—it was as if they
were very large engraver's tools, unexpectedly formidable
—one ring with a small green (jade) stone. I talked to
him about the recent book on him, written in English
by a Dutchman:[3] he was polite about it but obviously
not much thrilled by it. He had not read "the parts [of
his past] he remembered," but there were many things
he had forgotten. I then began to question him about
points in his work that I had never understood. His
memory about all this was perfect and his responses

immediate—showed how carefully he had planned every detail: I asked him about the procession of unidentified camel-like monsters that has simply the caption: Are we as welcome as ever? Those, he said, were "the friends of Edward VII"—then he went on rather slyly to explain the situation: the occasion for the caricature was the accession of George V; the friends were a couple of Rothschilds, a Sassoon, and a, I think, Lord Lawson[4]—after just a second's pause, he added about the new king, "Didn't need to borrow money so often, don't you know." He said nothing about these friends being Jewish, and since he rarely caricatured Jews, I imagine that this was the reason for his not having made the picture more explicit. He told us something about having started it and then finding that his hand went on drawing without his thinking about it—as if he were apologizing for it, wanting to make it out that the drawing had been done involuntarily. He confessed that the question posed by the young [Joseph] Conrad in "The Old and the Young Self"[5] was in a Polish he himself invented, but he remembered it verbatim. Why weren't his drawings collected? Oh, it would be impossible to dig them all up. He had had periodical exhibitions, and they had been bought by Tom, Dick, and Harry—I was very glad to sell them!—Tom had given his away, Dick had left his somewhere, and Harry doesn't know what became of his. —I asked about Walter Sickert[6]—the only one of Max's subjects who looks different in every picture— "He was protean," Frau Jungmann[7] put in—and Max gave me a little account of him: At first he had been completely Whistlerian, his painting had been all black and blue; but he was always having new ideas and deliberately changing his manner and he theorized too much, would perhaps have made a good critic. The painter should be "an impassioned eye" that sets down what he sees, or thinks he sees—but he later went on to complain about painters who set down things as nobody would see them. —The idea that he was the best English painter of his time Max thought was perfectly ridiculous. A question from Sam Behrman brought out that he preferred Wilson Steer.[8] —I reminded him of drawings and jokes, telling Sam about them, and he would chuckle, without any self-deprecation, as if they were by somebody else: "Oh, did I say that?" "Oh, is that in America?" [Marginal note: He indicated—he never stated things emphatically, strove to make points, as I do—that something similar had happened in the case of Pellegrini "Ape."[9] After a certain age, he had begun making excellent likenesses, which were no longer caricatures. "One fine morning, or, How they might undo me."] I asked him what the last caricatures were he had done—the album of *Bitter Sweet*?[10] These and a short series he had undertaken for the *Spectator*. He had found that he was simply doing very careful likenesses that expressed pity of the subjects—and then he had decided to stop: pathos (pronounced with a short *a*) was no quality for a caricaturist. I saw that this was true: the drawing of Noël Coward was an excellent likeness, which gently brought out his weakness but made him rather appealing. —So many of the drawings nowadays were ugly, he said (he had already, as I knew, in his foreword to a book of Ronald Searle's[11] made clear that he thought Searle was a distinguished exception to this) —now, his own things—"tho' I am perhaps not the one to say it—and I had nearly left it unsaid"—were very pretty drawings. "I venture to say that even the Milner" (which I told him of having seen in the common room of one of the Oxford colleges) "is not disagreeable to have around." —Another point I had asked him about was the additional passage to "The Mote in the Middle

Distance" that Gosse wrote him of having pasted in his copy [of *A Christmas Garland*].[12] That, he said, was a new and better ending that he had thought of afterwards—a more emotional ending, like those of *The Golden Bowl* and *The Wings of the Dove*. He recited a part of the conversation between Kate Croy and Merton Densher at the end of *The Wings of the Dove*—"Well she stretched out her wings, and it was to *that* they reached. They cover us . . . But she turned to the door, and her headshake was now the end. 'We shall never be again as we were' "—and one saw how much he admired it, that he really thought it beautiful (though it has always made me impatient). He said something pleasant that puzzled me at first about my dealing with *The Wings of the Dove* in *The Shores of Light*; and I asked him what he thought of the theory that the governess in "The Turn of the Screw" was intended to be a neurotic case. This aroused him: "Some morbid pedant, prig and fool." I pointed at myself and said, "I am the morbid pedant, prig and fool." I pointed out its analogy to other stories in which the narrator is deceiving himself but is not supposed to deceive the reader, invoked Leon Edel's opinion; but he asserted that it was simply a ghost story like several that James had written, talked about "Sir Edmund Orme." I gave the conversation a different turn by praising "The Jolly Corner," of which he said he had done a caricature,[13] with the businessman ghost of Henry James shaking his fist, from the foot of the stairs, at the real expatriate. He said that somebody had pointed out to him that a sentence must have been dropped out: the man in the "Jolly Corner" never gets to the foot of the stairs. —Another disagreement we ran into was about Bernard Shaw's phonetic alphabet, which he thought was an absurd and outrageous idea. The idea of thinking, etc.! Sam seemed to support him here. I pointed out that the liquidation of five letters of the old Russian alphabet in certain spelling reforms had encountered the same opposition. When England and America were communized, he said, they would doubtless have a phonetic alphabet. He was under the impression that Shaw had invented an alphabet himself and that he wanted it imposed by law. I tried to correct this, saying that he had never invented such an alphabet and that his money had been left for the use of any serious organization that had a project of this kind; but he denied this and reiterated his original statement. He said that Shaw had queered his chances of being buried in Westminster Abbey by making some démarche about it—he had insisted on getting the Webbs buried there, as they were, which had been entirely "inappropriate." Then in his will he had left instructions that his ashes should be sprinkled in the garden—a dreadful idea, you know, with dogs and cats about! I said that I did think it was rather absurd for Shaw to have left as a national shrine his apparently rather commonplace house—but that egoism like Shaw's was a disability like any other that you had to carry with you all your life like a physical disability. It had been all right when he was young, but in later years it became disagreeable, and one saw that it was compulsive and incurable. He described in great detail how Shaw had looked when he had first known him in London: he had had smallpox, which had left his complexion absolutely white, and he had straggling whiskers, which, as someone had said, was like seaweed on a rock; his eyes were very pale, too pale—later his eyebrows grew shaggy and shaded them, which somewhat improved the impression. Shaw perhaps hadn't liked Max's caricatures, but for him any kind of attention paid him was better than none at all. I said that Max had brought out the fact that Shaw's hands were well shaped. Yes: he had beautiful hands, the hands of a woman rather than a man. I said that Shaw had an erect carriage. Yes, and he moved well. He made a good impression in this way—unless one saw him from the back—the back of his head came straight down and made a line with his neck. At first nights, in his early days, he had been true to his principles—he had not worn evening clothes at the theater, but an old suit so shiny that, if you were behind him, you could see your face in it like a mirror. Later he became quite well dressed—I was rather sorry—I think people ought to dress according to their (personalities or inclinations understood). He had heard Shaw speak once at a meeting, at which, after his speech, he had answered questions and hecklers, with perfect readiness, without notes. "In a way it was better than what he wrote, you know. He was a wonderful debater—as (slyly) you see in his plays." —I felt a definite animus against Shaw—especially in the extra-illustrated copy of Archibald Henderson's life[14] that was shown me. He had sent this to William Archer,[15] and, after Archer's death, it had come back to him. One felt that it was not merely a question of kidding [the book]—Henderson's pompous and awestricken adulation—Max hadn't been able to stand it that Shaw should be attaining such fame. It had brought out in him everything that was most waspish and something that was a little ugly: by a most cunning use of ink, he had turned the photographs of such people as William Morris and Granville-Barker into horrible prognathous gorillas (there are a few examples of this type in his albums—notably in the drawings of imaginary celebrities of the '70s)—one felt that he wanted to degrade them. What bitterness did this arise from? (It may be that I always look for something harsh.) He had perhaps never been able to shake off a feeling of being always on the margin of things; and had sometimes been

unable to restrain himself from behaving like a bad little
boy who wants to spit at people. This is discordant with
his much-praised urbanity, and he has largely kept it
out of his published work; but I felt it again, when we
were taken to his study, to give him a brief rest, and
shown his library of tampered-with title pages. Belloc's
Cruise of the Nona[16]—which he told me later was a
lovely book—had pasted in on the title page a very
Victorian picture of a lady and a gentleman who seemed
to be seasick; Housman's *Last Poems* had a drawing of
a Wagner opera; a volume of Chesterton's essays was
covered by an expanding caricature by Max, in which
Chesterton covered the page and displayed in his open
mouth the printed words "thirteenth edition." I actually
found these rather shocking—when I came downstairs, I
told Max that my nerves had been shaken by them—
and I felt that there was something of envy in the
systematic way—for he had operated on quite an extensive scale—in which he had set about to depreciate his
friends' books by administering a kind of preliminary
kick, before one had got to the contents, to everything
they ever stood for. He seemed to treat Henry James with
more respect than anyone else—his admiration for him
was evidently immense—on the title page of one of his
books he had done a little drawing of him, getting
"wound up," as Sam said, to talk, leaning forward, with
his hands held up. —I was surprised to discover that
Max did not care for Virginia Woolf—her criticism was
the only thing that he had a (not enthusiastic) good
word for (after all, she had written admiringly of him).
He had just read her diary, which showed, he said, low
vitality and was "pettifogging" and overanxious about
things that concerned herself and not considerate about
anyone else. Leonard Woolf must have taken very good
care of her, and must have had a hard time taking her

over her reviews. "Poor soul!" he added. I said that I got the impression that she was some very peculiar kind of snob—without a social group to be snobbish with—she had been so extraordinary about Thomas Hardy, had apparently expected him to be like one of the old gaffers in his novels and had expressed surprise at his savoir-faire in offering Woolf a whisky and soda. Max did not like her novels, and expressed himself contemptuously and pettishly about the stream of consciousness: everybody has thoughts that go through their head, but it's absurd to try to make a novel of them. He liked to read a story, to have characters and see what they did. I stood up for *Between the Acts*, which he hadn't read, but didn't attempt to argue with him about the stream of consciousness. I felt it was a little frightening that age should make it impossible to react anymore to excellence in the art to which one was dedicated. I should have thought that for Max Beerbohm, with his exquisiteness of style, Virginia Woolf would have been the writer of her Bloomsbury generation in whom he would have been most interested. But he seemed never to have got beyond Lytton Strachey. He felt that the world he had loved had quite gone. The cities were not pleasant as they once had been. People in London, he said, are always in a crisis about something—about going somewhere or catching a bus. The old leisurely days were gone. It is certainly different, as I know myself, but is it really so different as he thinks? He must have come to Rapallo to live in 1910.

—At dinner, with Sam Behrman, I developed my idea that Max's work was a comic Divine Comedy,[17] in which the characters appeared and reappeared and played their appointed roles and were assigned certain moral as well as aesthetic values—this had been particularly inspired by seeing the little murals which he had done over the front doorway and facing it, as if he had taken his creations, his vision of the London world, with him into his long retirement of exile and continued to live with them there; Chamberlain and Asquith and Balfour; Chesterton and Kipling and Shaw; old favorites and friends of his, now relatively obscure: John Davidson and Conder and Cunninghame Graham.[18] That it was this part of his work, the caricature, that was instinctive and most imaginative was shown by what he had told Virginia Woolf, reported in her diary:

"About his own writing dear Lytton Strachey said to me: first I write one sentence: then I write another. That's how I write. And so I go on. But I have a feeling writing ought to be like running through a field. That's your way. Now how do you go down to your room, after breakfast—what do you feel? I used to look at the clock and say oh dear me, it's time I began my article . . . No, I'll read the paper first. I never wanted to write. But I used to come home from a dinner party and take my brush and draw caricature after caricature. They seemed to bubble up from here . . . he pressed his stomach. That was a kind of inspiration, I suppose."

So he said to me, when he was talking of having lost the impulse to caricature, that before, he would "dream" something in connection with people he had seen, and the result would be "good caricatures." I don't believe there has ever been anything else in art comparable to this world he has created.

I also told Sam that I felt in Max the pure dedication to art that was characteristic of artists of Max's period: whether James or Bernard Shaw, Whistler or Charles Conder. Sam had been telling me how poor Max had been and how hard it was to do anything for him: he had been offered a considerable fee for one television appearance—all you would have to do, Sam had explained, would be to appear and say something like "I am glad to be here tonight." "Would you have me begin with a lie?" said Max. It must have been hard for Sam, with his expensive tastes—always staying at the best hotels and having private cars at his beck and call—to understand that Max might take satisfaction in his simple enough little house—Sam had said to me: You'll see how he lives—how cold it is!—not making any bid for attention, scorning so much of contemporary life and gratified by the knowledge that he had done his best. —It was quite easy to see why he admired more, identified himself more with Henry James than Bernard Shaw—James had lived retired, never making any bid for publicity, never compromising his own standards.

His way of talking—quiet and unemphatic—words well and easily chosen—always trying to express what he thought, never trying to talk for effect. *10/31/10*

Second visit: We came at 4:30 instead of 3:30, and did not stay so long. Today he sat up at the table and presided at the tea. I saw now that his head was sunken between his shoulders and that his hair at the back of his bald domed head was uncut and hung over his collar. His looking up at you when he chuckled now seemed shy and a little deprecatory—reminded me of my poor cousin Sandy, as his drawing of himself with the flashlight on the cover of *The Poet's Corner*[19] had reminded me in my childhood of him.

He said that he had never been able to caricature Somerset Maugham, had tried to several times, then given it up; but that Sutherland,[20] in his recent portrait, had, he implied, made up for Max's failure, had "carried caricature as far as it could go." After painting this portrait, Sutherland had written Max, asking him to sit, and Max had replied that, though he had "made monsters of people himself," "the bully was always a coward," and that, having seen the Maugham portrait, he had decided to decline this offer. "Now that I'm old and afflicted-looking, I shouldn't want to be painted anyway, but even in my prime I don't think I should have wanted to be painted by Sutherland."

I asked him about Sem,[21] and he said that Sem had been able to do things that he couldn't do. He made sketches on the spot—which Max never did—sometimes an ear and an arm, etc., then would put them together, and there would be a perfect likeness. He was good at doing the types at the races and Monte Carlo: *"Tout Paris."* He came to England and drew people at the races and would then ask who they were. Max himself could not caricature people unless he had seen quite a lot of them—had heard their voices—and then the tone of their mind. His is certainly a highly reflective art: with spontaneity of physical imagination, he manages to combine thought. I spoke of Sem's Charlestoning album—so wonderful in its conception of how different kinds of people would move—and said that Sem's characters were always in movement, and he agreed that this was so. Frau Jungmann at once wanted to show me Max's caricature of Robert Trevelyan[22] walking, but I said that I had seen it. Max had lunched once with Sem at Dieppe, and people had thought: Two caricaturists lunching together; they must be preparing something. Sem had been good at mimicking people and had imitated Coquelin,[23] who was also there: *"Moi, je ne parle jamais de moi. [Pourquoi?] Parce que . . ."* and then there would follow an elaborate explanation [*Around Theatres* (1930), "Coquelin's Death"]. They had decided to send Coquelin a note saying that they had arranged for a window from which to see the fireworks that night and inviting him to share it with them. He hadn't answered. —"I think he must have been insulted," Max added with a certain complacency. Sem could caricature women, which Max had never been able to do. I said that he had done well with *Zuleika Dobson* in the new edition of the novel, and he replied that that was just "a caricature of a pretty girl." I think that the point is—since he has sometimes done imaginary women—that he is too much an old-fashioned gentleman to be willing to make real ones ridiculous.

I tried to draw him out about Hubert Crackanthorpe and St. John Hankin.[24] Of Crackanthorpe, he said that he had known him a little. His father had been a successful barrister, and he had sometimes gone to the parents' house. Hubert had thrown himself into the Seine and couldn't swim—some sudden fit of insanity, he supposed. His work had shown talent, but *le mot juste* had a way of coming between the lady and the gentleman that the story was about. Hankin he had known quite well. He had not been surprised when *he* committed suicide—he was rather a sad man. He was supposed to have been rather unhappily married. But Max did not throw any real light on these suicides of the end of the century, which seem to me a little mysterious. In what way, precisely, were they desperate? In what terms did they look at their situations? —This led him on, however, to John Davidson, who also had "thrown himself into the water and couldn't swim." I said something favorable about his verse, and Max at once asserted with warm conviction that he was the best English poet of that age. He had been a dominie, a schoolmaster, in Scotland, and had thrown it up and come to London. Once, in the Café Royal, he had set out to sing to Max a translation of the Psalms into Scotch, and had been requested by the headwaiter to stop, because he was annoying the other patrons. I tried to probe further by asking whether Davidson had been "poor and desperate." Yes, Max replied rather vaguely, but he had enough for himself and his family to live on.

—When we were going, I told him that I wanted to send two books: Angus Wilson's *Cloche,* which I said was the best thing of its kind since Harold Nicolson's *Some People*—though I wasn't sure that Wilson hadn't invented a genre of his own; and my essay on "The Turn of the Screw," of which I was just getting out a special phonetic edition, with which, however, a key was provided.

—Sam Behrman had told me about Frau Jungmann, who had for years been Hauptmann's housekeeper. She was intelligent and highly educated, spoke English perfectly. Max had said to her, When Florence dies, I don't know what will become of me. She had told him, I'll come to you, wherever you are. You can always reach me through this address. He had put it in a book and forgotten about it, hadn't been able to find it after his wife's death. But Elizabeth Jungmann had heard about this and came to him. Now she took care of him with just one maid where his wife had had three servants.

—While we had tea and sherry and something like Dubonnet, with cakes and hors d'oeuvres, he drank a single glass of something from a labelless bottle. While Frau Jungmann was out of the room, he sneaked an extra cigarette, and when she came back and saw him, she said, "Where the devil . . . !"

Apropos of somebody's conversation (first visit), I told about my conversation with Santayana in Rome,[25] in the course of which he had given me the remarkable disquisition about "Apollo with his golden arrows" and so on. I wrote it down after I left, and when I saw Irwin

Edman[26] in New York, who had read my *New Yorker* article, he asked me, Did he really talk like that? In complete rounded sentences? Since Edman had known Santayana well, I was rather surprised at his asking; but I realized later that this could not, indeed, have represented his regular habit when I found the whole thing was a passage in his then unpublished third volume of memoirs, which was not to come out till after his death.

—*First visit:* He showed us a little pink-and-blue watercolor drawing of Edward VII, and said something like: Now, that's a pretty little drawing.

—George Moore was very vulgar—which is so rare with the Irish. He was the vulgarest Irishman I ever knew. He sometimes talked well about landscapes.

—W. Sickert's transformations: had his hair cropped short at one point; at another, had himself made an enormous top hat, he must have found an ancient block —and wore trousers striped black and white in some very curious way. A great linguist; his French was wonderful, and he picked up the patois of Venice in only a few weeks. It was only after the first war had begun that his father became Danish, not German.

—*Second visit:* Bismarck had an astonishing high voice, like a woman's. Belloc, with his thickset figure, his square jaw, and his head set down between his shoulders, also surprised me by his voice. He used to sing French hunting songs in a sweet and exquisite way—it was a little like an enormous nightingale.

—Isaiah Berlin's story about meeting Max Beerbohm only once and having heard him make only one amusing remark. —I saw Lady Cunard the other day. —How was she? —Oh, just the same as ever. —(drily and quietly) I'm very sorry to hear it. —I repeated this for Sam's benefit, and Max chuckled. Oh, did I say that? —Sam then told a story about a Frenchman who had said of her, Well, one can see that she must have been ugly in her youth. —Max gave us a description of her: loud voice—came from Chicago—had married a conventional Englishman, who loathed her—it was always apparent that he loathed her, which made their parties particularly uncomfortable—much worse, he seemed to imply, than if it had been the hostess who loathed the host.

—*Second visit:* Max said that he never could read more than fifty pages of a book by P. G. Wodehouse—at first he would be entertained by the handling of language— almost like Cinquevalli[27] (this antiquated allusion is characteristic), but after fifty pages he lost interest.

He had found that in general it was now difficult for him to read novels: he couldn't believe in the reality of the things that were supposed to happen. Sam and I agreed about this.

—He said that Johnson, in Boswell, had said that there were two kinds of talkers: those who talked from a stream, of which Burke was the example, and those who talked from a tank. I think this was apropos of George Moore, who had talked from a stream, like so many Irishmen. —Later, when I asked him about Compton Mackenzie, he said that there was a man who wrote from a stream.

—*First visit:* Another of the books he had doctored, which he showed us, was Queen Victoria's *Leaves from the Highlands.* He had inscribed it, in an imitation of her handwriting, to the "much-to-be-studied Mr. Max Beerbohm" (I think) and written notes in her hand under each of the pictures. There were some such phrases as "very distressing and annoying," which he said was "very Victorian." He said that there had been something rather "bourgeois" about her. He has certainly always been fascinated by royalty. His poem on the Prince of Wales's visit to Thomas Hardy, of which David Cecil in Oxford had given me a copy. Frau Jungmann thought it was "bold" of him to have written this—everybody nowadays was so servile about the royal family.

—I said that my favorite poem of Max's was the sonnet about Henry James of which he and Edmund Gosse had composed alternate lines, mailing it back and forth. I recited the first line of the sestet, and he went on with it, reciting the rest, with much feeling for poetry, as he had done with the prose of *The Wings of the Dove*. Deep feeling for literature: excellence of some pages of *Zuleika Dobson*.

—Nuffield had kept a bicycle shop when Max was at Oxford. Almost nobody rode a bicycle then, he said: it was "the earmark of vulgarity."

—He thought that Belloc's poetry was sure to last—*The Cruise of the Nona* was a charming book.

Sonnet "To Henry James"[28]

[M.B.] Say, indefatigable alchemist,
[E.G.]   Melts not the very moral of your scene,
             Curbs it not off in vapour from between
          Those lips that labour with conspicuous twist?
          Your fine eyes, blurred like arc-lamps in a mist,
             Immensely glare, yet glimmerings intervene,
               So that your May-Be and your Might-Have-Been
          Leave us still plunging for your genuine gist.
          How different from Sir Arthur Conan Doyle,
          As clear as water and as smooth as oil,
             And no jot knowing of what Maisie knew!
          Flushed with the sunset air of roseate Rye
             You stand, marmoreal darling of the Few,
          Lord of the troubled Speech and single Eye.

NOTES

1. See *BBT*, pp. 41–63, which is largely taken from these pages.

2. S. N. Behrman was working on a book on Beerbohm (*Portrait of Max*, 1960). See note 17 below.

3. J. G. Riewald's *Sir Max Beerbohm* (1953).

4. In *BBT*, these friends are identified as "Sir Ernest Cassel, two Rothschilds, Lord Burnham and Baron de Hirsch" (p. 43).

5. "The Old and the Young Self," eighteen drawings in Beerbohm's *Observations* (1925).

6. Walter Richard Sickert (1860–1942), English Impressionist, most influenced by Degas.

7. Elizabeth Jungmann, Beerbohm's housekeeper and secretary. She had been Gerhart Hauptmann's secretary and Beerbohm met her when Hauptmann was in Rapallo.

8. Philip Wilson Steer (1860–1942), English painter much influenced by Turner and the Impressionists.

9. Carlo ("Ape") Pellegrini (1838–89), caricaturist for *Vanity Fair*.

10. Noël Coward's 1929 musical. Beerbohm's *Heroes and Heroines of Bitter Sweet* appeared in 1931.

11. Artist, illustrator, and author. Beerbohm wrote a prefatory letter to Searle's *The Female Approach, with Masculine Sidelights* (1949).

12. "The Mote in the Middle Distance," a parody of Henry James in Beerbohm's *A Christmas Garland* (1912). Edmund Gosse (1849–1928), biographer and poet, an influential figure on the English literary scene.

13. "The Jolly Corner" caricature is published in Sir Rupert Hart-Davis's *A Catalogue of the Caricatures of Max Beerbohm* (1972), p. 205.

14. Archibald Henderson (1877–1963), author of four books on Shaw, among them *George Bernard Shaw: His Life and Work* (1918).

15. (1856–1924), influential drama critic of the late Victorian years, author of the great success *The Green Goddess*, written to prove a critic could write a play.

16. Joseph Hilaire Pierre Belloc (1870–1953), prolific writer of novels, verse, biography, travels, and criticism; *The Cruise of the Nona* (1925).

17. See Behrman, p. 262, and *Letters on Literature and Politics*, pp. 707–8.

18. John Davidson (1857–1909), playwright and poet whose Fleet Street idiom influenced T. S. Eliot; Charles Conder (1868–1909), art nouveau artist and illustrator; Robert Bontine Cunninghame Graham (1852–1936), horseman, social reformer, and flamboyant author of exotic travel narratives.

19. A collection of cartoons the cover of which EW describes. Reissued by Penguin, 1943.

20. Graham Sutherland painted a famous portrait of Somerset Maugham in 1949.

21. George Coursat (1863–1934), French caricaturist. His "Charlestoning album" showed "*Tout Paris* doing the Charleston and the Black Bottom" (*BBT*, p. 53).

22. Beerbohm's portrait of R. C. Trevelyan had appeared as the frontispiece for Trevelyan's *Selected Poems*.

23. Benoît Constant Coquelin (1841–1909), the original Cyrano de Bergerac in Rostand's play.

24. The young writer Hubert Crackanthorpe (1870–96); St. John Hankin (1869–1909), author of four plays from 1903 to 1908.

25. See *The Forties*, pp. 56–67.

26. Irwin Edman (1896–1954), professor of philosophy at Columbia University. See *The Forties*, p. 58. EW's "Santayana at the Convent of the Blue Nuns" (*The New Yorker*, April 6, 1946).

27. "The great juggler of the last century, about whom Max had once written" (*BBT*, p. 54).

28. See Evan Charteris, *The Life and Letters of Edmund Gosse* (1931), in which the holograph sonnet is reproduced. EW copied the text into his journal.

11/2/10

ISRAEL AND THE DEAD SEA SCROLLS

[In pursuing his studies of Hebrew during 1952–53 at Princeton (see p. xxvii), EW became extremely curious about scrolls of the Essene sect recently found by Bedouins in caves near the Dead Sea. While certain scholarly papers had been written, EW was unable to obtain a coherent and sequential account of the discoveries. Sensing their importance, he induced the editor of *The New Yorker* to send him to Israel. The notes which follow, scribbled in various parts of the Holy Land, record first impressions and were amplified by him in his *New Yorker* series, which appeared in 1955, as well as later articles in the sixties. EW's book *The Scrolls from the Dead Sea*, a collection of these articles further revised, was published in 1955 by Oxford University Press. His essay "Israel," also derived in places from the entries which follow, was published in *Red, Black, Blond and Olive* (Oxford University Press, 1956). There was to be a second trip to Israel during the 1960s, but this occurred on the eve of the Israeli-Egyptian conflict, and EW had to beat a retreat. His writings from this 1967 visit were gathered as "On the Eve" (see also EW's

Israel letters to Elena in *Letters on Literature and Politics*,
pp. 671–76). All these writings were ultimately gathered
together as *Israel and the Dead Sea Scrolls* (1978), with
a foreword by Leon Edel.]

Athens, March 21. Grande-Bretagne Hotel: big square
tasteless rooms. —Strange feeling of nostalgia, though it
was only nine years ago, for days when I had waited for
Eva Siphraios in the dismal lounge. Greek columns with
yellow imitation-marble walls and that hideous hardly-
even-Victorian skylight of blue curlicues in brown in a
not-Greek key, with all the rest (?) brown or a dismal
gray-green—the war, the unexpected people there, meeting and talking to one another. It must have carried her
along in its excitement. —But strange that, at my age
now of fifty-nine, this should already all seem now like
a romantic youthful escapade—I was then fifty. —Bleak
and bad taste of this place—it has all been reorganized
since I was here—the big room in which, at breakfast,
I first read in the *Stars and Stripes* about the atomic
bomb is now empty, evidently now a ballroom. —Eva's
face has lost its Nausicaan look—her eyes are still cunning and have (?), but the lower part of her face has
hardened, though not necessarily in a bad way—I had
said to someone, when I was here before, that the Greek
women had soft recessive chins, and he or she had replied
that they were not at all weak, knew what they were
doing, got their own way. Certainly borne out by Eva:
I'm very motherly now, she said—had had a baby two
years ago—was now an official person; went to official
dinners, made official tours to Yugoslavia; but of course,
as she said, no one could tell much from what one saw
on an official tour. —That look of a sea nymph, she was
no longer that—met me in dark spectacles, in which at
first I had not recognized her. She is well-bred, though

in some relatively primitive semi-Levantine, non-French
and non-Western European way, combination of this
natural Greek-island old primitive good breeding with
the conventional respectability of the Frenchified bourgeoisie; her husband and mother-in-law. I suppose it was
and still is a good marriage. —Awful tasteless food of
the G.-B. Hotel: hors d'oeuvre—these (at least, some of
them) novel; sole meunière; compôte. Strange bleakness,
from our point of view, of Greece, which makes it impossible for them to go in for color—only form and
dimensions, which I suppose this dining room and its
doorways have in their uninteresting way. —Coming
into the Piraeus today, just before we passed Salamis:
the violet-blue sea, the silhouetted shadows of the mountains (Edward Lear,[1] in his sketches, has caught something about that part of the world)—the landscape in
March mist had something in common with the landscape
of summer, when I was here last.

—I walked with her to her door, made an effort to
find the American Classical School in order to locate
my archaeologist friend of 1945, Gladys Weinburg (?),
gave it up and bought a bottle of ouzo and, seeing it in
the store, a large cake of scented soap (thinking I might
need it in Israel), and took a taxi back to the boat. I
never even had a glimpse of the Acropolis—it was dark
when we got out of the restaurant. They were playing
Hecuba, she told me, and some other play of Euripides—
to which I could have gone. Electric signs in Athens, new
since '45: I made out a big one, with Eva's aid: Αστυρ—
which turned out to tell the passerby to lose no time in
getting his life insurance.

—Lados,[2] the Greek who had had the pet seal, whom
I met at the Gilroys' in Jerusalem, knew Siphraios (but
not Eva) and said that, though he looked like "an overgrown embryo," he was really a clever man—that the

royalists, piquantly enough, were now opposed to the King and Queen, because Papagos[3] was opposed to them; the Queen's attempts to govern had not been popular, and now she had evidently dropped them. Eva had told me, with a noticeable lack of warmth, that she "thought" the King was *"bon enfant,"* and that she "thought" that the Queen was clever. She had told me, when I said I was going to Cyprus, that I ought to go right to the headquarters of the Union with Greece movement. I should find myself at home there (referring to my supposed anti-British attitude). —Lados asked me if I knew his aunt, who was married to Sedgwick. I said that I had met them one evening and had with them a violent argument—he replied that he couldn't imagine seeing them without having a violent argument.

March 23. Israel: People on the dock at Haifa cheering the arrival of immigrants. Ride to Jerusalem in taxi: flock of black goats and flock of mixed goats, sheep and cattle grazing in unfenced fields, not even shut off from the road; red poppies and small yellow daisies. Woman, in the tourist agency, born in the Ukraine, with Zionist father and grandfather, who had brought the family to Palestine in 1920, after the Russian Revolution; very patriotic: "I always say I envy people when they come for the first time to our Jerusalem!"—had lived in Rehovoth when it was just a village, you went then in a cart, now it was full of cars; showed me the old rusted cars left beside the "Road of Courage" in memory of the men who had defended it; little stone castle on a hill, with a stone wall around it, that dated from the Crusades but had been used during the Arab war.

—It seems quite natural to hear them speaking Hebrew: a quick staccato language, made up of very short words.

—View from the window of the King David Hotel, looking over the walls of the Old City, reminded me of the view from my room in the Novaya Moskovskayo in '35, when I used to lie in bed and look over the walls of the Kremlin, not to be visited either, behind which the guards were smartly drilling. Absurdity of all these frontiers and restrictions, typical of the world today.

—Taxi driver who had come from Czechoslovakia twenty years ago: I asked him how he liked it: I like it—it is my country.

—When I spoke of the quietness of Jerusalem, Dr. Warburg said it was half dead. Tel Aviv was the clearing-house, and in Jerusalem the mud settled.

—In Europe, I think of New York with a nostalgia I shouldn't have expected. The restaurants in New York of all nations: French, Italian, German, Jewish-Roumanian, Russian, in which I have sat with friends who, by birth or in the second generation, derived from all those nationalities. We all had it in common that we were struggling with New York, stimulated by New York. More interesting, and perhaps more profitable—after all—than Europe. This is where the new culture, the new civilization, has really been being produced; the new American internationalism. —Bismarck herring and pickles, sauerbraten and beer, zimbalon music, cheese and apple, Orvieto in little straw-basketed flasks.

—Economist adviser to the government, had been in London, then Chicago; they are doing silly things, but they are doing things.

—Chronicles of the past as representing a confusion between present and past. —25,000 in Germany.

Joyce's little flowers. Zion:[4] From Zion came the Torah, from Jerusalem (?)—David's dubious tomb among cellar-like informal synagogues with pale bearded guardians;

path into this between snails of barbed-wire fencing off what must once have been yards but are now little long-grass-grown tracts full of red poppies and yellow daisies with sometimes cockeyed signs warning, in Hebrew and English, "Danger—Mines"; deserted private Arab house; David's tomb (report of Jewish traveler) covered with red cloths and silver vessels; walking through the empty and deserted stone monastery paths, walled all around and giving into barbed-wire-barred cul-de-sacs, to the Benedictine monastery and church;[5] German monks, new, apparently mainly from church built fifty years ago on the foundation of Crusaders' church, pictured gilt as-if-non-Byzantine ⌂ half-vaults from Germany; below, in crypt, for which he lighted candles, German altar for Chancellor murdered by Nazis, also Hungarian chapels with frescoes in a horned-toad Hungarian style; statue of the Virgin (she had died there), ivory face and some kind of marble or imitation marble the color of dried blood, lying stiff and rather impressive on her back lounging. Jew who hooked onto us and seized this opportunity to see the church, said to guide that it was forbidden (to enter a Christian church) but he wanted to see it once; was, the guide told me, rather impressed.

—Guide said that government had stopped their excavation of the third wall when they were coming to the conclusion that the real Calvary must have been between it and the second wall, would upset the Church of the Holy Sepulchre. —Why had Jerusalem never been excavated? They ought to dig out the Wailing Wall. —Mentioning rather pointedly that nothing archaeologically definite could be said about the New Testament places, he took me to the tombs of the Sanhedrin[6]— imposing with their high façades and their little rectangular entrances (to make looting, he said, difficult),

with large chambers, squared rooms inside, but all looted
and all empty. (Herod's tomb for his self-murdered
family full of old tin cans and crap, where a family had
once lived, its narrow underground galleries dark and
now unexplored.)

—The dogs' hospital, from which proceeded the barking—dogs and children blown up by mines—the big
"basin" of the valley made by Suleiman[7] into which all
the water drained, now overgrown by grass—the barbed-
wire fringes that are left (like the rusted wrecked cars
on the road out of Jerusalem) on purpose or through
negligence?—on purpose as a memorial and reminder?—
that Israelis are trained to ignore (depressing that they
always live among them. —A second round: F.G.'s
apprehension lest the old pattern may be repeated).

—Let us hope they have here combined their utopian-
ism with their practicality.

—Bareness of Jerusalem under its immense bright sky.

—Narrow concentration on Israeli interests: conversation Halkin's book.[8]

—dogs barking in night

—a good operation

—old bare Jerusalem, with its Catholics, Protestants,
Jews, and Mohammedans—compare Athens and Rome.
—Heine on the German kingdom of clouds—Germans
and Jews in some way too much alike—Germans and
Russians in war, tanks covered with canvas—dislike of
images, the work of the Jews has been done in the minds
and the spirit of men—in Judaism all the religions (including Marxism) to which the Jews have contributed—
Evelyn Waugh's account of midnight in the Church of
the Holy Sepulchre.[9]

—nationalist concentration

—anticlerical group

—Americanizing of Russia and Israel (collective farms,

kibbutzim)—to Americans, seems self-conscious but is it? —Artist I read recently (in *Commentary*?) on the *Narodniki** ideal and point of view.

—Man I met on the street while visiting Mea Shearim.[10] —Never had a quiet day in Poland—tennis match—man fell dead—had been here a year and a half but didn't seem so long—churches and barbed wire— long locks, fur hats (expensive), glossy coats with belts, long dull black coats (Polish costume), knickerbockers, white stockings and black stockings, little children with curls—a certain squalor—old man sitting on porch, beard and spectacles, cross-eyed bent man, the ones that are sallow and the ones that look quite healthy—they are mostly pale, these people. The woman are inconspicuous, I didn't notice any [illegible Hebrew]. Does every grad- uate of this Yeshiva dress this way? —Won't speak Hebrew, a sacred language; won't acknowledge rights of Israeli state, only the Messiah can establish Jewish state; take numbers of cars out on Sabbath and watch oppor- tunity to smash them, then have to be punished by state they don't recognize. Don't carry handkerchiefs on Sab- bath, twine them around their suspenders; beards trimmed with blunt scissors; milk drunk six hours after meat (by Ashkenazi in contradistinction to Sephardim?) so as to forestall the temptation of taking them together. (Caro[11] the great authority on observances.) Women walk behind men; can be divorced for burning food; shave heads and wear wigs, men cannot look them in face while having intercourse. Are fur hats mink?—hot in summer. Casuis- tical elaborations of observances. —Bastards disqualified for priesthood till tenth generation.

—barbed wire and mines, end knocked off the King David Hotel, Herod's tomb in which a family lived.

---

* EW's occasional use of Russian, in this case "populists."

—still getting on badly with their neighbors.

—Is the Talmud a vast morass that got the Jews through the Middle Ages but in which they can nowadays be bogged?

—demonstrate against conscription of women—in court —government will probably have to back down.

—work like Communist cadres—raise groups for demonstrations—infiltrate Talmudic schools—especially in contra-espionage on their own people (radio, chief rabbinate), mustn't be near top-hatted rabbi at funeral.

Mea Shearim Synagogue: brownish striped dressing gowns, old worn and dirty prayer books, prayers going on, black hats bobbing, responses, children, boy with red sidecurls and yellow torn sweater, stout smiling old man who offered us seat, slightly mad lean face with thin pointed beard, some well-curled and oiled brown earlocks, intellectual faces capable of exaltation, nibbling fingers and picking beard, not unhealthy-looking most of these people: rabbi had a good face, yet not unshrewd, one eye half closed, like Tur-Sinais'[12], as if from night-and-day study: just simple Jews who wanted to live as their ancestors had lived, fifth generation in Jerusalem, wouldn't recognize state of Israel, because it was not the real Israel (jolly old man said, They eat pork!), didn't deny story that they had gone to the Arabs with a white flag during the war, because, although it wasn't true, they had intended, or would have liked, to do it. —After prayers, they sat down at the table and had their noses in the Talmud. —They hung around the synagogue and gossiped. —Newsstand they had burned several times— women were not supposed to read novels—they thought the weeklies pornographic. —I asked if he hoped to get back to the Old City—he said, That would be God's blessing! —Their culture and civilization are all completely static, but their purity and courage are impressive. —Boarded-off gallery for the women. —Weissfisch[13] not his official representative. —Boys with clipped heads, little black cap, and sidelocks.

March 31. Conversation with Flusser:[14] he arrived with his briefcase, hatless. We sat down in the lobby as far away from the music as possible. Small and stocky, red hair, rimless spectacles. I said something about the controversy, and he said the important thing was not Zeitlin[15] (this was what he thought I meant by the controversy), but the large question of what was implied by the scrolls. He is dynamic, imaginative, passionately interested—soon began talking French. He produced from his briefcase a Greek Testament and the text of the scrolls (hymns and *Manual of Discipline*), and showed me the parallels, sometimes translating the Hebrew into Greek (the holy spirit = רוח, purification by baptism, righteousness—*dikaiosune*)—the similarities, he pointed out, were all with the Epistles and John: the doctrine of the elect—predestination thus originated perhaps with this sect, and you had the succession: Dead Sea sect–St. Paul–Spinoza–Calvin–Marx. Horrible the doctrine of predestination! He would smile slyly and drily and laugh with dry harsh laugh. He thought that the Master of Righteousness had written all the thirty hymns (as Licht, who had been working on them, also thought possible), and spoke to me of him later over our drink, with positive and emphatic admiration—a strong and courageous soul. But the doctrine of the sect— esoteric and underground—was the product of a people defeated, who hated their enemies. There was nothing of Jesus in this, since Jesus had preached love, and there was nothing of the Christian idea that salvation was to be found in believing in Christ, who would take all your sins away. In explaining all this, he became very intense and excited: at one point, when he was plunging into his briefcase, he began singing what he was saying to the tune of the familiar waltz that the orchestra was playing and that somewhat impinged on our conversation—I have never known anyone to do this before. Relation of the doctrine to the Gnostics: definite opposition between good and evil. [Marginal note: He would swell to a diapason—quite indifferent to the presence of the other people—the voice of a powerful lecturer.]

[André] Dupont-Sommer,[16] he told me, had been having *difficulties* over his views about the scrolls. *Les juifs sont dérangés aussi. Moi je ne suis pas dérangé!* —The people at the university had given me very positively to understand that the doctrine of the sect was something that had existed inside the Jewish world, but did *not* belong to Judaism.

Micah.[17] The second lot of scrolls: a fragment of another commentary like that on Habakkuk; a fragment of the Damascus document; two letters of Bar Kokhba:[18] *C'est drôle—c'est possible, mais c'est drôle. On les a publié dans un journal—on aurait dit qu'il les a écrit exprès pour ce journal.* —He reverted to this several times: *Je trouve que c'est un peu drôle.*

—At the Frumsteins', they had said that if you asked him a question, he would be likely to take three hours to answer it, but I found that he was not a boring or disproportioned talker. He took a long time to answer my questions, but each answer covered a subject, and when he came to the end, he flagged (*ceased* is not precisely the word). I asked him if he would have a drink, and he answered as we moved toward the bar. That was a difference between the Essenians and the Dead Sea sect. The Essenians practised abstinence, but the Dead Sea cult permitted drinking—in Talmudic times a *limonade* but in those times a real wine. —Over our drinks—he had already told me that he "had the *Finland Station* on his shelves"—he talked about determinism, Marxism—not a true religion, too easy to call it apocalyptic—quotation about *Die Freiheit*—the Marxists had the utmost difficulty in restraining themselves from becoming Messiahs. Then *la condition humaine*—he had begun by drinking to *le saint esprit*, that was, *l'esprit humain*—"*le saint esprit* in the sense that you and I believe in"—Nietzsche's saying, *Man muss müssen*, which he repeated with enthusiasm.

Comme vous voyez, je ne suis pas très patriote. —*C'est une petite nation*, but they were beginning to do real scientific work—an excellent edition of the Mishna, "punctuated" and with a commentary. He had come here three years ago, and it was interesting and valuable for him because it enabled him to study Jewish history, which he loved; but eventually he thought he would have to go to the U.S. or somewhere, where he would have a good medieval library—impossible for him in Israel to look up, for example, some edict of a medieval pope. His best language, he said, was medieval Latin. I asked him whom he spoke it with: The Jesuits. Had learned Hebrew only at twenty-two, was an assimilated Jew. *Les gens essayent à vous persuader de mille choses.* I asked him what he meant. *Que le noir est le blanc—le blanc est le noir.*

—I was rather surprised to find how strong in Greek these Jewish scholars were—Ben-Gurion has made a specialty of Greek, learned, I think, rather late in life. Simon Halkin, with whom I spent the following evening, told me that he read some Greek every day, along with his two chapters of the Bible—his "setting-up exercises" —now going through Thucydides. When I talked to him about the Old Testament, he, like Flusser, turned out to be rather on the humanistic side. It had always, with the ancient Jews, been a question of submission to God (walking humbly with your God, etc.); but in the *Crito*, for example—what could be more splendid?—you had Crito building up to Socrates the idea of his escape. Then Socrates saying to Crito, Which of us is going to die? —Why, you. —Then why are you cracking up? There was the human being standing on his own feet, deciding things for himself. Socrates's δαίμων, to which I referred to show that the Greeks resorted to God, was only a spirit that counseled him, a private and personal spirit.

—Halkin said, Flusser flushes. —Halkin has a touch of the fanatical, the narrowly concentrated Jewish type —from Russia originally, then taught "Judaica" in the U.S., had completely cockney *oo* sounds though he said that he had never lived in England.

—Flusser said, "The questions they would ask me—I can't imagine what questions they would ask!"—if he wrote about the scrolls?

April 2. The Warburgs—Abou Gosh—settlement (Kvutza): after the relatively crude (but edible and abundant) lunch at the common dining room, they took me to their little apartment, where they produced coffee and cake and various kinds of candy—some of the chocolates wrapped in gold or pink paper—with liqueur inside, and where I found myself surrounded by a very varied library—new books from Germany and England lying about the room. I had found her rather heavy going in English, which she did not know very well, so that she often had to ask me to repeat my question, but when I got her started in Russian, she was quite different:

the *milyi starik—ya yego lublyu* [nice old man—I love him]—and talked animatedly and rapidly—I saw that she was not without humor. —Both doctors, with no children—she from Riga, he from Berlin (he had had a year in Cambridge, England; she had come to Germany to study); they had lived in Berlin. I was very much impressed by him. He said that reading—though perhaps it was wrong—was for him a necessity of life, and living in the country, he had time for it. —What did I think of the young people? He felt that he understood them, but they spoke a different language. —When I had spoken to her about Germany, and the way that they were building themselves up, she was politely but markedly cold. When I later said the same thing to him, he said, Yes, they are good with things—good with things, but not with people. When I told him about the estrangement between Elena and her family, he said, Yes, those things can't be mended. —He took a more moderate view of Spender's book[19] than the other people I had met, agreed that they resented in Israel criticism of any kind—and they criticized themselves constantly, criticized one another. —The first two years he had been there, he had not felt himself at all at home, could easily have gone to America, but after three years, he had wanted to stay.

—Poultry yard kept by the children: ducks, geese, chickens, turkeys, peacock, sheep all looked extremely fat, as if they were pampered pets. —I mistook some small turkeys for guinea fowl, but they were going, he told me, to have guinea fowl, too—though guinea fowl were not kosher. He wasn't sure why this was, thought they didn't have a spur on their foot—he asked one of the boys about it—the boy said he didn't know. There are better rabbis than me! —Actually, they raised non-kosher animals: rabbits and guinea pigs, with the excuse that they were needed for the laboratories. The rabbis did not worry much so long as they did not bring in the pig.

—Lurie of the Foreign Office said that the anti-religious movement restrained itself in the interests of national unity, but that the religious elements did not.

—Mrs. Warburg told her husband to get back before dark on account of the Arabs. —Dr. Warburg thought that the English had still a romantic admiration for the Arabs as the Americans had for the Indians.

—Francis Quasher; Mrs. Maynes; mad rabbi; dinner at the Gilroys'; day at Rehovoth. 11/6/10

April 4. Story told by Greek [Lados] about seal (at the Gilroys' Sunday dinner): Seals are bad luck for fishermen—they raise their heads and say, Is Alexander living? —You must answer, He is living and reigning—otherwise, it is all up with you. —These fishermen had found two seals in their net—had let the mother go but kept the baby, but had been afraid to kill it out of hand, had been hedging it in a corner with a wall of stones, each laying a stone in turn, so that nobody would have all the blame. He had bought it from them, named it Panyaki. Found that it couldn't swim—when he put it in the water, head would sink and tail go up—the trouble he had taken teaching it to swim!, holding it under the chin—at last one day it had swum away, he had seen its little round head at a distance and thought he had seen the last of it, but then it came back grinning from ear to ear, delighted at finding it could swim. It is wonderful swimming with a seal—they come back underwater and nip your behind. He had also had to teach it to eat—when he had presented it with a red mullet, it had screamed like a soul in torment—how they scream! Didn't seem to like the smell of fish, though it smelled so much like a fish itself. Put milk in an empty gin bottle, but this also made it scream—the only way at first he could make it eat was by putting butter on its nose so that it would lick it off. Later it learned to take milk. Its fur was like having velvet skirts around. He had a hard struggle with the captain to be allowed to keep it on the ship. When it got older, it would bite his hand, and this became rather a nuisance: they don't have regular separate teeth, but a bony thing, I gathered, rather like the jaws of a trap without teeth. Bad luck began: they were fired on by another Greek vessel, and other disasters occurred. But when he got back to Athens, and the Communists were guarding the port, he was a little worried—being, I think, a royalist—but the seal— seals are very curious—would lean its flippers on the window of the taxi and look out. This interested the soldiers so much that they forgot about politics. He took it to his mother's apartment. Finding water in the bathtub and not knowing it was drinking water, kept there on account of the water shortage—he gave it a bath with soap so that it would not be so offensive for his mother. He soaped it on a table just under the window and the seal stuck its head out the window and attracted a considerable crowd. He would hold it out the window to show it. Then he had to go away and left it with his mother and it died. It was a very dear animal. He never discovered its sex.

—If the exclusiveness of the Jewish religion is tending to disappear in Israel, with the inevitable relaxation of its restrictions and rigors, it may be setting in, in another way, with the, for foreigners, all-but-impregnable wall of the Hebrew language, their all-but-encirclement by the Arabs, and their narrow concentration on their own problems.

—Bareness (nakedness) and meagerness of the "Holy Land"—the little valleys and hills that were the scenes of the savage Old Testament wars, the scenes, almost all humble and now hardly traceable, of the New Testament: strange to think how the riots of color of the Renaissance in nativities and annunciations, the towering crucifixes of Greece, the agonies and ecstasies of French and Italian, Germanic and Byzantine art, all sprouted from legends of these calm little hills sprinkled with stones and flocks, under luminous tranquil skies.

—livid and savage prophecies

—lightning—floods of prophesy, thunderous rejoicings

—Rather puzzling it must be to the Jew to hear the Christians singing about Israel, etc.—it must all seem rather a grotesque travesty. Amazement and amusement of the Frumsteins and their friend at discovering—on some occasion when one of them had happened to think to wonder about it—that the Bride of the Song of Solomon was for the Christians the Church and the Bridegroom Jesus Christ. —What can the Christians make of the Bible, what can they know about it? they must ask. For them, it is not the Bible, but the תנ"ך (Tanach)—it seems quite wrong, if it does not offend them, to see the order of the contents changed. It never occurred to me, till Frumstein suggested it, that the Old Testament is made to end with Malachi, instead of, as the תנ"ך (Tanach) does, with Chronicles, so that the prophets can lead up to Christ.

—Jerusalem and Israel as a whole in its present constrained and truncated state.

. . .

April 8–9. Grim and gloomy young man from Switzerland, a specialist in the medical aspect of law (*psi*chiatry), insisted on kosher restaurants and put on his little hat to eat, but was so horrified, at our Hotel Peer, by what another member of the party enjoyed as what they called a "Jewish breakfast": herring, sour pickles, sour cream, chopped carrots, olives and radishes, that he got up and removed them to the end of the table, where they would be out of his sight—did his best to get a simple French breakfast, coffee and bread.

April 8. Idyllic quality of the Lake of Tiberias—misted, with dim blues and greens, hills with skirtlike wrinkles, deep and calm dull water, when we came upon it from above not unlike the backgrounds of certain Italian paintings of Christian subjects, because the landscape a little resembled certain parts of Italy. I saw that Renan's descriptions, in *La Vie de Jésus* [1863], were quite accurate, though I had always suspected them before of being products of the French literary *paysage* tradition. It was not unnatural to interpret Jesus's life, as Renan did, in terms of these idyllic landscapes—*un charmant docteur* and the kind of thing that Proust parodies in his pastiche of Renan.

Dream about Margaret at Tel Aviv:[20] I thought I had gone, in New York, to the apartment of some California friend—it was only after a moment that I realized that the woman there was Margaret, very attractive and still young. We didn't communicate, the visit shifted. I had gone home, wanted to find her again; searched in the phone book under Canby and Waterman, then realized she would not be there, would be just in from the Coast for a visit as she had been when we first came together. I woke up as I was still trying to think how to reach her.

—What is the meaning of these still recurring dreams, in relation to my frequent dreams of alienations and separations from Elena? In these latter, it is not merely a question of fears, but also of the desire to assert my independence—yet the two are bound up together. My impulse to free myself from relationships with women had something to do with my letting Margaret go off to Santa Barbara, where she died. Now in dreams I want her back. I have Elena but dream of leaving her.

Grodzensky's story about Will Herberg:[21] When H. gave up Communism, after for years having worked on Lovestone's paper,[22] he tried to interest himself in Judaism, but found he couldn't respect their theology—he showed Grodzensky a long list of the authors he had read—and announced that he was about to embrace Christianity. Grodzensky rushed into the breach by lending him the works of Rosenzweig, which impressed Herberg sufficiently so that he accepted Judaism instead. Afterwards, Grodzensky heard him lecture and, in answer to some question from one of his hearers, found him saying in the dictatorial Communist manner, "Don't you know that that's a deviation from normative Judaism?"

—If you approach the Old Testament as I have from the Jewish point of view, it all seems so very Jewish and so intimately a part of the Jewish tradition that you wonder how the Christians and the Arabs were able to adapt it to their own minds and worlds. To the Jews, these foreign versions of their holy books must appear a desecration and a travesty. This especially apropos of Passover. What do Exodus and the prescriptions of the ensuing books mean to the Christians? They do not provide them with laws and observances, the ceremonies of their holidays (Easter is a Christian transposition of

Passover). Their way of attempting to assimilate them must appear rather ridiculous to Jews. —Reading Exodus, however, today, I can only wonder at the ignorance and credulity of "civilized" human beings in carrying along and continuing to swallow all this old nonsense. Voltaire, however obtuse to the spiritual values of the Scriptures, however unimaginative in his failure to put himself back into the origins of human culture (an omission repaired by Renan), did perform a useful service in pointing out the absurdities of the Bible stories. Let us slough off this ancient rubbish in proportion as we feel self-confidence in our new moral positions based on further experience of ourselves, of the world, of the universe. —The situation, in all this connection, of the Israeli of today is peculiar. How much is the old religion an essential part of Jewish character, how much should the ancient legends enter into present-day patriotism? (Tradition of being surrounded by bitter enemies, tradition of being defeated in the field—after rather short-lived victories— and resorting, for display of prowess, to affirming their religious supremacy.) —Will the whole thing evaporate in Israel, leaving only the orthodox ceremonies still kept up because people are used to them, somewhat as they are in Catholic countries? Importance of Israel in making it possible for the Jews to handle affairs—political, commercial, cultural—on a level of equality with the rest of the world. This is the main thing. The Zionist movement, though special, belongs to the same set of phenomena as the movements for Irish, Czech, Hungarian, Serbian, and Greek independence (Norwegian *landsmaal*; dialects of Swiss cantons, Romansh; from competing languages, each apparently with its culture, in Yugoslavia). The trouble is that these little states are always liable to lose their autonomy to the protection or oppression of some big state. Federations must be democratic. If they make possible the cultivation of various religions and languages, these will tend to disappear. The U.S.A., I should say, has, in spite of the problem of the South, been pretty successful from this point of view.

—The Jewish ban on images seems to have had its effect, not only in the blankness of pictures of orthodox Israeli homes but in the badness of the pictures in the others. They are in general weak on the visual side, as is seen in their cities and houses; yet I don't feel, as Stephen Spender does, that the Arabs are better off for the touches of prettiness in the windows or porches of their towns. I prefer the low white houses of the settlements, which always look both neat and easy—one, with roofs of a dim discreet pink, is charming.

—Conversation with the Passows and their guest (news distributor in the States, small industrialist here) about orthodox Judaism: a widow, it seems, is supposed to belong to her late husband's brother unless he repudiates her. He had had to appear as a witness in the case of a woman he knew, and had been rather horrified when he found that she was bound by rabbinical law to spit three times on her brother-in-law. He had heard about this in childhood, but had quite forgotten about it and was surprised to find it actually being done.

April 13. Session on the scrolls in holiday lectures for schoolteachers: Auditorium in school building packed, people standing up, crowding in and out, caps and beards mixed with moderns, hats and no-hats: man who made them all laugh showing, in a way that none of the scholars took seriously, that the Mosaic law was really Mosaic; Habermann[23] said that the Jews were leery of the scrolls for fear that they would upset the Masoretic text, and that they sometimes tended to take the attitude that it was something that was of more interest to Christians than Jews, yet Jews should be interested, too; tall rabbinical man with black fezlike hat and black beard and mustaches, who said that the Isadah scroll (American) was made of two fastened together, but whole thing executed in conformity to rabbinical rules; Licht; Flusser.

—At dinner, Flusser had said, *"C'est très désagréable pour tout le monde—sauf pour ceux qui s'occupent des apocalypses—ils sont contents!"* Pharisees not what the Christians thought: here was an anti-Pharisaic sect that kept to the strict observances (?). —After the lecture, he said, *Tout le monde est mégilotamène!*

—Tolman, with whom we walked to the hotel, told me he had published in *Biblia* a paper trying to show that the sect had changed the calendar and thus cut themselves off from the rest of the Jews.

—Flusser on errors as the constructive element in the development of civilization—got a rise out of Frumstein by asserting that apologetics were inseparable from science, were indeed its prime motivation; but distrusted especially people, like the first speaker of the evening, who began by disclaiming apologetic intentions. —It is as if he were the Devil's agent sent expressly to exploit the situation created by the discovery of the scrolls: subduedly flaming hair brushed straight up and not parted, modestly Mephistophelian eyebrows, little cold green eyes, a dry and harsh laugh, complete detachment from everything; yet I was told that he was shy and there was something about him of a rotund and gauche-bashful little-boyishness. There was "a scandal" about him, I was told—lived with a strong-minded sister-in-law, who made him do the baby-sitting and marketing. He would be seen reading Greek in a queue—I asked him why Ben-Gurion had gone in for Greek so late in middle age. I shall explain it very easily, he answered: the Jews from an early period had always gone in for Greek. He confirmed my own impression that they needed it to complement their own kind of culture. —The more Jewish a Jew became, like Ben-Gurion, the more he thought he needed Greek. —But *you* go in for Greek *tout de même*, I said. —It's perhaps the only respect in which *je suis juif*. —On Baer:[24] he felt in his presence as Aristotle did in the presence of Plato. Baer writing history of Halakah. Baer on Greek influence—felt first in Palestine, then reached Philo from there. He didn't agree but would rather go along with Baer, etc., quoted the Latin, but said he didn't want to be identified with Cicero.

April 14–17. Old Jerusalem: Church of the Holy Sepulchre—scaffoldings, Christmas-tree ornaments (bulbous brass lamps on chains), bad modern mosaics, black-gowned Armenian (?) priests, Russian inscriptions.

Working on scrolls, Rockefeller Museum: fragments of leather scrolls (a few of papyrus) like bits of autumn leaves under glass, ranging from dark brown to a rare, almost paperlike paleness. They put them in the humidifier (bell glasses and sponges), then go over them with a paintbrush dipped in castor oil or alcohol; when text too much effaced, they treated them with infrared rays and took reduced photographs of them, which they studied through a magnifying glass. —Only three men on it, Malik, Cross, Allegro,[25] in a room by themselves; enormous concordance of the Septuagint.

—Skeleton from Carmel 100,000 years old, between

Neanderthal and modern man—had taken years (?) to get it out with dental drills.

—The green copper scrolls, Hebrew words incised with stylus, read *silver* and *gold* from the other side.

—Tens of thousands of pieces—Bedouins would tear them in strips—having sold the first of these strips, they would ask more money for the second, etc.—so they finally adopted the policy of giving them baksheesh in proportion to the size of the pieces.

—$15,000 still needed to buy the rest

—Two new columns of the *Manual of Discipline*: a kind of communion rite: bread and wine; the master presides and each eats and drinks according to rank. *John* not a predominantly Greek but a mainly Jewish document, and definitely a product of the sect. —Priest-and-Messiah presides, the priest perhaps functioning for the Messiah, as in the Christian communion, and the whole thing a liturgical anticipation of something expected in heaven. —Note that Jesus, at the Last Supper, is evidently upsetting an accepted hierarchy.

April 15. Dead Sea: Père [Roland] de Vaux[26]—almost Jewish nose and eyes of the high-powered headlight variety behind the thick magnifying lenses of his glasses, teeth to match, long, regular, and always displayed, self-enjoyment, an eagerness almost greedy—*gusto* is the word I want—white flannel (?) Dominican robe with leather belt, what looked like blue golf stockings, a beret —always, with a certain smartness, smoking cigarettes— climbed the ruins like a chamois—in descending into cave 4, they had at first used a rope, but soon had got used to it and gone in and out as if it were a familiar staircase—energy and spirit. While he was camping there, they shot and killed a hyena—they hung it for two or three days, then boiled it and spiced it, very good.

[Marginal note: Had evidently (from his breath) just had some wine. —Beads at belt.]

Landscape without physiognomies, no faces of men, gods, or animals—Perowne[27] said, "Entirely monotheistic, no place for a nymph"—completely impersonal—brown-yellow-gray, fading grass of spring now looked simply like a mold on the amorphous leaves of the hills—or perhaps like humps of the camels, camel-color, tawny without warmth, dun hardly made rich by shadows—camels wandering, grazing, tawny with their dusty white calves—torn and black shelters of Bedouins, old watchtower from Jewish potash-working community, little inn fought over and destroyed during the war—finally looted by Bedouins (the Dead Sea fleet of two little boats, two little mongrel dogs, tea and cake), squatting figures of women, single camels and goats—flock of black goats blocking the hill. —Landscape of the sea itself (Edward Lear), descent below sea level stuns the ears (how many feet?) like coming down in a plane—dull blues and purples and yellows and browns that are not really any of these colors, dull pale blue of the water—you feel neither darkness nor light—the ground is dusted with streaks of some little reddish flower and brushed here and there with the plants of statice, a dreary little white everlasting—a hawk goes after a crow, which drops the small animal it has caught, the hawk circles about, the crow is loath to depart—a few scorpions. They killed several vipers. —They had explored 200 caves far above the ground level on the wall of reddish rock and had found traces of human occupancy in forty-five, none near the top of the cliff—nothing exciting will happen to this landscape, no exquisite violet or lavender like Greece—no fish in the heavy sea. [Marginal note: description of monastery.] The rains would run down in the trough of an angle of the mountains, caught by the sect in their cisterns—room where they wrote, benches, inkwells. They got their reed pens from the lake—mill to grind grain, found in two pieces; a kitchen with ovens, ovens to bake pots, great cisterns to which one descended by steps (for baptism?), refectory with 1,000 bowls and jars all stacked on shelves; long common room, where [?] was probably done, something like a dais for the pulpit—all made of rude gray stones—old Bronze Age Israelite wall of about 900 B.C.—gap between this and the buildings that began at 200 B.C.—graveyard with 1,000 graves, bones with no fixings, peculiar burial customs, community probably *four hundred*, women as well as men (perhaps a later development), in graves and mentioned by some document—people lived in the caves and forgathered at the monastery. —What a life! But no doubt no worse, probably better, than that of the saints in the African desert (did life in society in those days seem so much more precarious than now?). —Bits of pillars—used how and where?—two bases set too close together, must have been sawed-off fragment on which something was set—a round nest surrounded by stones: what was this for, a potter's wheel?—a yard at one end—the whole landscape and the sea, dull, are sunken, to live there itself a sort of burial.

—De Vaux knew the boy (now a man) who had found the first scrolls, Mohammed the Wolf—who had been looking for a lost goat and idly thrown a stone in the cave, ran away afraid, later investigated—they kept the scrolls around (perhaps a few weeks), would occasionally unroll them and show them to somebody.

—Sept. 1952, fragments brought, and offered at museum by antiquity dealer, sent secretary to L.H.[28] Must do something, H. called police, who sent squad—rat holes and rabbit holes

—*Discoveries in the Judaean Desert* (vol. 1)—Oxford

—Syrians went into cave secretly, nobody knows what they found

[Marginal note: fragments of Daniel now in hands of Syremal in N.Y., head of Fr. Bib. and Arch. School]

D[upont]-S[ommer] at Sorbonne

G. rue du Val-de-Grâce, Odéon 0848

Nouveaux aperçus

Vermès,[29] Desclée, *les manuscrites du désert de Juda*

Dead Sea: four large cisterns, seven smaller—twice in three years De Vaux saw water falling from hills—stored in winter water for all year.

—references to women and children in fragments

—skeletons like dust, some feminine bones—dug twenty tombs, bones of nine individuals only—one or two or three women—impossible to know about women —lying north to south

—Coins found only in big building, never in caves.

—Bedouins worked for the Department of Antiquities by day, did clandestine digging at night.

—£1.50 a square centimeter—£15,000 worth still in hands of Bedouins.   11/8/10

April 16. Tenebrae [services] at Holy Sepulchre. [Marginal note: narrow entrances to the parvis, as you leave the street.] The façade is propped with a metal structure, trimmed with barbed wire behind, that looks like the New York El: as you go in the church, you are confronted by a rectangular red stone on the floor, where Jesus is supposed to have been laid out—people knelt to kiss it; I saw one of the more fastidious women visitors wipe it with her handkerchief first: Christmas-tree ornaments: brass lamps and thurifers, round blue and red balls, tinsel stars; gigantic candles in candlesticks about the unction stone, "candles" had little bows of blue ribbon, little views of Jerusalem and other Christmas-card ornaments painted on them; fire of 1808, dome above the Sepulchre nearly effaced, because dome badly done and the paint had peeled off; archbishop in small red cap and fancy coat presided in a throne facing the Sepulchre (a kind of dark tower, walled in). [Marginal note: black-robed priests with flat-topped tall Greek Orthodox hats.] Mixture of brown-robed monks, white-coated choristers, visiting nuns, old women in black (one of whom went around the glass cases of reliquaries kissing the glass above every one), Christian Arab women with their children, at the "office" women kneeling on the floor and a nun with an enormous white winged cap praying in a niche, so that only her headdress was visible above her dark bowed figure, an occasional whiff of incense or of something like wine, man who looked like an Anglican clergyman who came out of the tomb in the end. —Above, very bad modern mosaics. [Marginal note: one column upstairs scrawled with names and addresses, among which the word *Dublin* shows black and clear.] —Abraham and Isaac and other subjects presumably the gift of the Franciscans; Greek chapel, with old bearded man talking to the pilgrims in their various languages in a very bad accent, apparently getting their signatures in a book—behind him, a row of half-fancy half-photographic pictures of the patriarchs or metropolitans; Russian embroidered pictures, much gold; Armenian inscription. —Whole place crowded, cluttered, designless, cathedrals within cathedrals, crypt approached by broad deep steps, a man hands you a candle with which you explore the spot where the true cross is supposed to have been discovered (what is in the further cellar?). [Marginal note: bulky giant statue that is probably Jesus but to which the little candles can't reach.] —Holy Sepulchre shrine is covered with wooden scaffolding that holds the pillars apart, little strips of glass are fastened to the columns that will break if a crack occurs; other walls are masked by scaffolding and their paintings completely concealed—which is probably no great loss, for the Church of the Holy Sepulchre probably contains more bad taste, certainly more kinds of bad taste, then any other church I have ever seen; a mess, a scramble of sects, with rites that blur and overlap, that interrupt one another. —I asked the French architecture student here what was going to be done about it. He said they were waiting for an earthquake to shake it down, and then they wouldn't have to do anything about it. As it was, they couldn't agree on what to do—you would have to build a new church. —Outside, as I was leaving, an Arab in a red fez and a brightly embroidered red jacket stopped and spoke to a lady. The people at the school thought he might have been a *kavass hagios* in front of important people, to warn of their approach and clear the way. —Whole place very claustrophobic—also claustrophobia of vulgarity. —Why was there relatively so little incense?

—Coming out, I saw the Père de Vaux striding out, a brown robe over his white one, leaving the church behind him, quickly outdistancing the crowd. —His almost biblical beard, but too well trimmed to be rabbinical Jewish, his face burned a brown brick-red, his rather wild-boarlike hair that was evidently not amenable to the brush—beard and eyebrows also—low but sure legs rather like a mountain goat's block-like hoofs.

April 14. When we came through the Mandelbaum Gate—amid the gashed and gutted houses, never restored since the war, the gaping arched Arab windows that so much suggested an easy life—we saw a squad of Arab soldiers standing at attention beside the gray blinded trucks of Israelis that were changing the guard at Mount

Scopus. They searched them and tested all the oil drums, had once found something contraband in one of them.

April 18. Samaritan Passover: Vertiginous trip up the mountain, a High Place indeed—on top a terrific wind, felt for the first time, that you almost felt might sweep you off—crowds of non-Samaritan children, following us, throwing stones, laughing at us when we slipped on the rocks: little morgue: like shrine of stone, base of a 5th-century Christian church. —Walked down to the ceremony—High Priest had been reading since morning and nearly finished Deuteronomy—he and two others in green, while everybody else wore white, white turbans with red tops, others sitting around with red tarbooshes— a little speech in Arabic which he read, one heard the word *Arabia*, and everybody applauded—they now began praying—there is only one God—and increased the volume and tempo, working themselves up to a climax. The general atmosphere—with all the visitors—was something like that of an Indian dance, but, except for the killing of the sheep, much more restrained and less colorful. Beside the priests and elders (?) another group of younger men, all with red tarbooshes, was doing more or less the same thing, with the fat brown-faced sheep waiting in the angle of a stone fence. Here was the altar, a ditch. I missed the moment of slaughter, thinking the sheep were to be led somewhere else—seven, one for each family—the High Priest, I was told, simply sawed their throats through with a knife. The Samaritans here rather excitedly prayed and uttered whistles and cries. When I saw them, pressing my way through the crowd with the little Lanven girl who turned out later to be Bob Chanler's granddaughter, the sheep were lying there heaps of wool, with blood around their necks. —We then went to the High Priest's tent—wine, arrack, matzoth, which we dipped in cheese and some sweet stuff—they sold us their literature, little scene about the price, young man snatched the booklets away when Muilenburg[30] tried to make him accept less than the stipulated price, High Priest (or leaner man in brown) drew back and looked angry—we sat on benches and beds—a woman, in the crowd, had just managed to rescue a ring as she felt it being slipped off her finger—a young theological student from Union had lost his fountain pen and his watch; but the High Priest said he would try to see that the police recovered them. —Sheep were slaughtered just as sun went down—a darkness like that out of which the voice of God had come in Exodus blotted everything out, sort of brown and dull, suddenly extinguishing the bright-shining moon—I have never seen darkness like this, remembered that in the Exodus passage it is doubtful whether to call it "deep darkness" or "mist." —Inbreeding had made them all look alike, not Arab but less pronouncedly Jewish than most Jews, nose definitely Jewish yet straighter, good features and well-grown bodies (though little girl thought their bones looked frail), perhaps a little lacking in character and yet of an exceptional purity. Women seemed to be lurking in tents. Man told me he had been surprised to hear one of the women speaking German, then discovered that a few had been allowed to marry Jews. High Priest said there were now 304, of whom 217 in Nablus. —When it was dark, we left the High Priest's tent and went up to where the sheep were being prepared—they were hung up by the hind legs to a rod stuck in holes in two uprights held by two men. They had separated the skin from the body by blowing it up with bicycle pumps (a non-biblical touch), and now the naked bodies had only their hoofs and their legs and their dangling, sometimes small-horned, heads. (First, however, they had been

scalded by having hot water thrown over them and the
remains of wool removed.) Near a fire, they were dis-
emboweled (see washing and salting of entrails), and the
rest of their insides removed—I saw one outfit with the
liver dangling—warm smell of excrement. It was the
young men who occupied themselves with this. Afterwards they roasted them for three hours or so, and ate
them about midnight. —Mrs. Muilenburg wanted to
stay long enough to see one over the fire—very feminine,
I suppose, goal and end product of all the preparations,
ceremony, slaughter, evisceration.

—*Reductio ad absurdum* of the Jewish point of view:
the Samaritans are being punished for sins committed
two or three thousand years ago ("syncretism," as Muilenburg said, with the heathen gods), they have kept the
race and the rites pure, but they know they are doomed
to extinction, and to this fate they are resigned (see
booklet). It is strange to see them setting up against the
Jews the same exclusive attitude that the Jews set up
against the Gentiles (Trotskyists and Stalinists, etc.).

—When I asked the Père de Vaux about the new MS.
of Petronius, he first laughed and said that this was
quite remote from his recent preoccupations, then said
that he believed he had heard of it—a papyrus.

April 18. Coming back through the Mandelbaum Gate,
after the usual brusque preliminaries, the man who was
attending to me asked whether I described myself as
"writer"—I wrote books. Then the man at the end of
the desks said, I am glad to see you—you are a world-
famous writer (he had evidently read the interview in
the *Jerusalem Post*)—I should like to talk to you about
the scrolls. I have my own opinion—they were written
in the second century. —The man who was evidently
the chief said, This is not the time, Mr. Friedman—

then to me: Some other time Mr. Friedman will have
an interview with you.

Back in old New Jerusalem, with almost the same
view from my window: still the real, the great Jerusalem
is all in the mind and spirit. Even the color, the exotic
quality, the fascination of the old is all the work of the
Arabs and the grandiose element is the work of Herod
and the Romans (the stalls under the temple where the
Templars kept their horses): Solomon's Temple has
disappeared. —"And we shall build Jerusalem in England's green and pleasant land."[31] —What they inherit
here is the dawn of New Jerusalem—the least bleak
part of which is the kibbutzim, etc.—quite right—it is
still a victory of the spirit. —Strange to come over from
the many religions, the colors and variety, of the Old
City, to the sobriety, the darkness, the quietness, the
seriousness, of the New City.

NOTES

1. Edward Lear (1812–88) was an accomplished painter in
addition to his writing of nonsense verse.

2. See p. 227.

3. Alexander Papagos (1883–1955) became Premier of Greece
in 1952.

4. "The red poppies and yellow daisies remind you of that
passage from Edgar Quinet that Joyce likes to play with in
Finnegans Wake: the wild flowers . . . through the wreckage
of civilizations . . . *'fraiches et riantes comme aux jours des
batailles,'*" *Israel and the Dead Sea Scrolls* (1978, hereafter
referred to as *DSS*), p. 88.

5. The Church of the Dormition and its monastery, completed
in 1910. The Austrian chapel commemorates Engelbert Dollfuss
(1892–1934), Federal Chancellor from 1932 to 1934, assassinated
by the Nazis.

6. The supreme rabbinic court in ancient Jerusalem.

7. Suleiman I (the Magnificent), Ottoman Sultan from 1520 to 1566.

8. Simon (Shimon) Halkin's *Modern Hebrew Literature: Trends and Values* (1951). Halkin was teaching this subject at the Hebrew University in Jerusalem. *DSS*, pp. 68, 80.

9. *The Holy Places* (1952).

10. Mea Shearim (Hundred Gates), a quarter of the New City of Jerusalem.

11. Joseph Ben Ephraim Caro (1488–1575), author of *Shulhan Arukh* ("the prepared table"), an important code of observances.

12. Naphtali Herz Tur-Sinais (1886–1973), Hebrew Semitic and Bible scholar.

13. Laibala Weissfisch, a "fanatical transcriber" of Torah scrolls. The rabbi speaking here (Rabbi Amram) belonged to the Guardians, a group urging moderation in relations with the Arabs. Weissfisch, before Arab representatives in the United Nations, had made proposals "prejudicial" to the interest of Israel. *DSS*, p. 57.

14. David Flusser, professor of comparative literature at the Hebrew University in Jerusalem. See *Edmund Wilson: The Man and His Work* (edited by John Wain, 1978), pp. 109–14.

15. Solomon Zeitlin, of Dropsie College in Philadelphia. *DSS*, pp. 209–10.

16. André Dupont-Sommer, professor of Semitic languages and civilizations at the Sorbonne, had published two books on the scrolls. *DSS, passim.*

17. The second batch of scrolls contained a commentary on Micah, a prophet of the 8th century B.C., similar to the Habakkuk commentary included in the first batch of scrolls and which EW describes thus (*DSS*, p. 174): "Ostensibly a commentary on the canonical prophet Habakkuk, it is in reality a history of happenings that were recent at the time it was written . . . chronicled . . . in terms of the assumption that Habakkuk was prophesying them."

18. Simon Bar Kokhba, hero and leader of the Jewish revolt against the Roman oppressors (131–35 A.D.).

19. *Learning Laughter* (1952).

20. Margaret Canby, EW's second wife; she died in 1932 in an accident in California. For EW's other dreams about her, see *The Thirties*, pp. 365–69; *The Forties*, pp. 128, 202.

21. Will Herberg (1909–77), author of studies in Judaism and 20th-century theology, often incorporating a Marxist perspective.

22. Jay Lovestone wrote and worked on behalf of labor and became AFL-CIO Director of International Affairs.

23. A[braham] M[eir] Habermann, librarian and author. This lecture is described in *DSS*, p. 193.

24. Yitzhak Baer, Jewish historian, then retired professor of medieval history at the Hebrew University.

25. J. T. Malik, a Polish Roman Catholic priest, Dr. Frank Moore Cross, Jr., of the McCormick Theological Seminary in Chicago and then Annual Professor at the American School of Oriental Research, and Dr. John Allegro, of Manchester University, were the only three scholars authorized to decipher and report on the scrolls. *DSS, passim.*

26. Père Roland de Vaux (1903–71), of the Ecole Biblique in Jerusalem. *DSS, passim.*

27. Stewart Perowne lived in Jerusalem and arranged EW's expedition to the Dead Sea.

28. G. Lankester Harding, of the Department of Antiquities of Transjordan. *DSS, passim.*

29. Géza Vermès, of Oxford University. *DSS*, pp. 276–78.

30. James Muilenburg, of the Union Theological Seminary, then director of the American School of Oriental Research in Old Jerusalem.

31. From William Blake's *Milton:* "I will not cease from Mental Fight, / Nor shall my sword sleep in my hand, / Till we have built Jerusalem / In England's green and pleasant land."

RETURN TO FRANCE

April 20–27. Return to France: I flew from Lydda to Orly—good weather and comfortable trip. Elena had left word at the Hôtel du Quai Voltaire that she was in the little Voltaire restaurant on the corner, where I found her dining with Petka; Helen was in bed. We had a bottle of Vouvray and went back to the hotel. She took a bath, and we made love—we both had a good deal of enthusiasm; but, after longing for one another and, as she said, idealizing one another, we began to fall out the next day. She had invited little Marina and, on top of that, had given in to Auntie Maroussia's insistence on coming to see us in the afternoon. The next day she had arranged to go out to the Russian home. It was thus impossible, Tuesday, on account of Auntie M.'s coming at 3:30, to do anything with the family or, because Auntie M. was counting on seeing me, even for me to take the little girls to a show. Auntie M., refusing our invitation to dinner, came with us "just to sit with us" and ended by eating an ample meal; and I got her off with difficulty on a train to St.-Michel-sur-Orges. At first she had seemed quite jolly, and I thought her not so bad as Elena had told me, but, when I got back from a short trip to the rue de Rivoli, where I had left my glasses to be mended, and found her still there and had a long conversation with her, I thought her perhaps worse. She complained about Antoinette, the widow of her nephew, a French woman, who ran the Russian home—A. the same type as Madeleine, whom she enormously admired—had said of her, *"C'est une ace!"* Three marriages she knew with French women—the wives were all bitches—succeeded in alienating husbands from their sisters and mothers. The French were all corrupt—the politicians—and they would cheat you if they could: you always had to check on bills and things. The Bolsheviks, like a cancer—the kind of thing that had to be dealt with the moment that it appeared—if you let it go, it infected everything. She loves this complaining and deploring, and it is horrible to see and hear her. Elena says that the family has always managed to live on other people. There are two kinds of women, Auntie M. told me, "the slaves and the queens." Olili was a slave, but she, Auntie M., had always been a queen. —Elena had told me how she loved to weep, and her memoirs bore this out. When I visited the Russian home and remarked that it looked— behind the building—like Russia (as it did, with its uncut grass and slim unkempt-looking trees), she made the "gesture," which must have been deliberate and practised, of momentarily bursting into tears, then wiping the tears away. Elena had told me of her and her daughter Masha, "One reads (aloud) and the other weeps." —But she sometimes shows signs of humor and a more normal point of view—said that what had happened at Johannisberg was a kind of thing you wouldn't believe if you read it in a novel—like something "in a bad novel."

—Aunt Elinka was, as Elena said, much more sensible

and sympathetic: in bed, only one lung, very frail, very pale. Much resembles Elena: blue eyes and large nostrils, and has expressions of childlike candor like hers. Old gentlemen in the home were bringing her flowers. Little Marina and other little girls were around—she said she sometimes preferred them to grown-ups. When I said that I had not been able to make any contact with Olili, she said that she had always called her *"le sphinx"*—nobody had ever known her. Elinka was unique in feeling that O. had not changed so much.

—Russian home, with its cramped little chapel, full of candles and ikons and stale Easter flowers—worse, if anything, than the Roman Catholic kind. Rooms downstairs with bad portraits and busts of the emperors and empresses. Memorial plaque to Elena's aunt Verinka, who had raised the money for the home from the benefactress Dorothy Paget.

—Masha's accident which had left her one eye out of line with the other (a man had ridden her down at night on a bicycle without lights and then ridden off without stopping) in her rather pretty refined old-fashioned (early 20th century) Russian face. —Petka's singing lessons at thirty-five (Auntie M. thought he was going to be another Chaliapin). —The old general, whose manner and appearance were still quite distinguished, did watercolors.

—Big Marina complained that the characters in Tolstoy were "vulgar," especially Anna Karenina. Elena said that her first husband, Vorontsov, had cleaned out a garage in Paris but had been treated by the other Russians as if he were the Dalai Lama.

—The trouble is that, when Elena and I are away from one another, we get so in the habit of independence, of arranging our lives for ourselves, that when we are together again, we try to go on doing the same thing, paying no attention to one another's desires and plans.

One evening when I was rather out of humor with Elena, I looked up Esther Arthur's address and went out, after dinner, for a walk along the quais—we were staying again in the Hôtel du Quai Voltaire—with a vague idea of looking her up. I actually found her, not far away, just off the Place St.-Michel at the rue Gît-le-Coeur (she explained to me that this, "the most beautiful street name in Paris," commemorated the grave, not of Louis XIV's mistress, as had once been supposed, but merely of his favorite chef). I went up in a little old elevator and announced myself as an F.B.I. man. It amused me to inquire for "Madame Arthur," as if she were the heroine of Yvette Guilbert's song.[1] We fell on each other's neck. There were two vague Austrians there—a small rather good-looking woman, who Elena thought must be Esther's current *amie*, and a young baron who was trying to go to Princeton (a grandson or something, as Esther explained with her usual historical gusto, of the Eulenburg scandal in which the Kaiser had been involved). It was wonderful to see her; I called Elena and tried to make her come, but she had gone to bed disgruntled. I needed to see an American, especially one of my own generation, and we sat drinking highballs and explaining America to Esther's two Austrians. Her explanations of the U.S. to the French ladies of her circle have long been a specialty of hers, and she and I performed admirably together, up-setting the Europeans' preconceptions and astonishing them at every turn. I explained that the South had been an occupied country for ten years after the Civil War— thirteen, Esther corrected—and had never been reconciled to the Union. Strange, said the young man; we think of

the U.S. as so homogeneous. Esther then went on to tell
us that the only two things accomplished by [President
Chester] Arthur in his rather uninteresting administration had been civil service reform and taking the troops
out of the South. (It is curious to think that, for Esther,
to have married the grandson of Arthur means almost
what it would have meant for Proust to have made an
alliance with the Guermantes.) But the conversation may
have been more enjoyable for us than it was for the
people we were talking at, for they very soon withdrew.

April 24, 25, 26. I saw her after that three times. We
went there to dinner one night; the next night she came
to the Café Voltaire and sat with us, Petka, and Masha
while we ate and she waited to go to dinner; and the
last night she dined with us and Petka, Masha, Auntie
Maroussia, big and little Marina, big Marina's son and
his friend young Davison (Davidson?), at the Café
Voltaire again. This last evening was very jolly. Two
bottles of champagne and many other drinks. Masha had
already told me that when she had seen me coming in at
St.-Michel-sur-Orges, she had felt that I was an old
Russian cousin that they were used to having around,
and they now always referred to me—as the Minors in
Charlottesville do—as "cousin." General atmosphere of
Russian hospitality and family *uyutnost* [coziness]. The
whole force of the Russians was enough occasionally to
cause intermissions in Esther's customary monologues—
though I had found her, I thought, less relentless in her
compulsive monologuing than she had sometimes been
in the past. She did not bore me, and was sometimes
quite brilliant. The celebrated adage quoted by Mme.
de Sévigné from her cook that *"il faut qu'une porte soit
ouverte ou fermée"*—Esther said, when I talked about
Malraux's formulations, that it was quite impossible for

the French to recognize any other interaction: they couldn't understand that the majority of doors were usually more or less ajar. She had seen Hemingway sometime fairly lately and had been astonished at the way in which he kept up his boyishness; remembered how, when he had said that he would like to die in the bullring, Zelda Fitzgerald had said, "You're more likely to die in the marble ring!" —There are so few of my old friends left that it does me good to see Esther and talk about the Fitzgeralds, the Seldeses, the Bishops, Muriel Draper,[2] Dos and Hemingway and all that. She said that the more she lived in Europe, the more American she became—would have to go back soon. It made me reflect on the difference, now, between Europeans and Americans. Esther and I, in conversation, have a much wider range, but probably don't go into anything as deeply as the intellectuals in England and on the Continent do. But they are all more provincial now than we. This is the great shift that has taken place during my time. I felt in connection with her, too, the special characteristics of our race of the twenties: habit of leisure and at least enough money (she certainly does not now live in luxury), freedom to travel and read, to indulge and exhaust curiosities, completely uninhibited talks, resistance to challenge of the right to play, to the idea of growing old, settling down to a steady maturity. We made fun of the puerility of Hemingway: yet when I read, on the boat going home, his article in *Look* on his African adventures, I couldn't help finding it stimulating. He lives in an adventure book for boys, but there is something in myself that responds to it. There may be an element of this in my pursuit of the Dead Sea Scrolls, my visits to Zuñi and Haiti, my love of acquiring new alphabets.

—Esther told us that Lorna Linsley, who had now

quite lost her memory, had just come back from Kenya. Esther and I have both arrived at the age when it is already very pleasant to find someone who can talk about old friends, laughing at some news or memory of what is characteristic, something that anyone who had not known them would never understand. —She told me how Margaret Bishop and she—who had gone to school together—had been allowed by their parents, when they were in their early twenties, to make an unchaperoned trip to Paris. They had seen, she said, nothing but other Americans. One evening, when dining together, they had decided to be daring enough to order liquor, but had thought it more decent and ladylike to confine themselves to Cointreau, of which they drank a whole bottle. —Esther's left eye is now partly closed all the time, and this gives her a perpetually waggish look— half of a jolly Irishwoman, half of an old New York clubman who is drinking with you and winking. Yet this age, when her brown hair is smoky with gray, is more favorable to her appearance than youth. Elena said that she felt about her exactly as if she were a jovial rather aristocratic old gentleman, but I never felt that she is masculine or even fundamentally lesbian (and she certainly has no pose of this)—I feel that she is always a woman, and am aware of her gawky girlhood, her dubious social position as an Irish girl in New York, her disappointment with John Strachey, the absurdity of her life with Chester Arthur, and her exile in California (about which she spoke one evening—did not interest her, did not suit her). She is perhaps more comfortable, happier, now—freer and more at ease—than at any other time in her life. This life must have been full of frustrations, failures to find sympathy, alienation from persons she loved; but I have never seen a sign of self-pity. Her talking, her devouring of history, is of course a release of energy; and the things she makes up, imagines, show that she has had partly to live in a fantasy not too close to reality.

Helen had written to Joan Rose: When I get back, I'll tell you about my good days and my not so good days on land and on sea. —To Johnny Frank she had written a long description of the making of wine, as explained to her at Johannisberg, ending: And the last thing is you drink it.   *11/16/10*

I took Helen to Sacha Guitry's[3] film, *Si Versailles en était conté.* Unintentionally, extremely funny: the wildest development I have ever seen of the kind of thing that V. Nabokov makes fun of in Aldanov's[4] novels and then Max Beerbohm parodies in "Savonarola Brown." Every possible historical character appears: Bossuet preaches, Barrault is Fénelon, Molière kisses Armande Béjart; at a masque ball of Louis XV, a series of masked couples all turn out to be famous people; Marivaux unmasks and exchanges with his partner a little marivaudage; another masker is Fragonard—Oh, says his partner—Pompadour, I think—you must paint me! Immediately, you see him painting her. Voltaire happens to be there, and when the King drops in on them, makes a few skeptical remarks. Lavoisier, André Chénier, and Robespierre all happen to call at the palace the same afternoon. They discuss with Louis XVI and Marie Antoinette the abolition of capital punishment, and all are agreed that they would not care to be executed. Louis XIV in his old age, as he is being wheeled out of court, takes a paper from the hand of a man standing by and, tearing it up, says, *M. de Saint-Simon, vous avez l'habitude déplorable de rapporter inexactement les paroles et les personnages!* D'Artagnan makes a gesture of bravery, which greatly pleases the King; Fersen is seen with Marie Antoinette; Orson Welles appears as Franklin and somehow makes him monstrous and sinister; Edith Piaf sang "Ça ira." Sacha Guitry plays the old Louis XIV (leaving the youthful one to somebody else) in a cold and monotonous manner that suggests that he is really playing Lucien, his father, playing Louis XIV, with modifications learned from Jouvet.[5] Claudette Colbert is Montespan with a thoroughgoing Hollywood vulgarity probably intended to facilitate the success of the film in the U.S.

Sartre's *Kean*: Adaptation of an old play, which, however, he had largely rewritten—much better, in its less ambitious way, than *Le Diable et le Bon Dieu* was. But he made Kean essentially comic (played by Pierre Brasseur)—and the whole thing was quite Sacha Guitry, with tradition of the younger Sacha Guitry. —Always wonderful time to see how the French actresses—here especially Claude Gensac as the Comtesse de Krefeld—deliver lines and use their hands—also their elegant coiffures and way of wearing their clothes. —Brasseur galloped through the performance, which deliberately and of course more or less appropriately went in for being lame.

Another evening Petka took us to *Crinolines et Guillotine*, in a pleasant little old-fashioned, red-plush-upholstered, somewhat Provincetown Players-like little theater in Montparnasse, La Gaîté Montparnasse—a series of dramatic sketches by Henry Monnier, the creator of M. Prudhomme—a sort of dramatic equivalent for Daumier and Gavarni, the effect of whose drawings was aimed at in the production. Early work of the bitter French tradition, exploitation of the sordid and banal, and quite suitable for the age of Sartre: we exclaimed at how modern they were. —This production and *Les*

Bonnes were certainly the most distinguished things that we saw in any country on this visit.

11/12/10

April 26. Second lunch with the Malraux: I enjoyed them even more than the first time—was not ill and the weather was no longer cold; and Malraux seemed more likable and human than on either of the two previous occasions I had seen him: full of enthusiasm and looked you in the eye. Helen was whisked away, quietly and efficiently, to have her lunch—under supervision, I think —in another room with the two boys, and we had a good conversation. I started out by asking him about Indochina, which he analyzed at great length, saying that the part played by everybody was *"ridicule."* In writing about our earlier visit, I described his present tic inaccurately—it is something like a snort from the nose, and when he becomes excited and voluble, it sounds like the exhaust from a car. —We talked about the Guitry film, which his wife had seen but not he. I told him that he ought to go, but he shook his head. He said that the idea of history of the ordinary Frenchman was that wars had occurred because the King had *couché* with somebody or other. —He talked about T. E. Lawrence, of whom, during the war, he had written a study.[6] He said that L. and his brothers were all illegitimate, and that this had affected his psychology. He thought he had a passion for "the absolute," thought that he had deliberately degraded himself by reducing himself to the ranks, in order to prove to himself that he was "invulnerable." *The Mint,* he said, was scatological but not obscene— the writing very much *"travaillé."* I told him that he had made Lawrence into *un personnage de Malraux.* —He started off with one of his usual formulations on the subject of the Dead Sea Scrolls. —There were arguments based on two kinds of evidence: historical and philo-

logical—but he dropped it when I made attempts to present the problem in different terms. —After lunch, when Mme. M. and Elena had withdrawn, he sat beside me on the corner of the chair or the desk, talking vehemently into my face. He was amusing about the publishing business—we were talking about Doubleday and Douglas Black. I don't know how it is in America, he said, *mais les éditeurs français ne sont pas drôles!* I asked him whether it were true that Genet had stolen Gallimard's cuff links. *C'est trop beau,* he answered; I said that Dos Passos had told me that Gallimard[7] was a character out of Balzac (though I believe what he really said was that the Gallimard office reminded him of Balzac). *Un personnage de Stendhal,* said Malraux. Gallimard was *un millionnaire timide* and wore ordinary buttons on his cuff. Mme. M. came back at this moment, and he asked her to corroborate this. —I had at moments, as I had had on the earlier occasion, the impression that it was part of his present role—*père de famille,* etc.—to say little conventional French things of a kind that must previously have been foreign to him. For example, when I expressed relief at his telling me that he would send me the proofs of the Michelet journals—so that I should not have to go to the library and could spend the afternoon with Elena and Helen—he said to Elena something like: Your good angel is presiding over you today.

It is always bracing to see him. Elena said that the afternoon with him and the evening at the Gaîté Montparnasse, where the young people were working sincerely, with however little means, to do something distinguished in the theater, had made her feel better about France. She had been struck by—what I had not noticed—the deterioration of the goods they turned out—had used to make things better than America, now this no longer true. This was apropos of my speaking of Dupont-

Sommer's inferiority to Renan, that there was just a touch of something cheap about him.

Since I do not believe I wrote at the time any account of my first meeting with Malraux in the fall of 1935, when I was passing through Paris on my way back from Russia, I may as well add a few notes now. —I first went to the apartment where his first wife was living. He came in, as it were, from the outside, as if he lived elsewhere. The impression I got is corroborated by the account in André Gide's diary, where he speaks of M.'s feeling, during the Spanish war, that he had to get away from his household. He never looked at you, was terribly tense—his current tic was a spasmodic winking. They took me to dinner in a restaurant. When I talked about Soviet literature, he made at once the distinction between the better writers, who were read by a kind of elite, and the popular writers, such as the poet—I can't now remember his name—who regularly appeared in one of the papers. I said that I had had the impression in Russia that the literary world was divided into two groups—those who thought that Alexei Tolstoy was the greatest living writer and those who couldn't hear his name mentioned.

I should have included in the account above of our second 1954 conversation that he talked, during lunch, about Stalin, whom he had met (on, I think, two occasions) while visiting Gorky. He said that Stalin was very "abstract." I objected that he was too primitive. He asked me why I assumed that a primitive man could not be abstract. I think he took Stalin's Marxism too seriously, underrated the political boss, the Oriental intrigues. He told us how, when Stalin was present, Gorky had told them a story about one of his visits to Tolstoy. Gorky liked to watch people when they thought they were alone —had followed Tolstoy on a walk in the woods (I couldn't help wondering whether Tolstoy had not been aware of this, and when I told Elena's Russian relatives the story, they were sure he must have been): Tolstoy had stopped to look at a lizard sitting on a rock, with his heart visibly palpitating, then had said, You are sitting on a rock in the sun, and your heart is beating—you are happy; but I am not happy! Stalin's response to this was simply to drop his hand, which he had been holding against his body. I asked whether Stalin had had Gorky poisoned, but Malraux said definitely not. Yagoda had done away with him. He had wanted to marry Gorky's niece, and had gotten rid of first her husband, then Gorky.

We came back on the *Ile de France*, sailing the 27th, arriving May 3. Except for one afternoon, when it became a little rough, another calm voyage. Tony and Ann Turano, in whose house we were married in Reno, turned up in the cabin class. They had been having a holiday in Italy. He has grayed somewhat, is clear-eyed and straight—a sound and healthy type (so is she), very proud of coming from some race of the Calabrian mountains, who, he said, had preceded Greeks and Romans and have outlasted everybody. He is a "liberal" and has read a good deal, and they find life a little dull in Reno, though they get away to San Francisco. Best type of American of immigrant stock—something of Felix Frankfurter about him: his father had been an old-fashioned anticlerical; and after his writing in the *American Mercury* (Tony, not the father) an article on birth control, the Catholics had tried to discredit him in connection with an article about something else—similar to my experience (because Paolo Milano last summer convinced me that that was what happened when *Hecate County* was suppressed at the masked instigation of [Cardinal] Spellman) after the Catholics had apparently gotten worried by my reviews of Catholic books—especially, no doubt, the review of Evelyn Waugh's *Campion*,[8] which had provoked a couple of letters from Jesuits.

—Helen has learned a little German. She likes to say *"Genug!"* and makes a quite mature gesture with her hand when the waiter is helping her to something.

NOTES

1. French cabaret singer and actress (1867–1944). See *The Twenties*, pp. 88–91.
2. The leftist hostess who had lived next door to EW in New York City in 1932.
3. Sacha Guitry (1885–1957), French actor and playwright; *The American Earthquake* (1958), pp. 54–55. The film is described further in *A Piece of My Mind* (1956), pp. 63–64.
4. Mark Aleksandrovich Aldanov (1886–1957), Russian author who wrote a trilogy of novels about the French Revolution.
5. Louis Jouvet (1887–1951), eminent actor and director. EW is contrasting the acting styles and productions of the turn of the century with the modernism of Jouvet.
6. In 1942 Malraux was writing a study of T. E. Lawrence (of Arabia, 1888–1935), which he destroyed. He published a short essay from it in 1946 ("N'était-ce donc que cela?"), and based Vincent Berger, the protagonist of *Les Noyers de l'Altenburg* (1945), on Lawrence.
7. Gaston Gallimard (1881–1975), the French publisher.
8. Edmund Campion (1540–81), a Jesuit priest executed for treason. EW's review of Waugh's life of Campion (1935) appeared in the essay "Lesser Books by Brilliant Writers" (*The New Yorker*, July 13, 1945), condensed in *Classics and Commercials*, pp. 357–58.

WELLFLEET AND TALCOTTVILLE

May 14. After my travels, I find Wellfleet something of a void—though for Elena it seems to be wonderful to clean house and plant the garden. I am just getting myself going again. Chilly weather, a late spring—I am writing on May 14—combine with my just getting back to create the illusion that it is earlier than it is. I have done no solid spring work and must get started with my Israel articles. Find myself weighed down again with family responsibilities and the need of making money. In Europe, what with money from publishers in England, Elena's money from Germany, and the expenses of my Middle Eastern trip all paid by *The New Yorker*, I had most of the time the feeling that money problems didn't exist. Now, back home, it is as if I had been swimming in salt water, which buoyed me up, and had gone into a freshwater lake.

I left Paris with a certain reluctance, had moments—under Esther's influence—when I could almost imagine myself, as I had never done before, becoming a mellow old expatriate discussing world literature and history, and explaining America to Europeans, in some comfortable familiar café. I had begun, before I left, to have again something of my old feeling for Paris.

—A few days in New York, followed by New Haven and Boston, with a visit to Reuel at school, had me back in the American jitters again—too many cocktails, too many engagements, too many things to do. I arrived in Wellfleet a wreck, with a remembrance of my Paris and Salzburg complaint. As soon as I arrived—even before— I felt that the tension at home was infinitely worse than anything in Israel, even with their troubles with the Arabs. Failure of Dulles at Geneva, the McCarthy investigation all over the papers and people getting it on radio and television. All messy and hysterical; makes no sense. Since I have been back, I have been feeling a little guilty at spending so much time on Hebrew, the Dead Sea Scrolls, and all that. When, in Israel, I read that speech of Eisenhower's about foreign relations that sounded so incompetent and panic-stricken, I had the impulse to publish a commentary on it, taking it up paragraph by paragraph and showing the confusions and absurdities of the assumptions on which it was based.

May 18. Boydens:[1] I went over to see the Boydens in the afternoon. I had watched the McCarthy investigation on television and wanted to find out from Bud about the legal issues involved. He had been following it very closely, making notes on it. As an elder retired lawyer, I gathered he had been suffering from feelings of frustration, imagining what he would do if he could only get his hands on McCarthy. He didn't see how the investigation could be sabotaged now—though the incompetence shown was terrible. The best that could be hoped was that the army lawyer Welch would get a chance to cross-examine McCarthy. Polly, now shrunken and very deaf, was making a lemon meringue pie in the kitchen.

She interrupted our conversation to say that she needed cream and could combine taking me home with going to Wellfleet to get some. I said that I didn't want to go home yet and suggested her borrowing some cream from Phyllis Given next door, which she did. —Bud looked rather bizarre with his thin legs in shorts—either these or his shirt was red—with his heavy "corporation" bulging out above them. His face has been softening up here— in the overripe-tomato direction—and somebody said about him, meeting in Wellfleet, that he looked like an old squaw. I got today a depressing impression of his having been impeded and demoralized in what might possibly have been a distinguished career by Polly's idiotic and infantile idea of living her own life, crusading against capitalism and war, keeping in touch with the higher values, becoming a writer, etc. I used to tell her that she ought to go back to Chicago and she would tell me how awful Bud's life was, the low level of their social world at Lake Forest. If she had had any sense, she might have helped Bud to do something more with his abilities. He went to Harvard and Harvard Law and has, I find, considerable grasp of constitutional problems. He might have become a New Deal official at the time when Polly was invading Harlan,[2] working for pacifist organizations, and sleeping with God knows whom. He is evidently very fond of her, protective toward her, has remarried her twice; and now, in the long run, she has had it her own way, for he is now decaying with her up here. First they drink together for days and weeks, then they go on the wagon and suck up Coca-Cola. —This is the kind of thing that is disgusting and dismaying in America—I notice it especially getting back. Good abilities degenerate, go to waste—I think of all the friends of my school and college years who showed promise and didn't pan out. There are moments when I feel like that myself. The vulgarity of life in the United States shows up in one of its very bad aspects in the inability of professional men to persist beyond youthful years in living up to any high standard of civic conscience or science or art. Since the standards are not there in clear sight, since they are not supported by a hierarchy, the individual has to make more of a moral effort, which, combined with the effort involved in mastering any field with its skills, is likely to prove too much for him.

—The Boydens are a perfect example of the selfish American woman sabotaging the activities of the male. This is the present typical situation, but it has developed from the earlier one of the crass and preoccupied business-man who left cultural interests to his women. The latter situation is what Polly of course imagines about herself and Bud. These American situations always appear in Chicago in coarser and plainer terms, and Chicago is always behind the times from the point of view of the East. The woman who abandons her household and drops her *terre à terre* husband for her freedom and higher things was already for us obsolete when Polly came to New York. The formidable career woman, the ruthless bitch, was already the order of the day. Poor Polly was not up to this kind of role, she was too fundamentally childish; and Bud, who was very fond of her and un-doubtedly worried about her, has had to come to rescue her and take her under his wing and has finally suffered the fate of being turned into the old mother hen that Polly refused to be. —Though she worried about Archie in the war, she was jealous of him when he published a book.

—The situation between the Adlai Stevensons sounds a little like this. She, one of the people who run *Poetry* magazine and full of cultural interests, decided that Adlai was not up to her and divorced him. She was furiously jealous when he ran for President and was said to have circulated malicious rumors about him.

—Polly came in and remarked with a giggle that she hoped that McCarthy would take over, because then she would have to leave America.

June 7. I had a letter from Celia [Goodman], dated the third, telling me that Mamaine had died three days before. The last letter I had from her was dated May 26. I had been afraid, from these letters, that she was not going to get well. I miss her: things keep coming to my mind that I want to write her or eventually tell her, then I realize that I'll never see her again. A part of the attraction of London is gone. But Celia, who has just been married, may now have a better chance to lead a complete and independent life. I hope she is not doomed, too. I always felt that the expression of one side of Mamaine's face was tragic, and I haven't felt this with Celia. —Elena's first reaction was to be sorry for having been disagreeable about Mamaine in Paris.

Story about *Auntie Maroussia:* she had been denouncing the liberals, and Elena had gently mentioned that Nina Chavchavadze was a liberal—whereupon Auntie M. burst into tears: "The cousin (or niece?) of His Imperial Majesty a liberal!"

I can't get over Mamaine's death. I had hoped to get to London again in a couple of years, but I realize, whenever I think of it now, how much of my interest in it depended on her being there. It is almost as if there were no more London for me. I cannot think about the place at all without this pang of pain and surprise.

· · ·

Feeling I had early in the summer about Elena's beautiful bare long slim legs, coming out from under that white patterned skirt, made of rather heavy material and wide so that it stood out around her (did it have a design of gold thread?), as she sat on the blue divan, with her legs a little sprawling and wearing her simple new sandals. How wonderful to have them around the house!

Talcottville: I arrived July 4.[3] Though I had left Wellfleet with Elena and me both in very bad states of mind and though I was still worried about her, and though I had done a good deal of drinking at Zoltán Haraszti's[4] the night before I left Boston, as soon as I started out with Bill Peck driving to Talcottville, my head became thronged with ideas for books. An idea for a Christmas card to be called *Wit and Wisdom of Rabbi Ben Edmund* soon turned into idea of a small book, for which I later got the title "Off My Chest." I began to revise my dream novel, "How Long I Slept (I do not know)."[5] The summer visitors at Wellfleet at once frustrate me and tempt me. In coming over here, I shake off a real oppression.

—This year I have hardly been aware of the past, which used to come down on me so, to surround me, as soon as I arrived here. It was probably that I was so much preoccupied with the subject of the second of my Hebraic articles, which I finished here, writing steadily morning, afternoon, and night, in the big stuffed armchair from Red Bank, Mrs. McGuire bringing me meals, which I ate on the same table. But it is also that I now feel I fill the house, that it has no relation to anyone but me. Last summer and the summer before I had my cousins here [Helen Augur and the Sharps], and felt that the place belonged partly to them. Also: getting the new screens put in and the obsolete wiring removed makes the place look fresher and cleaner, and it is possible thoroughly to air it. For the first time nothing smells musty. And having the good-natured Mrs. McGuire to get meals and sweep the floors, the Linck boy to mow the grass, and the Rice boy to dispose of the rubbish and bring the water from the spring, makes living a good deal easier.

New York visit, July 13–17. When I had finished the Jewish article, I took it down to New York, and had Elena meet me there. We stayed in Walther Mumm's apartment, and it was almost like a clandestine love affair. We made love madly the first two days—she had to go on the third—and that and finishing the article and selling it for a good sum made me thoroughly happy. Our relations are now restored. Our relations had been getting demoralized about her attitude toward Talcottville—the only important thing about which she has ever been perfectly unreasonable: I only ask her to come one month in the summer. Her threat not to come at all this year had seriously disturbed me, because I had arranged for Reuel to be here in August, and I always have a conflict about leaving her.

Walther's apartment is ornamented with a series of old prints of the Rhine, a series of old prints of horses, and innumerable photographs of women: photographs of his old girls and pictures he has clipped from magazines. In every room is a picture of his handsome daughter, who was killed in a motor accident. In the bathroom, she appears on the wall in a large photograph, taken with Billy von Rath, and again in the corner of the medicine shelf, with a small American flag on either side (her mother was an American). In the bathroom is also a full-page drawing clipped from *La Vie Parisienne*. The heading is *Ça Fond*. A naked woman and a man in pajamas are sitting on a bed. Near the bed is an Alpine picture, in which the snows are melting and trickling out of the frame. Underneath it says: *"Il va falloir nous modérer."*

(San Left) 11/14/10

July 17. Fern met me at the Utica station. I am always impressed by the change from her appearance in the cow barn with her great rubber boots to her attractiveness (not that I don't always find her more or less attractive) when she is dressed up. She was looking today very *pimpante* in a dress that she told me she had just bought —a gray upper part over a white lightly flowered skirt. She has been wearing glasses this summer, and she now told me that she had had a blood clot last winter and had temporarily lost the sight of one eye. She had felt stunned, as if somebody had hit her over the head, and had then had such a headache for nine weeks that she had only kept going with codeine, but had never stopped working. The doctor thought it was a belated result of her fall when the winter wind blew her off the bridge to the barn two or three years ago. She has also had a length of her intestine taken out, and, as Otis told me last fall, had a hysterectomy. It is wonderful how she remains so vigorous and able to do so much. It was impressive to see her, as I did last Sunday, throwing it on the enormous haying machine, with her enormous boys about her.

—I brought back two *Persian kittens* for Helen, and have now become more fond of them than I have ever been of any cats, including Pussinka. They were six weeks old when I bought them. They are supposed to be male and female, but I have not yet been able to tell which is which. They seem to me fine and rather fragile, as if they were pretty little butterflies or moths. They have short little kitten tails. Their color is café au lait, which verges, however, on orange, and their eyes, which seem rather weak, are pale and bluish—will no doubt become green. Their profiles seem flatter than most cats'. I was surprised that they were able to get up the stairs—bouncing lightly from step to step. When they first arrived, a mouse—the first I remember to have seen here—came out from under the hat rack, sized up the situation, and went back again. Unless I shut the door when I am working, they come in and crawl all over me and chew the things on my table. Sometimes one will go to sleep on the back of the chair and the other on the windowsill beside me. Yesterday morning, as I was reclining in a two-piece chair I just bought, one of them lay on my chest purring. Sometimes they scamper madly or roll one another around on the floor. Now that I come to think of it, I have never had kittens in the house before. In general, I don't really like cats, but a cat seems to be a necessity for Elena, and Helen has been yearning for a kitten. It is also a bait to bring them to Talcottville.

—Saw the orange-spangled pane;
    The orange filigree turned white;
    Chairs, bedposts, pictures now appear;
    The daytime room grows clear—
—The vines on the stone barn door that make a wreath of
    shadow in the moonlight.
—The darkening light that gilds the earth
—This house the old back log of all our family.
—Those old half-opened doors—
—Standing ajar with their doorknob eyes

Aug. 9. These last three notes made on whisky. After going to bed early on several whiskies, I woke up to see the white carved fireplace, one of the simplest of them, shining in the moonlit room. I had dreamed so many

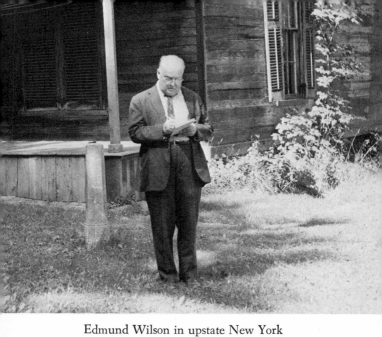

Edmund Wilson in upstate New York

The Stone House in Talcottville

Carl E. La Tray

times for so many years of coming back to this house and entering into possession; but in these dreams I seemed to be coming here only on a visit, had to go away again— always found things in disappointingly bad condition, sometimes had to drive away local people who had come in and were sitting around. But this summer, when we have got things in better shape and I feel that I have occupied the place myself, I had, at this moment, on waking up, the feeling—I think unique in my life—of a dream having literally come true—that is, the real experience—still under the influence of the drinks— corresponded closely with the dream, and was truly satisfactory as the dreams were not. I felt such satisfaction, such joy, that I could not help getting up—in the middle of the night—drinking some more whisky and walking around the house, delighted with everything about it. Of course, I was the worse for it the following morning, but I did not really regret it. *11/16/10*

Since my first entries above, since coming back from New York, I have felt that I now at last fully occupied the house. I do not feel the past as oppressive, do not feel that the families who have lived here are still present and crowding me out. Preoccupied with Israel and the Dead Sea Scrolls to the point that I was hardly conscious —writing or reading on these subjects morning, after-noon, and night—of the countryside around, and the very fine views from the windows had come to be like pictures hung on the walls. I had virtually been living in Palestine, and there was nothing here (there is so much at Wellfleet), even the past, to impede it. What was going on in my mind could expand in comfort and freedom, and take up as much room as it pleased. —But, with no exercise, hardly going outside the house, having my meals brought me by Mrs. McGuire at the table

where I worked, I began—with no visitors except Paul
Chavchavadze and Pozhidaev,[6] who just stopped over
a night, and the interlude of Louise and Henrietta[7]—by
the end of three weeks, to feel a little dotty and was glad
when the family came.

Elena, Helen, and later Reuel. Elena this summer has
got on somewhat better. She has installed an electric
stove and done over the dining room and the smaller
sitting room. I had sent some of the furniture to be recovered, and the "mohair" of the samples I chose proved
to be simply plush. She was horrified by it at first, but
then discovered that the darker pieces, which had a
gooseflesh-making sheen in the light of the living room,
looked all right in the duller dining room. It was a good
thing to eliminate the figured wallpaper, which completely killed the pictures. To our surprise, the old oval
landscapes for the first time looked quite handsome.
The blue skies came out quite attractively against the
new gray of the walls. (These came from Rufus Belere
in Utica—painted sometime in the 1840s?—perhaps
imaginary portraits from photographs, of European
scenes.) —Elena also likes the Sharps, who are living
in Aunt Addie's house, and we have cultivated the
Edmondses more, and met at their house Mrs. [Con-
stance] Robertson, the granddaughter of John Humphrey
Noyes,[8] and the Edward Roots of Hamilton College
(Root a son of Elihu Root).[9]

Aug. 31. We made an expedition to Clinton and Kenwood—had lunch with the Roots and visited the Oneida
Community with Mrs. Robertson. They had looked up
the records on my grandfather, Walter Kimball, when
he was a student at Hamilton. I found that he had missed
only his senior year, when, according to Mother's story,

his wallet was stolen, so he could not pay his tuition. Later, when he was practising medicine in Eatontown [N.J.], they made him an honorary M.A. He was in the class of '51; and I found in the lists of those years Knoxes, Wetmores, and Clevelands. Charles Dudley Warner[10] was a classmate of his. A John Jay Knox, of whom there is a portrait, was an important early trustee, and I discovered that Knoxville is quite near there. The Knoxes in the lists of those years all give their address as Augusta, a little town right next to Knoxville. The trustee of the portrait must have been the father of the John Jay Knox —father of the Seabright Knoxes—who was Comptroller of the Currency through several Republican administrations and only displaced on the advent of Cleveland. The Knoxes and the Kimballs must have known one another even before they lived next door at Monmouth Beach, and it was natural for them to intermarry. There was also a Martin L. Kimball from Leyden in one of those classes —I am not sure who he was.[11]

The Roots are real Henry James characters—not the timid Americans abroad of the New England Prufrock type, but New Yorkers from the [better] upstate towns —Mrs. Root from Albany, he from Clinton. (She always made a point of letting you know that the Roots had originally kept a tavern, the house they are living in, that Oren Root the grandfather had with effort got himself an education; she, from Albany, had, I was told, some sort of old Dutch name and a highly developed social technique.) One of the other ladies reminded me that James's "the American" came from Utica[12] and Daisy Miller from Schenectady. I enjoyed the old Albany of Mrs. Root—more worldly and flexible than Boston, very able intellectually, old-fashioned-snobbish, a little bleak; a gray, almost completely masculine face—she reminds me of Sybil in [Angus Wilson's] *For Whom the*

Cloche Tolls. Elena thought she greatly exerted herself to take an interest in her husband's collection of paintings and his activities in connection with the Utica gallery. He was deaf, wore a hearing aid, talked in a low voice; did not, I think, have very much real taste, and had obviously been sold a good deal of second-rate stuff by the various New York galleries from [Maurice] Prendergast, George Luks, [Arthur B.] Davies, Everett Shinn, through Peggy Bacon[13] to [Jackson] Pollock and [Mark] Tobey. He had even bought a [Saul] Steinberg drawing, and there was a mobile in the dining room, which was turned on at the end of lunch. There was still something rather Victorian about the house; Elena thought that the furnishings did not show much taste, but she has no feeling, no affection, as I have, for this sort of American thing. Mrs. Root inquired at lunch whether we wanted the light on or off. She was all for having it off, though she said that Edward liked to have it on: he thought it helped him to read people's lips—"a domestic issue." There was an old-fashioned butler in a dinner jacket, rather stooping and not very efficient. Mrs. Root got up to carve the roast, which was on a side table against the wall. Later on, in her long cape, she made a magistral figure. Back of the house, a great myrtle bank, winding garden paths, and woods—round the house, all the old-fashioned flowers. Next door lived the grandson of Grant, who had married Edward Root's sister.

Hamilton is a good little self-contained isolated specimen of the old-fashioned American "liberal arts" learning —originally, like Dartmouth, founded to educate the Indians. There was an Indian chief, a friend of the founder, buried in the college graveyard; but the last Indian had gone there in 1803. The reddish local stone— as the president said to me, taking me around the campus

Lillian Burnham, Dorothy Sharp, Huldah Loomis, Helen and
Rosalind Wilson; Edmund Wilson and John Gaus; Fern and
Otis Munn and Jane Gaus, Talcottville, 1955

—gave the various buildings their unity. There was also a purplish red shale that the Roots and other old inhabitants traditionally had on their drives, but which he seemed to disapprove of on the ground that it made a mess when it was tracked indoors. A "Languages" building and a "Philosophy" building. I was glad to see this place. Compact and self-sufficing, still maintaining a pretty high standard, it made me understand more solidly the Kimballs and the rest. I could imagine them going to their classes in the rather ugly yet not unimpressive old rectangular stone narrow-windowed buildings that look like the old halls at Princeton. There is a rather good white near-Colonial chapel that is peculiar in having three stories, the top one simply an attic.

11/17/10

I come to feel, when I have been here for any length of time, the *limited* character of upstate. It does not go very far back nor does it come very far forward. A period of American life is preserved here, and is still quite flourishing; and yet there is often about it a kind of cold-storage quality. There is something of this about Walter Edmonds.[14] His work—though I have only really read about the first fifty pages of *Rome Haul*—is a kind of historical fiction. There was much talk at lunch at the Roots' about how his invention had, as he said, been "flagging"—he had not been able to get started on anything new for something like nine years. His friends kept suggesting subjects. Oughtn't he to go abroad? The trouble is, I suppose, that his fiction has all come out of boyhood fantasies up here. He told me how *Rome Haul* was written as the result of a winter spent here—he had never really made the canal trip, had imagined almost the whole thing. His father, from Utica, acquired the farm as the result of the foreclosure of a mortgage (he has told me about this several times, and I feel that it is a little on his conscience). He had liked it here because he thought it was like Canada, had married very late (was a lawyer). Walter has a little of the look of the bric-a-brac, furniture, engravings, in one of those old Utica houses, with tall doors and windows and sober proportions but pleasantly ornamented, to a greater or less degree, with the decorous tassels and fringes of specially carved woodwork. For all his well-mannered dignity, his rather refined face, there is a touch of cold-storage about him—his pallor, his chiseled features. The people are nice here and decent (Boonville is a smaller edition of Utica); serious-minded, moderately cultivated; but there is no great liveliness of interchange, no density of the "spiritual" life. Religion hardly exists. Walter Edmonds has little contact with the modern world. He lives like a squire in a charming setting: big woods on the hill, big red barn, little stream that runs through the lawn, dark Adirondack-type lake artificially made by his father—but he is almost alone in his squirehood. The last contemporary event that seems to have interested him was the milk strike of 1933 (I think the date is right), and that is already now for him a historical event like the other events in his novels.

Mrs. Edmonds comes from Bangor, Maine, and says that her upstate New Yorkness is merely a kind of dream, that she is not unaware of the fact that there are other beautiful parts of the world besides upper New York State. Edmonds says that he is "completely unreliable about it," as, as a matter of fact, am I. —Elena thinks—what had not struck me—that Mrs. Edmonds looks unhappy. Elena still sullenly refuses to reply when you say it is a nice day or that the landscape or the sky is beautiful. One day, coming out of the Loomises', she said to me, "You see what I mean?" It turned out that she had already said to me that you expected here to breathe fresh air, and then what you got was the smell of cows—a novel point of view for anyone up here, for whom the smell of cows is fragrant. The children cannot help but be affected by her own negative attitude. Reuel took a bicycle trip to Canada, booked in a couple of square dances, then decided he wanted to go back to Wellfleet. Helen, dictating a letter, wanted to say it was "very dull here": when I remonstrated with her a little, she said, "Well, make it dullish." It is true that the high altitude and the breathlessness and heaviness of the midsummer days let Elena down and make her languid. She complains that she feels as if she could not breathe. Such weather merely makes me sleepy. She thinks, perhaps rightly, that in Wellfleet I am overstimulated, and that Talcottville keys me down to a point where I am steady and comfortable. —I induced her to give a party, which turned out to be quite a success and with which she was pleased herself. She depends very much on having people like her, and she now begins to feel that they do.

Elena and Helen went back Sept. 3, and I am staying on till the 9th or the 10th. I find it delightful for a while living here by myself. I understand that it is dull for the children. At Reuel's age (though as a younger child I had been so happy here) I did not want anymore to come to Talcottville at all: like him, I was meeting new people, visiting in livelier places.[15] But at my age, when my principal aim is to write, it is the ideal place for me to retire to. I have been sitting out on the lawn in the afternoons, giving the cats an outing, reading a little, looking out on the country, watching the repairs on the house and enjoying the changes in the weather—some days soft, warm, and dry, others on the verge of rain.

I never get over feeling how curious and piquant it is, to find a house so commodious and comfortable, designed with so much taste, even elegance, in the midst of what was once a wilderness and where now one looks out on a farmland that—with the blue Adirondacks in the distance—still merges with wild forests and hills. I also like having the life of the village around me—though sometimes I wish the road still ran, as Dorothy M[endenhall] says it originally did, just over the hill in front of the house, where the line of trees shows where it was. —A few days ago, from my bed, I looked out into a kind of great grotto of green made by the two high elms and watched the yellow leaves falling into it at intervals one by one. Today (Sept. 8), the trees are so thinned that the cavern hardly exists, and the leaves that have not fallen yet are growing yellow. In front of the house, the maple has been coming out in patches of orange-pink that first flared and are now fading. The lawn, which a few days ago was cleared up by Jim Linck, is covered again with leaves. —I should like to stay another week, but must go back on account of Reuel, who has to go back to school the 18th.

—When I think of *Mamaine* now, it is already with the pathos of something that belongs to youth—though it isn't ten years ago that I was with her in London and Rome—for though I never succeeded in getting her to Rome, she was present to me so much and so vividly (I never rode out in a fiacre without imagining her beside me) that when I remember it, she is usually there. —I can't bear to think of her shriveling up, losing her breath, alone in the hospital there—so much energy, brains, and charm—having had to divorce Arthur Koestler, repudiate him publicly in court, with Celia gone to her husband in the country.[16] I think that what she looked for from me was, as tended to be the case with her, something paternal; but I was not able to give her much of even this when she came over to Paris just after the divorce. I wish I could have seen her in the hospital. I never ever talked to her about Koestler—though I saw her occasionally for a meal alone. I never talked to her about anything personal.

Another illusion of the time sense: The first day that Jean Sharp was here, we all went to Flat Rock, but without her mother [Dorothy], and it all seemed perfectly natural—as if she were her mother at that age and as if I were again that age, too (actually she is older than her mother when I used to see her here). She very much resembles her mother—and seems to be a little bored with people telling her so—and is perhaps even prettier than Dorothy was.

Visit of Louise and Henrietta [Fort] (July 31–August 4): I was glad to have them together like this, and to restore my good relations with Louise. She was no longer debauched or hysterical, talked perfectly soberly and sensibly. I took her over to Flat Rock and we had, for the first time, a friendly middle-aged conversation. She said that Henri had (I think) multiple arthritis but wasn't allowed to know it, for fear it would affect her state of mind so that she would develop into a chronic invalid. Louise thought that it was partly psychological anyway—the result of the breakup of her marriage, the death of her little boy, her failure to connect with life in any practical way. The lack of coordination she had always shown—dropping things, getting things wrong— had lately become much worse. I was shocked, when I met her at Utica, at how sharpened, drawn, and aged her face was and seeing that—she said, from her fall at

Flair—she was still a limping cripple. She had gotten the time of both the trains wrong, and though she had told me on the phone that Louise's, from Chicago, got in later than hers from New York, was surprised that Louise was not here yet. When I went to meet Louise, I first mistook two other women for her. She had changed —grown much thinner and looked older, and looked, in a touching way, as if she had been through a great deal of suffering. She had had a hysterectomy a couple of years before and, before that, had been in a sanitarium to get over her narcotics and alcohol. In the midst of this sojourn she had tried coming out, but had run into Fern Insull and gone to a nightclub and found herself back in the terrible thirties, and voluntarily returned to the sanitarium; had given up having lovers, which had made her practice "duplicity" and go counter to her "simple nature" (or some phrase of the kind) and had been too much for her nerves—though she was born under the sign of Gemini and took some stock in astrology. (All this as we were walking through the pastures.) She had been highly successful as a receptionist at the advertising agency where she worked. A man from another agency had offered her more money if she would come to them; but, at a party where they had been discussing it, Peter had become jealous, had hit her and told the man that all advertising men were second-rate and dreadful and were spoiling the (??) Club. —Her doctor had told her she should take a job—not charity or anything of the kind, but something she would be paid for, and this had proved to be a sound suggestion—she was no longer dependent on Peter. What was sound and strong in her character, I saw, had reasserted itself. She had decided, from her talks with the doctor, that I had been right about the influence on both the girls of their father. The doctor's theory had been that she had loved him, Henri hated him. Since his death, after years of estrangement, she and H. and their brother Gerrit were all on good terms again. —Henrietta's current dominant girlfriend is Marianne Moore, about whom she constantly talks—much better than "Lady Esther," since she is both intellectual and entertaining and H. is not financially dependent on her. —The visit, in its way, was a great success. We renewed our old relation on a much less frenetic and childish level. I had always felt badly about Louise's last visit to New York. —But when they first arrived in Talcottville, I had been alone so long that I had difficulty adjusting myself to them—could not seem to hear what they said—though this was partly due to their still having the habit of talking for one another. I could not at first get myself out of Palestine, so gave them a little lecture on the scrolls—which H. declared was fascinating but to which Louise's reaction was that I was just a destructive character who liked to upset people. H. had been scared by her doctor and could drink nothing but what she called "white rum," preferably of some special brand which I wasn't able to get her in Utica; Louise drank nothing at home, but had two or three drinks here, and even these made her ill the next morning. It might have been better if we, none of us, had had any, but the habits of the 1920s and 1930s are still very hard to get rid of when old 20ers and 30ers meet.

—With Louise now, I always feel old: deaf, sodden, crotchety, arthritic, and woolly; with Elena—eleven years younger than I—despite irritability and gout, I seem a good deal younger. Yet Elena is so much more mature than Louise and is always complaining about getting old.

Louise supplied the explanation for Bud Boyden's retiring to Truro and ceasing to practice law. [It] perhaps

throws some light on Phyllis's[17] feeling that there was
something about him she did not like. Does not confirm
my theory of the Boyden situation as expressed a few
pages back. I suppose that Polly can't be blamed. Her
periodical revulsion may have been partly based on something bad in him. But does one know about any couple
—even one I know better than the Boydens?

I enjoy "galvanizing" this old house into life, as I
feel I have at last been doing, making it express at last
my own personality and interests, filling it with my own
imagination; substituting myself for Talcotts, Bakers,
Reeds, and my own parents, yet feeling a continuity
with them, basing myself, in some sense, on them—the
older I grow, the more I appreciate them. Intellectually
and geographically, I travel farther away from them, yet
also now fall back more on them, probably become more
like them; feel more comfortable and myself than probably anywhere else in the world.

Sept. 8. Last night Dorothy [Sharp] was showing me
Minnie Collins's collection of photographs. She passed
me a picture of the house here, with furniture that is
no longer here and the plates that I now remember
hanging on the wall, as the fashion was then, above the
big doorway in the double room. I said that I was going
to put it in my pocket, that the Loomises would never
do. She said sharply, I'm going to take it myself, I have
much more right to it than you. I said that I was making
a collection of pictures of the house, and she answered,
So am I. This was rather unlike her, and I thought it
was due to the fact that she had been somehow *froissée*
at dinner—I'm not quite sure how—by my attempts to
persuade Malcolm to come to Wellfleet and something I

had said about it to her. But her dignity at once asserted itself, and she said, Take it if you want it. We put it back in the box. —Not only did she lose her mother here at seven, but she undoubtedly has come to feel, from her grandmother's chagrin and her aunt Dorothy Mendenhall's love for the place, that her family have been dispossessed. Yet she tells me that her grandmother sided with the Bakers and they were, in consequence, ostracized by the Talcotts. —I hardly know Dorothy Sharp. Between the time in our teens when she was the first little girl I had loved and the time, so many years later, when I saw her in Chicago, the summer I was teaching there, was too long a gap, and now, after another interval, I find her here again, and I see her in a different light. Against my expectation and a little disappointingly, she is positive and trenchant like her grandmother and aunt, a little on the anti-men side; but I felt last night at dinner, in connection with the incident I've mentioned above, that she loved Malcolm and was somehow afraid of losing him and not living up to him or something. I wish I could make better connections with her, have done so a little better this summer than two summers ago: but I am shy about talking to her about her childhood here and all that. I asked her to write me a memorandum about her memories of the house, and she told me the next day that, after thinking it over, she couldn't bring herself to do it—some of her memories too harrowing—the night her father had come up for the 4th of July and set off all the fireworks over Sugar River. I couldn't bring myself to ask her why this was harrowing.

Oneida Community: high-ceilinged narrow halls; woodwork on the outside sometimes ugly, sometimes not bad; braided tapestries under glass that were faded and rather dismal; auditorium, with paintings on the ceiling of figures that we couldn't identify; photographs of various festivities, with the bearded John Humphrey Noyes, and much like other upstate gatherings of rural people; visitors inevitably try to imagine the breeding *esclavos*, but find themselves rather frustrated. Mrs. Robertson a little shy about this phase of the community. A crusader preacher at Hamilton had succeeded in putting it out of business, and it had only been very recently that the people of the original Oneida group would allow themselves —as Mrs. Robertson had for lunch that day—to come to visit the college. She told me that she had, as a child, never known any children who were not her cousins, and, when asked who the baby was in the painting of the Sistine Madonna, had said, Why, that's little Cousin Jesus. —Elena said that the place reminded her of a German sanitarium; and it is true that it, too, has something of the New York State cold-storage quality.

Fern and her children: She loves them, always knows where they are, feels that she must always look after them. On our way to the Antlers for dinner, she and Otis were saying that they would soon meet the boys coming back from the woods, and in the midst of the conversation in the restaurant, she was aware of it at once when they passed, one behind the other, in their trucks. Driving into Utica in the morning to take Elena and Helen to the airport, she said that they would soon meet Ann going in to work to Boonville from Stittville. When we passed her, the girl did not notice her mother. She complains that the boys don't take farming seriously and can't be left alone with the dairy. Chet is likely to drop everything and go to see his girl. If he marries her in the fall, maybe he will settle down there. Otis loses patience with the cows: if they won't let themselves be milked, he will smack them and shove them, and you can't do anything with them that way. Fern does have something animal and bovine that makes her good with both people and animals—*"Dans la fréquentation des bêtes."* She married Otis at eighteen; had been nursemaid to the Bests' daughter, and worked in the soda fountain. I like to hear her and Otis bantering one another; one feels in her, in spite of her brusqueness—or rather abruptness—a sound basis of good relations with everybody. I find that I like to have her around the house, painting ceilings, walls, and floors, as she was during my first weeks this summer. So different from poor Helen [Augur], who has no real relations with anybody, and is always trying to establish them or substitute for them by importuning people with attentions or complaints that make them pay attention to her. Yet I thought she was better this summer than last when she arrived the night before I left: California had done her good, and she was, I think, pleased by the favorable reviews of her book— displayed great packets of notes she had taken for her new book, was glad to get to Talcottville. I took her to the Sharps', where she showed off a little and was eagerly greeted by the Loomises. I thought the evening went well. —If Fern is going somewhere and sees her little grandson, she picks him up in her gruff way and takes him along. Coming to my house just after I had arrived with the kittens, the very first thing she did was go into the kitchen to see them: "The tuttin' little things!" She held one during our conversation.

At Kenwood (Oneida Community), Mrs. Robertson's cousin, the librarian, had a very pronounced form of the local accent: "Carloile," "surproise."

· · ·

Dreamlike purity, again: like the fairy tales (Beauty and the Beast) in which somebody lost in a forest finds a well-appointed castle, in which he is waited on by bodiless hands. Mrs. McGuire gets me meals and sweeps, Albert Grubel drives me, Jimmy Linck cuts the grass, Mrs. Failing does the laundry, Mr. Rice attends to the electrical arrangements, his boy Eddie brings water, burns the rubbish, and buries the garbage behind the house. They come and go, in and out of the house—I take them for granted, hardly think of them. Mr. Reber from Boonville mends the furniture, paints the hearths, reframes the pictures; the mail is brought to the box, without my being bothered to pay extra postage; a boy brings the Sunday papers. Mrs. McGuire gets groceries from the village store or supplies them from her own house.

Strange that the family, in its Talcottville connection, should now include mainly farmers, the Munns, who have largely lost their education, and rather "advanced" academic figures and writers: the Sharps and the Mendenhalls, Helen Augur and myself. There is no middle-class commercial element. The Loomises and Lillian Burnham are an intermediate group: both are farmers, but the Loomises all went to college, and Mrs. Burnham was once a schoolteacher.

At the end of our (quite successful) party, the people, all the "family" who stayed late, sat around the fire in the big north room. Otis and Mrs. Burnham talked about farming with feeling and expressed themselves well. Otis quoted the rhyme:

> Some folks say there ain't no hell.
> They've never been farmer—how can they tell?

But then they went on to advantages that offset the constant hazards: independence, freedom from office routine. Mrs. Burnham said that the idea of producing food gave her satisfaction. Even the Loomises, one feels—though they talk of it—are reluctant to sell their farm. I can see the satisfaction they derive from farming—dealing directly, in the magnificent setting, with animals and fields that belong to them. —Otis must lie awake nights—he so often returns to the subject—thinking about the 50,000 acres, including several Adirondack lakes, that the Munns once owned. He has bought a little of it back, but it irks him, as he told me this summer, to think that his boys are now trucking logs from land that once belonged to the family. He mentioned also that they had owned 10,000 acres in Texas before it became a state. He wishes he could find some defect in the titles of the present owners of the Adirondack land.

Otis, when Helen Augur had asked him how he had liked *Hecate County*, had answered, *"When Knighthood Was in Flower* is more my style."

NOTES

1. Polly Boyden, who had written one novel, and her husband, Bud, a retired Chicago lawyer. *The Thirties, passim; The Forties,* pp. 8, 221–22.

2. The Harlan County, Kentucky, coal strike. *The Thirties,* pp. 165–66, 177–78.

3. *Upstate,* pp. 105–36.

4. Zoltán Haraszti, librarian at the Boston Public Library.

5. Apparently an allusion to EW's unfinished novel. *The Forties,* pp. 10–46.

6. Dmitri Petrovich Pozhidaev, Soviet diplomat.

7. Louise and Henrietta Fort, longtime friends of EW. *The Thirties* and *The Forties, passim.*

8. John Humphrey Noyes (1811–86), the prophet of "perfectionism," established the Oneida Community in 1848, a eugenic experiment involving a central committee that regulated marriages within the group.

9. Elihu Root (1845–1937), Secretary of State, 1905–9; U.S. senator, 1909–15.

10. Charles Dudley Warner (1829–1900) collaborated with Mark Twain on *The Gilded Age*.

11. In *Upstate*, p. 123, EW identifies the John Jay Knox in the portrait as the Comptroller of the Currency under Presidents Hayes and Arthur. His daughter, EW's aunt Caroline, married Reuel Kimball, Walter Kimball's son. Martin Luther Kimball was one of Walter Kimball's uncles.

12. The lady was in error. James never gave Christopher Newman's place of origin.

13. EW's artist friend. *The Thirties* and *The Forties, passim*, and *The Shores of Light*, pp. 70–74.

14. Walter D. Edmonds, Utica-born novelist living in Boonvilie; *Upstate*, pp. 41–42, 129–31. *Rome Haul* (1929).

15. *A Piece of My Mind*, p. 213.

16. See Celia Goodman, *Living with Koestler: Mamaine Koestler's Letters, 1945–1951* (1985), p. 193.

17. Phyllis Duganne (Mrs. Eben Given), Truro resident who wrote short stories for *Collier's* and *American Magazine*.

1955–1959

AUDEN IN NEW YORK

March 21, 1955. Auden and his birthday party: I have
got to like him and usually see him when I come to
New York. When I was living with Rosalind in Henderson Place, he would devour in a headlong and hungry
way one of the colored cook's rather crude dinners. If
Rosalind came into the room when we were sitting
around talking, it would completely throw him off. He
has never learned how to behave with women. His father
was a doctor in Birmingham and his mother was a nurse,
and, as a doctor's family, he told me, they were consigned
to a position of social inferiority. He was sent away to a
"private" school at nine, then went on to Winchester
and Oxford. When he was out of the university, he went
back to the public schools to teach. He seems to have
grown up in these monastic institutions and never to
have had any chance to fall in love with a woman or
even to know women socially. I am not sure that his
homosexuality isn't all a dreadful mistake: but he is
certainly a homosexual chauvinist. He assured me that
W. S. Gilbert[1] was "queer"—on account, I suppose, of
his attitude toward stout aging women, which I should

put down merely to the general English boorishness about women. He enthusiastically encouraged the rumor that Eisenhower was homosexual, and after listening to a broadcast by Stalin with Nicholas Nabokov[2] said, "He's just an old queer!" He also told Harry Levin that Falstaff was "just an old queer." He himself takes a somewhat self-conscious aggressively masculine attitude toward his boyfriends, though Elena thinks he sometimes resembles a nice old English aunt.

He lives in a squalor of which I always thought till recently he was completely unaware. Spender was horrified when he saw his little house on Fire (Shelter?) Island; and Stravinsky said about him, "He is the dirtiest man I have ever liked." So he surprised me the other night by suddenly bursting out with "I hate living in squalor—I detest it!—but I can't do the work I want to do and live any other way." He had just said—in one of his hard-and-fast formulations—that the Americans had a sense of comfort but no sense of luxury. He liked spending the summer in Ischia, because there he had high ceilings and could have a barber come in and shave him. (Elena likes him but finds him a little hard to take on account of his boorishness. Once, in a previous winter, when I had gone out to buy liquor and left her alone with Auden, she said that the conversation stopped completely till I had come back. After his coming to dinner the other night, she said that he made her feel as if she were not there.)

Nonetheless, I have the impression now more than ever that, whether he knows it or not, he deliberately goes in for uncomfortable, sordid, and grotesque lodgings. A few years ago he was living on lower Sixth (?) Avenue. He had told me while we were dining in a restaurant that he was happy about his new apartment, which had an extra room in which he could put up Spender or

Isherwood.[3] The apartment turned out to be simply a floor in a building devoted to fur lofts. He told me, as we climbed several flights of stairs, that he had insured his typewriter and phonograph against theft. The place was completely without heat when we entered (it was sometime in late fall or winter), and Wystan started up some queer kind of little stove, but we sat in our overcoats and our breath went up in vapor. A long curtainless window gave a view on the shabbiness of Sixth Avenue with its cheap stores and small neon signs. The guest room was a thing like a doghouse built completely *inside* the loft (which was hardly or not at all divided by partitions into rooms), so that its roof was some distance below the ceiling. On one side of it were closets and drawers, which had been carpentered as part of the doghouse. When Lys Dunlap had first come over, he had offered, in his kindness, to put her up, and this was where he had proposed to put her. The loft belonged to a sculptor, from whom Wystan rented it, and the back part was strangely equipped with a compressed-air machine and other unrecognizable appliances, which I took at first to be furrier's machinery. He turned on the compressed-air machine to show me how it worked—with some difficulty, sprawling across something in order to get at the switch. It made a loud buzzing noise, but was not in the least interesting. He had even more difficulty in turning it off, and this held up the conversation for some minutes. There were some very unattractive statues—made, as I remember, out of some dark substance standing or lying about. When we returned to the front of the loft, which was littered with papers and books, he produced a bottle of hock from a case which he had laid in, which was lying right there on the floor, the bottles still packed in their straw. He then showed me a book on Victorian plumbing, a great favorite of his and Betjeman's, which B. told me later, when I saw him in London, really belonged to him but had been carried off to America by Auden. One of the high points was a picture of an evening party, at which the host was pulling the bell rope and getting no response. Beside it was a picture of the butler falling head first down the drain, some such caption as "Nobody answers the bell." This illustrated the importance of having sound covers on drains. (When I later described these lodgings to Katherine Raine, she told me that William Empson lived in a somewhat similar way.[4] He would invite people to dinner and give them simply the contents of a can, which he had just heated up; and on one occasion she had picked up a book that had the spine of a kipper for a bookmark.) Yet, as I looked out on the night of Sixth Avenue, I had something like a moment of wistfulness as I thought of my own independence in the poverty and responsibility of my one-room apartment on West 13th St. Many writers and artists have a phase of this, and it makes them feel their independence and helps them, in a sort of asceticism, to assert their virtue and power. It is a way of putting oneself to a test, makes a base for more prosperous days and guarantees one against compromises. But Wystan has condemned himself to this, so far as I can see, for all the rest of his life—as he has to homosexuality—and, in a puritanical way, seems to feel he is acquiring merit by living—with a touch of fantasy—in the most unattractive way possible.

—At some point before I married Elena, I went to a Christmas party of Wystan's. It was a very strange affair. His pansy friends sat around in a circle—they were extremely unappetizing. In one of his poems he speaks of making a point of being kind to "a Lideola," and these must have been Lideolas, whom he cultivated as part of the acquiring of merit—just as he told me once that he had to speak at a meeting to raise money for delinquent children. There were two or three anomalous women, a minority, broken in to the Lideolas. Throughout the evening he played Wagner on the phonograph, with the volume turned to full force. He gave everybody a present —me a reproduction of a Toulouse-Lautrec drawing of Yvette Guilbert, which I was very glad to have. He showed me an old metallurgical book, which he said was his bedside companion. He had originally intended, he told me, to be a mining engineer; and he had easily acquired an affinity for abstract inorganic phenomena. I felt that he was trying a little to explain the absence in his verse of human personalities and relationships. Later, he wrote the series—very characteristic of him—of geological poems, lakes, mountains, plains, etc.

For his birthday party this year, he sent out a printed invitation that imitated engraving and had in the corner "Carriages at 1." Elena had been ill and did not go—I think she resented a little, too, his bad manners of the other evening. Louise Bogan and I went together. We had written him a birthday sonnet, contributing alternate lines:

To Wystan Auden
On the Occasion of His Forty-ninth Birthday

Auden, that thou art living at this hour (EW)
   Delights us. How much duller wert thou not! (LB)
   And we have need of thee. A drear dry rot
Spreads its dank mould throughout the Muses' Bower;
Orc Tolkien* usurps Aladdin's Tower:
   The Groves of Academe are cold and bought;
   And countless other things have gone to pot.
Oh, Wystan, hear us! Implement our power.

* Or, if it is only two syllables: The orc Tolkien . . .

· · ·

How like some shaggy grampus, dolphin-finned,
    Sporting with smaller fish of lesser price,
Shaleing a spray that sparkles in the wind,
    Or diving to depth-pressures in a trice
—Unlike the salmon, never to be tinned—
    Thou hump'st a path through heavy seas of ice. (EW)
    Thou bear'st a banner with this strange device:

                                    Excelsior

I read this aloud, and he told us that he was going to
have it framed, as he had done a birthday card that
Stravinsky had made for him. He started to show it to
us, then snatched it away. Kallman removed something,
and Wystan explained—with much grinning and giggling
on the part of Wystan and Kallman—that a pornographic
drawing had been removed. At this point, I was much
depressed. There were only a few people—the same
unappetizing pansies and the two or three similar women.
The apartment in St. Marks Place had been that of an
abortionist who had died. There was dark early-19th-
century furniture of a third-rate machine-made Victorian-
ism: a high cabinet with a glass front on the shelves of
which were stowed away manuscripts and a long low
buffet, which now served as a bar. Above the mantel
was a dark painting involving large dull-red blossoms so
bad that it must have belonged to the abortionist, too.
He had somehow obtained from the American Institute
an old glass-topped case for exhibiting manuscripts, and
had sawed off the legs to make it low enough to serve as
a cocktail table and ornamented the top by putting under
the glass dozens of Italian postcards. We congratulated
him on the comfort in which he now lived, as compared
with his former quarters. Women in trouble who did not
know that the doctor was dead kept, it seemed, coming

around for abortions, and I feel sure that Wystan must rather have enjoyed this, since it at the same time meant the frustration of female fertility and enabled him to disappoint women. His boyfriend, Chester Kallman—of whom he is said to have said that he never felt such a passion for anyone—now resembles a tame goblin. He carries on self-effacingly—perfectly passive, a sallow-faced wife who is not supposed to be charming. Lys says that Wystan has prevented him from having any life of his own, will not let him take a job, since he wants to keep him always dependent, though this puts Wystan to double expense. He never says anything to me, never comes to see us with Wystan—from a distance he seems grisly, disgusting. In London, the homosexual circulates everywhere; but in New York he is much more condemned to inhabit an all-homosexual world; and this life of segregation is one of the disadvantages that Wystan has had to accept in coming to live in the United States. But he accepts it and celebrates "celibacy," and, as I have said, makes it a proof of his moral strength. —There was a barman handing out champagne in little tumblers. Wystan told me, in the course of the evening, that he had decided to give them champagne, because whisky often made people quarrelsome. I caught a glimpse of cases of champagne in a bedroom. Wystan himself for once had cleaned himself up, had his hair cut, and was wearing a newly pressed suit. His face has grown curiously parchmentry, almost leathery, and cracked with wrinkles, almost pachydermatous.

But then hordes of people arrived; the room became crowded and smoke-filled and the conversation deafening. Wystan went around with a camera taking flashlights of his guests. When he came to the group in which I was, I hung a handkerchief over my face at the moment he was taking the picture. At one point, he presented me to the Sitwells,[5] who were enthroned side by side, with an empty chair beside Edith to which people were brought one by one. I had never met her before, but she remembered that, in London in '45, I had sent her a letter from Tchelishchev that I had not been able to make use of—or rather, that I had not been eager to, since I did not much admire the Sitwells and had a feeling that they demanded much adulation. Osbert, who is said to have Parkinson's disease, sat red-faced, staring, and stiff. He was sallow with a line of the eyebrows that I imagine owed much to plastering. We talked about Tchelishchev a little; I said that I thought that he and George Grosz[6] were the two most underrated painters, because they were not sponsored by the Paris dealers. She replied that she regarded Tchelishchev as one of the three greatest living painters—of whom the other two were Picasso and Rouault. I said that I did not care for Rouault, and she answered that she did not like Rouault at all. I said that I would like to see something done about Ronald Firbank's[7] letters and papers. "Oh, we don't care about Firbank anymore—we think he's silly now." Then, turning to Osbert: "You don't care for Firbank anymore, do you?" I did not hear his curt reply, but it was evidently in the negative. Someone else was brought up, and I ducked away.

—Auden and Whitehead,[8] it seems to me, have been the two Englishmen of genius I have known who have embodied most authentically the strong creative English qualities—stout character, self-dependence, stubbornness in following their intuitions, combination of practicality with poetic and metaphysical thinking. And both have come to live in the United States. They have seemed of a different breed from the contemporary English don or London literary man. With Whitehead, coming to the States was partly due to logical positivism at Harvard and to his being made comfortable there, but partly perhaps to being old enough English to feel kinship with the old English on which were based the 17th-century Puritan and the 18th-century Revolutionary traditions. One felt in him the Englishman's awareness of his sturdiness, his special position in Europe, but not the complacency, the paramount need to put down all the other peoples. In Auden's case, there was something of this, and something of the reaction of the middle-class Englishman who does not want to be a toady or even to succumb to the fashionable attitudes that defend literary London against the hierarchy of England. He did not, he made it clear, desire to be a member of the Connolly literary family. Such surpassingly gifted men are uncomfortable in the British class system—Dickens and Kipling are also examples, but they could not endure democratic habits and manners, and eventually went back home. Auden is the first such man who has succeeded in adapting himself— though he still, he was telling us the other night, can't reconcile himself to seeing certain kinds of people— especially wearing the gaudy ties that he loathes—eating in restaurants that he frequents: "I feel that they're not gentlemen—they oughtn't to be there." (Elena says that this is a regular second reaction of enthusiastic foreigners who become naturalized citizens.) He is certainly the first writer who has succeeded in making a language that combines American with English—he is a great master of language; and he has produced, in poetic form, a comprehensive description of the whole English-speaking industrial-ugly, democratic-leveling-oppressive, urban and suburban world. He always claims that he is a monarchist, that our separation from England is a major disaster, that we should do much better under one king.

—When I was in London in '45, I saw Spender at Cyril Connolly's. Like everybody else, he was hoping that Auden was unhappy and that his work was deteriorating in the U.S. I always made a point of telling them the opposite. Spender, who was rather vain of his experience in the fire [bomb] brigade, said that he thought the most difficult thing for Auden would be to come back to England. Later on, when, after my first stay in Italy, I was in London again in midsummer, I had dinner with Spender and learned that Auden *had* come back to England and spent a few days there on his way to Germany, where he was to make a sort of "psychological" investigation. He had left his friend Stephen aghast, inarticulate with indignation. I asked what it was precisely that Auden had done. "There were several attitudes he could have taken," said Spender. "He could have taken the humble attitude—or the sympathetic attitude. But what he did was take the arrogant attitude." He had come to dinner with the Spenders and insisted on wearing his overcoat: did they mind his wearing it? London houses were so cold after the well-heated American houses. Spender spoke boastfully about the bombing (Mamaine said that people were "priggish" on this subject). "Oh, you haven't been bombed seriously," said Auden. "You don't know what bombing is. The Germans *were* really bombed and in far worse condition than you." They asked him if he thought of returning to England, and he said that he might come there occasionally to see the country—which was so lovely in summer. Spender said to me, "It made me so angry that I thought I wouldn't look him up when I went later to Germany myself." This story amused me very much. It was delightful to see an Englishman who had gone to live in the United States coming back and working on an Englishman at home the same game with which they were accustomed to put foreigners down. I told Mamaine about it and remarked that in America such a situation would have been impossible. The old friend in Spender's position would have said to the returned Auden something like "Another crack like that and I'll give you a sock in the jaw," and the incident would have ended in kidding, however hard-hitting and caustic; whereas all that Spender could do was to counter in an indirect way: snub him tacitly by not looking him up in Germany. Mamaine thought about this and said, No, there was no other possible course. I realized that the English must play these causes according to accepted rules: you must score by deliberate moves that cannot be directly declared: you may not have it out, as we do, in an open blow-by-blow quarrel.

—It has been one of the discomfitures of Spender's whole life that he is never able to catch up with Auden. When I saw him in New York, he was again aghast at the squalor in which Auden lived on Fire (?) Island and something he had just said about Yeats. Where Spender is a prima donna (a prima donna who really can't sing), Auden is a bold personality who is always knocking the wind out of his friend by his disregard of conventions and commonplaces; and his strong will does have an element of boorishness, as when I have seen him read through, with intent application, something written about himself that he had been given, interrupting the conversation and paying no attention to other people. There is a story of his going to somebody's rooms when the friend had not yet come back and reading avidly his correspondence. When the other man appeared, Auden demanded, "Where did you put the rest of that letter? I can't find it!"

Dos Passos, 1955: Two lunches with Dos—late February or early March. He seemed to be less keyed up, and I got along with him better. A publisher had asked him for a volume of his old manifestos and articles. He seemed to have been rather horrified by what he found when he looked at them. "I hadn't realized," he said, "how contentious I was." I told him he had not changed. —I said, in connection with Hemingway's *Old Man and the Sea*, that it was curious to take account of the pressure that, after the bad reception of *Across the River and into the Trees*, Hemingway had brought to bear on everybody to applaud his following book and to make this good enough little story appear a masterpiece. "I was fascinated by the 'operation,'" Dos said, "and his timing it so as to get the jackpot [by which he meant the Nobel Prize]: I was so fascinated by the 'operation' that I could hardly judge the story: it was like a magician's stunt—when he makes the girl float through the hoop, you don't notice whether she's pretty."

There are two kinds of women: those who move to make room when you sit on the bed and those who remain where they are even when you have only a narrow edge. Oddly enough, Elena in this follows the same procedure as Mary. Other women will at once roll or pull themselves away.

At my age, sex becomes less importunate, in the sense that you don't need it so often, and the impulse comes to seem less important. You even become impatient with this biological instinct, with its pleasure-bait, which asserts itself so much oftener than is necessary. It sometimes becomes nagging: you think, "Oh, yes: there you are again—I know all about it—you just want me to go to bed with some women so that more human babies will be born, and I have quite enough children already. I want to devote myself now to more intellectual and dignified things." Yet the sexual preoccupation, when it hits you, seems sometimes sharper, as if it were an elderly malady, like gout or enlargement of the prostate gland. —With what contempt at sixty do you look back at all the uncomfortable and unsatisfactory affairs of your youth, the transient episodes that meant nothing or had all-too-serious consequences, the sieges of women you could never have lived with, who would not interest you for a moment now, the complicated messes of entanglement with several girls at a time! Yet if I did not have Elena, I might still, at my age, on a more careful and temperate scale, be carrying on in this way. —Unlike some elderly men, I have no appetite for young girls; the women who occasionally attract me are invariably middle-aged married women. The women of my own age, however—or the age that corresponds with mine— are now too old to attract me: their breasts have collapsed, their hair is turning gray, they have gone through a change of life and are likely to have had hysterectomies that have left them unresponsive and juiceless. —And it is strange now to think that ten years ago, liberated from Mary, with whom I had spent seven years, there should have revived in me a capacity for falling in love of which I should not have thought myself capable: Mamaine, Eva, Anaïs [Nin], Elena (not all, of course, to the same degree).

The stories of Muilenburg and his colleagues at Union Theological Seminary about *the devices to which Catholic priests resorted* in order to get a *Nihil obstat:* Isaiah, Luther, made me realize that a Protestant has to be either honest or a hypocrite, whereas a Catholic does not have to be honest.

—But charming old Jesuit[9] met at the Strauses', a geologist who had spent fifty years in China and then left on account of the Communists; hopes to go to study in Mexico; in wrong with his church in France. When I asked him about his writings, he said, "I'm not allowed to print them." —"You're not allowed by whom? The Church?" "Yes, the Church—but I mimeograph a few dozen, and then these are copied—and [very mildly and sweetly] eventually there may be several hundred in circulation." I learned later that he was a great-nephew of Voltaire, and I wondered whether this underground circulation was a survival of the Voltaire tradition. I imagined he looked a little like V. When I asked him about the Dead Sea Scrolls and Dupont-Sommer, he said that he was interested in the subject, though he did not know much about it; that he did not know D.-S. personally, but had read his books with interest. "It looks," he said gently, "as if Renan had been on the right track, doesn't it?" Here was an honest Catholic. He apparently believed in God. —Soon after, we heard that he was dead.

Olga Loris-Melikov, the great-granddaughter of Pushkin, said to Elena, of some novel she had been reading: "I read through four hundred pages—it was very boring —to find that the hero has a little black blood—that's what the whole story has been about! Why should I be excited about that?"[10]

May 18, '55. We took a picnic to Duck Pond. Beautiful bright clear day with a little wind. Later on I always feel that the crystalline Cape Cod air is being polluted by the summer people, and the alcohol gets into the sunlight. Elena sat on the clean white sand—which she loves and which sets her off—with long slim bare legs stretched out a little apart and no panties on; blue skirt and black bathing suit. We drank some domestic *vin rosé.*

She said that the domestic wines were getting more and more "fruity," they sold them as soon as they made them, so that they tasted like simple grape juice gone a little sour. This is the kind of thing I never notice. We made love—I was slowed by the wine, and it lasted a long time, but was delightful, in spite of the fact that after a while the sand is rather hard on your knees—I finally put the towel under mine. Airplane overhead that swerved away. Elena said that at one point there was a bird of prey hovering over us. Afterwards, I walked around the pond, feeling perfectly happy—enjoyed the sight of a painted turtle swimming from the shore to the depths. I looked back toward Elena from time to time—she was taking a nap: I loved to see her—her bare legs and blue clothes (skirt and sweater)—and know that she was still with me, that we could still be happy together in the open air on the beach. When, coming back, I had almost reached her, she sat up, with legs together and knees bent, one on top of the other, pointed in my direction, tapering to her beautiful little feet, one on top of the other. —I drank most of two bottles of wine, yet seemed to remain perfectly clear-headed, but admired perhaps extravagantly the wavy grain of some roots in the path, as we were going back. Further on, Elena stopped to admire some sprouts of oak, of a red that was almost scarlet, in the middle of the path. She says that there are a great many varieties of scrub oak, and that the sprouts are likely to be quite different. —When I got home, I drank some whisky and was out like a light before six—put myself to bed above my study and didn't come to till three in the morning, when I had an awful dream that Elena was dead and went over to the other side of the house to find her. My sexual powers must be definitely flagging. I was sixty ten days ago.

Walther Mumm: When I was talking about the Bible the summer before last, I spoke of Jesus as a Jew: "You say Christ was a Jew?! He doesn't look like it in the pictures of him!" —This summer he and Elena were saying that they thought there was no French or German word for ticks because they didn't have them in Europe. I looked up tick in my small red English-German dictionary and found such words as *Scherflein* and *Zecke.* When I read these out to them, Walther said, "That's the Almanach de Gotha you've got there?" I told him that it was the best joke he'd ever made, and he said, "It wasn't an intentional joke."

Leverett Saltonstall[11] made the speech to the graduating class on Prize Day at Brooks (June 11, '55). His nephew was graduating and getting some honors. M. Ashburn a little too obviously doted on the Saltonstalls, introduced the senator by saying that there was a certain tendency nowadays to speak lightly of good breeding, old families, the old school tie, etc., but he believed that they deserved our respect—a brief sketch of the Saltonstall family followed. Leverett himself was a well-preserved specimen of the old Yankee breed. He talked informally, said "git" for "get," and had just a ghost, though no more, of the Boston *ar* sound. He is tall and bony, and has bird-lidded eyes that make him look like a wise old crow. His voice is flat and hard as nails, and it produced an uncanny impression as it seemed to come out of the summer trees on which the loudspeakers were hung: this was the voice of New England. His subject was the new horizons (though he used no such poetical phrase) opened up by the war; but these horizons for him were exclusively commercial and industrial. Who of us, before the last war, had realized the possibilities of trade with Indochina? Who, before the war in Korea, had known that they manufactured I forget what in the northern part of that country and raised I forget what in the southern part. When he talked about the careers that were open to them, he spoke of such activities as touched himself: business and politics—and he added that there was also a place for political commentators like Walter Lippmann and Arthur Krock.[12] They sometimes asked him at Washington why it was that, when his father and his grandfather (grandfather and great-grandfather?) had sat on the Democratic side, he was sitting on the Republican side; and he told them that the Republican side was where he thought he belonged. He said this with a great air of shrewdness, but did not explain the point. He concluded by telling us that one morning he had been waked up by a song on the radio—"Keep Smiling" or something of the sort. Somebody had recently said that optimism had become impossible, but he didn't see why this should be so: he thought it was a good thing to be optimistic. —Gardner Jencks,[13] who was with me, had evidently been horrified by Saltonstall, said he was "just incredible." For Gardner, he was simply a philistine, but I could enjoy him as a specimen of a certain type of New Englander in its purest form.

NOTES

1. Sir William Schwenck Gilbert (1836–1911), of Gilbert and Sullivan. *Classics and Commercials*, pp. 359–65.

2. Nicholas Nabokov (1903–78), cousin of the novelist, was a composer and musicologist. *The Forties*, pp. 76, 309.

3. Christopher Isherwood, the British novelist.

4. Katherine Raine, poet and critic, who wrote *Blake and Tradition* (1968). William Empson, poet and critic, author of *Seven Types of Ambiguity* (1930).

5. The English poet Dame Edith Sitwell (1887–1964) and her brother, Sir Osbert (1892–1969), writer of light verse, short

stories, essays, and novels. The Sitwells were much lionized during their postwar trip to America.

6. Pseudonym of George Ehrenfried (1893–1959), German cartoonist and book illustrator. *BBT*, pp. 586–89.

7. Ronald Firbank (1886–1926), the aesthetic and fastidious novelist, best known as the author of *Prancing Nigger* (1925). *The Shores of Light*, pp. 264–66.

8. Alfred North Whitehead (1861–1947), the philosopher. EW partly modeled Professor Grosbeake in *I Thought of Daisy* (1929) on Whitehead.

9. A marginal note by EW indicates that this was Pierre Teilhard de Chardin (1881–1955), the French geologist and paleontologist, regarded as a major voice in 20th-century religious thought.

10. Pushkin was said to have had an Ethiopian ancestor.

11. Leverett Saltonstall (1892–1979), U.S. senator from Massachusetts (1944–67).

12. Walter Lippmann (1889–1974), noted commentator on foreign affairs, and Arthur Krock (1887–1974), Washington correspondent for *The New York Times*.

13. Gardner Jencks and his wife, Ruth, were friends of EW on the Cape.

TALCOTTVILLE, 1955

Talcottville from June 17.[1] The day after getting Reuel
off to Europe, I came up here from New York. I got a
Pullman on the left-hand side of the Empire State
Express, leaving at nine in the morning, and it was
wonderful to sit and look out first at the Hudson, then
the Mohawk, and to see mountains rising above it.

The house was in excellent shape. Mrs. McGuire had
cleaned it, and Fern had done the upstairs hall, Helen's
room, and the little bedroom. It seemed to me quite
normal—that is, clean and sound. A few spots of decay
still left, but I hope to get these cleaned up this summer
—except getting the "kitchen chamber" and the back of
the house rebuilt, which will take more money than I
have got right now. —I have hardly felt the presence
of the past—it is now mostly as I have arranged it and
want it.

Dinner at the Sharps': Fascinating to see *Cousin
Dorothy* [Mendenhall] again. She is eighty-one. She still
wears her hair, which is remarkably still dark, in her
old kind of Phrygian-cap coiffure that always seemed to
present a challenge. She is now somewhat dumpy, has

acquired a figure more like my mother's. She had a bad accident just before or just after I saw her at Madison in '39, fell downstairs and broke both her arms and had to have her little finger amputated. She says that her knees are giving out, are "like water." She has pouches under her eyes, has to rest; in profile, her lower lip protrudes and her nose no longer seems handsome. I complimented her on her fine eyes, and she said that that was the Kimballs. It is true that she looks like a Kimball, something of my grandfather in her face—which I had not noticed before. (She told me of an early Kimball who had written a school grammar and surveyed, I think, Ohio, Illinois, and some other Western state—Indiana?) I felt that she was a little bit shy and ashamed of having grown old. Though I realize now that she and my mother are more alike than they ever used to seem to me—my mother, too, preserved a terrific morale—their cases are different in that Mother, in old age, suffered from physical infirmities, whereas Dorothy, except for her knees, seems to be perfectly sound. It is simply that her old shining presence, which made so much of her distinction, is gone, and old age is a humiliation to one who has been so challenging, so impassive, and so imperious. You only feel that rare dimension sometimes in what she says and in her handsome humorous smile. I am aware now of her accent and turns of phrase being more upstate than I ever was before, and I noticed New Englandisms—*lahst* and *bahth* and the way of ending a sentence (*have it*)—that the other people up here don't have. When I mentioned this, she told me that her father came from Lexington, Mass. She likes to wear purple, and, on one expedition to Hardy's Restaurant, wore white gloves, explaining, when she took them off at lunch, that she wore them only for the reason that she couldn't bear to have her hands dirty, especially couldn't eat with dirty hands. I told her that I couldn't write with dirty hands. She used to think she'd spend her last years traveling, but now hadn't the slightest desire to travel.

Birds and flowers: Red-winged blackbirds in the meadows—sprinklings of forget-me-nots in the brook. —The fields are full of flowers—I never remember to have seen them like this. The long green grass stained with yellow of buttercups and white of daisies, mixed marvelously with the bright rust of devil's paintbrush —other fields would be lovely with contrasting white mallows—fringes of blue bugloss, pools of blue iris— great fields of yellow mustard, which so much overpowered the grass that this only gave them a greenish tinge. Enormous brown dandelion tops, the biggest I've ever seen.

—Cousin Dorothy is the perfect type of the woman who has played the father. Her own father died before she was twelve; she and Bessie must have polarized as masculine and feminine in regard to one another: by the time she had become a young lady, she had put her mother on a budget; she emulated my uncles by becoming a doctor and cultivated their doctor's gruffness; then when Bessie died, she took over her children. Her brother Will evidently had no chance to become the man of the family: a black sheep, he disappeared, and used to write asking for money. D., who ran the family finances, finally refused to send him any, and then they did not hear from him anymore, and nobody knows what became of him.

—Her way of talking sounds now like my mother, and I realize that I have something of it: That looks like the postman t'me. I'll have a lot of money 'fore-uh go (when Malcolm had given her $50). Well, we got our face washed ennaway (when the garage had cleaned the windshield)—all on one frustrated trip to Highmarket, when we had to turn back on account of Dorothy Sharp's fear of thunderstorms.

—Her mother, my cousin Grace Kimball, was sent to Talcottville from Columbus, Ohio, at five when her mother died. She lived in the Stone House, and Aunt 'Phrone [Sophronia] Talcott and Jannett Daniels took care of her. (Mrs. Daniels, née Talcott and Aunt 'Phrone's sister, had married "a distinguished architect," who designed Druid Park in Baltimore, caught typhoid there and died; she was peppery and pugnacious, and it was she who brought the suit.) Of Aunt 'Phrone, Cousin Dorothy says sometimes that she was "fecked," sometimes that she was simply "dull." Grace went to the little red schoolhouse on the hill. When the stagecoach was coming, you first heard its horn. The passengers came into the house to get warm, and the horses were changed there (they did *not* put people up, says D.). Sometimes an Indian would come into the kitchen, get warm, say Ug, and go away. Nobody ever spoke to them. Then her father married again and she went back to Ohio. Jannett Daniels took her all the way by canal; it took a month, and she had an enchanting time. Then she used to come back in the summers. She married a man named Reed who manufactured shoes in Columbus. He was the son of a farmer in Lexington, Mass., a descendant of Anne Bradstreet and Governor Dudley. Dorothy thinks that members of her father's and her mother's families may have come over on the same ship. I am not sure when Reed died, but for some time before Dorothy was twelve, Cousin Grace and her three children, Dorothy, Bessie, and Will, were living in the Stone House, with Aunt Lan [Laura Ann Baker] and Aunt Lin [Rosalind Baker]. At that time there was a ballroom, with sheds underneath for the horses, that extended from the south side of the house almost to the stone barn. You could enter it from the house, but there were stairs that ran up outside, so that people who came to the balls and voted there did not have to go through the house. Aunt Lin was the postmistress then: the letters were sorted out into the compartments which can still be seen in the china closet in the dining room and handed out through the door in the wall (this never was a bar, as I thought it might have been). Upstairs, what is now the back southwest room was partitioned into three others—it was something like the group of rooms across the hall; and at that time the narrow bedroom was itself cut off from the window by a partition, the marks of which can still be seen. Two maids slept in this closet, and two more on the third floor in the closet between the two rooms. In each of these two upstairs rooms, and in each of the two front rooms on the second floor, there were two double beds. In winter it was so cold that you never went to your bedroom except to sleep. The only heat you could get was a warming pan. Dorothy and Bessie both had TB, and were "put out to grass" up here. They were supposed to keep out in the air. This must have been when they came back from Germany. They went over when Dorothy was twelve, and Bessie studied music in Berlin. They stayed for three years, then came back, but evidently continued to spend winters in Europe. Cousin Grace took Bessie to Russia one winter and sent Dorothy with some other girls to Copenhagen—rather strangely—to learn French. *Story of the bust:*[2] It was made in Rome. There used to be a button that you pressed to make it revolve. Cousin Grace would make Dorothy stand beside it and then make the bust turn around, calling attention to the profile. But Dorothy was sensitive about her nose, which had been broken at the age of four, when Bessie had pushed her downstairs. Bessie had kept her from telling what had happened by giving her a box of paints. She had come to loathe the bust and thought the pedestal would be nice for flowers. First it was in the house in Columbus, then in the Stone House. One day when the rest of the family were going to Lyons Falls, she pretended to be sick and stayed home. She hired two draymen to load it into their dray, carry it to the millpond, and drop it in. But Uncle Tom got it out of the draymen where they had put the bust, and he fished it out of the water. This Dorothy did not know till years later. When she was visiting the Stone House, she wanted to go into the large downstairs room. They did their best to prevent her, but, as usual, she had her way, and there was confronted by the bust. She tells me that she is now going to watch the house, and some day when she sees I am out, come and get it and throw it in the water again. She wrote me that Great-grandfather Baker was "a dreadful old man," and says that he sold the property piece by piece and drank it all up; yet she has just told me several times a story of an incident that seems to have made a great impression on her. When her mother, at the end of some visit, had come to take Dorothy and Bessie away, he had come downstairs with his eyes streaming, saying, "Don't take those little children away! Don't take those little children away!" I said that he must have been a not unamiable man. "Oh, he was very sweet! Lin and Lan adored him." She said that the ready-made portrait in the hall could not be Great-grandmother Baker, who was beautiful and a blond—it must be some member of Nelly Kent's (infinitely inferior) family. —*When they got back after their three years in Europe*, they found that the energetic Aunt Lan had taken down the rickety ballroom. She (D.) has never liked the house since the bathroom was installed on the bottom floor in what had previously been the dining room, and the dining room cut in two to make what are now the woodshed and the kitchen. This was done by Aunt Lan, too. She eventually worked herself to death, while Aunt Lin sat around and was waited on. The only piece of work she really did was make currant jelly once a year. Once when she was supposed to have broken her hip—which turned out not to be so—so that she could not get around, she lay all afternoon while Dorothy and Cousin Grace amused her by making her up little lace caps and trying them on her (but Cousin G. did all the sewing: D. cannot sew). At the end of the day, she said, "I don't know when I've had such a pleasant afternoon!" She had led them to believe that she was in considerable pain. Aunt Lan had had a lover who had ridden away and she never saw him again; but D. thought that Aunt Lin's romantic tale of a fiancé lost at sea was "buncombe." Aunt Myra and Aunt Jane (?) were the youngest of the girls, and they had not had the advantage of being trained to be young ladies by their mother. All the others were well-bred. These married Parsons and Augur. I know that Mother, too, looked down on them and did not willingly mention them. Poor Helen [Augur] and her father were never welcome when they came East. Nobody did anything nice for Helen when she was at Barnard. Dorothy says it is true that the Augur who married Aunt Jane was "a nut," but that Helen's father was fine. She is very loyal to everybody—because she takes everybody seriously.

Baker-Talcott feud: Dorothy's attitudes about this are contradictory. She always has Sir John Talcott at the back of her mind. He was sent over here by the King to fight in an Indian war. The Talcotts had been Tories, but had bought up here the land of dispossessed Tories. According to Cousin Grace, it had been a triangle of land that stretched from Bartle's Corners (where the old Bartle Tavern was—in my time it was old and abandoned, and we called it the Haunted House) to the Sugar River bridge. There was supposed to be a green in front of the house, which would have had, as in New England, a church and houses around it. When somebody had asked one of the Talcotts why his grandfather "had been such a fool as to build the house right on the road," the Talcott had replied, "Damme, my grandfather was no fool!" and explained the original plan. On the Talcott estate at that time, there were only two houses: the Stone House and Aunt Addie's. Cousin Dorothy still takes the attitude that the Talcotts had the right to keep the estate intact and not have it split up into lots and sold; yet if this process, as she says, began not long after Thomas Baker married Aunt 'Phrone, I do not understand how they could have possibly expected to get back the house. She says that the Talcotts were extremely English, that they practised primogeniture, were "patriarchal." They thus expected some male Talcott to inherit the house; but this does not seem to make sense. D.'s account does not satisfy Malcolm and me. He thinks that Aunt 'Phrone and Uncle Tom must have been fond of one another, and that the other Talcotts must have felt a sympathy for him. When the suit to break the will was brought at Mrs. Daniels's instigation, her own brother defended the Bakers for nothing. Cousin Grace was regarded as a renegade because she sided with the Bakers, and when asked why she did so, said, "I like them better." On this account, Dorothy was ostracized by the Talcotts. Her aunts would not speak to her on the street, and she was once, as a girl, ordered off some Talcott's place. She is personally loyal to the Bakers, had much admiration for the six (?) older women. The feeling—in spite of her remarks above—is all for Thomas Baker; yet in going through the house, she will dismiss even quite handsome things as "Baker," as if they could not be interesting.

There is some old English feudal arrogance in her, which must have been characteristic of the Talcotts: yet—like him, in spite of her gruffness—she is large-minded, not at all snobbish in her human relations and judgments. The only sign of pettiness I have seen in her is her story of her son Tom. Why, he asked her, did she always give all her good old things to John, never anything to him. She replied, "You have had three daughters, and you haven't named any of them after me. John has named his. Doesn't that explain?" I said, "Why, Cousin Dorothy!" "Dorothy," she said, "is a good old family name." —Her arrogance took the form, not of snobbery, but of the challengingly assertive attitude toward men and the patronizingly assertive attitude toward women who were content to be ordinary women that made her, to people like my mother—about ten years older than she —seem conceited and disagreeable.

—She has just been to her sixtieth reunion at Smith. If one of them hadn't just died, exactly half the class would still be alive. At college she had belonged to a group of girls who used to put on skirts very short for those days and go out for walks in the rain. They called themselves "the Rainy Daisies."

—She was married in this big side room, between the two windows at the front: 1906. "You couldn't see a fence post," the snow was so thick, and it was nip and tuck whether they could get married that day. They couldn't be sure they could get a minister then.

—Strange, she said, to go back and forth between the West and there.

—I said that I wanted to ask her later some more fundamental questions. She said, "All right, but if I don't know the answers, I'll make them up."

—Munn: Aunt Addie's husband had to have every morning for breakfast a cucumber fresh from the vine.

—She has had Hezekiah Talcott's tombstone put up again. It had fallen on its face in the graveyard on the hill.

—I have yet to see any evidence that the town was originally called Talcottville but then changed by Thomas Baker to Leyden—as Cousin Dorothy claims. The 1829 map I have here shows that it was then called Leyden. So far as I know, the name Talcottville was bestowed by Cousin Grace. Mother said that she told them triumphantly about having arranged the change. They could not be expected to rejoice, because they had known and loved the town as Leyden. It was always called Leyden in my childhood. [Marginal note: The County History shows that it was. The village of Talcottville was a part, as it still is, of the town of Leyden.]

—On our expedition to Hardy's Restaurant (on the outskirts of Watertown), Cousin D. kept giving directions to Huldah Loomis, who was driving. When we got to the restaurant and H. had parked and gotten out of the car, D. said, "You ought to park on the other side, Huldah, then you won't have trouble getting out." "You stay and show Huldah where to park," she said to Dorothy Sharp, and herself went into the restaurant. Dorothy protested a little, but she and Huldah obeyed. Similar scene on the way back: Huldah had been afraid, on our way there, that she was running out of gas; she had gotten some, but now Cousin D. insisted on her laying in some more. "Don't let her do those things to you!" cried Dorothy S., but Huldah succumbed. It was curious to see this, since among her sisters she was always the dominant one.

—Contrast between Dorothy Sharp and Dorothy Mendenhall on our frustrated trip to Highmarket: Dorothy S. afraid of the thunderstorm, didn't want to drive into the black cloud; Cousin D. said, "It's not going to do anything—it knows we're afraid of it." She kidded Dorothy but not unkindly and then acquiesced in going back. It is impossible for Dorothy S. to ask questions of how to reach some place; but Cousin D., like me, doesn't even understand the inhibition. She says that she enjoys getting into conversation with the people.

—Dorothy says that she thinks Cousin D. is having a very good time but that she is wearying to have in the house. Everything has to be done on the dot. At five-thirty every afternoon, she has one stiff drink of bourbon on the rocks, and she likes everybody to be there and drink with her. But after this ceremony, she acts as a brake on Malcolm's reckless pouring and consumption of liquor. But she rather resented it yesterday when I refused to come in for a drink at all, just as she had rebuked me the day I first came for appearing at six instead of five-thirty. The fact that I had told Fern to come in at that time was something that did not interest her.

There are some very fine birds around the house: a pair of Baltimore orioles and a woodpecker with red head and a round black spot on the breast (a flicker). Some bird has made a nest behind the floor of the upper porch.

Just before I left Wellfleet, Elena confessed for the first time the full story of the man who had looked in at the window. She had come downstairs in her nightgown, and seeing a little whisky left in a bottle, she had swigged it out of the bottle. (This seems very unlike her.) Then had seen the neighbor peering in.

Tour of the house with Cousin D.: She said at first, after a cursory glance, that the only things she recognized were the light cane-bottomed dining chairs; but when I took her from room to room, she told me that the Bo-

hemian glass bottles had always been there, that the
blue jar and the blue-and-white lamp base (the latter
had come from Germany) in the china closet in the
dining room had belonged to her mother. So had the bust
of Dante, probably left behind on account of its broken
nose. —There had been a companion to it: Beethoven,
they thought. The goblets were fingerprint goblets; the
big ones were celery glasses. What I had thought were
beer mugs were measures. The big pewter thing was
"Baker." What I had taken for a spit to roast marshmal-
lows was really a spit to roast corn. She was shocked by
my having given the melodeon to Carrie Trennam: it
had come from the church, as I thought, but had belonged to Aunt Lin, was rosewood. She was also rather
indignant over the disappearance from the porch of the
bittersweet vine—Bergen had stripped it away when he
repainted the porch and I was not here. I promised to get
cuttings from Mrs. Burnham and plant them. The little
white rose by the porch, that I did not remember to have
seen before, was Aunt Lin's damask rose.

Later tour of upstairs: In the southeast room, a door
went through where the corner closet now is: there was
a step up to the window opposite, and they walked out
of it into the ballroom, which was also accessible from
below by a staircase that made it possible to reach it
without going through the house. The southwest room
was divided into three small rooms, each with one of the
windows, and a corridor, which rose from the present
door. Across the hall was something similar, except that
what is now the narrow bedroom was a room that had no
window, in which two maids slept. My father, who put in
the bathroom, must have created the present arrangement.
Cousin Grace removed the partitions from the southwest

room in order to make a room for Cousin Dorothy. [Marginal note: Previous account of some of this is incorrect.]

—*The murder* occurred on the stone path along the south side of the house—a man chased his wife up the path and clubbed her to death there. The Reed children used to think that they could see a bloodstain there, about the middle of the walk. This was in her grandmother's time.

—How did they amuse themselves? They read, played the piano and sang, had balls, went for rides. "Bundled," suggested Malcolm. "You're just a scoffer!" —They didn't have cars and radios, and they had to do everything for themselves and to make more of everything they did. They would pay long visits that would last for two or three weeks. Usually, a brother and sister, the sister riding postilion, would go horseback to see some other family, and in the course of the visit it would be arranged that the others were to visit back.

—*Jesse Talcott*[3] was a gambler and drank. Cousin D. suspected him of having fixed up the marriage of Aunt 'Phrone. Later he went to Chicago, but eventually came back to Boonville. Dorothy and Paul Kimball [EW's uncle] once went to see him and found him living in squalor. When they left, P. said to D., "The wages of sin are death." She answered, "Or worse than death." They (D. and the Loomises) showed me a picture of him and pointed out his gentlemanly appearance. At the Boonville Centennial Fourth of July, his nightcap was exhibited in one of the windows.

—*Paul and Bessie:*[4] They had fallen in love. Neither family wanted them to marry. Not only were they cousins (though rather remote) but they both had TB (as did Dorothy herself). Paul went to Saranac and Colorado and came back cured. Bessie had been in

Berlin, in the pension with Alfred Rolfe,[5] Willard Furbish, and Malcolm's father, and had become engaged to Furbish, who could sing and was well-to-do, but was intensely disliked by D., who thought him stupid and spoiled (an only child)—I remember how disagreeable the family always thought him. When Bessie was back from Germany and Paul back from the West, he came up here to the Stone House to ask her again to marry him. It must have been terrible: she told him she had given her word and couldn't break it. "If I had been there," said Dorothy (she must have been at Johns Hopkins or M.I.T.), "I would have done something about it." When Dorothy was working at the Oceanic hospital, Paul asked D. to marry him. She laughed and told him she would just as soon think of marrying her brother. She knew that he only wanted to be near Bessie. —Here Mrs. Burnham's story. Bessie, with her three children, came back to the Stone House and died here (in the southwest room). The mill at Winchester outside of Boston that Furbish had inherited from his father burned down, and he had no insurance. Cousin D. had to raise money to educate the children. She lectured for the Department of Agriculture to the farmers' wives of Wisconsin. She had gone from pathology to pediatrics and began by lecturing them on the feeding of babies—formulas and all that—but discovered that their babies were all breast-fed. What they really wanted to know was how to avoid miscarriages, etc., so she gave them gynecology (I am not sure whether it was before or after this that she practised as an obstetrician—very tiring work, had to be up at all hours). She also lectured to the men—how to avoid rheumatism and focal infections. She traveled all over the state, got $100 a lecture. Her husband was very sweet to let her do it. She had her own two children at home— had seen one child killed, when he fell off the porch. She thus earned enough money to educate the Furbish children—Dorothy Furbish, like her, went to Smith.

—*Medical career:*[6] worked on Hodgkin's disease, which resembled TB (?) and was sometimes mistaken for it. She and a German pathologist, Sternberg, discovered more or less at the same time the distinctive Hodgkin's disease cell, which was named for them. Coming back to Johns Hopkins several years after she had left, she found them puzzled by an autopsy: the cause of death might or might not have been Hodgkin's disease. The presiding doctor put it up to her. She thought it *was* Hodgkin's but he thought not. She was dreadfully afraid she was wrong, when she set out to examine the tissue, which had been distorted by freezing; but identified the distinctive cell. She was evidently very proud of this.

Was one of [Sir William] *Osler's* favorite pupils, graduated third in her class. Holt would pinch a penny until it ached, but Osler was a prince. He liked to play practical jokes. On the occasion of a party at his house, he had seen his son carry off something, had chased him around the house, taken it from him, and dropped it in a vase. The vase was full of water and the parcel contained the slippers of one of the guests.

Gertrude Stein had thought that she could just sail through medical school. Dorothy said that she (D.) had average brains and had had to make a terrible effort. Stein had been swarthy and dirty, had displeased one of the head doctors, who was a Baltimore aristocrat. She was always stained up to her elbows in gentian violet, a spot of which on one hand was a disgrace. The affair of the model of the fetus finished her. She was flunked but does not say so in *Alice B. Toklas* and is guilty of a whopping falsehood when she asserts that her fetus model is still used at Johns Hopkins.[7]

Two girls who were roommates and cheated at exams.

Had roomed together at Smith and cheated. One was clever and rich, the other not bright and not well-off. She had copied from the brighter one, who did not go on to practise medicine, though the other one did on a rather low plane. Dorothy appealed to the head doctor. It was already so difficult for women to practise medicine that a scandal of this kind might kill the chances of other women students to be accepted. She prevailed on him against his better judgment—he told her later that he knew the girls were guilty, had seen them cheating himself. The class themselves had to vote on the case, and Gertrude Stein left town.

She was always called W. Reed.

Merwin Hart[8] had followed her to Baltimore, with the idea of becoming a doctor, but his father had gone after him and brought him back. Later, he was best man at her wedding. Now she finds it impossible to talk to him, as do I.

At one time there was an opening for a doctor at Bryn Mawr, and Cousin D. had gone on to see Carey Thomas.[9] Miss T. asked her what church she belonged to, and she said that she was agnostic. Miss T. said that it would look better for her to call herself a member of some church—all the Bryn Mawr teachers did. "I'm not easily intimidated, but she scared me—I knew that I could never get along with her."

—*Cousin D.'s accent* (see also above): Ohio, with certain mannerisms—when she is expressing her feelings emphatically—that are surprisingly like those of the Fort girls, must be something Middle Western; upstate New York, like my mother; Germanisms, such as *finger* pronounced like *junger*; and very old English pronunciations like *neve* for *nephew*.

These contrasts are part of the contrast between her old-fashioned English Toryisms and her American and professional (as a doctor) democracy. She loves the idea that Sir John Talcott would not stay in the Massachusetts Bay Colony because they would only allow people to own ten acres of land. For this reason, according to her, he went on to Connecticut (with Hooker). She still makes an issue of my great-grandfather Baker having broken up the Talcott land and sold it to mechanics (the property, her grandmother told her, extended from Bartle's Corners to the Sugar River bridge). She insists, with her children, upon "good breeding," and, on one occasion, when Tom wanted to get out of a date—with a friend and two girls, who were going out dancing—she told him that if he let them down, she would turn him out of the house, and, after putting up a stubborn resistance, he finally capitulated. Yet she makes a point of helping poor students who want to get an education, likes to talk to all kinds of people (is not too proud to ask the way, enjoys it, she says, because it gives her a chance to get into conversations with people), and allows her old servant to mutter behind her chair at dinner, "The old hag!" One principle involved here is the old feudal attitude. She had never, she told Elena, made a bed till 1940, can hardly cook, is physically lazy (though she got herself to Flat Rock once).

—Attitude toward men less virulent than that of the later career women. Likes to needle them in a teasing, but then makes up for it by special signs of affection— as she teased me about the Bakers, etc., when we were looking through the box of old photographs, then told me, as I was leaving, that she wanted to give me the root of the bunch of forget-me-nots she had just picked. She likes to read poetry, liked Eliot, but for some reason feels strongly against Dylan Thomas (obscurity, no doubt). —Her big scene with her son John: he had not done well at Harvard, had been flunking his scientific courses, then told her he wanted to study medicine—could she get him in at Johns Hopkins? She went up in the air, lost her self-control, as she shouldn't have—told him that he didn't have the stuff for a doctor, that he'd do better to think of going into business, and that he ought to be ashamed to ask her to get him into Johns Hopkins through pull. The result of this was that he got himself into Johns Hopkins and graduated, though she thought he was only a run-of-the-mill doctor. The Mendenhalls' Quakerism was very strong in Charles—he wouldn't accept prizes of money when he won them or even war compensation. He was reticent, never talked. Tom, on the other hand, was much more sociable, coached crew. I don't know whether she has hamstrung these sons, rather doubt it. In spite of her instinct to dominate, she has too much respect and affection for people. It is probably true that neither was ever potentially brilliant. The three men that composed her family were able, I imagine, to stand up to her. She said once, "The reason that I talk so loud is that for years I had to live with three men and assert myself against them." —But she had, while still a young woman, taken over the father's role. Her mother had been extravagant, "did not know the difference between capital and interest." She had put her on a budget, had been hard, as she admits, with her brother Will—up against his two sisters and his mother—had refused, at a given point, to send him any more money, and he was never heard from again after this, they do not even know what became of him. She had emulated my uncles by studying medicine, and then she played the role of uncle by taking over her dead sister's children.

—She is descended from Richard Kimball, the brother of "Priest" Reuel, so has no Mather relationship. (I find

from the Mather genealogy that I am closer to Increase
and Cotton than I thought. Hannah Mather, Reuel
Kimball's wife, was a first cousin of Cotton). He
(Richard) published a school grammar and surveyed
Ohio, Illinois, and Indiana. He was partly paid by the
government by being given forty acres of every four
corners. Hence his settling in Ohio. The Reeds were
direct descendants of Anne Bradstreet, and Cousin
Dorothy is now amusing herself by writing something
about her.

Dawn Powell's visit.[10] She was most appreciative,
knowing village life from Ohio. My stories became better
as I told them to her. —*Loomises* had the habit of swarming through any house, sticking their noses into every
room, the moment the door is opened to them; but
Huldah evidently suffers from feelings of frustration from
never having entered an octagon house, she is curious
about how the rooms are designed. (The look that comes
into her face when we talk about the Seiter house, in
which the unworthy Seiters have concentrated so many
of the most distinguished things of the Collinses, Bakers,
and Talcotts: an intense but restrained envy, a slyness
that is grave and thoughtful; something a little morbid,
a little disconcerting about it.) —Also, story about Mrs.
Burnham's secret—which turned out to be condensed
milk. Dawn said that, in this dairy country, it would be
the last thing that anyone would ever have thought of
using. —She thought Fern was "a beautiful woman,"
was impressed, as I have always been, by her walk—"as
if she were carrying a jar on her head," Dawn said.

4th of July 1955. Our champagne punch party, I
think, a success—though I did so much hopping around

from one person or group to another that I didn't get my teeth into any satisfactory conversation. —There was a wonderful full moon: coppery at first, then brightest white. After the guests had gone, I finished the punch sitting out on the back porch and watching it set steadily behind the big trees. I realized that Elena did not have much sense of the nobility and mystery of this country; reflected that champagne was a part of her essential personality—she has a natural affinity with anything that at all resembles champagne: the Cape with its dry and mild and exhilarating air, for example—she can *champagnieren* at Wellfleet: she loves to make things delightful, not sharp, not full-bodied, not emphatic, not Dionysiac. The loveliness of this country, its grandeur, the effort and ordeal of the past that life up here implies, scare her a little and put her off. She cannot imagine herself what she pronounces "a peeoneer woman," and is somewhat dismayed at my interest in someone like Harriet Beecher Stowe. It is silly as well as futile for me to demand her interest in something so alien to her. The punch she made tonight was a masterpiece—so perfect in flavor, so cool, so smooth, so well tuned to promote the amenities, to put people pleasantly out of range of the commonplaces of life. In coolness and smoothness and color, it resembled the coppery phase of the moon, and seemed in its way as perfect. But the moon moving through the trees brings out a romantic wildness that I have never felt, in America, anywhere else but here, and that I am always somewhat astonished still to find that I feel.

Elena says that, when she first comes here from Wellfleet, she feels as if she didn't exist.

Aug. 14   Champagne

—At morning and evening, those golden elms and fields . . .

—The blue Adirondack hills, still seeming unexplored . . .

—Gray-silver above deep rain-sated green . . .

                              —Adirondacks,

In which, in varying grays, the ridges show . . .

—Leaves on the maple at the front of the house already
turning orange-pink

And stretching, like a spaniel, paws and head,

As if appealing . . .

—The crescent moon like jewel-weed drooping in the sky

—Sorry you won't see our wild old moon rolling through the
sky.

Old Grand-dad: I feel at moments, when I'm living alone here, that it's all myself and nothing else—house, village, and Lewis County. I might get tired of the beautiful view from the door if I didn't feel it was also mine, a part of my habitat, imagination, thought, personality—of course, one can tire of these, but one cannot want to detach oneself from them any more than I want to do from the view.

—books and bookcases of my childhood.

Saturday night, Aug. 15. This kind of life, in the long run, does, however, get rather unhealthy. One evening (Aug. 13), I drank a whole bottle of champagne and what was left of a bottle of Old Grand-dad and started in on a bottle of red wine. I was eating Limburger cheese and gingersnaps. This began about five in the afternoon— I fell asleep in my chair, woke up when Beverly came, thinking it was the next morning, decided to skip supper, and felt queasy for the next twenty-four hours. Otis told me this afternoon (the 14th) that a brother of his mother's had died the next morning after a combination of home brew and Limburger at night.

.   .   .

I have read this summer at Talcottville: Barrett Wendell's biography of Cotton Mather; Mrs. Stowe's *Lady Byron Vindicated*; Peyrefitte's *Les Clés de Saint-Pierre*; M. L. Clarke's *Richard Porson*; Chapman-Huston's *Bavarian Fantasy* (skimmed); Faith Compton Mackenzie's *As Much as I Dare*; Siegfried Trebitsch's *Chronicle of a Life* (mainly the parts about Shaw); Gorki's *Na Dne*; went through *Brokenburn* and *Heroines of Dixie* for *New Yorker* article;[11] went through new volumes and papers on the Dead Sea Scrolls; *The Abominable Snow Man*, by Ralph Izzard; *The Loved and the Lost*, by Morley Callaghan; started *The Turgenev Family* by I. Zhitova and Litvinov's *Notes for a Journal*, but probably shan't get through them before I leave. [Marginal note: Aldous Huxley's *The Genius and the Goddess*.]

I read Helen *Juan and Juanita*, an old serial in *St. Nicholas* of 1887, which I had loved to hear at the Collinses'. She greatly enjoyed it, too. —We have read to her, also, from the volume of Andersen's fairy tales, now rebound, that Aunt Laura used to read to me under the tree in the field in front of the Collinses'.

—Rough river stones and elegance of house; human art in selection of view and designing of windows to frame it—my tendency to feel that the view is a series of pictures or panels, partly the result of the intention of the builders—all this rather rare in America—river stones roughly scratched and pitted in the course of prehistoric events—the fossils of Dry Sugar River—the gratuitous beauty of the fireplaces.

—The frame houses, like Carrie Trennam's, white and green, the windows green-marked like eyes.

Elena, since her change of life began, has sometimes been very much enraged by me. One day, in the kitchen here, she threatened me with the eggbeater, telling me to "go and join my ancestors"; at Wellfleet, when I was sitting in my chair, she came up and gave a terrific kick, a regular *moulinet*, which sent her shoe through the ceiling. Fortunately, we were just about to have it re-plastered.

11/26/10

Aug. 20. Went with Otis and Fern to the Lowville Fair in the evening. I was somehow touched and impressed. Fern, the day before, had been kicked by a cow in the back and found it uncomfortable to get around. When she had come to see me after work in the afternoon, she had at first thought she wasn't up to going at all, then decided she might as well. Face looks so heavy and coarse at times, so full of warmth and charm at others. Complained that Otis let her in for driving when he had promised to drive himself. —They examined the farm machinery, admiring the biggest ones. We threw away some nickels on the glassware game of chance, where the coins skim right out of the dishes, and there is no chance of winning anything except, as I once did, a glass, out of which they are not so likely to bounce. In the cattle tent, she couldn't resist petting the animals she liked. She gently prodded a Brown Swiss with her foot and made her get up, in order to admire her straight back and square build. At the end of the tent was an enormous black bull, for which the owner had paid $5,000. She patted him on the haunch. —We had hot dogs and iced tea, and went into the grandstand to see the drum corps competition. First there was a corps from Mexico, N.Y., who were rather strained and overanxious, would force themselves and hit false notes. Then a Canadian corps from Kingston—very military in khaki and much more effective—no drum majorette, but a leader with a long staff who marched with a strong and true beat but was soldierly to the point of burlesque, jerkily sawing the air with his arms as he walked and from time to time standing his men at attention and exhibitionistically saluting to an officer, whom he proceeded to the front to meet. These were much applauded. Fern, on a narrow seat in the bleachers, had no back to lean against, so I thought we had better go. [Marginal note: One before we went in could be heard playing *Put the Little Foot, Put the Little Foot*.] As we left, I saw the big swing that turns you upside down slowly whirling its blunt-ended bright-lighted spoke against the dark upstate sky, and there seemed to me something grand and wild about even this transient amusement park: the fun that the people were having against the immense dark sky in the mountain-horizoned countryside. A gaiety which, though healthy, was lonely and contrasted with their rural lives. Some, they told me, went every night. —But (this should go at beginning) the fair has not been paying lately. This year there was no horse racing, to save money for the purses put up by the town, and this has been greatly missed: "You can't have a county fair without horse racing." There is even some talk going around about not having it at all next year, but Fern says that there is a lot of money in Lowville and doubts that it will be discontinued. —Just before leaving, she bought some taffy—which they were making hot at the booth which had a delicious smell— to take home to her little grandchildren.

A cow groaning or shouting.

In account of fair above, I have omitted the show of wild animals in cages: a fine horned owl—evidently young, since Walter Edmonds tells me they reach a wingspread of six feet; great yellow eyes that looked as if they were made of glass; it ruffled up, put its head down, and glared; when a dog came near the cage, and when you got on one side of it, would turn its [head] almost all the way around, in the way which has sometimes made people think that it could actually revolve its head: what happens is that, when it has got as far as it can in one direction, it snaps it as far as it will go in the other direction. Walter told me that his guinea fowl began disappearing one by one; he would find some feathers and a piece of the windpipe. Then they saw a flock of crows which behaved as if they were after an owl; then he found a nest, from which a great horned owl peered down at them. He shot it, and the mate disappeared. It kills its prey by attacking the windpipe. He told me about another owl—wounded, I think, in the wing—which tried to attack the hunter, running down the snow slope with outstretched wings—brave as an eagle. There is something impressive about this owl.

There was also a wildcat in a cage: large paws, black hairs at the tips of its ears. I scrutinized it for several minutes, and this seemed to make it uneasy. Its short tail writhed—I hadn't known how flexible, mobile, this was. At last, it faced me and made as if to snarl; then, apparently realizing that it was helpless, walked to the other end of the cage. "And you felt embarrassed," said Walter. He was quite right.

There was also a red fox, curled up but attentive to everything—reminded me of the cub I wanted to buy from the Negro soldier at Le Havre.

Elena told me that Helen, walking on the beach at Wellfleet, had come out with the following little rhyme:

> Boys can have their bosoms bare,
> But little girls, they wouldn't dare.

The Affair of the Boston Rockers: When Elena arrived in Talcottville, she had the impression that some of the Boston rockers were gone—she thought four. We had said about them that they stood about like a herd of Lewis County cattle. I had had the impression myself that there was something unfamiliar about the furniture on the first floor. The big upholstered armchair that I had been in the habit of sitting in, in the corner of the big room, had been moved to a corner of the smaller room, and one of the highbacks (non-Boston) had also been moved into this room. I thought that this must have been done to cover up the disappearance of the rockers, and since the red barn had definitely been plundered, and the perfume I had bought two years before as a birthday present for Elena had never been found, and I thought that my Cruikshank *Peter Schlemihl*[12] had disappeared (though this turned up later), I at once rang up the state police. A young trooper arrived. We gave him a glass of champagne we were drinking, and he immediately attacked the problem. Soon he called me up to say that he thought he had found the chairs. Fern Munn had a brother-in-law, an antique dealer, who specialized precisely in Boston rockers. The trooper had gone to his place, found him out, but walked in and seen Boston rockers in process of being repainted. I had gone on the assumption that Fern was honest, and I liked her so much that it would hardly have upset me if it had really turned out she stole things; but Elena— who, I think, is a little jealous of the role she plays when Elena is not in Talcottville—said that she was like an animal and might very well do dishonest things, in a simple animal way, without being aware they were wrong. But I told the trooper not to question her. He had already questioned Mrs. McGuire; we said we were sure she had nothing to do with it. She talked to Carrie

Trennam, and Carrie had soon remembered that she had been in the house with Elizabeth [McGuire] and noted the absence of the rockers. The trooper had also talked with Carrie, and she had given him a whole dossier on Fern: she had been guilty of cooking the accounts at the dairy cooperative, for which she had lost her job; she and Otis had sold mortgaged cattle, and were planning to go South [to] live in order to escape the consequences. The trooper—I don't know whether from Carrie alone or from other sources as well, which he wouldn't divulge—in an astonishingly short space of time brought me this dossier. He had, as I found out only later, everything completely wrong. He said that there had been an investigation of the scandal of the dairy accounts, that Fern had still to appear in court. He named the considerable sum that had been stolen. All this was quite untrue. There had been no legal proceedings, there had never even been anything in the papers. But I didn't know that then, and the case against Fern was further confirmed by Mrs. McGuire's reporting that Fern had gotten the keys from her—not in spring, when she was working on the house —but much earlier, in January. The trooper complained that it was [not] possible to conduct the investigation properly if I wouldn't let him question Fern; so I told him to go ahead, but I first had her come to see me and talked to her about it. She was obviously surprised and shocked when I suggested that her brother-in-law might have taken the chairs. I unfortunately let it come out that Carrie had talked about her, and, a little while afterwards, from the window of my workroom on the second floor, I saw her advancing on and entering Carrie's with her firm and purposive step and her erect statuesque carriage, all charged with a terrific force of energy and indignation. She stayed in there so long that I became rather worried and blamed myself for provoking this row. She was, I learned, telling Carrie what she had just told me: her own story of the dairy scandal. She had noticed an enormous discrepancy between the amount of milk noted as received in the books and the amount of milk sold. This could mean only one of three things: either the scales were wrong; the milk was being watered; or the farmers were cheated when their milk was bought: they were paid for less than they brought. She had the weighing machine examined, and it was found to be all right. She took the matter up, not with the boss, but with another man just under the boss. He told her not to make a fuss—above all, to say nothing about the matter outside. Otis was one of the board of directors, and she talked to him about it. Presently she realized one day that, though no milk at all was recorded as having been bought that day, a certain number of pounds had gone out. She again brought the matter up. They told her to cook the accounts in order to conceal the discrepancies. The upshot of this was somehow—it was a little obscure —that they fired her and charged her with dishonesty, making her, she said, the scapegoat. I had already heard from Helen Augur—who had had it from the Loomises, never at all friendly to Fern—that she had been charged with watering the Munn milk for her and Otis's profit. I had never before spoken to Fern about this matter, which had happened since the summer before, and I now believed what she told me. After all, she had been able at once to get a new accounting job; she was a respected member of the Republican Party. But Carrie had told her that, after all, she had been the coöp accountant, and that she knew what she was doing, and should never have cooked the accounts at all; and Elena, in her gentle [way], implied the same thing when Fern mentioned the matter to her. On my part, I am afraid that a repressed desire for her made it, at moments, a satisfaction to feel that she was at my mercy. At such moments, I did suspect her, but I wanted to spare her, forgive. Yet I did—after telling her about it—let the trooper go to see her. The results of this were terrible. He walked into the house and accused her directly of having stolen the chairs: "We know it was [an] inside job—somebody who knew the house well! You heard them say that they had too many! You stole those chairs! He says that he won't prosecute." He made poor Mrs. McGuire a similar scene; and then came in to see me. While he was there, Fern arrived and denounced him with power and fury. She said that he had come into the house and behaved like the Gestapo, and that Americans didn't have to stand for that; that she was going to report him to the chief of police—which she did and elicited an apology. But Mrs. McGuire and Joe were so upset by this that they said it had brought on their old ailments, and they have never worked for us since. The younger trooper was extremely stupid. He had come to the conclusion that the chairs must have been stolen by either Mrs. McG. or Fern—though there were several other people in the neighborhood with dubious reputations. I regretted having gone to the state police and remembered the role they had played at the time of the milk strike in the early thirties.

One day, while this was going on, we went to have drinks with the Sharps. The Loomises were there, and Helen Augur, who was staying with them, had come up for the 4th of July. I found out, to my horror, from Helen that it was she who had moved the big chair—to a place where it would have more sun, and so not get moldy in winter; that she thought that it was we ourselves who had weeded out that room, that there were just as many Bostons as there had ever been. She and I went over to the house and tried to check. Elena remembered eight

Bostons, and we were able to reckon eight by counting the one upstairs (which I seemed to remember having moved myself in order to clear the living room), one that had had its rockers taken off, and two that had been painted gray. It is an unfortunate result of our long absences from T'ville that we lose track of the details of the place. On my way back to the Sharps', I passed the McGuires' and mentioned to Elizabeth, much upset by the trooper's visit, that it might be all a mistake, that the chairs might never have been stolen, and Helen— somewhat jealous of Elena, the real mistress of the house, though Helen has lived there so much, having the place to herself—at once seized upon this to take the attitude that the whole story was "a fabrication" on the part of Elena, who, she said, had the idea every summer that some of the sheets had been stolen, because she did not know how many there were. I invited her to come to dinner when the Loomises were driving me home— Elena having already gone home with Helen—and she made me a virulent little scene, declaring that she would not come to dinner with us, because we had slandered the McGuires, "who had been working for us for years." At dinner, inspired by the cocktails, I made out a perfect case against Helen as the person who had stolen the chairs. She had been alone in the house, had been poor, had heard us complain about too many Boston rockers. An antique dealer had come to the door—we knew from Elizabeth McGuire and Carrie that such people had sometimes asked about the house and looked in at the windows—and she had just sold him the chairs. Elena was sure that this could not be true, and she made a point of calling up Helen and saying goodbye before she left.

Fern told me afterwards about something that had happened at the 4th of July centennial of the incorpora-

tion of Boonville. An antique dealer had visited one of
the ladies who had exhibited old glass in the store
windows. She had shown him the pieces, and he had
asked her whether she had any others. She said yes and
went upstairs to get them, and he vanished with the
pieces she had left below. There is no question about
the depredations of the antique dealers lately. They drive
around the country in winter and break into old barns
and houses. But I am not sure that the theft of the rockers
was not wholly imaginary. Elena, who is naturally an
accurate observer with a strong sense of realities, has,
however, lately, since she has been having change of life,
a certain tendency to minor delusions.

—In *Toronto*, for the first time, I met *Morley Callaghan*, the Canadian fiction writer, a friend of Scott
Fitzgerald. I immediately asked him the truth about the
once-celebrated story of his boxing match with Hemingway.[13] He said that he had never before told the truth
about this, but that he would now proceed to do so. He
had been a student at the University of Toronto when
H. was working on the Toronto *Star*. He had known
him then, had been writing short stories, which he had
shown to Hemingway, and he intimated that he could
never be absolutely sure that H. had not got something
from them. First, H. had criticized them sympathetically,
then, at a given point, when Callaghan had sent him
some stories (published, I think), he had not written
him anything, and when C. had seen him again and
mentioned not hearing from him, had said, "I thought
you were going good—there was no need to write you
about them." —Later, they had met in Paris. The story
I had heard already was that, after the first dinner in
H.'s flat, he said to C., "Well, shall we go to a show or
shall we put on the gloves?" He did not know that

Callaghan, in Toronto, had had considerable experience in boxing. After that, they used to box at a gymnasium. "We had some rather distinguished referees," said C. "Miró used to referee us. He is a little man, and when we were walking together, Miró carrying equipment, people used to think he was H.'s servant. Hemingway didn't know who he was, and was taken aback when I told him: he always prided himself on being in the know about everything. One day Scott Fitzgerald refereed us." Scott at that time, he said, had been completely infatuated with H., had told Callaghan that H. was as good as young Stribling.[14] Callaghan had undertaken to enlighten him, had said, "Scott, you need to understand that H. is not as good as young Stribling—compared to the professional people, he and I are just clowns." H., he said, had very little science, he improvised his play. When Callaghan hit him in the mouth and made it bleed, Hemingway would stand there glaring at him, then spit out the blood in his face. He had not known quite how to take this, whether he ought to get angry and retaliate. He asked Hemingway why he did it. "That's what the matadors do," said H., "to show their contempt for the bull." On this occasion, Callaghan knocked him down twice. The first time, Hemingway stumbled over something behind him. The second (or first?) time, he said bitterly, "Well, at least you didn't push me over a (whatever it was)!" But this second time, according to C., Scott Fitzgerald was so dumfounded at seeing his hero knocked down that, sitting cross-legged on the floor with his watch in his hand, he forgot to keep time on the round and let it go on and on, with Hemingway getting the worst of it. When the contestants realized what had happened and stopped, H. said to Scott, "If you want to score off me and destroy me (wording probably not right), why don't you do it in the open instead of this dirty way?" He was furious, and neither Callaghan nor Scott knew how to pacify him; but fortunately—and this was the part of the story that Callaghan said he had not told before—a young man who had been looking on came up and said to Hemingway, "I've been watching you, and, if you don't mind, I'd like to say that the idea in boxing is to defend yourself." Hemingway said, "Oh, is that so?" "Yes," said the young man. "The object is to hit the other man without getting hit yourself." "Oh, that's very interesting. Would you like to show us your method? Demonstrate it with *him*," nodding to Callaghan. C. said that they could not be sure what they were up against; the young man did not look tough or strong, but Callaghan thought about Jimmy Wilde, a thin and wiry but formidable fighter. So he approached him in a gingerly way, and it was some time before he realized that the boy knew nothing about boxing. When he had established this fact, he drove him into a corner. Hemingway now offered boldly to take him on next, and spectacularly triumphed—much taller than he and with a longer reach—by simply standing with his left arm held out. When the boy tried moving around him, Hemingway would turn with him, holding out his arm. The young man now admitted with candor that it was possible to look on at sports and think that you understood them and that they were easier to do than you found they were when you actually tried to do them. The incident put Hemingway in such a good humor that he forgot about his earlier misadventure.

But later the story got around at home, and Isabel Paterson, in her literary column in the *Herald Tribune*, printed an incorrect version of it, which asserted that Callaghan had knocked Hemingway out. C. says that he

had already written to the paper to explain that this was
not the case when he received a wire from Hemingway
which said—as Max Perkins[15] or someone told me—
something like "I learn from the *Herald Tribune*. That
you knocked me out. Please wire when and where this
occurred." He wrote Hemingway that he (H.) might
have trusted him (C.) to behave in an honorable way.
"I've always," he said, "gone along with Hemingway's
publicity." He also brought pressure on Scott and bullied
him into making a statement which went so far as
actually to be false in its rehabilitation of Hemingway.
He was by that time on to H., and John Bishop or
someone told me that he was quite ashamed of having
allowed Ernest to bully him into this.

Another little rhyme of Helen's:

> Triumphant pages
> Escort me through the ages.

I'm not sure whether this is original.

Henry [Thornton] in Germany: They were directed
to paste on their army cars stickers that said, "Be smart.
Stay in." Henry had some similar stickers printed that
said, "Be smart. Get out," and put one on his own car.
He was immediately haled before his colonel and de-
moted. It was felt to be suspicious that the posters were
printed in pink, and also that he had more in his possession. The colonel asked what he had been going to do
with them, and H. replied he didn't know, which he
says is true. The colonel—who drank a good deal and
thought he had been to West Point—said, "I hope you
care sometime about something, Thornton, as much as
I care about the army!"

NOTES

1. *Upstate*, pp. 111–36.

2. It was a bust of Dante with a damaged nose.

3. Sophronia Talcott's brother. *Upstate*, p. 49.

4. EW's uncle Paul Kimball and Bessie Furbish. *Upstate*, pp. 56 ff.

5. Alfred G. Rolfe, EW's classics master at the Hill School. *The Triple Thinkers* (1948), pp. 233–56.

6. *Upstate*, pp. 59–71.

7. See EW's essay on Stein in *Axel's Castle* (1931), pp. 237–56. *The Autobiography of Alice B. Toklas* (1933).

8. A son of EW's aunt Lucy in Utica. *The Thirties*, pp. 447–48, and *Upstate*, pp. 66–67.

9. M. Carey Thomas (1857–1935), teacher, administrator, and crusader for women's rights, helped organize Bryn Mawr College and was its president from 1894 to 1922.

10. Dawn Powell (1897–1965), author of realistic novels about Westerners adapting themselves to New York City. *The Thirties* and *The Forties, passim*; *LLP*, pp. 397–99; and *BBT*, pp. 526–33.

11. "Three Confederate Ladies" (*The New Yorker*, November 5, 1955), revised and reprinted as "Three Confederate Ladies: Kate Stone, Sarah Morgan, Mary Chesnut" in *Patriotic Gore*, pp. 258–98.

12. The artist George Cruikshank's (1792–1878) illustrations to Adelbert von Chamisso's (1781–1838) *Peter Schlemihls wundersame Geschichte*.

13. The Canadian novelist Morley Callaghan; *O Canada* (1964), pp. 9–31. For Callaghan's account of his boxing match with Hemingway, see *That Summer in Paris* (1963).

14. William L. "Georgia Peach" Stribling (1904–33).

15. Maxwell Evarts Perkins (1884–1947), editor at Scribners. *The Twenties*, pp. 246, 459; *The Thirties*, pp. 311, 713.

11/27/10

WELLFLEET AND NEW YORK, 1955–1956

Drowning the young rats: I'm supposed to be sadistic, but I can't bear to do this. The garbage cans when they're empty are very effective as traps. The rats, if they are young, get in them and can't jump high enough to get out again. We have caught a good many this way. But then, the first thing after breakfast, I have to drown them in the swamp. Last year I held them under with the tongs, but now the tongs are in Talcottville. I have to catch them in the boxes that my writing paper comes in. I punch holes in the top and bottom and sink the rats in this. The water is icy now; yet sometimes when I open the boxes, the rats are still alive and manage to swim to shore. A couple have gotten away, and I am not sure whether or not I hope they survived.

Bad health: end of Oct. '55. I became so uncomfortable with panting and congestion in the head that I finally went to Dr. Niles of Osterville. I found that I could not climb stairs or even cross the room without getting into such a state that it took me some minutes, sitting still, to recuperate. He found that my ticker, as he called [it], was missing beats—though fundamentally sound, he said; that my blood pressure was 220; that I was very much overweight—over 200 pounds; and that my liver was slightly enlarged. He told me to cut down on alcohol and salt and gave me *Rauwolfia serpentina* pills. The effect of the pills was magical. In two weeks my pressure went down to 164 and my heart was regular again. I was able to get around without discomfort, unless I drank a lot of whisky, in which case the congestion set in again. —The *Rauwolfia*—now much used for high blood pressure and for people in overwrought states—is still rather mysterious to the doctors, and they are watching it for deleterious effects. It comes from India, it seems, a traditional empirical drug. In my own case, it has keyed me down as I have never in my life been before. I can't get used to my new plane of being. I rarely shudder and twitch—as I have been doing since the time of my breakdown at the end of the twenties; I do not fly into furies. On the other hand, it has relaxed my sexual impulses. I wake up often without an erection, and the need for sexual intercourse no longer works up to a periodical crisis as has always been the case before.

L'Engle, '55. Coming back, after Thanksgiving, from Boston, I met Bill L'Engle on the train. They had just come back from two months in Spain and France. Bill said he had not enjoyed [it], was so delighted to get back to Truro. Why had it been disagreeable? Why, being in Spain with no Spanish—though Lucy could get along. It had been a sentimental journey: they had looked up both the church and the registry office where they had had their "religious" and their civil marriages—Lucy had wanted to be married in church as well as to have the civil ceremony obligatory in France. I told him that I had never felt much interest in Spain except that I should like to see the Prado. He said that the Prado was too dark to see the pictures properly.

Christmas 1955. Elena made gingerbread cookies like a maniac—perhaps as a substitute for candy. They were supposed to be for the tree—cut up into shapes of men, angels, stars, and chickens—but the first batch was eaten so quickly that she made another and another, each somewhat different from the others and some made according to different recipes—more or less crisp and spicy, or rich in a vanilla way. They were garnished with little gobs of jelly or decorated silver balls or crumbs of colored sugar—the men had raisins for eyes, the angels little white frills—but we went on eating them just the same. One day—during the terrible cold spell, when there were only a few rooms we could live in—Helen said, as she was leaving for school: "I want to come back to a warm house, permeated with the smell of cookies."

Algonquin, New York, Dec. 26–Jan. 6–7, 1956. We had a suite, and I would sit in the living room and enjoy looking at Elena's little bare toes, the only part of her visible through the door, as she lay on the bed in the bedroom—she would flick up her big toe and drop it, as it were in rhythm with her reading. A luxury for me to watch it.

—I had no serious business to attend to, so enjoyed myself completely at first—read Turgenev's *Stuk, Stuk, Stuk* [*Knock, Knock, Knock*] and *Punin and Baburin*—reading Turgenev nowadays always puts me in serene good humor; then biography of Hugh Walpole,[1] an entertaining book, a pleasant reemersion in the gaiety and writing of before the first war and the twenties—I enjoyed hearing about all the money he made (now that

I am making a little myself on *The Scrolls from the Dead Sea*), without any real envy, because I shouldn't want to have written his books; *En attendant Godot*, not so good as some seem to think—really about the low state of Europe—Genet's *Les Bonnes* is better; then Coventry Patmore's essay on English metrics.

But, with hotel food and holiday drinking, I was soon full of gout and congestion and could hardly get around —most uncomfortable again.

Auden said that he had gone to the trouble of learning to say "inter*est*ing" over here, only to learn that this was "non-U" (Nancy Mitford's article in *Encounter*) and that the "U" pronunciation here was "int'resting."[2]

He came to dinner with us in New York the evening of Feb. 27 ('55) and we had dinner with him in St. Marks Place the evening of March 1. On this latter occasion, we found the apartment in even more of a mess than usual—they were painting, putting in a new bookcase: the furniture out of place and books all over the floor. Chester was struggling with lobsters, and dinner was very late—Wystan had just flown back from Toronto. As I came back through the kitchen from the bathroom, Chester asked me to "take a message" that "the cook would like a martini." I felt sorry for him and —what with the look of the kitchen and of Chester getting the meat out of the lobsters—did not look forward to the dinner, and at one point proposed going out. But it turned out to be unexpectedly good, because Chester is a good cook. He is, however, now most unappetizing himself. Elena referred to him as "that frog." —There is always a moment in the evening when Wystan drops off his shoes and sits in his stocking feet. When he came to our house, he did this and revealed bright blue socks with bright red soles that gave the impression

of ballet slippers. —He told us about his getting a medal
from the King. It was something that Masefield had
thought up, and Masefield escorted him there. He had
rented for the occasion a top hat and a dress suit. At the
palace, they waited in an anteroom, where there were
several lords about; then they were brought into the
King's presence; he was terrified and stammered. Wystan
said that if he had stayed in England, he wouldn't have
been able to withstand the pressure. I didn't understand
what he meant and was astonished when he explained
that he had doubted his own ability to stand up to the
British temptation to become a member of the governing
class, a public figure, clever and respected. America seems,
however, to have brought out his latent English snobbery.
He says he likes to read novels "about his betters," re-
grets that we ever broke away from the King, said to
Elena that Kingsley Amis³ was *"dritten Klasse."* He is
very much delighted about being elected at Oxford to
the Chair of Poetry against Harold Nicolson and Wilson
Knight; is planning to horrify them by mentioning that
the Oxford Movement began in America (he has found
out that Pusey⁴ was influenced by some American cleric);
wishes he could give the "Bronx cheer" on hearing something particularly silly (it is not so difficult to do, I am
sure he is prevented only by his own inhibitions). He
expressed the preposterous opinion that Robert Frost is a
better poet than Yeats. When I asked him whether he
was going to tell them that at Oxford, he said yes. He
boasts that among his supporters were a peer and a
prince. The peer was David Cecil, I forgot who the prince
was. —Auden and the Muirs both had the idea that Day
Lewis was grooming himself to be Poet Laureate. When
I asked how they knew, they said that he had been
writing ads to show how he could do it. Wystan said, "It
ought to be me—I can write occasional poems." Later,

when he got his Oxford appointment, I told him he would probably stay, get his citizenship back, and be made Laureate. He denied this, was afraid, on the contrary, that he might not be allowed to come back, which would put him in a ridiculous position in England; was very anxious about getting his return straightened out with the passport department. In becoming an American citizen, he had, he said, done the worst thing you could do in the eyes of the English now. Their way of dealing with it, he found, was to pretend it hadn't happened; they never asked him what America was like, what was happening there or anything.

The schoolmaster comes out in him in his impulse to discipline people of whom he disapproves. He is always full of moral indignation against Cyril Connolly, says he gets advances from publishers and doesn't deliver the goods—Wystan would like to flog him, only way to get him to work. Later, he was in favor of executing him, would like to perform the execution himself. Cyril, he said, didn't have the sound bourgeois idea about matters of money. Wystan himself, I am told, will not take any money for a book till he has actually delivered the MS. There is, I think, in this moral consciousness, something of compensation for his homosexuality. He is especially savage against Genet, who combines being homosexual with glorifying the thief and the murderer. He had told us, in an earlier conversation—in connection with *Notre-Dame des fleurs*—that, if he had been on that journey, he would have made short work of "that beauty," the hero; and now, when I mentioned Genet, he declared that he would like to see him guillotined. —Amusing to remember how Harry Levin, a little while ago, was all for having Wystan "prevented" from writing literary criticism—let him write his poetry, but not prose: he was letting the standards down. Harry was, in general, in one of his moods of wanting to have people put in irons. Here, too, this must be due to the schoolmastering spirit.

Wystan's hair today looks like a wig—a wig for a character part. Elena says it looks as if he were wearing a mop.

Look, March's brightness breaks the winter snow.

Blizzard of March 19, followed by weather almost springlike. But April here is always a letdown. You expect the spring, and it doesn't come. Cold, rawness, and grayness continue.

Rascoes:[5] We had the Rascoes to dinner in New York. I had thought, when I had looked them up before, that Burton was not so much off his head as Hal Smith[6] had told me he was; he had talked very intelligently about Cabell—his position in Richmond, etc.—when I had looked him up before. But I now saw he didn't make connections with reality. The Philip Hamburgers[7] were there, whom he had never met before, but he began talking about the suicide of his son immediately after dinner, said that he had been "a dead man" for a long time afterward; and bored us all on a crushing scale by talking about McCarthy and the Communists—he greatly admires McC.—and other subjects. He always did this more or less, however. The curious thing is that he should observe so intelligently and clearly and yet get so many important things wrong and apparently never know the difference—though he said to me—what appalled me— when I called him on them, that he had always made it a rule, in controversy with writers, "never to give a writer his head," even when he (Burton) was wrong. His persistence in delusion and his talking neurosis are,

I am convinced, defensive, acquired for the purpose of setting off some early disadvantage. —Hazel, though her hair is a little dimmed, still seems to me attractive, and I can't help wanting to hug her. I was pleased when she called me "dear." But she, too, as Elena noted, is now a little off-center. She occupies a good deal of time treating eye patients by Bates's methods, and her feeling about it seems mystical, her way of talking about it *exalté*.

11/29/10

Nightmare: My horrible nightmare at the beginning of April—the worst I have had since the little blue light.[8] I thought that I was back—alone, at night—in the old house at Red Bank (which I dream about constantly, near the one Mother bought after Father's death), with the corpses of two people I had killed. I propped them up at the dining-room table in the walnut-stained paneled dining room. I had turned off the lights, and the room was pitch-dark, and I lay back, a little way from the table, in the kind of chair in which one reclines. The body of the woman was facing me—I was vague about the other, a man. I thought, "This is Hell—can I stand it? A bottle of whisky might help—but how horrible to make oneself indifferent and cheerful in order to dull oneself to a thing like this!" But I decided I couldn't stand it and got up and made my way through the dark house. I was thinking on the way that there *was* a bottle—almost untouched—of whisky, and that I could always depend on that, could come back and drink it. I went out the front door and down the steps to the lawn; but I had hardly stepped off the bottom step when my mother appeared from behind me and stopped me. My state of mind then became that of a child. She led me back into the house, and into the dining room. She turned on the lights, and there was nothing there. I remembered that I had not, after all, left the bodies propped up at the table: I had decided to put them away. My mother went over to the cupboard under the left corner china closet—where she used to hide candy and cakes—and opened it. Inside there were simply large puppets of mine that I had put away, laying them on their sides. What I had thought was the corpse of a woman was simply a puppet-queen.

I think that the woman was Margaret and the male body my father (who was not in the house in the dream). I have felt guilty in connection with the deaths of both.

Dreams. Third week in April. I have sometimes been depressed of late years at realizing that I never have anymore the kind of ecstatic and delightful dreams that I used to have when I was younger—the arrival, for example, at a wonderful beach, bathed in summer sunlight, while the color of the sea is beautiful and everybody there is happy. But for the first time in years the other morning, I had two such dreams just before awaking. In the first, I was traveling in a motorboat, with Elena, from somebody's house in the country along a narrow waterway. At one point we seemed to skid and almost to skip water, but I did not after this look out the window. I settled down to wait the end of the journey in the rooms in which we were sitting—the boat had now grown in size, and had now the proportions of a yacht. I had no idea where we were going—somewhere that our host and hostess—and these young people— wanted to take us—and when I looked out again, I saw with surprise and pleasure that we were sweeping into a kind of lake, out of which opened, further on, a swimming pool as large as a pond, shallow, with a concrete bottom and sides built up with blocks. All around were solid summer houses, and on the edges were good-looking young people in bathing suits. It made me happy

to think that here was something that could be enjoyed
by both Elena and me. (It was a compromise, I suppose,
between the inland idea and the ocean.) We landed,
and I waded in. What I thought at first I should miss
was the animal life of the surf, but then I saw with
gratification that the pool was full of pond and marine
life: frogs, turtles, and little fish. There was a group
about a small dead flounder that was lying on the bottom.

In the dream that followed, I was staying, with the
family, in a house that was more than anything else like
my grandmother's house in Lakewood. A kind of truck
had drawn up in front of the house, beyond the deep
front lawn, and there was a man at the door, with a
German accent, who was telling us that his "stock" was
good. As I went down the path to the truck, I saw people
carrying birds away and assumed that he was selling
poultry, game. But when I came to the truck, I could
see that, on a kind of top story, which was opened by
removing the side, were all kinds of pet birds and animals. I climbed a small ladder to look at them. I called
to Helen to come out and see them. I was immensely
delighted myself, yet it seemed to me there was nothing
to buy. There were white guinea pigs, but I had had
guinea pigs—it seemed to me that Helen, too, had had
guinea pigs. I was fascinated by a baby moose, but it was
already extremely rambunctious, kept prancing forward
with its chest out—I had continually to push it back.
It had no antlers as yet, but when it got them, it would
be formidable, an impossible pet. Getting down from the
ladder was surprisingly easy. There was a moment of
apprehension of the kind that is familiar to me in dreams:
fear of falling from high places. But here—although I
somehow became detached from the ladder—I dropped
gracefully to the ground, almost as if I were wafted, and
at the same moment, in a deft gesture, leaned the ladder

back against the side of the truck, from which, in my descent, I had pulled it.

I regarded these dreams as good omens.

April 17. Wellfleet: At lunch—which was very gay—with the Nabokovs and Chavchavadzes, we had an orgy of naturalization stories. I have probably noted above the experiences of Auden, who was suspected of "premature anti-fascism" and asked in a suggestive [way] whether he thought "that the world could be made a better place." The story of Sasha Pietra's—Santa going with Eugénie Lehovich[9] and Walther. She had tried to make an impression by talking to Eugénie—with much dropping of names—about the Italian nobility. Eugénie had said, "You know I don't know those people." One question on the application blank was: Have you ever committed adultery. She asked Walther, What does that mean? It means, W. answered, when you do it with somebody under sixteen. —Paul told about a proud old Russian lady who, when asked who was the first President of the U.S., had replied with great self-confidence and emphasis, George Washington Bridge! When they asked about her children, she said, I have four daughters, and announced all their resounding married names, ending with Countess Wrangel. —Nina told about being asked whether she had any race prejudice. When she answered no, the man had said *sotto voce*, Of course you have—I'm a Southerner. She had repeated very emphatically, I have *no* racial prejudices! —When it came to the point where Paul would have had to forswear his title, he told them that it had been abolished in Russia.

At Wellfleet, this early spring, when I have heard the one train a day whistling in the afternoon silence, it still makes me think of Edna [Millay].

NOTES

1. Sir Rupert Hart-Davis's *Hugh Walpole: A Biography* (1952).

2. Nancy Mitford's essay distinguished upper-class English usage from middle-class usuage, "U" from "non-U."

3. Kingsley Amis, novelist and poet, best known for *Lucky Jim* (1954) and other satiric novels.

4. Edward Bouverie Pusey (1800–82), Anglican priest and professor of Hebrew at Oxford, was an important force in the controversial and widely influential Oxford Movement, which sought to revive the High Church traditions of the 17th century and stressed the compatibility of the English and Roman churches.

5. Burton Rascoe (1892–1957), literary critic and columnist, and his wife, Hazel. *The Thirties, passim,* and *The Shores of Light,* pp. 115–16, 397–402.

6. Harrison (Hal) Smith (1888–1971), then associate editor of the *Saturday Review of Literature. The Thirties,* pp. 188–89.

7. See *The Forties, passim.*

8. EW had introduced into his play *The Little Blue Light* (1950) an account of a nightmare in which the character who reports it, Gandersheim, enters an empty house and finds a "paralyzing unspeakable thing" hanging in the air above his head, "a little spark of blue light" that is, however quiet, "infinitely cruel." *The Twenties,* p. 230, and *Five Plays* (1954), pp. 481–82.

9. Eugénie Lehovich (1908–75), Russian-born American educator and author, associated with the New York City Ballet from its founding.

TALCOTTVILLE, 1956

Talcottville 1956—arriving May 21.[1] Strange to see
the landscape so denuded: the view clear to the Sugar
River and even to the barns on the other side, the
feather-duster elms only broom straws beginning to fledge
yellowish leaves. I found a little green-and-brown bird,
not yet quite able to fly, hopping across the pavement,
and a hummingbird who came to the bushes in front
must have found slim pickings. It was so cold in my big
room this morning that I took my table out on the porch,
where it was comfortably warm in the sun, and wrote[2]
with the birds and the village going about their business
around me, and the meadow in front of the house and
the newly ploughed patch for a garden giving me the
piquant sensation—which I always enjoy so much up
here—of living elegantly on a moderate eminence among
the fields and the forests. Orioles and red-winged blackbirds. Then, about noon, it clouded over, grew chill,
and I came back in, built a fire and—simultaneously—
made myself some soup, and went on writing all afternoon. Then it grew warm again, as I found when I

went outside. It excites me to see this country—I have never before been here at this time of year—in transition from its long naked coldness of winter to the rich and bright foliage of summer. I feel now that—in spite of the retarded spring, the almost-March winds and the April-type rain—it is going to come with a rush, that, unless I observe it quickly, it will be here before I know it. The buildings—Carrie Trennam's house and mine—seem more solitary, more sprinkled on the hills. How the snow and winter winds must sweep them!—without their deep summer setting. No flowers around her house, but it is pleasant to see her working the big patch for her corn and vegetable garden. I noticed for the first time today an effect—in the afternoon—of bright white *behind* my house, like the bright light in front in the morning. */1/30/16*

The house seems all mine now—I know it well and simply come in and find everything quite neat and comfortable. In this room, where I sat yesterday in front of the fire, the memory of how, in the evening, I used to sit here with my mother and read Michelet seems already very far in the past. I do not worry about the room where Cousin Bessie died and where Father slept before he died. I do, however, seem to myself here a little more than elsewhere like Great-grandfather Baker; but this, in some way—when I am alone here—I rather enjoy. Everybody so much more good-natured, and I am so much more at home with them, than at Wellfleet. Easier to get people to do things at this time of year than later when they have to do their haying. Laurence Kraeger is clearing out the field across the street—which will please Dorothy Mendenhall on account of the view and Carrie Trennam on account of the snakes. In my present clear view, the Adirondacks seem nearer and more like the

highland from which one is looking at them: a few
buildings are scattered among pastures and still half-wild
country. A square bed of daffodils and narcissi—somewhat clogged by dead leaves behind the house—that I
have never seen blooming before.

—Strong light green over ground, and in the background, along the river, the elm trees, not yet dark green
feather dusters, with their light yellowish leaves, and
below the still low Adirondack ridge, now a grayer blue.

—Much enjoyed sitting out on the porch, which was
warmer than the house, with my hat on, writing at a
card table, saying hello to the passing villagers and com-
menting on the bad weather: Do you think we're going
to have any spring? Very quiet now: no traffic, children
all in school. Also, season to get things done: Carrie
Trennam planting a garden and putting flowers in the
stone things in front of the house; Laurence Kraeger
clearing out the lot across the road; Billy Crawford coming
after school and holidays to mow and pick up the lawn.
I like to feel this activity about me, to visit them from
time to time and to be there in sight if they should need
me—also, like the companionship of the birds: since
the trees are so leafless, one can see what they are doing.
I have never had so good an opportunity to observe their
movments before. There is an oriole's gray baglike nest
hanging on one of the branches just in front of the porch.
The male has style and a smart way of flying—very sure
twinkling motions of the wings. He will sit on a twig
making a chirring sound, then visit the nest and give
cooing noises that sound full of affection for the family.
But there is also a less attractive starling or grackle, who
has a nest in a hole in the wall in the corner of the upstairs balcony. I see him (or her) bringing large bugs.
He is dark and untidy, makes a harsh buzz; looks more
vulgar than the orioles when flying.

—Kraeger's slender brown-and-white bitch is terribly jealous of his tractor and won't let anybody go anywhere near it.

—Torrential rains with thunder at night. One night and day, with wind, rain and cold, seemed almost exactly like autumn: the trees with their young yellow leaves might have been yellowed by fading.

Albert Grubel,[3] driving me to town, said, I guess there'll be quite a few killed tomorrow! Tomorrow was Memorial Day. —He often talks to me about people's accidents, and they do have some very bad ones up here. His mind dwells a good deal on accidents—a Boonville woman drowned on one of the lakes, etc.

June 7. I have never before seen the deep-purple lilac bush blooming at the northeast corner of the house. It reaches to my bedroom window.

Fern Munn gives me the impression of definitely having become grayer in the course of the last winter. She wrote me that she had had some trouble in her head.

Lorna Linsley's death: I read about it in the paper. Characteristically, one of the last things she did was look into the Mau Mau situation in Kenya. Elena told me over the telephone that she had come to the Cape just before her death; had cancer of the brain and was completely gaga: she had sat beside Brownie L'Engle and said to her, "I haven't seen Brownie L'Engle for years. What a dreadful bore she is!"

A Boston rocker has been stolen at the Parquet in Constableville. There was a wedding with a lot of guests, and afterwards a rocker was missing.

Reading at Talcottville, from May 21 (and during trips):

Turgenev: *Postoyalyi dvor* [The Inn] (finished). The familiar theme of unbridled badness: the man who makes the woman landowner sell him the other man's inn, making his wife steal his savings to pay her.

Jean Genet: *Pompes funèbres.* A work of genius, much better than Sartre; but though he makes homosexuality much more attractive than either Proust or Gide, to read about it at length gives an impression of futility and silliness—which they try to offset by brutality and dirtiness.

Mirsky:[4] *A History of Russia* (77 pages).

Norman Douglas:[5] *Alone* [1921]. This is the least attractive of the travel books of his I have read. He is usually mildly agreeable to read. But I don't think there is much in him. He is a dilettante at science; he has no idea whatever what is going on in the modern world. So much of this book is complaint about not being able to get good wine or the right kind of macaroni—who cares whether he gets them or not? He doesn't even care much about literature—was, I should say, not very widely read. How could he have spent some time in Russia and learned Russian as well as he apparently did without ever reading Russian literature? I have yet to find a single reference to any Russian writer. As for his learning, he has many odds and ends of out-of-the-way information. The problems of archaeology that he investigates are mainly trivial. Nor does he make his personal life at all interesting. Except for one instance in his book about the calling cards. They all take place offstage: but they were not all homosexual, so this cannot be the reason. He was obviously very narcissistic, adored himself as a boy—see the pictures of him looking at his youthful bust—and it must have been himself that he admired in his boyfriends. His books are full of petty sadisms—especially to animals. Though his admirers are always emphasizing his masculinity, there is about him something old-womanish. He is always fussing about something. He is always showing off his humanity, but one feels that he is naturally callous. He is always complaining of people's being disagreeable, yet the impression he makes is unpleasant. The thing that is most admirable about him is that he is not afraid to be himself. But he is always on the margin of things, so his moral example counts for little. *12/1/10*

Donald Elder: *Ring Lardner* (1956). Better than Mizener's *Fitzgerald* (1951) or either of the books about Mencken. It is depressing to read about Lardner—so unsatisfied as a writer, and actually inadequately equipped. It is the satirical fantastic side that is distinguished, but his mind is rather two-dimensional, as his physical appearance seemed incomplete. A good deal of life he doesn't understand—politics, etc., and his worst point of view is banal. He made a determined effort to live up to his obligations to his family, but this bored him, and his household probably bored him. Elder, of course, can't say this, with Mrs. L. and two of his sons alive.

Charles Angoff: *H. L. Mencken.*[6] I had never read anything by Angoff that I thought in the least interesting, but this book is at least interesting—though it gives you all that was coarsest and most brutal in M. Of course, he is trying to shock Angoff and pulling his leg a good deal of the time. Though Angoff writes about Mencken with a good deal of admiration, the effect is very much like that of [J.-J.] Brousson's[7] books about Anatole France. Such older men try to play up to these young secretaries, like to shock them, to boast about their sexual adventures. On the other hand, it is not much credit to either Brousson or Angoff that he elicited from the Master such low-grade stuff. Anatole France sounds entirely different when he is talking to Ségur, for example, and Ruth Jencks found Angoff objectionable, having never seen that side of Mencken, one of whose closest friends was her father, Raymond Pearl—said that you had a different impression of him if you saw him playing Beethoven at their Sunday-evening concerts: he would shout with exultation when they had finished a symphony. Angoff does admit that he was very much moved at hearing Mencken talk about Schubert. [Marginal note: Lardner and Mencken, after Turgenev and even Genet, seem rather vulgar and lacking in seriousness.]

I felt, after reading this book and Don Elder, that the twenties had been a squalid period. Ruth agreed with me about this, said that she had reacted against her parents, with their newly liberated ideas, had felt that they had no real moral basis. At the Baltimore parties then, everybody drank so much that she used to find herself, after the first few minutes, talking most of the time to Mencken's wife: they would be the only people who were making sense.

Cabell: *There Were Two Pirates*
      The Devil's Own Dear Son

Not bad, but not of his best—the two familiar themes: the bad man who accepts conformity, settles down to a comfortable marriage; the split personality, with the real half leading a commonplace life while the other lives in a dream.

Went through, without reading every word of, *The Meaning of the Dead Sea Scrolls* by A. Powell Davies, *The Qumrân Community* by Charles T. Fritsch, *Dublin's Joyce* by Hugh Kenner, and *Joyce* by Marvin Magalaner and Richard M. Kain. (*New Yorker* notes.)

Read part of Felix Frankfurter's collected papers. After Genet, it seemed quite fresh and bracing, and pleasantly brought back the days of liberal hope and faith, at the time of the founding of *The New Republic*.

George Scott: *Time and Place*. Read a good deal of this without expecting to when I picked it up: very interesting, illuminating—point of view of lower-middle-class Englishman, very young at the time of the war, given a taste of Oxford, where he was partly made to feel himself an outsider but got something from David Cecil: regards himself as a rebel but tried to go along with the Tories till he found they were doing nothing more serious than trying to perpetuate the old order. Corresponds to Kingsley Amis, whose horseplay, however, he rather deplores.

Angus Wilson: *Anglo-Saxon Attitudes* [1956]. His best book up to date, but I don't quite believe in his middle-aged heroes who get themselves muddled up and then make a moral effort to straighten themselves out. The characters seem more plausibly human and more subtly imagined psychologically in the first part of this book than in *Hemlock and After* [1952]; but later— when the Dance of Death begins—the catastrophes and the nasty scenes slip back into his satirical vein, which tends to be somewhat fantastic, and the characters no longer seem real.

Anthony Powell: *A Question of Upbringing, A Buyer's Market, The Acceptance World*.[8] A watered-down British Proust, the Proustian observations on human life are largely unsuccessful: the Latin of Proust's French style sounds pompous in English, and Powell is far from profound or poetic. These books are full of bad writing and even bad grammar. What is good in them is simply the rather lightweight comedy one finds in his earlier novels. Unlike Wilson and Waugh, he has no literary importance whatever. One is astonished by the state-

ments on the jacket—of Betjeman, Pritchett, Elizabeth
Bowen,[9] who talk about the "beauty" of the series, the
excellence of P.'s writing, etc.

I have been reading a few too many light British
novels lately—a holiday after finishing my book—they
are beginning to blur in my mind: elderly pederasts,
careerists who ring more or less false, nobility and gentry
who are losing their grip, discontented and rather fast or
bitchy wives, lower-class pansies and impudent spivs.

Compton Mackenzie: *Thin Ice* [1956]. A curious and
rather unsuccessful book. He has attacked the subject of
the pederast more seriously than in *Vestal Fires* [1927];
but it is hard to know what his intention is. Is this a
picture of the collapse of Imperialism or a tract against
the homosexuality laws? I suppose the idea is that Imperialism, like buggery, is a sterile assertion of power,
uncomfortable for the object. The friend who is telling
the story, adoring and apprehensive—though he believes
himself to be a liberal—is the passive obverse of Henry.

H. L. Mencken: *Minority Report*. I have been trying
to read this, but doubt whether I'll ever get through it.
Some of the paragraphs are effective; clear and crackling; but his ideas, stated boldly, are mostly stupid. It is
only when he embroiders them, sets them to music, that,
as Cabell says, one no more thinks to ask whether they
are true than one asks whether a symphony is true.

I read *Water Babies* to Helen.[10] It makes on me very
much the impression that it did when it was read to me
in my childhood. The satire on the professor—which is
both Rabelaisian and preachy—and unassimilable by
either child or grown-up. The moralistic fairies of virtue,
with their priggish names, are annoying, too. The escape
of the chimney sweep and his adventures with the water
creatures are charming. These parts are a pleasure to read

aloud, on account of the sound English rhythm and the vocabulary made up almost exclusively of Anglo-Saxon words—no Latin derivatives save such comparatively simple words as *interest*. Its moralizing prevents it from belonging to the same class as Carroll and Lear. Helen, however, loved it.

John Allegro: *The Dead Sea Scrolls*. So far the best book on the subject in English—am going to review it for the B.B.C.

Jean Genet: *Querelle de Brest*. Perhaps the best of the books of his I have read. Masterly picture of Brest: sailors, doctors, shipyard workers. Though he tells you that among his characters only the lieutenant is a pederast, they are all more or less homosexual. As in *P[ompes f[unèbres]*, an elderly woman who is made more or less ridiculous. In *Notre-Dame des fleurs*, you have the feminine homos, *les tantes*; here Querelle is supposed to be ultra-masculine—well muscled, audacious, and hard, has committed a series of murders. The people he kills are invariably weaklings—the young sailor, the American pansy—they seem to represent his own weakness, his homosexuality that comes out, in spite of himself, as passive in the episodes with the policeman and the brothel patron. As usual, the theme of betrayal—the point of it evidently is that it makes the heroes feel more alone, it is only in solitude that they feel their strength. Excellent psychology and descriptions of the episode of Gil hiding in the *bagne*—compare Tom Sawyer and Huckleberry Finn!

Started Turgenev's *Dva priyatelya* [*Two Friends*], but shan't be able to finish it before I go (finished on return from Europe—evidently reflects his unsuccessful affair with his second serf-girl mistress). Curious Sofka [Winkelhorn's] distaste for what she calls his stories about "provincial boys and girls in white organdie." This one, at the beginning, *is* a little dull when you have read a good many others; but she evidently has very little literary sense. I have been reading him straight through and have never lost my appetite for him, though I break off from time to time. She evidently cannot taste his quality, and she says that all his criticisms of Russia are an old story to her. The truth is that people like her and like the Chavchavadzes, not being particularly literary, do not want to read about the old regime—they never read Turgenev or Chekhov. What they like best is *Voina i mir* [*War and Peace*], heroic and aristocratic. They never read *Voskresenie* [*Resurrection*], which gives also a depressing picture of contemporary (with Tolstoy) tsarist Russia.

July 16, the day before I leave. The morning is simply marvelous, with its light and its cool live air. Walking out on the road was to find oneself in an element almost like water, flowing over the trees and the hills. Little clouds are drifting with it above the distant hills.

Sorry to leave the old house—when I have got it at last into such good shape—shut up for so long a time.

Before Elena left, Walther called her up to say that Light Ginger had little ulcers all over her stomach. When she went back [to] Wellfleet, she learned that he had taken her to the vet, who explained to him that the "ulcers" were simply her teats.

Talcottville Poem
Ambition, pride, and peace.

Coming back 1st, with Rosalind, Reuel, and Bill Peck, and seeing the trees, just outside Boonville, that gave me the old noble thoughts and finding the poor old house in such run-down condition.

NOTES

1. *Upstate*, pp. 137–47.

2. EW was writing *A Piece of My Mind* (1956).

3. A retired German farmer who frequently chauffeured EW.

4. Prince Dmitry Syvatopolk Mirsky, Russian critic and historian; *A History of Russia* (1927). *The Twenties*, *passim*; *The Thirties*, pp. 563–64 and *passim*.

5. Norman Douglas (1869–1952), British novelist, best known for *South Wind* (1917) and *Alone* (1921).

6. Charles Angoff (1902–79), *H. L. Mencken: A Portrait from Memory* (1956).

7. *Anatole France Himself* (1925), *Anatole France Abroad* (1928).

8. From Anthony Powell's sequence of twelve novels, *A Dance to the Music of Time*, which began with *A Question of Upbringing* (1951) and was completed in 1975.

9. V. S. Pritchett, novelist and critic; *Classics and Commercials*, pp. 419–22. Elizabeth Bowen (1899–1973), Anglo-Irish novelist; *The Twenties*, p. xiv.

10. Charles Kingsley's (1819–75) *The Water Babies, a Fairy Tale for a Land-Baby* (1863).

12/2/10

EUROPE, 1956

Crossing on Media *July* 20–28: I took along two volumes of Zola—*La Terre* and *Nana*—and we both read both of them. The neutral Britishers on the ship—so quiet and so generally dull—threw the novels into relief and made them rather prey on our minds. They were the only reading matter we had—our baggage having gone on the *Liberté*. Elena pointed out that they were influenced by, and quite in the atmosphere of, the French painters of the same period: Degas, Renoir, Manet, etc. —the sowing at the beginning of *La Terre* and the other country scenes, the Grand Prix toward the end of *Nana*, and the theater from in front and behind the scenes. There is more humor—of a grisly kind—than I had expected, and more insight into the characters' psychology; it is also better written, in spite of his repetition of favorite words, such as *ricaner*—something his characters are constantly doing; but at a certain point in each of these books, the acceleration of horrors begins to be implausible and absurd. He loses his grip on his reader. Yet in most ways it is much better than Maupassant, who struck me, when I read *Bel Ami* three or four years ago,

as not really so very much better than John O'Hara.
—Just having read Angus Wilson's *Anglo-Saxon Atti-tudes*, I was struck by the influence on him of Zola,
which is more in evidence, I should say, than that of
Dickens, to whom all the British reviews refer. The same
families which do not, like Dickens's, present variations
on the same theme but seem to have been invented solely
with a view to bad relations, quarrels, *engueulades*. Then
the disagreeable incidents accelerate and lose the belief of
the reader—the unpleasant party, which is followed by
John and his boyfriend falling over the cliff.

We went to the Palladium the afternoon of Saturday,
August 4. A vulgar and raucous vaudeville, which Elena
seemed to enjoy more than I did. There was one cockney
monologue by a woman so thick that I could hardly
understand it. Has cockney changed a lot since my
youth? She would say: "Here he cûms now." —But I am
almost always stimulated in the theater, and I think it
was here that I had the idea of a play that would end,
not with a neat curtain, a scene that ties up the whole
package, but with something fresh and unexpected that
goes on vibrating after the curtain, investing the whole
play with a new significance, suggesting a new dimen-sion. —I can't do this with the Talcottville play,[1] be-cause it must revert to the framework of the modern
people watching the past.

Elena left with Olili, the 6th, to struggle with Johan-nisberg.

Arriving in England is always relaxing. In spite of the
developments since the last war, the social system is still
largely taken for granted, and it is soothing for an
American to arrive in a place where everybody accepts

his function, along with his social status, and everything operates smoothly—officers on the boat, officials at the customs, conductor on the train, taxi drivers—the taxi drivers in New York talk your ear off unless you shut them up.

Early part of the trip from Liverpool reminded us both of Lewis County: black-and-white cows grazing, big trees in the pastures, fields of grain—but in New York State everything is wider and there are bigger hills in the distance.

Pleasant quiet, dim light, English beds, big bathtubs and old-fashioned trappings of the Basil Street Hotel.

Our whole trip (I am writing this in Paris, Aug. 18) has been much better this time. Better relations between both of us and Olili. Their visit in Johannisberg went off well, in spite of their apprehensions. Olili had not been there since February. Madeleine on some occasion had abused their mother and father, and O. had cleared out and remained away. Madeleine, when O. did not come back, sent Dorothy Paget an abusive letter, which O. had intercepted. When O. called M. up to tell her that Elena and she were coming, Madeleine gave her an *engueulade*—in this vein, Elena says, she goes on like the characters in Zola—saying that she supposed Elena had intercepted her telegram, and that when Olili came to Johannisberg, she would send Dorothy Paget some messages that would reach her. This so upset O. that she collapsed in bed for three days, and she remained at Hermit's Wood, and we did not see her. After O. and Elena had made their visit, and O. was staying here with us at Paris (Hotel Lotti, 7, rue Castiglione), Hermit's

Wood called O. up to say that a letter had come for
D.P. from Johannisberg and should they give it to her?
O. told them no, and again was much upset. —Elena
said that Bazata's position was bad, persecuted and bullied
by M. She thought their liaison was over. Brat was now
in a state of indifference in regard to Madeleine. Madeleine had now decided that Elena was charming. Elena
says that she always has to have someone as a scapegoat
for her bad conscience—they are lucky when Madeleine
has her sister there and takes it out on the sister. On
occasion she has called both Elena and O. *grues*—the
latter when she was having her affair with the cellist, the
sole love affair, I suppose, of her life—and at the time
Elena first returned after the war, she had called her
une sale renégate. —E. and O. had attended some merry-
making—an anniversary of the Mumm business—that
she said was completely feudal. I should like to have seen
this, but can't take the rest of it. Anti-Semitism is still
noticeable in O.'s conversation. She rather astounded us
in Paris by explaining that the occupying Germans had
been perfectly all right till living in France had made them
soft and then they had become corrupted. It turned out
later that she didn't know that the Germans had melted
up all (?) the metal statues in Paris. She commented on
the bright new gilding of the Jeanne d'Arc statue in the
rue de Rivoli without knowing it was a recent replica—
had not noticed the Voltaire statue was gone from the
Quai Voltaire. It is hard to handle all this. As E. [said],
you just have to avoid the war.

Returning to England—

Anecdotes: Evelyn Waugh went to the House of Lords
and said to an old gentleman he met there that it was
very interesting for a novelist to see it. Was he a novelist?

asked the old gentleman. How much did your last novel sell? —Thirty thousand. —My brother's sold three million. —It was Somerset Maugham's brother, now a law lord.[2] Waugh himself told Cyril Connolly this.

Sylvester Gates told me about an interview between Cocteau and Maurice Bowra, when Cocteau came to Oxford to receive his honorary degree. Bowra's French is pretty bad and after telling Cocteau about coming to France to receive the Légion d'Honneur, had ended, *Et à la fin, j'ai été baisé par le président de la République.* Cocteau did not bat an eyelash.

Aug. 9. Had lunch with Cyril Connolly and spent most of the afternoon with him; then later had dinner with him and Barbara and a young Irishman named Lindsay. A man named Alan Ross joined us. It is something to see Cyril examine a menu—will say, You have to be careful here not to get something too rich—hesitates over seafood and wine, always anxiously inquires of the waiter whether the fish he wants to order is really fresh. At lunch, he was surprised to discover that I did not know all the details of his recent experiences with Barbara. —It's been going on for a year! —He then proceeded to tell me—the story went on so long and had so many ins and outs that I more or less lost track of these. The main line was that B. had not at first liked Weidenfeld, Cyril's publisher, but then had. Weidenfeld had thought he wanted to marry B., had promised that he would do so as soon as the decree was made absolute; but as I gathered later from Esther Arthur, his respectable Jewish family, in conjunction, no doubt, with his Jewish wife, brought pressure to bear on him, and he let her down, told her that she could change her name to Weidenfeld by deed poll. In a fury she went back to Cyril in tears —I had the impression, though I am not quite sure, that he was still living in her cottage in Kent. He had evidently been thoroughly enjoying all this—she had, over a period of months, been shuttling between him and W.—and was now feeling rather triumphant over her now having returned to him. His account of all this to his friends was that his love affair with B. had gone rather stale, and that in order to revive it they had had to divorce and start all over again. But now she had written a book, and when she had been with him she had kept a diary about her relations with him, which she was now turning into a novel. It was intolerable to have this typewriter going all the time, and somebody in the house who took all the paper and pencils. In the meantime, she had confiscated and hidden a diary that he had kept about his relations with her. He knew where it was, however, and was going to break in and get it sometime when she was away. I said that I sympathized with his situation, suggested that he ought to get a different kind of woman, who would also take better care of him. Yes, he said, he should have either of two kinds of women: a woman who had some rather dim talent, who painted a little, for example, or a *"femme du monde*, like me." He did not bore me with this, however: he talks well, with amusing metaphors that he is good at carrying through. Lys had been a Shetland pony; B. was a lioness—her silvery hair and her greenish and feline eyes—her friends complained that she bit them, but then she would come back and rub against you and you'd think that she was a good lioness, that your friends might have been making passes at her. —In Paris, I read B.'s book, *A Young Girl's Touch*—no glamorizing, no self-pity—a flat and sordid account, occasionally rather funny, of her life in London during the war, adventures in Africa on war work (slept with a party kept by a king who is obviously Farouk), return to England and escape to somewhere else in order to get away from an old admirer. People come to grief on her account but she does not really care. She is sulky and selfish (her heroine), never seems to have any real fun, is not interested in what she sees. She is evidently neurotic (Cyril says that he has decided that B. is neurotic) and suffers from a feeling of inferiority. But explicitly there is nothing about class in her book. Nor is there anything about discipline in her account of the army, living up to British ideals of accomplishment, behavior, stamina. The girl is supposed to be bright, but does not bother with her work, is always fired. She has phases of loneliness and depression, but cares nothing about her men. The only thing she has to depend on is the power over men of her prettiness. When she has made proof of this, she repulses them. Something of Mary [McCarthy] in this, with less interest and force of character. She showed a lively interest in Mary's last book,[3] and I feel that her book about Cyril will probably show Mary's influence. —I do not get on with her, and when you talk to her, there is no response in her face, a simple narcissistic mask, petrified by a fundamental sullenness. This is only occasionally diversified by gusts of a flirtatious animation. —Elena says—rightly, I think— that all this wallowing in amorous difficulties is bound up with his luxury taste for literature, wine, and food. His friends are all, at any rate, bored with his tales about himself and B. When he found that I had not heard it all, he pounced upon me as a wonderful fresh listener. Sonia Orwell said that she had gone abroad to get away from it; then as soon as she got back to England, Cyril had called her up, and she had felt like leaving again. —Nevertheless, he has a wit and a distinctive, an innate, cachet of the artist that none of his contemporaries (whom I know) does. He talks so well that he did not bore me.

—My impression is—I get it from her book as well as from what I hear about her—that Barbara is really a bad lot. I was surprised to hear that she had written a book at all, and it was better than I expected; but she seems a destructive and empty girl, mischievous but not ever lethal on any very big scale. If, in her book, she exaggerates an importance at all, it is, I should think, in the destructive direction. Cyril, I imagine, likes to think of her as a fascinating and dangerous beauty over whom he has established some sort of hold. When I asked him why he didn't get someone else, he said, I'm still on the flypaper—I've got most of my legs loose, but I haven't yet quite got off. *12/4/10*

When I arrived in France, I found that Esther Arthur and Nicholas Nabokov knew all the same people that I knew in England, and simply went on gossiping about them. The gossip is certainly more amusing over here than it is at home. People are so scattered in the States that they may know very little about one another.

In England, I kept myself down to the English quietness and flatness and fell into the English conversational rhythm, in which, for example, in asking a question, one emphasizes the first word: *Do* you . . . ?, *Can* you tell me . . . ?, *Have* you read the program?, etc. We Americans emphasize the main verb: Have you *read* the program?, etc., which seems more natural from the point of view of the meaning. There is evidently, for the English, some principle of underemphasis involved. On the train from Boulogne to Paris, it was difficult to adapt myself to French, very quickly spoken and with the rhythm running the other way, final syllables accented. In Paris, when I saw Esther Arthur, the whole thing was broken up by our reversion to American methods, soon walking up and down the room and interrupting and shouting at one another. With Nicholas at lunch in the rue de l'Echelle, it was equally *mouvementé* in the different Russian way. If I asked about Roger Peyrefitte or the Russians at Oxford, *il se démenait*, seizing me by the arm and imitating the various characters at the top of his voice, attracting the attention of the people in the restaurant. —In Germany (I am writing this in Munich), the difficulty is to switch back out of French into a language with a rhythm more like English.

Two things about *Esther* that puzzle me: She repeats at length what people have told her, yet I don't know how she can have heard them say anything, since she is always talking herself. I have the greatest difficulty breaking into her monologue to tell her anything myself —even when she is talking about something or somebody —Sylvester Gates, for example, whom I had just seen in London—that I know more about than she. Janet Flanner[4] seems to think that she hears what people are saying when they are talking to other people, while she is talking about something else—says that she will read a book rapidly and be able to repeat passages from it, and at the same time listen to what is being said in the room. The second riddle: How is it that she has lived in France so long and still speaks French so badly? It seems to me that she actually gets worse: she aspirates the *h*'s in *hélas, Homais*, etc., and talks about *Madame Bovairy*. She is fluent in her rugged and rocky way and seems perfectly to understand spoken French. She will repeat long conversations in which her French interlocutors are made to speak as bad French as she does. She pays little attention to genders (I, too, get them mixed up). I asked Janet whether she thought Esther did it on purpose, as some English people seem to do, and she said that she didn't think that Esther did anything on purpose.

Esther had seen Lorna Linsley in Paris—just before her death—when she was on her way from Africa back to the States. Lorna had made an excursion by car into an African game preserve or reservation in which it was prohibited to go on foot. But Lorna had escaped from the car and immediately met a lioness. She had seen that the lioness was pregnant and knew that she might be dangerous: "I saw that the only thing was to go along with her"—so she walked along with the lioness, and then gently allowed their paths to diverge. Lorna was fined, I think, £20. —Esther's theory about Lorna is that she traveled all over the world looking for the Boston Tea Party, and she believes that Lorna's reason for doing this is that her great-uncle (I think) was a renegade to the Republic in the War of 1812—he was an admiral who made an attempt to betray Boston Harbor to the British. —In telling this to Janet Flanner, I said something about Esther's theory not necessarily being reliable. —"But," said Janet, "I'm sure it's brilliantly illuminating."

Esther still believes herself to be working on her book on Mme. de Maintenon, and that she is coming back home when she has finished it. This must have been going on for twenty years. I wonder how much writing she does. She reads up every angle of her subject. I love to hear her relapse into describing things in American terms: "When Mme. Guyon did her nosedive into Quietism—it must have been the same thing as Christian Science—she didn't stay very long!"[5]

She evidently still adores John Strachey; had seen him lately in Paris and quoted at length what he had said. It may be she does listen to him.

. . .

I have felt on this trip particularly the great difference between *Europe and America*, that we have always had something to build, to win, whereas they have too much to look back on. I can see with my own family—Talcottville and New Jersey—and my own career, how we have always been going somewhere. This involves a certain constant pressure, from which I relax when I come abroad—like my father in Carlsbad in 1908.

Ordinarily *Elena* seems tall and distinguished, and with, in her quiet way, a certain authority. I have seen her with only two women who gave her a different aspect: Elizabeth Bowen, whose Holbein-like figure and face made her seem a little less distinguished; and Maria Jolas,[6] beside whom she took on suddenly a lilylike fragility. We dined in a café on the Left Bank, where I sat next to a full-length mirror, so that every time I looked aside I saw myself, from head to foot, sitting at the table, and was horrified at the contrast between my big-bellied person and my red and swollen face, with a not too pleasant expression about the eyes and the mouth, and Elena's exquisite slimness and delicacy. She had just been vaccinated, and I thought she looked rather pale.

In Paris, we often made love. It was partly the atmosphere of Paris, partly the freedom and leisure of being away from home. She seemed more than ever divine. I still have a strong appetite for her, and I am grateful to her for not being disgusted with my being so heavy and flabby. But I have gotten over the soreness in my right arm which at one time made my embraces so clumsy; and I do not become congested and pant. I have not taken any *serpentina* pills since I left the States and have occasionally violated my non-salt diet, but I found

in Paris that I could take long walks and climb stairs
without much difficulty. It may be partly freedom from
anxieties, but it is certainly also due to the little hard
liquor I drink. From the American point of view, the
martinis here are thimblefuls, and a double scotch is the
equivalent of a single scotch at home. A bottle of Mar-
tell in our rooms did partially knock me out.

Aug. 8. From the English visit:
A day in Cambridge with Stewart Perowne. He is in
some ways rather a silly man, yet one cannot help in
other ways respecting him. I was rather puzzled at first
by the people he had asked to lunch: the Master of
Corpus Christi (Perowne's own college), a chemist; the
Master of Pembroke, formerly connected with the Cambridge University Press; the choirmaster of Trinity; and
Heffer of Heffer's bookshop (Heffer I understood). The
only thing they knew about me—except in the case
of Heffer—was that I came from the United States,
and the two Masters had been there; so they talked about
the differences in the prices of tobacco and gas between
England and the U.S. Since I neither smoked nor drove
a car, I couldn't contribute much to this. When I spoke
to Gates in the evening about this habit of English dons
of conducting long conversations about subjects in which
nobody is interested, he pointed out that it came from
the policy of not talking shop on social occasions—add-
ing that he himself thought that shop was the only thing
interesting to talk about. At one point, the Master of
Corpus Christi remarked that he thought that this period
was one in which people in general were particularly
well-off. I assumed that this was one of the paradoxes
which Cambridge is supposed to cultivate, but presently
inquired whether he didn't think that these wars were a
nuisance. "They're a nuisance," he said, "but they've

always had them." Before lunch, Perowne had taken me
to the Trinity Library, full of wonderful things—we
looked through a medieval Psalter, with a bestiary at the
end, mss. of A. E. Housman, Richard Porson, etc.—
and had had some of the treasures of the Corpus Christi
tableware brought out, drinking horn, apostle spoons,
etc. We had walked around a little. Cambridge must
be one of the most beautiful towns, if not the most
beautiful town, in England from the point of view of
grounds and buildings. It is much more attractive than
Oxford, with its unpainted Bodleian and its crumbling
stone. Here everything, since the war, has been polished
and scrubbed, and the gilt woodwork in one of the halls
has just been regilded. After lunch, the choirmaster of
Trinity took us through Trinity Chapel, bringing us into
the choir and behind the altar, where visitors were not
allowed; and the Master of Pembroke showed us a MS.
of the "Country Churchyard" and Gray's commonplace
book, taking us into a room that was accessible only
through doors that required five different keys, the idea
being that it could only be opened by three college
officials together. (He also produced a MS., which he
had bought for himself, of Housman's poetry lectures.)
I then realized that these men had been invited in order
to show me around. Since I had to get to London in time
for dinner and took a four-something train, I didn't
have time to do Heffer's justice. Most of the time I was
there I was being introduced to the heads of departments
and having tea in his office with Heffer. But I took
account, after I left, of the adroit and quiet way in which
Perowne had managed—as he had done in Jerusalem—
to show me a good deal in a very short time. I think he
enjoys this. —Cyril Connolly tells me that P., in his day
at Cambridge, was what was called "a great man," but
had never quite turned out. John Davenport was another

case. One of the *New Statesman* people described him
as "a half-successful *raté*."   *12/5/10*

Struck by the number of people in the literary world
of England who seem to be *illegitimate sons or the products of misalliances*. John Russell is, I believe, illegitimate. Pritchett told me at dinner that he was going to
order steak precisely because he was gouty, and that the
reason for his gout was probably that his mother had been
a barmaid; he had spent a good deal of his childhood out
of England—in France and Spain. John Davenport, I
was told, had some sort of mixed parentage. Wyndham
Lewis[7] is mysterious about his parents and has given
different people different accounts of his birthplace: he
told me Philadelphia, told Eliot (I think it was) that he
was born on a ship on the Atlantic between the U.S.
and England, the catalogue of his exhibition says he was
born in Canada—perhaps, as has been suggested, because
he wanted, during the war, to establish a residence in
Canada. Similar obscurity of Frank Harris's provenance.[8]
Elusiveness of the background of Bill Hughes, [George]
Meredith and his tailor grandfather. This is all a gesture
of the English system. Imagine Ezra Pound or Walt
Whitman concealing his parentage or birthplace! Lincoln seems to have hoped that he was an illegitimate
child, but everybody knew his background.

Angus Wilson seemed very happy over the success of
Anglo-Saxon Attitudes. Hair is quite white, face rosy; has
resigned from the British Museum, lives in the country
and writes, and has put on several "stone." Told me
that I ought to have met some of the young people of
the John Wain,[9] Kingsley Amis generation. Though
teachers of English in red brick universities, they had
done very little reading—knew little but the meta-

physical poets and Eliot; knew nothing of continental culture. No one had any interest in Shaw, whom A.W. thought a great man; would discover Nietzsche with astonished enthusiasm; greatly admired Carlyle. A.W., as someone else told me, had noticed Colin Wilson[10]— a young man in his twenties—exploring a variety of authors in the reading room of the British Museum, had made his acquaintance and encouraged him, and C.W. had dedicated his book to him. This book has made a considerable impression—highly praised by Cyril—but I doubt if I shall read [it], though, from an article of his I read in the *London Magazine*, I could see that he had verve, an appetite for ideas and literature—something rare in England just now. If he had been to this university, as someone said, he would have talked it all away.

Jean Genet: Angus Wilson agreed with me that there was something in Genet's life that he did not tell about in his books. In *Notre-Dame des fleurs*, the hero at one point goes away on a yacht, yet nothing is told about this. Nicholas Nabokov says that his friends in the country who know Genet say that he was once associated with somebody very cultivated and "erudite." I suspect him of interludes of luxury. Nicholas claims that Genet's argot and his waterside language are synthetic; says that his manners are good, not those of a *voyou*. —When I was over here before, I found that I rather embarrassed people or left them blank by saying that G. was a great French writer. Now everybody seems to have read him—the accepted attitude is not to be shocked. Completely different accounts of him that I get from different people. He had just been to England for the opening of *Les Bonnes* —which had not been a success; had taken the line that he didn't like London—having been there before at some time—and didn't care to see anything of it. [Marginal note: Elena had seen him and thought he was certainly a Slav.] John Raymond said that he was "horrible," wore a double-breasted suit and resembled a floorwalker at the Galeries-Lafayette. Angus Wilson had evidently not found him sympathetic either, said he was just like a petty crook—"which of course he is." Mme. Detourd, whom we met at Nelly de Vogüé's and who works at Gallimard's, told me that her husband knew Genet well, that G. put on a great show talking about his robberies—especially of rich South Americans. One of them had left out a silver cigarette box especially for G. to steal (I think this is in one of his books). Seeing that I was interested in G., Nicholas asked his friends about the possibility of my meeting him. He had answered, *"Qu'est-ce qu'il veut de moi? Un Américain— est-ce qu'il a de l'argent à me donner? Est-ce qu'il topé?"* When they told him probably not: *"S'il n'a pas de l'argent à me donner, je n'ai aucun intérêt à le voir."* He had been laying all his friends under contribution for money for his married boyfriend (and probably other boyfriends), whose family he helped to support. He had failed to persuade a boyfriend in Rome to accompany him to France; had looked in the window and asked Mme. Detourd whether he wasn't still good-looking. Since he was one of Gallimard's authors, she had to tell him yes. —She said that, after Genet's stock having gone way up—I suppose, as a result of Sartre's patronage —it was now extremely low. It surprised me to hear that it had ever been high and that G.'s books, in the NRF edition, had sold about 10,000.

At the reception of Cocteau at the French Academy, Jean Genet had been present and had sat beside Queen Elizabeth of Belgium. With all admiration for Genet, I do think it indicates a rottenness of Europe that he should be nowadays one of its great writers. —We went to see *En attendant Godot*, which I had thought pretty good when I read it but had not been tremendously impressed by. On the stage, it is, however, extremely effective—gives an impression of intensity and creates suspense, is conceived in completely theatrical terms; admirably acted in a revival at L'Hébertot. As a picture of squalor and despair, it reminded me of Genet's *Les Bonnes*. It did not succeed in New York as it has done in France, England, and Germany for the reason that we cannot accept this despair, this acquiescence in a low morale. —Elena says that after the war you felt that things were still stirred up, but that now they were simply stagnant: just pieces of the same old ideas and faiths floating around in the *pourriture*. In *Godot*, the only historical event of which they have any recollection is the crucifixion of Christ; but when they try to strike the pose they can't make it. Vladimir cannot remember how the song about it goes, the only features that are remembered are the thieves. The central characters in Angus Wilson are elderly stuffed shirts, long sunk in hypocrisy, who just manage a little—through the persistence in them of some old ideal of honesty—to straighten themselves out. The morality of Genet is completely perverse, antisocial, self-degrading, betraying his closest friends so that he can better feel his self-dependence.

I said to Cyril that *a passionate interest in women* was now very unfashionable in London—they had invented the word *womanizer*, a term of opprobrium, which means a man who likes women. I might have added that *heterosexual*—more uncommon than *homosexual*—gives the impression of referring to an aberration. He said, Yes, and the English have invented the word *uxorious*. Maurice Bowra, he said, talked contemptuously about *sex bores*.

—He said at lunch that the further back in h
he went, the richer he found they were—imp
the habit of having money was deeply ingraine
nature. He was expecting an aunt to leave him ─ good
£10,000 and worried because she was spending her
capital.

But this stagnancy and decadence, I suppose, is only
characteristic of the kind of people I know. I got the
impression in Paris of a kind of people swarming the
streets, the first Sunday I was there, who were not unlike the people in Moscow—not smart, not poor, fairly
comfortable, not referable to any class structure. Completely undistinguished, taking the freedom of the distinguished rue de Rivoli, drifting about the royal Louvre
and the classicizing Tuileries Gardens for their Sunday-
afternoon outings. So in England, Kingsley Amis is dealing with a kind of young people not unlike those turned
out by provincial universities in the States. Angus Wilson
called my attention to his having been the first writer to
describe, in *Anglo-Saxon Attitudes*, the kind of people
represented by the young garage mechanic and his wife,
who like to dine in little French restaurants. In Germany, the same kind of thing: Franz Höllering tells me
that the young people have no ideas: they are thoroughly
discouraged with causes and have no interest whatever
in politics, which they leave to the politicians. All they
care about are deep-freezes, television sets, and what
Beverly in Boonville calls "hot cars," in which they seem
to terrorize the people of such small towns as that in
which Franz lives. With all this—as I gather from the
movie *Schwarzwald Melodie*—which I have described
in a letter to Elena—a considerable awe of America. The
middle and working classes in Europe seem to be taking
over what is commonest and least interesting in the

United States—a new uniformity, which also assimilates us all to Russia.

On the part of the more intelligent people, there is a curious contradiction in the attitude toward America. On the one hand, they are always jumping you about what they consider outrageous happenings. When I was here before, it was McCarthy and the Rosenbergs; and the other day Petka queried us about a black-and-white bus incident in the South and, at the same time, the beating-up of Sumner Welles,[11] to which, it seems, the French papers had given some political significance. But, on the other hand, they expect America to do something wonderful for them, and they apply to us standards of integrity, humanitarianism, and political wisdom that they never would expect of themselves. They cannot seem to imagine that we are just like everybody else.

England: Great success of the *U and Non-U* discrimination of Nancy Mitford and her professor in Finland (articles in *Encounter*)—widely applied in ways that probably make N.M. squirm. A table in Zwemmer's bookshop had a sign that said, "U Books at Non-U Prices"; and Mark Gouldin told us that his son, a jazz enthusiast, would consider boogie-woogie "non-U." Intended by its inventor to distinguish between the English upper and the middle class, these terms seem likely to designate a single social distinction which has survived a general leveling—that is, a distinction between such people as are still more or less well educated and bred from those [who] are noticeably less so. They are already extending to America.

Auden was, it seems, very nervous about his appearance at Oxford; but he had a large audience, and every-

thing went off all right. He stayed at the Spenders
before going there, and Stephen talked about his behavior
there in very much the same way as when Wystan came
back to England after the war. He had been aggressive
and brusque; but after his lecture, relaxed. —Natasha
Spender had visited his place on Cornelia St., where I
had never been. They warned her to use perfume when
she went there. Somebody had tried to pull back the
curtains, and the whole thing had [come] down in his
hands. Wystan had said, Why bother about the curtains?
If you pull them back in the morning, you just have to
pull them to again at night.

I no longer feel much desire to see old churches and
things: I feel I have had all that, it has nothing more to
teach me. In the limited time that is left me, I must
occupy myself with the United States and with the
present state of the world. Yet I hope to do some sightseeing with Reuel. It pleases me that he has been doing
so much himself, has seen practically everything in Paris
and London that we suggested to him. —I shall make a
point of taking him to the Pantheon simply because my
father took me there in 1908—I don't think I have seen
it since. *He* was interested in it simply on account of
Zola. He admired his action in the Dreyfus case and had
been thrilled by his burial in the Pantheon in spite of
the demonstration at his funeral. I don't believe Father
knew what Zola's novels were like. So far as I could see,
he had only read the book on Lourdes [1894], which had
also interested him much.

—I dined with Elena at Fouquet's and ordered Châ-
teau d'Yquem, in memory of my enjoyment of it at the
end of the first war. I found that it sickened me now:
it is really what is called a "dessert wine," much too
sweet for my present taste. I had also loved Asti Spu-

mante. —I even went so far at Fouquet's as to order chicken croquettes, with the traditional tomato sauce, which I always ordered in my childhood——Father used to kid me about it. I found them equally insipid, and I shall never order either again. —It is really only fun, at my age, to do all the old regular things in London and Paris with a child.

Elena said she found Paris less beautiful than she had been remembering it——though it seemed to me as attractive as ever. She said that for the first time she no longer felt that Europe was the part of the world to which she belonged. I love to hear her expounding America and crying up its merits to people over here, and I am more impressed by her, as I was before, in comparison with her relations——her intelligence, initiative, character. Marina's son, Semyon (?) Vorontsov, has come to the U.S. really as a result of what she said to him on our visit of '54, and is happy and doing well in New York, she told her he was delighted to get away from France and to find himself free with a job. —Also, seeing her with her family stimulates my love in that it makes me feel I have chosen a wonderful human being who is peculiar, unique, something she has created herself and that I, in a way, have created. That is, the resemblances I see in her to the other members of her family, instead of making me feel that she is part of an animal brood, have the opposite effect for some reason of throwing into relief her individuality, which, I feel, is mine. It is not the family I love but the unique person Elena. This gives me an erection as I write. It is somehow associated with the unique products of art. Love is creative as well as art, and what someone like Elena grows up to be, what she makes of herself, is creative.

Conversation reported from Johannisberg: Madeleine said that what they needed in France was the restoration of the monarchy, the Duc d'Orléans or whoever the pretender was, who would be (?) Charles Something or Other. Olili was agreed that government in Germany, at least, could not be left to the low orders. Elena cried, *"A la lanterne!"*

Elena had already told me that, as children, they had usually made a point of talking some other language than that of the country where they happened to be. On the train on our way to Nicholas's, they began talking German, and Elena remarked that they tended to do this as soon as they came to France. The whole family habitually carry on conversation in English, German, and French, shifting from one to another. I noticed how they did this at Johannisberg (in '54) and thought that it was a kind of device for avoiding the responsibility of identifying themselves with any country. They could dissociate themselves from Germany by speaking French and for the moment pretending to be Frenchmen, and they could get away from the Continent through English. When we first saw Olili in London, she had brought up with her from Dorothy Paget's a very heavy old-dowager English, which Elena commented upon—it certainly removed her from Johannisberg, which she had left on bad terms with Madeleine and to which she had not been back since February; but this had entirely worn off by the time we got to Paris and had turned into an international English suitable for a young girl. When I told Elena that I thought it was a bad thing for them to be continually switching languages, she—rather to my surprise—agreed, said it saved them from facing things. —She herself, with her fluency in four languages—it

has taken me a long time to realize it—had grown up
with a queer discrepancy between what she thinks, feels,
and wills and the way she expresses herself. Due partly,
I think, to having been educated by governesses and
never having had the discipline of formulating the
answers to questions in school, she can often not put
plainly the simplest things. When I ask her how much
the mark is worth, she will say, You divide it four ways,
instead of A dollar is worth four marks, or Four marks to
a dollar. She seems to speak with perfect facility but
actually she rarely does justice to what is going on in
her head. Since my ordinary communications with her
are likely to be so vague and ambiguous, since I often
have to cross-examine her to find out what she means,
I forget how observant and intelligent she is, how she
notices and remembers everything and how interesting,
when stimulated, she can be; I am also thrown off my
guard, so that I may not be aware till a very late stage of
some combination or project that she has been develop-
ing. There is a mind and personality there that is really
camouflaged by her languages. Though she speaks and
reads Russian less well than her other languages, she is,
as she says, far more Russian than Brat or Olili. She has
never lost the Russian locution. We went to a movie
with so-and-so, meaning: So-and-so and I went to a
movie (*my s toboi* [we together], etc.), though it conveys
a wrong idea—that some other person or persons were
present—in any of her other languages; and when we
read Russian together, a Russian personality comes out
that is darling and quite absent from her personality in
English. In France, she becomes more animated, has
moments of a feminine coquetry I have never seen at
home. She told me the other day in connection with
Olili—whom she called "a great big lump of devotion"
—that she herself had no loyalty. I said, You mean

loyalty to Germany? —I mean loyalty period. She explained that she had no loyalty to anybody or any country that did something she didn't like. But the truth is, of course, that she is exceptionally loyal to the people and things she loves—forgives, overlooks faults, never forgets about them. She is likely, in fact, to go too far in the direction of pretending that things are all right when she ought to be grappling with the fact that they are wrong. This, too, is likely to deceive one. One is startled at some moment afterwards—perhaps a long time afterwards—to discover how sensitively she has sized up some situation or penetrated someone's motives.

Munich: Evening with Charley Thayer[12] and thoughts about the Germans in second letter to Elena.

Paris. Death of Allan Ross MacDougall:[13] He was with Janet Flanner and her sister Hildegarde; had just read them the fragment of a poem that was found after Edna Millay's death: "Today no one has died," that referred to Gene, and they had made him read it again. They got up and started moving across the room—was it in the Hotel Continental?—and he fell dead at their feet: a heart attack. Janet arranged to have him buried in an American Legion cemetery in Paris (I think—at any rate, a cemetery for American soldiers), so that there would not be any question of the perpetual upkeep of a grave in a French cemetery, with the possibility of the body's being eventually thrown out if the upkeep was not paid. He had left a little money to a boyfriend.

We took Olili and Messia to *En attendant Godot.* Olili sat rather tense and unsmiling, and told us in the intermission that she had seen during the war so much that was macabre that she didn't much relish it on the stage. She said that when the bombing was going on she had seen two little girls looking in the windows of houses and laughing with delight wherever they saw a corpse. To bodies laid out in the street they paid very little attention: they were not so much fun.

For Olili, the Nazi myth of the Jew has not yet evaporated. She talked about the "quality of Jewishness," which was not necessarily displayed by Jews—"something unpleasant and slimy." This showed that the conception of the Horrible Jew, hovering over Civilization, had become a complete abstraction, dissociated from real people.

Coming to Europe this year, now that London and Paris, from the visitor's point of view, have recovered their old charm, and even Munich—in spite of its neo-Piranesian ruins, already with bushes growing out of them—seems a pleasant city again, I appreciate better its amenities than I have done since the first year. I realize how much—unconsciously—the determination to make something out of America must have biased me against what was really good in Europe: attractively built cities, good and quiet manners, appetizing food, respect for the arts, and—in Paris, at any rate—feminine chic. Now that life in the cities and towns seems to me no longer exciting but rather repellent, I begin for the first time to be able sympathetically to enter into the feelings of the Americans of an earlier generation who chose to live in Europe. Yet an American, except to a limited extent or in the case of some special situation, has no business here.

I don't think it is the fact that I am over sixty that makes me find that the women in New York are no longer so attractive as they once were. I see many attractive women in Paris. But having Reuel with me puts them beyond me. When I see a pretty girl, I no longer have the impulse to make her acquaintance: I am blocked by thinking, I'm a fat old man: that kind of thing is for Reuel. I felt the old call to adventure in Paris, but would remember they cost money and could come to nothing. And how could I work up passion for another woman when I liked Elena so well?

Charley Thayer in Munich told me about going hunting with some royalty or nobleman. They sat in a boat in a river, which was held in place by a gamekeeper, up to his cheek in the icy water. Thayer had said, "If I wasn't afraid of demoralizing your feudal system, I'd buy you an anchor."

When Reuel got back to Wellfleet, he told Elena that he had been reading Edna Millay's poetry with enthusiasm. She said, You know your father knew her. —Did he know Emily Dickinson, too? —In Paris, where I had been talking to him about Dupont-Sommer and Renan, he had asked me whether I had known Renan.

Now that I am reading and reading up Goethe, I remember Volodya Nabokov's saying, "Horrible Goethe" —he made a point of mispronouncing it, as he did Freud. I can see now why Goethe, as a writer, would be inconceivable to him: his [Nabokov's] idea of a literary work of art is something in the nature of a Fabergé Easter egg or other elaborate knickknack.

Léger's poem in the *Nouvelle Revue Française*, "Etroits sont les Vaisseaux"—which I call *Opération Femme*. Reading it has upon me the usual effect of admiration combined with fatigue. I had complained to Katherine Biddle that there was no personal feeling in his poems— all rhetoric, no lyric voice; and she wanted to know whether I didn't think that he had here written something that was wonderfully personal; but the whole thing is still too much generalized and, like his other poems, runs too much to technicalities: the woman seems to be equipped with all the parts and accoutrements of a ship.

NOTES

1. EW never finished this play.

2. Somerset Maugham's older brother, Frederic Herbert Maugham, became Lord Chancellor in 1938.

3. *A Charmed Life* (1955), in which a character is partly drawn from EW.

4. Janet Flanner (1892–1978), who for many years contributed a regular "Letter from Paris" to *The New Yorker* signed Genêt.

5. Mme. Guyon (1648–1717) was imprisoned from 1695 to 1703 for her association with Quietism, a religious mysticism that Pope Innocent XII condemned in 1699.

6. Who with her husband Eugene Jolas edited *transition*, the Paris avant-garde magazine of the twenties. *The Twenties*, pp. 254–61.

7. Wyndham Lewis (1884–1957), the English artist and novelist.

8. Frank Harris (1856–1931), successively editor of the *Fortnightly Review* and the *Saturday Review* and a flamboyant figure in the 1890s.

9. John Wain, prolific poet, novelist, and critic. In 1978 Wain edited *Edmund Wilson, the Man and His Work*, which includes Wain's essay "The Daughters of Earth and the Sons of Heaven: Edmund Wilson and the Word" (pp. 131–48).

10. Colin Wilson, whose unorthodox volume, *The Outsider*, had had a sudden success.

11. Sumner Welles (1892–1961), Under Secretary of State (1937–43).

12. Charles Wheeler Thayer (1910–69), diplomat and author, U.S. liaison officer to the German government at Bonn, 1949–52.

13. Allan Ross Macdougall (1894–1956), screen and stage actor, author.

WELLFLEET AND CAMBRIDGE

Wellfleet, Oct. '56. Kenny Rose's wife (next door) is dying of cancer: all over her intestines and liver. They have given her only a few weeks to live. It is very sad and upsetting for us. Their two nice little children, Brian and Janet, play with Helen almost every day, and one feels for their mother and father a particular sympathy and interest on account of their being so fond of one another. He met her in New Zealand, when he was there in the army, married her and brought her back. She is pretty, speaks with a kind of cockney accent. His father—who just died—was a Portuguese, did not amount to much; the mother, rather better, is a Yankee. He sells ice and cleans cesspools, had been doing pretty well. She has been in the hospital in Boston. The day that Kenny heard the verdict, confirming the opinion of the Hyannis hospital, he broke it for the first time to his sister Eunice Ferrara. What with work, worry about Thora and her own and her brother's children, she had no sleep for three nights, and finally went to pieces. Her husband gave her a sleeping pill, and she came to our house to collect the children. She was obviously in such bad shape that Elena made her lie down in the little house, and, as Elena said, she began to *divaguer*. She was saying, Oh, God, if you will let Thora live, I'll bake an apple pie! Elena had her spend the night there, with one of her brothers in the next room. Elena had given Kenny a stiff drink of whisky when he came back from the hospital and told her, and had soon resorted to whisky herself. The next day Elena saw her in her car with a huge apple pie. The pie must have been for Thora, not for God.

Period of erotic revival: dates, I suppose, from the moment of getting Elena away from her domestic role, from the moment of going to Europe, but has continued since I have been back. One night we sat on the couch and listened to Stevenson on the radio, campaigning in Madison Square Garden. I began to feel her—she was half sitting up—and she opened her legs and loved it. The high-pitched speech and applause—heard from my study—created a sort of excitement. She thought it was due to the piquant combining of an immense public occasion with something so intimately private; but for me it was more, I think, the kind of thing we used to feel in the twenties: the stimulus of pressure and pace. It did not run very long, and when they cut it off, we went on to something more active. Nowadays I never can seem to get enough. Approaching from the side her lower lips, I like to bite them a little; but she doesn't like things that hurt her. —I said afterwards that this had been the ideal way to listen to a campaign speech, and she said that if everyone could have Stevenson like that, he would be overwhelmingly elected.

Nov. 30, '56. Helen's appendicitis: The *Gateses* came to see us Friday. I had a very good time with them, but since they arrived late, we sat up till 1:30: and Elena didn't hear Helen calling her. When she went to bed, she found that Helen couldn't sleep on account of pains in her side (as in Canada), so that Elena was up with her all night, then had to get meals for the guests and entertain them the next day—she looked haggard, but I didn't know [how] little sleep she had had. When Dr. Burke finally arrived rather late in the afternoon, he took a blood test, then telephoned us from Orleans that it looked like appendicitis and we had better take her to Boston right away. He lined up an ambulance, a hospital room (at the Faulkner Hospital near Jamaica Plains), and a surgeon. When the ambulance arrived at the door, Helen, now dressed, presented herself and announced, "I'm the patient." At the hospital, they took another blood test and found that the situation looked worse. The surgeon arrived and examined her and told me she ought to be operated on immediately. He said that she was "a peach," and I was impressed by her self-possession. As her mother said, "She's such a little woman!" They gave her a drug to put her to sleep but she took pride in the fact that, when they took her up, she was still wide awake. She discussed with the doctor what he was going to do to her, and afterwards she told her mother that the operating room was not what she had expected but more like the inside of a spaceship. The doctor said he had found "a red-hot appendix"—it would have ruptured in a little while, we had got her there just in time. She had not come out of the ether when we left. When she did clear up about seven, she rang for the nurse and asked for a television set. On her way to the operating room, she had noticed a sign that said that television sets were available. Later, she needed a bedpan and rang again, and when the nurse did not appear, got out of bed and sat on a chair, and her mother found her weeping—her only lapse of self-control. Elena stayed all of every day with her—there was only one nurse for the whole ward. When I was telling Nina about it, she said, "Let's face it: Elena is an excellent mother." Helen observed intently what was going on in the hospital and would retail the gossip to her mother. The first day they got her up to stand and walk about for a few minutes. She insisted on putting on her Japanese kimono, and when her mother asked her whether her wound hurt, she answered, "A child can stand a certain amount of pain." Later, when she could walk in the corridor, she [asked] whether she could get the kimono pressed.

Elena brought her back on Dec. 9—I had come the day before, picking up the animals.

The *Gateses* left Sunday noon—after having been entertained the night before by Rosalind and Reuel, who had arrived just the moment before we left in the ambulance—and I managed to spend a couple of hours with them in the Bellevue while they were waiting for the train to Toronto. When I called up the porter to find out what station the train left from, a bellboy told me wrongly the North Station. Then we had difficulty in getting a taxi, thought we were just making the train and found when we got to the North Station that it left from the South Station. Dash for a taxi—the driver decided "to do something irregular" and cut across the traffic when we came to the corner where the station was but got stalled in the middle of the road, holding up the other traffic. It was nightmarish—he had to get out and push; then got stalled again on the other side of the street, but backed up to the station door just in time for them to get on the train. As Sylvester said, it was like a movie.

Sylvester elaborated on the story of Bowra and Cocteau: it had been told him by a French professor who was present: *"Devant toutes ces dames françaises! —Moment inoubliable!"* —He says he has a horrible suspicion that Bowra wants to be made a Labour peer, is laying siege to Gaitskell[1] and writing letters to the papers about such matters as capital punishment in which he has never before taken any interest.

Barbara has married Weidenfeld, and Cyril has moved to London and stays in bed all the time. Barbara still shuttles between the two, occasionally bringing Cyril a bowl of soup.

At home I never hear any gossip—we have no literary world like the London one—so enjoy the gossip of English friends.

Cambridge: We moved into the Bloomberg house in Cambridge on the 16th and 17th (?) of January 1957— I came down first in a station wagon with Bambi, Dark Ginger, and most of the paraphernalia, and Elena, Helen, and Light Ginger followed the next day, in the same upholsterer's car, with the rest of the baggage.

Bambi is old, thirteen, I think, and moving upsets and depresses him. When he sees the suitcases come out, he is always afraid that we are going away and leaving him with someone else. In Cambridge, he just lies around most of the time; it was days before he got to the point of going out in the snow and sniffing for other dogs, and even now, Feb. 28, he never shows the eagerness to take a walk that he was still capable of doing in Wellfleet. Life must be dull for an old dog, suddenly moved into a suburb. —Dark Ginger—in the mating season—disappeared, and was only retrieved—by means of ads in the papers—at the end of ten days. He turned up at

Dunster (?) House three miles away, where the students had been feeding him and making a pet of him. He was in dreadful condition, quite gray with dirt, and had to have a drastic bath.

Elena Levin invited Elena and Helen, so that Helen could get to know little Sarah Frohock. The two little girls went upstairs together and got along like mad, Helen taking Sarah over. Presently Sarah came downstairs and said, Mummy, I want to have my appendix taken out!—as Elena said, a triumph of one-upmanship for Helen.

William James comes to see us and we call on him: he lives just at the end of this little street. He is touching, rather pathetic, when one remembers how his uncle Henry encouraged him and had hopes of his painting. When I first see him, I can't help looking in his face— his dark eyes are liquid and sensitive—for the lineaments of his illustrious family, and I suppose that many people do this and that it must make him rather shy. Conversation is made rather slow by his difficulty in summoning proper names.

The first afternoon that Elena was here I was sitting in the further downstairs room that opens out of the main living room and heard people come to call whom I could hear but not see. Since they did not sound at all interesting I let Elena receive them: elderly Cambridge voices—they lived across the street and wanted to know if there was anything they could do for us. They left without my having seen them. Several days later, when we had been having martinis with somebody, I took Bambi out for a walk in the dark. It was snowing, and his back was glistening with snow. As we passed a house across the street, I saw at the front window what I took, with my imperfect eyesight, for a beautiful young girl with bare arms, leaning on the windowsill. I looked at her again, and she waved to me. I went with Bambi to the door and was admitted to an old-fashioned entrance hall by an elderly lady in brown, with evidently dyed red hair, who cordially invited me in and asked what I would like to drink. I asked her what she had, and she answered, Whisky, gin, and vodka. I said that I had been drinking gin, and she immediately produced a bottle. Though she was perfectly correct, I had the impression that she had been hitting it up herself. She was the lady who had come to call on us. The house was a dark brown interior of the eighties, sitting room and hallway lined with books: I noted Oriental subjects, and there were Buddhas and things on the bookcases. I asked whether her husband taught at Harvard, and she explained that he was a public accountant—he was away on a trip at the present time—but that her father had for years been professor of Sanskrit and editor of the Harvard Series of Oriental Studies. She had been the only one of the children who had taken his Sanskrit course—she thought one of them ought to take it. She recited some Sanskrit poetry, and then translated it for me and made it sound quite attractive—the translation, no doubt made by her father, had the grace of the old-fashioned love of literature. Her father had built the house and insisted upon the omission of some of the features of the period, such as the usual colored-glass window. I explained that Bambi—to whom she had also given a cordial welcome—was thirteen years old, and she told me that they had had an Irish terrier which had lived to be seventeen. Her daughter had said that when she married, she wanted to take the dog with her, and her mother had replied that by the time she was married, the old dog would be dead; but actually her daughter had had three children before the dog died. The daughter was living in Concord with her husband, who was in television—they had their own younger set out there. In her father's day at Harvard, she told me, the professors had been paid very little. There was a self-portrait, a drawing, by Alexander James,[2] now dead—it made him look more like his father than the present William. Finally I took my leave. —Elena, a few days later, on her way to join me at the James house, also got into this house by mistake. She said that Mrs. Cushman was completely tight.

We are right in the midst of the residences of the old Cambridge professors: Child's house is just back of us, A. Lawrence Lowell's not far away. I enjoy it, because it is so quiet; but can easily imagine how [E. E.] Cummings must have revolted against it in his youth and can understand why he came to Patchin Place and never wanted to leave New York. I remember that he said to me once, I'm going to Boston Sunday—pray for me! But the whole atmosphere of Cambridge is more serious, and to me more satisfactory, than Princeton. One feels this even in a household of the younger generation, like that of Arthur Schlesinger, Jr., so much jollier and cleverer in a worldly way than the older generation could have been.

This has been for us a period of miseries: the income tax problem;[3] the death from cancer of our neighbor Mrs. Rose; weeks of painful dentistry for Elena; my bronchitis and laryngitis: I was in bed here with a temperature over 102, was cured by Acromycin and went on to New York to be at the rehearsals of *Cyprian's Prayer* [1954] at New York University, but had a relapse after the dress rehearsal and spent days in bed at the Algonquin—am not yet completely recovered, haven't got my voice back: *ya znayu* [I know]. I'm rotting, as Nina Chavchavadze says; in the meantime, Helen had something similar, though not to the same degree, out of which Hedwig nursed her while we were in New York; Elena began to show signs of coming down with the "virus" too, but has fought it off with vitamin doses. I have broken my father's watch, and this always gives me a feeling of helplessness; and the rewriting of *The American Jitters*,[4] besides being the worst kind of drudgery, gets me down by bringing me back to memories of Margaret and the period of the depression. Her aunt Elinka has died—whom she resembled in appearance and devoted affection. She paid $5, in New York, for a Russian *naseauxida* (mass for the dead) to be said for her. There has been constant snow since we have been here, and Cambridge never cleans the streets. When I came back from New York, the snow was gone, revealing a small stepladder in the middle of the yard and a crate beside the house. Today it is snowing again, and these are again being covered up.

Helen, when she wakes up in the morning, tells her mother her dreams. This morning (March 1), she said that she had dreamt that she had become very small, so that the cats were much bigger than she was: There were those great furry things, and I was quite tiny! Light Ginger had begun to claw at her, and she had said to her, Stop that! I'm still your mistress. —Then she added to her mother: This is partly fiction.

Dos Passos called me up in New York. He was in Boston and wouldn't be able to stop off in New York, he said: he had just bought a new bull and had to be home for its arrival, he giggled.

April 6. This winter, since we came to Cambridge, has been almost unmitigated hell. Constant nervous strain in connection with the income tax and with the struggle between me and Elena as to where we are going to live—we had only made love twice. My long illness and losing my voice; Elena's weeks of dentistry. Elena had a touch of the same thing as I, and also had to go to the dentist, lost a tooth. The teeth in my upper jaw have suddenly been falling out. Bambi died—he just faded out, his heart ran down. Reuel and I dug a grave in the corner of the backyard, and I buried him there the next morning, in a basket with a blanket around him. I had first bought him for my mother from Joan Colebrook (giving her books in return) when Mary and I were living in Henderson Place, but when I brought him to Red Bank, she wouldn't have him, said that spaniels were cowardly—so I had him with me in New York before and after my trip to Europe, and took him out every night for a walk in Carl Schurz Park— I was working up *The Little Blue Light* in my head. He was the cutest young dog I ever saw and a friend in those difficult days when I was breaking up with Mary. When people came to see us before she left, I would play with him and hold him in my lap. —Then poor Mrs. Rose died—Kenny and his sister and the two nice children came to see us over a Sunday night. Brian had broken the news that his mother was dead to the cat that she had been specially fond of. —One of my only consolations through this period has been hobnobbing with old William James. I felt that his wife's illness was affording him more freedom than he had had before. She kept a check on his smoking and drinking, and, I am told, used to finish his sentences for him as soon as he hesitated for a word—a habit caught perhaps from his

uncle Henry. I found that he was shy at first, hesitated
and could not remember names, but that he then became
much more confident and talked very interestingly about
his family and Cambridge personalities—also about
painting. He thinks that the trouble about modern art is
that humanity is no longer central to it, and believes that
Sargent[5] will eventually come back. Also his wife has
just died. —One night I drank four bottles of heavy
dark German beer, and just as we were finishing our
supper on trays, tried to recite to Elena Lizette Woodworth Reese's sonnet[6] "Tears." When I got to the sestet,
I began to weep, tried it again and got through it, but
broke down again after I had finished. I think it was
something about the last lines, "How each hath back
what once he stayed to weep: / Milton his sight, David
his little lad," which set up an association with Rosalind,
who—from vodka and an empty stomach—had had a
weeping fit at our house two days before. I had dinner
with her at Locke-Ober's last Thursday night and we are
going to have dinner together every Sunday. She has
been alienated from us since her going to the analyst, says
it upsets her to come to Wellfleet because Elena is so
unhappy—thinks Elena should go back to her painting,
something which I have often suggested. When Rosalind
and I spent our summers together, she was beginning,
especially at Provincetown, to mature and play the part
of hostess. Then my marriage to Mary set her back to
childhood—since Mary was herself so childish and com-
peted in a childish way with Rosalind. I shall never
forget one summer at Stamford when they were feuding
as to who should have the funny paper. Mary [McCarthy]
did her best to crowd her out of my life—till toward
the end, when she tried to make an ally of her. Then
afterwards, when Rosalind and I were living in Henderson Place and she was going to Columbia, it wasn't a

particularly happy arrangement either. I would have women and make her sit in the Columbia library till after they were gone. When I got back from Europe, she and Jeanie were living in the Wellfleet house, and when I went up there, I found it in a horrible mess. They had lost the key to the front door or something, had done nothing about it and had been living with it like that for weeks. After I was married to Elena—who, like Margaret, was perfect with her, but indulged her, as she does everybody too much—she had become so lazy and slatternly that I became worried about her and made her go out on her own. Some people thought I was being hard, but it was the only thing to do. I didn't want her to become a Henrietta [Fort] Holland—and the result was that she got her job at Houghton Mifflin, is popular there and is doing well. But then the awful blow of the breaking of her engagement. Since she has been to the analyst, it is as if she had schooled herself to indifference. I don't know whether she has anyone now. —The advantages I have in Cambridge are partly things Elena can't share: this study in the Widener Library, where conditions for working are perfect: never any interruptions, I take with me a sandwich and an orange and a bottle of ginger ale, and I am able to concentrate more steadily than I usually do at Wellfleet. If I want a little relaxation, I spend a little time in the periodical room. The only things that depress me are the window ledges covered with pigeon excrement, and the pictures of Charles Eliot Norton, one of them rather unpleasant, and of his brother with the muttonchop whiskers. I have taken the brother down. Then there are things like the Saturday Club, and the weekly dinners of the Fellows, to which women are not invited. Only really bright spots for Elena: Henry's passing his State Department exams and his engagement to Daphne Sellar.

Elena met her parents, separately, in New York, when I
was in bed in the Algonquin, and was quite cheered up
by the whole thing.

April 9 (written on that date, the following six entries).
Fellows' dinners; Saturday Club; Oppenheimer lecture
(April 8)—all really stimulating occasions, and much
above the level of Princeton, it seemed to me.

The *Bloomberg house* seemed comfortable and not unattractive when we first saw it, but it turned out to be
rather queer, gives you a kind of malaise. Dr. Bloomberg
seems to be one of those cases of the psychiatrist who
marries a favorite patient and then can never cure her.
The whole place has the unsatisfactory character of unsatisfactory relationships: one feels that the family has
never been real. There are queer unpleasant smells the
source of which one cannot put one's finger on. The
gate opens in instead of out, and many of the doors won't
latch: they pop open when one thinks one has closed
them. Elena hates the pumpkin walls of her room, and
says the kitchen is full of inconveniences: if one of the
cupboard doors is left open, you can't open the kitchen
door.

I have grown to hate *my bedroom*—with its popping
doors and its little bedside table which is a snarl of
electric light and electric blanket and telephone cords—
in which I was so horribly sick and in which I read every
morning such sickening news in the papers. I have the
worst *bad dreams* in it I have had in years. One night
after Bambi died I dreamt that Jenny was dead and they
were carrying her around in a carton. Before that I had
had one of my dreams of guilt. I thought I had poisoned
an old woman and was burying her. Afterwards I was

telling the story as if about someone else. There was something about a rambunctious Southerner who declared that he was going to investigate. I was imitating him and inventing the device by which the plan was to be discovered. Then I began to feel that I oughtn't to make a funny story of it and tell it as it had happened to someone else when I had committed the murder myself. This was undoubtedly derived from the trial of Dr. Adams in England, which I read about in the paper every morning. He was charged with killing old ladies by overdoses of narcotics after inducing them to leave him their properties.

One night when we had a quarrel—before I was sick —*Elena* came into my study and told me that she had always depended on *her beauty* to have people pay attention to her and do things for her—when she went into a store, for example. Now she felt that she was losing [it]—perhaps in explanation of her just having lost her temper. This surprised me—she is always so modest about herself and will not accept compliments; and she said that she had never told anyone that before. I saw that it accounted for her perfect poise combined with lack of authority. She has no authoritative tone, is unable to give orders to children or servants; she relies entirely on pleasing and this leaves her weak in some ways.

April 6. Dinner with the Gauses: good to see them, comfortable house—nice pictures, old-fashioned fireplace with fire splendidly burning—a great relief after the Bloombergs'. They had just come back from a trip to Prospect—had driven to Cape Vincent and passed my house, which looked so beautiful in the late March light with the trees all bare—John said to Elena that even she would have liked it. I asked him whether he was at all depressed about the state of the world, and he said that he had got, like me, so that he couldn't face the morning papers, had almost decided to stop taking them. He would say to Jane, "I still love you, and that's about the only good thing I can see."

We have had *a few better days* lately. Last Sunday (the 6th), Reuel drove us out to Concord. Most of the things were closed, but we saw the houses from outside and looked in the windows, explored Authors' Ridge in the cemetery, and visited the rude bridge that arched the flood. I am making Helen learn the poems I did with the other children. The cemetery is very touching—strange that those from families—Alcott, Emerson, Hawthorne, Thoreau—whose plots are all close together—should all have produced famous writers. And Channing is not far away.

Yesterday (the 7th), I stayed at home and had a very pleasant day with the family, only writing a few letters— finished reading to Helen the Edith Nesbit stories.[7] In the morning Elena and I made love, and it was wonderful. The nervousness was relieved that had been keeping me from sleeping, and I think Elena felt better, too. When I found her typing afterwards, she said she was trembling, and her anxious look seems to be gone. In the afternoon at 4:30, we went to hear Oppenheimer lecture. A lot of Harvard alumni had been making a fuss about it, threatening not to give money to Harvard, etc.; but the University—as I learned at the Saturday Club, where [McGeorge] Bundy, the dean of the faculty, and Judge Wyzanski, the head of the Board of Overseers, were present—did not make any explanation or statement. There were cops at the door but no demonstration. On the contrary, he was given prolonged applause both before and after his lecture, and many more people came than could be accommodated by Sanders Theater. The whole affair was tense and emotional. It made more of an impression on me than any other lecture I have heard. While Pusey, in his flat way, was telling about the William James lectures and introducing the speaker, Oppenheimer sat behind him, alone on the wide platform, nervously shifting his arms and feet in an ungainly Jewish way; but when he began to speak, he had the whole audience riveted, there was scarcely a sound throughout. He spoke very quietly but with piercing point. Extraordinary how terse and precise he was, speaking merely from notes—as in his description of William James, in which he touched on his relation to Henry. The opening was quite thrilling—he did nothing to make it dramatic, but he was raising terrific questions that were painfully in everyone's mind and one felt, as Elena said, his feeling of intense responsibility. We were both of us moved and stimulated. I love going to theaters and such things with Elena—she is so sensitive and responsive to everything, and her criticisms are always definite. This makes one of our best relationships. —Before we had left the house, leaving Helen with Mrs. Rinn, the Irish cleaning woman, I had given her the first two stanzas of the *Concord Hymn* to learn. When we were back and I asked her to recite them, it turned out she was shy about it: "Too many people," she said. I told [her] to come into my study, and she said, "Too few." What embarrassed her was Mrs. Rinn, waiting at the door for her taxi, but she wanted her mother to be there. —The day was marred at the end by my drinking too much whisky and stupidly reproaching Elena and in having a vision of Oppenheimer under a very depressing aspect: a brilliant man who had been beaten by the age,

who knew no more what to do about it than anybody,
who was as incapable of leading it as anybody; his
humility now seemed to me hangdog. Elena had been
telling me about Erich Kahler's *The Tower and the
Abyss*,[8] which she was reading. She went on reading it
in bed, and when I went in late to see her and tell her
I was sorry for reproaching her, she cried out that the
world just now couldn't be as bad as that, there must be
some love and goodness somewhere.

Stories by William James about his family.[9] He said
something to his uncle Henry about Anthony Hope, the
author of *The Prisoner of Zenda* [1894]. Henry James—
as if hurt—said he had seen Hope on the street not long
ago, and that this fabulous best-seller had cut him. William was surprised that his uncle should have thought
this incident worth mentioning. —A very short time
before William, Sr., died, Henry had come down to
Cambridge from Canada and complained to his brother
—who was lying on a couch—of the desolateness of the
Canadian country: "A wilderness of spruce forest, with
an occasional prehistoric swamp!" "Better than anything
in Europe!" said William. "Better than anything in
England!" "My dad was like a Westerner," explained
William Jr. —He did not like the way that Edith
Wharton had treated his uncle Henry in her memoirs;
and when I suggested that [Oliver Wendell] Holmes, Jr.,
had had a rather harsh side—Francis Biddle had told me
that he had "a streak of the mean Yankee"—William
said that Holmes and his father had been quite close as
young men but had later come to diverge;[10] that he himself had a rather unpleasant memory of Holmes's coming
to dinner at Lamb House—"He was horsing Uncle
Henry, you know, and I thought there was something
rather coarse about it."

He looks—one would judge from photographs—more like his mother than his father, and has perhaps caught his uncle Henry's attitudes rather than those of William. He was quite shocked in a quiet way when I said that I had opposed our entering either of the two wars, said he was surprised because he had always felt that England supplied our best standards, or something that amounted to that. When I talked about breeding a new elite, he remarked that, among young people, the conception of the "lady" had apparently disappeared; for the young girls, it didn't exist. —He also remarked that there used to be three classes in America: upper, middle, and lower, but you couldn't see it anymore.

In his youth, he had studied in Germany, at Marburg, and had hated the Germans. When he came back and told his father what he thought of them, his father remonstrated with him and said he didn't appreciate the richness of the German nature. Nothing they did afterwards surprised him: it was quite in keeping with his earlier impressions. It was only when the refugees from Hitler had come to the U.S. that he had seen the kind of Germans his father admired and understood what he had meant.

There seem to be traditional mannerisms for the Harvard intellectuals: Eliot, Dos Passos, and Robert Lowell (whom I have just met) all distinctly derive from the same established type. Characteristics: sticking the head forward, gesticulating vaguely with the forefinger, certain intonations and an amusing way of speaking without vehemence. Pleasant to see someone—Lowell—who is more like the friends of my youth and not like the *Partisan Review* et al.

Lincoln Kirstein also had these mannerisms—imitated, I used to think, directly from Eliot—in the days of his black clothes and what Nathanael West called his "shared coats."

Elena read Helen a fairy story in which it was a question of a princess's choosing between beauty, riches, and wisdom. Her mother asked Helen which she would choose: "Don't blame me, but beauty. If you have beauty, you can become rich—and education costs money, so you can have wisdom, too."

Republication of *William Wetmore Story*[11] and conversations with William James have made me think more about Henry. Stories that seemed rather pale and abstract when I first read them at college now look like indestructible crystals. I recently reread "The Liar" [1888], which had made no impression on me when I read it first, and saw how good it was.

Another painful incident of our stay in Cambridge. On the bottom floor of the Louisburg Square house in which Rosalind lives was a family of husband, very pretty wife, and three pretty little girls, with whom Helen made friends. The husband is in the curious business of providing housecleaning teams of energetic men, who will go anywhere and clean up anything. When he drove Rosalind over to our house and came in for a drink, I complimented him on his wife and daughters. Only a few days later, the wife committed suicide by an overdose of some narcotic. The girls will go to her mother's. This has affected Rosalind so that she has decided to move and has found a new apartment.

I spoke to Lowell of the shut-in character of Boston, which I thought had become so crowded by the suburbs built up around it that it was now only an enclave of old New England. But he said that he thought that the college had always had something of that atmosphere, it imposed a kind of constraint.

12/11/10

NOTES

1. Hugh Gaitskell (1906–63) had become leader of the Labour Party in 1955.

2. Alexander R. James was the youngest son of William James the philosopher and psychologist and, like his brother William, a painter.

3. EW had failed to send in income tax returns and was being questioned by the Internal Revenue Service.

4. EW was putting together his political and social reportage of the 1930s, *The American Earthquake* (1958).

5. John Singer Sargent (1856–1925).

6. Lizette Woodworth Reese (1856–1935). In the octave of "Tears" (from *A Wayside Lute*, 1909) Reese "wonder[s] at the idleness of tears," given the brevity of life. The sestet reads: "Ye old, old dead, and ye of yesternight, / Chieftains, and bards, and keepers of the sheep, / By every cup of sorrow that you had, / Loose me from tears, and make me see aright / How each hath back what once he stayed to weep: / Homer his sight, David his little lad."

7. Edith Nesbit (1858–1924), best remembered for her children's books. Her first stories about the young Bastables appeared in 1898.

8. Erich Gabriel Kahler, Czech-born cultural historian and educator who resided at Princeton, wrote *The Tower and the Abyss: An Inquiry into the Transformation of the Individual* (1957).

9. William James, second son of the psychologist William James, was still living in the late fifties and early sixties in the family house at 95 Irving Street in Cambridge. He had known his celebrated uncle, Henry James, during his studies abroad.

10. See EW's chapter on Holmes, with which he ends his Civil War book, *Patriotic Gore*.

11. See note 6, p. 67.

TALCOTTVILLE, 1957

Talcottville, May '57.[1] I arrived here the 17th, after
my now usual stopovers in Boston and Northampton.
Had attended a Phi Beta Kappa dinner that Charley
Curtis had invited me to. Before dinner, he said, I'm
presiding, the man who is presiding is the only person
who can't have enough cocktails. At dinner, he would
not drink wine or whisky, but continually ordered beer—
finally the waitress appeared with a large bowl full of
cans of Budweiser, which he drank up one by one. Phi
Beta Kappa dinners at Princeton were affairs of legendary
gloom—the boys were mostly professional friends and
were not likely to know one another. Charley was acutely
conscious of this and desperately anxious to have the
occasion convivial. In pursuance of this aim, he explained
to me, he had them all take off their coats, and by the
time of the speech of the evening—by the Nobel Prize
winner Purcell[2]—he was failing quite to make connections. The young physicist began with a few pleasantries,
but went on to a serious discussion of "the place of the
crank in Physics": Charley went on laughing uproariously

416

at everything he said, and seemed to lose track of the following discussion. He is a very sympathetic character. The Bostonians are so little notable for outgoingness and easy charm that the few who do have these qualities seem to develop them in a way which has been stimulated by the flatness and dryness of the background. They are irresistible and seem somehow miraculous. (E. E. Cummings is also a case of this.)

At Northampton, Helen Muchnic, Dan Aaron, and Newton Arvin[3] gave me an excellent lunch in the Faculty Club in an attractive private dining room. Afterwards we went to Dan's house and he produced a bottle of Mumm champagne, but I noticed that after this only later guests got any whisky and the bottle was never brought out. The next morning, when I saw her at breakfast, Helen told me that—to protect me from drinking too much—she herself had had the Aarons do this. —"You may have thought they were rather parsimonious," she said. She didn't know that, after she had left, Alfred Kazin and I had resorted, first, to the Northampton Inn, then, after this closed, to another place outside the town limits, where they served drinks till one o'clock. I had my first real talk with Alfred, who, though self-important, is shy and needs drinks to loosen him up. I said, I thought, some very good things. He told me—what I hadn't heard—that some kind of atomic laboratory had just blown up. I said that I couldn't cope with all that, that at my time of life I could only hope to get a few more books written. He said that the worst of the present situation was that everybody behaved like that—the young as well as the old. —I hope that the time will come when he gets over his basic lack of self-confidence and comes out with something really important.

. . .

On our way to Northampton, Bill Peck drove on the new state highway, the day after it had been opened, and we had the first accident. The front right tire blew out, and Bill steered the car to the side of the road, where, fortunately, it stuck in the soft shoulder and didn't go into the ditch. Three trucks stopped, one after the other: the first pulled us out with a chain, and the men from one of the others stepped in and energetically changed the tire, addressing Bill Peck as "Pop." He and I both tried to give them money, but nobody would take a cent. The men who changed the tire said that we might help them out someday. I [told] Dan Aaron about this, and he made the same comment that I was about to make: that that was the kind of thing that made you feel better about America. I have been so depressed lately about the country that I forget that such friendliness exists.

It was a little less exciting than usual to arrive in Talcottville this year—perhaps partly because, to write my novel, I shall have to put off my Talcottville play, so have not been thinking so much about it. But, besides, every year I come back, the place is more familiar and comfortable and reminds me less of the past. I am not at all haunted as I was before. Only when I saw the narcissus and the little white bells in the bed by the front door did I feel it was touching and queer that these flowers of Aunt Lin's should persist, should have gone on blooming among their weeds and seedlings from the trees—which I thoroughly cleared out last year—for years when there was no one here, and I had a little twinge of sadness when I found that nothing had come of the bittersweet that—in order to replace her own—I had planted by the front porch. Otherwise, I now have everything I need here and simply move in and start functioning. Everything is ready to my hand, and I fall into my old routine.

The first two days were cold and rainy. It poured more or less steadily for twenty-four hours. I burned quantities of wood in the fireplace. Then the morning of the 21st I was wakened by the burst of white radiance beyond my bedroom windows, somewhat milky in the moist air. Still cold in the house, but beautiful outside. In the afternoon, I had Albert drive me to the edge of the woods where the road goes in along Dry Sugar River. I found it far from dry where we usually go in—a torrent so deep off the rocks that I could not touch the bottom with my stick. I had to cross at a lower point. No very interesting flowers: yellow violets and the first forget-me-nots, some wild phlox, less purple than blue and with bigger, freer flowers than the garden kind; most showy were the coarse marsh marigolds. The most brilliant thing I saw was a bright red bird with black wings and a black tail, so little fearful of men that it would let me come quite close to it; but at last I gave a bogus birdcall, and then it flew away—aware of its beauty I thought. A smallish pretty chocolate-brown bird was sitting on a nearby tree—I wondered whether this were the mate.

May 22. Not so cold, but cloudy—in the afternoon it rained again. When the Munns and I were going to the movies the night before, Fern remarked that there were "mare's tails" in the sky.

May 24. I was interrupted in writing this, the day before yesterday, by the arrival of Gertrude Loomis. She had just been to the funeral of Tharett Best's[4] mother—who was ninety-one when she died. I said, Huldah isn't with you? and she said at once that she would go back to the house and release her—they had to take turns staying with Florence [their sister]. She is so used to having Huldah take all the initiative and do all the talking—and knowing no doubt that she bores people—that it was touching to see how she took it for granted that Huldah was the only one I would want to see. I made her come in and sit down and talk and have a drink—it was the first time, so far as I remember, that I had had a conversation with her alone. They have had a dreadful winter with Florence, who—the oldest of them, seventy-four—has hardening of the arteries of the brain and gradually becomes more deranged. They brought her back from Martinsburg, and she seemed all right for a time, but is now definitely getting worse. They have to dress her and feed her, and sometimes she tears off her clothes; likes to have Huldah read poetry with her, and sometimes recites German poetry. They don't want to send her to a state hospital, but she is wearing them down at home.

The trees, when I first arrived, had little feathery stitchings of leaves, like the backgrounds of Chagall's etchings. Since the rains, they have been rapidly enriched, and the ferns in front of the house have grown from little fringes to large fronds.

The orioles seem to be building somewhere in back of the house, instead of in the tree in front; I watch them while lying in the bathtub. The grackle, thank goodness, is baffled: I had the crack in the balcony filled up with concrete, so he can no longer make a mess on the porch.

Albert Grubel continues to regale me, on almost every trip to town, with his usual gruesome stories: A barn burned down in Constableville, and all the cattle were killed. They didn't get them out because they didn't know the fire had started. Then they was layin' there. I didn't go up to see 'em. —A boy had been drowned in one of the lakes. —A doctor in the Osceola hospital had gone out on a fishing trip—some place he had often fished—and never came back. They'd sent out blood-hounds to find him.

Moments when the taste of cold air and water brings me back to the Collinses'. —Pleasant lying in bed reading last night under that old distinguished pink-and-white checkerboard quilt, with, in the white squares, its varied patterns. The weather is not unlike autumn, and reminds me of lying in bed, in my youth, and reading the novels of Hardy.

NOTES

1. *Upstate*, pp. 149–53.
2. Edward M. Purcell, 1952 Nobel Prize for Physics.
3. All three were then members of the faculty at Smith College. See Helen Muchnic's "Edmund Wilson's Russian Involvement" in *Edmund Wilson, the Man and His Work*, pp. 86–109.
4. Tharett Gilbert Best, Boonville mayor and Oneida County historian.

12/13/10

VISIT TO NABOKOV

[The thrice-exiled Vladimir (familiarly Volodya) Nabokov came to the United States in May 1940. There had been the flight from Russia in 1918 to England and then France, and finally Germany; then from Germany to France to get away from the Hitler regime; and finally the flight from France when Hitler's legions overran the Republic. Edmund Wilson met Nabokov very soon after his arrival in America and helped him get reviews and access to various journals. They had much in common in their zealous interest in languages and the art of storytelling and translation. They also had many differences both temperamental and linguistic. They argued over points of language in English and Russian, Edmund's Russian and Nabokov's English, and carried on a running battle over how to render Pushkin from Russian into English. *The Nabokov-Wilson Letters, 1940–1970*, edited by Simon Karlinsky (1979), reveal the ups and downs of their temperamental friendship, as do the series of entries which follow. Nabokov had finally found a haven at Cornell University, where he was associate professor of Slavic literature. Two volumes of his Cornell lectures were published—*Lectures on Literature* (1980) and *Lectures on Russian Literature* (1981)—brilliant and unorthodox divagations on European as well as Russian masters, edited by Fredson Bowers.]

Visit to Ithaca, May 25–28.[1] George Munn drove me. He did not bring a coat and came to dinner at the Nabokovs in one of those floating fancy shirts he wears, which caused Volodya to tell him that he looked like a tropical fish. He does not know what to say, so doesn't speak unless spoken to, but he has dignity and is not embarrassed, runs true to the old tradition. I thought he would be bored by the literary and learned conversations, but he always seemed to be interested and afterwards told his mother that the thing he had got the most kick out of was an animated argument between Volodya and me—which almost became heated—on Russian and English versification. (We have been having this out for years: Volodya's point of view—that Russian and English verse are basically the same—is, I have become convinced, a part of his effort, inherited from his father, to believe that the two countries are, or ought to be, closely associated.) George was also much interested in Volodya's stories about the animals he had seen in the West. He encountered—in Montana—a long animal with claws that he thought was not a bear, and when he asked the zoologists about it, they immediately changed the subject. He came to the conclusion it was something they had been investigating but did not want to talk about yet. His theory is that it may be a giant sloth, of which prehistoric remains have been found out there.

George says that there are black bears back in the wooded region of Highmarket. There are lots of porcupines, which are hard to kill—I didn't know we had them there. Also, lately, many timber wolves. About the only amusements in winter are hunting and going to the movies, and nowadays, since they are married, George and his brothers don't hunt much anymore. I thought that people liked him. Morris Bishop's wife[2] took him all over the agricultural school. For Monday-evening supper he turned up in a good heavy brown shirt.

The first evening, when the Epsteins were there and Lange, the German professor, came to dinner, Volodya was playing the host with a good humor, even joviality, such as I had never seen him display before. The success of *Pnin* and the acclaim of *Lolita*, with the fuss about its suppression in Paris, have had upon him a stimulating effect. With no necktie and his hair *ébouriffé*, consuming his little glasses of "faculty" port and sherry (as Frohock at Harvard called it), he was genial with everybody, seemed full of high spirits. But when I saw him the next day after his two-hour examination—at which Vera had helped him—he was fatigued, rather depressed and irritable, said that he would never go back to Russia— [Roman] Jacobson[3] had been trying to induce him to pay a visit and lecture—that he had got so antagonized against it that it had become an obsession with him. He is undoubtedly overworked, had a hundred and fifty papers to correct. That night his nerves were still on edge but he exhilarated himself with drinks—in which I joined him in spite of my gout—and was at first amusing and charming, then later relapsed into his semi-humorous, semi-disagreeable mood, when he is always contradicting and always attempting to score, though his statements may be quite absurd—as when he asserts, on no evidence whatever and contrary to the well-known facts, that Mérimée[4] knew no Russian and that Turgenev knew only enough English to enable him to read a paper. These particular falsities, of course, are prompted by his impulse to think of himself as the only writer in history equally proficient in Russian, French, and English; and they are always hopping people for petty mistakes—such as Steegmuller's *verre de vin*[5] instead of *verre à vin*, in connection with *Madame Bovary*—when Volodya himself makes frequent mistakes in English, in French, and even, as Vera admits, in Russian. They would not believe me, two summers ago, when I told them that *fastidieux* in French meant *tiresome* and not *fastidious*, and Volodya swore up and down that *samodur* had nothing to do with *durak*. So he tried to tell me just how *nihilist* in English was pronounced *neehilist*. It is of course very difficult for him to have to function between two languages, and the difference between American and English usage is a further source of confusion. Our argument about metrics is a mare's nest, which I know how to straighten out but which he doesn't even want to. He seems to consider it a reproach against Pushkin that his verse is more regular than Shakespeare's, and even denies that Shakespeare ever achieved the flexibility that he did. Years ago he declared that the line from *King Lear* "Never, never, never, never, never!"—where all the iambs are turned into trochees—should really be pronounced so that the stress somehow fell on the last syllables, and now he says it is a line of prose. There are inversions, as he showed me, in *Evgeni Onegin*, but, he admitted, not anything like so many. Vera invariably sides with him and becomes slightly vindictive against people who argue with him. She did for me everything she could, brought me sandwiches for lunch, etc., but a little resented my gout, which made it necessary for me to eat with my foot up, so that she had to leave the table to serve me. She also resented *Histoire d'O*,[6] which I had brought on for Volodya to read. He agreed with me that, trashy though it is, it exercises a certain hypnotic effect. Vera, who had managed to look into it, became quite grim about it, and accused us of giggling over it, with a certain deadliness. She had precipitated the discussion of metrics, inquiring whether it wasn't true that I had said that *Evgeni Onegin* was written in syllabic meter, and when I answered that this was absurd, intimated that they had letters of mine which could prove the truth of this disclaimer. When I attack the subject of argument from some angle—such as Greek and Latin—about which Volodya knows nothing—he adopts a semi-ironical and patronizing expression. —The next morning, however, when I went to say goodbye, he emerged much calmed and refreshed (undoubtedly, the uncorrected papers had been on his mind the night before). I said, "How wonderful you look after your bath!" He leaned into the car and murmured, referring to *Histoire d'O*: "*Je mettais du rouge sur les lèvres de mon ventre.*" Vera had just asked me, "Did he give you back that little horror?"

I always enjoy seeing them—what we have are really intellectual romps, sometimes accompanied by mauling—but I am always afterwards left with a somewhat disagreeable impression. The explanation of this comes out in his work quite nakedly. The element in it I find repellent is the addiction to *Schadenfreude*—everybody is always being humiliated. The inward life of Volodya himself has had so much of humiliation that it would naturally be one of his themes. But there is also something in him rather nasty—the cruelty of the arrogant rich man—that makes him want to humiliate others, and his characters he has completely at his mercy. And yet he is an admirable person, a strong character, a terrific worker, unwavering in his loyalty to his family, with a rigor in his devotion to his art which has something in common with Joyce—who is one of his great modern admirations. The miseries, horrors, handicaps that he has had to face in his life would have degraded or broken many, and, after years of it, Volodya has achieved over here "life tenure" in a first-rate college and now a reputation as the author of brilliant books in English, besides being probably at the present time the most distinguished Russian writer. Even aside from his talent, he inspires more respect than Nicholas [Nabokov] for his fortitude and concentration, for the integrity of his family relations.

—Morris Bishop told me that at Harvard the pressure to publish was overwhelming, that was why they were all plugging at their books so hard. I suppose that I must have been responding to this when I shut myself up in the library and did six to seven hours a day almost without pause. Since I have been up here I have done nothing but this journal, the proofs on Turgenev,[7] and a letter to the Boonville *Herald* protesting against the proposed discontinuance of the band concerts Saturday night.

—One thing that has let me down here this spring has been, I suppose, the fact that I cannot afford this year to make any more improvements.

NOTES

1. *Upstate*, pp. 156–63.
2. Morris Bishop, professor of French at Cornell and a frequent contributor of light verse to *The New Yorker*.
3. Roman Jacobson, the philologist, had just returned from Russia.
4. Prosper Mérimée (1803–70), the novelist and historian, published studies and translations from Russian literature.
5. Francis Steegmuller, biographer of Flaubert and translator of *Madame Bovary* (1957).

6. Published by the Olympia Press in Paris and described by EW in *Upstate* as "that highly sophisticated and amusing pornographic work" (p. 161).

7. EW's introduction to Turgenev's *Literary Reminiscences* (1958).

12/13/10

TALCOTTVILLE AGAIN

June 1. Back from Ithaca (May 28), with horrible gout of the knee. Haven't been able to face the Wasson mushroom book[1] without my big reading rack, which has mysteriously disappeared, and spent a delightful day (May 31) sitting out on the lawn in the delicious sun and reading Joyce's letters, so dynamic, high-aiming, uncompromising, and so tragic at the end—bracing after Charles Godfrey Leland's memoirs,[2] in which I have rather bogged down—all one long boast and a desultory debauch of accomplishment and learning, with no high ambition and no directing purpose. —Sitting outside, I discovered that the grackles I had shut out from the front of the house had found a new nesting place right over the kitchen door and were making their usual mess below it. I am going to have this closed up, too—unless the female is already setting. It irritates me to see them return with what I take to be nest-building materials and perch warily for a moment on the edge of the roof, cocking their heads back and forth, before going into their crack.

The day before Memorial Day, Albert remarked as

usual that he guessed there would be quite a few accidents, then mentioned, the day after, that there *had* been quite a few people killed. Today he entertained me with the tale of an encounter with a skunk, which he had found caught in a trap and which had squirted right in his eye [?]. For a long time after this, when people said they smelled a skunk, he had to conceal it was him.

Days I spent crippled with gout after I returned to Talcottville. The drugs I had been taking to cure it must have contributed to making me dim. I would sit out on the lawn in a deck chair, and the gray south side of the old house would be pleasant to have there but *reculé* and unreal. Only on one occasion, when I sufficiently came to life to take a little walk in the village, did Talcottville, which is normally so vivid to me, come back in this way to my consciousness.

Driving me to Utica, George Munn told me about the pet fox they had had. One of his brothers had seen a fox on the place and thrown a rock at it. The fox had dropped something from its jaws, which turned out to be a baby with its eyes not yet open. He took it home, and they fed it with a medicine dropper. It became as tame as a dog—slept in a box, curled up in their laps, wandered about freely but always came back to the house to be fed. The dog paid no special attention to it. It was very playful, and they taught it to stand up and beg, to retrieve a ball, and to run and pull up a handkerchief, which they would bury in holes in the lawn. It would seize their hands in its teeth, pretending to bite like a puppy. It did not have a rank smell because it had never lived in a den, and it never barked, no doubt because it had never heard a fox bark—the only sound it ever made was a growl. It sometimes went out fox hunting with them, as if it had been a dog. It stayed with [them] eight years but eventually went away and never came back. It must have met another fox.

I hadn't realized how serious Fern's accident had been. A man had come out of a driveway without blowing his horn, and to avoid a collision she had swerved aside and run into the railing along the road. She was thrown right through the windshield and landed about twelve feet away from the car; was horribly cut under the knee, and her back was cut. She was in the hospital a week. The man had driven quickly away, without any attempt to help her, and the state troopers had not been able to find him.

Nostalgia since last summer for London and Paris. The point is that—except for Talcottville—it is only in London and Paris that I can find the things I knew in my youth. In New York, there is hardly a single house left that I went to in my college days, and in those days I hardly knew Boston. Of course, what is happening now in Paris and London is quite different from what was happening when I first used to go to Europe; but the streets and the buildings and the institutions *are* for the most part still there, and I haven't stayed long enough lately to be bothered by the social changes, the political atmosphere, etc. I revisit the scenes of my boyhood in England, of the war years in France and just after. I dream of taking the MS. of my projected American novel to France. After a short stay during March and April in England, at the Basil Street Hotel, I should get rooms at the Hotel Lotti in the rue Castiglione and spend the spring and the summer there making a final revision of it. I am beginning to feel about Paris the truth of all the clichés which since my Francophile phase have annoyed me: "gracious living," respect for literature, etc. Today it seems to me quite wonderful that there should be a rue Huysmans, and I remember that the effort to get Washington Place named for Henry James met with no success whatever. The places in which I feel most at home—since I am always somewhat at odds with Princeton—are thus Talcottville, London, and Paris.

I see that I have failed to note above my evening with Adelaide Walker[3] on one of my trips to New York when we were living in Cambridge. She got on the train at Cambridge, and we had the usual animated conversation, though it was hard for me to use my voice. I invited her to have dinner with me and go to the theater, and she said she would be delighted and got out of another engagement in order to do so. We had dinner at the Algonquin, then went to the Ziegfeld Follies. She said she hadn't done anything like that in years, and I said it was just like the twenties; but it was not really at all like the twenties. At the show, I was tired and dull: I realized that the Follies could not be revived, that Beatrice Lillie[4] was really too old, that I was really too old, and that the only person young was Adelaide. I afterwards had the idea of doing a *New Yorker* story with the title " 'This Is Just Like the Twenties,' He Croaked."

Visit to Mrs. Burnham, after I got back to Talcottville June 22. She was all alone in the house and lying on her back in a little bed in the dining room. She had had a bad fall when she went out one day to feed robins, and then had had another when she tried to walk around the house before she was ready to. She could hardly move her left arm. We spoke of the Sharps' accident, Dorothy Mendenhall's fall, and the Loomises. "Well,

Edmund," she said, with her sweet humorous look, "I guess all our good times"—and paused. I asked her what she was going to say. "I guess all our good times together are spoiled."

Beverly[5] turned up looking rather badly and more nervous, I thought, than ever. She couldn't get married, she said, till she had paid for her car—only saw her fiancé once a week, on the weekends at Port Leyden. Her teeth were in bad shape, one of them ached terribly —she would do as much work as she could for me so that she could make some money to pay the dentist, though most evenings she was tied up. The second time she came I saw that her jaw was swollen and urged her to go right away; but the next day, she said, she had to go to the beauty parlor in preparation for the 4th of July. I told her that it was much more important to get her tooth attended to. At last, on her fifth visit, she told me that her father had deserted the family about six months ago and gone to live in Utica with a woman— the wife of a fellow factory worker—who had deserted a husband and eight children. Elena and I had been struck by the appearance they gave of being a happy family: they played various musical instruments together and seemed fond of one another. The parents had been married twenty-three years. The other woman was not attractive, but she had run away with men before, and Beverly had hoped she might eventually go back to her family; but her husband now said he had divorced her. One of the children he had sent to a grandmother or aunt, and he had a niece come in to live with him to look after the youngest children, but this niece was out on the town a lot. The whole thing had shocked and saddened Beverly. She said that her mother had said that she could not go on living in the house—her husband only sent her

$25 a week: the grown-up ones who were not married would have to marry the people they were engaged to, and she would take little Paul, twelve, to live with her somewhere in rooms. The next time Beverly came here, she said that her father, very drunk and with his girlfriend, had come to the house and made them a terrible scene. He told his wife that he had never loved her and that he "hated all of us," but he tried to take Paul away with him. They didn't know what to make of him—the mother thought he'd gone crazy. —Beverly is getting worn out and bored with her work in the veneer factory, for which she has to get up at 5:30—though last year she was enthusiastic about it. *12/16/10*

This is a bad year for everybody. If the world goes on as it is doing—with ridiculous and impotent governments in the U.S., England, and France and the government of oafs in Russia, with gigantic taxes here for atomic weapons and foreign occupations and a foreign policy consisting of the ineptitudes of Dulles—I feel that there may be a catastrophe which will result in a kind of revolution that will make previous revolutions look orderly and rational—it will not be Marxist, and there are no signs at present of any new political philosophy. In the *Times* of July 3, one reads that the Senate has defeated an attempt to cut the President's appropriation bill for $34,534,229,000, that the Air Force has just granted a contract for "an undisclosed number" of guided missiles that will travel 5,000 miles and will cost $73,000,000, and that Dulles, in a press interview, has elaborated on his recent speech in which he declared that there had been no change in the administration's policy of not having any traffic with Communist China: "The Chinese Communist Party . . . came to power by violence," and we must not "betray" Chiang Kai-shek—

who also came to power by violence and was burning Chinese Communists alive. —I sit here brooding on writing a pamphlet or article, in which I should make an overall protest, explain that I had not paid my income tax and had no intention of doing so, and that the government was free to wipe me out or send me to jail. But I am too old for all the struggle and must not ruin the family, and my case, in some ways, is too weak.[6]

Margaret de Silver[7] and Dawn [Powell] came to see me—June 28–July 1. They, too, were rather the worse for wear; had been having particularly trying ordeals with their respective defective children. Margaret said it had done her good to get away. Dawn's mechanical jokes, always followed by her own "Ha-ha-ha," and the infantile remarks of Margaret had reached an extremely low level. Still we managed to have a moderately jolly time. I took them for dinner to Constableville and the restaurant near the ski ridge, and at the latter we played the jukebox all through dinner, I selecting familiar old numbers such as "Yes Sir, She's My Baby," and Dawn instructing me in the newer stuff, such as Belafonte.

Huldah Loomis invited me for dinner on 4th of July, thinking, she said, that we ought to do something to celebrate. She produced a bottle of New York State champagne, but avoided cocktails and highballs. Florence greeted me naturally enough, but dropped her eyes, knowing that I knew about her. She came to the table but hardly ate—they have to feed her, it seems. Her hands do not coordinate and she cannot see the things in front of her—her eyes are gray and dull. She upset them by knocking over her champagne glass, which fell to the floor and broke: "one of Aunt Martha's goblets." —"They'll cry over that all night," she said to me, when her sisters had gone to the kitchen. Through dinner she would unbutton her blouse and then, when they had buttoned it up, begin unbuttoning it again. She was very naughty, they told me—would go into the bathroom and soak all the towels and leave the water on. They couldn't leave her alone at the house. She said pathetically that she wanted to go to bed, but they got her into the car and off for a short ride after dinner. She and Huldah now have heavy mustaches. I was thankful to them for inviting [me]. They drove me through Collinsville— where Homer came from: houses of the Collinses and Deweys, some kept up and in good shape, some deteriorated: big old dark square Victorian house, in which had lived old Mrs. Dewey, that I should like to see the inside of.

Only cheerful event Henry [Thornton's] wedding (June 8). Everybody thoroughly enjoyed it. It was financed by Daphne's ninety-one-year-old grandmother, who was there and stayed all through the party, and all organized by Daphne, whose mother and father are quite incompetent. The mother said to Jimmy Thornton that she was so looking forward to meeting me. The father looked quite distinguished when he was giving the bride away, but soon afterwards [was back] in the limp and dim stage. He lives in Canada with another woman, couldn't stand having everything run by the grandmother. They didn't know where he was, to tell him about Daphne's getting married, but calculated that at that time of year he was usually at some place in the South. At the wedding dinner the night before the wedding (from which I tactfully absented myself), he asked Daphne's mother to remarry him, and she said that she would if he would stop drinking. Daphne, as Dawn said, came to the altar with an expression of triumphant satis-

(Seated) Elena, Helen, and Edmund Wilson; (standing) Reuel
Wilson; Henry and Daphne Thornton. Wellfleet, 1957

Edmund and Elena Wilson and Henry Thornton

Rollie McKenna

faction, and it was wonderful to see her afterwards bouncing around in her bride's dress, dancing with everybody. Henry also looked handsome and gratified. Helen was flower girl and made faces as she was going up and down the steps to the altar (St. James's, N.Y.), and Reuel was one of the ushers; they had all rented morning coats and striped pants. The reception was at the Colony Club, and the dancing went on for a long time after the bride and groom had left. Elena was cute in a gray dress and hat which, as she said, made her look like a matron. She was, as usual, so much afraid of making a show or putting on an act that she overdid the elderly thing. —The money in Daphne's mother's family seems in some way to come from Brown Brothers. My old friend Bill Brown[8] has just died. I am afraid, from the little that I had heard about him since my early days in New York, when I was going off the Greenwich Village end, that his career was rather mediocre. It is depressing to me that all these friends of my school and college days: Bill, Larry Noyes, Morris Belknap, David Hamilton, Ted Paramore, should all have petered out and have died relatively young. Stanley Dell is a hopeless neurotic. Charley Walker and Alfred Bellinger[9] at least keep on functioning at Yale, though neither is the poet he promised to be—Yale and Bones have kept them going. Phelps Putnam[10] did write some good poems, which neither Alfred nor Charley, though old Bones brothers, seems disposed to do anything to rescue. I suppose that, from the point of view of Bones, when you die that young—and with a slender body of work—you have failed. Bill Osborn works in metallurgy—he told me about 1936—and has or had his own laboratory; he said that he had done work of a certain importance. He seems to have been an exception, among my friends of this generation, in taking his social group with the utmost

seriousness, and he has probably been dominated all
his adult life, first by Peggy La Farge, then, no doubt, by
his present wife. John Amen is still decent, but partly
corrupted and cracking up—has evidently had a slight
stroke. In all this, I suppose I have got to an age when
my disappointment with old friends is tempered by a
certain satisfaction at outlasting and outworking them.
Paul Chavchavadze was telling me that his mother, who
is now very old, gloats, in a senile fashion, at news of the
death of her old friends: it is a game to see who will
live longest. I take a good deal of pride, however, in
having known Scott Fitzgerald and John Bishop, who
have left good work that will live; John Biggs, among
my friends, is probably a unique example of an improvement over his ancestors in public affairs. The rest
of them never panned out on account of the awful half-
bakedness of so many of the American "upper class"
families who had a tradition of intellectual activity—art,
science, "civic conscience"—too much watered down by
the combination of commercialism and genteel ideals that
submerged almost everything here after the Civil War.
So I am glad to be sitting here in Talcottville. Are even
the zoological Osborns[11] comparable to the zoological
Huxleys? I don't know: I used to think that Julian H.[12]
was a rather naïve Darwinian, but a review of his I
just read in the London *Sunday Times* made me think
he might have loosened up. I have been led to all this
both by memory of the Browns, who graduated from
their old-fashioned banking to theology, music, etc.—I
remember Bill's coming back from Russia with a Russian
copy of *Anna Karenina*, with which he said he had made
some progress and which made me swear to learn Russian
someday—and by the memory of "Aunt Martha," whose
goblet Florence Loomis broke and who comes back to
me, at the Talcottville Collins house, presiding over the

dinner table, to which no one could come late, under the Collins and Talcott family portraits, one of which she said, with an accent of dry skepticism, was said to be a Gilbert Stuart,[13] and she had always firmly believed it.

12/17/10

This afternoon (July 6) I sat out between the two trees on the lawn reading and watching, from my deck chair, the sky and the tops of the trees. Everything was so beautiful and interesting that I stayed till 8:10. There were chipmunks or small squirrels—I couldn't be sure which—chasing one another across the back roof and through the trees—swallows and other birds—a butterfly as high as the top of the elm, which looked a bright red when the sinking sun shone through its wings. I had never felt so much before that I had the freedom of that realm of treetop, roof, and sky; and I could look away toward the river, where the shadows were falling on the pastures. Later, when I was getting dinner, I looked again at this view through the open front door: deep blue and very dark green.

Albert Grubel: A man near Utica had been leading a dog on a chain. The chain had got into contact with an electric wire that was down and the dog had been electrocuted. The man tried to get him off the wire, but was electrocuted, too, when he took hold of the dog. The wife tried to come to the rescue but also got a shock and was now in the hospital. She has six children, between two and eight.

Near Silver Lake, two cars had a collision head-on and both burst into flames. Six people were killed, and the only survivor, a nineteen-year-old girl, was in the hospital in critical condition. He told me the whole story twice, on the way to Boonville and coming back, and said that it

ought to be against the law to go more than fifty miles
an hour.

Beverly's aunt, Mrs. Hutchins, drove me to Boonville
one day. It turns out that her grandfather was a Zimmer,
probably the one to whom Great-grandfather Baker sold
the farm across the road—since she says that he and her
grandmother were married in this house. She herself was
born in Twin. She is worried about Beverly and her
fiancé. The explanation of the $3,000 car is that Beverly
and the boyfriend agreed to buy it together, but lately,
at any rate, she has been making all the payments. Her
family think that when the car is paid for, the boy will
simply drop her, and she is terribly afraid of losing him.
She only sees him at Port Leyden on the weekends. At
one time he stayed with Beverly's family; paid them $10
a week and demanded pork chops and steak. —The car
is bright red, and Beverly likes to wear a bright red dress.
She came to clean today (July 30). It is her vacation
from the factory, and, she says, she is trying to get a job
at the state insane asylum.

Helen now—instead of playing with the Lincks and
the little girl at the store—goes every day to ride the
Coes' pony and play with Frances Coe. Frances (twelve)
has red hair and almost colorless eyelashes and eyebrows.
Helen is enchanted with the farm, helps to gather the
eggs, etc. The Coes have a good old stone farmhouse,
built about a hundred years ago, which is now in very
run-down condition, and the teeth of Charles Coe and his
wife are about the most battered I have ever seen. But
they are very good-natured and nice. They are somehow,
a long time ago, intermarried with the Talcotts, and
Cousin Grace knew Charles's father, Horatio. He tells
me that he has a compass that belonged to (?) Topping

(he calls it Toppen), the first settler in this part of the country. Helen rides around the alfalfa meadow—she practises riding bareback. Sometimes the two girls ride Topsy together.

The pale stone creeper-spangled barn—greenery by day, shadows by night.

Dorothy Sharp has perhaps aged, but her accident has given her a rest, and I somehow have found her, this summer, more attractive and more sympathetic. A moment comes with many women when they have resigned themselves to being elderly. She seems more distinguished and has more charm. It is partly that she as well as Malcolm is relieved that his Rosenberg book is out.[14] Elena had noticed before that they were both anxious about it. But having it published and taken seriously has given Malcolm more self-confidence. I am somewhat more impressed by his ideas this summer, though I think that his apologia for the businessmen and American capitalism is to some extent a kind of insurance against getting in too wrong with the academic authorities. As it is—as Elena says—he is so obviously, if a little bit morbidly and crankily, conscientious that no one can impugn his honesty.

—By hurricane or elm blight now brought low.

I have had to have two elms cut down, one across the road and the other at the corner of the stone barn.

August 19 or 20.

August?
The dark elms of dawn
In milky splendors melting.

John Gaus took Malcolm and me on an all-day drive to the just-opened Adirondack Museum at Blue Mountain Lake. Very strange to see simply a lot of things from what is to me the immediate past ticketed and carefully preserved in a streamlined modern museum: old stoves not nearly so interesting as the ones I removed from this house, footbaths less distinguished than our painted tin one with its pitcher; old spring wagons and surreys such as those that we used to use for such expeditions as Forestport; drawings scratched on fan-shaped tree lichens such as we used to make in our childhood. There was a set of little groups behind glass showing the early life of timbering. The early phases of the Blue Mountain summer-hotel registers and other relics dating no further back than the eighties and nineties, maple-sugaring, a beaver dam, etc.—you paid a quarter for a thing you plugged in under the tableau to listen to a little recorded lecture. At the end of this room was a window made of polarized glass or something through which Blue Mountain looked exactly like a picture postcard and a good deal less attractive than it really is.

—A couple of the big early landowners were beaten, Gaus said, by the country and committed suicide. Jacob or John Brown (see Hough's History) shot himself. He owned over 200,000 acres. —There is a sandy infertile patch in the eastern part of Lewis County, which must once have been under water. There are even distinguishable sand dunes.

—Prospect, where the Gauses live, a delightful little town considerably larger than Talcottville: two little hotels, one called Toper: children riding horses in the dirt streets, another set of children in a buggy or something of the kind, driving a white horse; a church or two, a few square solid residences. The Gauses' back lawn extends further as a field of goldenrod; people's lawns have no fences between them—on one side of them is a garden full of brilliant gladiolas, on the other are old-fashioned carriages with red-and-black wheels.— The idea of the Gauses' pretty little white house with, she says, its narrow doors and the little inland town so self-contained among its mild and rounded hills seems to give Elena claustrophobia, though to me it offers attractions which make me wonder whether it is nicer than Talcottville. I saw no house as interesting as ours, but no road humming with trucks runs through it.

Malcolm's story, which he says is Spanish: Somebody asks Khrushchev for a definition of capitalism. —"Capitalism is the exploitation of man by man." —"And what is Communism?" —"Why, Communism is just the opposite!"

Pleasant effect of wild vegetation creeping up to the house, yet feudal self-confidence keeps it from encroaching. Just now—at the beginning of September—there are goldenrod, bluebells, and purple asters all growing against the house. —Every year, though they dig them up, the Loomises are surrounded by the small black-eyed-like bushes of the cone plant (can't find it in *How to Know the Wild Flowers*).

One morning when I [got] up at six, the pane with the Nabokov poem in the upstairs door to the balcony came out in a beautiful way against the pink dawn, looking like a pattern of frost.[15] I told Volodya about this when I called him up and he produced one of his inescapable puns: "There's an English word for that: *rime*."

Independence River: Rosalind and I went there (August 22), when I explored it for the first time beyond the bend that is near the top of the first falls. It runs level for quite a stretch. There is a path through the woods, but it does not go far; it stops, and the whole thing becomes quite wild, except for, on either side of the river, single lines of rusty barbed wire, mostly on the ground. What could these have been for?—the forest is too thick for cattle. Many flowers at the edge of the water: closed gentian, turtlehead, asters, cardinal flowers, and a little white daisylike thing. I came within sight of the second falls—my next object is to explore beyond it.

I don't know whether I have noted looking up the Kimball genealogy when I was working in the Widener Library. There is a very pretty coat of arms, with a red griffin or something of the kind. The motto, I was delighted to find, is *Fortis non Ferox.* The College of Heralds supplied it to some inquiring Kimball but the compiler of the genealogy seems to think it is phony. The Heralds said the family came from Cumberland, but all the other information about them indicates they came from Suffolk. The Kimballs are supposed to have exceptional memories.

The maple in front of the house first got one spot of salmon pink, and now has a great pink streak, with the color somewhat faded.

This has been, from the point of view of weather, one of the best summers here I remember—hardly ever hot, never too long rains. After just a touch of cold, the last week has been warm and delightful.

. . .

Just before Labor Day, Albert G. said, Well, they expect that four hundred people will be killed. Labor Day morning he said, Several people have been killed already. The day after Labor Day, 440 people were killed.

Beverly finally turned up again, looking better and quite pretty in her red dress. She hadn't been able to come to see us during the week she was not working because she had had no car, had had to have the dents taken out of it. She now has a job as attendant at the state insane asylum in Rome. The hours are easier than at the factory, but the lunatics get on her nerves, and she doesn't know whether she can stand it. Her father went to the hospital for an operation and seems to have come out rather sobered. To their surprise, he turned up at her sister's wedding and gave the bride away. He told them that he was sorry for what he had done, he didn't know what had got into him; but he didn't want to come back to the family, because he was so ashamed of himself. They told him to forget about it, that he wasn't the only person who had ever done anything like that; but he said it wasn't only the family, it was the neighbors he couldn't face.

12/18/16

The Sharps, including young John and little Malcolm, had supper at Mrs. Burnham's. Afterwards I went out of the house and looked at the sky and the view. The gray clouded sky had grandeur, with the beginnings underneath it of the orange sunset, and I realized that all this in itself was something that kept Mrs. Burnham going and gave her her invincible dignity through her accidents, losses, disasters. Dorothy said that she thought it was the view that made her continue to run the farm.

She had a big plate-glass window installed when, after the fire, they built a new house. —Her earphone went wrong at the supper table, which somewhat threw out the conversation, since she likes to take an active part, even hold the floor, and we got somewhat at cross-purposes with one another; but she afterwards got it straightened out.

Loomis tells me that it is only in this generation that the Coe place has gone to pieces. Charles married the illegitimate daughter of a man who kept a greenhouse. She seems slatternly but in no worse order than he. Huldah doesn't know who is responsible. She says the inside of the house is appalling—all the furniture broken.

Talcottville has lately been improving. The Maredens in the old Smithling house have at least had a new roof put over the porch. Water Street is better kept up. The O'Donnells and the Walter Gieglers, who live next door to one another, have fine lawns with no fence between them: modern outdoor chairs and lots of zinnias and other flowers around the houses. An old lady belonging to the family who own the house adjoining the O'Donnells, Roffin, has moved in and is redoing the whole place, has graded the lot between her and the O'D.'s and is about to have it planted with grass. Huldah says she is a formidable character with black piercing eyes, but this hasn't prevented the Loomises from getting in and inspecting the house, which they say is being done in a modern style.

Looking out one day from my window on the third floor, I saw the change made here by autumn in the atmosphere and the landscape: they become more serious,

Nature warns, reassumes her august authority; the luxury of summer is being withdrawn.

I am leaving by car with George Munn and Lou early tomorrow morning (Sept. 4). With gout, non-production, and worries, I was in the doldrums the first part of the summer, but later got my energies back, got six chapters of the Civil War ready to be typed and did the chapter on Cable as a piece for *The New Yorker* apropos of Arlin Turner's biography.[16] Also did the mushroom article this summer.

Poor Florence Loomis would manage to take part in the conversation by always saying, Oh, that's it! when anybody explained anything, and *Wundershayne und wunderbar!* when anybody expressed enthusiasm.

Life at Wellfleet is pleasanter on account of my new room and bathroom—wonderful to get rid of the sordidness and stink of the woodshed and the old bathroom. The old windmill-body over the well has been moved down to where the grape arbors are, so that the view is now clear and I can see the big sunflowers and the sunset.

One thing I am doing now that I find extremely interesting and very strange is realistically to confront and examine things that have been with me from childhood as legends, imaginative entities, and to find out what they really are: Dickens, Kipling, Edna Millay, the Indians, the Civil War. More difficult to do with one's parents: there is probably still a good deal that I don't know about my father's career and, in writing about him in *A Piece of My Mind*, I may not have got rid of some elements of myth. Talcottville, in spite of my scrutiny of it, I have not yet got to the bottom of. But of course my special feeling about it—shared by others, Dorothy Sharp, John Gaus, and Walter Edmonds, from that part of the world—is due to something that really existed, is itself one of the data of history.

NOTES

1. *Mushrooms, Russia and History*, by R. Gordon Wasson and Valentina Pavlovna Wasson. EW reviewed it in "Mushrooms, Russia, and the Wassons" (*The Nation*, November 16, 1957), reprinted as "Mycophile and Mycophobe" in *BBT*, pp. 339–54.

2. Charles Godfrey Leland (1824–1903), author of the humorous dialect verses *Hans Breitmann's Ballads* (1857).

3. Wife of Charles Rumford Walker, a longtime Yale friend of EW's, internationally known for his expertise in labor relations and his translations of Greek plays.

4. Beatrice Lillie was appearing in the Golden Jubilee edition of the Ziegfeld Follies.

5. Beverly Hutchins, the niece of Mabel Hutchins; both worked for the Wilsons.

6. See *The Cold War and the Income Tax: A Protest* (1963).

7. See *The Thirties*, pp. 353, 650, 692.

8. EW's Hill School friend William Adams Brown, a member of the Brown Brothers banking family.

9. A Hill School classmate of EW's, where they worked together on the *Hill School Record* and collaborated on plays. *The Thirties*, *passim*; *A Prelude*, pp. 55–59.

10. Howard Phelps Putnam (1894–1948), poet. *The Thirties*, *passim*.

11. Henry Fairfield Osborn (1857–1935), paleontologist and author; Herbert Osborn (1856–1954), biologist.

12. Sir Julian Huxley (1887–1975), eminent zoologist who promoted a eugenic notion of evolutionary humanism.

13. Gilbert Charles Stuart (1755–1828), creator of American classical portraiture, and known especially for his portraits of George Washington.

14. Malcolm Sharp, member of the Rosenbergs' defense, wrote *Was Justice Done? The Rosenberg-Sobell Case* (1956). Bertrand Russell had reviewed it.

15. A windowpane in the Stone House. Certain of EW's guests were invited to scratch poems or autographs in the windows.

16. EW's review of Turner's *George W. Cable: A Biography* appeared in the essay "The Ordeal of George Washington Cable" (*The New Yorker*, November 9, 1957).

12/20/10

CAMBRIDGE AND ROBERT LOWELL

I went to see *William (Billy) James* on one of my visits to Cambridge this autumn. He couldn't bring himself, he found—in view of all the interest in his family—to destroy family letters; would take them out and look at them, then tie them and put them away. So much about the children's illnesses and the prosaic sides of living. —When he and Henry, as boys, had first gone to see their uncle Henry in Switzerland, William Jr. had found him somewhat formidable but at the same time very kindly. When the two boys were finally parting, one (I think) to stay in Switzerland, the other to go somewhere else, they shook hands in the conventional Anglo-Saxon manner; but their uncle Henry said, "You've been living in Cambridge, but now you're in Europe. I will turn my back and you will embrace." Later, William Jr. embraced his uncle Henry at the train, when he was either arriving in or leaving England, with the result that somebody standing by said, "Look at those filthy foreigners kissing one another!"[1] He had never told anyone that before, he said. —His brother Alexander's boy, who had been writing a novel, came in. He had decided to recoup his loss of earnings at the time he had been writing it by volunteering for one of those graveyard jobs—would be paid $80 a day for spending six weeks in the hospital—which, he thought, would give him time to read—getting inoculated to protect him from the diseases that one can get from dead bodies, then for moving the corpses in a Polish cemetery near Worcester, through which a new road was being put. He would spend something like eight months in quarantine. —He said that he was sure that neither his uncle Henry nor [John Singer] Sargent had ever had a real love affair—because they were so dedicated to their work that they wouldn't be distracted by a woman. In Sargent's case, he said, his indifference to women became a joke, and some of his friends, on one occasion, arranged to have a beautiful girl in his bed when he came back at night from some social affair. He simply made her get dressed and sent her about her business. I told him that Leon Edel had the theory that H.J. might have had an affair with Rhoda Broughton.[2] He said that he had been at Lamb House when R.B. was visiting there, and he couldn't see any signs of it.

Mrs. Gilbert, who types my MSS. and who bores me by talking too much—the truth is, she doesn't come from up here and finds it boring in the winter, so that she is eager to talk to somebody—startled me by saying that she liked doing the chapters of my Civil War book: "It's as if you were pulling the wings and legs off flies. When you put them together again they'll never be the same shining star."

Gladys Brooks, in Cambridge, told me that Mark Howe had said to her that he did hope his daughters' second marriages would turn out all right. The daughters were little girls.

Visit to the Lowells in November: I was so pleased to find someone who talked like an old friend of the twenties—I kept telling him that I was a man of the twenties, that he seemed to me perfect: accelerating conversations, going off in all directions, interrupting one another, range of interest and reading, flares of imagination, general freedom of the world. I didn't know that he was getting into his manic phase. He had just come back from a reading in the South and was very exhilarated. I think it was a bad time for us to have come: we prolonged the excitement when he should have rested. He also had a pretty little girl in Cambridge, who wanted to write poetry and with whom he had been going to bed. He told Elena and me both about her: "She looks like a Renoir"—and when I met her, I saw that she did. He wanted me to have lunch with them at Cambridge. He listened on the phone from his bedroom —as he afterwards explained to Elena—while she was talking to Hedwig in Wellfleet and making an appointment with Rosalind to have lunch at the Parker House. He told us that, apart from his income, he had about $50,000 to invest and that he was having lunch with his banker to consult with him about it. He arranged to go to the Parker House and there latched on to Elena and had her go around with him the whole afternoon, so that she had no chance to buy Christmas presents. They went to the Swetzoff Gallery, and called on a friend of Robert's, an artist, who was busy and couldn't see them. Finally, he took Elena to the very high Episcopal church to which he had gone as a child, and there they did some praying. When he came back—to Elizabeth's horror—he began telephoning in all directions and inviting people to dinner and for after dinner. Elizabeth had counted on only four people. He invited his little mistress, and other young people—I suppose, to cover her up. Elizabeth had made no provision for so many guests and succeeded in disinviting some of them. She was in a dreadful state of tension and apprehension, having realized that Robert was going off his trolley. It was already impossible for him to talk to everybody without flying off into a "free association." I had told him that I didn't much believe in Frost's poetry—in fact, that I thought him "a dreadful old fake"; but—or perhaps, in consequence—he called up the Frosts and invited them to dinner. He told Mrs. Frost over the phone that I was a great admirer of Frost's, and Mrs. Frost said that her husband would be so glad to hear it because he had thought I wasn't. When Frost was there, he kept shifting us around, on account of Frost's deaf ear, etc., in such a way as to make sustained conversation impossible, and said to Frost that I wanted to ask him how his reputation had become so exaggerated. He [Frost] looked like a clever old elephant. I realized, in talking to him, that as a writer he *was* serious. We talked about the New England poets, about whom he was quite good; greatly admired "Snowbound"; said that E. A. Robinson's favorite poem of his own had been "Flood's Party." I. A. Richards was there—told me afterwards that he could see already that Robert (L.) was getting perverse and mischievous. After dinner, Elizabeth went upstairs to her room and burst into tears, and the mistress remained with the younger crowd and stupidly tried to play hostess. The Schlesingers came in after dinner. Elena says that at one point I was lecturing young married people on artificial insemination while Robert was holding forth to a partly Jewish audience about what a great man Hitler had been.

In the morning, first Elena, then I had breakfast with Robert. He and I talked volubly both at the same time. Elizabeth, he said, was a Southerner and didn't understand people not talking in turn, but he and I understood one another though both were talking at once. After breakfast, I went up to my room to lie down, and Robert appeared, almost naked and covered with black hair, carrying an immense set of Macaulay's *History*, which he dumped on me—having discovered at breakfast that I had never read it—and announced that it was a present in return for the *Ingoldsby Legends* I had given him.

Elizabeth took him to the doctor's, and we did not see them again. He was in hospitals most of the time from then till March. When I saw him again, he was quiet and orderly. Elizabeth said she hoped he was good for four years more.

NOTES

1. EW here mixes two of Billy James's familiar anecdotes. One dealt with the novelist's urging his nephews to be affectionate with one another (see Edel, *The Middle Years* [1962], p. 328). The other is an old story James used to tell about James Russell Lowell seeing some continental friend off at a London railway station and, on their embracing, hearing an English bystander describe him as a "filthy foreigner."

2. EW seems to be confusing James's friend Constance Fenimore Woolson with Rhoda Broughton. Neither can be said to have been objects of James's affection, though both were good friends. See Percy Lubbock, *Mary Cholmondeley* (1928), pp. 38–41, for an account of James's friendship with Broughton. Miss Woolson's letters to James were published in Henry James, *Letters*, III (ed. Edel, 1980), 523–62.

12/20/10

THE IROQUOIS, 1957

[During the autumn of 1956, EW suddenly realized that he was surrounded at Talcottville by an Iroquois national movement—"not unlike Scottish Nationalism and Zionism." It startled him that in his preoccupation with the Stone House and Wilson family history he had been overlooking one of his deepest concerns of all his writing years—the plight of the American Indian—right on his own doorstep and within easy motoring distance of the upstate reservations. His compassionate writings about minorities, recently embodied in his volume *Red, Black, Blond and Olive*, included his early denunciation of the dictatorship in Haiti, his exploration of the Zuñi rituals, his pursuit of the plight of the Jews, his close inspection of the roots of European struggles for freedom embodied in *To the Finland Station*, and his vivid documentaries on American poverty and the depression of the 1930s in *The American Earthquake*. He took steps promptly to make himself acquainted with the leaders of the Confederacy of the Six Nations, the Iroquois.

"They have some legitimate grievances because they are losing their property in their reservations on account of the St. Lawrence Seaway," he wrote to Van Wyck Brooks. He visited the Iroquois first in October 1956 and found "some very strange things going on." He went again at the end of January 1957 when the Iroquois celebrated their new year. Out of these and other visits there emerged still another book, the fruit of his "up-state" incursions, which he titled *Apologies to the Iroquois*.

EW was fortunate to find at Albany a congenial and highly documented informant, William N. Fenton, whom he described as "the country's greatest authority on the Iroquois." Fenton, he wrote Roger Straus, was "brilliant and quite free from anthropological jargon." That freedom from the abstractions and formulae of high expertise had been one of the features of his story of the Dead Sea Scrolls, which he had lifted above the complexities of the scholars and religionaries. His notes in the ensuing pages on the upstate Indians in their state of decline and struggle are vivid and compassionate in their observed detail and careful objectivity.]

Oct. 15, arrived Amsterdam, N.Y.: *Trip for story about Iroquois Indians:* Beauty of the Mohawk Valley at this time of year (Berkshires also more interesting in their variegated colors instead of the dark solid green of summer): lemon, orange, rich gold, rich rust, more or less even heights that run along the river, the towns very well kept up, something of the Dutch tradition lingers, attractive little white houses, all different, and the more palatial dark square piles, also very individual, a little old red brick fort at Amsterdam, rather green brick and white frame churches, each a separate inspiration of some architect, and at Fonda a green little Gothic number in very much blackened stone, which is built right into a hill, in which the back part is embedded: stained-glass

windows at the front and back, all windows so narrow
that it must have been very dark to worship there—no
longer used as a church. When we looked through a
broken pane, we saw that it was now being used as a
combination of storeroom and dump; on the front, cut
out from the stone, simply "Zion 1866"—it is, it seems, a
reproduction, made by local Episcopalians, of an old
church in England. Fonda has a delightful old courthouse
and a very impressive new one, with portraits of worthies
and red leather seats in the courtroom. The leaves they
were raking off the pavement along the street where this
courthouse is had almost the look of chopped ham.

The Auriesville Martyrs' Shrine: I had seen this from
the train and the thruway and wondered what it was.
George Munn and I explored it. It turns out to be a
memorial to the French Jesuit priests who were captured
and tortured by the Mohawks. Their mission was on the
hill. The priests were canonized, and the Indian maiden
Tekakwitha, who was converted and had to escape from
her people and who is supposed to have led a life of
exemplary chastity, has the rank of "venerable." [Roger]
Peyrefitte, in *Les Clés de Saint-Pierre* (1955), says that
Rome does not want to make her a saint for fear of
having to have a Negro saint. The place is a large public
park with a wonderful view over the Mohawk and
benches from which to look at it. There is something of
the amusement park or circus. An immense "coliseum"
is a church with altars in the middle for the priests,
facing in different directions, a small marble statue of
Tekakwitha, a full-length wax figure of Our Lady as
bride, very pretty and well turned out American style.
There are seats all around the altars and confessional
boxes all around the wall. Outside it says, Press this
button if you want a priest to confess. A museum with

Indian relics and pictures of, and documents on, the Jesuits. A pietà in a sort of large grotto. Posts on which the signs seem to say that Jesuits' heads were impaled, though these can hardly be the actual posts. A tremendous Stations of the Cross, must be quarter of a mile long; begins in the middle of the park and goes on eventually up a hill, on top of which rises a cross. Every station is an eight-foot (?) monument, with a bas-relief picture of the incident involved. Near the first is a pile of light crosses, two unsmoothed poles tied together, which you are invited to carry with you.

County historian Edwin Sheean, very pretentious in his deadpan way, wanted to impress with his learning and part of his act in this was imparting it with the utmost reluctance. If you asked him a direct question, he would try to say something to puzzle and stop you. Very antagonistic to Standing Arrow:[1] Indians had been there simply to build [a] catwalk under thruway, then S.A. joined them, set up as their leader, tried to exploit the situation for publicity. Now the bridge was finished, the steelworkers were moving on, and the river would be swollen and wash away the shacks. Told me he was an honorary Seneca, the sachems all came to see him. Said that I wouldn't find many archivists in his position—it was a full-paid job.

(I afterwards learned from Fenton[2] that Sheean was a former policeman. His archivist job was not as secure as he thought. He was out by the time I came again. The other party was now in office. Fenton said that he exasperated the Albany Indian archaeologist.)

12/21/10

Standing Arrow was away the first day we went to see him. I was up against the old difficulty of talking to Indians. They don't like to answer questions. The two men I first asked about Standing Arrow said he was away; when I asked where I could find him, there was a long unresponsive silence, then: His wife lives over there. She was very handsome and dignified, seemed a pure Indian type—yet her skin was white and her eyes were blue. Same obstruction to communication. She said he might be back in the evening. I asked whether she meant night or later afternoon—should I come about five? Silence, then: You do that. But he wasn't there at five. I asked her whether they expected to spend the winter there. She looked at me in silence in a way that was almost fierce. As usual, I had to prime the pump and went on to say something about not seeing how they could keep warm if they stayed. We're aimin' to, she finally said, as it might have been Fern Munn. The children were just the same, did not answer Hi when you called to them, as other American children did. The only freely friendly person was a little mongrel dog, brown with a stripe on his back, who ran around madly and jumped up on us. At eight, he was still not at home, and Mrs. Standing Arrow suggested our coming next morning at nine.

We did. We were greeted by the dog but one knock brought no response from the house. A small boy was playing in the creek, but as usual did not greet or answer us. When I asked him the second time if there was anybody home, he finally replied, Um-hm, and disappeared. I knocked again at the door and, after waiting a few minutes, decided to leave. When we were just starting off in the car Standing Arrow appeared and waved to us. He was pleasant but I began by nettling him by saying that I thought his claims were not valid. Will you let me show you something? he said, and disappeared into the house, where he remained for some time. Then he invited us in. His wife and his children had been isolated in a little crate of a room annexed to the single room of what must have been the original shack. It was clean, as well kept as it could be. On the walls, a gigantic snapping-turtle shell, one of the guitar-shaped rattlers they use for their music, a feathered headdress of the familiar kind. He read me a long statement from an unidentified printed document of 1924 and produced a facsimile of the Treaty of Fort Stanwix. He was getting a little tough over this at first, explained that Washington had dealt with them as a nation, and that we had imitated their constitution. But he tried to pick us up with his charm, which is considerable and which he evidently depends on. Though fattish, he is quite fine-feathered except for a cast in one eye. I thought at first he had a touch of Mussolini, then saw that he strikingly resembled the pictures of the young Napoleon —gestures, perhaps based on French, that showed some skill at public speaking. He exerted a certain magnitude. In the meantime had entered another chief, who when we came had been fast asleep, contracted into a compact lump that filled up the back seat of a car. He was rather formidable-looking, dark beard, stocky shouldered, cigar-store-Indian features, piercing eyes open only a crack. He said to me, I will speak my language, and addressed some words in Mohawk to Standing Arrow. They had what used to be called a brief colloquy—I am falling into the language of old Indian fiction—then Standing Arrow said to me, You tell me you're a newspaper re-porter—can you show me your credentials. I explained to them exactly what I was doing, and we went on amiably enough. Standing Arrow had thought, I suppose, that my attitude was hostile. I asked if they had any souvenirs—I had promised to try to get some for Helen—and the second man produced some moccasins, bead dolls, and bead-embroidered handbags. He told me he had

been a steelworker like almost all the other Mohawks—
had worked on the Empire State Building, had even
worked on the tower. I came to like him, he had a sly
friendliness and humor. Standing Arrow showed me
some printed pages from some museum or anthropological
publication, with pictures of grotesque works called "false
faces," then he produced one from a bag: a hideous red
bugaboo, with a nose twisted around to the left in a
kind of curling sneer, almost like a Picasso or something.
He makes a terrible noise, he said. What kind of a noise?
You won't sleep afterwards. I turned it around to look
for a whistle. Don't put it on, he warned me, smiling.
We feed him. What? Corn. We had to help Mr. Fenton
out (at the New York State Museum in Albany). They
had one of these in a glass case—that's another thing we
don't like—and one night the watchman heard glass
breaking and he went in and found him on the floor.
They had a new glass put in, but the same thing happened again. The glass was broken, and they found him
on the floor. Then they told us about it, and we came
down and fed him. He has to be fed once a year. —He
explained the organization by clans. You have to marry
into a different clan, your children all belong to your
wife's clan. He was Turtle but his wife was Wolf, and
his children were all Wolf. The women elected the
chiefs, the clans voting as units. —He couldn't give orders
directly for somebody to move his house, for example.
He had to call a council first, then the orders proceeded
from the council. —I asked if the headdress on the wall
was his. No: it belongs to him (the steelworker); but I
wear it when the tourists are here. You know if you
don't wear one of those things, they don't think you're
a real Indian. He invited me to the council—the
Condolence,[3] I understood—at the Onondaga reservation
Saturday, for swearing in the new chief.

While we were waiting for Standing Arrow when he was getting ready to receive us in the house, we sat looking at Schoharie Creek. I tried to see how it had looked to the Mohawks in the days when this had been their home—Schoharie is a Mohawk name. The water was quite black in the light mist of morning—with a patch of blinding flashes near the stones on the higher shore beyond, in the yellowing trees of autumn, where it rose to a cradling hill. But what was scenery to me had been their real world. Later, at the council, the young Onondaga tried to explain to me in his imperfect English how much the Indians saw in surrounding nature.

Talcottville: After the warm days of sun and dryness, it became, on Friday, damp and misty. But the evening of my arrival at Talcottville, this had hardly begun. I felt the same emotion that I usually do when I looked out from the porch of the house. So this was how it had looked to *my* people at this barren time of year—I had never seen it before when the leaves were gone: the farms beyond the river visible, the black-and-white cows looking poorer for the poorness of their drying paling pasture, my lot across the road full of faded milkweed heads with a little red bush at the back, the mountains almost black in the background. The trees, they say, have lost their leaves just in the last few days; we are closer here to winter than in the Mohawk Valley, even around Utica, where you meet some golden foliage when you go down from the hills.

The next morning (Friday), on waking up: a gray day of slow rain among dulled yellow leaves . . .

The next day, Oct. 19, we went to the Onondaga council.[4] We were cordially greeted by Louis Papineau, the friend to whom Standing Arrow had sent us. He was

obviously working at "public relations," and I learned
that they were going to send a spokesman to appear before the Court of Claims in Washington (Feb. 4) and
make demands for land in the Ohio Valley, Pennsylvania, New York State, and perhaps Vermont. The young
men were getting together to try to promote a new
solidarity among the Six Nations,[5] to get them to take
action together, to evolve a concerted plan, and to put
their case to the government. The difficulty was to get
everyone who had enough education to deal with the
problems and present this case. The exploit of Standing
Arrow was only one feature of this movement. It seemed
to me that there was even an attempt to put new life
into the Longhouse religion,[6] which resembled the attempts of the younger Jews to revert to Judaism, and
the other phenomena of the kind. He said that it was
not correct to call the practitioners of the Longhouse
religion pagans: after all, they worshipped one God, the
Great Spirit. Those chiefs—we were waiting on the
Longhouse steps[7] for the procession of the chiefs to
arrive—were at that moment burning tobacco over the
fire—and that tobacco was incense—and praying to the
Great Spirit. They would arrive, each with his clan
mother, and they would mourn for the departed chiefs.
The last Tadodáho—supreme chief, who has to be
elected from the Onondagas, because they are the "fire-
keepers," connected with the divine origins of the group
—had died—they could, however, be deposed if it was
thought they were unfit for their function. He described
to me the ceremony and said that he would explain it
to me while it was going on. Afterwards they ate venison
and danced the rest of the evening. It was only on such
occasions, at intervals of years, that the chiefs with their
delegations from all the Six Nations got together. I said
that I was lucky to see it. He was a tree surgeon—a

nice-looking fellow, very serious and obviously honest and sincere and doing his best to be informative. Standing Arrow has something of the showman, the demagogue. I was surprised to find that, in general, they spoke Iroquois more easily than English, as Standing Arrow had told me, and that some of the older Indians could hardly speak English at all. They had some difficulty in explaining their theology and customs—sometimes used words out of English books which they did not know how to pronounce. Papineau said *line-age* for *lineage*. It is, I suppose, peculiarly difficult to explain, from one language to another, theology and social habits. They would sometimes misunderstand my questions and answer on wrong assumptions. I gathered that there was a certain disillusion, caused by religious differences. There were several Christian churches in the reservation: Episcopal, Seventh-Day Adventists, I forget what else. One man, a graduate of Dartmouth, in the St. Regis reservation, was a Mormon and an ardent proselytizer. He said that a large percentage were practising the old religion, though Sheean had told me there were very few. I mentioned Sheean and said he had told me that he had been made an honorary Seneca. When I had told Standing Arrow this, he had said, He's an honorary bullshitter! The Onondaga said, "There's no such thing." You either were a Seneca or you weren't. "It's only a mock honor." I commented on the beauty of their location, walled in by now golding hills. He explained that Onondaga meant "on the hills." Several of the ones I have talked to—like this one—had something of a British accent and turn of speaking—from being in or near Canada, I suppose.

The audience gradually gathered. The chiefs took a long time in coming, perhaps on account of the drizzling rain. I was surprised at the variety of type. If one knew the different nations well, one might, I suppose, recognize different breeds; but they are a good deal intermarried. Some are aquiline, some are round-faced, some are chin-less and have birdlike beaks. Some of the women with glasses reminded me of Xenia heads. Some of the older women looked like ordinary New York State farmer's wives, wore the same kind of clothes and had their hair done the same way; but if one looked, one saw some-times darker skin, sometimes rounder black eyes. When we had stopped at Papineau's house, his wife had asked us to take with us an old Indian who was going to the council. He was very tall, straight and stiff and quite gray, and his coloring seemed rather Nordic. He re-minded me of someone whom I could not place at first, then I realized that it was Walter Munn. I asked whether he spoke English; he said, Not much. What he did speak also seemed rather British. He thanked us very much when we set him down. He was the only person there in tribal costume, with one feather in the band around his head. He was not, I was told, a chief. Later on, when George [Munn] and I were standing on the steps of the Longhouse, he came by and said, You can't go in, you know. I said that Papineau had invited us. Louis Papi-neau? I'll ask. And he went inside. Nothing happened and, after an interval, we followed him. We [saw] him and Papineau in discussion. Papineau gestured to us to take a seat and went over to another old Indian, a giant, probably ninety, who P. had told us had been a football star. They, too, had an animated discussion, as George was aware, but not I, about us. Then the first old man came back and sat beside me, removing my hat from the bench and putting it in my lap. Presently he put his hand on my rear, gave me a gentle but firm push and said, You go out. George and I got up. Papineau came to remonstrate with the old conservative, but I asked him whether we oughtn't to leave and he nodded yes. He joined us outside and apologized. It's the result of ignorance, he said. I can't make him see that it will help us to have you as a witness that the Longhouse religion is still being practised by the whole Six Nations together. The old man at this point emerged, and Papineau began to scold him, so we withdrew and went to sit in the car. Just before that, a round-faced and amiable young man had introduced himself to me, asked my name, and explained that he was a Tuscarora. It was an attempt to make amends. And after we were in the car, another young man of the round-faced type, in a red-and-black lumberman's shirt and gloves, came up and said, "Old people, they don't understand nothing," then turned away and left.

We waited to see the procession, which was about three hours late, no doubt waiting for the rain to stop. The old man, perhaps insulted and refusing to attend the ceremony, took off his Indian costume, packed it in a small suitcase, got into the back seat of a car, and went to sleep. At last the chiefs arrived. No doubt on account of the rain, they were not wearing their headdresses and costumes. I am sorry not to have been able to see whether Standing Arrow, as I had read in a clipping, had been "dehorned" by the Turtle Mothers. The only woman among them was the widow of the late top chief, very middle-class-looking in checked middle-class clothes: white hair well taken care of, a small old lady's hat, and good shoes. She was accompanied by a corpulent man in the corresponding male clothes, whom I took to be her son. They looked somewhat pathetic in the rain, with their so varied features and builds and their varied American clothes, the remnants of the once mighty Iroquois. Some of the men were tall, dark, and lean with insolent wide-brimmed hats, rather in the

Western style. (I do not know why the Indians in general wear hats too small for them on the backs or the tops of their heads.) Then several cars drew up and women got out of them. These must have been the cult mothers, who had been allowed to—or rather had demanded, on account of the rain—to come in this way. A man in the front rank was howling a dirge. Of the houses in the reservation, some were on the shanty side, others like any small houses. Very strange to find this primitive civilization alongside our overpowering modern one, which itself contains so many primitive elements. When Standing Arrow was talking, I felt I was visiting a different country. One must realize that they have the conviction and the courage of a once independent people who have been decimated and pushed into a corner by an alien and unscrupulous race. Their surefootedness and other skills learned on the wild continent come out in their activities as structural steelworkers; and their spirit also survives. The steelworker was proud that the government had been glad to have the Iroquois (the Navahos, too) transmit messages during the war on account of their impenetrable languages.

Papineau had said yes when I asked him whether it would still be all right for us to come to the dance that night, but I felt that he had been a little hesitant, and on this account, since I knew that, the ceremony being so late, the dance would be beginning about ten, and since the day was very wet and I was suffering from gout in my leg, I decided to go back to Talcottville.

12/24/10

Talcottville: My first two days here were miserable. It was last May all over again. Dr. Sowles, in his knockabout way, had not yet got to the point of adjusting his perfect crowns in any condition which made it possible to chew with them. My new attack of gout was making it more and more painful to get around or even to sleep at night. It was raining as it always seems to do when I first arrive in Talcottville, and the house was again cold and damp. But last night, after getting back, I decided to spend the night at the Munns' and had the first good sleep for a week in a comfortable bed and warm room. I had had the doctor give me a shot, and I woke up this morning with my swelling gone down, so I am able, except for climbing stairs, to get around without pain. The weather is colder but bright, and I have had a delightful day in the Stone House writing up these notes in the big room beside a blazing fire.

Smell of the house when I first came back: old; this is the past—though somewhat musty, it charms me.

The lemon wisps of birch in the Mohawk Valley.

Talcottville: Last sight of the old house as I left. I had never seen it like that before—with no leaves or vines around it, looking out, with its windows glittering, on the paling green of the fields—denuded; it seemed more alone, facing squarely the wide spaces, dark mountains, a shelter erected by humans which still endured on its little eminence in that country where the Indians had hunted and from which they had now shrunk away.

One day, on the second floor, I looked toward the door to the balcony and saw that the panes were dark blue. I went closer and looked out at dark clouds, rather queer with creamy white tops.

The cold drove me out to sleep two nights at the Munns'. The bathroom no longer functions—though they characteristically did not mention this. They have been getting no water from the well in weeks, so the wash-basin and toilet are weak. There is not even a latch on the door. Only the long modern lighting on either side of the mirror works. They depend for water on the pump at the barn and for a toilet on the old-fashioned outhouse connected with the tenant's cottage. Otis Jr. and Helena have their water piped in from the barn; but the family of Otis Sr. have to bring it in in the morning in milk cans, and sometimes have to break the ice. It is difficult to get a bath, and a hot bath seems to be impossible. That is why poor little Lou always smells of dried perspiration. —The house, however, was warm, and after the first night—with the injection the doctor had given me—my gout was considerably better. But it got worse again the next day, and was most painful when Otis Sr. and I went on our trip to the St. Regis reservation. When we came back, I resorted to my own house—took a hot bath and went to bed with a pint of whisky. —The Munn house is not like any other house. They have no social life and no real family life. There are no pictures except on the bookcase a row of photographs of the children and their husbands and wives and in the dining room Doig's portraits of trout. The place is more like a bus station, a base where people come and go. At breakfast all the boys are likely to report, getting their orders from Fern—she tells them which trucks to use, etc., making decisions in a firm gruff voice. Ann occasionally calls up. Otis explained the whole economy of the family. Otis Jr. and Helena get their house and milk free; Otis works at Spayer's and drives a truck, one or more of which he owns. George drives a truck of Otis's and lives at home with Lou and the baby. He pays no rent and gets their food free, though he sometimes buys some himself. Lou does all the housework and never gets a bath, and is now in complete rebellion and bringing pressure to bear on George to get a house of their own. He had been saving up money and she thought she was going to get away, but then Fern persuaded him to put it all into the Spayer's project. Otis Sr. told me that George had been three years in Korea and didn't know whether he would ever see his home again and now didn't want to leave; but when he was in Wellfleet, he told Elena that he did. He is never able to save any money. He does not earn anything during the off-season for trucking, because, although he works on the farm, his father doesn't pay him anything, says that he can't afford to. At some periods he drives sixteen hours a day, at others twenty-one. He had lost seventeen pounds since I saw him last, and looked rather drawn and depressed. I said that he couldn't stand such hours, and he answered that you could for a while. I thought that he would welcome the opportunity of a day off between two of my trips, but he said that he would go crazy, wouldn't know what to do with himself if he took a day off. None of them except Otis Sr. ever reads or has any interest of his own (Helena is more bourgeois and better educated; she does occasionally read): they have to keep going all the time. Otis reads the New York and the local papers and keeps pretty well posted. There is a gigantic pile of old papers on one of the chairs in the living room. It seems queer to see books like *Zuleika Dobson* that I sent Aunt Addie for Christmas behind the glass of this bookcase. Otis did, of course, accomplish something, made, I suppose, a heroic effort, in rescuing the family from its degradation; but they are stuck at their present level, the children can't get above it—though perhaps the grandchildren may—Helena's little boy seems bright and sensitive. The worst of it is that—I suppose, through the dominance of Fern—they are all except Ann tied up together with no way of getting loose and doing anything for themselves. Otis and Fern themselves are always taking on new activities or shifting back and forth between beef stock and dairy farming, but it is always the same rather non-prospering enterprise. Even Chet, though he now lives in Constableville, works with his mother in Boonville at Crofoot's farm machinery salesroom. They are annoyed at his having had to turn Catholic to marry his present wife. They were not invited to the christening of his baby, and he has to go to confession. It seems that his mother-in-law was married to a Protestant, that her two other girls married Protestants, and that she felt she couldn't let the last one get away from the Catholic Church. Fern and Otis are talking now about going back to beef-stock-raising again, say they are getting too old for milking; but George told Elena that it wasn't possible to make money out of beef stock up there. They are all very well aware that the small dairy farmer is doomed, and they are somewhere between the big farmer and the small farmer. They have never yet succeeded in getting the whole house painted. It is as if the curse of Thad's life—he built it in the early 1900s—were still on it.

12/25/1

Trip to St. Regis:[8] I was suffering horribly from gout, could hardly get in and out of the car, the weather was cold, but what I found was so interesting it kept me going. First Indian I interviewed in the reservation expressed himself in English with difficulty. His house was on the water, and he was about to lose his property, as his neighbors to the west already had; but he wouldn't take money for it. For the Indians the earth was a mother, not to be bought and sold; but he seemed to intimate obscurely that he would somehow arrange to allow his children to benefit by the compensation. They had just lost their suit in the Utica court—the Six Nations against the state, as distinguished from the individual Indians who negotiated with the state. Each of them did his best for himself—they all hated one another. The clan chief no longer had any power; it was the state chiefs who were recognized by the authorities. The majority at St. Regis were Catholics, and they were run by a Catholic priest, a Canadian Mohawk. When, after fighting for the British, the Mohawks had taken refuge in Canada, they had been forced to accept Catholicism at the point of a gun. The Tadodáho from Onondaga had, without letting his people know it, been up there and appointed some Catholic clan chiefs. They despaired of getting justice or even a lawyer to defend them in these cases—couldn't get one in the state, perhaps not in the U.S.—aimed, if necessary, to bring their grievances before the U.N. He presently picked up a letter and read, so I gathered that the interview was at an end. I inquired about Philip Cook,[9] and he said I should by all means see him: he talked English better and could explain things better than he could. —The ceremony of the mask-wearers who visit the houses: the priest had tried to turn this ceremony into a sprinkling of holy water. They had discussed making such a démarche as Standing Arrow had attempted, but it was to have been carried out by responsible leaders. Now Standing Arrow had made a mess of it. On account of his inveterate crookedness, he would be sure to get into trouble. He had cheated and lied to people in his own reservation, and had had to go away, and, as chief of his clan, he had been dehorned. He (the speaker) had given money to Standing Arrow's wife when his children had had nothing to eat—was interested to know the wife and the twins were with Standing Arrow on Schoharie Creek: he had left them at one time in Syracuse. He had heard about the Mohawk steelworkers from Brooklyn building the catwalk under the thruway and had attached himself to them.

I had to wait for Philip Cook to get back from work in the aluminum factory, so we killed time—Otis Sr. and I—by driving around. Mrs. Lazore's admirable souvenir shop. She was part Indian, part white, and married to a pure Mohawk, who drove the school bus. He was concerned about the movement, but she told him not to worry about it: they had to find work to do and send their children to school in a white man's country. Indians from the Canadian half of the reservation constantly came over to our side, sold things at fairs, etc., but Indians from the American side were not allowed over there—Americans could not be given jobs in Canada; a Mohawk from Hogansburg who [had] gone to the other side had lately been bumped off by the Canada Indians.

I was much impressed by *Philip Cook*, who reminded me of Dan Aaron—talked English like an American (did not, in fact, speak Mohawk). A strong religious vocation of the benevolent not the aggressive kind—kindly and intelligent gray eyes. —Though a Mormon elder now, he supported the nationalist movement. When I asked how it could be effective, since the actual arrangements about everything were always made by the state chiefs with the white men, what could they do?, he answered, "Just show the white man a dirty face." He had been in court in Utica, and what had happened there was awful—I ought to look up the minutes. Their lawyer had been helpless and hopeless; the judge from the beginning had made clear his prejudice. He spoke of a local affair about which the other men had already told me in such a way that I had not understood it. The state was not supposed to have any jurisdiction inside the reservation, but a bad precedent had lately been created by the outside authorities stepping in to decide some question, I think, of title.

It grew cold in the backyard, so we went to sit in the car—he did not invite us into the house because his daughter was down with the flu. I asked him how he came to be a Mormon, and he told us the story of his life. He had been born in the St. Regis reservation, but had been taken by his parents all over the state—one of many children. They were evidently a family who were coming up—one of his brothers had been to Dartmouth. They had been Catholics from his grandmother's time, and the Catholic Church did its best to keep the Indians from knowing anything about their old religion, anything, in fact, about their past. But in every place he had gone he had looked up other Indians. Indians, he said, had a good time together. He had made friends and, even when he moved on, had kept them, had corresponded with them. They were presumably not all Catholics, since he had learned from them about Indian history. When he had come back to St. Regis again, he had been made a state chief, and thought then that he ought to know more about what the Mohawks were and how they had lived. He seems to have had access to the extensive Indian library of Ely Parker's nephew or grandnephew[10] and says he spent three and a half years reading in it. The official documents are misleading, he says: the early French and the English had their official line and always spoke of the Indians as "savages" or "pagans"; you get a much better idea of the white man's personal relations with the Indians and his actual impressions of them from reading the letters and diaries. He became very proud of his race, and when he realized how badly they had been treated, there came a time when he wasn't a human being—"I didn't have a heart here, I had a piece of lead—when I'd see a white man, the hair would stand up on my head." He gave up his office as state chief, and now at forty-four he realized he must break with the Catholic Church. His children went not to the Indian Catholic school but to the Irish school across the street. When he took them out, there was a big fuss. First two nuns were sent to see him; then the priest came and threatened to excommunicate him. But he persisted, and then he didn't have a friend in the reservation. At first he took an interest in the Protestant sects—the Methodists and the Episcopalians. He went to their functions, liked them at first: they were so friendly after the Catholics. But then when he found out they, too, went back to the early Catholic Church, he wouldn't have anything to do with them. He now studied the Longhouse religion, got someone to instruct him in it. [Marginal note: family came from Canada to teach him the Longhouse [Handsome Lake] code in 1948.] He saw that it was a wonderful thing. It was not correct to call the Iroquois pagans: they worshipped only one God. They did not worship the moon and other natural forces and objects, as the whites had sometimes said they did: they merely had celebrations about them. He had still retained some faith in Christ, and, traveling around the country on vacation, he had found that there was something like a legend of the ultimate coming of a Savior. He thought that the white men, when they first appeared, had been mistaken for this Savior. But when he set out to practise the Longhouse religion in the St. Regis reservation, he was handicapped by not speaking Mohawk. He had heard it spoken in childhood, and could understand it but not really speak it. He had furthermore found the Longhouse run by a stupid woman whose conception of the religion had nothing in common with his own. I had already learned from the man whom

I had previously interviewed at St. Regis that Cook had been kept out of the Longhouse by the man who had kept me out of the council at Onondaga and who was known as Rusty Oaks. It was his wife who dominated the St. Regis Longhouse. When I told Philip Cook this, he buried his face in his hands and moaned. He implied that it was too much that the first outside person who had taken an interest in the movement should have been kept out of the council by Rusty Oaks. He had plainly a religious vocation, and this had left him homeless for a church. Then two Mormon missionaries came to see him. He thought that it was just another Christian sect which would turn out to have split off from the Catholics. "I know what you're going to say," he said, "and I don't want to hear it!" But later he went out in his car and found them waiting to hitchhike a ride. He didn't like to refuse people who were hitchhiking, so he told them to get in, and then he explained to them the reasons for his prejudice against the Christian churches. But, they answered, we don't derive from the Catholic Church. The revelation came to Joseph Smith right here in New York State. Cook went on to explain that he wanted a church which would enable him to make some connection with the Indian religion. Mormonism, they declared, did connect up with the Indians. They didn't have the answers at their fingertips, but would look them up and let him know. Later they informed him that the Book of Mormon said that the Indians had come from Jerusalem and then gone to South America. It seemed to me strange that a man who had criticized Catholicism so acutely and approached Indian history in so scholarly a way should have been satisfied with this account of the origins of his own people. He had told me that he had realized the absurdity of the Catholic idea of salvation when he had found out that whole civilizations involving millions of people had existed all over the world before the Christian religion began—so what kind of a God was that who had allowed them to flourish and perish with no chance to save their souls? But his need for a religion in which to function must have been overwhelming, and Mormonism offered him a way out. He went to Utah and became a Mormon elder, and is now, I am told, a most effective preacher. *12/27/10*

William N. Fenton, authority on the Iroquois, formerly in the Indian Bureau, now director of the State Museum in Albany. They had come to see him and told him about their proposed démarche—he had asked them to let him know so that he could be present. Standing Arrow was in an old tradition. (Dan Aaron later told me that the type of the national hero, derived from the original Hiawatha, was invariably something of a rogue, so Standing Arrow's rascality may be part of his role!) The great leader was always expected. —I asked Fenton about the mask which was supposed to have jumped out of the case. There turned out to be this much of truth in it: that they had such a mask in the museum and that Fenton had invited the Senecas to come down and perform there the ritual of feeding it, which consisted of smearing its mouth with sunflower-seed oil and tobacco. But Standing Arrow, he said, had no business to talk as if this ritual were something that Mohawks could perform. It was in Seneca, a Seneca affair. The story they had invented, he said, was typical. —At one time, he had gone to Canada to study the Iroquois there and had found himself in the embarrassing situation—for an American state or government official—of communicating with an underground movement, which—since all of the Indians were supposed to be Catholic—was what the Longhouse religion was there.

NOTES

1. Standing Arrow, a former chief of the St. Regis reservation, was leading a group of Mohawks laying claim to land outside Amsterdam, N.Y., as property given them in a 1784 treaty. See EW's chapter on Standing Arrow in *Apologies to the Iroquois* (1960, hereafter referred to as *AI*), pp. 39–57.

2. William N. Fenton was then Assistant Commissioner for the New York State Museum and Science Service. See *AI* and *LLP*, *passim*, and Fenton's "The Iroquois in the Grand Tradition of American Letters: The Works of Walter D. Edmonds, Carl Carmer, and Edmund Wilson," in the *American Indian Culture and Research Journal* (5:4, 1981), pp. 21–39.

3. A part of the ceremony for mourning chiefs who have died.

4. The Onondaga reservation near Syracuse is the capital of the Six Nations.

5. The Iroquois people, comprised of the Mohawks, Senecas, Onondagas, Oneidas, Cayugas, and Tuscaroras.

6. The Longhouse religion was developed by the Seneca prophet Handsome Lake (1735–1815). Influenced in part by Quaker missionaries, and amidst the post-American Revolution demoralization of the Iroquois, he coupled ancient traditions with personal vision. He advocated self-control and abstinence and worshipped the Great Spirit.

7. "The temple, the center of the ancient religion, and the council chamber where decisions are made" (*AI*, p. 64).

8. *AI*, pp. 72–125.

9. *AI*, pp. 114–25.

10. The Indian general Ely S. Parker (1828–95), Commissioner of Indian Affairs under Grant: his grandnephew, Arthur C. Parker (1881–1955), an important Indian scholar: *An Analytical History of the Seneca Indians* (1926). *AI*, pp. 169–72.

INDIAN CEREMONIES

Expedition to western New York with William N. Fenton, Jan. 22, 1958. Mohawk Valley this time of year monotonous and grim, woods on the whitened hills now merely scratches of black, instead of the wonderful October colors.

Jan. 23. Tonawanda: Fenton had spent two years in Akron just outside the reservation. When he had been married to a girl from Salamanca who was teaching school nearby, the Senecas had given him a marriage celebration, for which he had provided the feast. They had presented him with a loaf in the shape of enormous testicles and a cane to get back from his honeymoon. What was *honeymoon* in Seneca?—*honey gă-gwä* (Morgan's spelling).

Nicodemus Bailey:[1] Extremely sly and clever old Indian politician—had played football at Carlisle, stooping now but had been a giant; dehorned for "being too bright," had wanted improvements; once had been told not to go to the Longhouse; they were threatening to beat him up, but he had put on his boots and gone, and nobody had said a word; had been to the last Republican convention but was now a Democrat; something of an Indian scholar, was at present working on some problem. Rather, I think, on the cynical side. Franklin John[2] had told me at Allegany,[3] with horror, that Nicky had brushed off talk of Allegany's right to oppose the federal government in the matter of the Kinzua dam[4] by saying that the Senecas were a conquered tribe. He had some old-fashioned New York State ways of saying things like those of the old people in Lewis County; but I was struck by his English, which was rather like that of an educated Russian or Oriental—unexpectedly felicitous and correct where a technical word was needed, though sometimes not otherwise correct. For example, he used the word *extant* correctly but made it *in extant,* having evidently hesitated over *in existence.* He said that the story of the hunter with which the Little Water cantata dealt was *mythic, a fanciful story,* and that it ended with a *flourish of the flute.* It ought, he said, to be given as an opera. I learned later that he played the piccolo and the flute, and had once been in Sousa's band. He had also a command of idioms. Fenton said that he had succeeded in getting someone to make a tape recording of the first of the four parts of the Little Water Ceremony, but had not been able to get the rest. I asked why, and Nicky said, You can lead a mule to water but you can't make him drink. —In connection with the messy and complicated situation of the Indian, he said, You have to be an Indian to know about it. People lift up the lid and look in, and then put it back on and go away. Some people dip in a spoon and take a spoonful. Bill knows about it, though I think he meant merely to be formally polite and was implying that Bill had merely a spoonful of knowledge.

When the New Deal began and John Collier was Indian Commissioner, Fenton, then only in his middle twenties, was offered the job of superintendent of the Iroquois. He had been somewhat dismayed and put it up to his father, whom he described to me as "an academic painter." His father had said, When they see you, they won't give it to you—but go down to Washington, present yourself, and they'll give you something else. This turned out to be correct: the moment the woman official saw him, she said, You don't want to look after all those Indians, do you?, and they sent him as a subagent to Tonawanda, where for two years he had a wonderful time. He kept a diary but after the first year didn't send in any reports to the Department. A man was sent out to check on him. The Indians said, You get out of the way and let us deal with this. They asked for the Washington man's credentials and completely confused and baffled him. Nicky, as he himself explained to me, had been profiting by Fenton's immense fund of information, which, as he said, had been always at his service, but when he [Fenton] got an offer of a job at St. Lawrence, he advised him to take it—"I threw him out of the reservation." They told him they were sad at his going: they had learned how to twist his wrist (evidently a great Indian expression: I heard Nicky use it), and they might not do so well with his successor. The only thing Fenton had done was to get the reservation electrified, and he wasn't sure this had been a good idea. [Marginal note: I asked Nicky whether he never wrote letters in Seneca. —Who would I write them to? —To your wife perhaps. —She would have to have an interpreter. —Fenton asked him why Indians made good soldiers, evidently entertaining the theory that they functioned better as part of an organization. Nicky replied that Indians were very adaptable and they also made very good burglars.]

At lunch they were singing the Little Water, telling

me how wonderful it was. About this Nicky was quite
sincere.

They always have good manners in their dignified
undemonstrative way—when they notice you at all, they
are not gruff or boorish like upstate farmers, though
these, of course, are amiable enough. It would be hard
to find among New York State whites anyone as subtle,
well instructed, and full of guile as Nicky. (His original
name, Billy, had been changed to Bailey.) They laugh
readily: you are all right with them when you get on a
laughing basis. He said that there was only one man in
Tonawanda who could really speak good Seneca—that
is, ceremonial Seneca.

Jan. 23–24. Gowanda: I had a crisis of gout—went to
the hospital for another shot (had already had one at
Geneva, where we spent the first night): spent the evening and next morning in bed, but didn't lose my time,
because I read up the documents on the Kinzua dam
that Edward O'Neill, the Senecas' Washington lawyer,
gave me. I had lunch with him, and he came to the motel
and briefed me. —In connection with Geneva, there
was a supposed Indian burial mound there. Nicky B. had
tried to get out an injunction to prevent the archaeologists
from opening it—had explained to Fenton that it wasn't
"a personal matter." He had been unsuccessful in this,
but when the archaeologists had got into it, they had
found it was not a mound but a limestone formation.
There were graves, to be sure, but these had been robbed
—nothing left but a few odds and ends.

O'Neill. Fenton said people at Washington hadn't
wanted to talk about him. Had been in the Department
of Justice and at the Nürnberg trials, had lost his
job when the Republicans came in. From Maine, I
take it, a relapsed Catholic—Irish New England

accent: he claims to have won a case by speaking
of "a hahlf glass of beer" ("Did you ever hear of anybody drinking a hahlf glass of beer?"—which was what
the defendant claimed to have done to show that he had
not been drunk)—one of the women on the jury, a
New Englander, thought that he must be right because
he came from New England. Rather hard-boiled, with
some wit and charm, probably capable of being unscrupulous; something of the McCarthy type, but more
sympathetic, reads history; instigated by his wife, had
read my *Dead Sea Scrolls*. Strikes me as a hard-hitting
Irishman who enjoys being in the opposition, would
love to win his case for the Senecas. Up here wears a
fur hat and rugged up-country costume. Thought at first,
when he took on the job, that it would take 50 percent
of his time, but it is more like 95 percent, hardly does
anything in Washington now, but gets back every ninety
days and takes his expenses living up here off his income
tax. Fenton thinks that the Indians still don't quite trust
him. He has antagonized the local lawyers—not because
he is corrupt, as they say, F. thinks, but because they
know that he is in earnest about winning his case for
the Indians. He had got off to a bad start with Fenton,
had come into his office in Albany with Cornelius
Seneca[5] and other Indians: "You claim to be the friend of
the Indian and . . ." "I never claimed to be the friend
of the Indian: I judge Indian undertakings on the merits
of the people in them." When O'Neill had left the
room, the Indians were discreet and dignified, indicated
an element of skepticism. Fenton went out in the morning and saw the arrival of the Bigheads or Uncles—deer-
skins and husk wreaths around their heads—while I was
in bed with gout.

Jan. 24. We drove on that afternoon to the *Allegany* reservation and put up at Salamanca, in the Waite Tour-O-Tel, which was moderately comfortable, though the tub hardly allowed one to sit in it, the toilet was so near the opposite wall that there was no room for one's knees in front and one had to sit sideways on it, and there was a heating system, run by gas, which interrupted one's rest, by going on with a roar at night when the temperature had sunk below a certain point.

We called upon Franklin John, one of the only three farmers of the reservation: a cornfield, a few cows, some ducks. A very nice and obviously honest man, who had once been president of the Seneca Nation. I asked him why the Indians didn't do well as farmers. Because they don't like it? —They don't like it. We talked about the strikes and the Dairymen's League. He said that what the dairymen needed was a John L. Lewis—thought, however, that the unions had become so powerful that the poor man could sometimes oppress the rich man.

Voting: Apropos of politics: Would you know it if somebody was telling the truth? Would you know if I was telling the truth if I told you how the Indians vote? Would you know if somebody told you something else that he wasn't telling the truth? —I answered that I thought I could. —Well, when the Indian came into the poll, there were two ballots on separate papers (Independent and New Deal parties), and first the voter would take $10 to be given one of these ballots, then $12 to be given the other. How is that different from the way you vote? —We only get paid once, said Fenton. Much laughter. O'Neill had tried to reform this system: he had had both ballots put on one paper—but the only result was that the bribers had to trust the voter, when he got inside the booth, to vote as he had promised to do. —Where did they get the money? He thought from

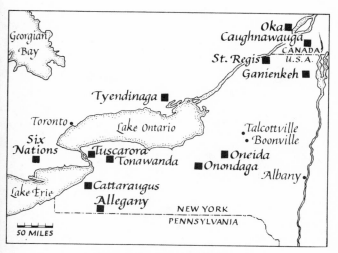

Eastern Iroquois settlements

The healing rite of the Falsefaces, from a painting by Ernest Smith, a Seneca artist of Tonawanda

Corney's [Cornelius Seneca's] travel expense account.
Since he himself had been president, the neighbors had
been suspicious whenever he had acquired anything new.
Even when he had repainted his tractor, they had thought
it was a new machine and said, So that's where the money
went that he got when he was president! —It was hard
to start farming now—you have to have $30,000 even
to begin. I said that small farming would soon be . . .
(hesitating how to put it). —Out of business, he filled in.

The Johns' house: Usual shabbiness and slatternliness
of the house—a hole in the wall stuffed with rags, like
the huge rectangular patch on the upholstered chair in
Nicky Bailey's house—of a quite different color from
the covering of the chair. Women's clothes in white and
bright colors hanging from the top of the door outside a
bedroom. Handsome wife, clever and a great kidder,
conscious of her attractiveness and used to challenging
the men. Told me I would have to dance in spite of my
gouty foot, and that when I started I wouldn't be able
to stop. There were three good-looking children: a fifteen-
year-old boy, naked to the waist, was playing solitaire; a
twelve-year-old girl with glasses, who looked a good
deal older, was studying a schoolbook, which, amusingly,
was called *How We Became Americans*; a younger girl,
also very big for her age—the Esquimau-faced type,
who was already well on her way to becoming one of
those immense cask-shaped squaws—was playing with
a toy model of a rocket missile that had U.S. Army on it.
The handsome and vivacious wife insisted on our staying for dinner; celery, bread and butter with jelly,
spaghetti and tomato sauce with meatballs, boiled potatoes, tea, canned jellied fruit salad, cheese and ice
cream and angel cake. She said that the only thing they
said to guests here was (the Seneca word for) Beware!
Spoke so quietly, with Seneca intonations, that I couldn't

always understand her. She had little Indian jokes for Fenton—said in some connection about times being bad that they would have had to live on (in Seneca) *ghost fried bread*—so called, it seems, because it is eaten at funerals. Took a cavalier attitude toward the Longhouse —knew only one Indian song: a lullaby. Her husband was a Christian. Good atmosphere of good humor and affection—which, in general, I felt in these families. I tried on the little girl the game of guessing which hand the coin was in, and she soon won it from me. He's a trickster, said her mother. You better watch him—he might be a pickpocket.

Franklin John grumbled that whenever the whites gave you anything, they took something away. They gave them the schools and the roads but they compelled you to send your children to Salamanca when he wanted to send his to Randolph, where, Fenton told me, Franklin banked and somehow had better standing. He and his wife sometimes spoke Indian, but they did not speak it generally in the family. After I went to bed Fenton attended the wake for the husband of O'Connell's[6] Seneca secretary. Shows definitely that they have abandoned the belief it is best to bury the dead during the new year's ceremonies.   12/31/10

Jan. 25. It was snowing, and Fenton imagined that the Longhouse was not yet dug out—which proved to be the case. They did not get the ceremonies started till the afternoon. When we drove up, the two men who were shoveling outside disappeared into the house, and Fenton was a little daunted because he had recognized one as Jake Logan, a man of about eighty-three, who was now the head of the Longhouse. There seems always to be an old man—like Rusty Oaks at Onondaga—who makes it his particular business to keep the whites out of the Longhouse. Jake's predecessor, Fenton said, had been mean, was always threatening to throw him out; and when Jake had become the head, he had made a fuss about Fenton's taking photographs and said he ought to get permission from him, Jake. But we were cordially enough received—though cordial is hardly the word for the reception you get from Indians. They do not look at you in public or show they are aware of you, but gradually I would bow to them and smile at them, and they would return my greeting and sometimes come over to shake hands with me. Jake had become quite mellow. I would have conversations with him while the rest, including Fenton—I did not go, on account of my foot— were off on their visitations. He was friendly, would smile, and he had in his eyes a look of shyness, almost of fearfulness. I couldn't always understand him. Remembered the old Longhouse and how it used to be—a great many more people there. —Once, when he had been working in Pennsylvania, his brother had sold to Bill Fenton's father a mask of his and a table.

The Longhouse is bigger than the one at Onondaga, but in considerably worse repair—very dirty and hasn't been painted for years (originally gray): high seats built along the wall with step-seats below, benches set in front of them—originally these had been painted red but most of this had been effaced—everything is worn and defiled; an equally dirty bench in the middle of the hall which must at one time have been white—on this the singers and drummers sit sideways or astride; a stove at either end in which they burn wood and which on a very cold morning may give even too much heat, and two cords with two bulbs hanging from either end of the ceiling naked; women at one end, men at the other —they rarely cross over to the other side; the cleanest objects visible are a couple of new brooms hung very high on the walls—they do not seem to have been much used, though I saw a man outside sweeping off snow with one; high windows with storm panes; a loft where the paraphernalia are kept and on which a trapdoor opens —they get into this without using a ladder: they upend one of the benches and a boy goes up it like a monkey simply by holding on to the back.

First day at the Longhouse: When he came in, Albert Jones was putting pinches of tobacco in the stove and murmuring prayers, so that he sounded very much like a Christian priest or minister: spectacles, gray hair, features not strikingly Indian—very sober, even when joking, rather monotonous delivery—the language sounded Oriental—only inflection of tone came at the end of a statement.

There are different physical types: some aquiline, some fat-cheeked and Esquimau. Fenton believes that the giants come from the Onondaga strain. Women have enormous bodies and tiny ankles and feet—so heavy you wonder they can dance. One had what looked like acne of the nose, which gave her something of an African appearance—she had a cunning and very bright little eight-year-old boy, who took part in the dancing with earnestness and energy, holding his mother and father by the hand. I amused him with the handkerchief trick; mother Geneva Jones, Albert's wife, always sat on the higher bench near the door on the women's side. She was enormous—bosom and belly, and legs like great columns—and only took part in the dancing a little on special occasions. She tried to hold the little boy on her lap so that she was more or less holding him in the air, and he bawled loudly and steadily. Her face was, however, not proportionately fat. During the war, she had worked as a boilermaker, and there were stories of her prodigies of strength.

They had formerly visited seven houses when they carried the baskets around for corn, but now visited only two. Bill Fenton went around with them as they waded across fields in the snow. I had conversations with Jake Logan, who said, Come around here in ten years' time and the Longhouse will be empty. Fenton scouted this, told me that there were four young men of about his own age who would be able to take over from their elders. One of them, a husky broad-shouldered fellow, had been with the army in Europe. He often sang and led the dances. We talked to him outside the Longhouse one day when they were getting more used to me. He said that in Europe he had been under Eisenhower and had had to do everything that Eisenhower said. Now —apropos of the dam—he thought that the thirty-fourth President might be expected to redeem the promises made by the first. This all in a tone of quiet joking.

This first day a rather dull fellow who lived in Salamanca had "put up" a dance and a feast for himself. The feast was on a small table at the women's end of the room. There were only twelve people.

In the evening we went to the Dark Dance,[7] accompanied by this man, who consented to take us in. Unfortunately we got there late. The darkened unpainted house looked quite spooky as we approached it and stumbled through the snow. They were singing only three of the four parts, but we missed the whole of the first, and had to listen to the end of the second standing outside the back door in front of the outhouse. Then the light was turned on and we entered. They were sitting around the wall in a large kitchen. An enormous boiler of corn soup was keeping hot on the stove. We had seen, outside on the porch, a pile of cans from which the corn had come. In the intermission, a saucepan with strawberry syrup and canned strawberries floating around in it is passed around, and in a ritual manner, everybody takes some on a paddlelike wooden spoon. In the next room, very incongruously, some young people and some older people were watching television: comedians and commercials. When the singing of the Dark Dance was going on, one could still see the crack underneath the door. The legend: The Great Little People. They are summoned by the dream, and when they arrive—which we missed—they are supposed to stumble over people in the dark, and the performers shuffle their feet. The effect of the singing and the drumming in the dark (accompanied by the snapping-turtle rattles) is eerie and quite wonderful. It made me feel that oratorios probably ought to be sung in the dark. It is a cycle of 168 songs, each of which is short—lasts only a little while. They seem to suggest the stanzas of ballads, and have nonsense refrains like ballads. (When the Little People themselves are speaking, they use a gibberish language that nobody understands.) You feel that you are being taken back to a very primitive world. The songs work up to a climax, but slow and quieter sections sometimes follow the more rigorous ones. I presently became aware that the bulks of large bodies had been interposed between me and the crack of light from the room with the television. At this point they do some stamping. The voices are effective in the dark in a way that they would not be with light. They seem to fill the room; you become aware of the texture of the music. In the end, the Little People go back to their rocks, over the hills, beyond the sky. (The songs sometimes come in pairs, with only a word or a phrase changed in the second.) "Ten overnights" (literally hearths) "they take." —Finally the lights were turned on, and the old lady who was "putting up" the feast came from the next room, where she had been watching television all the time. She sat in a chair against the wall, and the women paraded around a chair, sat in the middle of the room, and paid her a kind of homage doing special steps as they approached. The sound track of the television had been turned off, but the people in the next room went on watching it. The women are likely to laugh when they work up to the spurt of the climax of their short little dances, and one will take another by the shoulders and try to make her be more active. Then Amos Johnny John came in—he had also spent the whole evening watching TV—and made a set speech thanking the singers and dancers. Then a platter of meat was handed around, which the Indians ate with their fingers, and everybody was given a pail of soup.

Fenton says he believes that the singing here is better than anywhere else in "Iroquoia."

Jan. 26. We picked up Armstrong, who had accompanied us the night before, and took him over to the Longhouse. I asked about the War Dance. He said it wasn't much done anywhere—only occasionally when people asked for it. I asked how the war whoop sounded, and he gave it in a very gentle way, remarking, I ought to have a tomahawk. This dance, it seems, involves long speeches, and bores the younger people; but it is perhaps rather embarrassing nowadays, quite out of key with their present lives.

I asked Jake Logan about the White Dog,[8] and he said, smiling in his rather sad way, that they didn't make this sacrifice anymore, that they never had within his memory, though he knew it had been done before his time. He added that it was difficult nowadays [to find] a pure-white dog that didn't have black spots. (They used to pull out the black hairs.) Fenton had told me that the practice had been dropped on account of the protests of the Buffalo Humane Society, because the special breed of white dogs had died out, and perhaps because the Indians had become more "squeamish."

I think that this was the day of the Bear and Buffalo Dances.[9] In the former they walk around with a heavy stamping step and make noises which are evidently conventionalized versions of the growls and the grunts of bears. There is a saucepan of berry syrup or a plate of honey set on the bench with the drummer and singer, and they help themselves to this while they are dancing. One of the features of the Bear Dance is that the dancer may become possessed by the bear and fall greedily on the sweets, pawing them with his hands. Women especially gave way to this. Fenton says that an Indian once told him that he had watched these performances for years and always thought the women were putting on an act, then, noticing that they were likely to be nervous and high-strung personalities, had finally come to the conclusion that the hysteria was not deliberate. Nothing of this kind occurred except that one young man, at the end of a dance, sat down on a bench and perhaps rather ostentatiously finished up the syrup in the saucepan. This dance, also, was taken around to the houses. Fenton did not participate, and when the Longhouse had been emptied of everyone else except ourselves and Jake Logan, the latter complained to Fenton that everybody had to take part in the Bear Dance, otherwise they would be poisoned by their food. Fenton explained that he made a point of not taking part in the ceremonies of the medicine societies—which the Bears were: After that, you're a fellow traveler, and then you're on the mailing list. I didn't understand this at the time, but it dawned on me in a later conversation that in the so largely Irish Catholic city of Albany he was afraid, in even this connection, of getting into trouble for taking part in heathen religious ritual. We were talking again about the Gagón-sah mask which, according to Standing Arrow, had leaped out of its case at the museum. It was true he had invited the Senecas to come down and feed the mask, but had later been dubious about it, since he realized that it would never do to have the Catholics know about this. (The breaking of the glass case, he now told me, had actually occurred, but it had not been the mask that did it but a workman who had fallen through it. He said that the Indians were likely to think that their objects which had been put in museums were unhappy, and they would sometimes try to get them back. Jesse Cornplanter[10] had given him a drum, which Fenton had given the museum. Then Cornplanter wanted it back to use in the ceremonies. Fenton had difficulty in explaining that it was now the property of the state of New York. Cornplanter had said, You say you want to help us to preserve our ancient rites, and you actually, by refusing to let me use my drum, prevent us from practising them.)

They did the Bear Dance a number of times but the Buffalo Dance only once. The leader tossed his head, buffalo fashion, at a little boy who had come too near.

We had been invited to the Crouses' for dinner, and we walked along the road in front of the house to see the boys and the young men playing the snow-snake game. (It had snowed almost every day and seemed to be constantly getting colder.) The snakes are like javelins of white basswood, with slightly raised snake heads. They are likely to be owned by the older men, who polish them and press them with the greatest care—their ways of preparing them are secret and have implications of magic—and then get the young men to throw them. A long groove—half a mile or more long—has been made in the snow by dragging along a log fastened to a pole which two men hold at either end walking on either side of the track. They throw from behind a deadline. One man always did a somersault in the snow. It is quite a trick even to get the snake to run along in the groove, and often they jump out at an early stage. A great deal of betting goes on—the Iroquois are passionate gamblers. Fenton says that you sometimes see them at the contests flourishing rolls of bills. A couple of boys were drinking beer out of bottles, the first signs of liquor I had seen.

Myrtle Crouse, sixty, the equally good-looking but less vivacious sister of Mary [Mrs. Franklin] John, who also has a slight touch of coquetry. When I said something complimentary about Maxine's looks, without having mentioned her name, she said "I thought you meant me!" The house was very clean and comfortable—her husband's father had built it in the 1880s. Piano with music on it in a kind of darkened extension of the living room. Two couches facing one another with a low long table covered with magazines—*Time, Life, McCall's*—and newspaper clippings about the dam. Crouse came in from shaving and looking quite distinguished, very clean in a gray (nylon?) shirt, with no necktie but well-brushed iron-gray hair. He, like many of them, worked on the railroad (the Erie runs right beside the reservation). Some of their vowels have a singsong drawl that makes them sound Scandinavian; their way of saying *No* and *Oh, yes* in a short and positive way I had thought at Onondaga was British, but it may be something peculiar to that part of the world in general. He seemed to me rather European, his face more expressive and more subtle than most Indians'. Afterwards I learned that he was one of the descendants of a white captive, a Pennsylvania "Dutchman," named originally, I suppose, Kraus. The dinner was eaten in a dining room and a little more sophisticated than in Mary John's house: very clean tablecloth, pot-roast beef, mashed potatoes, frozen peas, pickles, jellied fruit salad, celery, with other things I forget, and ending in a wonderful lemon pie. —After dinner, very discreetly, Fenton ventured to draw her out on the Dark Dance. Curious how difficult it is to get them to answer questions about these matters. For one thing, it is a secret; for another, they don't know how to translate, to explain things in the white man's terms. It was strange to see this attractive woman—so natural with white people, and for an Indian so up-to-date— immediately become silent, cease to laugh, and apparently be carried back to something very ancient, of the substance of childhood imaginings and not very well understood. Her father had been in the habit of "putting up" the Dark Dance because he felt a special debt to the Little People. His uncle, when a boy of ten, had disappeared in the forest and not turned up for a month. They thought he had been lost or killed. Then he appeared again; he never was able to remember what had happened to him during this month. The Little People rescued children from misfortunes that they knew to be imminent by taking them to live with them till the danger was over. She told this with complete solemnity, as if she had gone back into that older world. Her only acknowledgment of the difference from the world in which we were sitting was to say, "It was wild here then." (I found afterwards that this was a traditional story, evidently based on the legend itself, in which the boy, like the child who has been stolen by the fairies, comes back to find his village abandoned and he himself some years older.) —Fenton asked her about specific lines— which, invariably after some thought, she would try to elucidate. From an analogy with other Indian folk tales, he had thought that there was a crow involved, who acted as a messenger for the Little People and was referred to in the last lines as following them "over the hills, beyond the sky." She told him that the word or words in question did not refer to a crow but simply meant "Let's eat." Something else she explained as meaning "You are about to go," then, after a moment's thought, it means "Get out!" He now took up the delicate matter of the charms, the amulets involved in the section which had not been sung the night we heard it. Certain people had handed-down amulets about which they never spoke, yet people knew who they were, and this section of the cycle could be sung only when such people were present. The connection with the Little People was that they had given the boy a little bundle which was also an amulet. Fenton had told me that these charms were supposed to go back to the world of prehistoric monsters: there were a scale of the giant serpent, a horn of the horned serpent, a feather of the exploding wren—a bird that looked like a wren but was enormous and would burst out of its hole in a tree and rush away through the air "like a jet plane"—and a paw of the giant otter. He tried to get her to give some account of the animals from which the charms were derived, and after her usual pondering, she said, "Mostly bears, I think." In the meantime, her husband had closed his eyes, and I said that we had put him to sleep, and it was time for us to [be] going. "I've had a long day," he said, opening his eyes, "but I wasn't asleep—I was listening. Those are things that I don't know much about." —Then daughter Maxine came in with a young man: very well poised and pretty—bun-shaped, the Esquimau type, which neither of the parents seemed to be—black dress in good taste but worn with red-leather high-heeled shoes. She had a young man with her: spectacles, crew cut, yellow sweater, in some ways a typical American boy but dark and unmistakably Indian. They had something to eat quietly in the dining room. She was a teacher, and told us that she wanted to get a scholarship for Teachers College at Columbia, to train herself to deal with "exceptional children." Fenton said he would recommend her and tell them how strong she was, how she had handed him the day before a staggering rack of potatoes as if it had been nothing at all. She said later, when her application was being more seriously discussed, Don't you dare say anything about those potatoes! This whole family are obviously superior people. There is another sister, whom I haven't met (though I saw her later at the dances). All three sisters seem to have "married well." —Fenton agreed with me that Indians, unlike Haitian mulattoes, for example, do not become bourgeois. If they are relatively well educated and prosperous, they may improve their standard of cleanliness and even of communicability; they don't put on genteel manners. The ordinary ways of living and talking which you find in any rural household in up-state New York are always based on Indian bedrock. They are not a natural growth out of Western pioneer life.

They spoke of the adventure of Myrtle's sister's son, Basil, sixteen years old, about a year ago with a bear. He had been out hunting in the snow—had begun sliding down a slope without being able to stop. He saw that he was headed for a bear, which at the bottom was eating some small animal. He shot at it and hit it in the neck but did not kill it. When he was close to it, he fired again, but again did not injure it vitally. When he came up to it, the bear knocked the gun out of his hand and began to try to get his arms around him in order to squeeze him to death. The boy had a police dog with him, and the dog would fly at the bear and distract him whenever he seemed to be getting the boy into his paws. (As someone said, the dog saved his life: he was clever enough to take this tactical advantage. Almost any other kind of dog would have rushed at the enemy and been immediately killed.) Then the boy would slug the bear in the head with his fists. The bear tore his legs and his torso badly, and the boy finally fainted. When he came to, the dog was standing above him, whining and licking his face. The boy got home and was taken to the hospital. The dog was also badly hurt, but survived. I saw Basil's father the big night of the ceremonies, and he told me that he had dragged in the bear, and that it weighed 600 pounds. They skinned it and ate it. As Basil's aunt said, it was the kind of story you could hardly believe. One of Fenton's son's had been so excited about it that he wrote a story called "Basil and the Bear," which he tried to get published in the papers. I also saw Basil on the big night—he was over six feet tall and obviously very strong.

Fenton says that they are interested in names and choose their white names with care. There is a Cecil as well as a Basil, and they are often pronounced Ceecil and Beesil. One child, he says, is called Beverly Joyce. These white names never make sense from our point of view, but the Indian names do. These Indian names are given to all the children that have been born in the previous six months at the Longhouse on the day before the ceremonies proper begin.

The women of this family are rather remarkable—

they belong to the Beaver clan and exert a good deal of power. When I asked Fenton just what this consisted of, he answered, That would be hard to say. It's a question of how they influence their men. One of Myrtle's nieces had fallen in love with a young man that their mother and aunts disapproved of—rightly, according to Fenton —and they had mercilessly ridiculed him. He came from the mountains, and they called him a "hillbilly." But the girl had resisted them and married him—was still living with him and had several children. I said that I suppose that these women had nothing that corresponded to our organized women's activities. Yes: they were active in connection with the Presbyterian Temperance Society. When I said something to the father of Basil about the women of the Beaver clan, he said, Yes: eager Beavers. A tall lean good-looking man—had once done a certain amount of drinking. Fenton told me that the husband of one of the Beavers had always intimidated him—big and strong and so silent and impassive that he gave an impression of hostility. But when his, Fenton's, wife had been taken into the Beaver clan, this man, to his surprise, came to him. He said, I think we ought to get to know one another. We belong to that unfortunate group of men who are married to Beaver women.

Jan. 27. In the morning just after breakfast we went to see *Charlie Congdon,* a lawyer in Salamanca, who, Fenton said, had made a career out of the Indians, working sometimes for them, sometimes against them. A typical old-fashioned provincial lawyer: lean, sallow, dry, black clothes and black shoes; costive but shrewd, humane: seventy. The family had come from New England—I saw their house in a neighboring town, a square white New England affair, but with Greek Revival trimmings. He had gone to Hamilton College, and had Greek and Latin Loeb Classics and Scartazzini's Dante on his shelves, had once read Fenton Horace Bleak old-fashioned lawyer's house: many bookcases, photographs of children (his wife was dead, and he seemed to be living alone), piano, a big engraving of Heidelberg, which he had visited. He began by suggesting that O'Connell really wanted to sell the Indians out —an impression we did not share—Fenton said afterwards that he was afraid that the hostility to O'Connell of the local lawyers was due to the fact that he was perfectly sincere. When we demurred, Congdon changed his line and said some complimentary things about O'Connell. He knew at once that we were up to something, after something, and was trying to find out our line. He successfully defended Jesse Cornplanter's claims for veteran's compensation, which were somehow being impeded by his having taken a second wife when his first wife was still living. He told how Jesse had come to him, and "the little Beaver was curled up there in the chair" (the little Beaver was the second wife). He was amusingly cynical about the profits that Salamanca would derive from the dam. There had been people who had been making a living for years estimating the probable flood damage—had inspected every cellar and outhouse, "every orifice." In his study, he had a considerable collection of masks, hanging high on the wall: some old ones, traditional Falsefaces;[11] others brand-new and glossily glazed. One was a blond face of a hula-hula girl, made by an Indian who had been in the Pacific in the last war. Some of them had been made by Congdon himself—he made them in the basement. When Fenton spoke of our having been present at the ceremony of stirring the ashes,[12] he asked if they had had paddles. It turned out that he had made the paddles.

Salamanca had originally been called Hemlock, but
had been renamed when the Duke of Salamanca had in-
vested in the Erie Railroad, and in the restaurant of the
Torges Hotel, along with the den and moose heads, was
a poster of a Salamanca bullfight. A town of 10,000
people. It is one of the "Congressional Villages" that
have to be leased from the Indians, at a dollar an acre,
I think. The people in the town had got into the habit
of not paying this, and as a result of some action—on
the part of the Indians (?)—the town had adopted the
policy of not collecting from the inhabitants individually,
but of paying the Indians a lump $15,000, and itself
collecting from the population. Fenton confirmed O'Connell's impression that Salamanca was somewhat sour as
a result of leasing from the Indians: it had "made the
inhabitants neurotic and had made the Indians gentlemen."

This was rather an off day at the Longhouse.[13] They
played the peach-pit game, but with only five or six
balls. The game leads off with a war whoop, quite blood-
curdling in its suddenness, though given by only one
man. One from each "moiety" plays. They squat, rattling
the wooden bowl briskly on the floor to make the pieces
change sides, while the onlookers stand bending over
them, uttering cries that keep the excitement keyed up.
All the pieces must have their dark or their light sides
up. If there are many it may take a week. One wonders
whether there is any technique for getting the desired
result. This, too, is taken around to the houses. —After
this game, the Longhouse is supposed to be thrown open
to the dreamers. The general name for the festivities is
Ondinnonk, which F. says means They Are Demented.
The French Jesuits called it the Feast of Fools and—
Morgan, II, notes[14]—tell of the extravagant way that
the people at that time behaved. Fenton says that in his

experience it was like one of those guessing games in
which you have to guess who somebody is supposed to
be by what they say about themselves or how they per
form some dictated action. The other person is challenged
to guess the dreamer's dream, and is given hints to help
him guess it. Then, when the dream has been guessed
the guesser must the next day fulfill the dream—either
literally or symbolically. Example given by Fenton: if
somebody has dreamed about a deluge, the successful
guesser may give him a little wooden boat. But today
as long as we stayed, the Longhouse received no dream
ers. We left about lunchtime, and had the impression
that, though somebody, presumably, had to stay there
they were not expecting anybody that afternoon.

We drove two young girls into Salamanca. They said
that the visits of the Falsefaces might be expected that
night, and that, since Albert [Jones] was the master of
ceremonies, they would be likely to begin with his house
Fenton had promised Albert to try to straighten him out
about the moons (months) of the year, so he used that
as a pretext to call on him after dinner. We walked
through a large kitchen, in which the grandchildren were
swarming and a daughter was standing over the stove
into an extremely messy and rickety sitting room, the
worst kept-up family house I saw. Albert and Geneva
were sitting against the wall side by side. Opposite was a
wood-burning stove—We're old-fashioned, he explained
we burn wood—with a pile of wood beside it. Geneva
had in front of her an old-style sewing machine, but was
sewing with a needle. Albert and Fenton discussed the
months: all seasonal descriptions of things: snowshoes:
they croak a little, or a few croak, for the frogs of early
spring; then they are shouting. Falling leaves in the
autumn. There was supposed to be a thirteenth moon,

which sometimes occurred, but nobody could remember what it was called. The old couple, when we did not prompt them, sat silent with their eyes lowered, but responded to our questions with answers and to our laughing remarks with smiles. Geneva showed us photographs of her two boys by a former husband, who had been killed—I think—one in the Korean, one in the other war. A younger son was now in Germany but she didn't know exactly where. She and Albert exchanged remarks in Seneca, and when a little dirty-faced and tow-headed grandson was fooling with the logs in the pile, she warned him off, first in Seneca, then amplified this in English, saying he would get spli-i-inters in his hands. When I asked her, she said that he could understand her Seneca but could never be able to speak it. In this general connection, I think, Albert said that when they were gone, there would be no more Longhouse ceremonies. Fenton asked him whether he wouldn't make some tape recordings of his speeches in the Longhouse and encountered the usual lack of eagerness, but presently Albert said, If I had known you wanted to do that, we could be doing it this evening. The children went to bed, and we could hear them on the floor above, only thinly cut off from us. (They did not do their tamping dances in the houses now for fear the floors would collapse.) We stayed and stayed but no False-faces appeared. We learned from Albert next day that only one arrived, at 11:30.

On our way home, I said to Fenton that I thought that intercourse between such a pair must present quite a problem of engineering. He told me that after his wife had been admitted into the Beaver clan, they had begun to tell her the gossip. Albert could no longer get into Geneva, and occasionally returned to his former wife,

whom he would take to the movies or out to dinner.
asked what they had done with the $20,000 that Geneva
had received from the government for the death of he.
sons. He said that he had never known and didn't dare
to ask. They had bought a new car, he knew, and he
imagined they had suffered immediately from "an in
festation of relatives." They had probably eaten up a
good deal of the money. The Indians all overate.

Jan. 28.[15] This was the big night of the ceremonies
There were over a hundred people. We came at six and
stayed till twelve, when it ended.

This was the first time we had run into any antagonism
Two youngish men were sitting back of us. They were
tight and smelt of some low-grade kind of alcohol. One
was ugly. The other rather good-looking, had grown a
narrow black mustache in imitation of Ronald Colman
or somebody. He leaned down and said, How'd you like
to be scalped? I asked him if he wanted to scalp me. The
other man asked me if I knew what *hon-hon* meant—*a
white man*. I asked him what *Indian* was, and he told
me. They asked for cigarettes, and I gave them one of
the packages of Winstons I had bought for the Ga-gón
sah and they said thank you in Seneca. This ribbing
went on for some minutes, then the first fellow asked me
if I belonged to a clan. I said that I didn't but Fenton
did. Fenton, who hitherto had been rather pointedly
disregarding the conversation, now turned around and
told them in Seneca what clan he had been adopted into.
The good-looking one said that the ugly one was half
Polish, that he was a Ga-gón-sah (Falseface) without a
mask. [Marginal note: The Pole would first address me
as "white man."] I then saw that he was behaving like a
low-class Pole (Polish workers I had seen in Chicago),

not at all like an Indian—garrulous, boastful, and boring, offering to explain anything about the ceremonies, explain anything that was being said—"What do you want to know? I'll tell you anything!"—being aggressively ingratiating. They asked Fenton whether he knew who they were, and he told them both their names. The non-Polish one kept saying, "Why don't you dance? Go ahead: dance." Fenton pretended alacrity, as if responding to an invitation to dance with the Indian. The Indian got to his feet, but his idea was to perpetrate a joke, get Fenton to dance alone, which he finally did with his usual competence, paying no attention to the others' withdrawal. When he came back, the Indian said, I was kidding. But the truth was that he wanted to dance himself, would get up by himself and do the steps; was perhaps afraid to take part on account of being drunk, and not drunk enough yet not to care. He went out from time to time to take another drink and finally did join the line. In the meantime, I talked to the Pole, who said he had just "retired" from a railroad job. He said that he spoke Polish, and I tried him in Russian, asking him whether he understood it. He tried to reply, *Nemnozhko* [a little]. I have something of an impression that it intimidates Slavs of this kind to spring some Russian on them. Later the Pole disappeared, and the other man sat by Fenton and talked to him in a friendly way, thickly. At one point he had said to me that he had never seen a bald Indian. I told him that I had been scalped. He now asked me whether I was a politician, and when I tried to explain why I was there, he said, as if taken aback, "You're a reporter?!"

Fenton told me afterwards that at first he had been somewhat alarmed. He had seen some nasty brawls at the ceremonies. They would eventually throw out a drunk, but it was nobody's particular responsibility to deal with situations like this, and things sometimes went too far. Fenton said that it would really have to be somebody like Geneva who would take the matter into her own hands. She had called to Fenton, when he was dancing, to take off his hat and at one moment had come down onto the floor and removed the hats of the singer and drummer and put them on the bench beside them. —Otherwise, everybody was friendly. In the dance for which the women choose their partners, Maxine came over and said to F., "May I have the honor of this dance?" Later, toward the end, her mother came over and sat beside her for a little tattle—the first time I had seen any visiting between the sexes in the Longhouses. It was felt by both Fenton and the Indians that the evening was especially successful. When I spoke of it later to Amos Johnny John he had answered, "I'll say!" Fenton wasn't sure whether our presence hadn't spurred them to special efforts.

Albert's admonishment: Albert, in one of his speeches, admonished them, I was told, that they must come out to the ceremonies—"otherwise, how will the Great Spirit know that you're Indians?" —It had been curious to hear them switch from the solemnity of their primitive chants to colloquial New York State English. One day Johnny John said to me after a strenuous dance, "It's a great life if you don't weaken!"

Johnny John had to sing the Bear Dance tonight fifteen or sixteen times. His voice pretty well gave out.

The Fish Dance is a young people's dance—men and women both take part. They take first a few steps to the right, then a few steps to the left. This, as I understand, is supposed to represent the technique of salmon swimming up a stream.

The Naked Dance, now known as Shaking the Bush. Originally they actually danced naked—to the horror of the early Jesuits. They dance in couples, two boys, two girls—alternately headed in the same direction, and then facing one another. It used to be followed by grabbing a girl and taking her to one of the houses. The clan taboos were off: you could go to bed with anybody you wanted.

The Huskfaces burst in three times, but on the first two occasions they go through in a flash: they are merely to herald the great arrival that takes place at the end of the evening. A banging is heard at the door—"Watch that door! Watch that door!" said the drunken young man behind me, feeling himself some of the excitement —then it opens partway but closes again, though not completely—then the same thing occurs again—then the doors are flung violently open, and two of the biggest men available, one appearing from the men's door, the other from the women's, come charging through the Longhouse, each holding out a long staff before him, cross each other (there is a Seneca word for this), and each goes out the opposite door, closing it behind him. Before their next appearance, which will not take place for at least an hour (and I believe that the actors will be two different men), the Ga-gón-sah will have appeared as clowns (I am not sure this hasn't first happened before the Huskfaces' first appearance). They herald their advent not by banging at the door but by scraping sticks on the boards. Some are men, some women—I thought that I could distinguish them by looking at their feet, then I realized that the men also had small feet and ankles. Fenton said he could identify some of them—one of them was one of the girls we had driven back to Salamanca. It is striking how much the conventional personalities of these folk-beings impose themselves. The

Falsefaces cannot speak—they can only make a noise like *Hon-hon-hon,* and only the experts can do it well. The clowns do it amateurishly. First they come to you and make this noise, holding out a gloved paw, with the fingers apart, for cigarettes. They take the cigarette with the left hand, lift it sharply up with a kind of jerk, and stick it between two of the fingers of the other hand. The second cigarette goes between two other fingers, so that they are holding them as you hold the balls in the multiplying-billiard-ball trick. Then the snapping-turtle rattle is proffered to someone with another *Hon-hon-hon.* The person who is being invited takes it and beats time on the bench, and the Falseface does a grotesque and energetic dance—surprisingly effective, they love this. One or two of the clowns wore masks of the traditional kind, but one was a Chinese, one a kind of hooligan with a grinning mouth, a derby hat, and an old tail coat worn with pajama bottoms, one a bogus Indian, a white man's Indian parodied from a road advertizement, and one a luscious paleface beauty parodied from such Hollywood favorites as Jayne Mansfield and Marilyn Monroe upholstered with enormous bosoms. Something sexy about all this: the boldness of the masquerading girls, offering the rattle to men that they want to have make them dance (they began on the men's side, but later, I think, gave a show for the women); the impossibility of telling whether the Hollywood beauty is not a boy; the accelerated breakdowns they dance, the women do the men's steps and vice versa. This amuses the audience, who smile, but nobody ever applauds. They pretend to steal cigarettes from the pockets of one another's pants—this is done with conventionalized gestures like the taking of the cigarettes. Presently they depart, and the regular dances resume. A genuine effort is made, it seems, by the dancers to disguise themselves. Sometimes they exchange costumes between two appearances. They, as well as the Huskfaces, wear big covered handkerchiefs around the tops and backs of their heads.

Just before the second appearance of the Huskfaces, three of the clowns appeared, the bogus Indian, Marilyn Monroe, and one of the traditional Ga-gón-sah. When the banging comes at the door, they pretend to be terrified. M.M. throws her arms around the neck of the Indian, but he is as frightened as she, and the three huddle together in a corner. The two enormous Huskfaces burst in and disappear as before. The suddenness, swiftness, and straightness with which they move are of the essence of their doing the role well. As soon as they are gone, the cowardly Indian advances to the middle of the floor and makes brave and threatening gestures toward the departed Huskfaces.

At the first appearance of the Falsefaces, a little boy who sat back of me with his father was scared to death and howled through the whole act. It worried me but the father did not worry—he had his arm around the boy but I did not hear him try to comfort him. Fenton said to me that it was probably his grandmother, masquerading as a Ga-gón-sah, that was frightening him. When the Ga-gón-sah had done their stuff, the child's mother came across the floor and took him over to the women's side.

Again the regular dances resume. At the end of each of these, the dancers can demand an encore. Hence the Bear Dance so many times.

Then the traditional rite of the Ga-gón-sah. This time, at the women's end, they come in—only two or three—crawling on their knees. These are accomplished performers who make the Ga-gón-sah noise so that it sounds absolutely weird, like the bubbling of a cauldron of liquid iron. I thought this must be done with some instrument in the mouth, but when, two days later, I had the temerity to ask Amos Johnny John how it was done, he said reluctantly, after the usual moments of silence, "With the voice." They are wearing the regular masks, with the long black hair made from horses' tails and the crooked nose and pain-twisted mouth from the impact of the mountain on their father.[16] They stir up the ashes in the stove, then rub them into the hair and along the arms of the man who is playing the symbolic sick man. So long as the Falseface actors are playing their roles, it is supposed to [be] impossible for the hot coals from the stove to burn them, and when they are seen the next day with blisters or bandages around their hands, they will not admit the damage.

Now at last, not long after the departure of these, the great arrival of the Huskfaces occurs. This time a terrific banging takes place on all sides of the Longhouse, as if the place were being bombarded. Then the two heralds appear. The Huskfaces cannot talk, they can only make a blowing sound. They must kidnap someone to speak for them. Usually they come to his house. Nicky Bailey told us that he had been drafted several times, and evidently had thoroughly enjoyed it. I imagine that he gave them something clever. But tonight they simply took old Albert. They make him go out the door with them, supposedly to impart to him their message. Then he reenters alone and delivers a long speech—with his usual sobriety: he was surely not the ideal person and had, besides, as master of ceremonies, been working hard for days. The Huskfaces tell the assemblage that they come from the Country of Stumps. This at first, when Nicky explained it, had meant to me a burnt-out and desolate place; but I found now that it meant the opposite: a place of stumps was a place that had been cleared (see their old method of charring the trees at the bottom) and in which their corn could be made to grow—in fact, a place of abundance. Their spokesman tells the audience how high their corn grows and of the other wonderful things they raise. It is a wonderful, a fabulous country, where everything is bigger and better. They have fine gardens there, said Albert, and we plant no parsley at all. He also told them that in the Huskface country the children were always obedient and did not make themselves a nuisance. They had been running around the floor and getting in the way of the dancers, and I noticed that after this a certain silence and self-consciousness descended on them. I tried to get the young man who had been kidding me to explain this speech while it was going on, but by this time he was too far gone. "I understand it," he said, "but I don't know how to explain it." He made a clumsy attempt to interpret the part about the children; Fenton did better later. The speech over, the Huskfaces appeared en masse. The men were all dressed as women and the women as men, and did one another's steps. This was the big final dance. Each Huskface would draft a partner. Taking him by the arm (I didn't see what was going on at the other end, don't know how the sexes worked out in this), they would gently but strongly propel him to the floor. The lines swell, there are now two circles, this is the biggest dance. Apparently tired and relaxing, stopping at the end of every bout, they start up again and become more vigorous. The challenge is how long they can keep it up. Tonight they seemed constantly to be gathering strength. When it ended, everybody seemed satisfied, even set up and happy. Everybody felt: Long live the Huskfaces, the inhabitants of that marvelous country, who encourage us to live in ours! The people who play the Huskfaces are glad to have encouraged the others, the others are grateful to have been encouraged.

Attractiveness of the Huskface masks—the one (one of the masks that I have, one of the run-of-the-mill ones) that looked like an old five-foot Englishman in a mackintosh, toddling about his routine.

Jan. 29.[17] In the morning the big costume dance took place: the Feather Dance; a large attendance for this but not so large as the night before. The men wore their headdresses and coats. The headdresses at their handsomest are made of eagle feathers, white at the ends, brownish further down, and with smaller rusty-red feathers stuck in at the base. But there are also gaudier ones, partly white, partly dyed pink or orange. They get the feathers from a plume company, it seems. The women wear blouses over skirts, and under the skirts trousers at the bottom split a few inches in front. All these garments are embroidered—usually, I think, with beads at the lower edges. The little boy with whom I had made friends also wore a chief's headdress and danced holding his mother's hand. When he passed me, I would smile or wink, but his face remained as unresponsive as that of any other Indian. Altogether it was a very fine display. —A feast was being prepared in the cookhouse that stood near the Longhouse: two enormous cauldrons in an enormous hearth, with soup bubbling in them—one beef and one pork: the large pieces of meat made it almost as much like stew.

Albert had told F. that he would try to come to the motel at three that afternoon to do some tape recording. To the surprise of Fenton—who, as he told me, had often been "stood up by Indians"—he turned up at three sharp to explain that he could not make the recordings. The women had sent him to do the shopping for the Longhouse, and he was thoroughly worn out besides

So Fenton took me to see Oscar Nephew, the brother of the Beaver ladies. His house was snowed in and they were digging it out, so we went to talk, across the street, in a store kept by whites, where a fine stock of Indian-made baskets was hanging from the ceiling. He was more the Esquimau type, like Maxine, and did not seem so clever as his sisters, but I learned that this was not the case. I learned for the first time from him that the family were descended from the same stock as Corn-planter[18] and Handsome Lake. When Cornplanter had signed one of the treaties, a nephew had signed *Nephew* underneath. Hence the family name. He indicated that, though he belonged to the Seneca Nation, who had got rid of their chiefs in '48, he was proud of the distinction of the family and felt that he had a certain rank. We talked about the dam. I had forgotten what Fenton had told me about him and assumed that he did not want it, but after we left Fenton reminded me that Oscar had been quietly buying up all the property he could lay his hands on, evidently with a view to disposing of it to the government in the event of the dam's going through.

Jan. 30. We went to say goodbye to the people at the Longhouse and found them with the benches drawn around the stove getting ready for the tobacco ceremony. A younger man had taken over from Albert as master of ceremonies. Amos Johnny John took me to his house and sold me a drum and two Huskface masks: "Don't say nothing about it." His shack—his wife had died, and his children did not live with him—was the last word in squalor. Fenton said that it "wasn't easy to get a place into such bad shape as that." It had formerly been occupied by the worst housekeeper on the reservation.

On our way through the Cattaraugus reservation,

Fenton stopped off at Cornelius Seneca's house to return the tape recorder he had borrowed. The little house was as neat and spotless inside as out: piano, phonograph, bookcase, photographs of Cornelius himself, with headdress, which made him look handsome and impressive, one of them—with his gaze lowered—even tragic—no trace of the ironic humor one found in him in conversation. One of the pictures had been taken in Washington for purposes of publicity in connection with the fight against the dam. He was very much interested in recordings and played us some Seneca versions of Christian hymns. I should like to have met his wife, who had obviously a feeling for the amenities unusual among Indian women.

I persuaded Fenton to get off the thruway at Fonda and go to see Standing Arrow. They had an eviction notice against him. He had moved from the bank of the creek. The trailer was next to a house, in and about which were a good many children, and in the house was a youngish man. After a little conversation, I seemed to inspire him with enough confidence so that he told me where Standing Arrow now was: a little distance down the road, just beyond the bridge under the thruway. We found the place, some way from the road: an old gray barn and two or three shacks, with smoke coming out of one of them. We did not discover the path, so, following where someone had been before, we stumbled through the snow—an arduous walk for me with no shoes under my galoshes. I hurt my gouty foot and was quite out of breath by the time I got to the top of the slope. The pretty Mrs. Standing Arrow appeared from her house and said that Standing Arrow was away but might be back any minute. She sent a child to call Angus, the dark steelworker cigar-store Indian whom I had met when I had been there before. Fenton was interested in a little cart to haul wood they had made, said it was a traditional thing. She could not find Angus, but just as we were about to go, he appeared from the other direction. He had, he said, just come back from the ceremonies at Onondaga. They were going to have a council there Saturday to decide what was to be done about the eviction. They were also applying for an interview with the governor or, failing that, his secretary. It was just getting dark, and those Mohawks seemed comfortless and miserable there. They showed us the path back, and, to our enormous relief, it proved quite easy to get back to the road.

Fenton told me that a man he knew from St. Regis— half Irish, half Indian—had spoken of Standing Arrow with a bitterness that he had never known him feel about anybody else: said that Standing Arrow was "evil," would go away and leave his wife and children locked up in the house.

Details omitted:

They dance in any kind of shoe they happen to be wearing—often galoshes.

Dance in which the women carry ears of corn—I think one of the costume dances. The song is the voice of the corn, which says it is glad to be home.

Some of the dances involve two concentric lines.

Ed Coury: He was present and very active during the first few days, then went to visit his children. Except for a bent Indian nose, he seemed so completely like a non-Indian upstate New Yorker—with his spectacles, his square face, and his straight graying hair that would come down over his forehead—that it was actually a little embarrassing to see him howling the Indian music. I learned that he was partly white.

At the beginning of either the Big Night or the costume dance, Albert passed around a corncob pipe, and everybody took a whiff.

In English, they always referred to the ceremonies as the "doin's."

NOTES

1. See *AI*, pp. 186–89.

2. Often Allegany's president, then its lone working farmer.

3. Derived from the same Indian word as Allegheny River; there are two other spellings of the word—the Allegany reservation and the Alleghany Mountains (*AI*, p. 191).

4. On August 30, 1957, the Senecas brought action against the Kinzua dam project on the Allegheny River, whose resulting lake would have flooded 9,000 acres (three-fourths) of the Allegany reservation. *AI*, pp. 190–97.

5. President of the Seneca Republic. *AI*, pp. 184–85.

6. The Senecas' lawyer.

7. One of a class of rituals performed not in the Longhouse but in private homes, a set of song sequences sung in the dark. *AI*, pp. 202–12.

8. The Sacrifice of the White Dog had been the central event of the midwinter rites. *AI*, pp. 424–25.

9. *AI*, pp. 222–23.

10. Well-known Seneca artist and author of *Legends of the Longhouse* (1938).

11. The wooden Ga-gón-sah masks with twisted, grotesque features were used by the Falsefaces in medicine ceremonies. *AI*, pp. 239–44.

12. Persons who were healed by the Falseface society might have their cure renewed by being smeared with hot ashes. *AI*, p. 242.

13. *AI*, pp. 227–33.

14. Lewis H. Morgan's (1818–81) *League of the Ho-de-no-sau-nee, or Iroquois* (2 vols., 1851, reprinted 1954).

15. *AI*, pp. 233–46.

16. According to tradition, the Stone Giant, the last of a race of such giants, challenged the Creator to a mountain-moving competition. Giving a command, the giant moved the mountain a few inches. When it was the Creator's turn, "the giant felt a rush behind him, and, quickly turning his head, he was hit by the mountain" (*AI*, p. 240). The noise the Falsefaces make is the one by which the Stone Giant had attempted to dismay the Creator.

17. *AI*, pp. 246–47.

18. Handsome Lake's half brother.

WELLFLEET, NEW HAVEN, NEW YORK, 1958

Mary Meigs and Barbara Deming:[1] They bought Mary's old house on the Pamet Point Road. Mary paints; Barbara writes. They are so quiet and apparently so shy that they did not at first make much impression on me; then I began to feel that they were touching, almost heartbreaking. We invited them more and more—there have been so few people here this winter—and went to dinner with them. Their household seems peculiarly bleak: any number of cats, which they always have castrated or spayed. Rather dark rooms and difficult silences. One evening, in my cups, I kissed them both (at our house). Then Barbara had to go away to do something about her family, and I began to feel a strange attraction exerted by Mary and a tendency, when sufficiently exhilarated, to kiss her. She is the stronger and more interesting of the two—though sometimes rather liberal-minded and not so intelligent about literature as Barbara. I decided that her effect on me—with snub nose, her glittering blue eyes, her square face, boyish cheeks, straight up-and-down figure, and "sensible" unfeminine shoes—was actually homosexual. I did not feel

that her attraction for me was that of a woman. I thought
that this experience was unique in my life till I learned
that she was a "not identical twin" and tied it up with
the attraction for me of Mamaine Paget, the less feminine
of her and Celia, and wondered whether it had some
connection with my own early relationship with Sandy. I
had realized from the first that there was something
morbid about it. I said to her one evening, "You're entirely a lesbian, aren't you?" "I wouldn't say that," she
replied. The next time I saw her, I said to her, "Are
people always falling in love with you?" She said, "Yes,"
and added some matter-of-fact remark about it which I
am sorry I can't remember. She was not at all embarrassed by such questions, though she sometimes blushes
in the old-fashioned way. I realized that she was not
so much shy as extremely well controlled. But Barbara's
shyness is real: she has a strangulated voice like Léonie
Adams's.[2] It turned out that they both knew Léonie, and
I seemed to feel the existence of a semi-lesbian college
girls' world in which Léonie was an idol and a model.

When Elena and Helen were in Boston having Helen's
tonsils out (April 8–14), I had dinner with them three
nights running, three times at their house. Once I took
them to the Orleans Inn and went to a movie afterwards.
I found that Elinor Wylie[3] and Edna Millay were great
heroines to them, and that they liked to hear about them.
I told them that the twenties had in some ways been a
dreadful wasteful time, and Mary said she didn't see
how anyone had survived but that she would like to
have gone to those wild parties—"just as a looker-on." I
showed them the *bouts-rimés* sonnets that Elinor Wylie
and I had written together, and Mary was all for playing
this game, so we did on the last evening. Mary produced
two extraordinary things: one directed against her mother,
the other against her twin sister. I saw that there was a

good deal of violence behind her somewhat wooden mask. I had felt this already at the Anna Magnani which she had just already seen in Washington but was willing to see again. It was a trashy affair, though well acted, with lots of slugging that alternated with heavy kissing. (I had not been able to interest her in Lizette Reese and E. A. Robinson. The American poetry of that period seemed, I think, rather thin to her, after her favorites, Shakespeare, Keats, Hopkins, and Yeats.) Barbara was covered with embarrassment when it came time for her to read her sonnet, said she hadn't been able to write one, had finished it, and crumpled it up, that it had been Mary who wanted to play the game. I made her go into the dining room and finish it, and it turned out that she didn't know how to write a sonnet—it was the difference between Bennington and Bryn Mawr—had no idea of English metrics and could only write a kind of vers libre. She thought that the octet and the sestet were supposed to be two different poems. I had been talking about Genet at dinner, and one of [the] girls had contributed the rhyme word *crime*, and both their poems struck a criminal note. —Barbara seems to me frozen. Elena says she is scared of life. I am afraid, having seen her verses —very pale—that she has not enough talent to do much with writing. They are so different from the old Cape Cod artists and writers—in either their more bohemian or their more respectable phase—yet it is evidently partly the glamor of this past which has made them want to live here. Never saw women who are interested in the arts display so little emotion in conversation, and I find that I cannot talk to them as I do to other women. But I have become, unexpectedly, fond of them.

[E.W. added to this account the texts of the two *bouts-rimés* verses of Meigs and Deming.]

Mary Meigs's fine sonnet in our *bout-rimé* game:

> Imagination, once upon a time,
> Gathered its sublimated energy
> And darkly brooding over jasmine tea
> Committed an imaginary crime,
> Its character infernal and sublime,
> Something that made the universe debris,
> And forced the great Jehovah to his knee,
> And froze the Styx and covered Hell with rime.
> My mother, when she heard it, hit the ceiling.
> "Monster," she said, "I've raised you from the cradle.
> May there from this day be a total blank
> Where you are and an absence of all feeling!"
> And now I sipped my jasmine from a ladle
> And said, "Mama, I've only you to thank."

Barbara Deming's octet:

> A criminal, once upon a time,
> Had too little energy
> To drop into his victim's tea
> Enough poison to make it a crime.
> He hungered to be sublime,
> And pile debris upon debris,
> But see him, listless, on his knee,
> Scrawling naughty limericks in the rime.

During February and March in Wellfleet it is like being on a long ocean voyage with Elena—Helen and Mrs. Daley are with us, but there are no other passengers. Strong winds are blowing against the ship and make it difficult to go on deck. Everybody we know is away, even Bill Peck, and it is for me as if there were, outside the house, nothing but the sea.

New Haven, April 19–20. My first visit to New Haven for years. Arrived in the middle of the afternoon after a bad trip. Helen had been sick in the car and, embedded in the Saturday traffic, we got lost and went through town without finding Prospect Street and then had to go back. Bill Peck tired and nervous and irritated with Mrs. Peck. Elena had been a week in Boston with Helen's tonsil operation, which had been fairly serious: she had been on the operating table an hour.

At the Walkers', Elena and Helen rested. I did some magic with Danny. He is my only sleight-of-hand pupil, had been performing the tricks I showed him years ago. —The Walkers had asked for dinner a large and varied company and had to use Charley's study for a second dining room: Alfred and Charlotte Bellinger; Tom Mendenhall[4] and his wife; Red Warren and Eleanor,[5] with Lewis Galantière, who was staying with them. Alfred seems nicer and less pompous; had had to sell his grandfather's Delphic Classics, had no room for so many books; said he couldn't really read Greek and Latin easily, could read French but didn't quite know how he had learned it. I was interested to hear that, like me, he had never learned to read Latin verse at Yale—had had, like me, to pick it up later for himself. Charlotte has still from the Gunnery[6] some of the mannerisms of old-fashioned New England schoolteachers, says, "Shall you" do so-and-so. I was amused, when Alfred and I went to get our buffet dinner together, at his cutting short the conversation after somebody had handed me a furnished plate, telling me that I ought to go back to the table and not wait for him. Very characteristic and reminiscent of our early days. Tom Mendenhall told me that his mother was now in a nursing home near New Haven. When I started to celebrate her—telling about her nostalgic account in Talcottville of the autopsy on her return to Johns Hopkins—he impatiently, as he always does, pulled away. He has heard all those stories too many times, has been bullied by her, no doubt, all his life. —I talked to Lewis Galantière about the new text of the Goncourt diaries, avoiding Radio Free Europe, for which he works and of which I disapprove. He said about pansies that one was all right, two were even all right, but when there were three you became an outsider and couldn't understand anymore what they were talking about. —Late in the evening, I began talking to Warren about the Civil War. His ideas are closer to mine than those of anybody else I have seen. I had forgotten that he had written a book about John Brown.[7] He feels that it is a myth which will never be cleared up. I told him that I was going to try to dispel it.

The next morning I looked up Louisberg—just around the corner—the young student of Iroquois language about whom Fenton had told me. Oneida is the language he has been studying, because he has lived in Wisconsin, to which most of the Oneidas went. —Lunch at the Gilbert Troxells'. His Rogers groups of scenes from plays, featuring old American actors; her Rossetti collection—drawings, paintings, and death mask. I always make a point of seeing the Troxells at their own house, because at the Walkers' I know that they won't talk freely—be funny, tell gossip, etc. I said to Adelaide that, with Bones and non-Bones, Yale was Disraeli's Two Nations.[8] At lunch, sure enough, somebody was telling about a social evening which had been desolated by the arrival of a man who had sat down at the piano and "played *Parsifal* all through." "A Bones man!" said someone else; and this started them off on the inevitable ribbing of Bones, a good deal at Alfred's expense. Gilbert said that he had seen the letter that Alfred wrote opposing his admission to the Elizabethan Club, and he cautioned me not to show Alfred—I don't quite know why: is it sacrilege for someone of whom Alfred disapproves to write about the Club at all?—a paper he had written on its history, of which he gave me a copy. Gordon Haight[9] and his wife had been asked because Haight was the only person who knew anything about De Forest. His wife had been an archaeologist who had seen something of Alfred in Greece, and when Haight was about to marry her, Alfred had strangely appeared to him and told him that "if he didn't treat that little girl right, he would have him (Alfred) to reckon with. I thought it was the biggest piece of impertinence I had ever known in my life. That old bottom-pincher!" (I learned later that he was supposed to have had a flirtation with a woman who worked in the library.) They talked about De Forest—who had never, it seems, been "accepted" in New Haven. Though the De Forests were very rich, they lived "on the wrong side of Orange Street." A torrent of New Haven gossip. There had been years ago a scandalous adultery, and when the wife of the offender filed for divorce, the neighbors had appeared in court and testified to the things that they had heard the guilty saying to one another on the party line in a day when there were few telephones. The delinquent husband was named Trowbridge; some highly respectable New Havenite had afterwards said with pride that he had managed to spend years without ever having had to shake hands with a Trowbridge. When the ladies withdrew to the other room, Elena said they were terribly boring with their domestic conversation about people she didn't know; but I was thoroughly entertained, when the men and women were together, by the dense New Haven atmosphere. —Isabel Wilder, Thornton's sister, was there; she lives with him, has recently been with him in Germany, where he and Thomas Wolfe seem now to be the great American authors. Harry Levin says that, when he comes to the U.S., he is more and more like a European dramatist whose works are sometimes done in translation here.

We then paid a brief call on the Bellingers. I had been surprised to hear from Alfred that his mother was still alive. She had always seemed so wispy and frail, with her square high-foreheaded bespectacled face. She will be ninety on June 13. Has to stay in bed and cannot see, so is read to by phonograph records. But she seemed to have all her faculties and was even able to execute her old-fashionedly amusing conversational exploits. She said that you got to the point where you forgot which people you knew belonged to which generations and to what phases in your life. —The Bellingers seem long ago to have taken the stand that, without being at all unfriendly, they would never read my writings. I never heard of Alfred's reading anything of mine except one of my *New Yorker* articles against detective stories. He wrote me a note about it, confessing that he was an addict and that he had once planned to do something about it in the vein of De Quincey's *Opium-Eater*. I had struck at the end of the article a half-burlesque moral note—it must have been this that fetched him. At dinner the night before he remarked that, while on a visit, he had found one of my books in his room and read my essay on Housman,[10] was surprised that I had not included the story of his after-dinner speech at Cambridge—which, besides being a chestnut, had no relevance to what I was saying.

After this, to the library, to take out some De Forests. Back to the Walkers' for another gay drinking conversation—though Charley now is for him burning rather low—he has some queer disease (unclear?) rare in adults and does seem to be rather wasting away. When I told

Adelaide that De Forest had not been accepted, she said, "None of us are, you know!"

Altogether a tumultuous, amusing, and, for me, very profitable visit—Yale at what I used to think its most characteristically dynamic. Elena felt more freedom and space than at Cambridge.

We went on to New York Sunday night.

New York, April 20–May 4. Wystan Auden was sailing for England on Thursday, but came to dinner on Tuesday. He looks now, as Elena says, like an old tree. He got a large money prize from Italy and has bought a villa outside Vienna, which Chester seems now to be getting ready while Wystan does his eight weeks at Oxford. He gave Christ Church an electric refrigerator and this induced them to let him live there; says he likes the weather report that the scout gives you in the morning, "Rather rainy, sir," etc.—I remember that the scout did this at All Souls. He had wanted to put up an American sergeant and had told the scout to make a bed for him, and the scout, resisting this, had said, "I don't know his year, sir." He had introduced two Americanisms —one of them *gotten*—into his last lecture. I told him that, if I were in his place, I should go to Europe and never come back. He said that, even after weeks at Oxford, he did not feel that it was where he belonged, that he belonged over here. I then gave him a tirade about how horrible America was now, said that I had been working in it all my life and was now extremely fatigued. He said that of course it was "hell," that things were "always wrong," but that "the dream" was always there. I replied that the "American dream" was a sickening propaganda phrase, and that the glorification of the American past that had recently been going on was of a kind that made me uneasy, that it reminded me of the glorification of the ancient Roman virtues that became official at a time when they were probably disappearing. He nodded a certain assent, but attempted to raise my morale. "You must remember we depend on you," he said. "Who are we?" "I do. You have to go on even if you die with everything still just as bad." He is very moralistic about all this kind of thing. When I told him that I was going to give up giving pep talks to Cyril Connolly since he had told me that he wanted to fail, he declared that Cyril's attitude was very wrong; and when Elena was talking about the people in Boston who would have themselves committed to McLean for a week or so when they [happened] to have a bad hangover, he said that that was very bad behavior. I told him that I had been in a sanitarium for a couple of weeks in the early thirties,[11] and he said, "That was very naughty: an Auden doesn't do that, a Wilson doesn't do that." But after Elena had quietly gone to bed and we had become further advanced with our gin-and-lemon drinks, he began somewhat to go to pieces himself. He had told me that he was glad that a telegram from Guy Burgess had reached him in Italy instead of here, where he might have had the F.B.I. after him; and he now said that he should like to write something about E. M. Forster—in a tone which suggested that, if he did, something rather dark would be revealed—but that he was afraid to because he didn't want to lose his passport. He said, "I'm queer," and became, I thought, a little incoherent. We had talked at length about differences between English and American usage. He had learned to say *áddress* in America, I told him that no educated American pronounced it this way, but he insisted that in certain quarters he would otherwise not be understood. Actually, when he first came in, it seemed to me that he had reverted to the Oxford way of speaking to an extent that made him partially unintelligible.

At the time when Elena and Helen had been in Boston having H.'s tonsils out, Billy von Rath had called me up to say that he had called Walther up at his apartment several times and had not been able to get him. I suggested that he ought to get the janitor to let him in. They found Walther unconscious. He had been packing to go to Germany. He hadn't wanted to go, though Elena and Billy had decided it was the best thing he could do—and he had just had a blow when Lehmann Brothers had told him that they didn't want him in the office. He also felt that the family didn't want him in Germany. Billy and Carol von Radowitz, who had just arrived, representing Moët et Chandon, got him into the Beth David Hospital. He was unconscious for three days, then came to in a state of complete confusion which is sure to become worse. At first, he thought he was in Germany, talked German and asked to be sent back to New York. When I saw him, he didn't know that he was in a hospital, seemed to think it was a hotel where the service was not very good. He has arteriosclerosis of the brain—like Florence Loomis—and has had a cerebral hemorrhage. Billy von R. went back to Germany, and Elena had the whole responsibility and, during the two weeks we spent in New York, was able to do little else except attend to Walther in the hospital, dispose of the things in his apartment—many photographs of nude girls and memorials of the Gordon Bennett balloon race, which he had won in his youth—and make legal arrangements with Chuckie Walker so that she could deal with Walther's finances. She said that Walther had succeeded in charming the middle-aged bespectacled Jewish social worker by kissing her hand and, when she said good night, telling her, "Think of me often but never trust me!" Elena realized that he must have been saying that to women all his life. The hospital was something very strange and characteristic of recent New York. It was brand-new, so clean and well equipped, but as yet made very little sense. The doctor was a low-grade Italian who could hardly speak English; the nurse a Puerto Rican who couldn't speak English at all. The special nurse that Elena got for Walther was a pretentious Negro boy who claimed to be able to speak French when Walther resorted to that language. The orderlies and nurses were mainly black; the administration was Jewish. They first told Elena that he would have to go to a state hospital, then, after a psychiatrist had seen him, told me that it would be much better to put him in a nursing home. So we had him sent to Hyannis in an ambulance. But he got violent with a nurse the first night and wanted to walk out and go to his bank or his office. They said they could not have him, so Elena, going with him, had him taken to McLean in Boston.

This made our New York visit gloomy but it would have been so in any case. People seemed run-down, apartments allowed to go to pieces. Dawn Powell's husband has lost his job and is on employment relief. Sofka Winkelhorn looked terribly tired. Jason Epstein is gloomy and Barbara is very thin, overworked with the baby.

Thurber had wanted to see me to talk about Ross and *The New Yorker*, about which he is doing a book.[12] We arranged to have lunch at the Algonquin, and I invited Dorothy Parker.[13] Helen Thurber had been rather annoyed with her because several years before they had invited her to dinner and Dorothy had been an hour late,

giving them as an excuse that she had had to walk her
sister's dog, so when she wasn't there at one, we left word
with the man at the desk and went into the dining room.
She, however, for once arrived on the dot, was not recognized by the man at the desk, and waited for some time
in the lobby before she looked in the dining room and
found us. It was like, as we said, a reunion of Civil War
veterans. The G.A.R. —Raoul Fleischmann was sitting at
the next table and offered to join the rally. Dorothy had
somewhat deteriorated, had big pouches under her eyes.
Thurber seems blinder than ever, one eye is quite gray,
and his hair is completely white. I totter around with
gout. We at once burst into a confused but animated
conversation about *The New Yorker*, the kind of thing
of which nobody listening would have been able to
understand a word. Elena and Helen joined us, and
since the case of Walther was then at the stage when it
was thought Elena would have to commit him to Wel-
fare Island, Elena was under a strain. It depressed me to
think we were sitting in the room where the Round Table
had once been and where I had arranged for Dorothy to
meet the Fitzgeralds for lunch, when Dorothy, on that
or some other occasion, sitting at one of the tables along
the wall that have chairs on only one side, said that we
looked like "a road company of the Last Supper." And
I used to bring Mary Blair there, and afterwards, when
Rosalind was a little girl, it had always been her favorite
place to be taken to lunch. Some of Dorothy's stories had
been lately rejected by *The New Yorker,* and some of
Thurber's pieces also. They regarded *The New Yorker*
in its present phase as something alien to them. Since
we never got around to the purpose of the luncheon,
to reminisce about *The New Yorker*'s past, it was agreed
that we should reassemble at our apartment late in the
afternoon. I invited them to come there now, but Dorothy

said she had to walk her dog. I told her she wouldn't
come, and she said, "I will, too!" But when the Thurbers
and we were there, she sent a telegram excusing herself.
The Thurbers and I, however, gave *The New Yorker* a
thorough hashing-over. Helen Thurber is extremely good
at handling Jim—steers him by the elbow and guides
his hand when he is shaking hands. He makes a point of
looking at the person he is talking to, so you forget he
doesn't see you; and it is as if she made a point of having
her own eyes especially responsive in order to make up
for his blindness.

On Saturday afternoon, after Elena left, I called
Dorothy up and went to see her at the Hotel Volney,
in the hope of getting her to write one of her poems on
a Talcottville pane. This, too, was rather depressing. I
was glad to see all the evidences of her having returned
to her old kind of writing: a typewriter with manuscript
beside it, piles of books she is reviewing for *Esquire*. But
it is just the same kind of life that she used to live in
New York before she spent so many years in Hollywood.
It is as if her work in Hollywood and her twice marrying
Alan Campbell had counted for nothing—she might as
well have been in fairyland. Bob Benchley is dead,[14]
Campbell has left her again. She lives with a small and
nervous bad-smelling poodle bitch, drinks a lot, and does
not care to go out. I found her, when I came in, so
much in the phase of difficult utterance that I despaired
of getting her to write on the pane. She complimented
Helen's complexion and told me three times about a
remark of hers at luncheon. I had said that Dorothy had
discovered me as a writer,[15] and H. had piped up: "But
he married Mummy." She gave me a number of drinks,
as was inevitable in this atmosphere of the twenties, and
later we seemed to talk more sensibly. I asked if it were
true that Seward Collins[16] were dead: "Why, I think

so—there was nothing else for him to do." We discussed Sybille Bedford[17] and Esther Arthur. At last, I did get her to do the poem on glass, though the writing is a little undulant: the quatrain about John Knox and Helen,[18] which is, she says, the only poem of hers she cares for. She showed me an omnibus volume of the American Beat generation and the English Angry Young Men, which she was going to review for *Esquire*. —I asked her what she thought of J. D. Salinger: she didn't like *The Catcher in the Rye* [1951] but did like his short stories. Mary McCarthy, of course, it turned out hated him.

I had had lunch with Mary—she had somewhat aged, I thought, but also perhaps matured. It must have been a year and a half since I had seen her. It is unfortunate, and I must arrange to see her more often, because Reuel, failing a real collaboration between his parents, has been getting somewhat out of hand: his trip through the Abruzzi with a borrowed car last summer, when he had gone against Mary's wishes—and soon come to grief, been robbed and smashed up the car.

Jason Epstein surprised me by saying, without my giving him any cue, that Mary Meigs "brought out the homosexual in all of us." He added—what I hadn't felt—that somewhat the same sort of thing was true of Odette Walling.

Red Bank, May 4, '58. I went down to Red Bank Sunday morning and came back in the afternoon. I found Jenny so aged and emaciated that I could hardly have recognized her. One of her legs is apparently paralyzed, and she is now completely bedridden. One of her neighbors occasionally comes in and carries her. She cannot read, and the radio is out of order. She has nothing to do, she says, but lie there and look at the ceiling. Margaret Rullman told me that Jenny, when she had been in the hospital again last winter, had been quite depressed when she had realized that she was well enough to go home again and had to go on living. Margaret is going to bring her a radio and try to get her better glasses. It is strange, after visiting Walther, to find that Jenny, though so much worse off physically, has still all her mental faculties. I talked to her about Talcottville, and she remembers everybody and everything perfectly. As usual, she talked about my mother, what a wonderful woman she was.

I had lunch with the Rullmans. They had had a trip to Europe, which I gathered had been something of a trial. The trouble is that Walter is not interested in anything but operations—cares nothing about sightseeing and is discommoded by dining away from home: nothing is further from his taste than exploring foreign restaurants as Margaret likes to do. He sold his canaries when he left, but has kept the other pseudo-mynah bird. They told me two gruesome pieces of news. My mother's old cook Gerda Holst had had syphilis all her life. It was hereditary: she had had two blind sisters in Sweden. Walter discovered this when he delivered her first baby. The husband at first had been furious, thinking it implied loose living. In her last years, she had really been out of her head, should have been in an institution. Finally she hanged herself. I had always supposed that the removal of my father's gallbladder was a necessary operation; but Rullman says not. It was one of his hypochondriacal obsessions that gallstones or something was wrong with it, but Rullman and the other Red Bank doctors had told him that it was perfectly normal. Since he persisted in his delusion, Rullman sent him to a doctor in New York, and this doctor told Rullman that the idea that he ought to have his gallbladder out had become such a mania with Father that he was afraid he might go insane unless he had it done. So the operation was performed. Rullman says that my mother knew was not needed. —The Rullmans' son, now married, living in New York, working in an architect's office Margaret feels as I do that the city has become uninhabitable, and that life—with the bomb and the rest—is getting us all down. What is going on in New York is reflected in Red Bank, she says. People are feeling queerer. She and Walter had pneumonia last winter. Their son, she says, is always telling them about the mistakes they made in bringing him up. The mother of Henry's friend Ritchie from Rumson who had just committed suicide is a friend of Margaret's. Henry had just been to his funeral the night we had dinner with him and Daphne. He told Elena that it was something about a girl, but said to me that he didn't know why he had done it. Margaret seemed to have heard that he was worried about his marks at college; but, she said, at twenty-six you don't commit suicide about your marks.

Visit of the Bellingers to Wellfleet, May 30–June 1. They motored up from New Haven and arrived at seven Friday. Alfred seems to me more agreeable and human now than I have ever known him at any time. He was genial and funny and gave no signs of that annoying moralism that he used to have. It amused me that he and I, who in our younger days had diverged so in ideas and literature—I being avant-garde and subversive and he very reverent of accepted values, denouncing the "unnecessary unpleasantness" (I think his phrase was) of Ibsen and condemning Anatole France as "unsound"— should now be getting together and shaking our heads

ver the young people of the present not being properly
ducated and not knowing how to write and the de-
oralization of scholarship by the Rockefeller and Ford
undations, etc. He told me what I already knew, that
the people who ran these foundations were likely to be
second- or third-rate English teachers. Before and during
dinner, we talked about archaeology, a field in which he
was easily able to score off me. He has worked in Turkey
and Greece. He told me many amusing academic stories.
He had known Roman Jacobson at the Dumbarton Oaks
thing. I said that he was a typical linguistics man: he
couldn't speak any language. Harry Levin had told me
that when Roman called him up on the phone, he would
hear him gasping in an effort to prepare himself to
speak English, then he would hear: "Je Roman." Alfred
said that when one of Franz Boas's[19] pupils had come
to him and said of some language he was studying that
he didn't have enough vocabulary, Boas had said, "Vocabulary? Sentimentality!" I told Alfred that it seemed
to me strange that we should now agree about so many
things and he said that his tastes were now "less limited."
Yet I occasionally ran into the old solid walls. Apropos
of Housman, I told him about an article in one of the
English weeklies in which the writer had said that, having once had the text of Manilius[20] along with him on
some sojourn or journey, he had read it and discovered
that M., so far from being dry and an inappropriate subject for the labors of Housman, was actually an excellent
poet who had a good deal in common with him. No,
Alfred replied, he thought that the accepted opinions
were correct. And when I mentioned the bad aspects of
the academic life, Alfred seemed to deny that there were
any. I said, "You're probably above all that," and he
answered, "Well, not entirely." Curious though nowadays typical story of his wanting to give some of his

students Virgil in Dryden's translation. Dryden seemed
to him particularly readable, but one of his colleagues
told him that he had tried this but found that it was
almost as impossible for them to deal with a poem in
heroic couplets as it would have been to read the Latin
original. He is not nearly so much a pedant as I had
expected to find from the report of Thornton Wilder and
the attitude of the Walkers; he is, on the contrary—
though he likes to jump people for scholar's inaccuracies,
men who had confused Dionysius with Dionysus[21]—
apparently rather anxiously concerned about the absence
of literary appreciation in the teaching of the classics.
—Charlotte, whose hair is quite white and who seems
somewhat bowed, is sturdier than she seems. When she
went to one of the ponds with Rosalind, she surprised
her by doing some vigorous swimming. Reminded me of
Mount Tom. We talked about the Corlers' camp and
Mrs. Will Brinsmade, who made such a perfect chap-
erone.[22] (I read the *Oxford Book of Victorian Verse*
there and discovered William Johnson Cory, Meredith's
Love in the Valley, and other things. Arthur Jackson's[23]
swan dives.)

We had a picnic the next day at Higgins Pond with
the Bellingers and Barbara Deming. I suffered with my
gouty foot. —That evening the Walkers and the Jenckses
came to dinner, and we had quite an uproarious time
reverting to school and college. I produced an old Yale
anthology of poetry, in which I had found poems by
Henry Luce as well as Alfred, Charley, and all the rest.
Charley said that I was like William Lyon Phelps,[24]
who one day when Frank Bangs came to see him, held
out a book and said, "I've just been reading a story of
John Kendrick Bangs—your father, you know!"[25] Alfred
astounded me by confessing that—though partly op-
pressed by a feeling of guilt—he had once stayed away

:om a football game to read in the Hill Library—some-
ling that, much though I hated those games on the
old autumn afternoons, when the cheering would jar
le in my wool-gathering, I should never have dared to
o. Gardner [Jencks] told about the honors of Hotch-
iss—authorized hazing—at which he had not finished
ut to which Alfred had sent a son or sons. Alfred also
urprised me—after the virtuous loyalty of his school
ays—by giving evidence of having reached a point at
·hich it was possible for him to be sufficiently critical
f Hill to say that he had "swallowed the whole thing."
Ve had a long conversation about dreams. I made A.
epeat a story he had told me about having dreamed that
e had the greatest difficulty in finding some book in a
brary. The woman librarian had said, "What can you
xpect of a library where *matrimony* is filed under
mbiguity and *fame* under *graveyard*?" We talked about
reams of flying. Charley leaps from window to window
f skyscrapers; Elena glides through the air—making,
n her way to Wellfleet, a neat easy turning of the
orner just beyond Payne's garage; I used to swim with
breaststroke, astonishing people by flying to the ceil-
1g, but it is something of an effort: I cannot stay up
idefinitely. John Bishop used to tell me that he did it
y a certain kind of step: you would prance along and
oon be soaring. Charley and I both have dreams of
ppearing on the stage; but whereas I never know my
nes, can't imagine why I ever undertook the part, and
ventually have to withdraw, Charley is a great success:
n one occasion, people said to him, "I don't know how
ou were able to take up all the cues when you had never
een the script!" He then showed us how bad he had
een when they had been trying out his play *Crazy
American*—he had always declaimed to the audience
ven when he had been supposed to be making love to

a girl. He had somehow been roused to high spirits from the sinking of his queer illness. —Alfred said, when he and Adelaide had left, "He's not very different from when we first knew him." Alfred reminded me—I was surprised that he should have remembered it when I had forgotten it myself—that I had told him of hearing my father say in his sleep, "It was a long dark flight of stone steps. Up these stole a youth." I don't know whether I understood it then, but I can see now that the whole morbid side of my father's life must have seemed like this.

The next day we had lunch at the Walkers': all the local people: Chavchavadzes, Jenckses, Edie Shay (looking thinner and much better than before she got her foot attended to). Paul had been reading the translation of Turgenev's literary memoirs. There was something about T. that Paul didn't quite like—agreed with Dostoevsky that he shouldn't have gone to see Tropmann guillotined[26] and then continually complained that he didn't think he ought to be there. This is something that is felt by Russians: Helen Muchnic and Sofka Winkelhorn as well—but not by foreign readers. When I finished reading him through the winter before last, I felt only a certain regret at parting with Ivan Sergei- vich, whose company I had so much enjoyed. —Charley was still in high spirits and plugging the collegiate line. When I drove off in the car with the Bellingers, he was giving us *Brekekekex, ko-ax, ko-ax.* I asked Alfred whether they still sang "Boola-boola"; he rather coldly replied that they didn't—though Daphne, who has a brother at Yale, told me that they always still did. (Alfred had even blas- phemed to the point of saying that—due to having roomed with Kenneth Simpson[27] and having had to answer the telephone for him—he had grown to loathe the Yale *News.*) Charlotte was inspired by this to burst

Elena and Edmund Wilson and Leon Edel, picnic at Slough Pond, Wellfleet, 1958

to the Vassar version of a Princeton football song. I
undertook to sing the Princeton version:

> Crash through the line of blue—
> Send the backstop round the end—

but Alfred interrupted by explaining that *backstop* was
impossible, it was "send the backs around the end." So
far as I can remember, I had always thought it was the
other way. I insisted later to Daphne that there was at
least a backstop in baseball but she explained that it was
a shortstop.

Reuel and Rosalind were there with the Bellingers.
Henry and Daphne arrived just after they left. I had
my usual disrupted relations with Elena, who hates to
have me go to Talcottville, though I should think she
would be glad to get a rest from me. Henry had to go
back to New York to take his final oral exam for the State
Department. He thought he did well and was told that
he had done better than most, but wasn't chosen—only
fifty out of five thousand were taken. Disappointing and
depressing to everybody, though Elena, over the telephone to Talcottville, tries to pretend that neither she
nor Henry much cares. She says that he will have to get
a job in a German-American importing firm or something.

Reuel and I started out on the 12th. I got my final
crowns put in in Boston, so that at least is over and I
am able to talk and chew. Northampton: Helen Muchnic
and Dorothy Walsh;[28] a lot of people after dinner, too
many to deal with satisfactorily. Afterwards drove to
Williamsburg—a porcupine crossed the road on the way
—and spent the night at the Linscotts'. Bob now looks

rather old but has a handsome and pleasant wife from Chicago. For years, it seems, she had a job in Hyannis promoting Cape Cod as a summer resort, and now, she says, as a result, is hated by many people. She has buried herself here with Bob in this relatively remote part of Massachusetts. He has now completely retired, never goes near the Random House office, reads books and plays the phonograph as usual. He imported a pair of beavers and put them in a small stream that runs past his house. They have multiplied and built dams and lodges, flooding the meadow and killing the trees. He says that they come out in the morning and spend some time looking over their estate, just as a farmer does. I was sorry not to have had a chance to see more of them but was short-breathed, gouty, and giddy from the night before, could hardly balance myself on the remnants of a stone fence to get a view of a beaver lodge.

NOTES

1. See Mary Meigs's autobiography, *Lily Briscoe: A Self-Portrait* (1981), pp. 13–16, 18–20, 22–23.

2. See *The Twenties*, pp. 95–96, 199.

3. See *The Twenties*, *passim*, and *The Shores of Light*, pp. 392–96.

4. Dorothy Mendenhall's son.

5. Robert Penn (Red) Warren and his wife, the novelist Eleanor Clark. *The Thirties*, p. 76.

6. A private school in Connecticut.

7. *John Brown: The Making of a Martyr* (1929).

8. An allusion to Benjamin Disraeli's *Sybil, or The Two Nations* (1845), a novel describing "The Two Nations of England, the Rich and the Poor."

9. Gordon Haight, professor of English at Yale and biographer of George Eliot.

10. EW's "A. E. Housman: The Voice, Sent Forth, Can Never Be *Recalled*" in *The Triple Thinkers* (1948), pp. 83–99.

11. EW actually went to the Clifton Springs Sanitarium in 1929. See *The Twenties*, pp. 493–95.

12. James Thurber's (1894–1961) *The Years with Ross* (1959).

13. See *The Twenties*, *passim*.

14. Robert Benchley (1889–1945), drama critic, humorist, and actor. *The Twenties* and *The Thirties*, *passim*.

15. Dorothy Parker had helped bring EW to *Vanity Fair* in 1920.

16. See *The Twenties*, *passim*.

17. Sybille Bedford, novelist and authorized biographer of Aldous Huxley (2 vols., 1973–74).

18. "Partial Comfort" in *Sunset Gun* (1928).

19. "The Father of American Anthropology," noted for his work in Canada among the West Coast Indians and the Inuit.

20. A. E. Housman's five-volume edition (1903–30) of Gaius Manilius. See *LLP*, pp. 242, 458.

21. Dionysius, Syracusan tyrant (430–367 B.C.); Dionysus, the wine god.

22. At the Hill School in summer students went to camp on Mount Tom in Massachusetts. *A Prelude*, p. 55.

23. Arthur Jackson, old New York friend of EW. *A Prelude*, p. 166.

24. William Lyon Phelps (1865–1943), Yale professor of English and author of the column "As I Like It" in *Scribner's*.

25. John Kendrick Bangs (1862–1922), editor of *Puck* (1904–5) and other humorous magazines, author of extravagantly farcical tales.

26. See *Turgenev's Literary Reminiscences* (1958), pp. 244–71, for his account of Tropmann's execution.

27. Kenneth Farrand Simpson (1895–1941), Hill School classmate of EW's and New York lawyer. *The Thirties*, p. 299.

28. Dorothy Walsh, author of *Literature and Knowledge*. See *LLP*, pp. 702–3.

ST. REGIS AND ONCHIOTA

Talcottville, arrived Saturday, June 7th:[1] It is cold—
as cold as it was in mid-May when I came up here last;
but my gout is nearly gone, and my new teeth make life
easier. And in general I am not so depressed. Having
Reuel with me is very pleasant. He has moods, when I
am making him do something which he does not like,
when he withdraws into somewhat sullen silence; but he
is almost always helpful and amiable. We have long
conversations. I am surprised at how much Russian he
has learned in a year. Last night (June 14) he plodded
through a few pages of Chekhov's *Spat Khochetsya* ["I
Am Sleepy"]. He has spaded most of the garden, unearth-
ing large tree roots and stones, which hadn't been removed before.

It is likely to seem rather empty when I first come up
here, but then the world soon fills in around me, and
it comes to seem far more real than Wellfleet. A little bit
sad this year: Huldah and Gertrude Loomis have been
upset by Florence's death; Lou Munn has gone home to
her father and then come back again, and is, I suppose,
as hardworked as ever—it seems that her father has mar-

ried again, and that there is no place for her down there
—she couldn't take a job on account of the baby; Carrie
Trennam is so tied up with arthritis that she can't even
cross the street or visit her neighbors; Fern has had
another blood clot but seems just as energetic as ever.
(While I have been writing this, George and Lou have
come in. They look pale and thin, and seemed to us a
little constrained from the recent crisis.) Poor Beverly
has suffered exactly the fate that her aunt predicted to
me last fall and tried to warn her against. She paid all
the installments on the car that had been registered in
the name of her fiancé. When he began to go out with
other girls, she asked him to let her put it in her own
name; but he refused, telling her that it made no difference, since they were going to get married. Then, when
the car was all paid for, he took it away and sold it. She is
out $2,000. When he sees her now, he will not speak to
her—though, she says, it ought to be her who won't
speak to him. She is now paying for another and cheaper
car, but has succeeded in getting her teeth attended to.
She works in the Park Market, then comes over here
after six and gets dinner and eats it with us. She, too,
is more self-conscious, and nervous—amiable as ever but
sometimes seems troubled.

Trip to St. Regis and Onchiota (June 12–13). What
with my talking and Reuel's inattention, we must have
driven a hundred unnecessary miles by keeping on when
we should have turned off or taking the wrong turning.
—I first went to see Alec Gray and had the usual difficulty communicating with him; sometimes we were talking at cross-purposes. But he told me that it was impossible that Standing Arrow could have been Tonto's
brother,[2] because he had nothing but sisters—Ray Fadden later confirmed this. He had simply lied to Fenton

when Fenton had thought he recognized him as Silverheels. All his adherents had dropped him when he
accepted the land that was offered him because they
would have to pay taxes on it, and taxes are the great
issue. He had again abandoned his wife and children,
leaving them with his mother-in-law in Syracuse. There
was about to be a big council at Onondaga, to which
Alec Gray had been summoned—even Indians from
Grand River were coming. He said that Rusty Oaks was
crazy, and Philip Cook told me later as a great joke that
the evening of the same day when Oaks had had me
expelled from the Longhouse, he—having discarded his
feather—was himself expelled from the Longhouse by
a drunken Onondaga who thought he was white. Gray
always speaks of the Catholic Church as the Seventh
Nation, thinks the proportion of Longhouse to Catholics
about 300 or 400 to 1,700. There was trouble about the
Canada boundary line: several Canadian Indians were
now living on the U.S. side just across the line and
working here. I asked whether it wasn't true that our
Indians were not allowed to work in Canada—asked him
twice but he didn't answer. When I left, I wished him
luck, and he pointed above his head and said, "I don't
expect people to help us, I only hope for help from the
Creator—I even thank Him for the water from the
tap!"—pointing to the kitchen sink. Outside I found a
very drunk Indian, slobbering at the mouth, talking to
Reuel in the car. A contrast to Alec Gray, a serious,
earnest man. —The Cooks confirmed my impression—
they can't always understand him either. He is so much
still in the Indian world that it is hard for him to make
contact with the white world, whereas Cook, as somebody said to me, is handicapped by his lack of Mohawk
in getting his ideas through to the Indians.

At the place where we had beached, a group of Indian boys came in and played one of the games at the front of the restaurant. One of them had his head shaved, in the traditional way, with a strip of hair down the middle ending in a scalp lock. This was a challenge to the enemy to come and get the scalp "if he was man enough." He could strip it right off. Is this a sign of reviving nationalism?

When we arrived at the Cooks' at five, they had already sat down to supper at a table on the back lawn: Cook and his wife, three daughters, son and his wife, with two little grandchildren playing around on the outskirts (one of them looking more Indian in the Esquimau way than either parents or grandparents), an old rather smart-alecky and boring Yankee from New Hampshire or Vermont, and three young men, one Indian, one non-Indian Middle Westerner, one of dubious stock, all the last four of whom had come to work at the big new aluminum plant (Reynolds) at which Cook was now foreman of the ironworkers. (With the new plant and the Seaway, Massena is being transformed, filled with new little modern houses that look more or less like motels.) Cook's wife, she told me, is Armenian—competent and bright, I thought. The son, who is studying geology at Brigham Young University in Utah, says he is usually mistaken for an Italian or a Jew. The pretty eldest daughter is at Albany State College, studying to teach Latin—talked about the Latin poets. We had spaghetti and salad and rhubarb and "fried cakes" (very good) for dessert. Cook is affectionate and friendly, the family seem very harmonious. The aluminum workers seemed all to be lodgers. Cook, after supper, held up one of the grandchildren by the feet while the child stood up straight to demonstrate to me what he calls the "uncanny instinct for balance" of the Mohawks, which makes it possible for them to walk along steel beams. His likeness to Dan Aaron struck me less: he has a stronger face and natural air of authority. He is evidently a kind of magnetic figure. People all through the evening are coming to see him: a man from Texas and his wife, who were looking for a house to live in, a young man who had just graduated from Hamilton and was looking for a job. His brother also appeared: like Philip, a deconverted Catholic, who had helped him and Fadden, in 1948, compose the leaflet protesting against the bills that were to deprive them of their jurisdiction. —When he was driving us around, he showed us the great gray mound of subsoil that had been left along the shore where they had been digging for the Seaway. It is only on the reservation, he said, that this had not been cleared away.

The next day we went on to see Ray Fadden at Onchiota near Paul Smith's. His wife directed us to the school where he is teaching. His father was Irish, and he has red hair and blue eyes and a great gift of gab. Fenton had described him to me as "a professional Indian," and what has happened is that he has canalized into the cause of the Six Nations all the eloquence, wit, and spirit which the old professional Irishman used to direct against England. His England is the U.S. government. He says—not, I think, without some reason— that if the government can get away with disregarding the Indians' rights in the interests of large government projects, they will go on to do the same thing with the rest of us. It is the first time—this last year—he says, that he has taught in a white school—science. He seemed to be popular there—everybody knew him, and the girl students would smile at him and joke with him. He decided to play hooky (had apparently no classes that afternoon) in order to go home and show me his museum[3]—told somebody that he was going, but said he didn't want the principal to see him—drove me back in a tiny French car, talking volubly all the time, while Reuel followed behind. His wife looks much more like an Indian than he does. I couldn't tell whether she had white blood. The boy was working on one of the tepees, was studying art at college. He and his father build everything. There are longhouses, lodges, tepees, all supposed to be accurate for their various tribes. A pet porcupine, caged in, having his daytime sleep in one of the Indian houses. Fadden talks too much and too glibly for an Indian, and he has performed in a great piece of beadwork an exploit in picture writing which is a good deal too fancy for an Indian and evidently derives somewhat from comic strips: the admonition against drinking is represented by a bottle on its side with the whisky running out of it, the Spirits of Good and Evil radiating lightning at one another—and little figures that seem adopted from the Navaho cloths.

Salamanca, 8 p.m., June 20. Beefeater martinis at dinner. Looking out from front window of Hotel Dudley (which Bill Fenton says his children used to call the Hotel Deadly)—typical old New York State hotel, tall and narrow, a few modern improvements mainly consisting of an elevator to take the place of the long staircases with dark wooden rails and fluorescent (?) lamps over the beds which no longer work. On the right, the old long dark-roofed red brick station, and the railroad tracks of the Erie, which still runs three trains a day between Chicago and New York, and of the Baltimore and Ohio, which nowadays runs only freight—crescents of pink, white, and robin's-egg-blue cars on both sides of road to the station. I have seen two women who are either pregnant or the barrel-shaped type of Indian women leading little boys along this road toward the town. In front and on the left old brick buildings for stores with tall narrow ogive windows. A steeple beyond green trees. A taxi stand on the right, a liquor store on the left, and a clock surmounted by a sign, "Mortgage Loans Savings Accounts," and a neon sign, "Fenton Insurance Agency," a sort of false-Dutch high-peaked façade: "1882 BANK"—hills beyond: those Seneca hills, comfortable, wild and green and now at evening misty. I don't mind all this, in spite of the noise of the trains and railroad yards at night, nearly so much as the modern development of Niagara Falls and the Seaway, with their impermanent-looking new houses for the people who have come to work there, like toys set out on a lawn. The food in the dining room tastes very good and in spite of the universal lobster tails (listed as coming from Maine but undoubtedly from elsewhere, from South Africa)—not quite the same as all the other such places, with its high ceiling, wide space, and silence, it seems to depress Reuel but rather pleases me. I have a certain tenderness for all this part of the world, though the New York State cities northwest of here are horrid—though settled considerably later than our section, some of the towns have the New York State neatness and decent self-assured tranquillity. The Indians, too, in their nest of hills—where, as in Onondaga, they have been living for thousands of years—make an extremely agreeable winterland. I hope they may never be disturbed.

Reuel and I left Talcottville Monday the 16th—Syracuse two nights (Serta Shavalov and Onondagas), Niagara Falls one night (Tuscaroras), then Salamanca three nights; spent night of the 22nd with the Mulligans;

returned Talcottville Monday the 23rd; Reuel left as soon as he could, early in the afternoon.

I left for New York the next day and did not return till Wednesday, July 2.

NOTES

1. See *Upstate*, pp. 179–80.
2. The television Tonto, played by Jay Silverheels.
3. The Six Nations Museum at Onchiota.

DJUNA BARNES[1]

My dream in New York about Mary Meigs: She and
I had made an expedition, with several other people, to
a more or less wild island in the Mediterranean, where
Spanish was spoken. We had advanced from a town on
the shore a little way into the interior, where we were
picnicking or camping or something among some big
brownish rocks (it may be that Edward Lear's travel
books, which I had been lending her, had something to
do with this). We left the party for a short exploration,
and got lost. She had a man's bicycle, and I decided to
try to save the situation by having her ride behind me on
the bicycle, "pillion"—not on the handlebars—so that
we could make better speed. (This has obviously something to do with my recurrent dream of long bicycle
rides, with a companion, in which we go shooting down
hills and successfully navigate rough roads and sometimes discover, in the backcountry of New Jersey, a
little half-French town, which derives from my rides at
Princeton with Bill Osborn and Stanley Dell and my
later rides in France with Dave Hamilton and John
Anderson.) As usual, the ride was a great success, though,

as sometimes happened in the older dreams, we did not reach our destination—did not get back to our party. But after we had got through some bad going, had emerged from the rocks and the scrubby growth, we went rolling down long steep slopes—now completely at a loss as to where we were—and at last arrived at a town. We went to the inn—I here forget the transition—and were soon in a bedroom, in which a small white-haired man, not particularly old and with clever eyes, was lying in bed, attended by a kind of secretary or stooge. I asked the way to get back to the place where we had left our party, and he answered in very good English that he would have to explain in Spanish and we shouldn't understand it. There was about him something perverse. "He knows many languages," said the stooge. I thought to myself, "So do I—I don't speak them very well," but refrained from saying this. In any case, I didn't speak Spanish, so there we were trapped. We couldn't get back to our party. Would we have to spend the night at the inn? —Then I woke up. It had had certain aspects of one of those worrying dreams, to which I am so much addicted, but—what I did not realize while dreaming— it was pressing to a desired conclusion: it was not in the least nightmarish, but vivid, consecutive, coherent—it was, in fact, a kind of short story. I liked afterwards to think about it. What I feel for Mary Meigs is love. I am not in love with her but what I feel for her is something unexpected, not something that has grown out of previous admiration—I thought at first she was pale, a little of a bore—or out of some close nonsexual relationship. It is rather queer, not, I think, like anything I have ever experienced before. The only two women, since I have been married to Elena, who have attracted me at all strongly have been Mary and Sofka Winkelhorn. But I am too closely bound to Elena and enjoy making love to her too much to be seriously tempted by other women. Besides, I think my sexual energy is ebbing, and at my age irregular love affairs are far too much of a nuisance.

I went with the Epsteins to a party that the Kazins were giving for their wedding anniversary. When I came in, I asked Anna what anniversary they were celebrating. "Sh!" she said. "It's the first time he's remembered it." It turned out to be their sixth. —Ralph Ellison[2] was there, back from Rome, where, having won some prize, he had spent two years—very glad, he said, to get back to America, away from all those ruins. The Edels were there. At one point I talked about our conversation at Wellfleet with the Bellingers and Walkers about flying dreams. Only two had such dreams. Ellison said that he dreamed about starting down a certain slope in Oklahoma and taking off—it was just a soaring, but he could guide himself like a bird. At the end of the evening, Ellison and Alfred became involved in one of those long futile and frustrating arguments—I have engaged in them, in my early days, playing Alfred's role, in which the novelist or dramatist is trying to explain that he feels that the way he is writing his books is the right way for him to write them while the critic is arguing some kind of a case which implies that he somehow knows better. Leon Edel, who did not intervene in the discussion, was sitting between the two, very much the more intelligent and amiably ironic Frenchman, looking down and subtly working his eyebrows.

Louise Connor and John Amen:[3] John is still somewhat paralyzed, but says that he has now found out that the whole thing has been due to a stomach ulcer, which he is apparently having treated. He now drinks nothing but milk. I told him I was on the wagon, but, when I last

saw him at his apartment, succumbed to highballs. He
said rather morosely, I thought you were on the wagon.
Marion went to the kitchen to get him supper. The
German lady was not in evidence. —Louise had suddenly left home—in February or March?—and had descended upon John, saying she wanted a divorce. He had
the impression that she had been taking drugs, was quite
out of her head. She says she wept and that he also wept.
He says he made her leave the office, but that later she
became much more reasonable, and that he was arranging
a Mexican divorce. Pete, as usual, was trying to get her
back; but she had succeeded, by going to law in Chicago,
in getting a settlement of money. —I had her come to
dinner at the Princeton Club and thought at first, like
John, that she now made no sense at all. I spent the
whole dinner trying to find out what had happened. She
had been to a sanitarium, it seemed, and had been going
to a psychiatrist—whom she called a "therapist"—and
got off on an anti-Semitic track, telling him that his
whole point of view was affected by the fact that he
was Jewish—in the sanitarium, she insisted, with no very
obvious point, about a third of the patients were Jewish.
John afterwards told me the reason her children had
"turned against her," as she said, was that they thought
her crazy and irresponsible, that, after she left the sanitarium, she still went to the doctor one day a week, and
that she thought they were planning to send her back.
She suffers somewhat from delusions of persecution,
thinks that Pete is having her spied on. John thinks that
she is definitely headed for a divorce, but I am not sure
that she is. She seemed to me a little unconvincing when
she said she was going to Mexico. Yet I have now learned
that women like her—Louise Bogan and Helen Augur,
for example—that one thinks should not leave their
husbands turn out actually to be much better living alone.

She has evidently calmed down in her little apartment in the Hotel Irving, and is about to move into an independent one, which she insisted on taking me to see, though she found that she could not get in. She says she is schizoid—I suppose she is. She must be well through the change of life, since she says that her interest in sex is dead. I need drinks to get through all this—she is evidently making a point of not drinking—though I always find excuses for them, I guess. —She had left all her clothes when she went away, and now was making dresses for herself.

June 29. I went with the Epsteins to see *Ulysses in Nighttown*[4] in what used to be the Minsky Theater at Houston Street and Second Avenue. As I went up in the elevator, I thought about going there with Magda and Margaret Canby. Joyce came out better than you might expect. We were in the front row, and beside us was an elderly man with a woman who looked like the Red Queen. I thought it was *Djuna Barnes* and spoke to her in the intermission. It was Djuna, and the man beside her was Harrison Dowd, whom I had seen in Boston playing with the Lunts in *The Visit.* He is old, lean, and gray now, and I had never before noticed how New England he was. Strange to think how I had once resented him as one of Edna Millay's pet pansies, who used to intrude on what I regarded as my time. After the show, we all went to a Greenwich Village restaurant, where we had various kinds of spaghetti, which seemed to me very good. When I saw Djuna close up and not in profile, she no longer resembled the Red Queen. Instead of having grown, as I feared, spare and sour—she had almost never smiled during the show—she was broader and seemed gentler. She was dressed in black and wore a little black three-cornered hat, in imitation

of Jane Heap.[5] She has had some kind of bad accident—
a fall, I think, and injury to her back, has some difficulty
in walking and uses a cane. When I put my hands over
my eyes, she began to worry about me. I said I'd never
known her so considerate, and she replied that she was
trying to be a kind old lady. I told them how I'd tried
to get her to go to Italy with me in Paris in the summer
of 1921 and she had turned me down. She said she had
never told anybody about that. She said that she had
refused because of my dinner with her, when I had
talked to her about Edith Wharton.[6] At the end of my
little lecture, she had said something like "If there's
anybody I loathe it's Edith Wharton." She now explained
her refusal: "I thought *Ethan Frome*: no!" The restaurant
was on Montmartre, and I remember that I afterwards
took her to *L'Enfer*, which had amused me in my army
days, but she hadn't liked this either. I inquired about
all the old lesbians: Jane Heap, Margaret Anderson.
She told me something—I forget what—about Henrietta Metcalf, whom I had known on *Vanity Fair*,
when she was the wife of Metcalf the painter, a good
deal older than she, and seemed strongly interested in
men. I had forgotten that she had eventually become a
lesbian. I am always a little surprised that, though
lesbians are likely to see a lot of their male opposite
numbers, they seem to feel a certain contempt for them
(Janet Flanner has this tone, too)—I suppose they think
them too feminine. Harrison Dowd was less loyal to
Edna than I should have expected him to be—thought
some of her short poems were good, didn't care for the
way she read her poems: too much of the elocutionist
about it. There is something in this, and it is the reason
that some people find her records embarrassing; but she
and her poetry meant, and still mean, so much to me
that I don't mind it at all. Besides, this deliberate grand

manner united them. Djuna was always jealous of Edna, who had had a brief affair with Thelma. Thelma could not have meant much to Edna, but it was tragedy for Djuna when, after living with her, Thelma left her. I have always thought that Djuna was pathetic. I used to think, years ago, that she might not be a lesbian, that she was not really happy in that role. And—though Edwin Muir and Eliot admire *Nightwood*—I have never thought she had real talent (have not read the new play in verse[7]). She seems doomed to live alone, and I was impressed to see her growing old with dignity and good humor.

I remember her attacking me years ago for insisting that American writers should stay in the United States. Why shouldn't they live in Paris, where it was so much pleasanter? Today I detest the American cities and would gladly spend a good deal of my time in Paris.

NOTES

1. Djuna Barnes (1892–1982), novelist and short-story writer, author of *Nightwood* (1937). *The Twenties*, pp. 79, 85–86.

2. Ralph Ellison, author of *The Invisible Man* (1952), held a Rome Fellowship of the American Academy of Arts and Letters from 1955 to 1957.

3. Louise Fort, once engaged to John Amen, later married Peter Connor. *The Thirties*, pp. 243 and 457.

4. Padraic Colum (1881–1972) had adapted for the theater the phantasmagoric "nighttown" section of James Joyce's *Ulysses*.

5. Jane Heap, editor with Margaret Anderson of the *Little Review*, which attempted to serialize *Ulysses* in 1918–21 but was suppressed.

6. Edith Wharton (1862–1937), the novelist. See EW's "Justice to Edith Wharton" in *Classics and Commercials*, pp. 412–18.

7. *The Antiphon*, 1958.

1|18|11

TALCOTTVILLE, 1958

Talcottville again:[1] The 4th of July was rainy, so one quite forgot the holiday. I took the Loomises to dinner at Constableville, and they told me all the gossip. One of the great topics of talk of the winter had been the Munns' heifers. They had let them get loose and wander all over. First they had fed in other people's pastures, then when the pastures were covered with snow, they would come to the barns to be fed. Various people called up the Munns, but they didn't do anything about it. The heifers finally got to be such a nuisance that the state police had to intervene. The Munns then sold them to a man from the South, but they were so wild that he wasn't able to catch them and finally had to shoot them and pile them in a truck. I don't know whether he had originally wanted to sell them for beef. —Lillian Burnham is now eighty-eight or eighty-nine, too deaf and infirm to keep on running her farm in the way that she has been able to do. The Sullivan boy has either been married or is about to be and has proposed moving in and living in the back part of the house, but Mrs. B. won't have this. Huldah said that Lillian nowadays "got in her hair," so that she tried to avoid seeing her. At the time of Florence's death, they had wanted to buy a plot in the Talcottville cemetery, of the administration of which Mrs. Burnham is president. They examined a blueprint map, which Mrs. B. thought the Loomises wanted to take away. A terrible scene seems to have taken place. The only plot available was one under a large tree, which the Loomises didn't want—I suppose because it was too much hidden away and Huldah pointed out that in most cemeteries the large trees were trimmed. It was this that precipitated the scene. Since then, Mrs. B. has had the cemetery kept locked, and has had to be notified—at the instance of the L.'s—that the law was that cemeteries had to be kept open. They finally buried Florence—where there were other Loomises buried in a little graveyard on one of the side roads. Yesterday, when she told me all this, Huldah had just left a basket of strawberries—Lillian not being visible—at Mrs. B's house.

Dorothy Mendenhall is getting bored with her nursing home and wants to come up here and stay with the Loomises; but they won't have her. Huldah says that she has spent a good deal of her life looking after old ladies and is not going to do it anymore. Dorothy, she says, would need two or three attendants and somebody to cook for them.

Coming back along the Boonville road, Dorothy Sharp said to me that she had never known who lived in the houses beyond the Collinses'. She meant in Talcottville, but I thought she meant between the Collinses' and Boonville—she said afterwards she didn't know anything about these either—so I asked Albert Grubel about them. He said that Mrs. Sweeney lived in the first house but "she don't live with Mr. Sweeney—she lives with a man named Overrider." Across the road lived the Edicks: "They don't live together no more. She'd go away with other men and then come back and have a baby." Her husband got tired of this and got a separation. She was up north somewhere now. I asked whether any of the children were his. *"Why, I think so—right on the start."*

When the Sharps, before coming up here, had gone to see Dorothy Mendenhall in the nursing home, she had said to Malcolm, "You're the head of the house"—which seemed to imply that she had before considered herself the head of the house—that is, of the family of her two sons and of Dorothy's family and Dorothy's brothers. Malcolm was now the senior male. A little later in the conversation, Dorothy [Sharp] remarked, in connection with his having done or having offered to do something for somebody, that he was always so good-humored. "Weakness, I call it!" said Aunt Dorothy.

Alternate appetite and tiredness; desire still for more falls and summers and willingness at last to call my life a day.

The world is dimmer now—books on the shelves I'll never read. —*Dreimäderlhaus* first heard over and over at the Stadttheater in Trier, now also played on the phonograph when I am alone here in the summer, but becoming rather decayed and funereal. In this place, gray and plain and elegant (Aug. 30).

> June was cold and August cold:
> Log fires when the day was bright;
> Old pink and patterned quilts enfold
> And stupefy my sleep at night.
> . . . Happy among the Boston rockers.
>   mockers
>   lockers
>   shockers
>   knockers

Drinks in the morning just after the Brookses left.

> Whoever set our house to face the East
> Displaying trees and river in the dawn
> Under the bright triumphant sun,
> Seen from between white columns,
> Had something of the Jeffersonian touch
> That makes our human habitations
> Ignite with the earth and shine
> . . . Raw day and the dairy world begins
> But sad and old and dead.

Visit of the Van Wyck Brookses, Friday–Sunday, August 1–3.[2] Gladys has certainly been much softened—though she said some characteristic things. Her first remark when they arrived was "This house is so much better than I thought it was going to be!"; later on, in her very quiet way, "Wouldn't it be possible to do something to keep the whole place from collapsing." Van Wyck seemed to enjoy himself and be much interested in everything, likes to tell you about people he knows and the interconnections he loves to discover between well-known figures; was delighted that, through the Meads of Vermont—McKim, Mead and White—he should be related —or connected by marriage—both to Howells, whose life he is writing,[3] and to the Noyeses of the Oneida Community, to which I took him. He discussed this with old Pierrepont Noyes, the son of John Humphrey, and was, I think, thrilled by the Noyes family. (They gave us an excellent lunch in the Mansion House.) He is nine years older than I am, but it seemed to me his memory was better, and I was afraid that too much drinking was damaging mine. His mother's family—I think it was—were Platts of Plattsburg and had a big old house there, which now belongs to someone else. He loves everything connected with the world of the arts and is obviously proud of having known so many artists and writers. Resents the treatment he has lately had on the part of the academic world, told me that he and I were the only men of letters left. Anthony West's article about me in the London *Sunday Times* apropos of my Eliot article[4] arrived when the Brookses were here, and I said that I'd just received a ferocious attack, and he said he'd like to read an attack on me: I'd been "getting all the laurels" lately. He underrates his reputation as well as, apparently, his profits. He likes to talk literary shop, about which he is rather naïve; pays attention to all the reviews, knows who got every prize. He has just done a book on Americans in Italy[5] and is now working on his life of Howells. I have a feeling that these books are sedatives and that he has really been taking literary sedatives ever since his breakdown in the twenties. The night before he left I gave him a little pep talk on putting into his present work more of the psychological insight of his *Ordeal of Mark Twain* [1920] period. He does not want nowadays, I think, to explore below the surface. He is at the same time very opinionated. He still can't see much in Henry James, against whom he confesses to a special animus, and is extravagant in his hatred of Eliot. Jack Wheelock told me that when he said to Van Wyck that Eliot had been very ill, he had startled him by replying, "I hope he dies in agony!" Issues of patriotism involved, I think, in the cases of both James and Eliot. The trouble with Van Wyck as a critic is that he doesn't understand great literature. His conception of it seems to be based on the writers he admired in college. Tolstoy is the great writer that he expects other writers to measure up to, and I feel that Tolstoy in his mind is somehow associated with Wells. He is childish about "form" and "content," said to me angrily at Wellfleet that Eliot was the person responsible for emphasizing

form rather than content and thus misleading the young
I keep off modern literature with him, but he gave
Malcolm his usual line: Proust and Joyce were haters of
life, etc. Malcolm had denied this, and he considerably
bewildered Van Wyck by his unexpected opinions. I
told Malcolm after they left that Van Wyck had thought
Malcolm was pulling his leg. "I was just telling him a
few simple truths," said Malcolm. It is curious that a man
who writes so well, who is very much an artist, should
not understand style and form in other writers. It must
be due to his imperfect education in French and his
ignorance of Italian and the classics. —We all had a
very good time, and I felt let down when he left.

Dinner with the Edmondses: The day the Brookses
left I have never seen Walter so animated and talkative
He made such a fuss over Elena—who had remarked
before we went that he was "rather a drip"—that she
decided she liked him somewhat better. His new wife is
no longer self-conscious about being in her predecessor's
place, and the whole atmosphere is easy and pleasant.
Improvements made in the house—a new study for
Walter at the back where some maids' rooms used to be
Walter has a kind of refrigerated upstate New York
gentility—rather like my Utica relatives, the Harts—
which can't be expected to appeal to Elena, and though
it somewhat repels me, as the Harts do, also has a certain
interest for me. Walter is a museum piece: his feudal
estate and establishment, his way of pronouncing *o* as *ao*,
his ostentatious satisfactions in his brandies and wines
"laid down" by his uncle or father, his sense—in spite of
his winters in Cambridge, a sense that in my own way I
share with him—of being remote, half dissociated, from
the rest of the American world but supreme in his little

domain, which belongs to a dreamlike world that those
outside it do not really know about. His books, so far as
I have sampled them—though he knows well enough
in a practical way what is going on in this part of the
world—all seem to take place in a juvenile New York,
something imagined in boyhood that was nourished, however, by the real romance of a beautiful and impressive
environment, and are in consequence invariably juveniles,
whether intended for adults or children. His feudal New
York State gentility—which is sometimes a little jarring
(see my conversation with Merwin Hart at the time when
he was coming under the spell of fascism. I hope I recorded this[6])—appeared in his telling us that the lower
classes had sometimes as good instinctive manners as
"any of us." The man who looks after things for him and
who lives there all the year around ordinarily walks past
the screened porch but when they are talking there, he
is careful to give it a wide berth.

For several years now there have been supposed to be
timber wolves around—the hide of one was displayed in
a window at the time of the Boonville centenary. But
Walter insists that they are not timber wolves but a cross
between coyotes and police dogs. The coyotes escaped
from a train which was taking them to a zoo. The
Edmondses' place is now infested with them. We heard
somebody firing at one, and they have lately been coming
so close to the house—one of them had just calmly walked
past—that they were afraid to have Helen and Marcia
[Roch] play out of sight or go to swim alone. Walter
calls them coydogs. I told Dan Aaron about this, when
we were on our Indian trip. He is so absorptive of everything that he took it in with all the Indian lore and
immediately, he said, had a dream in which he thought
he saw Indian dogs who were holding a bow-wow.

Aug. '58. Last summer I was going through the Goncourt journal at the same time as G. W. Cable, and this summer I read the Stravinsky conversations in the midst of plodding through De Forest. In both cases, the same reflection: that the artistic background for the Goncourts and Stravinsky is so much richer and more interesting; artistic poverty of the air that Cable and De Forest had to breathe. With Howells, Mark Twain, and Henry James, there was more interest in serious writing in the 1870s and early 80s than later when the pressure to turn out popular romances became virtually irresistible.

On a walk toward the Coes' along the East Road, Elena and I saw a large red fox, the only one I have ever seen wild. He would let us get fairly close to him, then run on a little way, moving his long graceful tail, as Elena said, like the rudder of a ship. It was delightful to watch him running, springing so lightly over the ground—made me think how depressing caged animals were. Elena can't bear to see anything caged (hence her resistance to restraining Button). When we got to a certain point, he went into a field and watched us from the top of a large boulder. At the point of the road in which he had evidently been interested, there was the leg of a woodchuck carcass.

Indian trip with Dan Aaron, Aug. 15–18. Elena and Helen left the same Friday. Niagara Falls (Grossman, Mad Bear).[7] Fort Niagara (unexpectedly very much worth seeing, but why the devil must the boy in the garage slap a sticker on the front of our car saying "See Fort Niagara"? When I had it taken off and asked whether people didn't complain, he said, "Quite a few do"). Nicodemus Bailey at Tonawanda. Tried to see

Howard Manley, but found he was away—Syracuse (where we drove round and round for a maddeningly long time trying to get the car headed in the right direction to stop at the Hotel Syracuse, only to find it full up with a convention)—went on to Talcottville that night, arriving late and rather groggy, drinks and inspired conversation about the Indians.

Mad Bear and Stanley Grossman, the Tuscaroras' lawyer, stopped off and had dinner with me on their way back from St. Regis, to which the Confederacy Chief had asked them to come in connection with the income tax crisis.

Dan [Aaron] took the occasion of our trip to ask me about the radicals of the twenties and thirties—he is writing a book about them.[8] The whole thing seems to me so stale that I couldn't imagine anybody wanting to write a book about it, but we ran over the personalities, and I told him a lot of stories. It seemed to me like that grisly museum that I had had him visit at Niagara Falls: old stuffed two-headed calves, moth-eaten panthers attacking a moth-eaten stag, dried-up corpses from Indian graves and Egyptian mummy cases, old bags made of rubber tires in which people had tried to shoot the falls—and all around it an all-powerful industrial life that nothing could stop, that had spoiled the landscape of the river and crowded everything else out. Everything connected with the Indians seemed to me, on the other hand, very interesting, lively, and fresh. But they were being overwhelmed and crowded out, too, by the encroachments of the Power Authority.

Lou Munn said that she couldn't be in favor of desegregation because she had grown up in South Carolina, where a Negro was not allowed to come to the front door. Her father had beaten one up because he had come to the front door—"I got a big kick out of that."

Good days now at the end of August—after all the days of rain—mornings when everything is painted in the good strong New York State colors. —Wonderful calm sweep of the great green country, blue in the distance and tinged in the foreground with yellow fields, when Malcolm drove me to Watertown (Aug. 29).

NOTES

1. *Upstate*, pp. 181–82.
2. *Upstate*, pp. 182–86.
3. *Howells, His Life and World* (1959).
4. " 'Miss Buttle' and 'Mr. Eliot,' " *The New Yorker* (May 24, 1958), reprinted in *BBT*, pp. 364–402. Anthony West, son of H. G. Wells and Rebecca West.
5. *The Dream of Arcadia: American Writers and Artists in Italy, 1760–1915* (1958).
6. EW did not record this conversation in his journals but incorporated it in *Upstate*, pp. 67–68.
7. Stanley Grossman, the Tuscaroras' lawyer in their struggle with the Power Authority over construction of a Niagara Falls hydroelectric plant on reservation land (*AI*, pp. 137–59), and Wallace P. "Mad Bear" Anderson (1927–85), a champion of Native Indian civil rights (*AI*, pp. 160–63).
8. Daniel Aaron, *Writers on the Left* (1961).

1/18/11   2↙

DEGANAWIDA'S PROPHECY

Deganawida's Prophecy, as told me by Mad Bear (Wallace Anderson) August 31, 1958:[1]

When Deganawida was leaving the Indians in the Bay of Quinté in Ontario, he told the Indian people that they would face a time of great suffering. They would distrust their leaders and the principles of peace of the League, and a great white serpent was to come upon the Iroquois, and that for a time it would intermingle with the Indian people and would be accepted by the Indians, who would treat the serpent as a friend. This serpent would in time become so powerful that it would attempt to destroy the Indian, and the serpent is described as choking the life's blood out of the Indian people. Deganawida told the Indians that they would be in such a terrible state at this point that all hope would seem to be lost, and he told them that when things looked their darkest a red serpent would come from the north and approach the white serpent, which would be terrified, and upon seeing the red serpent he would release the Indian, who would fall to the ground almost like a helpless child, and the white serpent would turn all its attention to the red serpent. The bewilderment would cause the white serpent to accept the red serpent momentarily. The white serpent would be stunned and take part of the red serpent and accept him. Then there is a heated argument and a fight. And then the Indian revives and crawls toward the land of the hilly country, and then he would assemble his people together, and they would renew their faith and the principles of peace that Deganawida had established. There would at the same time exist among the Indians a great love and forgiveness for his brother, and in this gathering would come streams from all over—not only the Iroquois but from all over—and they would gather in this hilly country, and they would renew their friendship. And Deganawida said they would remain neutral in this fight between the white serpent and the red serpent. At the time they were watching the two serpents locked in this battle, a great message would come to them, which would make them ever so humble, and when they become that humble, they will be waiting for a young leader, an Indian boy, possibly in his teens, who would be a choice seer. Nobody knows who he is or where he comes from, but he will be given great power, and would be heard by thousands and he would give them the guidance and the hope to restrain them from going back to their land and he would be the accepted leader. And Deganawida said that they will gather in the land of the hilly country, beneath the branches of an elm tree, and they should burn tobacco and call upon Deganawida by name when we are facing our darkest hours, and he will return.

Deganawida said that as the choice seer speaks to the Indians that number as the blades of grass, and he would be heard by all at the same time, and as the Indians are gathered watching the fight, they notice from the south a black serpent coming from the sea, and he is described as dripping with salt water, and as he stands there, he rests for a spell to get his breath, all the time watching to the north to the land where the white serpent and the red serpent are fighting. Deganawida said that the battle between the white and the red serpents opened real slow but would then become so violent that the mountains would crack and the rivers would boil and the fish would turn up on their bellies. He said that there would be no leaves on the trees in that area. There would be no grass, and that strange bugs and beetles would crawl from the ground and attack both serpents, and he said that a great heat would cause the stench of death to sicken both serpents. And then, as the boy seer is watching this fight, the red serpent reaches around the back of the white serpent and pulls from him a hair which is carried toward the south by a great wind into the hands of the black serpent, and as the black serpent studies this hair, it suddenly turns into a woman, a white woman who tells him things that he knows to be true but he wants to hear them again. When this white woman finishes telling him these things, he takes her and gently places her on a rock with great love and respect, and then he becomes infuriated at what he has heard, so he makes a beeline for the north, and he enters the battle between the red and white serpents with such speed and anger that he defeats the two serpents, who have already been battle-weary. When he finishes, he stands on the chest of the white serpent, and he boasts and puts his chest out like he's the conqueror, and he looks for another serpent to conquer. He looks to the land of the hilly country and then he sees the Indian standing with his arms folded and looking ever so nobly that he knows that this Indian is not the one that he should fight. The next direction that he will face will be eastward and at that time he will be momentarily blinded by a light that is many times brighter than the sun. The light will be coming from the east to the west over the water, and when the black serpent regains his sight, he becomes terrified and makes a beeline for the sea. He dips into the sea and swims away in a southerly direction, and shall never again be seen by the Indians. The white serpent revives, and he, too, sees this light, and he makes a feeble attempt to gather himself and go toward that light. A portion of the white serpent refuses to remain but instead makes its way toward the land of the hilly country, and there he will join the Indian people with a great love like that of a lost brother. The rest of the white serpent would go to the sea and dip into the sea and would be lost out of sight for a spell. Then suddenly the white serpent would appear again on the top of the water and he would be slowly swimming toward the light. Deganawida said that the white serpent would never again be a troublesome spot for the Indian people. The red serpent would revive and he would shiver with great fear when he sees that light. He would crawl to the north and leave a bloody shaky trail northward, and he would never be seen again by the Indians. Deganawida said as this light approaches that he would be that light, and he would return to his Indian people, and when he returns, the Indian people would be a greater nation than they ever were before.

Mildred Garlow, the head clan mother of the Seneca Nation, who lives on the Tuscarora reservation, first told Mad Bear this prophecy. It foretold that the Indian would someday be back again on his feet and his nation would be revived by a miracle. The people of the Longhouse would be strong again. Wherever the Iroquois people were, the prophecy had been told; it had remained in the Longhouse many years but had not been understood. But Mildred Garlow had had a dream that the people were right. Jesse Cornplanter knew the legend but regarded it as a fairy tale. See Morgan on Gaiwiio—he mentions it; and there is also an allusion to it in Arthur Parker's *Myths and Folktales*. But it has never been brought out because the Longhouse felt it ought not to be published—it had simply been kicked around for years. Corbett Sundown had heard of the prophecy as a little boy. Aline Frost, the sister of Jonas Green, had told him part of the prophecy: the white serpent would come down and choke the Indian people and another serpent would come to attack the white serpent and release the Indian. They had always been told that the confederacy would be strong again. The Son of God had promised these things to the Indian people. Then at Onondaga, George Thomas, Sr., had told him the prophecy in detail, except for the red serpent's leaving a bloody trail northward—and the land of the hilly country he called the rocky land. His version was almost the same as a Grand River version, which he had heard, I gathered, from Howard Sky and Joe Logan. Alec General had heard of the prophecy but did not know it in detail. (Some

thought that the light across the water was the white
man's god.) At Deseronto he had heard the same story
at St. Regis the same story in detail.

The white serpent is the white race; the red serpent
Soviet Russia; the black serpent the Negro race. The
white hair that flies through the air is Eleanor Roosevelt
who spoke to the black serpent. When the news of the
Mau Mau rebellion[2] reached the shores of this country
the black serpent was infuriated into making a stand for
himself, and Eleanor Roosevelt was exalted like a god by
the colored people.

Chronology: The prophecy covers a period of five years.
The red serpent appeared among us when the immigrant
from Hungary came, following the Hungarian revolt
bringing Communism among us. The battle between the
red and the white serpents is thus now in its third year.
The colored people will fight the whites this coming fall.
It will take the Indian people four years to gather in the
hilly country (they are not sure where it is). The Russians will bomb this country, and the United States, after
a great war, will come to an end in 1960. The Tuscarora
themselves will be bombed. But in 1960 a great light will
come back to the Indian people.

He said that the expectation of this savior was common
among the Indians generally.

The various explanations of Standing Arrow's having
been abandoned by his adherents: I had heard that they
had left him because, since he had paid a dollar for the
land offered him, they would now have to pay property
tax on it, and that taxation was a vital issue; but also that
the others were sure that Standing Arrow would take the
land all for himself. Mad Bear now told me that he had
heard that Standing Arrow had bought the land in his
own name, not in that of the Mohawk nation. He had

also been accused of calling himself Deganawida. He came to see them not long ago in Tuscarora but then disappeared—had probably gone back to Baltimore, where he has work with a paint company. He has parked his wife and children with his mother-in-law in Syracuse.

Story of Indians who were lured to Ohio (?), then poisoned with blankets infected with germs. I asked Fenton about this and he told me it was true that Lord Jeffrey Amherst[3] had suggested that the Indians might be got rid of by infecting their blankets with smallpox.

At the Onondaga council from which I was expelled last year, the inauguration of the new Tadodáho, he said they had done nothing but quarrel. There had not been full representation, because there was no Cayuga there, and one of the Oneidas had come "intoxicated"—which Mad Bear thought a disgrace.

An Indian can't get a loan under the G.I. Bill of Rights because he lives on a reservation. Mad Bear had wanted one. He had been five years in the navy—all through the Pacific war: Saipan and Okinawa; had driven a truck in the Seventh Amphibious Fleet landing craft. Now spent every winter in the merchant marine, ninety days a year.

He thought that Ely Parker had had a Tuscarora mother. He had had a round face like Clinton Rickard,[4] before Rickard's face had caved in with age—and of course, as he did not say, like Mad Bear himself. The Tuscaroras, with no Longhouse and always kept a little subordinate, like evidently to think that this great man was one of them. The feeling of inferiority that the T.'s have always had may even be acting as a spur to incite Mad Bear to aim at a position of leadership. He tells me that since the T.'s have no Longhouse, he has never been properly given an Indian name. Mad Bear is simply what his grandmother—or his mother?—used to call him when he was headstrong and reckless as a boy. I felt, at Grand

River, when they were waiting for him at the Sunday games, and later, when he was summoned to St. Regis over the Mohawk income tax crisis, a suggestion of the atmosphere created by the presence or expectation of the great man.

There was, he told me, a movement at Grand River to get the White Dog back. It seems to be felt on the part of this faction that Handsome Lake diluted the old religion, that the White Dog was more efficacious. Nelson Mount Pleasant, an Onondaga living on the Tuscarora reservation, says that he has seen the ceremony at either the Onondago or the Cayuga Longhouse at Grand River. It was performed a little way from the Longhouse. They wrapped the dog in bright ribbons and put wampum around his neck. The officiating functionary had cleaned him and now caressed him, then slowly choked the life out of him, and he died "without even a kick or a flinch." The dog knew he was going to die and wanted to die. They burned him, and there came up a high wind blowing thirty or forty miles an hour, but the smoke was not affected. They dropped the tobacco into the fire and the smoke went straight up like a ray of light, and it never even shook when it hit the high wind above the trees. Mount Pleasant claims that the Indians watched the smoke until they couldn't see it anymore. He tried to leave the fire, and something was pushing him, and he couldn't see exactly what it was. The Indians prayed with tobacco, and they asked the Creator for something and it was granted to them. The smoke took the message directly to the Creator. Mad Bear asks me not to write about the sentiment for reviving the White Dog rite for fear it might get them into trouble. (Fenton says he has known old men who claimed to have seen the rite. One told him that the dog was choked by two men on either side pulling ropes.)

He says that Eleanor Roosevelt went to see Ernie Benedict[5] when he was in prison at Malone for resisting the draft. She asked him not to add to the President's troubles, talked with him an hour and a half. As a result, he consented to serve. Benedict had said nothing about this when I talked to him on the subject: he said that it was Pearl Harbor which had changed his mind.

He said that he had heard the story—told me by Nick Bailey—that the wearing by the Iroquois of war bonnets dated from their first sight of Pontiac,[6] but he did not believe this. He thought that it dated perhaps from the eighties. (Fenton thinks that it did not begin till the early years of this century, when they took part with the Sioux in Wild West shows and realized that they would have to have them in order to make an impression.)

While I was taking dictation from Mad Bear, Malcolm Sharp, in the other room, was talking law and law schools with Stanley Grossman. I said to Grossman that these cases over Indian property claims were confusing, and he replied, "That's the understatement of the evening. The lawyer who's defending the Indians in one of these cases can always be sure that his adversary is as much at sea as he is."

Grossman said that, besides the tentative overtures of the Communists, operating through a cell in Ottawa, somebody in Pennsylvania has been writing to Mad Bear and proposing that the Tuscaroras should infiltrate the labor unions and engage in acts of calculated violence. Grossman thinks that the writer of the letter is not a Communist but merely a crank.

We drank some more beer, and Mad Bear, seeing the checkerboard, asked me if I played checkers. We played a couple of games, in which he easily and slyly beat me. I thought of the sly under-eyelid look from his sharp bright and black eyes that he had given Dan Aaron—as

Dan was intent on the pipe—when Dan was about to smoke the peace pipe that Mad Bear had made of an ancient unearthed pipe bowl by fitting to it the conventional long stem. I had heard that Indian tobacco was supposed to be terrifically strong, and Mad Bear had said, with his mischievous glance, "There's a lot of marijuana in this." Yesterday they asked me how Dan had enjoyed our expedition, and Mad Bear had said, "He's game. He wasn't afraid to smoke that pipe"—in which there was actually no marijuana.

Sept. 1, Labor Day. Albert Grubel, on the way to Boonville, as usual commented on the traffic accidents, as he had read about them in the paper: "Twenty-six people killed, and others drownded and other things."

Sept. 1.[7] After a stormy evening and rainy day, the gray clouds moving toward the east. Wonderful day of work, writing down Mad Bear and Grossman's visit, and long relaxed morning's sleep, ending in bad dream about Elena and front room at Wellfleet.

6:45. Receding storm clouds beautiful, deep darkish blue, with a whitening low row of cloud; foreground of country green with yellow strip, brightly lighted, and even Carrie Trennam's gray unpainted barn with a bright slice of light across its top. The big trees that give the country its unsuppressible strength. The bushes in front of the house have now grown high enough again partly to screen us from the street—but no vines. While I was writing this, the bright light faded. Now the whole landscape is duller, but the top edge of the white cloud-ridge is lighter. —I still rather write in a vein of old-fashioned landscape writing. The aviators already see different cloud-landscapes, we may lose this view of things altogether. I have now become incapable of writing poetry based on this—though the country here still thrills and uplifts me—later also the thick gray was thinned out, leaving a tender light color drifting away to the east. Close relation of people to the weather here—not romantic, but romanticism derives from this relatively primitive relation of people to country they live in. Nobler country here, nobler people—part of the whole moral foundation of my life.

Beverly talks about people being "real common," meaning that they are not pompous but friendly. She said this about Fenton and Grossman; the latter several times walked into the kitchen and asked her how old the house was, how it felt to work for an author, etc.

Reuel arrived in Talcottville Sept. 12 and drove me back to Wellfleet the 16th. I found Susan Wilson here. We talked the segregation crisis, and I told her that, in studying the Civil War, I had come to understand better the Southern point of view. I found her, as usual, somewhat divided between the attitudes of the North and the South. She supported Byrd's "massive resistance,"[8] yet when I talked to her about the delusion of the North that God was behind them and meant them to win, I discovered that she believed this. Some Southerners, after the war, of course, came to share this view; but I think that in Susan's case our Grandmother Wilson was prompting her.

Oct. 16–22. New York State trip to see Penberthy[9] in Utica, go to the Little Water Ceremony at Tonawanda, and close up Talcottville. Fenton had had it from the master of the Tonawanda ceremonies, Corbett Sundown, that the Little Water Ceremony was to be on the 18th. I called up Nick Bailey, and he said he would take me in his car, and if they didn't want me inside, we sit in the car and hear it from the window. On the morning of the 18th at Talcottville, I got a wire from him saying that it had taken place the Saturday before. Same story as at Allegany, where Ed Coury told me the same thing. I imagine that they are giving me the runaround—also Fenton, who has been trying to get them to let him wire-record the Handsome Lake code. We went to Onondaga, however, where I talked to Davis Grieg and Henry Rockwell, the ninety-year-old Oneida, who had come on to visit his son. He claims to have a one-man reservation. All the other Indians had been driven off when a mortgage was foreclosed; but Rockwell (the son of a white man of a family that is well known locally—there is a Rockwell Street in Syracuse) went to law about it—Indian lands are not supposed to be "encumbered"—and succeeded in getting reinstated. Very vigorous for his age, talks with emphasis and will go on any length of time. He repeatedly failed to approve the recent document in which the Six Nations had tried to draw up their claims, and they had finally put in a younger Oneida. I could see, from his ignorance of situations in the more distant reservations, that he was out of touch with the present movement. The bitter and declamatory old-fashioned Indian attitude—always putting rhetorical questions—alternated with humor and charm. Educated at the Negro college, Hampton Institute. His story about coming back to New York from Hampton and being asked to tell his experiences by a woman schoolteacher who had invited people in to hear him. He made up a story, told them that at first they had thought he was a savage, that he had climbed up a tree and refused to come down. Then they had made him sit in a chair and had pulled three Iroquois feathers out of the back of his neck. They had asked to see the scars. He thought that this was a great joke, that people who were supposed to be educated should behave in this way. He makes out a very good case for the hypocrisy of the whites in calling the Indians barbarians. "Do Indians put on shows like television? —'You leave town in twenty-four hours!' Stick a revolver at somebody: Bang bang! Do Indian boys kill their fathers and mothers?"

On the way back, we stopped off to see Constance Robertson. The more I see of the Community people, the more I realize how special Constance must be, continually embarrassed by the reputation of the Community for loose living. She is likely to explain to people who do not know anything about it that they were under the strictest kind of discipline—"my grandfather would have probably thrown me out on my ear." They are dignified, straight-bodied, well educated, intelligent, but a little at an angle to the rest of the world, and rather inbred among themselves. She says that they are given to "ancestor worship." I see that it is another case of the upstate New York thing—the anachronism that is solvent, that is going strong, that is beautifully kept up, like the Mansion House and Walter Edmonds's place, and that is yet a kind of dream from the spell of which one does not want to escape. We talked about this. She said that Walter had still not got over his writing block. I said that I thought he lived in a boyhood fantasy of New York State, that his books had all been written out of it, that he had become too old for it now but hadn't been able to find out what else to do. She said that she was making a desperate attempt to get away from historical novels—she has done one about the Community—and write about modern life. Her publishers wouldn't like it, because they expected her to go on producing reliable historical fiction. I told her about my own feeling for the country, that I couldn't see it objectively, from an outsider's point of view. She said that she couldn't see Oneida objectively—and ended, "All right, then: we're a lot of Brontës!" I get to like her more and more. When other people are around, she stiffens somewhat on account of Community consciousness, the official explainer and guide, but when I drive with her alone in her car, she always loosens up and laughs and becomes amusing.

So cold in the Stone House that we spent a night with the Loomises. Jannett Talcott's old album, with Sophronia's verses. The next night it was warmer, so I went back to the house, but Rosalind stayed with the Loomises. We took them out for dinner at the place we had discovered at the Constableville crossroads, when we came back late from the trip and found all the other restaurants closed. They were all excited, had heard about it but had never been inside—"a place where girls meet men illicitly." It was disappointingly quiet because we had come so early. Little boy who played accordion, reading the music on the piano—so loud it made conversation difficult—I finally gave him a dollar and asked him to stop. Huldah drank two vodkas—she had never had any before. I warned her about them, but she held them very well, slightly piqued at my apprehensions. She wouldn't let Gertrude have one, made her stick to her usual daiquiri. There seem to be signs that Gertrude is going the way of Florence, gets names mixed up, etc. A depressing prospect for Huldah, whose morale has evidently been somewhat shaken.

> To Jannett—
>> Sister, I know you will little expect
>> From one whom the muses and science neglect;
>> But wishing and praying in your best behalf,
>> I leave in your Album my own autograph—
>>> Leyden, May 8th, 1833, Sophronie B. Talcott

Talcottville: Brown, gold and green
 The rose and smoky West
 Diminished to a blade of gray

 The cold house with its (dead and) dying bees,
 Who hoped to find some warmth within—

 Those insects don't know—cold crickets—
 that there's a family living here, who call themselves Talcott, Baker, Wilson.

NOTES

1. The prophecy also appears in *AI*, pp. 163–68, in almost the same form as here. "I took it down as he told it and give it here in his own words" (p. 163). Deganawida was an Iroquois prophet and statesman who helped found the Six Nations.
2. A violent uprising against British colonialism in Kenya resulting in a state of emergency from 1952 to 1959.
3. Lord Jeffrey Amherst (1717–97), British commander-in-chief in North America (1758–63).
4. A Tuscarora chief, co-founder of the Indian Defense League.
5. Ernest Benedict had been active in Mohawk resistance to certain New Deal Indian reforms.
6. Pontiac (1720?–69), Ottawa chief, leader of the 1763 uprising against the British.
7. *Upstate*, pp. 189–94.
8. Harry Flood Byrd (1887–1966), senator from Virginia (1933–65). He supported Virginia's radical segregationists in their strategy of "massive resistance" to court-ordered integration.
9. Francis Penberthy, EW's lawyer.

1/20/11

WELLFLEET

I am always resisting the mechanical age, sticking to old ways of living, liking things made by hand; yet I cannot help, in reading about early travel by foot and by horse-drawn vehicles, about manuscripts sent to the printer, about the cavalry battles of the Civil War, involuntarily wondering, "Did they really do it like that? How crude! How could such fine results have been achieved without modern methods?"

Night of Nov. 11–12, 1958. In the evening, I made love to Elena on the blue divan in the middle room— delicious and wonderful. I find that it takes longer nowadays from the moment my orgasm is launched to the moment the emission begins. We loved each other afterwards.

Feeling peaceful and satisfied, I went to bed, finished Mosby's memoirs,[1] reread a good deal of Graham Greene's *The Lost Childhood* [1951], and went to sleep without a sleeping pill. Just before I woke up in the morning, I was having one of my typical anxiety dreams. I was supposed to lecture at some college, but didn't have time to get the lecture ready. I wrote down the first part, then

wanted a quotation from "Chatham"—some quatrain he
had used in a speech. It was old-fashioned ringing verse,
and I thought I could recite it effectively. First I went
back to my hotel—these hotels and their elevators have
become a regular feature of these dreams. I couldn't
remember the number of my room nor even whether it
was in the main building or the annex, which had different elevators—I didn't find it. Then, realizing my time
was short, decided to look for the book I wanted in a
bookcase in one of the hotel sitting rooms—on one of
the upper floors, however, so that it had to be reached
by elevator—in which I thought I had seen it; but when
I got there, I couldn't find it and was told that the books
had been moved. There was no time to look further, so
I went back to the college building, trying to remember
the quatrain. There was, I found, a moderate-sized library just beside the room in which I was supposed to
lecture. The librarians were a dreary and dingy young
man and a typical elderly librarian spinster. The young
man was not at all helpful, couldn't find the works of
"Chatham." I said that the poem had appeared in the
Anti-Jacobin Review, which he said that they did not
have, seeming to doubt that any such thing existed. He
made a couple of grumbling disagreeable remarks to the
effect that if I had consulted the catalog "according to
the rules," I should have been able to look for the books
myself. Then, since I was keeping the audience waiting,
I was escorted into the lecture room—with my lecture
only partly written out and not even the notes completed
—where about thirty people were scattered, with gaps,
among the back rows of seats. I had been looking at the
title of the lecture, which had been supplied me by
whatever professor had invited me and which struck me
as a typical absurdity of the academic mind when it tries
to think up a general subject. All I can remember now

is that it contained the word Guilt (no doubt derived from Graham Greene). At the point of mounting the platform I woke, but in my partly wakened imagination the fantasy of the dream continued and changed its character from anxious to comic, so that I was presently laughing hysterically. (The lecture in Amis's *Lucky Jim* was evidently the influence here.) I began by pointing out the absurdity of the title; then explained that I had not been able to find the quotation, reciting a vague version of it with the blanks filled in with "something," "something or other." I told them about the librarian who had not been "particularly cooperative," but said that I could quite understand his bad humor, since he had to live among all those greasy and shabby and partly dilapidated books that make up a college library. I said that I had not been able to finish writing out my lecture, but read them a few sentences at the beginning, saying in a more or less disparaging way, "That's the kind of thing I would have given you." I then produced three arrows, tied together with string at the ends of the shafts, and explained that, failing a lecture, I would show them how to throw these. "It is like darts," I said, "but requires extreme skill." I threw them against the back wall, and they fell to the ground. "The target," I said, "must be less resistant." I switched to something else. "Since I have forgotten the verses I meant to recite, I will recite to you the only poem that I know by heart: 'The Ride of Paul Revere' "[2]—and I told them about reciting it, in my childhood, in the basement of the hotel at Atlantic City in which I was staying with my mother, in an entertainment that other children and I got up. These children were from Philadelphia and (this whole incident really took place) when they discovered that I came from Red Bank, they went and whispered to their mothers, and I heard one of them say, "He may be a

very nice little boy even if he doesn't come from Philadelphia." I now told them that I had come to see that
this poem was not usually recited as it should be:

> On the eighteenth of April, in Seventy-five;
> Hardly a man is now alive
> Who remembers that famous day and year.

It is obvious that the speaker is very old, and that his
senility should be brought out in the rendering. I took
out my handkerchief and hung the ends over my ears in
such a way as to give myself a beard; then I began to
recite the poem in a quavering yet still vigorous voice in
the manner of Lionel Barrymore in his last years. By
this time I had many of them laughing and I wanted to
have them in stitches. At the end of the next stanza:

> And I on the opposite shore will be,
> Ready to ride and spread the alarm
> Through every Middlesex village and farm . . .

I stopped and explained that in my childhood, having
learned the poem by rote (this was also true), I had
imagined that there was here an enumeration of three
things, that it read "Through every Middlesex, village,
and farm"—I had never understood what a Middlesex
was. "Little did Boston know," I added, "that the tutorial
system was coming at Harvard!" (Reuel had been complaining about pansy tutors.) My delivery now became
more ringing as the old man was caught up by the spirit
of the tale. When I came to the lamp in the old North
Church, I snatched my handkerchief off and waved it
like a signal. Just before this, however, I had said, "I
shall skip a few stanzas here. Not that I think the poem
is too long, but personally I am rather tired of it." —At

some point before this, the professor who was presiding —who rather resembled the photographs of J. B. S. Haldane[3]—thinking I was out of my head or drunk, came up to the platform to turn me off. "Back, Bruce!" I ordered him. "Down, Bruce!" "My grandparents," I said to the audience, "had a big black shaggy dog named Bruce" (also true). —Having done with my recitation of "Paul Revere," I made the handkerchief disappear by the method I use after the mouse trick, produced a pack of cards from my pocket and went on to the "Fastest Card Trick," summoning a girl in the audience to come down to a nearer row, though warning her, "But not so close as to be in danger of getting spattered by my saliva" (some of my teeth have come out, and I have lately been afraid of this). I gave them the routine with the patter written in at the back of the pamphlet, "I wouldn't let a knight go out on a day like this!" By this time, I had waked up sufficiently so that I had begun to consciously invent rather than experience the thing imaginatively. The conclusion was that the presiding professor came up on the platform smiling—since I had ended by captivating the audience—and my saying to him, "I hope I didn't offend you by saying you looked like a shaggy dog, but"—to the audience—"he does, doesn't he?" "Since I haven't given you the lecture you wanted," I said to the shaggy professor, "I don't want any fee for this." "I have the check right here," he said, producing it from his pocket. "Thank you," I said, taking it. I pocketed it and walked off the platform.

After breakfast, feeling calm and cheerful, I sat, with my feet up, reading *The Bull of Minos*,[4] which took me back to Greece and enchanted me. I became sleepy again and went to lie down. I must have been aware during my nap of Elena's starting off in the car to take Mrs. Daley back, because I had one of those recurrent and tiresome dreams in which I imagined that she was abandoning me. I was back—as so often—in the old house at Red Bank, lying in bed upstairs, and I realized that Elena and Helen and Button were getting into a small carriage and about to drive away. I came down the stairs in a hurry and asked Elena where they were going. She and Helen and Jenny were sitting against the side of the house. Elena and Jenny laughed, they had some joke between them. I confronted them, looking angry and brutal—then woke up.

The rest of the day was delightfully relaxed. I made little attempt to do anything but go on reading *The Bull of Minos*. Barbara and Mary came over before dinner and we played a game of Great Painters with Helen, then had dinner at the Orleans Inn, talking about travel in Greece, then came back and played Chinese checkers and made the shapes of the Anchor Puzzle, a red sandstone set which Mary had found, after her mother's death, among the family's things in Washington. There was a mother-of-pearl one in Red Bank that had belonged to my Wilson grandparents—I haven't been able to find it here—and Elena said that she, as a child, had had one, too, but had never been able to see the point of it. Quite an old-fashioned family evening. But the fact that I was worried by my lapsing potency was shown by the dreams described above. I thought about Frank Crowninshield's story[5]—which he told me at lunch at the Coffee House, the last time, I think, I ever saw him. A man says to his doctor, "I can't do it twice anymore." "The thing to do," advises the doctor, "is just to take a nap after the first time. You'll find that that will refresh you." The man tries to follow this advice. When he wakes up, his girl has gone, and he finds that it is almost noon. He calls up his secretary at the office and says that he has overslept—calls up the people he had appointments with and apologizes. "It's all right about this morning," she tells him. "You didn't have any appointments. But where were you yesterday?"

Nov. 16, '58. One of my bicycling dreams—on a trip in which western New York (probably on the basis of my dislike of Syracuse) became confused with memories of Detroit—which later became a dream of writing: I was composing a built-up enumeration. The words came, and as the phrases went by I tried to have them make sense but failed. The only item I was able to hang on to, since it came at the moment of waking, was "a maddening want of mad (sic) that restraint should collide with partition."

Dec. 4, at the end of nap in chair:

In pigs once the unfortunate offer of furs unfurled.
In pigs once the unfortunate offer of furs unfurled
    (puns unpurled).
In pigs once the unlucky offer of furs occurred.
In funs once the impertinent (impermanent) proffer of
    puns (perns) appearled.
In plume once the impermanent passion of pearls im-
    pugned.

Jan. 19, waking up in morning:

Kit entourage, my dear, and sibling hisn't fair.

Miss Freeman and bloodhound: Young bloodhound bitch of Miss Freeman's occasionally comes to see us. She came into the middle room and rather intimidated Elena, who called Miss Freeman. When Miss F. arrived, she reproached the dog and rubbed noses with her, as was apparently her custom. The dog's name was Siglinda, and Miss F. called her Siggy. Elena says she rides around with one bloodhound beside her and the other in the back seat.

Visit to Cambridge—in March, I think. I went to arrange about Harvard job and was put up at Lowell House by Elliott Perkins. I asked him whether he had contributed years ago to the Humanist Symposium, befoggedly confusing him with a man whose last name was Elliott, spelled in that way. He replied that he didn't know of any other Boston Perkins of whom that could have been true, and I soon realized that he was a professional Bostonian, who put on for me such a complete Boston act that I thought he must not be quite genuine or not quite well in the top drawer. He always talked about "a fellow"—which, with the accent and the brusqueness and gruffness, is a distinguishing mark of the old-fashioned Bostonian. His wife (an Englishwoman, I'm told) was not there, and I found that we were sitting, though side by side in two chairs that diverged at an angle, so that, instead of talking face to face, we were facing somewhat away from one another. When he saw I was ready for another drink, he put the whisky bottle on the floor and shoved it in the direction of my chair; then, after a moment, the bowl of ice. He talked good sense in deploring the lecturers who came from outside and merely chatted to the students; if you were hot about something, you could put it over. I said something about professors who insulted the students (thinking of Kelly Prentice at Princeton and Brooks's stories of Barrett Wendell), and he said that the most serious way in which the professor could insult the students was by not giving them something worthwhile. He said presently, consulting his watch, "I'll have to hurl you into outer darkness. I have to meet a group of freshmen." I had been discussing with him the question of how much I ought to give my students to read, and, as I left, he said, "I'll send you my reading list, which will show you how one fellow has handled this problem."

I was telling Charley Walker about this, and he came up with two wonderful Bostonian anecdotes. Reese Alsop, when a student at Yale, once went to a Boston Cotillion. The young men, approaching in line, were received by a hostess as follows: "Mr. So-and-So, you're in college? (Yes.) Harvard? (Yes.)" When it came Reese's turn, he had to say, "Yale." A pause: "How exciting!" When Charley was living in New York, he had entertained a Boston friend. When the friend had seen the big electric signs, he had said, "This must be Broadway." When they had come to the Times Building, with the headlines running around it in electric letters, he said, "This must be Times Square." Charley said, after a moment's thought, "You must have been in New York before." He answered, after a silence, "I suppose I have." Charley said that when he had worked on *The Atlantic Monthly*, he found that he was being groomed for a regular position in Boston. But when he began to feel that Boston was closing in on him—having come from New Hampshire and graduated from Yale—he pulled himself together and left—wrote his not very good labor novel. —This reminds me of Frank Crowninshield's story of going back to Boston and having lunch at some place like the Somerset Club. After using the urinal, he asked where to wash his hands, and received the scornful reply: "Oh, you New York dudes."

Robert and Elizabeth Lowell had been telling us, when we saw them last, about Allen Tate's attitude toward Boston since he had become engaged to Isabella Gardner. He would wink at Elizabeth and say, "These

people have no manners—you know what I mean!" and
she would say, "Yes, I know what you mean." To
Robert, he would say things like "Ten generations of
commercial activity!"

NOTES

1. John Singleton Mosby (1833–1916), Confederate cavalry
leader known for his exploits as a ranger. *Patriotic Gore*, pp.
307–29. *Mosby's War Reminiscences and Stuart's Cavalry Campaigns* (1887).

2. The poem is actually called "Paul Revere's Ride" and is
included in H. W. Longfellow's *Tales of a Wayside Inn* (1863).
See *A Prelude*, p. 45.

3. J. B. S. Haldane (1892–1964), British geneticist, pioneer
in population genetics and evolution. He became a Marxist in
1930.

4. Leonard Cottrell's account of the discoveries of Schliemann
and Evans (1953).

5. EW had worked under Crowninshield at *Vanity Fair*. *The
Twenties*, pp. 32–44.

TORONTO

Trip to New York State and Canada;[1] *April 12–18.*
Trip from Boston to Utica: Black trunks and purplish
bushes, with the gray-blue flowing streams, dashed with
the small white rapids—patches of straight pines. —Desolate Boston-and-Albany brick building. —Under the
influence of the whiskies I had drunk in the South
Station, I was deeply and rather unhealthily moved by
the landscape along the Mohawk and wrote down ecstatic
notes which I now can't decipher. Made two excursions
to the lounge, where, contrary to my usual custom, I
spent almost the whole journey talking to people there:
A rather nice Swede from Chicago who worked for the
Pullman Company—they now have to make something;
a working-class fellow who was—I got the impression—
going somewhere to break a strike. "I'm going to be
working for you," he said to me. He evidently thought
I was a capitalist, said later, "You're worth a couple of
million!" He went to sleep on his beer and dropped out
of the interchange. There was finally a general conversation about the next election. A pale and plain woman
who, I thought, came from Boston was evidently bursting

with a rancor against the Catholics which she didn't dare express, and when I said that I should vote for Kennedy, if he ran, she could do nothing but give me terrible incredulous looks. The Swede said that people oughtn't to make any distinctions of creed, nationality, or color.

Ella Worthington: When I arrived in the Royal York railroad hotel in Toronto, I noticed, as I was checking in, a good-looking woman in the lobby, rather smartly dressed in gray, and, remembering the Stratford festivals, said to myself that it was true that there *were* some handsome women in Canada, turned out in a dignified way. I was glad to see her turn in my direction so that I was able to get a better look at her, and she immediately presented herself as the lady with whom I had been in communication and who had engaged for me the rooms at the Royal York. She had left a letter for me, which she now handed me, but had apparently been unable not to linger. The letter said she was "gorgeously thrilled" that I should have thought it worthwhile to come up there. I told her that I had just been admiring her and took account of her well-done graying hair and chic little gray hairband across her head. In spite of the marvelous compliments with which, in the course of my stay, she buttered me up from time to time, she had never, so far as I could see, read a word that I had written and had only heard dimly about *Hecate County* and the *Dead Sea Scrolls*. Later on, when I mentioned being sixty-three—she caught me up: "I know how old you are—I looked you up on the library slip," and told me she was fifty-three. She at once produced a reporter and photographer from the Toronto *Star* and had a flashlight taken of me in the lobby. After that, we went into the lunchroom, where I talked to the *Star* people about the Iroquois. At one point, when I said something

about their claim to be a sovereign nation, she poked my
foot under the table—explaining afterwards that, in the
handling of the case,[2] by their attorney Malcolm Montgomery and herself—she was helping him out by looking things up—they had decided not to argue for
sovereignty. She apologized for kicking me, as she afterwards did for contradicting me: "That I should contra-
dict you!" etc. Since I had told her that I wanted to see
Morley Callaghan, she had called him up and arranged
it—though she did not know him at all—and we went
round there, she protesting that if I would let her come
she would be perfectly quiet, she just wanted to listen
to us. She was soon, however, intervening—the first
time, she checked herself: "Oh, I'm supposed not to
talk!" and maintained a slightly sullen silence while
Morley and I talked about Hemingway and Scott Fitzgerald, about whom she did not seem to know anything
but then sailed in and talked incessantly, opinionatedly
arguing with Morley about Canadian economics and
politics. She advocated a return to the classical econo-
mists—something which Morley evidently recognized as
representing some current line. They were soon at it
hammer and tongs—he calling her "darling." I was
presently calling her "darling," too. The phrase for her
that eventually came into my head was "a big operator
with the soul of a child." After the death of her second
husband, she had studied political science at Columbia
and taken a master's degree.

The next morning, as we were driving out to Brantford—though I tried to get some information about the
Six Nations Reserve situation—she talked about herself
most of the way; would from time to time break off and
say, "But why should we talk about me? Let's talk about
you"; then return to the subject again. She had been
born on Lake Champlain but had spent most of her

life in Canada. Her father and mother were both Baptist preachers. She had married a Canadian who taught Institutional Management—that was why so many of the employees knew her in the Royal York—they were old students of her husband's—she hoped they had given me a good room as she had told them to. But she had started up a business of her own on Manitoulin Island in Lake Huron, had built a summer resort which had become a considerable success—Franklin Roosevelt used to come there. Hadn't let her husband know how profitable it was—because with a British man it undermined their self-confidence if his wife was doing too well for herself. She spent the money on schools for the children and clothes. There were 7,000 Ojibways on Manitoulin, and apparently her idea about them was that she had dominated them and had them eating out of her hand. She had adopted two boys, and both had been killed in the war. One Indian who was working for her had brought to live with him the wife of someone else who was away, and she had had a showdown with him. "I showed him who was boss!" was a favorite phrase of hers. One night when she was alone, a big black Indian —he was partly Negro—had come out of the woods. He had asked if Tony was there. —No. —I wanted to see him about a job. —I do the hiring here. —Are you all alone? —Yes. —Aren't you afraid? —No. —She gave him some tea, and he faded away in the woods. —When her husband died, she married a surgeon, whom she first described as thirty-five years older, then, later, as thirty years older, than she. (She had lost, she said, two husbands in, I think, four years.) "You're a good deal older than I am," she had said when he asked her to marry him. —I'm a good deal older than you—we'll let it go at that. —But he had given her a date for his birth which, after his death, she found out to be false—she had, however, had it put on his tombstone. He had taken her out to Vancouver—that was a very rigid closed little society, to which her husband belonged. They would fly seventy miles to go to a cocktail party. He had wanted to show her off. But then she had gone on a whaling cruise: we got a whale—a male, seventy-one pounds, it was white. Later on some of the crew turned up, and she shocked the proper Vancouver set by letting them see how chummy she was with these rude men. When she came back from the cruise, she had stunk— you could smell me a mile off. Then her husband had died and had evidently left her some money—though she had never let him pay for her children. She had been so full of "grief" that she had gone to Europe and driven around by herself for two years, exploring out-of-the-way countries: Finland, Yugoslavia, East Germany. In the Communist-dominated countries, she had defied the police—"It did them good! I wasn't afraid of them—I'd just drive right through." Now she wanted to run for Parliament from the riding where Manitoulin was, and displace Lester Pearson.[3] Just before I left, when I was trying to sum up her project, I said, "And you count on the votes of those seven thousand Ojibways," and she leaned across the table and said emphatically, "I think I can get in without them!" —In the course of one of our drives, she told me that she belonged to a family who for sixteen generations (she always had the figures on everything, figures were one of the features of her conversation) had had six fingers and six toes—"poly-dactic," she called it. She showed me the scars where her superfluous fingers had been removed. In the case of one of her sons who had had this, she had had the superfluous fingers but not the toes taken off. She did not, however, think these superfluous, but rather a sign of superiority, and she had for this phenomenon both a mythological and a biological explanation. The mythological one was that some creature with six fingers had got at Eve in the Garden of Eden—I forget exactly how this went. The other explanation was that there had always been a biological tendency for six fingers to appear—there was especially a six-fingered salamander. Presumably some anthropoid or primitive man had developed six fingers and toes, which had given him a great advantage in climbing and general dexterity—so much so that his five-fingered fellows had ganged up on him and wiped out this breed. I think that actually her polydactylism was something that she had had to live down and that the necessity she was under to assert her superiority—in brains, ability, love—must partly have been due to this. She had turned a deformity into a boast. In spite of her aggressiveness, her egoism—she had something of Helen Augur, with more good looks and good sense—I was touched by her and, though annoyed by her, liked her.

At Brantford, she at once called up the local paper and wanted to have reporters and photographers in. I blew up about this, and she took the attitude that I was selfishly refusing to help her good cause. Having had to be somewhat brutal, I felt, when we went in to lunch at the Kirby, that I ought to do something to make it right, so I said—the dining room was quite dark and the tables lit only by lamps—that in that light she looked very pretty. "I don't care anymore," she answered, "whether people pay me compliments or not. If people didn't notice I was good-looking, I'd call their attention to it." I was tired with the ride after the evening with Callaghan and at one point during lunch covered my face with my hands. I at once felt a soft hand clasping my wrist. She was trying to feel my pulse. At times I would escape from her, and when she found me again,

she would say things like "Getting independent, eh?"
Both evenings in Brantford we went to the movies. The
first evening I asked what I could do to entertain her,
and she said, "Nothing except talk to me—you speak
in such exquisite prose," but I knew that she would
do all the talking, so I took her to a picture about
Houdini, which was preceded by one about Attila and
the Huns descending on Rome. I had never been to the
movies with anyone who took them as she did. She
never laughed at anything ridiculous or in bad taste, but
believed in everything that happened. She thought that
the fourth-rate old Hollywood hacks who played the
Roman ladies were "exquisite," and when thick red
paint was doing duty for blood, she couldn't bear to look.
She suffered as much from anxiety over Houdini's narrow escapes as his wife in the picture was supposed to do.
(I had told her that I thought she was an extravert, and
she had answered, "I'm very well integrated!") The next
night we went to a super-Western called *The Great
Valley*. When two of the characters were glaring at one
another, she said in dismay, "Oh, they're behaving like
men! Why do men have to behave that way?" In one
scene, after a terrific fistfight, the hero turned up the
next day with no signs of having been battered. I remarked on this, but Ella said, "I've been in lots of fights.
The hands go before the faces do." Later I tried to get
her to enlarge on this, and she told me about giving an
Indian a sock in the jaw—"It showed him who was boss."

I had to scheme to get away from her. "Getting independent, eh?" The first day of the hearings, an old lady
named Miss Doyle fastened [herself to me]. She had
once been a newspaper editor; she wrote books and was
a friend of the Indians. "They admit me to their coun-
cils." She was a frightful old bore, would maunder along
endlessly in her quiet genteel voice; and she was one of

those women, like Mary Vorse,[4] who make people do
everything for her. She would sit in the hotel lobby
waiting for us to drive her or take her to meals. I said
something to Ella about Miss Doyle's being a bore, and
she immediately came back with "Do you think I'm a
bore?" She explained that, on account of her political
ambitions, she had to be nicer to Miss Doyle. At a break
in the hearings, Miss Doyle began explaining to me that
she had both come over on the *Mayflower* and been one
of the original settlers of Canada. She later elaborated on
this when we were driving back to Toronto and gave us
to understand that most of the *Mayflower* people had very
soon gone to Canada. Ella, who had immediately claimed
Pilgrim ancestry, got rather tired of this and said suddenly, "I'm a descendant of Anne Boleyn. She had six
fingers." —While I was talking to a reporter in the
courtroom, a rather tense and feverish white woman
sitting behind me volunteered the information that the
Indians, when they went to school, were not allowed to
talk their own languages. During one of the intermissions, she spoke to me, told me she was English and had
come to Canada eighteen years before. She had married
an Indian and lived on the reservation, but now had
been compelled to leave on account of the row. Miss
Doyle, who seemed to feel that she had a monopoly on
talking, quietly got between us and asked to speak to me
a moment aside. She said, "I just want to warn you not
to believe what that woman says. She's a regular pest."

Ella on her love life: A Jewish advertizing man had
been "courting" her in New York. He had said, "If I
married you, I'd take your name. I could do anything
with a name like Worthington!" She had had a short
affair with a writer from Canada. He was married and
had been impotent, but Ella had got him going again
and had sent him back to his wife "healed." She had

said something about not wanting to live in the country alone, though she had a house somewhere, so I said later that she ought to find herself a husband. But this was not at all her idea. To live in the country with a *man!* would be worse than living alone. The solution for her was not to get married and not to live in the country. At dinner they brought the wine in a bucket filled with a new kind of non-cubic ice cubes. Ella at once produced a joke about them. One man says, "Have you seen the new ice cubes? It's a lump of ice with a hole in it." The other man replies, "I've been married to one for years." "You can see I've led a sheltered life," she added.

The last night, when I was taking the train, we had dinner at the Royal York. I asked her if she had ever drunk vodka: "Oh, yes. They brought me a Bloody Mary when they carried me out of that canyon in the Klondike. Do you know what the Klondike is?" She neither smokes nor drinks. I asked whether religion meant something to her. She said it did and asked whether I could guess her religion. I correctly guessed Christian Science. She said that it had done a lot for her, had given her self-assurance. Before, when she had been married to her second husband, she had been "vain and idle —yes, I was vain"—she had just been "a body," had just worn clothes, apparently for the admiration of her husband and his friends.

Mad Bear: The Mounted Police were supposed to have threatened to run Mad Bear out of Canada if he showed himself again; but he turned up the second day of the hearings. He was in full regalia but regalia of a kind that seemed to be of his own creation and that was bound to be embarrassing to us friends of the Indian. The few of the local Indians who were not wearing ordinary clothes were dressed in the conventional buckskin. But Mad Bear had a coronet of feathers and wore a masked-ball arrangement of yellow and blue that left a whole fat arm and shoulder bare. It unfortunately tended to confirm the rumor that he was homosexual. He waved to me beamingly in court, and at a recess, outside the courthouse, the newspaper photographers wanted to take us together, but I wouldn't let them. This seemed to hurt his feelings, but I explained to him that I had just testified in a purely historical way, and that, as an "American" (as they call us up there), I couldn't be plugging his movement in Canada. It would make us both "foreign agitators." I did, however, have lunch with him and two of his lieutenants. I presently realized that the only other people in the restaurant beside ourselves were the judge and someone he was lunching with. Mad Bear's two companions were an Onondaga, who spoke English fluently but with such an accent that he was difficult to understand, and a young Mohawk from St. Regis, who was perfectly white and showed Indian origins only in a trace of accent and a long nose that was somewhat hooked. This boy was evidently a fanatical nationalist, and reminded me of a young Israeli. They had just been to Utica, baiting Judge Brennan, and were going on for a big all-night condolence for the dead to be held at St. Regis. I mentioned the White Dog and said that I understood that this was no longer done. The Onondaga winked at Mad Bear, who explained that they were fattening up two dogs on the Six Nation Reserve. He spoke of this sacrifice as a "crucifixion."

1/23/u

NOTES

1. **EW** was visiting the Six Nations Reserve near Brantford, Ontario, the largest of the Iroquois reservations and the only one that includes groups from all the Six Nations.
2. Supporters of the Iroquois Confederacy had attempted to

make the Six Nations Reserve completely independent of Canada, paying no taxes and organizing their own police force. The Mounted Police had "raided" the reservation, and the issue was now in court. *AI*, pp. 252–69.

3. Lester Bowles Pearson (1897–1972), Canadian Prime Minister from 1963 to 1968, was then leader of the Liberal opposition in the House of Commons.

4. Mary Heaton Vorse, the veteran libertarian and trade union writer. *The Thirties, passim.*

WELLFLEET, NEW YORK, TALCOTTVILLE

Talcottville, April 19, 1959.[1] They had had the worst winter in forty-one years; snow on the ground since Thanksgiving, and even now I find part of a dirty drift still against the big kitchen window. The steps of the Stone House are covered with an unpleasant and unfamiliar crumbly mud that looks as if it had been digested by earthworms. And the whole country looks as if it had had the life smothered (crushed) out of it by the winter-long oppression of the snow—no color, no relief, everything neutral; the very grand old elms like gray broom straws. Carrie Trennam's house a blank, all the shades drawn—she is in the hospital. —House in good shape except the ceiling of my upstairs workroom, from which the paint, put on last September, was peeled in patches. The mice, as usual, have eaten the soap and left their little rice-grain turds all over the bathtub and the kitchen sink. —The people are like this, too. Beverly looks sallow and awful, has to work till ten tonight. I felt she was glad to see me, but didn't want to show it, much in fear of the boss. —House not so terribly cold and damp. —Even the Adirondacks seemed dim and flat. —George Munn, who brought me from Niagara Falls here, is worn down, pale, not robust—not a full face, but a, for him, sharp profile. —A few birds active.

On my way to New York, I reflected, looking out the train window at the *monotonous modern cities*, that it was fortunate one's moods, at least, change, so that taking such a trip as this was not always exactly the same.

Dinner with Wystan Auden: His hair now looks like a yellow wig, and he has become rather portly and old-man-of-the-world, like somebody in an 18th-century coffeehouse. I said, when we had left the dining room and were sitting around in the room, something about [the Marquis de] Sade in connection with Gorer[2] (whom Wystan seems to be unique, among the people I know, in liking), and he suddenly began telling us that he was no good at flagellation: "When they say, 'Stop, stop!' I always stop, when what they really want is to have you go on. And I don't like to say abusive things unless I'm angry." He said that it was significant that in one of Sade's books, when some *partouze* is being arranged, that the parties are forbidden to laugh. To laugh would make the whole thing impossible.

Elena at the Algonquin: I so seldom see Elena get dressed and undressed in Wellfleet that I enjoyed lying and watching her in our room at the Algonquin. She has a splendid and still very firm body. On account of her trouble with the veins in her legs, she lies a few minutes every morning with her legs up and her feet against the wall. This shows off her beautiful legs and always arouses me. I kiss her first between them, then fuck her in that position. I go straight in without impediment, and this excites me very much.

Elena at Wellfleet: Back at Wellfleet, there is quarreling about Talcottville and about going to Cambridge for the winter. One morning she told me she hated me, I was "a scorpion that wants to destroy."

Beginning of May '59. We have discovered Lieutenant's Island, first time we were ever there. A handful of little houses, with nobody in them yet and nobody for miles around. A wonderful high cliff that looks over the bay. The tide was out, the first time we went, and there were lovely effects of silvery blue, with the faraway mewing of gulls. It reminded me of my days with Margaret at Peaked Hill bar. We made love near the edge of the cliff, moving back so we shouldn't fall over. It was marvelous. Her blue clothes and white body made a harmony with the seascape. Afterwards I was thankful that love was lasting for me so long and remaining so satisfying—that I still had a woman I enjoyed so much.

This was followed by more scenes about Talcottville and Cambridge. I am never able to make any plans with her, because she is always so evasive and puts everything off. If there is anything looming which will discommode her, she seems to think if she waits, it will go away. So she leaves me in uncertainty till the last moment, when she acts, as it were, under protest and then complains, as long as we are away from Wellfleet, of the place or the accommodations. She finally went to the Chavchavadzes and complained about my drinking, so I called up Nina from town and got her to meet me at the café by the bayside shore. She told me, as she had before, that Elena had usually been dissatisfied with wherever she was— except Wellfleet, where, for the first time in her life, she had been able to make herself a home—Canada, Binghamton, apartments in New York. Nina, when she visited Binghamton, had said that it was a most attractive little town, and Elena had said, "Oh, how can you say that!" Nina offered to come to Talcottville. She told me that it was true that nowadays I didn't hold my liquor so well as I used to do; was likely to become quite stupefied. Our conversations with Nina relieved the strain. We made love and parted on affectionate terms.

Trip to Talcottville, May '59. I drove down to Boston (Friday, May 22) with Mr. Shahani from Pakistan and England and had lunch with him and Reuel at St. Clair's. Max Hayward joined us later and we went over for a few minutes to the table where Arthur Schlesinger was having lunch with a good-looking blond girl. Rosalind and I got to Cummington successfully enough (last fall we found we were headed for Canada) and spent the night with Helen Muchnic and Dorothy Walsh; next night the Linscotts and their beavers; next day (Sunday) lunch with Bill Fenton in Albany. He says that Ella Worthington, from my description of her, was typical of a certain kind of Toronto women: their husbands, who still have something of the pioneering spirit, are away a good deal of the time, and they—very aggressive and energetic—go in heavily for causes or social activities. The anthropologist's point of view.

We arrived here Sunday night in time to have dinner in Constableville. Afterwards a call on the Loomises. I had asked Rosalind if she would like to see the L.'s, and she said, "Do you hear the castanets clicking and see the flash of the shawls?"

Carrie Trennam is back from the nursing home. The store has made some improvements. George and Lou, it seems, are at last to have a house of their own, somewhere near Oneida Lake. The countryside has all come to life since April, though everything has been very late:

lilacs and lilies of the valley were only just beginning when I first arrived. A little light brown bird has built her nest in the grass just at the edge of the garden and pops up whenever I go near it—five little brown speckled eggs. The orioles I have not seen, but Mrs. Crofoot says she has a pair at her house, probably the same ones. For once a good spell of weather when I come in the spring —delightful the last few days—the bright green land- scape from the front door, with the yellow streak of mustard in the middle.

Rosalind left on Monday. We had a very jolly trip. She seems quite self-confident and cheerful. The money from her grandmother and the red-lined dreamboat of a car she has bought with it have, I think, done her a lot of good. She speaks of "irons in the fire," which she has to be in Boston to attend to, but she does not tell me what they are. I seem only to get at all close to her and Reuel when they drive me around like this.

Bob Linscott's beavers: He ordered a pair from the state, and they sent someone to interview him and his wife to make sure they were responsible people—as if they were adopting a baby. There are a staff of some twenty people in Massachusetts in charge of beaver con- trol—they bring them and, on request, they take them away. Bob had had several removed. Their operations there were most impressive. The original pair had built a huge dam which caused the little woodland stream to produce a large pond in which was what Bob called "the ancestral lodge," a gray igloo of branches protending from the water. The trees—partly birches—were but broken- off sticks rising out of the water. All about were trees they had felled, with the bark wholly or partly gnawed off, and stumps with pyramidal tops. There were three other dams below the ancestral one. They have only one baby a year, and there are rarely more than two or three in a lodge. They only come out at sunset and do all their work at night. The beavers—like the porcupines and skunks—are not afraid of anything; they will swim right up and look at you. They insolently slap their tails on the bank. Bob had to destroy one dam eleven times—they are hard to break, you have to take a pick—before he discouraged the beavers. They evidently decided that the current was too strong. As soon as a leak occurs, they rush to repair it. They cannot be out of the water for long and die if they are forced to be dry. When the beaver-control people are moving them, they have to stop at filling stations and wet them. Robert Moses[3] and his power projects: the blind will to build dams, indifference to the landscapes, leaving devastation all around.

Up here even the movies in Boonville and the radio broadcasts one hears in cars seem natural and not too strident, a part of American country life, assimilable, not unenjoyable.

Beverly had a boring winter, wrote us at one time a nostalgic letter. What did they do in Boonville in winter? "Just work, eat, and sleep, that's all!" If it was snowing, they were afraid to go to a dance: might not be able to get back.

I sometimes wake up in the morning with a little plaintive whistle in my nose. It annoys me extremely and is hard to get rid of. I summon my forces to snort but this does not always dispel it. What makes it seem something perverse that goes on independently of the rest of my organism is that the whistling always goes on much longer than the breathing itself seems to warrant. I have to rouse myself and blow my nose.

Another symptom that I now dislike is the spasmodic twitching of my hands or whole body when I am sitting in a chair or in bed. This dates from my breakdown about 1930, just before I married Margaret. I thought at the time it was caused by the rebellion of certain instincts—reluctance to divorce Mary, affection for and a sense of duty toward her—against something imposed by my will: the divorce and later my left politics and labor reporting, the latter of which, besides being difficult for me, involved my taking a high moral stand in regard to social questions which I did not always feel I was entitled to (tried later to get this into the open by showing how Marx's animus against the exploiting bourgeoisie was derived from his own exploitation of Engels). This twitching still reminds me of that period and, when I am lying in bed with a hangover, depresses me. I feel a compulsion just afterwards to remember and count the number of times—usually four—that my hands have twitched.

9:15, Memorial Day. The feathery filigree of an elm against the gray-blue of the sky and the flat dark blue-gray of the hill behind, on which loomed the darker silhouette of another, more distant elm. I thought that the old race of New Yorkers were more worthy of the landscape than the present ones.

Albert Grubel the day before Memorial Day said that the papers predicted about 260 car accidents for the holiday. The day after he asked me whether I knew how many there had been—from the paper, he gathered that they had been runnin' double. Then he told me that in April two women had gone out in a car and disappeared, and then they found them at the bottom of a lake under two feet of water.

.   .   .

Drive with Otis and Fern to St. Regis (June 1): Fern, whose father was a cheese manufacturer, couldn't resist stopping off at a big cheese factory on our way. She bought a great paper bag of yellow cheese curds, which they ate on the way like popcorn. Fern said, "It squeaks good," and Otis said, "It squeaks good." They were talking about the sound you can feel it making when you bite it, which means that it is of the right consistency for cheese. —I asked them about the Little Hotel, the roadhouse at the corners which Rosalind and I had discovered last October and to which we had taken the Loomises. They told me that it used to be called the Little Whoretel, but was now under different and respectable management. I asked Fern where they got the girls: "Oh, local girls." They told me that the McGuires in Talcottville had for some time had a pair of field glasses for the purpose of watching the neighbors, and that now Carrie has a pair.

Later bulletin from Albert: 287 people had been killed in car accidents on Memorial Day and 41 had been "drownded"—328 in all. A party had gone out to pick flowers, and one of the girls had strayed away, and they hadn't found her yet and had set bloodhounds after her. A little boy had also strayed and had bloodhounds set after him.

This morning (June 3) Albert told me about a man who had "committed suicide the hard way." He had filled his mouth with gunpowder and lighted it. This reminded him that once he had killed some skunks and skinned them and hung them up; but there was some of the stuff left in one of them and he smelled so bad near the place where they were making maple sugar that he burned some gunpowder around them, and it took all the smell away.

June 4. I sit at my little card table on which I write, on Mother's old heavily upholstered chair, and look up, after work—6:30—at the old framed map on the opposite wall. It just frames the window behind me now—the white curtains, the white net that holds the panes, the June green of the lilac bushes—with myself, head and shoulders at the bottom, dim but rather darkly ruddy, with the line of the mat going through my chest.

Beverly, as her aunt says, is a good girl. I tried to kiss her one night, when elated with drink, and she very determinedly squirmed away. I said I was sorry that I had got to the age when I wanted to kiss young girls, but that she had certainly learned how to resist. She evidently thought she ought to apologize and told me that it was just that she was nervous. I had kissed her on the cheek in an innocent way before, but the other night I must have seemed more aggressive.

NOTES

1. *Upstate*, pp. 195–96.
2. Geoffrey Gorer, British anthropologist.
3. Robert Moses (1888–1981), chairman of the New York State Power Authority (1954–63). *AI*, pp. 137–59.

TONAWANDA

[The following account of the Little Water Ceremony which EW attended was used by him in *Apologies to the Iroquois* (pp. 293 ff.) with, as always, a certain number of revisions.]

Tonawanda, June 6, 1959. Fenton and I went first to Corbett Sundown's. He was out manuring his garden. He seemed to me the most authentic Indian I had met, in the sense that he resembled what one imagines them to have been before their blood had become mixed and before they became partially adapted to the white civilization. He has a very strong Seneca accent. One would not think he had any white blood. He is not tall, but very handsome—a proud look that is characteristic of these Senecas of Tonawanda. He is evidently top man of the reservation, handsome and quite formidable—although his face at moments melts into charm. Indoors he made many jokes, at which he violently laughed. I couldn't help feeling that that must be the way in which, in the early days, they had laughed to see their enemies tortured. His wife was working in the kitchen, a coffee-colored woman with most of her upper front teeth out.

She was cooking, and did not greet us. The only son, a little adenoidal, was lying on the bed and watching television. His father said, "That's *his* culture. He grew up with it." The boy peeked into the room where we were sitting to see who was there, then went back and lay face down on a rug on the floor. I wondered about his growing up in Tonawanda with his head full of trashy white doings that he was watching and hearing on television. Sundown and Fenton discussed the ceremony, some of which, having made a recording of it, the latter knows by heart. I learned that each song sequence is started low, then gradually pitched higher and higher. On one occasion, Sundown told us, the first singer started off so high that he did not leave them enough scope for this progression, and they had to stop and start over again. They laughed about a man who had left the reservation, on which the Tonawandas congratulated themselves. He was always roaming from one reservation to another; and he was always disorganizing the ceremonies. He would arrive and decide that something was wrong, and soon nobody would know what to do and everything would be in a mess. Corbett Sundown had been on the expedition to Washington with Holdridge and Mad Bear. Fenton had said that Sundown was a "conservative" chief (he is one of the hereditary chiefs and his title means something like He Has a Broad Brow), but he had been collaborating with Mad Bear and Holdridge. We tried to find out what he thought of the latter, but he was rather noncommittal. He said that the "Commies" had been buzzing around them at Washington. They knew everything they were going to do, everything the F.B.I. was going to do. They would tip the Indians off to what was going to happen, and so were useful to them. Fenton asked how they knew they were Communists. "They told us." Referring to the St.

Regis shooting and the state troopers, he said, "There's one less now." Somebody had stolen a car and left it on the reservation, and a trooper had come onto the reservation and tried to arrest an Indian boy. Sundown had called up the local chief of police and told him to call the trooper off, which he had. He said that they could have ambushed him and shot him easily, and nobody would ever have known who had done it. I asked him if the Indians had no police. "No—and no [mental] institutions—and no jails. When the white man discovers something," said Sundown, "you read about it in the papers. When the Indian discovers something, you don't hear about it. Penicillin. It's nothin' but mold." The Indians had always used mold. He said that ordinary offenses by white men were not featured in the Buffalo papers, but if an Indian was guilty of anything, it appeared on the front page.

Just as we were taking our leave, his wife said we mustn't go: she was just getting supper ready; so we sat down to the most primitive and Indian meal that I had yet had among these Iroquois: fried gray Indian corn bread, which I at first mistook for slices of some kind of meat loaf, very tough sliced fried meat, with a bowl of greasy watery gravy, mashed potatoes, bread, and green tea in glasses without sugar. We ate in the kitchen, which was not so primitive, with white modern refrigerator and towering deep-freeze. The boy came to the table but wouldn't eat—went away but his mother made him come back and cut up a piece of meat for him. Sundown told about going somewhere and having to explain that he was not legally married to his wife. He had told them that among the Indians you lived with a woman, and if you didn't like her, you got another one. But these unions were now recognized: she was Mrs. Sundown now. (It had been one of the issues in the

Six Nations Reserve to get Indian marriages recognized in Canada.) Like Philip Cook and all the serious Indians I had met (though Mad Bear had offered us beer), he much disapproved of Indian drinking. When it had been against the law to sell an Indian liquor, the excuse for their debauchery when they got it had always been that it was demoralizing to have to beg it and smuggle it from the white people. But now—from, I think, about five years ago—they had been able to buy liquor anywhere, so why must they still be making hogs of themselves? Why couldn't they learn how much they could hold?

We then looked up Ely Parker's house and found an old lady living there, a niece of his maternal grandmother. The house unpainted and in bad repair. Fenton said that she "used to keep quite a neat house," but it was almost squalid now (though one never feels that these Indians are dirty, no matter how sloppily they live). She was almost eighty, and she was living alone with a big friendly white dog with black markings. Her son was supposed to live with her, but he was away, we learned, a good deal of the time. The lace window curtains were yellow, the shades tattered; drawers were half open or closed with the contents sticking out of them; there were faded cloths like coverlets thrown over some of the chairs, clothes lying around on others. But the old lady was full of dignity of a Queen Victoria kind: dumpy, coffee-colored, with jowls and no neck. She sat in an armchair and answered my questions about the Parkers. She had, it seems, been adopted by the branch of the family that lived in that house. She also had that proud Seneca gaze, would partly drop her eyelids and look at you straight from under them. Her English was good and literate. She told us that they had put the historical marker for the ford by which Washington had crossed in the French and Indian Wars at . . . [left blank by EW]. I have found that when you first meet these Indians, they are likely to be stiff and unsmiling—though with no formalities of speech—and conversation will be broken by silences; but they will presently make deadpan jokes. You have to smile or laugh the first, and then they will laugh. We got to this point when she said about someone that Fenton knew about who was living in a certain house: "She thinks she owns it." When Fenton laughed and said, "You can never be certain of anything," she laughed in a jolly way, and this kind of thing continued. When we left, she said that our visit had livened up her evening.

We then visited a household in which the wife had a good deal of white blood and not so much of an Indian manner. The husband was a sweet old man with spectacles, liquid brown eyes and high arched bushy black eyebrows, who had just had a stroke and was sitting in a wheeled chair. He would open and close one hand to show that it was growing more flexible; was quite cheerful, did not seem worried. The Indians believe that to eat a turtle or be splashed with turtle blood is bad luck: you will die a lingering death, because it seems, it takes turtles a long time to die; and he said jokingly that he was going to die like that. He had been chief petty officer in the navy, had been to New Guinea, the Galápagos, and other places and spent a great deal of time in Cuba. He and his wife both come from the reservation. He had looked her up in Seattle on one of his voyages, and they had been married there. Their son was in the army—a photograph of him in uniform on the wall in the next room. In the room in which we were sitting,

on the table and one side of the floor, the many toys of
their little granddaughter.

He told us that his brother had been the head of the
Little Water Society, but would never answer his questions when he asked him what it was all about. I thought
that it was very queer that Fenton and I should be admitted and the brother of a member kept out, but Fenton
told me that our host was a Christian, and that they
never could have admitted to such a sacred ceremony a
man whom they regarded as an apostate. Apropos of the
unwillingness to communicate secrets: Fenton had been
telling Sundown of having tried to find out something
from an Indian and having been only answered, *"Digwa."*
He did not know the root of this word, called it "a vague
negative." Sundown explained that it was something you
said "when you wanted to be evasive." Fenton had once
asked an Indian what it meant, and he had answered, "I
don't know, I didn't heard."

The ceremony: We went a little before the time that
Corbett Sundown had told us, ten, to the house where
it was being done: Nelly somebody's. Nobody as yet had
come, and the hostess's son told Fenton through the
screen door that he would have to check with Corbett
Sundown. We drove off and engaged two rooms at a
motel. When we returned, Corbett Sundown was there,
with two or three of the singers, to whom he introduced
us. The room was a big kitchen, as in the case of the
Dark Dance, with a stove, a washing machine, and a
white modern sink; a big box of corn flakes standing on
a shelf. The singers straggled in and took their seats on
two benches along the walls, which made a right angle
with one another. The materials for the ceremony and
the feast arrived. Two or three boxes of fresh strawberries,

from which Corbett Sundown removed the stems, and several cans of canned ones. These were put into two white enameled pails. A great modern container for the soup, which evidently worked on the principle of a thermos bottle, was set on the sink at my elbow, and I could hear some disturbance in it from time to time— still bubbling, I suppose. The pork for it, loosely wrapped, was put on the stove. I had expected the traditional pig's head, but these seemed to be simply cuts of pork. The rattles were brought in a big white bag: they are pale yellow polished gourds of various sizes, some of them pretty big. Three reed flutes were laid side by side on the table. Fenton had told me that they had no stops, but one of them, we noticed, had three; in the case of the others, we could not see. The medicine in two quite modern boxes was laid on the same table and covered up with a cloth. No cigarette smoking is permitted, and no one can come in who has liquor on his breath. No menstruating woman is allowed to come anywhere near. In Parker's diagram of the layout, a place for women members was indicated, but here no women were admitted. During the ceremony, the hostess and another woman sat in the next room, hearing it through the door. Everybody, including ourselves, brought in a small package of Indian tobacco, which was handed to Corbett Sundown on entering. This tobacco is mixed in a single receptacle, and little piles of it are made on the table, two rows of four each—for the Senecas' eight clans, to show that the medicine has been given for everybody. There were ten men in the room, not counting us. The hostess and her son entered only to make preparations for the feast.

A good deal of joking went on before the thing began, as afterwards between the sections. Fenton says that they talk about the ceremony and their roles in connection

with it, not about one another as individuals. The conversation was all in Seneca, with the exception of a few
remarks exchanged with us; but they refer to the time
in English: "eleven o'clock," etc. Their voices are low
and their speech is rapid compared to those of the other
upstate New Yorkers. Corbett Sundown, who prays and
presides, seemed usually to spark off the jokes, laughing
in his somewhat coercive way. The mosquitoes were
thick outside, and every time the door was opened a
fresh eager flock came in. Insects always go for me, and
I was slapping my ankles and the top of my head. "If
you don't bother them, they won't bite you," said a quietly
grinning round-faced man with spectacles. Fenton told
me that the mosquitoes at Tonawanda had always been
notorious. Somebody had said that they were tri-motored.
He told me an Indian story about a gigantic mosquito
that had once existed there. It had been chasing a man,
who was running for his life and who dodged behind a
tree. The mosquito's proboscis pierced the tree, and,
swollen with blood, she exploded. From the myriad drops
of her blood had sprung the present breed of mosquitoes,
smaller but equally fierce. This started up an Indian from
Canada, the only man present who wore a tie. He gave
us a different version, in which the insect had been shot
with a bow and arrow, and, evidently a great storyteller,
he went on to tell us three more. An Indian had met a
bear and, getting a tree between him and it, had seized
with either hand a paw of the bear on either side of the
tree. There was nothing more he could do: he had to
stand there holding the bear. At length his brother came
by, with another man, and he called out for them to
help him. "Have you had your breakfast yet?" asked the
brother of his companion. "Yes." "Then you help him:
I haven't had mine yet." —In Canada, a Member of
Parliament was eating at a lunch counter beside an

Indian. The Indian ate a stack of pancakes. "I wish I had your appetite," said the Member of Parliament. "I never have any appetite." "Take it," said the Indian, "why don't you take it?" "What do you mean?" said the Member of Parliament. "You've taken my land, you've taken my freedom, you've taken my women," said the Indian. "You might as well take my appetite, too." —"I was traveling in the South and I tried to thumb a ride, and there was a man and a woman that wouldn't pick me up because they thought I was a nigger. I went into a bar, and I asked for a drink, and then the man and woman came in. Then a policeman came in and said that I wasn't allowed in the bar. 'I'm an Indian, not a nigger,' I said. 'Then you're not allowed to drink. Who gave this Indian this drink?' I told him the man and woman, so he arrested the man and woman and took them away to the station house."

At a quarter past eleven, preliminaries to the ceremony began. Corbett Sundown arose and, with his eyes closed and with his hands held down and clasped, made a twenty-minute speech in Seneca—with many repetitions, Fenton told me—announcing what they were going to do tonight. There were two volunteers, who had come to help them. This was true in Fenton's case, since he knows much of the ceremony by heart. Then the food and the musical instruments were all placed on the stove or beside it, and Corbett Sundown, taking off one of the stove lids, began dropping into the fire pinches of Indian tobacco, as he thanked, by the usual formula, the Creator and all his deputies and blessed to the use of the ceremony the objects required for it. Then the rest of the tobacco was put into pipes, which for a few minutes were smoked in silence. Then the strawberry pails were passed to the members of the company, including us, in a ritualistic order. This is done in the same way at the end of each intermission between the five sections of the ritual. Everyone drinks from a ladle. And they jokingly spoke a word which I did not understand but which reminded me of the ritual *"Gorko, gorko!"* that they cry at Russian weddings. This, it seems, is the word for "You're welcome." It is a ritualistic joke. The point seems to be that—somewhat as the English have abbreviated "Thank you" to "Kyou"—the Senecas have averted it altogether by saying "You're welcome" first. A few preliminary cries of this word eliminate the repetitive interchange. I had noticed that I was the only person present who said "Thank you" when I had had my draught of strawberries. (The hostess and one or two other people were sitting there—this time no television.) Now the door to the next room was closed, the light was turned off, and the ceremony proper began. The room and the performers had vanished; in the darkness, a completely new atmosphere is established by the very first sounds. The single beat of a rattle is heard in the sudden blackness like the scratching of a gigantic match, and it is answered by other such flashes that rip in the darkness as startlingly as large-scale electric sparks. Then one of the soloists sets the rhythm, which is picked up by the company in unison, like the jogging sound of an express train as it is heard by the passenger inside. This is kept up, without raggedness or flagging, for something like an hour. Parker says that the pace is 150 a minute. I do not know whether this applies to the first section or the even faster parts of the later ones. The songs to which this is an accompaniment are sung to a slower rhythm. The structure and nonsense refrains of these songs have something in common with those of old English and Scottish ballads, as well as something of their wistful accent, as of human beings alone with nature, singing to unpeopled spaces. But there is also a mighty choral element. Fenton said rightly that if the Dark Dance was Debussy, the Little Water Ceremony was Beethoven. The music consists of a couplet, of which the first and the second lines differ only, as in the Dark Dance, through the change of a single word. In this case, whether dealing with human beings or with the animals who have contributed to the medicine, the first line refers to the female—since the Iroquois always put women first—the second to the male. In the first section, which deals with the search for the medicine: "She went into the field (or wherever)," "he went into the field," etc. Each of these is sung twice, then taken up by the chorus, who sing each one twice (? and do the soloists sing with the chorus?). The search proceeds all through this section, and in the last couplet the man and woman go to the top of the hill, and there they stand under the clouds. In the second section, the rhythms of the rattles are different. While the soloists are singing the couplet, the rattles go so fast that they seem to weave a kind of screen or veil—a scratching almost visible on the darkness—that hangs before the lyric voices, but when the chorus takes the song up, this changes to a slow heavy rhythm that has something of the pound of a march. This shift is enormously effective and, contrary to our convention, the animation of the big shimmer begins before the chorus is quite ended, so that you know that in a moment a fresh song will be quickened to life. In a similar way the pound of the chorus commences before the soloists are quite finished. This second section deals with the animals and birds: "The she-owl came and joined the song," "the he-owl came and joined the song," etc. Toward the middle, the creatures begin to speak, as they are mentioned one by one in the couplets. They are mimicked by one or more singers, while the others are singing the songs. The effect of this is startling and weird. The crow, the Ga-ga, caws;

the bears and the panthers roar; the owl has a beautiful four-note hoot, not unlike "Tu-whit, tu-wu." There are archaic words in the ritual that nobody understands—among them some of the names of the birds. When one of these unidentified birds was mentioned, the cackle of a hen who has just laid an egg was heard from the prehistoric darkness, and was followed by fresh laughter. A climax of animation occurs toward the end of this section with the arrival of the she- and he-wolves, who are heralded as running through the meadows. These wolves do not howl; since they are running, they bark like wild dogs. A queer kind of excitement is created here. All the animals are supposed to be present in the dark, and Parker says that the adepts believe they can see them. The medicine is also supposed to become luminous. I could not, however, see that the boxes containing it were ever opened. Nor was I conscious of another phenomenon that Corbett Sundown had warned me to expect. "You'll hear a woman's voice," he said, "and there's no woman in the room." Fenton said that he could hear feminine "overtones."

It was delightful to go out in the intermissions. One was here in the cool June night of the green Tonawanda woodland. There was a fragrance of something blooming. The back lawn, where the grass was cut, was revealed by a bulb with a reflector behind it, which directed the light down from the top of the house, and one could see strips of asphalt shingling in imitation of brick that were peeling away from the wall. The Indians smoked and talked a little. The real hoot of an owl was heard, and a nighthawk flew through the area of light toward the forest that made the background.

The third section is the climax of the symphony. Now the medicine at last is found. Each of the sections is opened and closed by Nick Bailey's "flourish of the flute."

This is the whippoorwill, whose cry is thus imitated. It is a kind of leitmotif (like the bird in *Siegfried*), for it guides the questers to the medicine and it now for the first time (?) is heard in its pivotal role in the action. This section is more complicated and difficult to sing. The melody and shape of the songs of the two preceding sections has been uniform from beginning to end of each. But now the songs begin on unexpected notes and follow unconventional courses. This is magic, a force beyond nature is tearing itself free. There is a passage of reiteration that sounds as if some phenomena were being enumerated one by one, a litany of praise perhaps. A great structure is raised by the rattles that is neither the big shimmer, the express train, or the grand march. And a paean is let loose; it fills the room with its volume. One finds oneself surrounded, almost stunned, as if the four walls of the room had become the cylinder of a pipe organ and as if one were sitting inside it, immersed in a sustained diapason. How strange when the lights are turned on—strange apparently for the singers, too, who are blinking and dazed at first, having to bring themselves up short in this kitchen, in this new electric-lighted world—to find oneself there in the room with ten men who work during the day in the gypsum mines and plants, dressed in their unceremonious clothes; an assortment of physical types, some handsome, some not so handsome, some young and some old, some fat and some lean, some sallow, one almost black, some with spectacles, some with their teeth gone, who have just given body in the darkness to a projection that absorbed them all. A car had driven up to the house; its headlights had glared through the window. I saw the profile against it of a man turning round to look; but the singing was not interrupted, and the driver, who had heard it, withdrew.

I found in the intermission that Fenton was somewhat baffled as to what had been going on in this section. I had noticed, in his previous conversation with Sundown, that he had expressed unclearness about it and that Sundown had not helped him out. He told me, also, that—since the versions somewhat differed in the various Seneca reservations, and even in the same reservation in relation to different orders of illness (the version we were hearing was intended for people who had suffered accidents)—he had never heard it sung in quite that form. He now questioned Corbett Sundown—who said laconically, "Everything has a meaning"—and some of the singers when we were standing outside. One man who had little command of English pondered long and at last brought out, "He goes to the swamp . . . He goes to the swamp . . . He (I do not know whom he referred to) explained it all to us." I thought he did not want to tell us, but Fenton said that the difficulty was that he did not know how to express the meaning in English. One man said he was covered with sweat; I should think they would all have been. I have noticed the comparative odorlessness of Indians. Though they sometimes live in squalor, they do not seem dirty.

The fourth section is a relaxation. The music is the same as in the second. The animals and birds are thanked pair by pair, and they acknowledge it in their various voices. There is an atmosphere of calm jubilation. The fifth section is not often sung in connection with the other four sequences. It is the sequence of the ceremonial that is used in the actual curing of a patient. Instead of animal cries, there are interpolated shrieks and groans, which I took to be the agonies of the patient, but Fenton thought them rather the cries of the singers now laboring and yet keeping up their spirits through the final phase of the cycle. This, too, needs a good deal of strength and produces a powerful impression. Everybody is limp at the end, the listeners as well as the performers. But a great affirmation has been made. Whether or not the patient at whom the fifth section is aimed may have been redirected by it toward life, the Senecas have asserted their vitality, their will, and their force to persist. Ten men in a darkened kitchen, with an audience of four or five about whom the celebrants hardly care, make a core that sustains a people.

I knew that the Little Water Ceremony—representing death and resurrection—was supposed to end just at dawn, and I wondered how accurately they would time it—when the lights were turned on, it was half past four. I had already been aware, glancing out of the torrent of sound, that the windows were becoming less dim; but when I thanked Corbett Sundown and wished him good night, he answered, "Not good night, good morning," and when we went out of the house, I found that it was indeed dawn. The birds were now tuning up, and the roadside was already green in the first soft and misty light.

TALCOTTVILLE, 1959

Beverly and Fern both have only one way of respond-ing to anything astonishing you are telling them—as when, while we were waiting in the Boston airport for the Provincetown plane, I described the Little Water Ceremony to Beverly: by shaking the head (though I believe that Fern sometimes makes a sound)—the sign for hearing something outlandish is the same as for dis-approval.

Dinner at the Biddles': Very pleasant, nobody else here—I thought perhaps because Francis was rather subdued—I was reassured, remembering Uncle Reuel, to see how well he had survived his prostate operation—and wanted to draw me out rather than do the key talk-ing himself. He had two very good Boston stories of the same kind as Charley Walker's. While watching Isadora Duncan dance, one man had said to another that she was like a naked Cabot, to which the other replied that Cabots were never naked. And some Bostonian had said to Francis that he never read the *New York Times* because he found it confused him. This reminded me of

George Biddle's story about the Philadelphian who said, at a party of Philadelphians, "I don't understand about Mrs. ————: there's something there that's not quite right." To which another Philadelphian replied in a low voice, "Her mother was a Bostonian." —Francis and Katherine had just spent the afternoon with the Conrad Aikens, and had for the first time heard the word *catamite*. They wanted to know if I knew about this.

Nina drove Beverly and me back to Talcottville—we made it in about seven hours. Elena and I parted affectionately; but when she called me up after Nina had left, and I told her, as I had before, that I couldn't struggle with her anymore about Talcottville: she would have to decide for herself, but that I didn't want her to come here for two short stays—which was what she had proposed to do—she began to weep and said I didn't love her. Then she wrote me a letter and said that she loved me but wasn't coming to Talcottville this year. She had already told me that she was "jealous of Talcottville." I had been more or less expecting this and received the news with relief and a new sense of freedom. She suffers and complains so much here and inhibits me from growing into New York State as otherwise I tend to do. But she is terribly run-down and ought to have a vacation, went this weekend to the Sellars' at Newport, where Daphne and Henry and the twins are. At Wellfleet, she insists on doing everything, and is upset if I make any arrangements for myself. The result is that I become dependent on her and take no responsibility. Here I attend to everything and am quite free to make my own routine and thoroughly enjoy it. I drink less and get more work done. The bad thing is that at my age and with my self-preoccupation I don't seem to have quite enough energy to do all I should for Helen after I have

ished work. If I drink, I am likely to slump and
arrel with Elena. Here there is nobody to quarrel with,
d I don't have to do anything for anybody—though it
ves me a pang to look into Helen's room, with its little
ings that belong to her, and know that she isn't here.

Tension with *Elena* now relieved. She is going to meet
e at Pittsfield—with her new car, which evidently
rills her—and we will go to some music at Tangle-
ood, then visit the Winkelhorns at West Cornwall, then
rhaps the Brooks and Dells, then come back up here.
hen we discussed it over the telephone, she said, "This
where we came in." We had gone to the Tanglewood
estival before we were married and stayed at a hotel
gether.

Albert's story about the woman in Boonville, who shot
er good-for-nothing husband when he came home drunk
d kicked her in the stomach at the time she was
regnant. "They say he was layin' on the bed when she
ot him. They didn't do much of anything to her."
On another of our rides to Boonville, he seemed about
run over a boy on a bicycle. He didn't turn aside till
yelled to him. Then he said, "They're supposed to stay
the side of the road."
He made his usual prediction of accidents the day
efore the 4th of July, but I don't remember his men-
oning it afterwards—I suppose because there were
wer accidents than the newspapers had prophesied.

Conversation with Beverly after the Fentons left. She
ad said last summer that Bill was "real common," and
ow said the same thing about Olive. I asked her what
e meant by this, and she found it hard to explain: the
est she could do was "people who are rich." I asked her

to name people in Boonville that she thought were r
common: Mr. Pratt and Colonel Best—"I don't thi
you're quite common."

1/27/11

The old Dewey house at Collinsville.[1] Seeing it so da
and Victorian among its gigantic elms, I had always be
curious to go inside. Now old Mrs. Dewey is dead a
her son wants to sell it for $10,000 with everything th
is in it. I went over with the Loomises to see it, and I
wife took us around. It has not been painted lately a
has an ironlike neutral color. It is one of those squa
affairs (built in 1852) and perhaps what is meant
Hudson River Bracketed, for the long upstairs windo
have ornamental supports. The roof of the porch has
kind of row of teeth that give it a sinister look, and t
porch itself, with slender pillars that are joined at t
top with arches, is masked by a great growth of spru
and a spread of Virginia creeper that hangs from the to
At the back of the lawn a gray stone smokehouse a
more or less enveloped in greenery; and, parallel wi
the house, a stable, on top of which—one can't imagi
why—is a flat square turret with windowpanes. Woo
beyond this and a stream—Dewey's Glen—on whi
used to stand a gristmill. The gate is an ironwork gri
the black bars and spikes of which give it, too, a fe
bidding look; a narrow stone-paved path leads to t
broad stone steps of the house. The interior is most u
attractive but a not uninteresting example of the tas
—the bad taste—of that period, since little seems to ha
changed since it was built. It has a curious unlived-
air. The Brussels carpet with a rose design that co
pletely covers the floor of the enormous living room o
the left as you come in the door is faded and worn
the end toward the front but this was done, it seems, I
skiers—to the indignation of old Mrs. Dewey—w

nted the house one winter and gave a good many
rties. This room has upholstered Victorian chairs, in-
uding one covered in dark red plush with elaborate lace
lies from which long tassels hang protecting the arms
d back; an ottoman near the fireplace, with em-
oidered flowers on the top. Extravagant drapes on the
indows—one set at the opposite end of the room has
the top a scalloped canopy and, hanging from below
in the middle, a kind of great tongue of cloth and, at
e sides, august curtains which are caught up, near the
ottom, with ropes. To one side of this is a whatnot with
nch shells and china ornaments. Facing the fireplace a
ano with an old-fashioned black piano stool, above
hich hangs a large boxed picture, painted in 1876 by
meone with a foreign name and supposed to have origi-
lly hung in the house of a New York City Dewey. This
cture is called *A Musical Party* and shows a group of
dies, one of them seated at a piano, in the hats and
stled gowns of the seventies. Other pictures are un-
lored family portraits that have almost the look of
gravings but must be monstrously enlarged photo-
aphs; a few small more modern photographs; an en-
aving of a village blacksmith; and a painting of a horse
hich was made by a relative (there are other horses
d cows by this artist in some of the other rooms). A
hite marble fireplace and a great low-hanging wide-
reading gilt-and-black gas chandelier, which has been
ted with two tiers of bulbs. There is a cornice of gilt
aves. (In one of the bedrooms there is a frieze of wall-
per which, it seems, is as old as the house: classical
gures in blue and white—unpleasing like everything
se in the house.) The front room across the hall is
mehow especially disgusting: a mantel of black marble
ith white mottlings, perhaps imitation marble, on top
which, beside the mirror, rises a dark structure of

wood which cannot be seen to have had any use, un
possibly to contain ornaments; a blue velvet and wic
chaise longue; a low bookcase darkly crammed with ch
sets of Scott, Bulwer-Lytton, and Thackeray; the
two-volume edition of Grant's memoirs was lying on
floor. In the next room, a larger bookcase with glass do
and shelves of old rubbish, some 19th-century series
children and worthless novels of the early nineteen h
dreds. Upstairs in one of the bedrooms, a small bookc
of books on agriculture. The only attractive feature v
the hallway when you came in the door: there wa
pretty little gilt mirror, and the old red-and-yellow s
carpet ran rather steeply up to an ornamental wind
with a scrolly design of yellow and brown and wh
clouded glass, through which the afternoon light—
only bright thing in the house—fell on the old sta
When I first came into the house, I thought it was go
to be enchanting, and that if there were to be a sale
the things there were some I should like to have,
the more closely I looked at them, the less I wan
them. Even the little gold mirror came to seem seco
rate. The second time I went—with the Fentons—
effect of the place was actually sickening. I do not w
to go there again.

Huldah Loomis tells me that old Mrs. Dewey is s
posed to have been rather loose in her youth before
was married—that Homer Collins, who was related
her, did not like to be kidded about her. She is suppos
to have had a baby by a man in Boonville, and the m
is supposed to have bribed his wife to bring up the
as her own. The bribe was a grand piano, which it v
noticed that she acquired soon after the appearance
the baby.

The house in which the present Deweys live was bu
in the 18th century and afterwards added to. Mrs. Dew

showed us around it and offered us a drink. Everything was very decorous, and I refused a second highball. A few days later I took the Loomises to dinner at the summer hotel on Brantingham Lake. Everybody on the porch studied us as we went in the screen door. A rather low-grade lot of people. Smorgasbord sloppily served. Mr. and Mrs. Dewey and two of their daughters. Mrs. Dewey came over and sat at our table and announced that she was tight. She started to say something about her grandchildren, then explained to me, "I've got more goddam grandchildren!" I asked how many, and she held up all the fingers of her right hand and one of her left. I said that I was sending some people to look at the house but I didn't think they would buy it. She said, "They goddam well better!" Later, when her daughters came over, she said, "I've got more goddam daughters!"

Beverly says she has always said "youse" and "witjus" (with you), and she doesn't know where she got it. People notice it in Boonville as well as in Wellfleet. When she was going to school, they tried to correct it, but did not have any success. She used to write it in compositions, and it helped her get low marks. She spelled it "you'se."

Old Reber, now in his eighties, can do anything. He undertook to paint my ceilings. His wife forbade him to do it, but he cheated by getting an old Texan from Boonville, then working with him. He called the old Texan "grandpa," also calls me "grandpa." I think he likes to call people "grandpa" in order to bring out how young he is himself for his age.

A rainbow on the left; on the right, rather dry gray-blue clouds. —Later, green goldenrod in the foreground, where the edge of the roads has been cut—then sky all dry gray and white, and the gray Adirondacks in the background.

Vista in the house I like best: to sit in the long chair in its new location and look across the hall into the smaller living room, at the slim legs of the chairs and of the phonograph table—with the patch of plush from the upholstered rocking chair, the gray floor and gray shadow behind the white curtains, where the shade is down. —Dark in that room: chairs and tables dark, even the gray floor, the curtains, below the shade, only glowing dully—8:15, August 8.

This summer, in relaxation from the historical and anthropological reading that I do on the Indians and the Civil War, I have fallen into going to bed or beguiling breakfast with books on the literary life of the late eighteen and the early nineteen hundreds, the period in which I suppose I am most at home. It rests me and entertains me. I have read in the Max Beerbohm volumes that I have here, Shaw's correspondence with Ellen Terry, have read Lionel Stevenson's biography of Meredith, Edward Marsh's reminiscences, *A Number of People*, and Christopher Hassall's biography of Marsh. I met Marsh once or twice in London in 1945 and found him likable. These books about him are delightful: good and well-bred English style, background of classical studies, background that combined the political nobility with the accomplished professional class, personality good-humored, conscientious, generous, great love of poetry and painting, the best of the life of the English upper classes in the period before the first war—he goes on rounds of visits to country houses and makes all the great people sound charming—good living, good stories, good jokes, attractive eccentricities. Marsh had had serious illness at the moment of adolescence, and neither his voice nor his sexual organs had ever matured, so he never had to worry about love or a family. His crushes on Ivor Novello and Rupert Brooke were passionate in their way but do not seem to have involved him deeply. He worked, as a civil servant, under Liberals, Tories, and Labour—Churchill, Thomas, and the Duke of Devonshire—without, apparently, ever worrying seriously about politics. When he comes to the first war, he says, in effect, "I don't want to bore you, so shall skip it." In regard to other events, he says, "It is written in the Book of Chronicles."

Jenny's death: Margaret Rullman called to say that Jenny was in very bad shape and would have to be moved to a nursing home. I went down on Sunday and learned the next morning that she had died that night. She had been in great pain; it was impossible for Helen to move her, and she could no longer even use a bedpan. On Friday the Rullmans got her into a nursing home. They didn't tell her about it and she protested, but when she got there and they had cut and washed her hair and bandaged up her bedsores, she found that she was much more comfortable. She died Sunday about 10:30. They found she was seventy-nine—she had never been willing to tell her age, but it was given in a certificate of baptism. The funeral was not till Friday: the first Catholic funeral, and the least depressing, I had ever attended. They make of it a social occasion. Jenny was on view as if on a bed, and had been made to look far better than when I had last seen her. They had filled out her cheeks and smoothed her wrinkles. Something came out in her face that I had not noticed before: a kind of Irish family profile that seemed masculine. The people at the Catholic funeral parlor had induced them to buy a new dress for her, and a rosary was entwined in her fingers. The relatives came and admired her and talked about old times. Each knelt and made a prayer on a rail beside her resting place. The funeral was at St. James's at nine the next morning. I don't think I had been in the church since my nurse Ellen Cavanagh had taken me there. They gave her a high mass, which lasted about forty-five minutes. The singing of the choirboys had nothing doleful; the little bell rang to mark the stages of the mass. Jenny's casket was set in the aisle, and the priest came down and sprinkled it with holy water: one could hear almost nothing he said. At the grave, he merely mumbled the Latin. Strange to hear so perfunctory a rendering; but, as Margaret says, the great thing is that they feel they have been able to do something; they pay for something for Jenny, and they feel that they are getting their money's worth. —Poor Helen was as much of a wreck as Jenny had been after my mother's death. She has been having a similar collapse, and was too ill to go to the funeral.

Sunday night I had dinner with Dawn [Powell]. It depressed me to go to the Village, where she had Katharine Anthony's[2] apartment on Bank Street for the summer. Male and female beatniks in the streets, the girls in trousers, the men with beards. It depressed me that Dawn should be now in such straits that this apartment, with all its shabby Greenwich Village things—old furniture, pictures, and books—should seem to her quite wonderful. But she and Joe were worrying about where to go next. She had never really lived in the Village. As she said, her old East Side address was relatively uptown. This was a community all to itself—lower prices, more neighborly relations. It reminded me of my days at 8 Bank Street in an apartment equally shabby—visits of

Frances and Margaret. I went there again on another evening and found Cobey Gilman,[3] who couldn't drink because he had "a swollen liver." Dawn was serving him a swordfish dinner. This depressed me, too, as did the next time I saw her, when she and Joe, Friday night, came to dinner with me at the Princeton Club. He no longer has a job. He said that one of the days I had been there, he had been taking their spastic son for a walk.

The heat in New York and in Red Bank was horrible. The Rullmans were also depressing. Margaret said that Walter was "failing" fast, that the young men at the hospital were brushing him aside. He told me that he could no longer perform "long operations." M. didn't know what to do with him: he has no hobbies, does not read, isn't interested in what she has to say—"All he can do is think about people's insides." Red Bank is now even more unattractive than before. The trees have been cut down on Front Street and the road widened; the old brick Episcopal church has been painted a light mud color; the road to Shrewsbury has a great supermarket. The state wants to build "jug handles" along it and make parking illegal—which would eliminate the 17th-century "old Allen house" and encroach to some extent on the churchyard; but there is a strong local protest and they have a gimmick which may avert it: nothing can be done by the state unless the locality passes an ordinance against parking. We went on to Eatontown. The Corlies place is still in good order—it has been bought by a fairly high-grade Italian family. The smokehouse is still there, with the same trumpet vine whose flowers I used to put on my fingers. But the farm has all been cut off—I wondered what has become of the little brook with willow roots and watercress that used to run through it, how the menace of Fort Monmouth looms right behind them. I thought of how bored poor Aunt Laura used to be after she had finally married Charlie Corlies and they would sit at night on the front porch, silent, she unhappy and he sulky. —Margaret's sister Charlotte has just lost her husband, and her daughter has just had one breast removed. The daughter has a hydrocephalic child.

I tried to amuse myself in New York by going to three foreign movies, all of them disappointing. Monday night I had dinner with Eugénie Lehovich and took her to *La Plume de ma tante*. The first part was very amusing, but then, after the intermission, it turned out that, because part of the company had gone back to Paris or for some other reason, the second part of the show consisted of the songs and skits of a group of tough and shrieking Americans. I enjoyed seeing Eugénie, however, and I think that she enjoyed herself. We went to the Algonquin afterwards and talked about Pasternak, Russia, etc.

[Reading] Edward Marsh helped me through it all— and the satisfaction of finishing the Indian book and having it approved and scheduled by Shawn.[4] —Was glad to get back to Talcottville, where, though people were complaining about the heat, it was nothing like the hell of New York.

Elena's uncle Walther died the day after Jenny.

Huldah Loomis has finally succeeded in getting to see the inside of the Constableville octagon house. It has a spiral staircase in the middle.

Arrival in Cambridge in early hours of Sept. 12. Written Nov. 3. Hilliard Place: Cambridge at its darkest brown claustrophobic; short narrow street, narrow sidewalks be-

tween Mount Auburn and Brattle. Yet house very satisfactory, modern, well equipped, well built, plain but
solid, dark woodwork, egg-shaped sharp-ended newel
posts on bannister; reminded me a little of old Red Bank
house probably built a little before. Theater being put up
at corner on Brattle Street but otherwise my room at the
front very quiet, except at the beginning of the week
when the garbage-removers are wrestling the garbage
pails. It was depressing and so characteristic of Cambridge
to find them, on our first arrival, obstructing the narrow
pavement. —I have since been enjoying the house, as
Elena has been making it more attractive—as if it were
a little "town house" such as I have always wanted. Only
thing lacking a nice little maid to go in and out the
swinging door between the dining room and the kitchen,
and now we have coming tomorrow a young Irish girl
who has just come over—I didn't know that this happened anymore.

Reuel did not do well with the Congress for Cultural
Freedom in Paris last summer. Nicholas Nabokov is
almost never there, so did not give him any guidance,
and he made mistranslations in the matter connected
with the Tolstoy celebration. They soon let him go, so
he ended by doing just what I thought he wanted to do:
bumming around Italy on a motorcycle. He and his
roommate Doc Lowell remind me of how passive and
moony you are up to the end of college. I have remembered what a shock it was to start in in the office of the
Evening Sun,[5] where nobody introduced you to anybody
—you gradually made their acquaintance and found out
who they were—and from which you were sent out on
assignments which were never in any way explained. I
was sent to find out about something that had happened
at Coenties Slip, a place I had never heard of. I was too
timid to do more than ask a few questions of people who

were standing around, realized how hard it was to get down to the truth about anything. If you just go to prep school and college, everything is fed to you, you are simply receptive; the moment you get out and work at a job, you have to find out for yourself how things are done. I told Reuel that if he had been a different kind of person, he would have taken over the office in Nicholas's default and displaced him as the head of the Congress.

One of Reuel's stories of his adventures: He had ridden about fifty miles, was tired and evidently thirsted for companionship. A French girl, also on a motorcycle, had to stop beside the road because something had gone wrong. He pulled up and offered to help her. She replied in a harsh voice, *"On regarde le paysage!"* He had told me this as an illustration for his opinion that the French girls were hard-boiled.

Elena went to Wellfleet the weekend that I went to the Iroquois experts' conference at the Allegany State Park. She saw Brownie L'Engle at Peggy Day's. When Elena told about her little twin grandchildren, one of whom was already walking, Brownie exclaimed, always true to form, "That's too early—it will make her bow-legged!"

Sept. 7. [Written later] The day before the Crostens left, they took us to the place they had been telling us about where Sugar River, after going underground, gushes suddenly out of the earth. This was a great revelation. I had always assumed that its reappearance was the trickle that runs toward Boonville and goes under the condemned bridge, eventually to merge with the Black River; but actually the main stream turns sharply east and runs for about a third of a mile completely concealed under-

ground. Just before you get to the spot, going toward
Boonville, where the road along the dry bed of the river
merges with the bed itself, you get through the barbed-
wire fence on your left and, just below the old quarry,
walk through a queer terrain which turns out to be
basically the same as Dry Sugar River proper: the same
great square blocks of stone with deep straight-cut crevices between them, but from a distance disguised by the
fact that they are much grown over, like a field, so that
the crevices have grassy lips. This formation continues
through a woodland, in the open places sprigged with
everlasting—after which you come to a clearing partly
framed by big maples, but on one side lined by a row of
cottonwoods—"popples"—diffusing a pleasant fragrance,
that grow on the edge of a great pit from which rises a
strange rock pyramid, made of more or less square-cut
blocks. One cannot tell whether this pyramid is natural
or erected by human hands—somehow in connection with
the quarry. Traversing this field to the left, you soon hear
the sound of the river. You find yourself at the top of the
glen at the bottom of which it gushes forth in what is
at first a small torrent. But when you look down, you
find that the trees that grow out of the walls conceal it.
You descend by a kind of flight of wide stone steps that
present themselves on the slope at intervals—you cannot
tell about these either whether they are man-made or
natural. On the left of the path are large rocks speckled
with black lichens; on the right a higher wall of ledges,
with rusty ferns growing out at the base, somewhat as
at Flat Rock. At the bottom, you stand on the edge of
the water, but you still, on account of the bushes and
trees and the lively bends of the stream, cannot see—
what makes it even more mysterious—exactly what it
gushes out of: you would have to wade up to the mouth
of the cave. On one side, in a little cove, there is a pool,

brown and flecked with foam. But the river is active: it twists and turns, spreads out into a wider bed. It goes under a crude bridge, over which, as one can see from the layer of manure, a herd of cattle pass. It is propped up by trunks of small trees, some with the bark still on them; it has at one time been faced with concrete, but has no railing; the edges are grassy. Just below this, some gaps in the rocks of the bank have been filled in with crudely cut stones. The stream turns so often and so sharply that one can never see ahead where it is going. (It, too, I find, eventually runs into the Black River.) There are the ruins of an old stone mill, which is roofless and which one can enter through a low door like the entrance of an Egyptian tomb. Not far away, sunk level with the ground, is a very large old millstone, grooved from the center with curving rays. There is also an old rickety picnic table with benches, knocked together from old gray boards, leaning askew but with small boulders against the legs to keep it from collapsing too easily. It cannot have been used for a long time, because when I tried to sit down, it wouldn't hold. There is a fenced-in pasture this side (to the right) of the stream, where the bank becomes steep and high and the fence runs along its top. Along the fence is a great bank of lilacs that must have been planted years ago, and beyond this one comes to a collapsing barn, with an old-fashioned stone foundation, inside which the ancient hay drips down through the cracks of the windows. I looked inside through the planks that barred the door and saw a carriage wheel of large circumference standing upright embedded in the dirt floor.

Strange that, with all the times we have picnicked at Dry Sugar River, I have never known about this place, which is hidden just across the road. Crosten says that he doesn't believe that very many people in Boonville know it exists; he and Mary discovered it when they [were] camping on the Black River and used to take long walks of exploration. It seemed to concentrate an essence of the romance that we feel about this part of New York —a fragment of survival from the past, not so long ago still prehistoric, then humanized and lived, then abandoned except for the cattle and in any case disregarded. Nobody seemed to know who owned it now—a modern silo could be seen beyond the trees. Crosten said that the people who farmed in that part of the world or who had their businesses in Boonville were mostly too much occupied by their work to pay any attention to the landscape. Yet most of them like to go fishing and camping. I had been saying that the living in a romantic dream was something characteristic of upstate New York which one did not find at all in New England—Walter Edmonds, Constance Robertson, John Gaus and myself, even Bill Fenton. For myself, I was a little troubled, in connection with this romantic spot, by the feeling that I had found it too late—too late for children's picnics or for youthful love affairs. What could I do about it? Perhaps my children or grandchildren may someday enjoy it more.

1/30/11

NOTES

1. *Upstate*, pp. 199–203.
2. Katharine Susan Anthony (1877–1965), American biographer.
3. See *The Thirties*, p. 627 and *passim*.
4. EW's articles on the Iroquois, which had been scheduled for early publication by William Shawn, the editor of *The New Yorker*. (October–November 1959).
5. EW worked on the *Evening Sun* in 1916. *A Prelude*, pp. 154–56.

INDEX

645